PIRANDELLO POINTS OUT IN AN ESSAY INCLUDED IN THIS ANTHOLOGY THAT IT WAS BOCCACCIO'S RIBALD ADVENTURES OF COMMON PEOPLE THAT FIRST PROVIDED THE IMPETUS FOR ITALIAN DRAMA. COMEDY—ROMANTIC, SATIRIC, REALISTIC—HAS SINCE THEN BEEN THE SPECIAL PROVINCE OF THE ITALIAN PLAYWRIGHT.

The Follies of Calandro, a sixteenth-century drama that bases its principal character on a figure from the *Decameron*, is as wickedly revealing as the controversial works of Henry Miller. De Filippo's uproarious play *Filumena Marturano*, the story of an ex-prostitute who tricks her aging paramour into marriage, is soon to be seen on film as *Marriage, Italian Style*. Giordano Bruno's *The Candle Bearer* is a great comedy by one of the greatest Italians of all time. Pirandello is one of the foremost artists of this century; many critics consider his tragicomedy *The Emperor*, reprinted here in full, his best work. In the day of Fellini and Antonioni the sheer theatricality of the Italians need hardly be proved; these seven plays reaffirm it as the heritage of the Italian playwright for four hundred years.

Commentaries by Goldoni, Castiglione, and three modern critics are included.

Other MENTOR Drama Anthologies

The Genius
of the
ITALIAN
THEATER

EDITED BY

Eric Bentley

 MENTOR

A MENTOR BOOK

Published by THE NEW AMERICAN LIBRARY

MENTOR TRADEMARK REG. U.S. PAT. OFF. AND FOREIGN COUNTRIES
REGISTERED TRADEMARK—MARCA REGISTRADA
HECHO EN CHICAGO, U.S.A.

MENTOR BOOKS are published *in the United States* by
The New American Library of World Literature, Inc.,
501 Madison Avenue, New York 22, New York,
in Canada by The New American Library of Canada Limited,
156 Front Street West, Toronto 1, Ontario,
in the United Kingdom by The New English Library Limited,
Barnard's Inn, Holborn, London, E.C. 1, England

PRINTED IN THE UNITED STATES OF AMERICA

EDITORIAL FOREWORD

The New American Library is putting the title *The Genius of the . . . Theater* on a whole series of books, but it happens to be especially suitable to the present one, because the Italian theater did have a "genius" in both principal senses of the term, and because what had this genius *was* the theater, and not dramatic literature. Italy has never known such a great age of drama as the Greeks enjoyed in the fifth and fourth centuries B.C., the English and the Spaniards around 1600, the French around 1650. Nonetheless, so strong has been the Italian sense of theater that theater itself, in our Western world, is to a very large degree Italian theater. Gordon Craig tries to convey his sense of this fact in the short essay beginning on page 538. Pirandello conveys his sense of it with unrivaled eloquence in the essay which is the real introduction to the present book. Once the reader has acquired this same "sense" he will read the texts that follow in a different way. And I do not mean he will read them as mere illustrations of a thesis. I mean that he will be more sensitive to the kind of life that is them, the life of the Italian theater, the life, indeed, of the Italian people. That there is no Shakespeare here, no Sophocles, no Molière will not then be a depressing thought. This is dramatic literature of high quality and it is imbued with a sense of life which is that of the most theatrical of temperaments and the most lovable of peoples.

E. B.
New York, 1963

Contents

THE ESSAYS

The Genius
of the
ITALIAN
THEATER

Introduction to

THE ITALIAN THEATER

by

Luigi Pirandello[1]

(TRANSLATED BY ANNE PAOLUCCI)

It is difficult for us to realize the importance of the
Theater in the civic life of a people, after having sat
through the usual sort of play being offered the public
these days—and not only here in Italy.

I ask you, therefore, to return in thought to the times
when truly civilized human societies—such as existed
in ancient Greece and Rome, and, as far as we know,
much earlier in India, and later, during the Renaissance,
in Rome again but above all in Ferrara and in our own
thriving Florence—celebrated the Theater as a religious
or quasi-religious rite; that is, as a genuinely "vital act"
that united all the spectators in a reality expressly created
by the poet to exalt their feelings.

One could then still feel, almost palpably, what the
Theater in its innermost essence really is: a form of life
itself, existing even among lower animals who, though
irrational, are yet capable of playing and offering their
play as a spectacle for others; and much more among

[1] Luigi Pirandello, "Introduzione al teatro italiano," *Storia
del Teatro Italiano,* a cura di Silvio D'Amico (Milano:
Luigi Pirandello. Translation copyright © 1965 by Anne
Paolucci.

men, who in their instinctive need to see themselves in
action are moved to represent their own lives, to judge
and thereby understand themselves better in relation to
others—that is, before the immediate sense of a Whole,
of which they rightly think and feel themselves to be
inseparable parts, component elements. Out of such
natural necessity the Theater is born among all peoples.
It is born when a people sing joyfully or tearfully in
religious feasts and one among them rises, exalted or
grieving, to commemorate a god or a hero, the rest
attending him in chorus, and then two or three or more
separate themselves from the crowd to personify, in a
truly authentic representation, punctuated by the measured sequences of the chorus, the fortunate or tragic
adventures of the god or hero.

That one might do without the Theater was then in-
conceivable. Every year there came a day—and more
than once each year—when the Theater was the solemn
fulfillment, not so much of the particular day, as of
a longed-for and necessary expression of communal
life, an example which that life offered itself; and the
word of the poet found its place much more visibly
among the highest ideal values of those human societies.

But someone will say: those societies are not ours, which
is so much more civilized, so much more vast and complex; and, on the other hand, the Theater of those times
is a far cry from ours, which has become, alas, so much
tinier, so much more futile and—we might almost say
—useless. In that vast complex of values that is the
civilized nation of today, what importance can there be
in a representation of the fictitious adventures of an
amateur detective trying to unmask a criminal in the
least suspect character of a comedy?

Today, the Theater can be no more than the pastime
of an evening for persons who, having worked all day,
want to enjoy some honest relaxation before going to
bed.

And who might these persons be, who, having worked
all day, can still have the desire, the time, and the
means to relax after dinner at the Theater before going
to bed?

Can we honestly say they are "the people"?—"the
Community"?

No. Only some few from the wealthy and middle
classes, and an occasional tradesman.

Let us at once admit, therefore, that if it ever had great value in the life of a people, if it was ever capable of having such great value, the Theater has lost it today; it is no longer performed for the people as a whole, nor, in conscience, would it be worthy of such performance, in its present state. Today it is merely a pastime, and less entertaining than many other pastimes.

Admittedly, this seems to be what we call a realistic argument, one that accepts facts as they are, stripped of rhetorical embellishments, and draws the inevitable conclusions—ugly and wretched as they are—calling a spade a spade. Instead, it is a cheap sophism, a sop for that miserable instinct of lazy indifference with which we have allowed ourselves to regard things of the spirit, responding momentarily with enthusiasm only when they are blatantly presented to us with the pressing enticements of rhetoric.

Reasoning about it with intellectual honesty, one is bound to see that the Theater today has not lost, and could not have lost, any of its real value, because that value is an intrinsic part of its very nature and, therefore, impossible to lose. What a people, coming en masse to the solemn spectacles of religious feasts, made of the Theater in the past—that is, a vital, communal act of the highest spiritual value—the Theater today, in and of itself, by its own virtue, insofar as it is truly Theater, makes of its audience, howsoever composed, howsoever sparse. What I mean to say is that when, in a half-empty hall, before a few scattered spectators, a real work of art is presented, those few, that evening, by virtue of that magic power which poetry acquires when its characters take on flesh and come to life on the stage, have become nothing more or less than "the People." And so much the worse for whoever stayed away; he missed the chance to participate in an experience of spiritual life actually and wholly realized within the circle of the community of which he is a part, and there can be nothing to boast of in his having turned his back on it.

But what in essence is the Theater? What is that value which is intrinsic to it and which, therefore, can never be lost?

I spoke of it on a recent occasion and I repeat it now in the same words: by giving voice to feelings and thoughts which are altogether evident in the lively play

of passions represented, and which, because of the very
nature of this art form, have to be spelled out in terms
as clear and precise as possible, the Theater offers
what might properly be called a public trial of human
actions as they truly are, in that pure and everlasting
reality which the imagination of poets creates as an example and warning for our commonplace and confused
natural life—a trial both free and human, which spurs
the consciences of the judges themselves to an ever
loftier and more rigorous moral life. This, in my judgment, is the value of the Theater; and I wanted to state
it in advance to assure you that in undertaking now to
speak of the first and foremost Theater of the world,
which is the Italian, we are dealing with a serious matter.

I fear, let me admit, that someone among you may
have marveled at my saying "the first and foremost
Theater of the world, which is the Italian." My hope is
that, after reading these pages of mine, marvel will give
way in his spirit to a less prejudicial and more
considerate regard for the ideal values of which even
he, as an Italian, is a depositary—established values,
renewed and augmented, age after age, by those who
shaped this great nation of ours.

The time has come to make amends, good people,
even in this area, for that damnable pleasure we take
in disparaging the value of our own things and belittling
them in comparison with their foreign counterparts.
After so many centuries of indulgence, that damnable
pleasure has become a sort of comfortable niche for
spiritual indolence and a cheap excuse for personal and
collective irresponsibility regarding these values, which
instead of accepting we rejected so as not to have to
defend and preserve them later—an attitude which,
prior to that most sacred renewal of public life brought
on by Fascism, could well be considered one of the characteristic traits (among the least attractive) of the
Italians. And it must be acknowledged, painfully, that
perhaps the only ones immune to it were our humble
peasants and artisans, who, as often as circumstances
matched them against foreign peasants and artisans, felt
and knew and had the heart to declare themselves
openly to be superior to the others, more skillful, more
capable of work; while our "intelligentsia," in the schools,
in the newspapers, in books, in conversations, in spirit,
out of intellectual poverty, out of narrow-mindedness,

often out of ignorance, always for want of conscience (for that is what the absence of right judgment, true culture, and broad sensibility amounts to in matters involving personal responsibility), took pleasure in ridiculing, with polished skepticism, every genuinely Italian literary expression: or, when ridicule was out of the question, took similar pleasure in hedging on their dutiful concession of meager praise by searching breathlessly to discover, as a necessary justification, where, why, and to what extent—granted it was a beautiful thing, a beautiful comedy, for example—we might at least consider it somewhat French . . . or, if French is really out of the question, at least somewhat German, or, desperately, for want of anything better, at least somewhat English; there! for it is always possible to detect a Shakespearean influence whenever there is an elevation of tone in any of our theatrical works, beginning with those of the fifteenth and sixteenth centuries, which Shakespeare—fortunately for him—knew so well. Well worth his knowing! And were they not also familiar to Molière, and Calderon, and Lope de Vega? Vivacious, loquacious, bursting with strange and picaresque experiences just then gained in an adventuresome world all their own, they revealed all their secrets to extremely attentive ears. . . .

But we must not anticipate. It might be worthwhile, first of all, to recall a point of fact, which is, in fact, a point of time.

The European Theater is not really as old as, in its confused totality, it may appear to one who neglects to verify the chronology of his facts. The medieval Theater is, for a long stretch of time, a desert in which every now and then, instead of an oasis of life, we may come upon, at most, some tiny place where the only vestiges of human existence are a few squalid tombs— never a mausoleum. What I mean is, there is actually nothing for centuries, and when, at rare intervals, we do find something, it is a stillborn babe. There was much talk, at one time, about the poetess-nun Roswitha, as if hers were a living voice coming to us out of that darkness; but, really, even hers is a voice of death, resounding coldly out of a poor shriveled corpse laid to rest in its final peace. Much time has yet to go by before we hear in Italy—while a few learned scholars announce with a thrill of excitement the glorious recovery of Sen-

eca, in the midst of the fresh prattling of the new sweet-
sounding language—a first living voice, a voice that is
no longer artificial, no longer pitched to the timbre of a
sepulchral tradition, a voice from human hearts overflowing with emotion, a *present* voice, revealing and
vitalizing an age that appears to us inhabited, at long
last, by a new people, moving with ease in the intimacy
of their homes, at work, in their fields, gathered together
to pray in their churches. And indeed it seems as if
the world of man were revived in an act of prayer of
boundless gratitude for the beautiful sun of Italy that
warms and illuminates it. The place where for the first
time Christ finally moves like a living person among
men, a sign of heartfelt faith, a voice of poetry resounding from the heart and no longer a dogmatic
formula mouthed in an already forgotten language, the
place where Christ appears as the first sublime character
of the Theater of the new Christian world, is Italy.
Here the fancy of ingenuous poets makes Him talk,
as a man, with the Madonna, His Mother, and the Saints
—and as He talks with them, all coldness is thawed,
the infinite distance between earth and heaven having
given way.

A great mental deafness has heretofore afflicted our
learned professors of literary history, who presume to
compare the contemporary *mistères* of France— in which
the inner spirit does not yet move or give even the slightest sign of disentangling itself from the abstract rigidity
of medieval intellectualism—with our vitally human
expressions of Umbrian devotion.

Expansive warmth as opposed to sententiousness;
spontaneous turns, ingenuousness of surprise and dis-
coveries as opposed to an almost impassive repetition of
formulas hardly capable of anything other than a slight
variation of words—this is what they should have felt, in
that comparison; they might then have been prevented
from committing so lightheartedly that offense against
truth, that offense against ourselves, which we find in the
so-called impartiality with which, one after the other, in
their textbooks and manuals, they repeat monotonously,
"Contemporaneous with that of the French *mistères* was
the development of our own Umbrian devotions," and
stop there.

The essential vitality of this first dramatic expression
of ours is clearly revealed to us by the way it eventually
develops into the organic complexity of the sacred repre-

sentations of the Passion, or of the Christian legends associated with this or that saint, which are and will remain imperishable artistic monuments of the natural religious birth of the Italian Theater.

It is a rare pleasure to notice how this religious poetry—guided by a sure instinct to appropriate the boldest expressions of dramatic narrative and the purest of the lyric, upon which all truly theatrical language is founded and sustained—from another point of view (that is, with respect to what we might call content), takes nourishment, in its thirst for a human element, from the purest sources, such as seem to conform least with its religious nature but are in fact most suited to give it the warmth and movement of life, and with that, the possibility of art: and for that very reason, a genuine power to uplift human hearts. Having given present-day life to those great Personalities whose acts and feelings it exalts as an example and comfort to men and no longer merely as an abstract exercise in rendering praise, it surrounds them with an assembly of other living personalities of the time, who, in the background of the mythical action, retain their first and last names, their habits, their inner world, and all those limitations that serve to define personalities. The poet thus has discovered for himself the same device of the painter, who, on the altarpiece commissioned of him, depicts his pious patron kneeling in the midst of his family and friends, the curate of the church, the hunting dog, capturing them in gestures and expressions of daily life—the dog barking and frightening the baby, the mother comforting it in her arms, the neighbor anxiously gesturing for silence lest the absorption of the *paterfamilias* in his adoration of the Sacred Images be disturbed; and these Images, alive, breathing the same air, but not otherwise embodied or dressed than the human figure, glow nevertheless with greater beauty, nobility, and grace. This alone distinguishes them from the figures drawn from life, raises them above the others, guards them against all earthly baseness, in an aura of happiness that seems to derive from their own surpassing beauty—the only evidence the artist is now able to supply of their divine essence.

It is the bursting forth of life within a confining pattern. The professor of literature—his own mind a series of rigid patterns—will see in all this nothing more than naïveté, absence of logic, crudeness; and to spare himself the subtle irritation of things not understood, he will dismiss them as "crude aspects of popular art," to discourse leisurely, instead, on the "regular forms," those aspects of culture where one may hope to find more seriousness, a greater sense of responsibility.

But, alas, the Italian Theater is not a field for professors of literary history. Incredible as it may sound, they do not succeed in understanding even the "regular forms," as they call them. For these forms, although deriving, for tragedy, from classical imitation of Seneca (and later, with the Greek renaissance, from imitation of Aeschylus, Sophocles, and Euripides), and for comedy, from Plautus and Terence, nevertheless—how shall I say?—can hardly be called serious: they, too, insist on exposing themselves to the contamination of life, and with the same crude arrogance of the sacred representations force their classical pattern to accommodate a mass of characters never encountered before, dangerously uneducated, involved in the strangest intrigues.

The evidence is irresistible: both the sacred representation and the imitation of Classical Theater, both popular art and cultured art, have inexplicably absorbed something that seems made of air, and inflates them, and makes new characters breathe in them.

What can it be?

But it's obvious: it is our very life, newly conceived; our new substance, unadulterated and altogether original; our new life as it appears in the tales of Boccaccio.

It is the spirit of romance.

The Italian Theater could not have originated otherwise than by absorbing this spirit of romance, already alive in another of our literary forms, which had become, one might say, a daily household reality among us. But we must insist: among us only; as we must also insist that the European Theater at this time is still something far off, yet to come. And this is understandably so, for even the European Theater, when it arrives, will have as its sole substance that same spirit of romance, which is *ours*, undeniably *ours;* and it will have to wait for our Theater to provide it.

Try to imagine what this spirit of romance must have meant to a world grown incapable of detaching itself from intellectual concepts. It meant life; it meant liberation from the tyranny of a mind grown subtle, made constantly more pointed, abstract, and dry by its mania for logical distinctions. Opening the heart to the spirit of romance will be like depriving logic of voice and passing it on to the imagination. And thus we see men of sheer intellect rediscovering that they have senses: legs that can carry them to far-off countries, and eyes and ears with which to see and hear true and strange and wholly unexpected things, which discourage any attempt to probe for syllogisms and must be drawn simply for what they are—adventures. So many adventures! How complicated human affairs have suddenly become! If we remember the sort of complications—intellectual complications—that until then men had been used to, we realize at once the reason for that farrago of interconnected, entangled, crowded happenings of the sacred representations, which leave us almost breathless.

Now, it is in Italy, in the tales of Boccaccio, that this spirit of romance manifests itself for the first time as wholly free, content within itself, heedless of all else. To provide the impetus for the modern Theater, to become a suitable leaven for such a development, it had first to discard completely all its cold traits of intellectualistic exemplarism (retaining which—and this is a necessary distinction—even if present elsewhere, as in the French *fabliaux,* that spirit could serve no real purpose since it remained merely an instrument of ratiocination). And, having acquired the magic of life in its objective reality through the creative genius of the great Boccaccio—true father *ante literam* of the humanistic renaissance in the still medieval European world—it had next to find someone to lift and carry it, in its entirety, from the *novella* (which is like the mirror of one solitary consciousness placed before another, silent, consciousness, that of the reader) into the Theater—that is, into the midst of social life, which by its very nature is bound to respect all conventions, including literary ones. It is natural for such emancipation to take place first in isolated individuals, in those of keener sensibilities, while society as a whole is still tied down by its ancient rules and, though secretly desiring it, fears all that is new, believing itself incapable of controlling it, should it accept such novelty in its midst. Who will take on the task? Who will accomplish, with the Theater, this decisive test of strength?

Italian society, with the Italian Theater.

It will come into being as soon as it is possible and *insofar* as it is possible to represent in action, without

narrative supports and before popular audiences, those
new, thoroughly human, and romantic adventures that
already were being felt in our midst, above all among
the common people. This change takes place among us as
a spontaneous and happy one, on a popular level. Once
it has taken place, the task is accomplished: everyone
now can see how it is done. And the European Theater
has been shown the way.

The germ and many of the subsequent stages of
growth of the modern European Theater are already
present in our sacred representations.

Among us, the discovery brings, from the very first
moment, such a sense of relief that we feel an impulse to
be humorous even in the company of saints; and the
comic is freely introduced into the sacred representations.
The lesson will be used to advantage by Shakespeare,
later.

Divine providence—called thus so long as it governed
every detail of a life incapable of movement—relaxes
the chains of its absolute governance, reveals itself often
enough as chance, blindly agitating mortal creatures,
and as fortune, thrusting them into all sorts of adventures; and only in the happy or tragic ending of the
representation does it come again to be considered the
polar star by whose light—but as an afterthought only—
a moral is drawn regarding all that has happened among
these people left thus almost entirely on their own,
guided in their conduct by natural ethics rather than
precepts, by sentiments rather than the constraints of
reverential fear. Lope and Calderon will make use of
all this to give vigor and movement and human excitement to their religious dramas.

Considering the importance of the result attained,
the time required will not seem excessive: with the
sacred representation, we find ourselves beyond the
second half of the fifteenth century, well into the sixteenth; and yet the suggestive power of expression in
these masterworks of ours, the sheer intensity of their
tragic and lyric motifs, still retain the ingenuous freshness of the beginning. Indeed, that same spirit of romance out of which they were born made possible, two
centuries later, an almost miraculous revival in them,
or rather a second flowering, of our fourteenth century.
It is a new test. And interestingly enough, many who
rely more on the promptings of their own sensibilities
than on dates take them actually to be works of the

fourteenth century; while some learned scholar who, instead, relies heavily on dates and external evidence will begin to suspect that the ingenuous, frank representation of Saint Uliva, which enchanted and edified us all a short time ago, might well be a late work—as late, perhaps, as the sixteenth century. He is probably right; but so are we in saying: fourteenth century.

In the light of this esthetic intuition, which for me is beyond all doubt and which rests, after all, on abundant factual evidence, we can assert with complete conviction that the culminating outburst of the Theater, in all Europe, in the seventeenth century—Shakespeare in England, Lope and Calderon in Spain, Molière in France —is a direct outgrowth of the Italian matrix. Molière alone was frank enough to admit: *"je prends mon bien où je le trouve,"* in answer to those who remarked that perhaps he had gone too far in appropriating not only situations and characters but entire scenes from our *commedia dell'arte;* and he was right in shrugging off such remarks, considering the narrow point of view reflected in them. The truth is that all these great authors, these originators of the European Theater, had appropriated—without being aware of it—something quite different: the very spirit of our Theater.

That Theater seemed to them to be the only original and living form of expression from which one could take his bearings; just as today, of all the works of that time, only theirs seem original to us. A perfectly natural attitude, then as now, for the awareness of originality is much clearer, much more compelling in connection with foreign works; while a much more cultivated taste is required to recognize it in our own writings, in which the greater their originality, the more unassuming their appearance. To those on familiar terms with them they seem perfectly natural and not especially noteworthy. Do we ever make a fuss over the plain, ordinary drinking water we use every day? But no sooner do we move to another town, and water, than we notice the change in taste. Now, the specialist in literary history ought to be able to distinguish it with unerring precision; he should have, in other words, an esthetic taste so cultivated as to enable him to recognize, in the unassuming plainness that seems so natural, the vital originality of certain works. And should he have the good fortune of discovering such a work in his own backyard, so to speak, he ought to publicize it, acknowledging its true value and

studying carefully the things around it, both near and
far, to determine just how, where, and when its appearance changed and directed subsequent artistic activity.

Reputations have first of all to be established at
home. And that of the Italian Theater suffers from the
fact that those who first concerned themselves with it
failed, from the very outset, to recognize the new values
which that Theater was bringing into the world. Attention was regularly diverted from those works, as being
merely "popular," that is, of no account (on the basis of
God only knows what distorted values and tasteless prej-
udices); and there was chronic complaining over the
alleged ruin wrought by classical imitation in what the
professors call the "regular" forms—forms which, on
the contrary, immediately expanded to admit the popular
element, so that they too absorbed and made their own
the spirit of romance, reflecting all the contingent interests of the society of the time. The very trunkline of
our Theater was thus neglected; as a consequence, its
history must be retraced from the beginning, in order to
credit it with the enormous importance it once had
and still has.

What was missed, to be perfectly clear, was the very
essence of the development of our Theater.

Why, and how, does the *Commedia dell'arte* come
into being?

The assignment of so much weight—so much crushing
weight—to the imitations of Latin and Greek models in
order to justify a hasty and utterly stupid condemnation
of them (a condemnation by no means applicable solely
to the products of the Italian Theater) served, on the
one hand, merely to conceal the true value of what was
lively and timely in those classicizing works, and, on
the other, to give a semblance of authority to that
paradoxical notion that, of all people, we who had re-
discovered the humanistic spirit in the recovered masterpieces of the classical world had made use of these only
as literary models and academic exercises. Nothing of
the sort ever happened, except in the minds of our professors of literary history. Classical forms had anything
but a stifling effect on Poliziano's *Orfeo;* Buonarroti the
Younger remained untouched by them in his teeming
and popularesque *Fiera* and *Tancia;* while that spirited
rough hewer of types and scenes, Giovan Maria Cecchi,
and the great Machiavelli in that masterpiece which is

the *Mandragola* (*The Mandrake*), profited greatly from a liberal use of those forms, as Aretino also did, and Ariosto, whose *Negromante* should be considered, in the final analysis, not as a descendant of those Latin models but as the primogenitor of *Tartuffe* and *Rabagas;* until, finally, the boundless, irrepressible humor of Giordano Bruno's *Candelaio* altogether shattered them, preannouncing the coming of romanticism—and all this in the course of little more than a century. But in those same sixteenth and seventeenth centuries an entirely different current of popular Theater was also running its course. There, by the side of a nobleman like Alioni d'Asti, who observes and describes in his farces the manners of the lower classes, or the *litterati* of the Neapolitan court, who do the same in their farces about the people of Cava de' Tirreni, we begin to run into the type of theatrical personality who is at once author, actor, and producer of comic works: Ruzzante, first and foremost, whose works, translated into French by Mortier, won new acclaim a few years ago through the efforts of Jacques Copeau; the Sienese artisans of the *Accademia dei Rozzi,* celebrated for their rustic farces, which they were invited to perform at the court of Ferrara as well as that of the Pope; the Neapolitan school of comedy, out of which a little later came the remarkable production of Antonio della Porta; the Venetian Andrea Calmo, who began to introduce local dialects in his many comedies; finally, Andreini, who tours half of Europe with his famous troupes and, gifted with a solid talent and high ambitions, writes, in addition to licentious farces, sacred dramas of vast design.

The *Commedia dell'arte* emerged, little by little, precisely from theatrical personalities such as these, who, as actors, knew the pulse of the public and, as authors, also indulged their own personal tastes and ambitions: thus Ruzzante was drawn, for example, to the naïve world of the fields, while Colmo was attracted by that crucible of races and interests that was Venice. But they were also well acquainted with the output of the *litterati,* and as producers took out options on those works, performing them with their own, or revising them to suit their purposes. It is absurd to imagine in this an accidental discovery of mere actors. Anyone having even the slightest acquaintance with the way an actor works on stage, with the precise directions he requires if he is to take a step to the right instead of the left, will readily see that the idea of improvising their performances could never have occurred to actors.

The *Commedia dell'arte* is born, on the contrary, out of authors who are so deeply involved in the Theater, in the life of the Theater, as to become, in fact, actors; who begin by writing the comedies they later perform, comedies at once more theatrical because not written in the isolated study of the man of letters but in the presence, as it were, of the warm breath of the public; who then take up the task of adapting for their own performance and that of their troupe the comedies of other authors, old and new, in order to supply the pressing need for repertory, constantly revising these adaptations, after having tried out on their audiences the effectiveness of certain flourishes added as an outlet and vehicle for the particular talents of some actor of the company. And as their fellow actors gradually become skilled in keeping up the already-familiar repartee of the middle episodes, they will write only the exits and the outline of the action.

In other words those authors must have lost all their serious artistic pretensions: the transitory, impassioned life of the Theater must have taken such full possession of them that the only interest left to them was that of the spectacle itself—a complete absorption in the quality of the performance and communication with the audience.

They are no longer authors; but they are no longer even actors, in the true sense of the word.

What are they, then?

By now each one of them has become a *type*, with a completely defined stage life of its own; so that finally a theatrical convention is established whereby with ten of them, ten such types—no more, no less—a complex and varied spectacle can be put on that will provide full satisfaction for the audience—an audience already familiar with these conventions, with the rules of the game, and passionately interested in how their favorites carry on, how far each succeeds in giving prominence to his part.

And where do these types come from?

That ancient ambition of authorship which had spurred Ruzzante, for example, to write his bitter comedies gradually wore itself down, turning from the creation of an entire comedy to the creation, or rather to the recopying of one of its characters, that of the country bumpkin, at once simple and shrewd: Zanni. And this figure thus made his entrance into a world no longer his own; out of his natural element, he found himself, still in his characteristically tight-fitting clothes, on the bare boards of a stage during the performance . . . of a comedy about somebody else! One by one the rest of these figures, or—at this point—the rest of these types, found themselves on the same stage in the same predicament. And the comedies from which they had come were also all there together on that stage: all . . . and none. For, that passionate love of the Theater that wanted to see them all exhibited there together had dried up their vital sap, thus destroying their form. What remained, concentrated in those types, was their sheer movement.

It was now a question of reducing all these movements into some kind of order. These various types, each distinguished by its unmistakable dress and speech—here, with Zanni, is Pantalon de' Bisognosi, and with them, the terrible Capitano, and Arlecchino and Brighella and Doctor Balanzon and the little maidservant and the pining sweetheart and the gallant cavalier—had now to be assigned a role in some sort of intrigue within a more or less logical pattern of development which the classical forms, long emptied of their content, easily provided.

It is impossible to conceive of greater contempt for the classical literary world on the part of those who first brought it to light, those same people whose creative powers—the professors of literary history would have us believe—were paralyzed and suffocated, with regard to the Theater, precisely by imitation of those models.

We who recovered from them what was living and restored it to the world were also the ones who, very early, transformed their characters into types so that the labor of sterile imitation might not be prolonged *ad infinitum*: transformed into types, they continued to provide entertainment—for us and for the entire world.

Only Italy, with its Theater, can thus boast of having drained the recovered classical world of all that it had to offer.

Because of the exceptional skill of its traveling comics (the so-called *improvvisi*), the *Commedia dell'arte*—which, as we have seen, was perhaps a more vulgar and practical, perhaps a quicker and more prudent way, certainly a more decisive way, of profiting from all the material of classical comedy (something which the literary writers, in other ways and for other reasons, were themselves striving for)—enjoyed universal acclaim and throughout that entire period was regarded, outside of Italy, as synonymous with the Italian Theater itself. Meanwhile, perhaps to console somewhat the professors of literary history, Tasso was creating that admittedly Italian but also undeniably literary genre: the pastoral drama. In it, those who cannot feel the power of the Theater may enjoy themselves at leisure with the harmony of the verse and other such charms and, after much waiting, may expect as much of quite another kind of esthetic enjoyment from the delicately ornate dramas of Metastasio, where, one cannot resist saying, the poetry is genuine enough and superabundant, but the Theater has slipped out through the service entrance.

With the *Commedia dell'arte*, on the contrary, our Theater led the way—in France, especially, but also in England and Spain. It emerged triumphant in its aggressive vitality wherever the local Theater, not having covered the same course as ours, still lingered in pure and simple imitation of those classical models that we already had reconsidered, and struggled vainly to infuse new life into those very forms that we, instead, had rid ourselves of, to experiment freely and impetuously with all the theatrical movement that could be gotten from them.

In life, a spirit of romance; in the Theater, a sense of movement.

This was the definitive and timely lesson that our Theater offered the European Theater; nor can we complain of the students who made use of it. Shortly thereafter, we find among the graduates of that same school our own Goldoni.

Here, too, our literary histories seem to be apologizing that the Italian Theater, having reached at last the possibility of bringing forth a great author, should have given us, with Goldoni, simply a minor version of Molière.

Here again we have failed to recognize the novelty and originality of our own native works. Goldoni is rightly celebrated, of course, for having relaxed the rigidity of the masks in their strained and artificial laughter and for having reanimated the now flexible muscles of the human face with the natural laughter of a life caught in the midst of the most vivacious and, at the same time, most exquisite and incomparably graceful activity. But the vitality of his creations, entrusted for all time to the first direct and natural language ever to be spoken on the stage, does not spring from the fact that he has given new form, human form, to the movement of masks and types of the *Commedia dell'arte;* that had been marvelously done by both Shakespeare and Molière. That effort had transformed types into characters. And we will never discover the true Goldoni if we fix our attention on the characters that, according to the fashion of the time, he too tried to create—the good-natured boor, the grumbler, the miser, etc. They are indeed marvelous; but in the comedies in which they appear as protagonists the truly great new author reveals himself, on the contrary, in the subordinate characters, one of whom—the little housemaid, for example—suddenly becomes, like Mirandolina, the center of a comedy of her own; and many others come forward, en masse, to stand there and bicker freely in the streets of Chioggia.

What has happened?

Simply this: the Theater has taken, unexpectedly, such a long leap forward that it can hardly believe it, and for a time, beginning with Gozzi, it will try, in its confusion, to turn back.

Goldoni has transcended "character," and has seized —with an unapproachable facility, with an astounding lightness of touch—all the volubility, the fluidity, the contradiction, the spontaneity of life in action, and has thus, with the stroke of a magic wand, opened the way for the contemporary Theater to come streaming forth out of the massive rock in which the "characters" of the seventeenth century had been rough-hewn, not yet great, as they appear to us now, but simply big.

At this point, having seen how false it is to hold that the Italian Theater before Goldoni was simply a desert or cemetery, and having touched briefly upon (what surely deserves a fuller discussion) the true greatness of Goldoni's genius, which is far greater than we Italians as a rule acknowledge it to be, I would like to talk about the grave sin we commit in allowing such riches to lie inert and forgotten—riches which, if taken up boldly with a revitalizing spirit altogether legitimate in the Theater, would constitute our glory and prestige in this field.

The Theater is not archaeology. Unwillingness to take up old works, to modernize and streamline them for fresh production, betrays indifference, not praiseworthy caution. The Theater *welcomes* such modernization and has profited by it throughout those ages when it was most alive.

The original text remains intact for anyone who may want to reread it at home, for his own edification; those who want to be entertained by it will go to the Theater, where it will be put on for them rid of those portions that have lost their freshness, brought up to date where its language is outworn, readapted to the tastes of today.

Why is this legitimate?

Because in the Theater a work of art is no longer the work of the writer (which, after all, can always be preserved in some other way), but an act of life, realized on the stage from one moment to the next, with the cooperation of an audience that must find satisfaction in it.

If this were realized, we would have tangible proof of all I have said.

And I seem to have said what matters most. At this point it would be a simple task for me to indicate what approach to follow in building up—after Goldoni, down to our own time—the living repertory of the Italian Theater; but I don't think it would serve any purpose to spend further energy illustrating my premise with additional arguments—reaffirming, in other words, that even when this Theater of ours came under the influence of the foreign Theater, and especially the French, our productions yet stand out, in contrast with those others, in their greater realism and their greater fidelity to life; that there emerged, as in the *Commedia dell'arte*, regional characters and forms of expression—Milan or Venice, Piedmont or Naples or Sicily—by means of which our theatrical productions, too, move in the great current of that constant reaction against intellectualism that is, after all, one of the greatest contributions of our genius to civilization; that, finally, after the long quest of the last century, the movement of our new Theater led happily and suddenly to the discovery of a virgin field, particularly suited to our dramatic talent, and found a true voice for the expression of new conflicts, abandoning all psychological study or indulgence, all normative aims, in order to realize without further ado the direct and free expression of those genuine emotions that are present and striving in the soul of every man, without fear of the contradictions that prevail in the emotional life, in the imagination, and in the will —contradictions that, until then, had been scrupulously avoided as incapable of being assimilated within the moral and esthetic integrity of the character. Out of this came, indirectly, the most caustic criticism of contemporary society ever articulated by writers of any age. It was nothing less than an illumination of the psychological state of man in our time; and it was recognized at once as characteristic and true, not only of the Italian soul, but also of our universal culture, in all those countries of the world that share in it. This explains the expansive force of the new Italian Theater, which has brought substance and spirit back into the work of so many European and American dramatists, directing their art to that vast virgin world of the unexplored life of human personality: something for which the creative artists of our time evidently must have felt a pressing need, since with the first suggestion provided by our creative, original Italians, those others—almost to a man—have turned to confront that world with the most varied means and from the most diverse spiritual points of view.

THE PLAYS

Bernardo Dovizi da Bibbiena

THE FOLLIES OF CALANDRO

(Calandria)

The Follies of Calandro was one of the first prose comedies in Italian, and the first Italian comedy, in prose or verse, to achieve a wide popularity. But it is interesting for other reasons as well. In the characters of Polinico, the foolish pedant, and Ruffo, the magician-swindler, Bibbiena created types that were to become familiar fixtures of the genre that came to be known as *commedia erudita*—comedy based on Latin models. The influence of *The Follies of Calandro* can be traced in at least seven important Italian Renaissance comedies (Ariosto's *I Suppositi*, Aretino's *Il Marescalco*, Machiavelli's *The Mandrake*, Giancarli's *La Cingara*, Groto's *Alteria*, Belo's *Pedante*, and the anonymous *The Deceived*) as well as in the Elizabethan comedies for which some of these served as models, like Gascoigne's *Supposes* and Jonson's *Silent Woman*.

Bibbiena's own sources were Plautus' *Menaechmi* and Boccaccio's *Decameron*. From the former he took the central situation, changing the sex of one of the twins, and from the latter the character of Calandro, whose name is a variant of Calandrino, the foolish husband who appears in Volume II. (Such was the popularity of

Boccaccio's book that by 1512, when Bibbiena presumably wrote his play, the name Calandrino had already come to signify, in the popular language, simpleton.) Other Boccaccian influences are seen in Fulvia's long monologue (III, v), which is an almost word-for-word translation of a speech that Donna Vergellesi utters (Third Day, Fifth Story), and in the incident (III, iii) where Fessenio revenges himself upon Calandro by making him carry the trunk, which is strikingly similar to one related in the Second Story of the Seventh Day.

The author of *The Follies of Calandro*, Bernardo Dovizi da Bibbiena, became in his youth the secretary of Cardinal Giovanni dei' Medici. He early showed signs of political astuteness, and his maneuverings are said to have been chiefly responsible for the election of his master to the Papal throne in 1513 as Leo X. Leo rewarded him by making him Papal Treasurer and, a few months later, a cardinal. It is difficult to exaggerate the power he wielded in these capacities ("He is the Pope," wrote Mario Equicola in 1513), and he was intimately acquainted with most of the artists and literary men then in Rome, an extraordinarily brilliant group which included Raphael (whose portrait of him hangs in the Pitti Gallery), Michelangelo, and Baldassare Castiglione, author of *The Courtier*. He died rather mysteriously in 1520: there was a rumor, probably unfounded, that Leo himself, resentful of his popularity, had had him poisoned.

The Follies of Calandro was written when its author was forty-two, just before he took up residence in Rome with his patron. It was given a most spectacular first performance at the court of Urbino on February 6, 1513. Castiglione arranged the details of the production, even writing the prologue himself when the one sent by Bibbiena—who was away on a diplomatic mission—failed to arrive in time for the actor to memorize it. (Castiglione's is the better of the two, and appears in most editions instead of the author's own.) The sets were painted by the court artists (Timoteo Viti and Girolamo Genga); there were concealed singers and musicians; and the hall was hung with garlands and with candelabra constructed specially for the occasion. Four *intermezzi*, consisting of elaborately staged ballets on mythological subjects, separated the five acts; and at the end of the performance a Cupid recited verses explaining their allegorical significance.

The following year, when Isabella d'Este Gonzaga of Mantua visited Rome, Leo X gave the play an almost equally lavish production upon his private stage in the Vatican, with sets by Baldassare Peruzzi. Two other notable performances of it occurred in the winter of 1520 at the court of Mantua, with Castiglione once more in charge, and in 1548 at the court of Henry II, King of France, and Catherine dei' Medici.

For his indispensable assistance in translating this play, I wish to thank Professor Rufus S. Crane, Jr., of the Romance Languages Department of St. Mary's College, South Bend, Indiana.

O. E.

THE FOLLIES OF CALANDRO

(1513)

Bernardo Dovizi da Bibbiena

ENGLISH VERSION WITH NOTES BY OLIVER EVANS

Characters

LIDIO, *an adolescent youth*
SANTILLA, *his sister*
FANNIO, *servant to Santilla*
FESSENIO, *servant to Lidio*
POLINICO, *a teacher*
CALANDRO
FULVIA, *his wife*
SAMIA, *maid to Fulvia*
TIRESIA, *maid to Santilla*
RUFFO, *a magician*
SOFILLA, *a prostitute*
A PORTER
CUSTOMS OFFICIALS
BROTHERS TO FULVIA

THE PROLOGUE

by Baldassare Castiglione

Today you will be the spectators of a new comedy, called *Calandria*, written not in verse but in prose; not in Latin but in Italian; not ancient but modern. Calandria comes from Calandro, a character whom you will discover to be such a fool that you will find it hard to believe him one of nature's creations. But if you have seen or heard of similar things (especially concerning Martin of Amelia, who believed the star Diana to be his wife and himself Amen, able at will to become a woman, a god, a fish, or a plant), then it will not seem strange to you that Calandro is so credulous and does so many stupid things.

Depicting, as this play does, things commonly said and done, its author has thought it best not to use verse: remember therefore that he is speaking to you in words that are free and natural. That it is not ancient should displease no one of healthy taste, since things that are new are always pleasing and delight an audience more than things which, seen so often, have become flat and stale. The reason it is not in Latin is that the author, desirous of pleasing you to the utmost and wishing for himself as large an audience as possible—since not everyone is a scholar—wished therefore to write it in Italian, so that, understood by everyone, it would be enjoyed by everyone: besides which, the language given us by nature and by God ought not to be less esteemed among us than Latin, Greek, or Hebrew, compared with which ours would not be inferior if we would only exalt, obey, and polish it with the same diligent care as the Greeks and other ancients. That man must be reckoned an enemy who esteems another language over his own. I know well that my own is so dear to me that I

35

would not exchange it for all the other languages now in use: I believe you are of the same sentiment. Therefore you should be pleased to hear the play spoken in your own language—or rather, in our language, not yours, for it is we who will do the talking and you who must be quiet.

As for those who will claim that the author has stolen certain things from Plautus, we shall say merely that Plautus deserves to be robbed, the snot-nose, for leaving his things to the world without either a key or a watchman. The author swears upon the holy cross, however, that he has not stolen so much as this (*snapping his fingers*) from Plautus and wishes to be compared with him in his own right. Anyone who doubts this can look up Plautus' works; he will find that nothing is missing from them. If that is the case, and Plautus has not been robbed, then no one can say that the author is a thief. And if someone should be so stubborn as to insist that he is, we pray that at least he will not curse him openly, threatening him with the Bargello, but that he will go and whisper it secretly into Plautus' ear.

Now here is the man who will recite the argument of the play; prepare to give him your very closest attention by opening wide the cavities of your ears.

THE ARGUMENT

Demetrius, citizen of Modone,* had a son named Lidio and a daughter named Santilla. They were twins, so similar in form and appearance that they could not be distinguished except for their clothes: this you will not find hard to believe, for, among the many such examples that we could cite, it is sufficient to mention those highborn Roman brothers, Antonio and Valerio Porcari, who were so similar that everybody in Rome mistook the one for the other.

As for our own twins, they have been fatherless since they were six: the Turks seized and burned Modone, killing anyone they found in the streets. Their nurse and their manservant, Fannio, in order to save Santilla, dressed her as a boy and called her Lidio; they believed her brother had been massacred by the Turks. Leaving Modone, they were captured and sent as prisoners to Constantinople, where they were rescued by a Florentine

* In Greece.

merchant named Perillo, who took the three of them to
Rome and installed them in his house, where, over the
years, they picked up the local language and customs.
And now Perillo wants to give his daughter in marriage
to Santilla, whom everyone calls Lidio and believes to be
a boy.

The real Lidio, her brother, escaped alive from Modone with his manservant, Fessenio. Coming to Italy,
he settled in Tuscany, where he too learned the language
and customs. When he was nearly eighteen, he came
to Rome, where he fell in love with, and was loved by,
a married woman named Fulvia. In order to accomplish
his purpose with her, he frequently visited her in female
dress. After many mishaps, Lidio and Santilla finally
learn each other's identity. Take care now, open well
your eyes so as not to mistake the one for the other, for
I warn you that both are of the same size and general
appearance; both are called Lidio; both dress, speak,
and laugh alike; both are in Rome today; and presently
both of them are going to appear before you. Don't imagine, however, that they have come here* from Rome,
so quickly by means of witchcraft: this platform *is* Rome,
which, when it was in its glory, was so large that it
contained many cities, towns, and rivers; but now it is
so reduced in size that, as you see, it fits comfortably
into our own city. And so it is with everything that was
once great and powerful.

ACT I

Scene I

Fessenio, *alone.*

Fessenio.   How true it is that man makes one plan and
    fortune makes another for him! Just when we thought
    we were quietly settled in Bologna, my master Lidio
    learned that his sister Santilla was alive and in Italy,
    and immediately his love for her was revived—a
    love stronger than ever brother felt toward sister,
    since, being twins, they were so alike in appearance,

* Urbino was the site of the first production of the play in
the early spring of 1513.

in speech, and in manner that at Modone, if Lidio
were dressed as a little girl and Santilla as a little
boy, their own mother and nurse could not tell them
apart, let alone strangers. God Himself could not have
made them more alike, and it was only natural that
each should love the other more than himself. Therefore Lidio, who had thought his sister dead, has now
set out to find her. Four months ago, coming to Rome
to look for her, he met the Roman lady Fulvia and
fell in love with her. So as to have his way with her,
he had her husband Calandro hire me as a servant,
and with her consent I immediately arranged it so
that the lovers could meet whenever they wished by
having Lidio visit her dressed as a woman answering
to the name of Santilla. But lately, fearful that they
should be discovered, he has shown himself increasingly neglectful of her, and pretends that he wants to
leave Rome. Fulvia is so upset about this that she can
scarcely control herself, and has been consulting
soothsayers and magicians; she has come to me about it,
and has even sent her maid, Samia, who is in her confidence, to Lidio with prayers, with gifts, and with
promises to give her son in marriage to his sister,
should Lidio succeed in finding her. All of this has
been done so openly that if her husband were not
more of a sheep than a man he would have known
about it long ago—in which case I would have had
to take all the blame: it's a good thing that I know
how to take care of myself. I am in an impossible
position: it's bad enough to serve two masters, and
I am trying to serve three—tne husband, the wife, and
my own master. I never have a moment's rest. Oh,
well, I don't mind too much: a man who has nothing
to do is as good as dead, and if it is true that a good
servant is never idle, why then I am the best, for I
never even have time to clean my ears. And speaking
of Lidio, here he comes with Polinico, his teacher.
When you see a dolphin, as the saying goes, you
know a storm is brewing. I am going to step aside
a moment and listen to what they are saying.

Scene II

Polinico, Lidio, Fessenio.

Polinico.   I never would have thought, Lidio, that you

would waste your time on idle love affairs. You are
becoming an utterly worthless person, and I blame
it all on that rascal Fessenio.

Fessenio (*apart*). Aha!

Lidio. You shouldn't say that, Polinico.

Polinico. Ah, Lidio, I am wiser than you and that
wretched servant of yours.

Fessenio (*apart*). We shall see about that.

Polinico. A prudent man always thinks of what may
happen in the future.

Fessenio (*apart*). Here we go with the lessons again.

Polinico. Should this affair of yours become known,
you would not only be in danger of your life but
would lose the respect of everybody.

Fessenio (*apart*). Stupid pedagogue!

Polinico. Nobody has any use for a playboy. And to
think that you have been carrying on with one of the
most respected women in our city! Take my advice,
Lidio, and get out of it before it is too late.

Lidio. Polinico, I am young, and young people have
always been ruled by love; older people can afford to
think of more serious things. I must do as love commands, and it has bidden me to love the lady Fulvia
even more than I love myself. And I believe that many
people, even if they knew, would not hold it against
me, for, just as it is a sign of common sense in a
woman not to love a man in a higher position, so it
is a sign of merit in a man to love a lady of higher
birth than himself.

Fessenio (*approaching*). Well said, my master.

Polinico. These are arguments that you have learned
from that miserable Fessenio.

Fessenio. You are the miserable one.

Polinico (*to* Fessenio). Actually I'd be surprised if you
didn't try to spoil the good things that people try to
do.

Fessenio. I'm not planning to spoil anything of yours.

Polinico. Nothing is worse than to see the lives of
wise men governed by the sayings of fools.

Fessenio. I have always given him better advice than
you.

Polinico. No one can give good advice who has bad
habits. If I had known you better, Fessenio, I would
not have recommended you so highly to Lidio.

Fessenio. Did I ever ask you for any favors?

Polinico. Now I know that when a man praises another

he is often deceived; when he criticizes another, he
never is.

Fessenio. The more fool you, for praising someone
you did not know well. For my part, I know that when
I speak of you I am never wrong.

Polinico. Have you spoken evil of me?

Fessenio. You have spoken evil of yourself.

Polinico. I must be patient. I am not going to argue
with you; it would be like shouting at the thunder.

Fessenio. You won't because you know you are in the
wrong.

Polinico. I am trying to avoid other means besides
words.

Fessenio. And what harm could you ever do to me in
a hundred years?

Polinico. Never mind, never mind. You would soon
find out.

Fessenio. My, my! I'd better be careful. Wild beasts
can be dangerous.

Polinico. I don't want to argue with a servant.

Lidio. That's enough, Fessenio. Come off it.

Fessenio (*to* Polinico). Don't threaten me. I may be
just a servant, but even a fly has his rages, and even the
smallest hair casts its shadow. Do I make myself
clear?

Lidio. Be quiet, Fessenio.

Polinico (*to* Fessenio). Let me continue my conversation with Lidio, if you please.

Fessenio. Oh, he'll do anything for the sake of peace.

Polinico (*ignoring* Fessenio). Lidio, God has given us
two ears so that we can hear well.

Fessenio. And only one mouth, so as not to talk too
much.

Polinico (*to* Fessenio). I am not speaking to you.
(*To* Lidio). A bad habit is easy to cure when it
is new, but not when it has had time to grow old.
Get rid of this passion, I tell you.

Lidio. Why?

Polinico. Ah, me, don't you know that the companions
of love are anger, hatred, enmity, disagreement, ruin,
poverty, suspicion, worry, pernicious diseases in the
souls of men? Avoid love, avoid it.

Lidio. Ah, Polinico, I cannot.

Polinico. And why?

Fessenio. Damn you anyway, with all your whys and
wherefores!

Lidio. Everything is subject to the power of love, and there is no sweetness like that of fulfilling one's desire: without love there is nothing perfect, nothing virtuous, nothing good.

Fessenio. No one could have said it better.

Polinico. There is no greater vice in a servant than flattery. And you, Lidio, do you listen to him? Listen to me instead.

Fessenio. Yes, listen to him; he's such a pretty piece of merchandise.

Polinico. Love is like fire, which, when sulfur or some other vile substance is sprinkled over it, sends off evil odors that suffocate a man.

Fessenio. And when incense, aloes, and amber are sprinkled over it, it makes a fragrance that will revive even the dead.

Lidio. Aha, Polinico is caught in his own trap.

Polinico. Return, Lidio, to what is worthwhile.

Fessenio. What is worthwhile is adjusting to the times.

Polinico. What is worthwhile is what is good and honest. I warn you that this affair is going to turn out badly.

Fessenio. The prophet has spoken!

Polinico. Remember that a virtuous soul is not moved by greed.

Fessenio. Nor discouraged by fear.

Polinico (*to* Fessenio). You also do wrong when you know it is arrogance to ridicule the advice of wise men.

Fessenio. At the same time that you call yourself a wise man you christen yourself a fool: you know there is no folly like that of attempting the impossible.

Polinico. It is better to lose, speaking the truth, than to win telling lies.

Fessenio. I tell the truth as well as you, but I don't go around criticizing everything and everybody the way you do: just because you know a few words of Latin you think everyone except yourself is an idiot. You are not Solomon, you know. You never stop to consider that what is right for an old man may not be right for a young one; that what is right in time of danger may not be right at ordinary times. You, who are old, cling to the kind of life that old men remember, but you must allow Lidio, who is young, to lead the kind of life that is proper for young men nowadays, and adjust yourself to the idea.

Polinico. It is certainly true that the more servants a man has, the more enemies. This fellow will lead you to the gallows, Lidio, and even if you had no other troubles you would always have a remorseful soul, for there is no torture so great as knowing the mistakes that you have made. Therefore leave this mistress of yours.

Lidio. I can no more leave her than a form can leave its shadow.

Polinico. Indeed, it might be better for you to hate her than to leave her.

Fessenio. Oh, oh! He can't even carry a calf and you want him to carry an ox.

Polinico. She will leave you soon enough.

Lidio. Oh, all women are not the same.

Polinico. They may not look the same, but they have the same nature.

Lidio. You are wrong there.

Polinico. Lidio, don't be blind: they are all alike, and you cannot believe one even when she is dead.

Fessenio. Now I am beginning to see the light.

Polinico. What's that?

Fessenio. You are adjusting to the times.

Polinico. I am merely speaking the truth to Lidio. What are you driving at?

Fessenio. I mean that you have made an adjustment to the modern fashion.

Polinico. How so?

Fessenio. In disliking women, as almost everyone at this court does. But when you speak of them in this way, you do them an injustice.

Lidio. Fessenio is right. I cannot approve of what you have said about women; they are the greatest source of goodness and comfort in the world, and without them we would be useless, inadequate, harsh, and like the beasts of the field.

Fessenio. Is it necessary to say all this? Everyone knows that women are so desirable that nowadays all the men go about imitating them and would willingly become women both in body and in soul.

Polinico. Such comments do not deserve a reply.

Fessenio. You mean you can't think of one.

Polinico. Remember, Lidio, that you can still get out of this if you try. For your own good, I beg you once more to do so.

Lidio. Polinico, there is nothing in the world that heeds

advice less than love, whose nature is such that a man
will allow himself to be consumed by it rather than
give it up because someone tells him to. So that if you
try to make me give up this woman it is like trying to
catch a shadow or snare the wind in a net.

Polinico. And this worries me very much. You used to
be as easily molded as wax, and now you are headed
for the worst kind of trouble. You don't know what
this woman is really like, and I warn you once more:
this is all going to end very badly for you.

Lidio. I don't believe it, and even if it were true, haven't
you taught me in your lessons that the man who dies in
love dies happy?

Polinico. Well, I have warned you. Do as you please,
and listen to this jackass instead of me: you will soon
find out the damage that love can cause.

Fessenio. You have said enough, Polinico. Do you know
what damage love causes?

Polinico. What, jackass?

Fessenio. Like a truffle, it causes the fortunes of young
men to rise, and old men to fart.

Lidio. Ha, ha, ha!

Polinico. Ah, Lidio, you laugh about it, and pay no attention to what I am trying to say. Well, I shall leave
you on your own, and go about my business.

           Exit.

Fessenio. What a pity. Did you notice how pious he
pretends to be, as if we didn't know he's the world's
biggest hypocrite? I haven't been able to get a word
in edgewise, and I have good news about Calandro.

Lidio. Let us hear it. It may take some of the sting out
of Polinico's words.

Scene III

Lidio, Fessenio.

Lidio. Well, now, tell me what has been going on.

Fessenio. Fulvia's husband, Calandro—that sheep whom
I pretend is my master and whom you are cuckolding
—seeing you dressed as a woman and calling yourself
Santilla, has been completely taken in and has ap-
proached me to see if I could arrange for you to sleep
with him: I have arranged it for this very evening.

Lidio. Ho, ho! This is really something. And now that
   you mention it I remember that the other day, as I was
   returning from Fulvia dressed as a woman, he followed
   me for a short distance—I never guessed the reason.
   Let's lead him on, shall we?

Fessenio. Leave everything to me. I'll make him think
   I've done miracles for him, and you may be sure he
   will believe everything I tell him. I tell him the wildest
   things in the world and he never once doubts me; he is
   the world's biggest simpleton. I could give you a thousand examples, but to make a long story short I will
   simply say that there is so much nonsense in him that
   a single speck of it, found in Solomon, Aristotle, or
   Seneca, would be sufficient to discredit all the wisdom
   of those men. And the funniest thing of all is that he
   thinks himself so handsome and so charming that he
   imagines every woman who sees him falls in love with
   him, as if he were the most dashing young fellow alive.
   He is such an ox that it wouldn't surprise me to see
   him eat hay, and for this reason it will be easy for us
   to lead him where we like.

Lidio. Ha, ha, ha! I am going to die of laughter. But
   tell me, what's going to happen when he comes up to
   me, thinking I am a woman?

Fessenio. I'll take care of that; leave it to me. But look,
   I see him now, coming our way. Go quickly: he mustn't
   see us together.

Scene IV

Calandro, Fessenio.

Calandro. Fessenio!
Fessenio. Who's calling me? Oh, it's my master.
Calandro. Tell me, what about Santilla?
Fessenio. You say, what about Santilla?
Calandro. Yes.
Fessenio. Well, let's see. . . . I don't know for sure, but
   I think she is wearing a skirt, a blouse, an apron, a
   pair of gloves, and a pair of slippers.
Calandro. You idiot, I don't want to know what she is
   wearing, but how she is.
Fessenio. Oh, I see. You want to know how she is.
Calandro. If you please.

Fessenio. Well, when I saw her a few minutes ago she was . . . wait, let's see . . . she was sitting with her hand up to her chin, listening while I talked to her about you. Her eyes and mouth were wide open, and her little tongue hung out slightly, like this.

Calandro. That's more like it. So she listened willingly, eh?

Fessenio. Indeed she did. And I have prepared her so that before long you will have your wish.

Calandro. Good for you, dear Fessenio.

Fessenio. I hope it will be.

Calandro. Never doubt it. Oh! Fessenio, give me a hand: I'm afraid I don't feel very well.

Fessenio. Why, what's the matter, master? Do you have a fever?

Calandro. No, of course not, stupid. It's Santilla.

Fessenio. Did she hit you?

Calandro. Oh, what a fool you are! I mean I am so much in love that it hurts.

Fessenio. Well, you will soon be with her.

Calandro. What are we waiting for? Let's go to her now.

Fessenio. Not so fast. There are still a few details I have to attend to.

Calandro. All right, but be as quick as you can.

Fessenio. I will; don't worry.

Calandro. Don't forget, now.

Fessenio. I won't. You'll see. (*Exit* Calandro.) Ha, ha, ha! This is quite a situation: both husband and wife are in love with the same person. And now I see Fulvia's servant, Samia, coming out of the house. Something is going on; I can tell by the look on her face. I'll talk to her: she knows everything.

Scene V

Fessenio, Samia.

Fessenio. Samia, Samia, wait a minute!

Samia. Oh, hello, Fessenio.

Fessenio. What's going on inside?

Samia. Nothing that's good for my mistress.

Fessenio. How do you mean?

Samia. She's in a bad way.

Fessenio. Why, what's wrong?

Samia. I'd better not say.

Fessenio. Not say what?

Samia Well, frankly, she's too anxious.

Fessenio. To do what?

Samia. Well . . . to enjoy herself with Lidio. Do I make myself clear?

Fessenio. Oh, I knew that as well as you.

Samia. But there is something else you don't know.

Fessenio. What?

Samia. She is sending me to someone who will make Lidio do as she wishes.

Fessenio. Oh? How will this "someone" make him do that?

Samia. By means of songs.*

Fessenio. Songs?

Samia. Yes, sir.

Fessenio. And who is this musician?

Samia. Who said anything about a musician? I said she was sending me to someone who would make Lidio go back to her, or die in the attempt.

Fessenio. Who is this fellow?

Samia. Ruffo the magician, who will do whatever needs to be done.

Fessenio. How does he do that?

Samia. He has a linguistic spirit.†

Fessenio. You mean a familiar spirit.

Samia. I don't understand all these words. All I'm supposed to do is tell the magician to come to my mistress. Good-bye, and don't tell anyone what I've said.

Fessenio. Don't worry; I won't. Good-bye.

Scene VI

Samia, Ruffo.

Samia. It's too early to catch Ruffo at his dinner; I'd better look in the piazza to see if he's there. Oh, what luck! I see him. Ruffo, Ruffo! Don't you hear me, Ruffo?

Ruffo (*turning around*). I hear someone calling me.

Samia. Ruffo, wait a minute.

* A malapropism involving the similarity between *canti* (songs) and *incanti* (charms).

† Another malapropism involving the similarity between *favellario* (linguistic) and *famigliare* (familiar).

Ruffo.   Who can this woman be?

Samia.   Oh, I am all out of breath.

Ruffo.   Well, what is it?

Samia.   My mistress begs you to go to her right away.

Ruffo.   Who is your mistress?

Samia.   The lady Fulvia.

Ruffo.   Calandro's wife?

Samia.   Yes, sir.

Ruffo.   What does she want from me?

Samia.   She will tell you.

Ruffo.   That's her house over there, isn't it?

Samia.   Yes, it's only a few steps. Shall we go?

Ruffo.   You go ahead and I'll follow. (*Aside.*) Could this be one of the many foolish women who think I am a magician and have a familiar spirit, as they call it? I think I know what she wants, so I'll go to her house before this fellow who is coming this way gets here.

Scene VII

Fessenio, Calandro.

Fessenio.   Now I see that the gods have their jokes as well as human beings: here is love, who is accustomed to dwell in noble hearts, sticking so firmly to this sheep Calandro that it's impossible to dislodge him. He must not have much to do, to visit such a baboon.

Calandro.   Fessenio, oh, Fessenio!

Fessenio.   Who is it? Oh, it's you, my master.

Calandro.   Have you seen Santilla?

Fessenio.   I have.

Calandro.   How do things look?

Fessenio.   You will have your way, and what a morsel! You certainly have good taste. You must do everything you can to win her.

Calandro.   I'll get her, even if I have to go nude and barefoot.

Fessenio (*aside*).   Just listen to this, all you lovers.

Calandro.   If I get her, I shall eat her up.

Fessenio.   Eat her up! Ah, Calandro, have a little pity. Wild beasts may eat one another, but men don't eat women. You're supposed to drink them, not eat them.

Calandro.   Drink them?

Fessenio.   Yes, drink them.

Calandro.   But how?

Fessenio.   Don't you know?

Calandro.   I'm afraid I don't.

Fessenio.   What a pity that a fine-looking fellow like you doesn't know how to drink women.

Calandro.   Come, tell me how.

Fessenio.   All right. When you kiss one, don't you suck her lips?

Calandro.   Yes.

Fessenio.   And when you drink something, don't you suck it also?

Calandro.   Yes.

Fessenio.   Well, then: when you kiss a woman, you suck her lips, so you are drinking her.

Calandro.   It does seem so, and yet I have never drunk Fulvia, though I have kissed her many times.

Fessenio.   Ah, but that's because she was kissing you, too. She was sucking your lips at the same time that you were sucking hers, which is why neither of you was drinking the other.

Calandro.   You are a clever man, Fessenio. It is true that I never once kissed Fulvia without her kissing me in return.

Fessenio.   There, you see?

Calandro.   But tell me. I used to know a Spanish girl who was always kissing my hand: did that mean she wanted to drink it?

Fessenio.   I'll tell you a secret. When a Spanish girl kisses you, it isn't because she loves you; it's because she wants to drink your hands—or rather to suck the rings on your finger.

Calandro.   Fessenio, you know more about women's secrets!

Fessenio (aside).   Especially your woman's.

Calandro.   That Spanish girl drank two rings of mine. I swear before God that from now on I will never let anybody drink me again.

Fessenio.   A wise decision.

Calandro.   And I'll never let anyone kiss me unless I kiss her at the same time.

Fessenio.   Yes, do be careful, because if a girl should ever drink your nose, or one of your cheeks, or an eye, you would be the ugliest man in the world.

Calandro.   I'll be careful, all right. But be sure to fix it so I can sleep with Santilla.

Fessenio.   Leave it to me. I'll bring it off.

Calandro. And be quick about it, won't you?
Fessenio. I'm going to see her now, and I'll be back soon.

Scene VIII

Ruffo, *alone.*

Ruffo. A man should never give up hope: fortune sometimes comes when it is least expected. Fulvia, as I thought, believes I have a familiar spirit. She is passionately in love with a young man, and, every other means having failed, has come to me to see if I can arrange to have him go back to her dressed like a woman. She has promised me money if I can do this, and I think I can because the man she loves is Lidio, a friend of mine from my home town. I also know his servant Fannio, so I shouldn't have too much trouble. But I haven't promised her anything; I wanted to talk with Lidio first. The lady Fulvia can make both our fortunes if things go right. I'll go up to Perillo's house now, where Lidio is staying. It's about dinnertime, so he should be there.

ACT II

Scene I

Santilla as Lidio, Fannio, *a nurse.*

Santilla. Men are certainly more fortunate than women, and I can bear better witness to this than most women: ever since that day when Modone was burned by the Turks and I dressed as a boy and took my brother's name, things have gone very well for me. Whereas if I had let it be known that I was a girl, the Turks would have kept me as a slave and not sold me to Perillo, and perhaps Perillo would not have bought me if he had known I was a girl. And now, because he has always been pleased with my behavior, he wants me to marry his only daughter, whom he plans to leave everything to when he dies. He wants the marriage to take place right away, and therefore I have come to you, nurse, and to you, Fannio, to discuss this thing, which, as you can imagine, causes me some concern.

Fannio. Shh, quiet!—or this woman I see coming toward us will hear.

Scene II

Samia, Santilla *as* Lidio, Fannio.

Samia. My mistress really has it bad. She says she saw Lidio from her window, so she has sent me to talk to him. I'll see if I can draw him aside. Good day, sir.

Santilla. Good day.

Samia. May I have a word alone with you, sir?

Santilla. Who are you?

Samia. You ask me who I am?

Santilla. Naturally, since I don't know.

Samia. Well, you'll find out soon enough.

Santilla. What is it you want?

Samia. My mistress begs you to love her as she loves you and says you are to feel free to come to her whenever you wish.

Santilla. I don't understand. Who is your mistress?

Samia. Ah, Lidio, you want to make fun of me.

Santilla. It is you who are making fun of me.

Samia. It's certainly odd that you pretend not to know either me or my mistress. Come, what shall I say to her?

Santilla. I am not going to answer you until you explain yourself.

Samia. So you don't understand me, eh?

Santilla. I don't understand you; neither do I know you. Nor do I have any desire to. Please be on your way.

Samia. You certainly are discreet. I'll tell her that much.

Santilla. Tell her what you like, as long as you leave me alone. I'm tired of looking at you.

Samia. You are, are you? You miserable Greek, you'll go see my mistress if it costs you your life, because she is sending me to the magician, and his spirit will make you do whatever he wants.

Exit.

Santilla. Ah, me, this only proves what I was saying: sad indeed is the fortune of us poor women! Things like this only serve to make me realize it.

Fannio. I wish we had got more out of her; it couldn't have done any harm.

Santilla. My mind was on something more important. But if she had been more willing to talk, I would have shown myself more willing to listen.

Fannio. I know who she is.

Santilla. Who?

Fannio. The servant of Fulvia, a noble Roman lady.

Santilla. Oh, I know who you mean. And Fulvia is a good name for her.*

Scene III

Ruffo, Santilla *as* Lidio, Tiresia, Fannio.

Ruffo. Hello there!

Santilla. Whose voice is that?

Ruffo. I have been looking everywhere for you.

Fannio. Hello, Ruffo. What is it?

Ruffo. Good news.

Fannio. Let's hear it.

Santilla. Wait a minute. (*To* Tiresia.) Tiresia, go to the house, see what Perillo is doing about this wedding of mine, and when Fannio comes there, send him back to me so I can find out what's going on. Today I am going to keep out of sight: I want to see if there is any truth in the old saying, "As long as there is time, there is hope." Go quickly now. (*Exit* Tiresia.) Now, Ruffo, tell me your good news.

Ruffo. Though I have known you and Fannio only a short time, I have grown quite fond of you. After all, we are from the same home town, aren't we? And now something has come up that can work to our mutual advantage.

Santilla. We are fond of you, too, Ruffo, and will be happy to help if we can. But what is it?

Ruffo. I'll be brief. Lidio, a certain woman has fallen in love with you and wants you to return her love. Other means having proved unsuccessful, she has come to me; this is because, since I know a few tricks and can read palms, I have the reputation among women— you know how credulous they are—of being a magician. They think I have a familiar spirit by means of which I can do or undo anything I want. I have al-

---

* The name Fulvia suggests fire, therefore passion.

lowed them to believe this because sometimes it has
proved both useful and pleasant—as it will in the case
of this woman, if you cooperate. She wants me to
persuade you to go to bed with her, and I, thinking you
would be agreeable to the idea, have given her some
hope. This is all you have to do—it will make us both
rich, and you will have the pleasure of sleeping with
her as well.

Santilla.   Ruffo, this is a pretty tricky business, and as I
have no experience in such things I could easily be
made a fool of. But, because I trust you, I will not say
no at once. I'll think it over and discuss it with Fannio.
But tell me: who is this woman?

Ruffo.   Her name is Fulvia. She's rich, of noble family,
and also beautiful.

Fannio.   Oh! The mistress of that woman we were just
talking to.

Santilla.   Yes, she's the one.

Ruffo.   Her maid spoke to you?

Santilla.   Just a few minutes ago.

Ruffo.   And what did you say?

Santilla.   I sent her away with strong words.

Ruffo.   Too bad. Well, the next time you talk to her you
must be more agreeable, if we are to bring this off.

Santilla.   I will.

Fannio.   Tell me, Ruffo, when would Lidio have to go
to her?

Ruffo.   The sooner the better.

Fannio.   By day or by night?

Ruffo.   By day.

Santilla.   Oh, someone would be sure to see me.

Ruffo.   She has thought of that. She wants me to have
the spirit make him go in the form of a woman.

Fannio.   And what good would he be to the lady Fulvia,
if your spirit changes him into a woman?

Ruffo.   I think she meant dressed like a woman. Anyway,
that's what she said.

Santilla.   How very extraordinary! Don't you think so,
Fannio?

Fannio.   I do indeed. As a matter of fact I like the idea.

Ruffo.   Are we agreed, then?

Santilla.   We'll let you know in just a moment, after
we've talked it over.

Ruffo.   Where shall we meet?

Fannio.   Right here.

Santilla. And whoever comes first will wait for the other.

Ruffo. Good enough. See you soon.

Scene IV

Fannio, Santilla *as* Lidio.

Fannio. This makes it easier for you to keep out of sight today, just as you wanted: no one would think of looking for you at Fulvia's house. And knowing she is a whore, you can buy her silence as often as you please. But what I like best is the humor of the situation. You are a woman, and she wants you to go to her dressed like a woman: thus in satisfying her you will also be disappointing her.

Santilla. Shall we do it?

Fannio. By all means.

Santilla. Very well. Now go home, find out what's going on, get me the necessary clothes, and meet me at Franzino's shop. We'll tell Ruffo we'll do as he says.

Fannio. You'd better go, too. Here comes someone. Maybe Perillo has sent him to look for you.

Santilla. He's not one of our men. But you're right; I mustn't show myself. Good-bye for now.

Scene V

Fessenio, Fulvia.

Fessenio. There's the lady Fulvia over there. I'll go and tell her Lidio is determined to go away, just to see how she takes it.

Fulvia. Welcome, dear Fessenio! Tell me, what news of Lidio?

Fessenio. He doesn't seem to be himself today.

Fulvia. Oh? What's the matter with him?

Fessenio. He's taken it into his head to go look for his sister Santilla.

Fulvia. Ah, me. He wants to leave Rome?

Fessenio. He seems set on it.

Fulvia. Dear Fessenio, if you are interested in your own welfare, or in Lidio's, and if mine means anything

to you, you must urge him, persuade him, beg him not
to leave on this account. I will search all Italy for this
girl, and if we succeed in finding her, I give you my
word that I will give her in marriage to Flaminio, my
only son.

Fessenio. Do you want me to promise him this?

Fulvia. I have given my word, and I will keep it.

Fessenio. I'm sure he'll listen willingly to this; it's a
thing that's certain to please him.

Fulvia. Unless you can help me I am desperate. Plead
with him to save my life, for it belongs to him.

Fessenio. I'll see what I can do. For your sake.

Fulvia. For yours, too, dear Fessenio! Remember that.
                                                    Exit.

Fessenio. Well, well, may God have pity on her. It's a
good thing that Lidio is planning to pay her a visit
today, dressed like a woman as he always does at such
times. Though she doesn't know it, he's as hot for it as
she is. But first I have to attend to Calandro, and there
he is now. I'll tell him everything is ready.

Scene VI

Fessenio, Calandro.

Fessenio. Greetings, master! You are in luck, for I
bring good news. Give me your hand.

Calandro. My hand—and my foot.

Fessenio (aside). My, how witty we are today!

Calandro (grumpily). What's this news of yours that's
supposed to be so good?

Fessenio. What is it? Why, man, the world is your oy-
ster.

Calandro. What do you mean?

Fessenio. I mean that Santilla loves you even more than
you love her, because I told her how generous you are,
how good looking, and how wise. And now she is as
eager for the bed as you are. I no sooner mentioned
your name than she got all excited: you're going to be
the happiest man in all the world.

Calandro. Are you telling me the truth? Ah, I can't
wait to suck those red lips and lovely cheeks, the color
of wine and cottage cheese.

Fessenio (aside). Blood and milk—his favorite diet.

Calandro. Dear Fessenio, you shall name your own reward.

Fessenio (*aside*). Such kindness, all of a sudden!

Calandro. Let's go to her now.

Fessenio. Oh, no, you can't do that! Do you think she's a common whore? You will have to do this thing properly.

Calandro. Well then, how am I to go to her?

Fessenio. On your feet.

Calandro. I know that, but in what manner?

Fessenio. If you went there openly, someone would be sure to see you, so we have decided that you must hide in a trunk and let yourself be carried into her room: in that way you can best fulfill your mutual desire.

Calandro. Ah, so I don't go on my feet after all.

Fessenio. I can see you are a shrewd one. That's right.

Calandro. It won't be too uncomfortable, will it, Fessenio?

Fessenio. No, no.

Calandro. Will the trunk be big enough that I can get all of me inside?

Fessenio. What difference does that make? If we can't get you inside in one piece, we can do it in little pieces.

Calandro. Little pieces? How do you mean?

Fessenio. Just so. Little pieces.

Calandro. But how?

Fessenio. Why, don't you know?

Calandro. I do not.

Fessenio. If you had ever sailed on a ship, you would. Because when there are hundreds of people that have to be fitted into a boat, the only way it can be done is to take a leg from one, an arm from another, and so on until they are all neatly stowed away like any other kind of cargo. That way they don't take up so much room.

Calandro. But what happens after that?

Fessenio. Why, when they get into port, each person claims the part of him that has been taken away, and sometimes, whether through carelessness or malice, a man will take a limb that belongs to someone else: that's bad, because it's either too big or too small, which makes him look crippled and lopsided. Now do you understand?

Calandro. I do, and I shall take care that my member* is not exchanged for someone else's.

Fessenio. If you don't exchange it yourself, no one else

---

* *Membro* signifies both limb and the male organ of reproduction.

is going to: that's for certain. Anyway, you'll be all alone in there. Of course you may have to be divided up before we can fit you in.

Calandro. Where are the best places to divide a man?

Fessenio. Why, wherever you see a bulge or a prominence of some kind, like up here, or down here. Would you like to see how it's done?

Calandro. If you please.

Fessenio. There's nothing to it, just a bit of magic. You have to repeat what I say, but in a low voice, because if you should shout, everything would be spoiled.

Calandro. All right.

Fessenio. First we'll start with your hand. Give it to me, and repeat after me: Ambracullac.*

Calandro. Anculabrac.

Fessenio (tugging his arm). You said it wrong. Try again: Ambracullac.

Calandro. Alabrucuc.

Fessenio (again tugging his arm). That's even worse. Ambracullac.

Calandro. Alucumbrac.

Fessenio. No, no, no! look, say: Am.

Calandro. Am.

Fessenio. Bra.

Calandro. Bra.

Fessenio. Cul.

Calandro. Cul.

Fessenio. Lac.

Calandro. Lac.

Fessenio. Stupid.

Calandro. Stupid.

Fessenio. Ox.

Calandro. Ox.

Fessenio. Now.

Calandro. Now.

Fessenio. You're.

Calandro. You're.

Fessenio. Going.

Calandro. Going.

Fessenio. To.

Calandro. To.

Fessenio. Get it! *(Twisting his arm violently.)*

Calandro. Ouch! Oh, my poor arm.

Fessenio. Didn't I tell you not to raise your voice? I

---

* Literally, amber-ass. A humorous variation on *Abracadabra*.

never saw anyone with such a short memory and so
little patience. Now you have broken the spell.

Calandro.   And you have broken my arm.

Fessenio.   It's no use. We won't be able to divide you up.

Calandro.   How shall we manage, then?

Fessenio.   I'll have to find a truck big enough to hold
you as you are.

Calandro.   I hope you can, because I don't like all this
dividing. My arm is killing me.

Fessenio.   I'll go look for one now.

Calandro.   And I'll go to the marketplace and come right
back.

Exit.

Fessenio.   Now I must find Lidio and tell him about this:
it's so funny we'll be supplied with laughs the rest of
the year. I'm going now because I don't want to have to
talk with Samia, whom I see over there muttering to
herself.

Scene VII

Samia, Fulvia.

Samia.   Ah, me, such is life! It hasn't been more than a
month since Lidio wanted to spend every minute with
my mistress, and now, when he sees how much she is
in love with him, he pays her no attention. If we don't
find some way out of this, I don't know what Fulvia
will do; she might cause a scandal, and I have a feeling that Calandro's brothers already suspect something.
Heaven knows it's obvious enough: all she thinks about
is Lidio. How true it is that he who has love in his
heart has spurs in his side!

Fulvia.   Samia!

Samia.   Coming!

Scene VIII

Santilla *as* Lidio, Fannio.

Santilla.   Tiresia told you this?

Fannio.   Yes.

Santilla.   They are taking the wedding for granted?

Fannio.   They are.

Santilla.   Does Virginia seem happy about it?

Fannio.   She can hardly wait.

Santilla.   They are getting everything ready, then?

Fannio.   Yes, indeed; they have turned the house upside down.

Santilla.   They think I am pleased?

Fannio.   Evidently.

Santilla.   Ah, me! What causes others to be happy causes me nothing but pain. The affection that Perillo and his wife have for me hurts like a sharp arrow: I can't do what they want, but neither can I do what would be best for myself. Oh, if God had only given me death instead of life, and a grave instead of a cradle when I came out of my mother's womb, then this situation would never have arisen: my fortune would have ended where it began. Oh, my poor brother, you who met with such an untimely death in our fatherland (or so at least I believe), if only you were here to advise me! What is poor Santilla going to do now—since henceforth I must call myself Santilla and not Lidio? I am a woman, yet I must also be a bridegroom! If I marry Virginia, they will find out I am a woman and not a man: they will turn me out and might even have me put to death. And if I refuse to marry her, they will also turn me out, with their curses. If I reveal myself now to be a woman, I would only bring harm upon myself. I can't stand much more of this, though. A cliff on one side, wolves on the other!

Fannio.   Don't give up hope; something may yet turn up. I think you are right to keep out of Perillo's sight, and this idea of Ruffo's for you to go to Fulvia in women's clothes is a good one. I have them all ready for you. We must do one thing at a time, as they come.

Santilla.   I wonder what is keeping Ruffo.

Fannio.   Remember what we said: whoever came first was to wait for the others.

Santilla.   We'd better not stay here, or that fellow over there might see us. He may have been sent by Perillo, though I doubt it.

Scene IX

Fessenio, Calandro.

Fessenio.   Things couldn't possibly work out better. Lidio is dressing up as a woman, and Calandro is waiting for him in a room on the first floor of his house. Lidio, looking simply irresistible, will visit him there, and then when the old fool's back is turned, we'll slip in a prostitute through the back door to take his place. He's such a fool that he can't tell a nightingale from a jackass, and will never know the difference. Here he comes now; see how happy he looks. God bless you, master.

Calandro. And you, too, dear Fessenio. Is the trunk ready?

Fessenio. Yes, and it's so big you won't even get your hair mussed.

Calandro. That's fine. But tell me something.

Fessenio. Yes?

Calandro. Should I stay awake in the trunk, or go to sleep?

Fessenio. What do you mean, awake or asleep? Don't you know that when you are on a horse you ride, when you are in the streets you walk, when at table you eat, when in bed you sleep, and when you are in a trunk you die?

Calandro. Die? What do you mean?

Fessenio. Just that. Die. Why?

Calandro. Damn! That's not so good.

Fessenio. Didn't you ever die before?

Calandro. Not that I know of.

Fessenio. Then if you've never been dead, how do you know it's so bad?

Calandro. Did you ever die?

Fessenio. Oh, yes! Thousands of times.

Calandro. Does it hurt?

Fessenio. No more than sleeping.

Calandro. Do I absolutely have to die?

Fessenio. Absolutely, when you get in the trunk.

Calandro. But who will kill me?

Fessenio. You will have to do it yourself.

Calandro. And how do I go about it?

Fessenio. There's nothing to it. But since you don't know, I'll tell you.

Calandro. If you please.

Fessenio. You close your eyes, clench your hands together, twist your arms, and then keep very still and very quiet. Finally you neither see nor hear anything.

Calandro. I see. But how do I come back to life?

Fessenio. That's one of the greatest secrets in the whole world; hardly anybody knows it. I wouldn't tell it to anyone but you, and you must swear not to repeat it to a single soul.

Calandro. I swear I won't tell it to anybody, not even to myself.

Fessenio. Oh, it's all right to tell it to yourself—but only to one ear, not to both.

Calandro. Promised. Now tell it to me.

Fessenio. Well, Calandro, you know that the only difference between the dead and the living is that the living move around and the dead do not. And if you do exactly as I say, you will come back to life all right.

Calandro. Tell me how.

Fessenio. First you must raise your head and spit straight up in the air, then you give your whole body a shake. Next you open your eyes, say a few words, and move your arms and legs. That always chases death away, and you may be sure, Calandro, that whoever is able to do this is never dead. Now you are in possession of one of the world's greatest secrets.

Calandro. I appreciate your confidence. Now I can die and come back to life whenever I like.

Fessenio. That you can, master.

Calandro. And I'll be careful to do it exactly right.

Fessenio. I'm sure you will.

Calandro. Shall I try it once, just to make sure?

Fessenio. A good idea. Are you ready?

Calandro. Yes.

Fessenio. Make an ugly face. Uglier still. There! A fine corpse if ever I saw one. There's nothing like a little know-how. Who would ever have thought this man would learn to die so well? At least he looks dead on the outside: if he's as dead on the inside as he is on the outside, it's a perfect job. We'll see. (*Makes magical motions.*) Calandro! Oh, Calandro!

Calandro (*weakly*). I'm dead. I'm dead.

Fessenio. Come back to life, Calandro. Spit in the air.

Calandro (*sighing*). Ah, ah. You should have let me alone.

Fessenio. Why?

Calandro. I was just beginning to see the next world.

Fessenio. You'll have plenty of time to see it in the trunk.

Calandro. I can hardly wait.

Fessenio. That's the right spirit. Now that you know how to die and come back to life so well, we mustn't waste time.

Calandro. That's right. Are we ready?

Fessenio. Not quite. We have to make sure that your wife doesn't suspect anything. You tell her you are going to the country, and go instead to Menicuccio's house. I'll have everything ready and meet you there.

Calandro. All right. I'll do it now, since the beast is ready.

Fessenio. It's ready, is it? Let's have a look. (*Inspects Calandro's lower parts.*)

Calandro. Ha, ha! I mean my mule is ready.

Fessenio. I knew what you meant; I was only joking.

Calandro. It's been a long time since I was in the saddle, but I'd do anything for that little angel that's waiting for me up there.

Exit

Fessenio. Angle, eh? Today we're going to see stupidity joined to filth. He's gone now to mount his mule, and I'll go tell that pretty little prostitute to get everything ready and wait for me. There is Calandro, already in the saddle. What a lot of strength there must be in that little mule to carry such a stupid old elephant!

Scene X

Calandro, Fulvia.

Calandro. Fulvia! Oh Fulvia!

Fulvia. What is it?

Calandro. Come to the window.

Fulvia. What do you want?

Calandro. I'm going to the farm, to see Flaminio.

Fulvia. When are you coming back?

Calandro. Maybe tonight sometime.

Fulvia. All right. Good-bye. (*Exit* Calandro.) And bad luck! A fine husband my brothers married me off to! I can't stand the sight of him.

ACT III

Scene I

Fessenio, *alone.*

Fessenio. Ladies and gentlemen, we have here the spoils of love: whoever wants to acquire politeness, insight, and knowledge need only buy these clothes and wear them awhile. They belong to Calandro, who took them off when he got into the trunk—a man so clever that he has fallen in love with another man, believing him a woman, and so powerful that he can die and come back to life as he chooses. Let whoever wants to buy them show the color of his money: I can sell them with a clear conscience as they belong to a dead man. Ha, ha! And now Lidio, dressed as a woman, is waiting merrily for this handsome lover, who, to tell the truth, is uglier than Bramante himself. I ran ahead to meet the prostitute that I made an appointment with; she is going to cooperate. Here she is now, and there is the porter with the trunk, which he believes is full of precious merchandise: he doesn't know that it contains the vilest stuff on earth. Doesn't anybody want these clothes? No? Well, good-bye then. Be of good cheer: I am going to lead the gelding to the mare.

Scene II

A prostitute, Fessenio, *a porter, two or three customs inspectors,* Calandro.

Prostitute.   Here I am, Fessenio. Let's go.

Fessenio.   Let the trunk go first. No, porter, not that way. Over here.

Prostitute.   What's inside?

Fessenio.   Something for you, pettikins.

Prostitute.   What is it?

Fessenio.   Silks and fine clothes.

Prostitute.   Whose are they?

Fessenio.   They belong to the man you are going to entertain, my dear.

Prostitute.   Oh, will he give some of them to me?

Fessenio.   Yes, if you do what I said.

Prostitute.   I will. Don't you worry.

Fessenio.   Remember that your name is Santilla, and everything else I told you.

Prostitute.   Leave everything to me.

Fessenio.   Otherwise you won't get a penny.

Prostitute.   I said don't worry. What do these customs inspectors want with the porter?

Fessenio.   Quiet! And listen.

Inspector.   Tell me, what's inside that trunk?

Porter.   Why, what's the matter?

Inspector.   Have you passed the customs?

Porter.   No, sir.

Inspector.   What's inside?

Porter.   I don't know.

Inspector.   Better tell the truth.

Porter.   They told me it was silk. Dresses and such as that.

Inspector.   Silk?

Porter.   Yes, sir.

Inspector.   Is it locked?

Porter.   I don't think so.

Inspector.   Set it down.

Porter.   Ah no, sir.

Inspector.   Set it down, stupid. Do you want me to hit you?

Fessenio.   Oh, oh! Our plan is spoiled. He is going to find out everything, and we shall all be ruined.

Prostitute.   What's the matter?

Fessenio.   Our plan is spoiled. (*To* Prostitute.) Sofilla, you must help me.

Prostitute.   What can I do?

Fessenio.   Cry, shout, tear your hair, as if you were mourning for someone.

Prostitute.   But why?

Fessenio.   You will soon find out.

Prostitute (*weeping loudly*). Boohoo! Boohoo!

Inspector.   What's this? Somebody dead?

Fessenio (*approaching,* to Inspector). What are you looking for?

Inspector.   The porter told us this trunk contained dutiable merchandise, instead of which it seems to contain a corpse.

Fessenio.   That's right. It does.

Inspector.   Who is it?

Fessenio.   It's this poor woman's husband. Don't you see how hard she is taking it?

Inspector.   Why are you carrying him in a trunk?

Fessenio.   To fool the police, if you must know.

Inspector.   To fool the police? Why?

Fessenio.   Because no one would have anything to do with us if they found out the truth.

Inspector.   What is the truth?

Fessenio.   This man is dead of the plague.

Inspector.   The plague! Oh, and I touched it!

Fessenio.   To your harm, I fear.

Inspector. Where are you taking him?

Fessenio. Someplace we can bury him, or drop him in the river.

Calandro (sitting up in trunk). You want to drown me, do you? But I'm not dead, you rascals. I'm not dead, I say!

Fessenio. Oh, everyone is running away, and no wonder: this is the work of the devil. Run, Sofilla! Run, porter! Run, everybody!

Scene III

Calandro, Fessenio.

Calandro (emerging from trunk, striking Fessenio). So you wanted to drown me, did you, you wretch?

Fessenio. Why, master, what's the matter? Why do you want to hit me?

Calandro. You want to know why, do you?

Fessenio. Yes, sir.

Calandro. Because you deserve it, you scoundrel. That's why.

Fessenio. This is what comes of trying to do a good deed. Are you angry with me because I have saved your life?

Calandro. And how did you save my life, may I ask?

Fessenio. Why, I kept you from going to the custom-house, didn't I?

Calandro. And suppose I had gone there, what would have happened?

Fessenio. What would have happened? I should have let them carry you there—then you'd have seen.

Calandro. What the devil do you mean?

Fessenio. You act as if you were born yesterday. You were being smuggled: they would have sold you just as they do everything that's smuggled.

Calandro. Well, then, you did right after all. Forgive me, Fessenio.

Fessenio (arranging his clothes, which Calandro has rumpled). Next time I hope you think twice before you get angry. *(Aside.)* I'll get even with him for this.

Calandro. I will. But tell me, who was that ugly-looking woman who ran away just now?

Fessenio. Ah, don't you know her?

Calandro. No.

Fessenio. That was death, who was with you in the trunk.

Calandro. With me? What do you mean?

Fessenio. Just that. With you.

Calandro. I didn't see her there.

Fessenio. You don't see sleep either, do you, when you are sleeping? Or thirst when you drink, or hunger when you eat? You don't see life either, for that matter, although you are alive. But it is with you just the same.

Calandro. It's true I have never seen these things.

Fessenio. Exactly. And when you die, you don't see death.

Calandro. H'm. Why did the porter run away?

Fessenio. He was afraid of death. So I'm afraid you won't be able to see Santilla today.

Calandro. Then I might as well be dead.

Fessenio. I don't know how I can arrange it now— unless you are willing to do a little work.

Calandro. Fessenio, I'll do anything to see her. I'll even go to bed barefoot.

Fessenio. Oh, no, nothing like that.

Calandro. What, then?

Fessenio. You'll have to be the porter yourself. Nobody will be able to tell the difference: you've already taken off most of your clothes, and since you've been dead for a short time, your face has changed somewhat, too. I'll pretend I'm the carpenter who made the trunk. Don't worry about Santilla. She'll put two and two together immediately: she's a regular sibyl.

Calandro. A good idea. I would do anything to gain Santilla's love.

Fessenio (*aside*). Did you ever see such an anxious lover? (Calandro *lifts the trunk with difficulty.*) Look out, you're going to drop it! There, that's it. Steady, now. Are you sure you're all right?

Calandro (*groaning*). Fine.

Fessenio. Well then, carry it to her house. I'll follow and meet you at the door. (*Exit* Calandro.) That jackass's load is becoming to him. Now I have to find the prostitute and lead her into the house by the back door. I'm afraid Lidio may have to let Calandro kiss him, but no matter—Fulvia's kisses will then seem all the sweeter. Here comes Samia. She didn't see Calandro talking with me—fortunatley.

Scene IV

Fessenio, Samia.

Fessenio.   Where have you been?

Samia.   To Ruffo the magician. My mistress sent me.

Fessenio.   What did he say?

Samia.   That he was coming to see her.

Fessenio.   My, my, women are so silly. Well, I have to
     go find Lidio and tell him what your mistress asked
     me to.

Samia.   Is he at home?

Fessenio.   Yes.

Samia.   What do you think he will do?

Fessenio.   Frankly, I'm not too hopeful. But I can't
     say for sure.

Samia.   Things certainly don't seem to be turning out
     very well for my mistress and me. Well, good-bye.

Fessenio.   Good-bye.

Scene V

Samia, Fulvia.

Samia.   My mistress is not going to like this. Neither
     Lidio nor Ruffo's familiar spirit has given her much
     encouragement.

Fulvia.   Why were you gone so long?

Samia.   I wasn't able to find Ruffo until just now.

Fulvia.   What does he say?

Samia.   That the spirit answered him . . . how was it?
     I don't remember.

Fulvia.   You goose-brain, you'd better remember!

Samia.   Oh, yes, now it is coming back to me. He said
     he made an amgibuous reply.

Fulvia.   You mean ambiguous?

Samia.   Yes, that's it. Ambiguous.

Fulvia.   He said nothing else?

Samia.   That he was going to try again.

Fulvia.   Anything else?

Samia.   That he was at your service and that as soon
     as he had anything good to report, he would come
     here right away.

Fulvia.   Ah, me! That's not so good. But what about
     Lidio?

Samia. He thinks about as much of you as he would a pair of old shoes.

Fulvia. Did you find him?

Samia. Yes, and talked with him, too.

Fulvia. Well, what did he say?

Samia. You won't like it.

Fulvia. Ah, me! Tell me anyway.

Samia. He pretends he never met you.

Fulvia. What are you saying?

Samia. That's the way it is.

Fulvia. How could you have understood him to say such a thing?

Samia. He spoke to me in a way that frightened me.

Fulvia. Maybe he was joking with you.

Samia. No, my lady. He was insulting.

Fulvia. Maybe you didn't talk to him right.

Samia. No, my lady. You should never have sent me.

Fulvia. Maybe someone was with him, eh?

Samia. I took him aside.

Fulvia. Maybe you talked too loud.

Samia. I whispered into his ear.

Fulvia. But what did he say?

Samia. He drove me away.

Fulvia. He doesn't love me anymore, then. Is that it?

Samia. No, nor respect you either.

Fulvia. You really think so?

Samia. I know it.

Fulvia. Alas, can I believe my own ears?

Samia. You can, my lady.

Fulvia. He didn't ask you how I was?

Samia. He said he never heard of you.

Fulvia. So he's forgotten me, has he?

Samia. You're lucky that he doesn't hate you.

Fulvia. How unhappy I am! I know now for certain that Lidio is unfaithful. How sad is the destiny of women! And how few women find lovers who are completely satisfactory! Poor me, I loved too deeply and gave so much of myself that I am no longer my own mistress! Cruel heavens, why don't you make Lidio love me as I love him, or let me run away from him as he runs away from me? But what am I thinking of?—Not to love Lidio, and to run away from him? Ah, no, I can't do that, nor do I want to. On the contrary, I am going to seek him out. Why, since he has come to me so often in women's clothes, shouldn't I, just this once, try going to him dressed like a man? It's reasonable enough, and he might even appreciate my going to such trouble on his account. Why don't I do it then? Is there any reason why I should pine away like this? There is no pain like that of a woman who has wasted her youth, and whoever thinks that once it's gone you can get it back is mistaken. When will I ever find another Lidio? A man like that is worth any amount of trouble. And now is the right time, because he's at home and my husband is away at the farm. Who dares to stop me then? My mind is made up; I shall do it. I didn't think that magician was going to do much good anyway. The best way to get something done is to do it yourself. Others do it at their own convenience and never take the same interest. If I go to him myself, he will see my tears, hear my sobs, and listen to my prayers: I shall throw myself at his feet, hug him around the neck, and pretend to die. No one could be so cruel as not to take pity on me then. No one hearing words of love spoken straight from the heart could possibly be indifferent to them, and in love all things are possible. Therefore I am going to dress myself up like a man and go to him. Samia, you stay here at the door and don't let anyone linger in front of the house: if somebody sees me coming out, they might recognize me.

Scene VI

Samia, Fulvia.

Samia. How unhappy we poor women are! When we fall in love, we are done for. Fulvia, who was always so prudent, doesn't know what she's doing now that she's in love with Lidio. Since he won't come to her, she has decided to go to him dressed like a man, never thinking of what might happen if she were discovered. Well, she ought to be satisfied now: she's given him everything, including her honor and her body, and he thinks no more of her than of the dirt under his feet. Our sex is truly to be pitied. Here she is already, rigged out in men's clothes. It didn't take her long.

Fulvia. Well, Samia, I am off to find Lidio. You stay here and keep the door locked until I come back. Do you understand?

Samia. Yes, my lady. But do be careful.

Scene VII

Fulvia, *alone.*

Fulvia. Love can make a person do anything. I used to be so timid I was afraid to leave my room alone, and now, moved by love, I don't even hesitate to leave the house alone in men's clothing. I am going straight to Lidio's house, though it's a good distance, and I'll make him listen to me. No one will be there except the old woman who waits on him and maybe Fessenio, who knows everything anyway. No one will recognize me; I don't have anything to worry about. And even if someone found out, it's better to act and be sorry than not to act and be sorry: nothing ventured, nothing gained.

Scene VIII

Samia, *alone.*

Samia. She is gone to seek her pleasure. I was wrong to blame her, for he who is indifferent to love is no better than a beast of the field. I am never so happy myself as when I am with my lover Lusco, who is waiting for me now in the courtyard. We'll have the whole house to ourselves. I'll follow my mistress' example: a person's a fool not to take his pleasure when the opportunity comes along. (*Calling.*) Lusco! Oh, Lusco!

Scene IX

Fessenio, *alone.*

Fessenio. Calandro is with the prostitute now; they'll have some pretty secrets between them. I must tell Fulvia what's going on—she will die laughing. And no wonder! It's enough to make a dead man laugh.

(*Approaches* Calandro's *house, knocks.*) H'm. The door seems to be locked. Hello there! Anybody home?

Scene X

Fessenio *outside* Calandro's *house,* Samia *inside.*

Fessenio (*knocking*).   Anybody there? Can't you hear me? Open up!

Samia.   Who's knocking?

Fessenio.   It's me, Fessenio. Let me come in, Samia.

Samia.   Wait a minute.

Fessenio.   What's the matter? Why don't you open the door?

Samia.   I'm trying to put the key in the lock.*

Fessenio.   Haven't you got it in yet?

Samia.   I'm trying. Oh, it's no use. I can't do it.

Fessenio.   Why not?

Samia.   The hole is stopped up.

Fessenio.   Blow on the key.

Samia.   I'm doing the best I can.

Fessenio.   Why are you taking so long?

Samia.   I have it nice and wet now; it ought to do the trick.

Fessenio.   Well, hurry up.

Samia.   There, you hear? It's unlocked now; you can come in.

Fessenio.   Why do you have everything locked up like this?

Samia.   My mistress' orders. She wanted the door locked.

Fessenio.   Why?

Samia.   With you I can talk freely. She has gone to Lidio dressed like a man.

Fessenio.   Samia! You don't mean it?

Samia.   I do indeed. I'm supposed to stay here and keep everything locked up until she comes back.

---

* This speech and the remainder of the scene puns erotically on the word *chiave* (key). The infinitive *chiavare,* in colloquial Italian, means to engage in sexual intercourse. Samia is presumably entertaining Lusco when Fessenio knocks on the door, which explains her delay in opening it and gives a double meaning to her words throughout.

Scene XI

Fessenio, *alone.*

Fessenio. Truly there is nothing too dangerous or too foolish for a lover to attempt: here Fulvia has gone to Lidio's house, not knowing that her husband is also there. He is bound to believe the worst, seeing her there alone and dressed like a man. He'll be so furious he may notify her relatives.* I'd better hurry to see if there is something I can do. Oh, heavens, here comes Fulvia now, and she has Calandro with her, leading him by the collar. I'll step aside and listen; that way I'll find out what has happened.

Scene XII

Fulvia, Calandro.

Fulvia. So you were going to the farm, were you? You miserable creature, don't you have enough to do at home that you go prowling around like this? And to think that this is the man I have given my love to and remained faithful to all these years! Now I know why you have been keeping away from me the last few nights: you've been saving your energy. I don't know how I keep myself from tearing your eyes out. Did you think you could pull the wool over my eyes so easily? I heard about it before this, and that's why I dressed myself up like this—to find out for myself if it was true. And now I'm leading you by the collar, like the dirty dog you are, so that all the world can see and take pity on me who have had to put up with your outrages. Do you suppose that if I were like you, and didn't care what I did, I couldn't have a good time, too? I'm not as old or as ugly as all that. And it's only because I have some self-respect that I didn't revenge myself on that woman I found you with. But

* Who had arranged the match (Act II, Sc. x). In Roman society a husband could divorce his wife by the mere act of sending her back to her family.

I'm not finished yet: I'm going to get even with you both.

Calandro. Have you finished?

Fulvia. Yes.

Calandro. Then, damn you, I'm the one who ought to be angry. I was enjoying a paradise on earth when you came along and spoiled everything. You are not worth one of her old shoes, for at least she knows how to make love. Her lips are sweeter than wine, she shines brighter than Diana, and she has the wisdom of a Fata Morgana. And if you do her any harm, you had better watch out.

Fulvia. That's enough out of you. Inside the house! Inside, I say!

Scene XIII

Fessenio, *alone.*

Fessenio. Well, well, live and learn. O love, how great is your power! What poet, what doctor, what philosopher can hope to rival you as a teacher? All knowledge, all doctrine is secondary to yours. What else but love would have enabled Fulvia, in so tight a spot, to act so intelligently? I never saw anything like it. There she is over there, standing in her doorway. I'll say something encouraging to her about Lidio— that'll cheer her up. Poor thing! I feel sorry for her.

Scene XIV

Fulvia, Fessenio, Samia.

Fulvia. Ah, Fessenio, see how unlucky I've been—to find, instead of Lidio, that wretched husband of mine. But I got out of it all right.

Fessenio. I know; I heard everything. Don't show yourself too plainly—somebody might see you in those clothes. There, that's better.

Fulvia. You are right. I don't seem to be able to think about anything but Lidio. Tell me, dear Fessenio, have you seen him?

Fessenio. Yes, my lady.

Fulvia. Recently?

Fessenio. I have, my lady.

Fulvia. What does he say?

Fessenio. He's not going to leave Rome right away.

Fulvia. But when will I be able to speak with him?

Fessenio. Maybe today. I was on my way to talk with him when I saw you and Calandro.

Fulvia. Try once more, dear Fessenio. For us both.

Fessenio. I'll see what I can do. Meanwhile try not to worry.

Fulvia. Try not to worry, eh? That's a good one. I won't have a moment's peace till you get back.

Fessenio. Good-bye, my lady.

Fulvia. Good-bye, Fessenio, and don't be long. (*Exit* Fessenio.) This suspense is killing me. Samia, tell me what I ought to do.

Samia. Maybe Ruffo's spirit will be able to think of something.

Fulvia. He's certainly taking his time about it. Samia, go and see the magician again.

Samia. Very well, my lady.

Fulvia. Remind him that we are waiting, and come back at once.

Samia. Just as soon as I find him, my lady.

Scene XV

Samia, Ruffo.

Samia. Oh, what luck! There is Ruffo. God bless you, sir.

Ruffo. Hello, Samia. What is it?

Samia. My mistress is dying to know if you have any news for her.

Ruffo. I believe everything is going to be all right.

Samia. But when?

Ruffo. I am going to make a complete report to Fulvia.

Samia. All this is taking so long.

Ruffo. Samia, there are some things that can't be rushed. The stars have to be just right, and I have to find the right magical words; then I have to gather herbs, rocks, and water from various wells. Finally I have to summon my familiar spirit. All these things naturally take time.

Samia. Well, as long as it works in the long run.

Ruffo.   There is every reason for hope.

Samia (looking offstage).   Oh, oh! Do you know who her lover is?

Ruffo.   Not for sure.

Samia (pointing to Santilla *as* Lidio, *who has just appeared).*   It's that man over there.

Ruffo.   Do you know him well?

Samia.   I should think so. Less than two hours ago I was talking with him.

Ruffo.   What did he have to say?

Samia.   He acted as if I were some sort of criminal.

Ruffo.   Go try again: see if the spirit hasn't softened him up a bit.

Samia.   Shall I?

Ruffo.   By all means.

Samia.   Well, I'll try.

Ruffo.   After you talk with him, go back to Fulvia and tell her I'm coming to see her right away.

Samia.   Yes, sir.

Ruffo (aside).   I'll step aside and listen to this conversation.

Scene XVI

Fannio, Santilla *as* Lidio, Samia.

Fannio.   Oh, Lidio, here is Fulvia's maid coming toward us. Remember that her name is Samia, and be nice to her.

Santilla.   I intend to.

Samia.   Well, sir, are you still upset?

Santilla.   No, no, not at all. Samia, I hope you'll forgive me. The last time I saw you I had something on my mind; I wasn't my usual self. How is my beloved Fulvia?

Samia.   Do you really want to know?

Santilla.   Indeed I do.

Samia.   She wants you to give her your heart.

Santilla.   I can't do that.

Samia.   Why not?

Santilla.   Don't you know that it already belongs to her?

Samia.   God only knows if you are telling the truth. First you couldn't even remember her, and now you want me to believe that she is your only love—as if I didn't know that you don't love her and don't want to go near her.

Santilla.   On the contrary, until I see her again I am as good as dead.

Samia.   The spirit certainly seems to have done a good job. So you will go to see her as usual?

Santilla.   As usual? How do you mean?

Samia.   Why, dressed as a woman.

Santilla.   Ah, yes, of course. Dressed like a woman. Yes, of course. Tell her that.

Samia.   Oh, sir, that will make her so happy! I'd better not linger here any longer, and I'll take the back street home. It wouldn't do for anybody to see me talking to you and then going back to Lady Fulvia. Good-bye, sir.

Santilla.   Good-bye.

Scene XVII

Santilla *as* Lidio, Fannio, Ruffo.

Santilla.   Did you hear that?

Fannio.   Yes, and I heard that "as usual," too. It's obvious she's mistaking you for someone else.

Santilla.   It seems so.

Fannio.   We'd better tell Ruffo about this. Here he is now.

Ruffo.   Well, gentlemen, have you made up your minds?

Santilla.   You don't think we'd let something like that slip through our fingers, do you?

Ruffo.   Aha, our friend has reconsidered. Well, you are right, Ruffo, because she's a great beauty.

Santilla.   I know all about her.

Fannio (*to* Santilla).   You are sure to gain some pleasure from it.

Ruffo.   And profit as well.

Fannio.   Ruffo, if I understand you correctly, you said that Fulvia came to you, other means having failed, from which I gather that she has tried other means. From something that happened today, we have reason to believe that Lidio has been mistaken by her—and by her maid as well—for someone else. Therefore it will be necessary, as a precaution, for you to tell her to make no reference to what has happened in the past. Otherwise she would find out everything, and there would be a terrible scandal. Be sure to warn her of this.

Ruffo.   You were wise to think of this precaution, and

I'll not forget to do as you say. Well, we're wasting time here; let's get this thing started. I'd better go to her first.

Santilla. We'll meet you here when you come back.

Fannio. Lidio, you go ahead. I'll be along in a minute. (*Exit* Santilla.) Ruffo, let me have a word with you.

Fannio. I'm going to tell you a secret. You'd never guess it, no matter how hard you tried. But you must promise not to tell it to a single soul.

Ruffo. May God deny my every wish, if I ever breathe a word of it.

Fannio. If you do, I will be ruined, and you would not gain the reward you expect.

Ruffo. Don't worry. What is it?

Fannio. My master, Lidio, is a hermaphrodite.

Ruffo. A herphramodite. Well, what of it?

Fannio. Not herphramodite. Hermaphrodite. Heavens, how dense you are!

Ruffo. What does that mean?

Fannio. Don't you know?

Ruffo. No; that's why I ask.

Fannio. A hermaphrodite is someone who is half man and half woman.

Ruffo. Is Lidio like that?

Fannio. He is.

Ruffo. You mean he has the sex organs of a woman and the sex organs of a man, too?

Fannio. Yes, sir.

Ruffo. Come to think of it, I always thought there was something a little effeminate in his voice and manner.

Fannio. This first time, therefore, he will use only the woman's organ with Fulvia. She will think that this is because she asked him to come in the form of a woman; she'll think the spirit did this to please her, and she'll have so much faith in his power that she will worship you forever, for being his master.

Ruffo. This is one of the best schemes I have ever heard: we stand to make a fortune.

Fannio. Is the woman generous?

Ruffo. I should think so! True lovers, you know, share everything they have—money, clothes, livestock, everything. A woman who loves as deeply as the lady Fulvia would even give her life.

Fannio. What you say pleases me.

Ruffo. As what you have told me about that herphramodite pleases me.

Fannio. I'm glad you can't pronounce that word, because even if you wanted to repeat it you couldn't.

Ruffo. Better go to Lidio's now and get yourselves dressed up. I'll tell Fulvia she can expect him.

Fannio. I'm to go as my master's maid. Right?

Ruffo. Right. And be sure to be ready when I come back.

Fannio. I will. It's a good thing I have the necessary clothes.

Scene XVIII

Ruffo, Samia.

Ruffo. So far things couldn't have worked out better. By now Samia has probably spoken with Fulvia, and she'll be waiting for me. I'll tell her the spirit has arranged everything; then I'll give her this image and tell her to say certain words and make certain gestures before it, that this will bring about what she wants, and I shall warn her not to say a word about it to anyone except her maid. Ah, I see Samia now, standing in the doorway.

Samia. Come in, Ruffo. My mistress is waiting for you downstairs, because her sheep of a husband is upstairs.

Scene XIX

Samia, Fessenio.

Samia. What is it, Fessenio?

Fessenio. I have to see the lady Fulvia.

Samia. She can't see you now.

Fessenio. Why not?

Samia. She's with the magician.

Fessenio. Let me in anyway.

Samia. No, I can't.

Fessenio. Women are such fools.

Samia. Maybe yours are.

Fessenio. It's a good thing I know how to hold my temper. I'll take a walk and come back later.

Samia. That's a good idea.

Exit.

Fessenio. If Fulvia knew what I knew, she wouldn't
worry about spirits. Lidio yearns for her even more
than she does for him; he wants to see her this very
day. But I want to be the one to tell her this, because
I know she'll give me something. I'm not going to let
Samia do it; that's why I didn't tell her anything. But
I must go now: if Fulvia were to see me, she might
think I came to see her magician, who must be that
man I see coming out of the house.

Scene XX

Ruffo, *alone*.

Ruffo. Everything is going beautifully. Fulvia has given
me a nice sum of money; at this rate my fortune will
soon be made, and then good-bye to these rags. What
a stroke of luck! This is a rich woman and, unless I
am badly mistaken, more in love than she is wise.
She'll have need of me again, unless I miss my guess.
Isn't it strange how people's dreams sometimes come
true? Last night I dreamed I caught a pheasant. I
pulled the pretty feathers from his tail and stuck them
in my cap. If the lady Fulvia lets herself be caught
like this, as I think she will, I'll pluck her likewise.
Then I'll be well off for a while, at least, and I'll know
how to make the most of that. But who is that woman
I see waving to me? I don't know her.

Scene XXI

Ruffo, Fannio *in women's dress*.

Ruffo. Fannio! Your disguise is so good I didn't recog-
nize you.
Fannio. Am I pretty?
Ruffo. Yes, indeed. And now go and console the lady
Fulvia.
Fannio. I'm afraid she won't get much consolation—not
this time, anyway.
Ruffo. Why, yes she will. Lidio is going to use the
female organ with her.
Fannio. That's right. Well, shall we go?

Ruffo. Yes. Is Lidio ready?

Fannio. He's waiting for me nearby, and he's done such a good job that no one would ever guess he wasn't a woman.

Ruffo. Wonderful. Well, Fulvia is expecting you, so get Lidio and go to her. I'll wait here and see what happens. I see she is standing on her doorstep now, waiting. It didn't take her long to get ready.

Scene XXII

Fessenio, Fulvia.

Fessenio. No need to worry anymore, my lady.

Fulvia. What do you mean?

Fessenio. I mean that Lidio is more anxious to see you than you are to see him. No sooner did I tell him what you asked me to than he got himself ready: he's on his way here now.

Fulvia. Dear Fessenio, this is the kind of news I like to hear, and you shall be rewarded for it. Listen to Calandro upstairs, asking for his clothes so he can go out again. Better not stay, or he'll see us together. Oh, how glad you have made me! Things are really looking up now. As soon as I have let that buzzard out of his cage, I shall feel free.

Exit.

Fessenio. These lovers are going to make up for lost time, and if Lidio is wise, he'll forget about his sister. Calandro won't be at home; they will have lots of time to enjoy themselves. I can afford to take a walk now. Ah, Calandro is coming out. I'd better go, because if he stops to talk with me, he might see Lidio, who ought to be here any minute.

Scene XXIII

Calandro, Lidio *as Santilla, Santilla in woman's dress accompanied by* Fannio *in woman's dress.*

Calandro. I see I am in luck: no sooner do I step outside the house than I see my beloved coming my way. Heavens! What shall I say to her? Good morning? No, it's not that early. Good evening? No, it's not that late. God bless you? No, too casual. Mistress of my soul? But that's not a greeting. Heart of my body? No, too commonplace. Angel face? Too vulgar. Divine spirit? No, that's not right either. Oh, my, here she is now. Spirit, heart, angel: which shall I say? Oh, damn, what a fool I am! I was mistaken; this isn't Santilla—there she is over there. (*Addresses* Santilla.) Good morning . . . that is, good evening. Oh, no, she's not the one. It must be the other one after all. (*Approaches* Lidio.) No, I think it *was* the other. No, it must be this one. No, it's the other. Damn!

Lidio. This madman thinks I am a woman: he has fallen in love with me and will follow me all the way to his house. I'll go home, change, and go to Fulvia later.

Calandro. It's the one across the street. I'll go follow her. (*Follows* Lidio.)

Santilla (*to* Fannio). He's gone the other way. Quick, now—let's slip inside before he comes back. There is Fulvia, waiting to let us in.

ACT IV

Scene I

Fulvia, Samia.

Fulvia. Samia, oh, Samia!

Samia. Yes, my lady.

Fulvia. Come down here right away!

Samia. Coming.

Fulvia. Faster, for God's sake. Faster!

Samia. Here I am. What is it?

Fulvia. Go quickly, find Ruffo the magician, and tell him to come here at once.

Samia. Let me go upstairs and get my hat.

Fulvia. Forget your hat, stupid. Go as you are. There's not a moment to lose!

Samia (*grumbling*). What the devil is she so angry about? She's on fire about something, and Lidio doesn't seem to have quenched it.

Exit.

Fulvia. O false spirits and stupid human beings! How I

have been deceived! How unhappy I am! I have harmed
not only myself but also him whom I love even more
than myself. Miserable me, who have what I asked for
and found what I wasn't looking for! If the spirit can't
help me, I am ready to kill myself: suicide would be
better than a life of misery. Here comes Ruffo; soon I
shall find out what my fate is to be. No one's in sight,
so I'll talk to him out here. That's better than indoors,
for even walls have ears.

Scene II

Ruffo, Fulvia.

Ruffo.   What is it, my lady?
Fulvia.   These tears, even more than words, show you
   how I feel.
Ruffo.   But what is it? Don't cry, my lady.
Fulvia.   Ah, Ruffo, I don't know if it's my ignorance or
   your treachery that's to blame.
Ruffo.   What are you saying, my lady?
Fulvia.   Whether it was my afult, or whether the heavens
   willed it, or whether the spirit acted maliciously—I
   don't know the reason, but Lidio has been changed
   from a man into a woman. I discovered this when I
   was feeling him over. And though I have been deprived
   of my pleasure, I do not weep for my own sake so
   much as for Lidio, who because of me has lost that
   which he prizes most. Now you know the reason for
   these tears and will be able to understand what I want
   you to do.
Ruffo.   My lady, if I did not see these tears, which would
   be hard indeed to feign, I would have trouble believing
   you; but seeing that they are real, I can assure you
   that you need weep only for yourself. I remember you
   asked that Lidio visit you in the form of a woman, and
   now it occurs to me that the spirit, wishing to follow
   your instructions to the letter, sent your lover to you
   as a woman both in dress and in body. So cheer up,
   because he who could change him into a woman can
   change him back again into a man.
Fulvia.   This explanation makes me feel better already.
   If you can return Lidio to me whole, you shall have
   money, clothing, anything that is mine to give.
Ruffo.   I know the spirit will do as you wish, so I can

promise you that he will change your lover back into a man immediately. However, in order to avoid making another mistake, state your wishes clearly this time.

Fulvia. First, that he be given back the dagger for my sheath. Do you know what I mean?

Ruffo. Quite.

Fulvia. And that he visit me in the dress of a woman, not in the body of one.

Ruffo. If you had said this earlier, this mistake would not have happened. But I'm glad it did, because now you know how powerful my spirit is.

Fulvia. Ruffo, I beg you to relieve my suspense. I won't have a moment's peace of mind until I see him.

Ruffo. You will be able to touch him as well as see him.

Fulvia. When? Today?

Ruffo. It's late now. He'd only be able to stay with you a short time.

Fulvia. He wouldn't have to stay. I would just want to make sure he was changed into a man again.

Ruffo. Ah, my lady, that would be like a thirsty man going to a fountain and being unable to drink.

Fulvia. He'll come tonight, then?

Ruffo. If you wish. You can wait for him just inside the door.

Fulvia. That's not necessary. As long as he's dressed like a woman, no one will know he's not one.

Ruffo. As you wish.

Fulvia. Be of good cheer, Ruffo. You'll never want for anything again.

Ruffo. No more will you, my lady.

Fulvia. And he'll come right away?

Ruffo. The moment I get home.

Fulvia. I'll send Samia along so you can let me know what the spirit says.

Ruffo. Do so, and don't forget that the lover, too, must have his reward.

Fulvia. Don't worry; he'll have money and jewels aplenty.

Ruffo. Go in peace. (*Exit* Fulvia.) Love is painted blind with good reason, for he who loves never sees the truth. This woman is so blinded by her passion that she believes a spirit can make a person male or female at will, as if all that had to be done to make a woman out of a man was to pull out the root and replace it with a crack, and then, to turn him back into a man, sew up the mouth down there and replace it with a

peg. Oh, the credulity of lovers! Ah, here comes Lidio
and Fannio; I see they have already changed their
clothes.

Scene III

Ruffo, Santilla *as* Lidio, Fannio.

Ruffo.   You must get dressed up again.
Santilla.   Why?
Ruffo.   To go back to Fulvia. Ha, ha!
Fannio.   Why are you giggling in that obscene way?
Ruffo.   Ha, ha, ha!
Santilla.   Come, what is it?
Ruffo.   Ha, ha! Fulvia, believing the spirit changed Lidio
into a woman, wants him to change back into a man
again and revisit her.
Santilla.   What did you tell her?
Ruffo.   That it would be done right away.
Fannio.   You said the right thing.
Ruffo.   When will you go back then?
Santilla.   I don't know.
Ruffo.   You don't seem very enthusiastic. Don't you want
to?
Fannio.   Yes, we'll go.
Ruffo.   You must be sure to do so, because I told her
the spirit promised you would.
Fannio.   Don't worry. We'll go back.
Ruffo.   When?
Fannio.   Just as soon as we finish our errand, we'll dress
up again and go back.
Ruffo.   Don't fail to do so. I see her maid standing in
the door; I don't want her to see me talking with you,
so good-bye. Oh, wait! Fannio, let me have a word
with you privately. This time, see that our dainty
gentleman uses his pestle instead of his mortar with
the lady Fulvia.
Fannio.   I'll do that. Good-bye.

Scene IV

Fannio, Santilla *as* Lidio, Samia.

Fannio.   Samia is coming out. Let's step aside and let
her go by without seeing us.

Santilla.   She is talking to herself.

Fannio.   Be quiet, and listen.

Samia.   This is what comes of meddling with the spirits: just see what they've done to Lidio.

Fannio.   She's talking about you.

Samia.   First they made a woman out of him, and now they want to make a man out of him; this is a hard day for him and for me, too. But if they succeed, everything will be all right. I'll soon find out, because my mistress has sent me to ask the magician. She is so sure of the outcome that she is getting together a sum of money to give to Lidio.

Fannio.   Did you hear that about the money?

Santilla.   I did.

Fannio.   Then let's get ready to go back.

Santilla.   Fannie, you must be out of your mind. I don't know what you could have been thinking about to promise Ruffo that we'd go back there.

Fannio.   Why can't we?

Santilla.   Silly man, as if you didn't know I am a woman.

Fannio.   So what?

Santilla.   So what, he says! Don't you know, stupid, that if I reveal my sex, I'll bring harm to myself, disappointment to Fulvia, and cause Ruffo to lose his standing with her? How can you prevent that?

Fannio.   You ask how?

Santilla.   Yes.

Fannio.   Where there are men, there are means.

Santilla.   But where there are only women, like her and me, the means are lacking.

Fannio.   Don't worry. When I promised Ruffo that you would revisit the lady Fulvia, I knew what I was doing: I had it all figured out.

Santilla.   How?

Fannio.   Didn't you tell me it was dark in her bedroom?

Santilla.   Yes, it was.

Fannio.   And that she did not talk with you but only felt you with her hands?

Santilla.   That's right.

Fannio.   Well, I'll go there with you, the way we did before.

Santilla.   Yes?

Fannio.   That is, I'll go as a maid.

Santilla.   Well, and then?

Fannio.   Dressed as a woman, like yourself.

Santilla.   I understand that. But then what?

Fannio.   When you get in her room, pretend you have
   something to say to me. Come out of the room and
   take my place outside while I go inside and pretend to
   be you. She won't be able to tell the difference in the
   darkness. She'll think the spirit has changed you back
   into a man: we shall have all the money we want, and
   moreover I'll be able to enjoy myself.

Santilla.   Fannio, I never heard of a cleverer plan than
   this.

Fannio.   So you see I was right to tell Ruffo we would
   go back.

Santilla.   Indeed you were. But in the meantime it would
   be a good idea to find out what's going on at the house
   about this wedding of mine.

Fannio.   As to that, I see no way out: better not think
   about it in advance.

Santilla.   Putting things off is not going to solve them.
   They won't look any better tomorrow than they do
   today.

Fannio.   Who can say? One thing at a time. Where the
   lady Fulvia is concerned we stand only to gain.

Santilla.   All right, but first go to my house and find
   out from Tiresia what is going on. Come back quickly,
   and then we'll go to Fulvia's.

Fannio.   I will.

Scene V

Fessenio, Samia.

Fessenio.   What seems to be the trouble?

Samia.   My mistress has the devil in her.

Fessenio.   Ah?

Samia.   The magician changed Lidio into a woman.

Fessenio.   Ha, ha, ha!

Samia.   You think it's funny?

Fessenio.   Indeed I do.

Samia.   It's the gospel truth.

Fessenio.   You're not serious, are you?

Samia.   Of course I am, stupid. And whether you believe
   it or not, that's what's happened. My mistress felt of
   him and found out he was a woman.

Fessenio.   Well, what's she going to do now?

Samia.   You don't believe me, so I'm not going to tell
   you.

Fessenio. I swear I do. Tell me what she's going to do next.

Samia. The spirit is going to change him back into a man. I have just been to see Ruffo; he has given me this note to take to my mistress.

Fessenio. Let me read it.

Samia. Oh, no! Something might happen to you.

Fessenio. Even if I should drop dead, I want to see it.

Samia. Fessenio, be careful. Don't meddle with the spirits.

Fessenio. I'm not afraid. Show it to me.

Samia. Don't, Fessenio. Or at least cross yourself first.

Fessenio. Come, let's have a look.

Samia. Well, all right . . . but you must promise to be as silent as the grave. If anyone found out I let you see it, it would be bad for both of us.

Fessenio. Don't worry. Give it here.

Samia. Read it out loud.

Fessenio (*reading*). Greetings from Ruffo to Fulvia. The spirit, when he learned the effect of what he had done, was much amused. No one was to blame but yourself, but rest assured that he will restore to your lover the part that is now missing and send him back to you right away. He says moreover that Lidio loves you more than ever, so much so that he will never again give his heart to anyone else. But that you are not to speak to anyone of this, or a dreadful scandal might result. That, finally, you are to send money to him and also to the spirit, to show your gratitude both to him and to me. Be of good cheer, and do not forget your faithful servant Ruffo.

Samia. Now you see it is true there is nothing the spirits do not know and cannot do.

Fessenio. I can hardly believe it.

Samia. I am anxious to bring this good news to my mistress.

Fessenio. Go, and God be with you. (*Exit* Samia.) Good heavens, am I to believe that Lidio has really been changed into a woman by magic, and that he will never love anyone again except Fulvia? Only God could work such a miracle, and yet Samia says that Fulvia felt him carefully. I intend to see this miracle with my own eyes, before he changes into a man again, and then, if it's as she says, I'll worship this magician forever. I'll go to Lidio now; I may find him at home.

ACT V

Scene I

Samia, Santilla *as* Lidio, Lidio.

Samia. How true it is that women do to money what
the sun does to ice: they consume it completely. My
mistress no sooner read Ruffo's note than she gave me
this bag of money to take to Lidio. There he is now.
Now, Lidio, you will see how the lady Fulvia keeps her
word. (*To* Santilla.) Come, here it is. Take it.

Santilla. Here I am.

Lidio. No, give it here.

Samia. Oh, I made a mistake. (*To* Santilla.) Excuse me,
sir. I wanted this gentleman, not you.

Santilla. Now you *are* mistaken. Come, do your business
with me, and let that gentleman go.

Samia. You are right; I'm sorry. (*To* Lidio.) Good-bye,
sir. (*To* Santilla.) You come here.

Lidio. What do you mean good-bye? Here, look at me.

Samia (*to* Lidio). Oh, yes . . . it is you after all. (*To*
Santilla.) It's this gentleman I want. You may leave us.

Santilla. Leave you? What do you mean? Am I not
Lidio?

Samia. Why, yes, I think you are. (*To* Lidio.) *You* go
away, sir.

Lidio. What's the matter with you? Look at me carefully. Am I not the one?

Samia. Why, of course. I'm sorry. You *are* Lidio. (*To*
Santilla.) *You* leave us, please.

Santilla. You fool, *I* am Lidio; he's not.

Samia. Well, well, you are right. (*To* Lidio.) Do please
leave us alone.

Lidio. What are you trying to do, you bitch? You know
the money belongs to me, yet you want to give it to
this fellow.

Santilla. What do you mean, yours? Give it to me.

Lidio. No, to me.

Santilla. Why to you? You are not Lidio; I am.

Lidio. Give it here.

Santilla. Here!

Samia. Don't touch it, either of you, or I'll scream. Let
me have a good look at you both. Good God, what a
miracle! These two resemble each other more than

87

snow resembles snow, or one egg another. I don't know
which of you is Lidio: first it seems the one, then the
other. But I know how I'll find out. Tell me, is either
of you gentlemen in love?

Lidio. I am.

Santilla. And so am I.

Samia. Which one?

Lidio. I.

Santilla. I.

Samia. Where does this money come from?

Lidio. From a lady.

Santilla. From my sweetheart.

Samia. Oh, heavens! Still not clear. Tell me, who is this
sweetheart?

Lidio. Fulvia.

Santilla. Fulvia.

Samia. Which of you is her lover?

Lidio. I am.

Santilla. I am.

Lidio. What do you mean, you are?

Santilla. I mean I am.

Lidio. You're not. I am.

Samia. Ah, me, what is all this? Which Fulvia are you
talking about?

Lidio. Calandro's wife.

Santilla (to Samia). And your mistress.

Samia. Still no light. Either I have lost my mind, or
these men are bewitched. Tell me, how were you
dressed when you went to her?

Lidio. As a woman.

Santilla. As a young lady.

Samia. This is too much. But oh, now I will find out.
When did my mistress want her lover to visit her?

Lidio. By day.

Santilla. At midday.

Samia. What the devil! This is certainly a fiendish plot
of some kind, thought up by that damned spirit. I'd
better go back to my mistress with this money and let
her give it to whomever she wishes. Gentlemen, I'm
sure you understand—I don't know which of you to
give it to. My mistress will surely know who her lover
is, so whichever of you is Lidio go to see her and you
may be sure that she will give it to you.

Exit.

Lidio (aside). My own reflection in the mirror looks
less like me than does this fellow; I shall soon know

who he is. Such adventures don't happen every day,
and Fulvia may change her mind. This is quite a lot
of money. I'd better go pay her a visit, the way I used
to.

Exit.

Santilla. That must be the man that I was mistaken for.
I wonder what is keeping Fannio? If he were here, as
he said he would be, we could go to Fulvia's and
maybe collect a lot of money. But he's not, and I have
to do something about this wedding I'm supposed to
be in.

Scene II

Fessenio, Santilla, Fannio.

Fessenio (apart). I couldn't find Lidio anywhere.

Santilla (apart). What am I going to do now?

Fessenio (apart). If I don't get to the bottom of this,
and find out if it's true that Lidio has been changed
into a woman, it won't be my fault. Oh! Is that him
over there? No, I don't think so. Yes, it is. He does
seem changed.

Santilla (apart). Ah, me!

Fessenio (apart). He is talking to himself.

Santilla (apart). What a mess all this is!

Fessenio (apart). I wonder what's the matter?

Santilla (apart). Must I be ruined so soon?

Fessenio (apart). What ruin is he talking about?

Santilla (apart). Because of too much love?

Fessenio (apart). I wonder what he means by that.

Santilla (apart). Will I have to stop wearing these
clothes?

Fessenio (apart). My, my, his voice certainly has become feminine. What a pity!

Santilla (apart). And lose all the freedom I have enjoyed?

Fessenio (apart). Well, it's true, all right. There's no
longer any doubt about it.

Santilla (apart). Now everyone will know I'm a woman.
I'll never be able to pass for a man again.

Fessenio (apart). True enough. The harm's been done
now.

Santilla (apart). From now on I must call myself Santilla, and not Lidio.

Fessenio (apart).   Sad but true.

Santilla (apart).   I'd be better off if they had let me die the day Modone was captured.

Fessenio (apart).   Oh, cruel fate! He's taking this very hard. If I hadn't heard it from his own lips, I'd never believe it. I'll speak to him. (*To* Lidio.) Oh, Lidio.

Santilla.   Who is this wretch?

Fessenio.   Why do you call me a wretch, as if you didn't know who I am?

Santilla.   I never knew you and I don't care to.

Fessenio.   So you don't know your own servant anymore?

Santilla.   You my servant?

Fessenio.   If you don't want me, I'll be someone else's.

Santilla.   Please leave me alone. I have no time for drunkards.

Fessenio.   Either you are drunk or you have lost your memory. But don't think you can hide from me, because I know all about your little accident.

Santilla.   What accident?

Fessenio.   When the magician changed you into a woman.

Santilla.   I a woman?

Fessenio.   Yes, a woman.

Santilla.   You are mistaken. (Fessenio *approaches, attempts to feel her.*) You wretch! What are you trying to do?

Fessenio.   I want to make sure.

Santilla.   How dare you touch me, you brute?

Fessenio (persisting).   I'll find out or die in the attempt.

Santilla.   Miserable creature, don't you dare! Help! Fannio! Help!

Fannio.   What's going on here?

Santilla.   This impudent fellow claims that I am a woman, and is trying to feel me against my will.

Fannio.   How dare you do such a thing?

Fessenio.   What right have you to come between my master and me?

Fannio.   Your master?

Fessenio.   Of course. Why?

Fannio.   My good man, you are mistaken. I know for a fact that you are not his servant, nor he your master, because I am his servant, and he is my master.

Fessenio.   That cannot be. I am his servant, and he is my master. You are both lying.

Santilla.   I'm not surprised that you speak with such arrogance, since you acted with such presumption.

Fessenio. Nor am I surprised that you have forgotten who I am, since you have forgotten your own identity.

Fannio (*to* Fessenio). Mind what you say to him.

Santilla. I don't know my own identity?

Fessenio. My lord, or rather my lady, if you knew who you were, you would know who I am.

Santilla. I know well enough who I am, but as for you, I have no idea.

Fessenio. Say rather that in losing yourself you have found someone else.

Santilla. And who is it that I have found?

Fessenio. Your sister Santilla, for now, since you have changed into a woman, she is in you; and since you are no longer a man, you have lost yourself. You are no longer Lidio.

Santilla. Lidio? Who is Lidio?

Fessenio. Poor fellow! He doesn't remember a thing. Come, master, don't you remember being Lidio of Medone, son of Demetrius, brother of Santilla, pupil of Polinico, master of Fessenio, lover of the lady Fulvia?

Santilla. Fannio, did you hear that? Oh, yes, I know the lady Fulvia.

Fessenio. He remembers no one but Fulvia; it's obvious he's been bewitched.

Scene III

Lidio *in women's dress,* Fessenio, Santilla *as* Lidio, Fannio.

Lidio. Fessenio, oh, Fessenio!

Fessenio. Who is that woman waving to me? (*To* Fannio.) You wait—I haven't finished with you yet.

Santilla. Fannio, if I dared to think that my brother was still alive, I would be full of hope. That person (*indicating* Lidio) must be the one they have mistaken me for.

Fannio. You are not sure of your brother's death?

Santilla. By no means.

Fannio. For now I am quite certain that that is indeed our lost Lidio, and now it seems to me that I also recognize this man as—Fessenio!

Santilla. Oh, God, I begin to feel my heart grow light with joy.

Fessenio (*to* Lidio). I'm still not sure if you are Lidio or if the other one is. Let me have a better look at you.

Lidio. What's the matter with you? Have you been drinking?

Fessenio. Yes, you are Lidio all right, and you are a man, too.

Lidio. I am on my way to see the lady Fulvia.

Fessenio. That's right; she's waiting to give you the money.

Santilla. What's that you said?

Fessenio. If I've said or done anything to offend you, I beg your pardon, for now I realize that you have been mistaken for my master.

Santilla. Who is your master?

Fessenio. One Lidio of Modone, and he looks so much like you I thought you were he.

Santilla. Dear Fannio, everything is clear now. (*To* Fessenio.) What is your name?

Fessenio. Fessenio, sir, at your service.

Santilla. Now there is no longer any doubt of it. Oh, how happy we are! (*Embraces* Fessenio.) Dear Fessenio, you are mine!

Fessenio. What are all these caresses for? And why do you say I am yours? When I said I was your servant a moment ago, I was lying: I am not, nor are you my master. I have another master, so you must seek another servant.

Santilla. You are mine, and I am yours!

Fannio (*embraces* Fessenio). Oh, my dear Fessenio!

Fessenio. What does all this mean? Something's going on here that I don't know about.

Fannio. This is Santilla, your master's sister.

Fessenio. Our Santilla?

Fannio. Shh, not so loud. Yes, it is. And I am Fannio.

Fessenio (*embraces* Fannio). Fannio! My dear fellow!

Fannio. Not here; someone's coming. Don't say anything about it.

Scene IV

Samia, Fessenio, Santilla as Lidio, Fannio.

Samia. Boohoo! Boohoo! My mistress and I are done for. Ruined! And out of a clear sky. Boohoo!

Fessenio. What's the matter with you, Samia?

Samia. Oh, my poor mistress!

Fessenio. Why, what's the matter?

Samia. Oh, my dear Fessenio, we are done for.

Fessenio. But what is it? Come, speak up.

Samia. Bad news.

Fessenio. How so?

Samia. Calandro's brothers founds your master Lidio with my mistress. They have sent for Calandro and for her brothers, too. They are going to denounce her to them and maybe kill Lidio.

Fessenio. What's this? Oh, my poor master! Are they holding him prisoner?

Samia. No.

Fessenio. Why didn't he run away then?

Samia. Because of my mistress. She is in hopes that before Calandro and her brothers get to the house, the magician will change Lidio back into a woman. That way he'll keep his life and my mistress her reputation: if he saved himself now, by running away, she would surely be ruined. That's where I'm going now—to see Ruffo.

Fessenio. Wait a minute. What part of the house is Lidio in?

Samia. Both he and my mistress are in the bedroom on the first floor.

Fessenio. Isn't there a window in the rear of that room?

Samia. Yes, he could escape easily enough if he wanted to.

Fessenio. That's not why I asked. If someone were to slip in through that window, would he be noticed?

Samia. Probably not.

Fessenio. Samia, this magician business is a lot of nonsense. If you want to save your mistress, go back to the house, and if there's anybody in the hall, try to get rid of them.

Samia. Well, all right. I'll do as you say, but I hope you know what you're doing.

Fessenio. Don't worry. Run along now.

Exit Samia.

Santilla. Ah, me, Fessenio, it looks as if fate has arranged that I should no sooner find my brother than I should lose him again; no sooner does he come to life than he must lose it.

Fessenio. Now is no time for tears: this situation calls for quick action and clear thinking. No one is looking now, so swap clothes with Fannio. Quickly—that's it.

Don't worry; I'm coming with you. Fannio, you wait
here. Now, Santilla, I'll tell you what you must do.
                              Exeunt Fessenio *and.* Santilla.
Fannio. What a strange predicament this brother and
sister find themselves in! This will either be the happiest or the worst day of their lives, depending on how
it ends. It seems that heaven made them similar not
only in their appearance but also in their fortunes:
each of them is now in a position where what profits
one profits both and where what harms one harms the
other. Until I can see further ahead I am unable either
to rejoice or despair, fear or hope. I pray heaven that
Lidio and Santilla will somehow find a way out of all
this. In the meantime, I'll step aside and wait for the
outcome.

Scene V

Lidio *alone.*

Lidio. I have been delivered from great danger, and I
scarcely know how it happened. While I was in that
room, bewailing the misfortune that overtook my mistress and me, someone sent by Fessenio jumps into the
room through the rear window, dresses himself in my
clothes, and gives me his. Then Fessenio told me to
slip out the window, saying not to worry, that everything would turn out all right. Just a few moments ago
things couldn't have looked worse; now I am pleased
with the way they seem to be working out. Fessenio
stayed behind to tell Fulvia something. I'd better wait
here to see what happens. Oh, there is my mistress
now, standing on the threshold. She looks happy, too.

Scene VI

Fulvia *alone.*

Fulvia. This has been quite a day for me, but everything has turned out for the best, thank heaven. I
couldn't be more pleased: my reputation has been
saved and so has Lidio's life. And now it will be easier
than ever for me to see him as often as I like. Whoever
wouldn't be satisfied with that wouldn't be human.

Scene VII

Calandro, *accompanied by two of* Fulvia's *brothers,* Fulvia.

Calandro. Wretched woman, what are you doing at that door? How can you stand there and wait for me like that, knowing you have hung horns on me? I don't know how I can keep myself from beating the breath out of your body, but first I want you to see me kill the man you have in that room, you slut, and then I'm going to tear the eyes out of your head.

Fulvia. Alas, my husband, what is the meaning of all this? Why do you act as if I were guilty of something, when I am not? What is the reason for such cruelty?

Calandro. Shameless woman, how can you keep pretending, as if we didn't know you have a man in there, dressed in woman's clothes?

Fulvia. My brothers, this wretched man wants to expose what I have always kept hidden, and that is my patience and the many outrages I have suffered at his hands. There is no wife in all the world more faithful than I, nor treated worse. And he dares to say that I have made him wear horns!

Calandro. It's true, you miserable creature, and now I'm going to prove it to your brothers.

Fulvia. Go on in, all of you, and see who it is I have in my room that this miserable little worm says he is going to kill.

Scene VIII

Lidio *alone.*

Lidio. Fessenio said everything would be all right, but it doesn't look that way, and I'm beginning to be suspicious. I didn't know who that was he made me swap clothes with. I don't see Fessenio, and Calandro has gone in the house, threatening Fulvia. He is beside himself with rage and may hurt her. If I hear any trouble, I'll go inside, no matter what, and either protect her or die for her. No true lover was ever lacking in courage.

Scene IX

Fannio, Lidio.

Fannio.   There is Lidio over there, or rather Santilla.
Let's change again. Give me back my clothes, and I'll
give you yours.

Lidio.   Why, what do you mean?

Fannio.   It's been such a short time since Fessenio made
you change clothes that you can't have forgotten.
Come, give me those and take these.

Lidio.   Certainly I remember changing clothes, but those
aren't the ones I gave you.

Fannio.   What's wrong with you? Do you think I'd have
gone and sold them?

Lidio.   Don't make me angry. Oh, there is Fessenio.

Scene X

Fessenio *alone.*

Fessenio.   Ha, ha, ha! They thought that under that dress
they'd find the young man they suspected Fulvia of
amusing herself with: they were going to kill him and
denounce her, but when they found out it was a girl,
they quieted down and apologized to Fulvia, saying
she was the most virtuous woman in all the world.
Now her reputation is secure, and so is my own happiness. They have let Santilla go; I see her coming
out now. And there is Lidio, too.

Scene XI

Santilla, Fessenio, Lidio, Fannio.

Santilla.   Where is my brother, Fessenio?

Fessenio.   There he is over there, still wearing the
clothes you gave him. Let's go to him. Lidio, do you
know who this is?

Lidio.   Not for sure. Tell me.

Fessenio.   The one who saved you by taking your place
at the lady Fulvia's, and for whom you have been
looking so long.

Lidio. Who?

Fessenio. Your Santilla.

Lidio. My sister?

Santilla. I am your sister, and you are my brother.

Lidio. Are you really Santilla? But I see now that you are. Oh, my dear sister, for whom I have wished and searched so long! Now at last I am satisfied; now I have gained my wish; now I am the happiest man alive.

Santilla. Beloved brother of mine, though I see you and touch you, I can scarcely believe you are really he whom I thought dead and for whom I mourned so long. Now that I find you are alive, my joy is as great as my grief was then.

Lidio. And I, my dear sister, love you all the more because of what you did for me today: if it hadn't been for you, I wouldn't be alive to say this.

Santilla. Now that I have recovered somewhat from this shock, allow me to present to you our servant Fannio, who has always served me faithfully.

Lidio. Dear Fannio, I remember you quite well, and in having served one of us you have served us both. You shall be rewarded for it.

Fannio. My greatest reward, sir, is to see you alive and rejoined with your sister.

Santilla. Dear Fessenio, why are you looking at us so hard?

Fessenio. Never in all my life have I seen a man resemble another man so much as you and your brother resemble each other. I understand now the reason for all these strange mistakes.

Santilla. They have been strange indeed.

Lidio. And more numerous than either of you realizes.

Fessenio. We'll have time to talk about that later. Right now the most important thing is this: when I told the lady Fulvia that this was your sister Santilla, she was greatly pleased and said that, if everyone is willing, Santilla would become the wife of her son Flaminio.

Santilla. Now I understand why, when we were in the room together, she kissed me tenderly and said: I don't know which of us three is the happiest; Lidio has found a sister, I a daughter, and you a husband.

Lidio. It could all be true, too.

Fannio. I know of a better plan still.

Lidio. What is that?

Fannio. As Fessenio says, you two are so much alike that you would fool anybody.

Santilla. I know what you mean—that Lidio should take my place in the marriage with Perillo's daughter.

Lidio. That's settled then?

Santilla. As settled as the weather.

Lidio. How fortunate we are! After so fierce a storm, how beautiful a calm! We shall be even better off than we were in Modone.

Fessenio. As much better off than Italy is worthier than Greece; than Rome is statelier than Modone; and than two fortunes are better than one. We shall all be gainers.

Lidio. Come, let's get started.

Fessenio (to audience). Good people, the weddings will take place tomorrow. Whoever wishes to see them should stay, but whoever wishes to avoid the inconvenience of waiting till then, let him go about his business, as we are finished with ours. VALETE ET PLAUDITE.

Anonymous

THE DECEIVED

(Gl'ingannati)

In his book *Italian Comedy in the Renaissance* (Urbana: University of Illinois Press, 1960), Marvin T. Herrick writes:

> Among the best known and most influential learned comedies is *Gl'ingannati* [*The Deceived*], first performed at Siena in 1531, written by a member of the Sienese Academy of the Intronati. This play has attracted unusual attention outside Italy because it offers a parallel to and a possible source of Shakespeare's *Twelfth Night*. . . . *The Deceived* is one of many comedies derived from the twins in Plautus' Menaechmi and doubtless owes something to Bibbiena's *Follies of Calandro* as well. . .

The play was translated, in an abridged form, by the great English writer, Thomas Love Peacock, who introduced his text as follows:

> A girl assumes male apparel and enters as a page into the service of a man with whom she either previously is, or subsequently becomes, in love. He employs her as a messenger to a lady, who will not listen to his suit. The lady falls in love with the supposed page and, under the influence of a mistake, marries the girl's twin brother. The lover transfers his affection to the damsel, who has served him in disguise.
> I propose to translate the scenes in which these four characters are principally concerned and to give a connecting outline of the rest.

99

The original has no stage directions, and the scenes have no indication of place. I have inserted some stage directions and have indicated the places of the action, on what appeared to me probable grounds.

The house of Virginio is too far from the house of Gherardo to be shown in the same street. This is apparent from several passages, especially from *Act IV, Scene VII*, where Virginio asks Gherardo to take in his supposed daughter because he cannot take her to his own house without her being seen in male apparel by all the city.

The house of Gherardo is near the hotels.

The house of Flaminio is in a distinct locality from both. It is clearly not under observation from either.

I have, therefore, marked three changes of scene:

A street, with two hotels and the house of Gherardo.

A street, with the house of Flaminio.

A street, with the house of Virginio.

E. B.

THE DECEIVED

(1531)

Anonymous

ENGLISH VERSION WITH NOTES BY
THOMAS LOVE PEACOCK

Characters

GHERARDO FOIANI, *an old man, father of* Isabella
VIRGINIO BELLENZINI, *an old man, father of* Lelia *and* Fabrizio
FLAMINIO DE' CARANDINI, *in love with* Isabella
FABRIZIO, *son of* Virginio
MESSER PIERO, *a pedant, tutor of* Fabrizio
L'AGIATO, } *rival hotelkeepers*
FRUELLA, }
GIGLIO, *a Spaniard*
SPELA, *servant of* Gherardo
SCATIZZA, *servant of* Virginio
CRIVELLO, *servant of* Flaminio
STRAGUALCIA, *servant of* Fabrizio
LELIA, *daughter of* Virginio, *disguised as a page, under the name of* Fabio
ISABELLA, *daughter of* Gherardo
CLEMENTIA, *nurse of* Lelia
PASQUELLA, *housekeeper to* Gherardo
CITTINA, *a girl, daughter of* Clementia

The Scene is in Modena.

ACT I

Scene I: A street, with the house of Virginio.

Virginio *and* Gherardo.

(Virginio is an old merchant, who has two children, a
son and a daughter, Fabrizio and Lelia. He has lost
his property and his son in the sack of Rome, May,
1527, when his daughter had just finished her thir-
teenth year. The comedy being performed in the
Carnival of 1531, the girl is in her seventeenth year.
Another old man, Gherardo, who is wealthy, wishes
to marry her, and the father assents, provided the
maiden is willing. Gherardo thinks that the father's
will ought to be sufficient and that it only rests with
him to make his daughter do as he pleases.)

Scene II

Virginio *and* Clementia.

(Virginio, having shortly before gone on business to
Bologna, in company with a Messer Buonaparte and
others, had left Lelia in a convent with her Aunt
Camilla, and now, in the intention of her marriage,
desires Lelia's nurse, Clementia, to go to the convent
to bring her home. Clementia must first go to Mass.)

Scene III. A street, with the house of Flaminio.

Lelia; *afterward* Clementia.

Lelia (in male apparel). It is a great boldness in me
that, knowing the licentious customs of these wild
youths of Modena, I should venture abroad alone at

this early hour. What would become of me if any one
of them should suspect my sex? But the cause is my
love for the cruel and ungrateful Flaminio. Oh, what
a fate is mine! I love one who hates me. I serve one
who does not know me: and, for more bitter grief, I
aid him in his love for another, without any other
hope than that of satiating my eyes with his sight.
Thus far all has gone well: but now, how can I do?
My father has returned. Flaminio has come to live in
the town. I can scarcely hope to continue here without
being discovered: and if it should be so, my reputation will be blighted forever, and I shall become the
fable of the city. Therefore I have come forth at this
hour to consult my nurse, whom, from the window, I
have seen coming this way. But I will first see if she
knows me in this dress.

Clementia enters.

Clementia. In good faith, Flaminio must be returned to
Modena: for I see his door open. Oh! If Lelia knew
it, it would appear to her a thousand years till she
came back to her father's house. But who is this young
coxcomb that keeps crossing before me, backward and
forward? What do you mean by it? Take yourself off,
or I will show you how I like such chaps.
Lelia. Good morning, good mother.
Clementia. I seem to know this boy. Tell me, where can
I have seen you?
Lelia. You pretend not to know me, eh? Come a little
nearer: nearer still: on this side. Now?
Clementia. It is possible? Can you be Lelia? Oh, misery
of my life! What can this mean, my child?
Lelia. Oh! If you cry out in this way, I must go.
Clementia. Is this the honor you do to your father, to
your house, to yourself, to me who have brought you
up? Come in instantly. You shall not be seen in this
dress.
Lelia. Pray have a little patience.
Clementia. Are you not ashamed to be seen so?
Lelia. Am I the first? I have seen women in Rome go in
this way by hundreds.
Clementia. They must be no better than they should be.
Lelia. By no means.
Clementia. Why do you go so? Why have you left the
convent? Oh! If your father knew it, he would kill you.

Lelia. He would end my affliction. Do you think I value life?

Clementia. But why do you go so? Tell me.

Lelia. Listen, and you shall hear. You will then know how great is my affliction, why I have left the convent, why I go thus attired, and what I wish you to do in the matter. But step more aside, lest anyone should pass who may recognize me, seeing me talking with you.

Clementia. You destroy me with impatience.

Lelia. You know that after the miserable sack of Rome, my father, having lost everything, and with his property my brother Fabrizio, in order not to be alone in his house, took me from the service of the Signora Marchesana, with whom he had placed me, and, constrained by necessity, we returned to our house in Modena to live on the little that remained to us here. You know, also, that my father, having been considered a friend of the Count Guido Rangon,* was not well looked on by many.

Clementia. Why do you tell me what I know better than you? I know, too, for what reason you left the city, to live at our farm of Pontanile, and that I went with you.

Lelia. You know, also, how bitter were my feelings at that time: not only remote from all thoughts of love, but almost from all human thought, considering that, having been a captive among soldiers, I could not, however purely and becomingly I might live, escape malicious observations. And you know how often you scolded me for my melancholy, and exhorted me to lead a more cheerful life.

Clementia. If I know it, why do you tell it me? Go on.

Lelia. Because it is necessary to remind you of all this, that you may understand what follows. It happened at this time that Flaminio Carandini, from having been attached to the same party as ourselves, formed an intimate friendship with my father, came daily to our house, began to admire me secretly, then took to sighing and casting down his eyes. By degrees I took increasing pleasure in his manners and conversation, not, however, even dreaming of love. But his continuous visits, and sighs, and signs of admiration at

* This count makes a conspicuous figure in Guicciardini's *History*.

last made me aware that he was not a little taken with me, and I, who had never felt love before, deeming him worthy of my dearest thoughts, became in love with him so strongly that I had no longer any delight but in seeing him.

Clementia. Much of this I also knew.

Lelia. You know, too, that when the Spanish soldiers left Rome my father went there, to see if any of our property remained, but, still more, to see if he could learn any news of my brother. He sent me to Mirandola, to stay till his return, with my Aunt Giovanna. With what grief I separated myself from my dear Flaminio you may well say, who so often dried my tears. I remained a year at Mirandola, and on my father's return I came back to Modena, more than ever enamored of him who was my first love, and thinking still that he loved me as before.

Clementia. Oh, insanity! How many Modenese have you found constant in the love of one for a year? One month to one, another month to another, is the extent of their devotion.

Lelia. I met him, and he scarcely remembered me, more than if he had never seen me. But the worst of it is that he has set his heart on Isabella, the daughter of Gherardo Foiani, who is not only very beautiful, but the only child of her father, if the crazy old fellow does not marry again.

Clementia. He thinks himself certain of having you, and says that your father has promised you to him. But all this does not explain to me why you have left the convent, and go about in male apparel.

Lelia. The old fellow certainly shall not have me. But my father, after his return from Rome, having business at Bologna, placed me, as I would not return to Mirandola, in the convent with my cousin Amabile de' Cortesi. I found that among these reverend mothers and sisters love was the principal subject of conversation. I therefore felt emboldened to open my heart to Amabile. She pitied me and found means to bring Flaminio, who was then living out of the town, in a palazzo near the convent, several times to speak with her and with others, where I, concealed behind curtains, might feast my eyes with seeing him, and my ears with hearing him. One day I heard him lamenting the death of a page, whose good service he highly praised, saying how glad he should be if he could find such another. It immediately occurred to me that I would try to supply the vacant place, and consulting with Sister Amabile, she encouraged me, instructed me how to proceed, and fitted me with some new clothes, which she had had made, in order that she might, as others do, go out in disguise about her own affairs. So one morning, early, I left the convent in this attire and went to Flaminio's palazzo. There I waited till Flaminio came out: and Fortune be praised, he no sooner saw me than he asked me, most courteously, what I wanted and whence I came.

Clementia. Is it possible that you did not fall dead with shame?

Lelia. Far from it, indeed. Love bore me up. I answered frankly that I was from Rome and, that being poor, I was seeking service. He examined me several times from head to foot so earnestly that I was almost afraid he would know me. He then said that if I pleased to stay with him, he would receive me willingly and treat me well; and I answered that I would gladly do so.

Clementia. And what good do you expect from this mad proceeding?

Lelia. The good of seeing him, hearing him, talking with him, learning his secrets, seeing his companions, and being sure that if he is not mine, he is not another's.

Clementia. In what way do you serve him?

Lelia. As his page, in all honesty. And in this fortnight that I have served him, I have become so much in favor that I almost think appearing in my true dress would revive his love.

Clementia. What will people say when this shall be known?

Lelia. Who will know it, if you do not tell it? Now what I want you to do is this: that, as my father returned yesterday, and may perhaps send for me, you would prevent his doing so for four or five days, and at the end of that time I will return. You may say that I have gone to Roverino with Sister Amabile.

Clementia. And why all this?

Lelia. Flaminio, as I have already told you, is enamored of Isabella Foiani; and he often sends me to her with letters and messages. She, taking me for a young man, has fallen madly in love with me, and makes me the most passionate advances. I pretend that I will not love her unless she can so manage as to bring Flaminio's pursuit of her to an end: and I hope that in three or four days he will be brought to give her up.

Clementia. Your father has sent me for you, and I insist on your coming to my house, and I will send for your clothes. If you do not come with me, I will tell your father all about you.

Lelia. Then I will go where neither you nor he shall ever see me again. I can say no more now, for I hear Flaminio call me. Expect me at your house in an hour. Remember that I call myself Fabio degl' Alberini. I come, signor. Adieu, Clementia.

Clementia (alone). In good faith, she has seen Gherardo coming, and has run away. I must not tell her father for the present and she must not remain where she is. I will wait till I see her again.

Scene IV

Gherardo, Spela, *and* Clementia.

(In this scene, Clementia makes sport of the old lover, treating him as a sprightly youth. He swallows the flattery and echoes it in rapturous speeches, while his servant, Spela, in a series of asides, exhausts on his folly the whole vocabulary of anger and contempt.)

Scene V

Spela *and* Scatizza.

(Spela, at first alone, soliloquizes in ridicule of his master. Scatizza, the servant of Virginio, who had been to fetch Lelia from the convent, enters in great wrath, having been laughed at by the nuns, who told him all sorts of contradictory stories respecting her; by which he is so bewildered that he does not know what to say to Virginio.)

ACT II

Scene I: The street, with the house of Flaminio.

Lelia (*as* Fabio) *and* Flaminio.

Flaminio. It is a strange thing, Fabio, that I have not yet
been able to extract a kind answer from this cruel, this
ungrateful Isabella, and yet her always receiving you
graciously and giving you willing audience makes me
think that she does not altogether hate me. Assuredly,
I never did anything, that I know, to displease her;
and you may judge, from her conversation, if she has
any cause to complain of me. Repeat to me what she
said yesterday, when you went to her with that letter.

Lelia. I have repeated it to you twenty times.

Flaminio. Oh, repeat it to me once more. What can it
matter to you?

Lelia. It matters to me this, that it is disagreeable to you
and is, therefore, painful to me, as your servant, who
seeks only to please you; and perhaps these answers
may give you ill will toward me.

Flaminio. No, my dear Fabio; I love you as a brother:
I know you wish well to me, and I will never be wanting to you, as time shall show. But repeat to me what
she said.

Lelia. Have I not told you? That the greatest pleasure
you can do her is to let her alone; to think no more
of her, because she has fixed her heart elsewhere: that
she has no eyes to look on you; that you lose your
time in following her, and will find yourself at last
with your hands full of wind.

Flaminio. And does it appear to you, Fabio, that she says
these things from her heart, or, rather, that she has
taken some offense with me? For at one time she
showed me favor, and I cannot believe that she wishes
me ill while she accepts my letters and my messages.
I am disposed to follow her till death. Do you not
think me in the right, Fabio?

Lelia. No, signor.

Flaminio. Why?

Lelia. Because, if I were in your place, I should expect her to receive my service as a grace and an honor. To a young man like you, noble, virtuous, elegant, handsome, can ladies worthy of you be wanting? Do as I would do, sir: leave her and attach yourself to someone who will love you as you deserve. Such will be easily found, and perhaps as handsome as she is. Have you never yet found one in this country who loved you?

Flaminio. Indeed I have, and especially one, who is named Lelia, and of whom, I have often thought, I see a striking likeness in you: the most beautiful, the most accomplished, the most courteous young person in this town: who would think herself happy if I would show her even a little favor: rich and well received at court. We were lovers nearly a year, and she showed me a thousand favors: but she went to Mirandola, and my fate made me enamored of Isabella, who has been as cruel to me as Lelia was gracious.

Lelia. Master, you deserve to suffer. If you do not value one who loves you, it is fitting that one you love should not value you.

Flaminio. What do you mean?

Lelia. If you first loved this poor girl, and if she loved and still loves you, why have you abandoned her to follow another? Ah, Signor Flaminio, you do a great wrong, a greater than I know if God can pardon.

Flaminio. You are a child, Fabio. You do not know the force of love. I cannot help myself. I must love and adore Isabella. I cannot, may not, will not think of any but her. Therefore, go to her again: speak with her: and try to draw dextrously from her what is the cause that she will not see me.

Lelia. You will lose your time.

Flaminio. It pleases me so to lose it.

Lelia. You will do nothing.

Flaminio. Patience.

Lelia. Pray let her go.

Flaminio. I cannot. Go, as I bid you.

Lelia. I will go, but——

Flaminio. Return with the answer immediately. Meanwhile I will go in.

Lelia. When time serves, I will not fail.

Flaminio. Do this, and it will be well for you.

Scene II

Lelia *and* Pasquella.

Lelia. He has gone in good time, for here is Pasquella coming to look for me.

Lelia *retires.*

Pasquella. I do not think there is in the world a greater trouble, or a greater annoyance, than to serve a young woman like my mistress, who has neither mother nor sisters to look after her and who has fallen all at once into such a passion of love that she has no rest night or day, but runs about the house, now upstairs, now down, now to one window, now to another, as if she had quicksilver in her feet. Oh! I have been young, and I have been in love: but I gave myself some repose. At least, if she had fallen in love with a man of note and of fitting years: but she has taken to doting on a boy, who, I think, could scarcely tie the points of his doublet if he had not someone to help him: and every day, and all day, she sends me to look for him, as if I had nothing to do at home. But here he is, happily. Good day to you, Fabio. I was seeking you, my charmer.

Lelia. And a thousand crowns to you, Pasquella. How does your fair mistress?

Pasquella. And how can you suppose she does? Wastes away in tears and lamentations that all this morning you have not been to her house.

Lelia. She would not have me there before daybreak. I have something to do at home. I have a master to serve.

Pasquella. Your master always wishes you to go there: and my mistress entreats you to come, for her father is not at home, and she has something of consequence to tell you.

Lelia. Tell her she must get rid of Flaminio, or I shall ruin myself by obeying her.

Pasquella. Come and tell her so yourself.

Lelia. I have something else to do, I tell you.

Pasquella. It is but to go and return as soon as you please.

Lelia. I will not come. Go and tell her so.

Pasquella. You will not?

Lelia. No, I say. Do you not hear? No. No. No.

Pasquella. In good faith, in good truth, Fabio, Fabio, you are too proud: you are young: you do not know your own good: this favor will not last always; you will not always have such rosy cheeks, such ruby lips: when your beard grows, you will not be the pretty pet you are now. Then you will repent your folly. How many are there in this city that would think the love of Isabella the choicest gift of heaven!

Lelia. Then let her give it to them: and leave alone me, who do not care for it.

Pasquella. Oh, heaven! How true is it that boys have no brains. Oh, dear, dear Fabio, pray come, and come soon, or she will send me for you again and will not believe that I have delivered her message.

Lelia. Well, Pasquella, go home. I did but jest. I will come.

Pasquella. When, my jewel?

Lelia. Soon.

Pasquella. How soon?

Lelia. Immediately: go.

Pasquella. I shall expect you at the door.

Lelia. Yes, yes.

Pasquella. If you do not come, I shall be very angry.

Scene III: A street, with two hotels and the house of Gherardo.

Giglio (*a Spaniard*) *and* Pasquella:

(Giglio, who is in love with Isabella, and longs for an opportunity of speaking to her without witnesses, tries to cajole Pasquella into admitting him to the house,* and promises her a rosary, with which he is to return in the evening. She does not intend to admit him, but thinks to trick him out of the rosary. He does not intend to give her the rosary, but thinks to delude her by the promise of it.)

Por mia vida, que esta es la Vieia biene avventurada, que tiene la mas hermosa moza d' esta tierra per sua ama. O se le puodiesse io ablar dos parablas sin testiges. . . . . Quiero veer se puode con alguna lisenia, pararme tal con esta vieia ellacca ob alcatieta que me aga al canzar alge con ella.

Scene IV: The street, with the house of Flaminio.

Flaminio, Crivello, *and* Scatizza.

Flaminio. You have not been to look for Fabio, and he
does not come. I do not know what to think of his delay.
Crivello. I was going, and you called me back. How am I
to blame?
Flaminio. Go now, and if he is still in the house of Isabella, wait till he comes out, and send him home instantly.
Crivello. How shall I know if he is there or not? You
would not have me knock and inquire?
Flaminio. I have not a servant worth his salt but Fabio.
Heaven grant me favor to reward him. What are you
muttering, blockhead? Is it not true?
Crivello. What would you have me say? Of course I say,
yes. Fabio is good: Fabio is handsome: Fabio serves
well: Fabio with you: Fabio with your lady: Fabio
does everything. But——
Flaminio. What do you mean by but?
Crivello. He is too much trusted: he is a stranger, and
one day he may disappear, with something worth taking.
Flaminio. I wish you others were as trustworthy. Yonder
is Scatizza. Ask him if he has seen Fabio: and come to
me at the bank of the Porini.

(The scene terminates with a few words between Crivello and Scatizza.)

Scene V

(Spela soliloquizes on the folly of Gherardo, who had
sent him to buy a bottle of perfume; and some young
men in the shop, understanding for whom it was
wanted, had told him he had better buy a bottle of
asafetida.)

Scene VI: The street, with the hotels and the house of
Gherardo.

Crivello, Scatizza, Lelia, *and* Isabella.

(Crivello and Scatizza are talking of keeping carnival at the expense of their masters, when Gherardo's door opens, and they stand back. Leila and Isabella enter from the house of Gherardo.)

Lelia. Remember what you have promised me.

Isabella. And do you remember to return to me. One word more.

Lelia. What more?

Isabella. Listen.

Lelia. I attend.

Isabella. No one is here.

Lelia. Not a living soul.

Isabella. Come nearer. I wish——

Lelia. What do you wish?

Isabella. I wish that you would return after dinner, when my father will be out.

Lelia. I will; but if my master passes this way, close the window and retire.

Isabella. If I do not, may you never love me.

Lelia. Adieu. Now return into the house.

Isabella. I would have a favor from you.

Lelia. What?

Isabella. Come a little within.

Lelia. We shall be seen.

Scatizza (*apart*). She has kissed him.

Crivello (*apart*). I had rather have lost a hundred crowns than not have seen this kiss. What will my master do when he knows it?

Scatizza (*apart*). Oh, the devil! You won't tell him?

Isabella. Pardon me. Your too great beauty and the too great love I bear you have impelled me to this. You will think it scarcely becoming the modesty of a maid; but God knows, I could not resist.

Lelia. I need no excuses, signora. I know too well what extreme love has led me to.

Isabella. To what?

Lelia. To deceiving my master, which is not well.

Isabella. Ill fortune come to him.

Lelia. It is late. I must go home. Remain in peace.

Isabella. I give myself to you.

Lelia. I am yours. (Isabella *goes in.*) I am sorry for her and wish I were well out of this intrigue. I will consult my nurse, Clementia; but here comes Flaminio.

Crivello (*apart*). Scatizza, my master told me to go to him at the bank of the Porini. I will carry him this good

news. If he does not believe me, I shall call you to
witness.

Scatizza. I will not fail you; but if you will take my advice, you will keep quiet, and you will always have this
rod in pickle for Fabio, to make him do as you please.

Crivello. I tell you I hate him. He has ruined me.

Scatizza. Take your own way.

Scene VII: *The street, with the house of* Flaminio.

Flaminio *and* Lelia.

Flaminio. Is it possible that I can be so far out of myself,
have so little self-esteem, as to love, in her own despite,
one who hates me, despises me, will not even conde-
scend to look at me? Am I so vile, of so little account,
that I cannot free myself from this shame, this torment?
But here is Fabio. Well, what have you done?

Lelia. Nothing.

Flaminio. Why have you been so long away?

Lelia. I have delayed, because I waited to speak with Isabella.

Flaminio. And why have you not spoken to her?

Lelia. She would not listen to me; and if you would act
in my way, you would take another course; for by all
that I can so far understand, she is most obstinately
resolved to do nothing to please you.

Flaminio. Why, even now, as I passed her house, she
rose and disappeared from the window, with as much
anger and fury as if she had seen some hideous and
horrible thing.

Lelia. Let her go, I tell you. Is it possible that in all this
city there is no other who merits your love as much as
she does?

Flaminio. I would it were not so. I fear this has been the
cause of all my misfortune; for I loved very warmly
that Lelia Bellenzini of whom I have spoken; and I fear
Isabella thinks this love still lasts, and on that account
will not see me; but I will give Isabella to understand
that I love Lelia no longer; rather that I hate her, and
cannot bear to hear her named, and will pledge my
faith never to go where she may be. Tell Isabella this as
strongly as you can.

Lelia. Oh, me!

Flaminio. What has come over you? What do you feel?

Lelia. Oh, me!

Flaminio. Lean on me. Have you any pain?

Lelia. Suddenly. In the heart.

Flaminio. Go in. Apply warm cloths to your side. I will
follow immediately and, if necessary, will send for a
doctor to feel your pulse and prescribe a remedy. Give
me your arm. You are pale and cold. Lean on me.
Gently—gently. (*Leads her into the house, and returns.*)
To what are we subject! I would not, for all I am
worth, that anything should happen to him, for there
never was in the world a more diligent and well-man-
nered servant, nor one more cordially attached to his
master.

Flaminio *goes off, and* Lelia *returns.*

Lelia. Oh, wretched Lelia! Now you have heard from the
mouth of this ungrateful Flaminio how well he loves
you. Why do you lose your time in following one so
false and so cruel? All your former love, your favors,
and your prayers were thrown away. Now your strata-
gems are unavailing. Oh, me, unhappy! Refused, rejected, spurned, hated! Why do I serve him who repels
me? Why do I ask him who denies me? Why do I
follow him who flies me? Why do I love him who hates
me? Ah, Flaminio! Nothing pleases him but Isabella.
He desires nothing but Isabella. Let him have her. Let
him hold her. I must leave him, or I shall die. I will
serve him no longer in this dress. I will never again
come in his way, since he holds me in such deadly hatred. I will go to Clementia, who expects me, and with
her I will determine on the course of my future life.

Scene VIII

Flaminio *and* Crivello.

Crivello. And if it is not so, cut out my tongue and hang
me up by the neck.

Flaminio. How long since?

Crivello. When you sent me to look for him.

Flaminio. Tell me again how it was, for he denies having
been able to speak with her.

Crivello. You will do well to make him confess it. I tell
you that, watching about the house to see if he were
there, I saw him come out; and as he was going away,
Isabella called him back into the doorway. They looked
round, to see if anyone were near, and not seeing anyone, they kissed together.

Flaminio. How was it that they did not see you?

Crivello. I was ensconced in the opposite portico.

Flaminio. How then did you see them?

Crivello. By peeping in the nick of time, when they saw
nothing but each other.

Flaminio. And he kissed her?

Crivello. I do not know whether he kissed her or she
kissed him, but I am sure that one kissed the other.

Flaminio. Be sure that you saw clearly, and do not come
by-and-by to say that it seemed so; for this is a great
matter that you tell me of. How did you see it?

Crivello. Watching with open eyes, and having nothing to
do but to see.

Flaminio. If this be true, you have killed me.

Crivello. This is true. She called him back, she went up to
him: she embraced him; she kissed him. If this is to
kill you, you are dead.

Flaminio. It is no wonder that the traitor denied having
been there. I know now why he counseled me to give
her up: that he might have her himself. If I do not take
such vengeance as shall be a warning to all traitorous
servants, may I never be esteemed a man. But I will not
believe you without better evidence. You are ill-dis-
posed to Fabio and wish to get rid of him; but by the
eternal heaven, I will make you tell the truth, or I will
kill you. You saw them kissing?

Crivello. I did.

Flaminio. He kissed her?

Crivello. Or she him. Or both.

Flaminio. How often?

Crivello. Twice.

Flaminio. Where?

Crivello. In the entry of her house.

Flaminio. You lie in your throat. You said in the doorway.

Crivello. Just inside the doorway.

Flaminio. Tell the truth.

Crivello. I am very sorry to have told it.

Flaminio. It was true?

Crivello. Yes; and I have a witness.

Flaminio. Who?
Crivello. Virginio's man, Scatizza.
Flaminio. Did he see it?
Crivello. As I did.
Flaminio. And if he does not confess it?
Crivello. Kill me.
Flaminio. I will.
Crivello. And if he does confess it?
Flaminio. I will kill both.
Crivello. Oh, the devil! What for?
Flaminio. Not you. Isabella and Fabio.
Crivello. And burn down the house, with Pasquella and everyone in it.
Flaminio. Let us look for Scatizza. I will pay them. I will take such revenge as all this land shall ring of.

ACT III

Scene I: The street, with the hotels and the house of Gherardo.

Messer Piero, Fabrizio, *and* Stragualcia.

(Messer Piero, who had been before in Modena, points out some of its remarkable places to Fabrizio, who had been taken from it too young to remember it. Stragualcia is a hungry fellow who is clamorous for his dinner.)

Scene II

L'Agiato, Fruella, Piero, Fabrizio, *and* Stragualcia.

(L'Agiato *and* Fruella, *two rival hotelkeepers, dispute the favor of the newcomers.*)

L'Agiato. Oh, signors, this is the hotel; lodge at the Looking-Glass—at the Looking-Glass.
Fruella. Welcome, signors: I have lodged you before. Do you not remember your Fruella? The only hotel for gentlemen of your degree.

L'Agiato. You shall have good apartments, a good fire, excellent beds, white crisp sheets—everything you can ask for.

Fruella. I will give you the best wine of Lombardy: partridges, homemade sausages, pigeons, pullets; and whatever else you may desire.

L'Agiato. I will give you veal sweetbreads, Bologna sausages, mountain wine, all sorts of delicate fare.

Fruella. I will give you fewer delicacies and more substantials. You will live at a fixed rate. At the Looking-Glass you will be charged even for candles.

Stragualcia. Master, let us put up here. This seems best.

L'Agiato. If you wish to live well, lodge at the Looking-Glass. You would not have it said that you lodged at the Fool.*

Fruella. My Fool is a hundred thousand times better than your Looking-Glass.

Messer Piero. Speculum prudentiam significat, juxta illud nostri Catonis, Nosce teipsum.† You understand, Fabrizio.

Fabrizio. I understand.

Fruella. See who has most guests, you or I.

L'Agiato. See who has most men of note.

Fruella. See where they are best treated.

L'Agiato. See where there are most delicacies.

Stragualcia. Delicacies, delicacies, delicacies! Give me substance. Delicacies are for the Florentines.

L'Agiato. All these lodge with me.

Fruella. They did! but for the last three years they have come to me.

L'Agiato. My man, give me the trunk, it seems to gall your shoulder.

Stragualcia. Never mind my shoulder, I want to fill my stomach.

Fruella. Here is a couple of capons, just ready. These are for you.

Stragualcia. They will do for a first course.

L'Agiato. Look at this ham.

Messer Piero. Not bad.

Fruella. Who understands wine?

Stragualcia. I do; better than the French.

* In the sense of *fou,* not of *sot.*

† The looking-glass signifies prudence, according to the saying of our Cato: "Know yourself."

Fruella. See if this pleases you. If not, you may try ten other sorts.

Stragualcia. Fruella, you are the prince of hosts. Taste this, master. This is good. Carry in the trunk.

Messer Piero. Wait a little. What have you to say?

L'Agiato. I say that gentlemen do not care for heavy meats but for what is light, good, and delicate.

Stragualcia. This would be an excellent *provedore* for a hospital.

Messer Piero. Do not be uncivil. What will you give us?

L'Agiato. You have only to command.

Fruella. Where there is plenty, a man may eat little or much as he pleases; but where there is little, and the appetite grows with eating, he can only finish his dinner with bread.

Stragualcia. You are wiser than the statutes. I have never seen a landlord so much to my mind.

Fruella. Go into the kitchen, brother; there you will see.

Messer Piero. *Omnis repletio mala, panis autem pessima.**

Stragualcia (*aside*). Paltry pedant! One of these days I must crack his skull.

L'Agiato. Come in, gentlemen. It is not good to stand in the cold.

Fabrizio. We are not so chilly.

Fruella. You must know, gentlemen, this hotel of the Looking-Glass used to be the best hotel in Lombardy; but since I have opened this of the Fool, it does not lodge ten persons in a year, and my sign has a greater reputation throughout the world than any other hostelry whatever. The French come here in flocks, and all the Germans that pass this way.

L'Agiato. That is not true. The Germans go to the Pig.

Fruella. The Milanese come here; the Parmesans, the Placentians.

L'Agiato. The Venetians come to me, the Genoese, the Florentines.

Messer Piero. Where do the Neapolitans lodge?

Fruella. With me.

L'Agiato. The greater part of them lodge at the Cupid.

Fruella. Many with me.

Fabrizio. Where does the Duke of Malfi?

Fruella. Sometimes at my house, sometimes at his, sometimes at the Sword, sometimes at the Cupid; accordingly as he finds most room for his suite.

---

* All repletion is bad, but that of bread is the worst.

Messer Piero. Where do the Romans lodge, as we are from Rome?

L'Agiato. With me.

Fruella. It is not true. He does not lodge a Roman in a year, except two or three old cardinals, who keep to him from habit. All the rest come to the Fool.

Stragualcia. I would not go from hence without being dragged away. Master, there are so many pots and pipkins about the fire, so many soups, so many sauces, so many spits turning with partridges and capons, such an odor of stews and ragouts, such a display of pies and tarts, that, if the whole court of Rome were coming here to keep carnival, there would be enough, and to spare.

Fabrizio. Have you been drinking?

Stragualcia. Oh! And such wine.

Messer Piero. *variorum ciborum commistio pessiman generat digestionem.**

Stragualcia. Rus asinorum, buorum castronorum pecoronibus†—the devil take all pedants. Let us go in here, master.

Fabrizio. Where do the Spaniards lodge?

Fruella. I do not trouble myself about them. They go to the Hook. But what need more? No person of note arrives in Modena but comes to lodge with me, except the Sienese, who, being all one with the Modenese, no sooner set foot in the city but they find a hundred friends, who take them to their houses: otherwise great lords and good companions, gentle and simple, all come to the Fool.

L'Agiato. I say that great doctors, learned brothers, academicians, virtuosi, all come to the Looking-Glass.

Fruella. And I say that no one who takes up his quarters at the Looking-Glass has been there many days before he walks out and comes to me.

Fabrizio. Messer Piero, what shall we do?

Messer Piero. Etiam atque etiam cogitandum.‡

Stragualcia (*aside*). I can scarcely keep my hands off him.

Messer Piero. I think, Fabrizio, we have not much money.

---

* The mixture of various foods causes the worst possible digestion.

† Mock Latin.

‡ It is to be thought of again and again.

Stragualcia. Master, I have just seen the host's daughter, as beautiful as an angel.

Messer Piero. Well, let us fix here. Your father, if we find him, will pay the reckoning.

Stragualcia. I will go into the kitchen, taste what is there, drink two or three cups of wine, fall asleep by a good fire, and the devil take economy.

L'Agiato. Remember, Fruella. You have played me too many tricks. One day we must try which head is the hardest.

Fruella. Whenever you please. I am ready to crack your skull.

Scene III: The street, with the house of Virginio

Virginio *and* Clementia.

Virginio. These are the customs which you have taught her. This is the honor which she does me. Have I for this escaped so many misfortunes, to see my property without an heir, my house broken up, my daughter dishonored: to become the fable of the city: not to dare to lift up my head: to be pointed at by boys; to be laughed at by old men, to be put into a comedy by the Intronati, to be made an example in novels, to be an eternal scandal in the mouths of the ladies of this land? For if one knows it, in three hours all the city knows it. Disgraced, unhappy, miserable father! I have lived too long. What can I think of? What can I do?

Clementia. You will do well to make as little noise as you can and to take the quietest steps you can to bring your daughter home, before the town is aware of the matter. But I wish that Sister Novellante Ciancini had as much breath in her body as I have faith in my mind that Lelia goes dressed as a man. Do not encourage their evil speaking. They wish her to be a nun, that they may inherit your property.

Virginio. Sister Novellante has spoken truth. She has told me, moreover, that Lelia is living as a page with a gentleman of this city and that he does not know that she is not a boy.

Clementia. I do not believe it.

Virginio. Neither do I, that he does not know that she is not a boy.

Clementia. That is not what I mean.

Virginio. It is what I mean. But what could I expect, when I entrusted her bringing up to you?

Clementia. Rather, what could you expect when you wanted to marry her to a man old enough to be her grandfather?

Virginio. If I find her, I will drag her home by the hair.

Clementia. You will take your disgrace from your bosom, to display it on your head.

Virginio. I have a description of her dress: I shall find her: let that suffice.

Clementia. Take your own way. I will lose no more time in washing a coal.

Scene IV: The street, with the hotels and the house of Gherardo.

Fabrizio *and* Fruella.

Fabrizio. While my two servants are sleeping, I will walk about to see the city. When they rise, tell them to come toward the piazza.

Fruella. Assuredly, young gentleman, if I had not seen you put on these clothes, I should have taken you for the page of a gentleman in this town, who dresses like you, in white,* and is so like you that he appears yourself.

Fabrizio. Perhaps I may have a brother.

Fruella. It may be so.

Fabrizio. Tell my tutor to inquire for he knows whom.

Fruella. Trust to me.

* Viola, in assuming male apparel, copies the dress of her brother:

"He named Sebastian: I my brother know
    Yet living in my glass: even such and so
    In favour was my brother; and he went
    Still in this fashion, colour, ornament;
    For him I imitate."—*Twelfth Night, Act* iii., Scene 4.

Scene V.

Fabrizio *and* Pasquella.

Pasquella. In good faith, there he is. I was afraid of having to search the city before I should find you. My mistress says you must come to her as soon as you can, for a matter of great importance to both of you.

Fabrizio. Who is your mistress?

Pasquella. As if you did not know.

Fabrizio. I do not know either her or you.

Pasquella. Oh, my Fabio.

Fabrizio. That is not my name. You are under some mistake.

Pasquella. Oh, no, Fabio. You know, there are few girls in this country so rich and so beautiful, and I wish you would come to conclusions with her: for going backward and forward day after day, taking words and giving words only, sets folks talking, with no profit to you and little honor to her.

Fabrizio (*aside*). What can this mean? Either the woman is mad, or she takes me for somebody else. But I will see what will come of it. Let us go, then.

Pasquella. Oh! I think I hear people in the house. Stop a moment. I will see if Isabella is alone and will make a sign to you if the coast is clear.

Fabrizio. I will see the end of this mystery. Perhaps it is a scheme to get money of me: but I am, as it were, a pupil of the Spaniards, and am more likely to get a crown from them than they are to get a carlin from me. I will stand aside a little, to see who goes into or out of the house, and judge what sort of lady she may be.

Scene VI

Gherardo, Virginio, *and* Pasquella.

Gherardo. Pardon me. If this is so, I renounce her. If Lelia has done this, it must be not merely because she will not have me, but because she has taken somebody else.

Virginio. Do not believe it, Gherardo. I pray you, do not spoil what has been done.

Gherardo. And I pray you to say no more about it.

Virginio. Surely you will not be wanting to your word.

Gherardo. Yes, where there has been a wanting in deed. Besides, you do not know if you can recover her. You are selling the bird in the bush. I heard your talk with Clementia.

Virginio. If I do not recover her, I cannot give her to you. But if I do recover her, will you not have her? And that immediately?

Gherardo. Virginio, I had the most honorable wife in Modena. And I have a daughter who is a dove. How can I bring into my house one who has run away from her father and gone heaven knows where in masculine apparel? Whom should I find to marry my daughter?

Virginio. After a few days nothing will be thought of it. And I do not think anyone knows it except ourselves.

Gherardo. The whole town will be full of it.

Virginio. No, no.

Gherardo. How long is it since she ran away?

Virginio. Yesterday, or this morning.

Gherardo. Who knows that she is still in Modena?

Virginio. I know it.

Gherardo. Find her, and we will talk it over again.

Virginio. Do you promise to take her?

Gherardo. I will see.

Virginio. Say yes.

Gherardo. I will not say yes: but——

Virginio. Come, say it freely.

Gherardo. Softly. What are you doing here, Pasquella? What is Isabella about?

Pasquella. Kneeling before her altar.

Gherardo. Blessings on her. A daughter who is always at her devotions is something to be proud of.

Pasquella. Ay, indeed. She fasts on all fast days and says the prayers of the day like a little saint.

Gherardo. She resembles that blessed soul of her mother.

Virginio. Oh, Gherardo! Gherardo! This is she of whom we have been speaking. She seems to be hiding or running away for having seen me. Let us go up to her.

Gherardo. Take care not to mistake. Perhaps it is not she?

Virginio. Who would not know her? And have I not all the signs which Sister Novellante gave me?

Pasquella. Things are going ill. I will take myself off.

Scene VII

Virginio, Gherardo, *and* Fabrizio.

Virginio. So, my fine miss, do you think this a befitting dress for you? This is the honor which you do to my house. This is the content you give to a poor old man. Would I had been dead before you were born, for you were only born to disgrace me: to bury me alive. And you, Gherardo, what say you of your betrothed? Is she not a credit to you?

Gherardo. She is no betrothed of mine.

Virginio. Impudent minx! What would become of you if this good man should reject you for a wife? But he overlooks your follies, and is willing to take you.

Gherardo. Softly, softly.

Virginio. Go indoors, hussy.

Fabrizio. Old man, have you no sons, friends, or relations in this city whose duty it is to take care of you?

Virginio. What an answer! Why do you ask this?

Fabrizio. Because I wonder that, having so much need of a doctor, you are allowed to go about, when you ought to be locked up and in a straitjacket.

Virginio. You ought to be locked up, and shall be, if I do not kill you on the spot, as I have a mind to do.

Fabrizio. You insult me because, perhaps, you think me a foreigner; but I am a Modenese and of as good a family as you.

Virginio (*taking* Gherardo *aside*). Gherardo, take her into your house. Do not let her be seen in this fashion.

Gherardo. No, no; take her home.

Virginio. Listen a little, and keep an eye on her, that she does not run away.

(*They talk apart.*)

Fabrizio. I have seen madmen before now, but such a madman as this old fellow I never saw going at large. What a comical insanity, to fancy that young men are girls! I would not for a thousand crowns have missed this drollery, to make a story for evenings in carnival. They are coming this way. I will humor their foolery and see what will come of it.

Virginio. Come here.

Fabrizio. What do you want?

Virginio. You are a sad hussy.

Fabrizio. Do not be abusive: for I shall not stand it.

Virginio. Brazen face.

Fabrizio. Ho! ho! ho!

Gherardo. Let him speak. Do you not see that he is angry? Do as he bids.

Fabrizio. What is his anger to me? What is he to me, or you either?

Virginio. You will kill me before my time.

Fabrizio. It is high time to die when you have fallen into dotage. You have lived too long already.

Gherardo. Do not speak so, dear daughter, dear sister.

Fabrizio. Here is a pretty pair of doves! Both crazy with one conceit. Ha! ha! ha! ha!

Virginio. Do you laugh at me, impudence?

Fabrizio. How can I help laughing at you, brainless old goose?

Gherardo. I am afraid this poor girl has lost her wits.

Virginio. I thought so at first, when I saw with how little patience she received me. Pray take her into your house. I cannot take her to my own without making myself the sight of the city.

Fabrizio. About what are these brothers of Melchisedech laying together the heads of their second babyhood?

Virginio. Let us coax her indoors; and as soon as she is within, lock her up in a chamber with your daughter.

Gherardo. Be it so.

Virginio. Come, my girl, I will no longer be angry with you. I pardon everything. Only behave well for the future.

Fabrizio. Thank you.

Gherardo. Behave as good daughters do.

Fabrizio. The other chimes in with the same tune.

Gherardo. Go in, then, like a good girl.

Virginio. Go in, my daughter.

Gherardo. This house is your own. You are to be my wife.

Fabrizio. Your wife and his daughter? Ha! ha! ha!

Gherardo. My daughter will be glad of your company.

Fabrizio. Your daughter, eh? Very good. I will go in.

Virginio. Gherardo, now that we have her safe, lock her up with your daughter, while I send for her clothes.

Gherardo. Pasquella, call Isabella and bring the key of her room.

ACT IV

Scene I: Scene continues.

Messer Piero *and* Stragualcia.

Messer Piero. You ought to have fifty bastinadoes, to teach you to keep him company when he goes out and not to get drunk and sleep, as you have done, and let him go about alone.

Stragualcia. And you ought to be loaded with birch and broom, sulfur, pitch, and gunpowder, and set on fire, to teach you not to be what you are.

Messer Piero. Sot, sot.

Stragualcia. Pedant, pedant.

Messer Piero. Let me find your master.

Stragualcia. Let me find his father.

Messer Piero. What can you say of me to his father?

Stragualcia. And what can you say of me?

Messer Piero. That you are a knave, a rogue, a rascal, a sluggard, a coward, a drunkard. That is what I can say.

Stragualcia. And I can say that you are a thief, a gambler, a slanderer, a cheat, a sharper, a boaster, a blockhead, an impostor, an ignoramus, a traitor, a profligate. That is what I can say.

Messer Piero. Well, we are both known.

Stragualcia. True.

Messer Piero. No more words. I will not place myself on a footing with you.

Stragualcia. Oh! To be sure; you have all the nobility of the Maremma. I am better born than you. What are you but the son of a muleteer? This upstart, because he can say *cujus masculini,* thinks he may set his foot on every man's neck.

Messer Piero. Naked and poor go'st thou, Philosophy.* To what have poor letters come? Into the mouth of an ass.

---

* Povera e nuda vai, Filosofia.—*Petrarca,* p. i. s. 7.

Stragualcia. You will be the ass presently. I will lay a load of wood on your shoulders.

Messer Piero. Furor fit læsa sæpius sapientia.* For the sake of your own shoulders, let me alone, base groom, poltroon, archpoltroon.

Stragualcia. Pedant, pedant, archpedant. What can be said worse than pedant? Can there be a viler, baser, more rubbishy race? They go about puffed up like bladders because they are called *Messer* This, *Maestro* That. . . . (Stragualcia *ends with several terms of untranslatable abuse.*)

Messer Piero. Tractant fabrilia fabri.† You speak like what you are. Either you shall leave this service, or I will.

Stragualcia. Who would have you in his house, and at his table, except my young master, who is better than bread?

Messer Piero. Many would be glad of me. No more words. Go to the hotel, take care of your master's property. By and by we will have a reckoning.

Stragualcia. Yes, we will have a reckoning, and you shall pay it.

Messer Piero. Fruella told me Fabrizio was gone toward the piazza. I will follow him.

Exit.

Stragualcia. If I did not now and then make head against this fellow, there would be no living with him. He has no more valor than a rabbit. When I brave him, he is soon silenced: but if I were once to knock under to him, he would lead me the life of a galley slave.

Scene II

Gherardo, Virginio, *and* Messer Piero.

Gherardo. I will endow her as you desire; and if you do not find your son, you will add a thousand golden florins.

Virginio. Be it so.

Messer Piero. I am much deceived, or I have seen this gentleman before.

---

* Wisdom frequently injured becomes fury.

† Workmen speak according to their art.

Virginio. What are you looking at, good sir?

Messer Piero. Certainly, this is my old master. Do you know in this town one Signor Vincenzio Bellenzini?

Virginio. I know him well. He has no better friend than I am.

Messer Piero. Assuredly, you are he. *Salve, patronorum optime.**

Virginio. Are you Messer Pietro de' Pagliaricci, my son's tutor?

Messer Piero. I am, indeed.

Virginio. Oh, my son! Woe is me! What news do you bring me of him? Where did you leave him? Where did he die? For dead he must be, or I should not have been so long without hearing from him. Those traitors murdered him—those Jews, those dogs. Oh, my son! My greatest blessing in the world! Tell me of him, dear master.

Messer Piero. Do not weep, sir, for heaven's sake. Your son is alive and well.

Gherardo. If this is true, I lose the thousand florins. Take care, Virginio, that this man is not a cheat.

Messer Piero. Parcius ista viris tamen objicienda memento.†

Virginio. Tell me something, master.

Messer Piero. Your son, in the sack of Rome, was a prisoner of one Captain Orteca.

Gherardo. So he begins his fable.

Messer Piero. And because the captain had two comrades who might claim their share, he sent us secretly to Siena: then, fearing that the Sienese, who are great friends of right and justice and most affectionately attached to this city, might take him and set him at liberty, he took us to a castle of the Signor di Piombino, set our ransom at a thousand ducats, and made us write for that amount.

Virginio. Was my son ill treated?

Messer Piero. No, certainly; they treated him like a gentleman. We received no answers to our letters.

Virginio. Go on.

Messer Piero. Now, being conducted with the Spanish camp to Corregia, this captain was killed, and the Court took his property and set us at liberty.

---

* Hail, best of masters!

† Remember that such things must be more sparingly objected to men.

Virginio. And where is my son?

Messer Piero. Nearer than you suppose.

Virginio. In Modena.

Messer Piero. At the hotel of the Fool.

Gherardo. The thousand florins are gone; but it suffices to have her. I am rich enough without them.

Virginio. I die with impatience to embrace him. Come, master.

Messer Piero. But what of Lelia?

Virginio. She has grown into a fine young woman. Has my son advanced in learning?

Messer Piero. He has not lost his time, *ut licuit per tot casus, per tot discrimina rerum.**

Virginio. Call him out. Say nothing to him. Let me see if he will know me.

Messer Piero. He went out a little while since. I will see if he has returned.

Scene III

Virginio, Gherardo, Messer Piero, *and* Stragualcia; *afterward* Fruella.

Messer Piero. Stragualcia, oh, Stragualcia, has Fabrizio returned?

Stragualcia. Not yet.

Messer Piero. Come here. Speak to your old master. This is Signor Virginio.

Stragualcia. Has your anger passed away?

Messer Piero. You know I am never long angry with you.

Stragualcia. All's well, then. Is this our master's father?

Messer Piero. It is.

Stragualcia. Oh, worthy master. You are just found in time to pay our bill at the Fool.

Messer Piero. This has been a good servant to your son.

Stragualcia. Has been only?

Messer Piero. And still is.

Virginio. I shall take care of all who have been faithful companions to my son.

Stragualcia. You can take care of me with little trouble.

Virginio. Demand.

---

* As far as it was available, through so many accidents and disastrous chances.

Stragualcia. Settle me as a waiter with this host, who is the best companion in the world, the best provided, the most knowing, one that better understands the necessities of a foreign guest than any host I have ever seen. For my part, I do not think there is any other paradise on earth.

Gherardo. He has a reputation for treating well.

Virginio. Have you breakfasted?

Stragualcia. A little.

Virginio. What have you eaten?

Stragualcia. A brace of partridges, six thrushes, a capon, a little veal, with only two jugs of wine.*

Virginio. Fruella, give him whatever he wants and leave the payment to me.

Stragualcia. Fruella, first bring a little wine for these gentlemen.

Messer Piero. They do not need it.

Stragualcia. They will not refuse. You must drink too, master.

Messer Piero. To make peace with you, I am content.

Stragualcia. Signor Virginio, you have reason to thank the master who loves your son better than his own eyes.

Virginio. Heaven be bountiful to him.

Stragualcia. It concerns you first and heaven after. Drink, gentlemen.

Gherardo. Not now.

Stragualcia. Pray then, go in till Fabrizio returns. And let us sup here this evening.

Gherardo. I must leave you for a while. I have some business at home.

Virginio. Take care that Lelia does not get away.

Gherardo. That is what I am going for.

Virginio. She is yours. I give her to you. Arrange the matter to your mind.

---

* The reader may be reminded of Massinger's *Justice Greedy*:—

"*Overreach.* Hungry again! Did you not devour this morning
A shield of brawn and a barrel of Colchester oysters?"

"*Greedy.* Why, that was, sir, only to scour my stomach—
A kind of a preparative."

New Way to Pay Old Debts, Act iv., Scene i.

Scene IV: The street, with the house of Virginio.

Gherardo, Lelia, *and* Clementia.

Gherardo. One cannot have all things one's own way.
Patience. But how is this? Here is Lelia. That careless
Pasquella has let her escape.

Lelia. Does it not appear to you, Clementia, that Fortune
makes me her sport?

Clementia. Be of good cheer. I will find some means to
content you. But come in and change your dress. You
must not be seen so.

Gherardo. I will salute her, however, and understand how
she has got out. Good day to you, Lelia, my sweet
spouse. Who opened the door to you? Pasquella, eh? I
am glad you have gone to your nurse's house; but your
being seen in this dress does little honor to you or to
me.

Lelia. To whom are you speaking? What Lelia? I am not
Lelia.

Gherardo. Oh! A little while ago, when your father and
I locked you up with my daughter Isabella, did you
not confess that you were Lelia? And now you think I
do not know you. Go, my dear wife, and change your
dress.

Lelia. God send you as much of a wife as I have fancy
for you as a husband. (*Goes in.*)

Cle.nentia. Go home, Gherardo. All women have their
child's play,* some in one way, some in another. This
is a very innocent one. Still these little amusements are
not to be talked of.

Gherardo. No one shall know it from me. But how did
she escape from my house, where I had locked her up
with Isabella?

Clementia. Locked up whom?

Gherardo. Lelia; this Lelia.

Clementia. You are mistaken. She has not parted from
me today; and for pastime she put on these clothes, as
girls will do, and asked me if she did not look well in
them?

Gherardo. You want to make me see double. I tell you
I locked her up with Isabella.

---

* *Cittolezze (zitellezze),* equivalent to *fanciullaggini.*

Clementia. Whence come you now?

Gherardo. From the hotel of the Fool.

Clementia. Did you drink?

Gherardo. A little.

Clementia. Now go to bed and sleep it off.

Gherardo. Let me see Lelia for a moment before I go, that I may give her a piece of good news.

Clementia. What news?

Gherardo. Her brother has returned safe and sound, and her father is waiting for him at the hotel.

Clementia. Fabrizio?

Gherardo. Fabrizio.

Clementia. I hasten to tell her.

Gherardo. And I to blow up Pasquella for letting her escape.

Scene V: The street, with the hotels and the house of Gherardo.

Pasquella, *alone*.

(Pasquella, who had only known Lelia as Fabio and did not know what the two old men had meant by calling the supposed Lelia, whom they had delivered to her charge, a girl, has nevertheless obeyed orders in locking up Fabrizio with Isabella, and now, in an untranslatable soliloquy, narrates that the two captives had contracted matrimony by their own ritual.)

Scene VI

Pasquella *and* Giglio.

(Pasquella, seeing Giglio coming, retires within the courtyard, through the grated door of which the dialogue is carried on. Giglio wishes to obtain admission to Gherardo's house without giving Pasquella the rosary he had promised her. He shows it to her and withholds giving it, on pretense that it wants repairs. She, on the other hand, wishes to get the rosary and give him nothing in return. She pretends to doubt if it is a true rosary and prevails on him to let her count the beads. She then cries out that the fowls are loose and that

she cannot open the door till she has got them in.
Giglio declares that he sees no fowls; that she is im-
posing on him. She laughs at him: he expostulates,
implores, threatens to break down the door, to set fire
to the house, to burn everything in it, herself included.
In the midst of his warth, he sees Gherardo approaching, and runs away.)

Scene VII

Pasquella *and* Gherardo.

Gherardo. What were you doing at the gate with that
Spaniard?

Pasquella. He was making a great noise about a rosary.
I could not make out what he wanted.

Gherardo. Oh, you have executed your trust well! I could
find it in my heart to break your bones.

Pasquella. For what?

Gherardo. Because you have let Lelia escape. I told you
to keep her locked in.

Pasquella. She is locked in.

Gherardo. I admire you impudence. She is not.

Pasquella. I say she is.

Gherardo. I have just left her with her nurse, Clementia.

Pasquella. And I have just left her where you ordered her
to be kept.

Gherardo. Perhaps she came back before me.

Pasquella. She never went away. The chamber has been
kept locked.

Gherardo. Where is the key?

Pasquella. Here it is.

Gherardo. Give it me. If she is not there, you shall pay
for it.

Pasquella. And if she is there, will you pay for it?

Gherardo. I will. You shall have a handsome present.

Scene VIII

Pasquella, Flaminio: *afterward* Gherardo.

Flaminio. Pasquella, how long is it since my Fabio was
here?

Pasquella. Why?

Flaminio. Because he is a traitor, and I will punish him; and because Isabella has left me for him. Fine honor to a lady of her position, to fall in love with a page.

Pasquella. Oh, do not say so. All the favors she has shown him are only for love of you.

Flaminio. Tell her she will repent; and as for him, I carry this dagger for him.

Pasquella. While the dog barks, the wolf feeds.

Flaminio. You will see.

Exit.

Gherardo. Oh, me! To what have I come! Oh, traitor, Virginio! Oh, heaven! What shall I do?

Pasquella. What is the matter, master?

Gherardo. What is he that is with my daughter?

Pasquella. He? Why you told me, it was Virginio's daughter.

(Gherardo has discovered the clandestine marriage and gives vent to his rage in untranslatable terms.)

Scene IX

Gherardo, Virginio, *and* Messer Piero.

Messer Piero. I wonder he has not returned to the hotel. I do not know what to think of it.

Gherardo. Ho! ho! Virginio! This is a pretty outrage that you have put on me. Do you think I shall submit to it?

Virginio. What are you roaring about?

Gherardo. Do you take me for a sheep, you cheat, you thief, you traitor? But the governor shall hear of it.

Virginio. Have you lost your senses? Or what is the matter?

Gherardo. Robber.

Virginio. I have too much patience.

Gherardo. Liar.

Virginio. You lie in your own throat.

Gherardo. Forger.

Messer Piero. Ah, gentlemen! What madness is this?

Gherardo. Let me come at him.

Messer Piero. What is between this gentleman and you?

Virginio. He wanted to marry my daughter, and I left her in his charge. I am afraid he has abused my confidence and invents a pretext for breaking off.

Gherardo. The villain has ruined me. I will cut him to pieces.

Virginio *goes off*.*

Messer Piero. Pray let us understand the case.

Gherardo. The miscreant has run away. Come in with me, and you shall know the whole affair.

Messer Piero. I go in with you, on your faith?

Gherardo. On my faith, solemnly.

ACT V

Scene I: Scene continues.

Virginio, Stragualcia, Scatizza; *afterward at intervals,* Messer Piero, Gherardo, *and* Fabrizio.

Virginio. Follow me, all; and you Stragualcia.

Stragualcia. With or without arms? I have no arms.

Virginio. Take in the hotel something that will serve. I fear this madman may have killed my poor daughter.

Stragualcia. This spit is a good weapon. I will run him through and all his followers, like so many thrushes.

Scatizza. What are these flasks for?

Stragualcia. To refresh the soldiers, if they should fall back in the first skirmish.

Virginio. The door opens. They have laid some ambuscade.

Messer Piero. Leave me to settle the matter, Signor Gherardo.

Stragualcia. See, master, the tutor has rebelled and sides with the enemy. There is no faith in this class of fellows. Shall I spit him first, and count one.

Messer Piero. Why these arms, my master?

Virginio. What has become of my daughter?

Messer Piero. I have found Fabrizio.

Virginio. Where?

Messer Piero. Here, within. And he has taken a beautiful wife.

Virginio. A wife? And who?

* To return with arms and followers.

Messer Piero. The daughter of Gherardo.

Virginio. Gherardo! It was but now he wanted to kill me.

Messer Piero. Rem omnem a principio audies.* Come forth, Signor Gherardo.

Gherardo. Lay down these arms and come in. It is matter for laughter.

Virginio. Can I do it safely?

Messer Piero. Safely, on my assurance.

Virginio. Then do you all go home and lay down your arms.

Messer Piero. Fabrizio, come to your father.

Virginio. Is not this Lelia?

Messer Piero. No, this is Fabrizio.

Virginio. Oh, my son, how much I have mourned for you!

Fabrizio. Oh, dear father, so long desired!

Gherardo. Come in, and you shall know all. I can further tell you that your daughter is in the house of her nurse, Clementia.

Virginio. How thankful I am to Heaven.

Scene II: The street, with the houses of Virginio *and* Clementia.

Flaminio *and* Crivello; *afterward* Clementia.

Crivello. I have seen him in the house of Clementia with these eyes and heard him with these ears.

Flaminio. Are you sure it was Fabio?

Crivello. Do you think I do not know him?

Flaminio. Let us go in, and if I find him——

Crivello. You will spoil all. Have patience, till he comes out.

Flaminio. Not heaven itself could make me have patience. (*Knocks at the door.*)

Clementia. Who is there?

Flaminio. A friend. Come down for a while.

Clementia. Oh, Signor Flaminio, what do you want with me?

Flaminio. Open, and I will tell you.

Clementia. Wait till I come down.

Flaminio. As soon as she opens the door, go in, and if you find him, call me.

* You shall hear the whole affair from the beginning.

Crivello. Leave it to me.

Clementia. Now what have you to say, Signor Flaminio?

Flaminio. What are you doing in your house with my page?

Clementia. What page? How? Are you going into my house by force? (*Pushing back* Crivello.)

Flaminio. Clementia, by the body of Bacchus! If you do not restore him——

Clementia. Whom?

Flaminio. My boy, who has fled into your house.

Clementia. There is no boy in my house.

Flaminio. Clementia, you have always been friendly to me, and I to you; but this is a matter of too great moment——

Clementia. What fury is this? Pause a little, Flaminio. Give time for your anger to pass away.

Flaminio. I say, restore me Fabio.

Clementia. Oh, not so much rage. By my faith, if I were a young woman and pleased you, I would have nothing to say to you. What of Isabella?

Flaminio. I wish she were quartered.

Clementia. Oh, that cannot be true.

Flaminio. If that is not true, she has made me see what is true.

Clementia. You young men deserve all the ill that can befall you. You are the most ungrateful creatures on earth.

Flaminio. This cannot be said of me. No man more abhors ingratitude than I do.

Clementia. I do not say it for you; but there is in this city a young woman who, thinking herself beloved by a cavalier of your condition, became so much in love with him that she seemed to see nothing in the world but him.

Flaminio. He was a happy man to inspire such a passion.

Clementia. It so happened that her father sent this poor girl away from Modena, and most bitterly she wept on her departure, fearing that he would soon forget her and turn to another; which he did immediately.

Flaminio. This could not be a cavalier. He was a traitor.

Clementia. Listen. Worse follows. The poor girl, returning after a few months and finding that her lover loved another and that this other did not return his love, abandoned her home, placed her honor in peril, and, in masculine attire, engaged herself to her false lover as a servant.

Flaminio. Did this happen in Modena? I had rather be this fortunate lover than lord of Milan.

Clementia. And this lover. not knowing her, employed her as a messenger to his new flame, and she, to please him, submitted to this painful duty.

Flaminio. Oh, virtucus damsel! Oh, firm love! A thing truly to be put in example to all coming time. Oh, that such a chance had happened to me!

Clementia. You would not leave Isabella!

Flaminio. I would leave her or any one thing else for such a blessing. Tell me, who is she?

Clementia. Tell me, first, what would you do if the case were your own?

Flaminio. I swear to you, by the light of heaven, may I never more hold up my head among honorable men, if I would not rather take her for a wife, even if she had no beauty, nor wealth, nor birth, than the daughter of the Duke of Ferrara.

Clementia. This you swear.

Flaminio. This I swear, and this I would do.

Clementia. You are witness.

Crivello. I am.

Clementia. Fabio, come down.

Scene III

Clementia, Flaminio, Crivello. Lelia *in female dress; afterward* Pasquella.

Clementia. This, Signor Flaminio, is your Fabio; and this, at the same time, is the constant, loving girl of whom I told you. Do you recognize him? Do you recognize her? Do you now see the worth of the love which you rejected?

Flaminio. There cannot be on earth a more charming deceit than this. Is it possible that I can have been so blind as not to have known her?

Pasquella. Clementia, Virginio desires that you will come to our house. He has given a wife to his son, Fabrizio, who has just returned, and you are wanted to put everything in order.

Clementia. A wife? And whom?

Pasquella. Isabella, the daughter of my master Gherardo.

Flaminio. The daughter of Gherardo Foiani?

Pasquella. The same. I saw the ring put on the bride's
finger.

Flaminio. When was this?

Pasquella. Just now. And I was sent off immediately to
call Clementia.

Clementia. Say, I will come almost directly.

Lelia. Oh, heaven! All this together is enough to make me
die of joy.

Pasquella. And I was to ask if Lelia is here. Gherardo has
said she is.

Clementia. Yes; and they want to marry her to the old
phantom of your master, who ought to be ashamed of
himself.

Flaminio. Marry her to Gherardo!

Clementia. See, if the poor girl is unfortunate.

Flaminio. May he have as much of life as he will have
of her. I think, Clementia, this is certainly the will of
heaven, which has had pity no less on this virtuous
girl than on me; and therefore, Lelia, I desire no other
wife than you, and I vow to you most solemnly that if
I have not you, I will never have any.

Lelia. Flaminio, you are my lord. I have shown my heart
in what I have done.

Flaminio. You have, indeed, shown it well. And forgive
me if I have caused you affliction, for I am most re-
pentant and aware of my error.

Lelia. Your pleasure, Flaminio, has always been mine. I
should have found my own happiness in promoting
yours.

Flaminio. Clementia, I dread some accident. I would not
lose time, but marry her instantly, if she is content.

Lelia. Most content.

Clementia. Marry, then, and return here. In the meantime I will inform Virginio, and wish bad night to
Gherardo.

*Scene IV: The street, with the hotels and the house of
Gherardo.*

Pasquella *and* **Giglio**.

(Pasquella again befools the Spaniard, who goes off, vow-
ing that this is the last time she shall impose on him.)

Scene V: The street, with the houses of Virginio *and*
Clementia.

Cittina.

(Flaminio and Lelia have been married and have returned to Clementia's house. Cittina comes out from it
and delivers an untranslatable soliloquy.)

Scene VI: The street, with the hotels and the house of
Gherardo.

Isabella *and* Fabrizio; *afterward* Clementia.

Isabella. I most certainly thought that you were the page
of a gentleman of this city. He resembles you so much
that he must surely be your brother.

Fabrizio. I have been mistaken for another more than
once today.

Isabella. Here is your nurse, Clementia.

Clementia. This must be he who is so like Lelia. Oh, my
dear child, Fabrizio, how is it with you?

Fabrizio. All well, my dear nurse. And how is it with
Lelia?

Clemeentia. Well, well; but come in. I have much to say
to you all.

Scene VII

Virginio *and* Clementia.

Virginio. I am so delighted to have recovered my son that
I am content with everything.

Clementia. It was the will of heaven that she should not
be married to that withered old stick, Gherardo. But
let us go into the hotel* and complete our preparations.
                              (*They go into the hotel.*)

Stragualcia. Spectators, do not expect that any of these
characters will reappear. If you will come to supper
with us, I will expect you at the Fool; but bring money,

---

*It would seem that the nuptial feast is to be held at the
Fool. Stragualcia had previously said, "Let us sup here this
evening."—*Act* iv., *Scene* 3.

for there entertainment is not gratis. If you will not come (and you seem to say "No!"), show us that you have been satisfied here; and you, Intronati, give signs of rejoicing.

Torquato Tasso

AMYNTAS

(*Aminta*)

John Addington Symonds' *Renaissance in Italy* contains what is still the best introduction to the drama of that time and place. His pages on the two principal pastoral dramas, *Amyntas* and *Il Pastor Fido*, can fitly serve as preface to Leigh Hunt's translation of the former. (*Il Pastor Fido* is the play Cardinal Bellarmin said had done more harm than the Lutherans.)

We have traced the pastoral ideal from its commencement in Boccaccio, through the *Arcadia* of Sannazzaro, Poliziano's *Orfeo*, and the didactic poets, up to the point when it was destined soon to find its perfect form in the *Aminta* and the *Pastor Fido*. Both Tasso and Guarini lived beyond the chronological limits assigned to this work. The Renaissance was finished; and Italy had passed into a new phase of existence, under the ecclesiastical reaction which is called the Counter Reformation. It is no part of my program to enter with particularity into the history of the second half of the sixteenth century. And yet the subject of this and the preceding chapter would be incomplete were I not to notice the two poems which combined the drama and the pastoral in a work of art no less characteristic of the people and the age than fruitful of results for European literature. Great tragedy and great comedy were denied to the Italians. But they produced a novel species in the pastoral drama, which testified to their artistic originality, and led by natural transitions to the opera. Poetry was on the point of expiring; but music was rising to take her place. And the imaginative medium prepared by the lyrical scenes of the Arcadian play afforded just that generality and aloofness from actual conditions of life, which were needed by the new art in its first dramatic essays.

It would be a mistake to suppose that because the form of the Arcadian romance was artificial, it could not lend itself to the presentation of real passion when adapted to the theater. The study of the *Aminta* and the *Pastor Fido* is sufficient to remove this misconception. Though the latter is the more carefully constructed of the two, the plot in either case presents a series of emotional situations, developed with refined art and expressed with lyrical abundance. The rustic fable is but a veil, through which the everlasting lineaments of love are shown. Arcadia, stripped of pedantry and affectation, has become the ideal world of sentiment. Like amber, it encloses in its glittering transparency the hopes and fears, the pains tnd joys, which flit from heart to heart of men and women when they love. The very conventionality of the pastoral style assists the lyrical utterance of real feeling. For it must be borne in mind that both *Aminta* and the *Pastor Fido* are essentially lyrical. The salt and savour of each play are in their choruses and monologues. The dialogue, the fable and the characters serve to supply the poet with motives for emotion that finds vent in song. This being conceded, it will be understood how from their scenes a whole world of melodrama issued. Whatever may have been the subject of an opera before the days of Gluck, it drew its life-blood from these pastorals.

The central motive of *Aminta* and the *Pastor Fido* is the contrast between the actual world of ambition, treachery and sordid strife, and the ideal world of pleasure, loyalty and tranquil ease. Nature is placed in opposition to civil society, the laws of honour to the laws of love, the manners of Arcadia to the manners of Italy. This cardinal motive finds its highest utterance in Tasso's chorus on the Age of Gold:

O bella età dell' oro,
Non già perchè di latte

Sen corse il fiume, e stillò mele il bosco;
Non perchè i frutti loro
Dier dall' aratro intatte
Le terre, e gli angui erràr senz' ira o tosco:
Non perchè nuvol fosco
Non spiegò allor suo velo,
Ma in primavera eterna,
Ch' ora s' accende, e verna,
Rise di luce e di sereno il cielo;
Nè portò peregrino
O guerra, o merce agli altrui lidi il pino
   Ma sol perchè quel vano
Nome senza oggetto,
Quell' idolo d' errori, idol d' inganno,
Quel che dal volgo insano
Onor poscia fu detto,
Che di nostra natura 'l feo tiranno,
Non mischiava il suo affanno
Fra le liete dolcezze
Dell' amoroso gregge;
Nè fu sua dura legge
Nota a quell' alme in libertate avvezze
Ma legge aurea e felice,
Che Natura scolpì, 'S' ei piace, ei lice.'

The last phrase, "S' ei piace, ei lice," might be written
on the frontispiece of both dramas, together with
Daphne's sigh: "Il mondo invecchia, E invecchiando
intristisce." Of what use is life unless we love?

Amiam, che 'l sol si muore, e poi rinasce;
A noi sua breve luce
S' asconde, e 'l sonno eterna notte adduce.

The girl who wastes her youth in proud virginity
prepares a sad old age of vain regret:

Cangia, cangia consiglio,
Pazzarella che sei;
Che 'l pentirsi da sezzo nulla giova.

It is the old cry of the Florentine *Canti* and *Ballate,*
"Gather ye rosebuds while ye may!" "Di doman non c'è
certezza." And the stories of *Aminta* and *Pastor Fido*
teach the same lesson, that nature's laws cannot be
violated, that even fate and the most stubborn bosoms
bow to love.

Of the music and beauty of these two dramas, I find it difficult to speak. Before some masterpieces criticism bends in silence. We cannot describe what must be felt. All the melodies that had been growing through two centuries in Italy, are concentrated in their songs. The idyllic voluptuousness, which permeated literature and art, steeps their pictures in a golden glow. It is easy enough to object that their apparent simplicity conceals seduction, that their sentimentalism is unmanly, and their suggestions of physical beauty effeminating:

> Ma come Silvia il riconobbe, e vide
> Le belle guance tenere d' Aminta
> Iscolorite in sì leggiadri modi,
> Che viola non è che impallidisca
> Sì dolcemente, e lui languir sì fatto,
> Che parea già negli ultimi sospiri
> Esalar l' alma; in guisa di Baccante,
> Gridando e percotendosi il bel petto,
> Lasciò cadersi in sul giacente corpo;
> E giunse viso a viso, e bocca a bocca.

This passage warns us that an age of *cicisbei* and *castrati* has begun, and that the Italian sensuousness has reached its final dissolution. Silvia's kisses in *Aminta*, Mirtillo's kisses in *Pastor Fido*, introduce a new refinement of enervation. Marino with his *Adone* is not distant. But, while we recognize in both these poems—the one perfumed and delicate like flowers of spring, the other sculptured in pure forms of classic grace—evident signs of a civilization sinking to decay; though we almost loathe the beauty which relaxes every chord of manhood in the soul that feels it; we are bound to confess that to this goal the Italian genius had been steadily advancing since the publication of the *Filocolo*. The negation of chivalry, mysticism, asceticism, is accomplished. After traversing the cycle of comedy, romance, satire, burlesque poetry, the plastic arts, and invading every province of human thought, the Italian reaction against the middle ages assumes a final shape of hitherto unapprehended loveliness in the *Aminta* and the *Pastor Fido*. They complete and close the Renaissance, bequeathing in a new species of art its form and pressure to succeeding generations.

E. B.

AMYNTAS

(1573)

Torquato Tasso

ENGLISH VERSION BY LEIGH HUNT

Characters

LOVE, *disguised as a shepherd*
DAPHNE, Sylvia's *friend*
SYLVIA, *loved by* Amyntas
AMYNTAS, *in love with* Sylvia
THYRSIS, Amyntas' *friend*
SATYR, *in love with* Sylvia
NERINA, *a messenger*
ERGASTO, *a messenger*
ELPINO, *a shepherd*
CHORUS OF SHEPHERDS

PROLOGUE

Love, *disguised as a shepherd.*

Who would believe that in a human form,
And underneath these lowly shepherd's weeds,
There walked a hidden God? and he no God
Sylvan, or of the common crowd of heaven,
But the most potent of their greatest; one
Who many a time has made the hand of Mars
Let fall his bloody sword; and looked away,
From the earth-shaker Neptune, his great trident;
And his old thunders from consummate Jove.

Doubtless beneath this aspect and this dress,
Venus will not soon know me—me, her son,
Her own son, Love. I am constrained to leave her,
And hide from her pursuit; because she wishes
That I should place my arrows and myself
At her discretion solely; and like a woman,
Vain and ambitious, she would hunt me back
Among mere courts, and coronets, and scepters,
There to pin down my powers; and to my ministers
And minor brethren, leave sole liberty
To lodge in the green woods, and flesh their darts
In bosoms rude. But I, who am no boy,
Whate'er I seem in visage or in act,
Would of myself dispose as it should please me;
Since not to her, but me, were given by lot
The torch omnipotent, and golden bow.

Therefore I hide about; and so escaping
Not her authority, which she has not in me,
But the strong pressure of a mother's prayers,
I cover me in the woods, and do become
An inmate with its lowly populace.

She follows me and promises to give,
To whomsoever will betray me to her,
Sweet kisses, or a something else still dearer!
As if, forsooth, I knew not how to give,
To whomsoever will conceal me from her,
Sweet kisses, or a something else still dearer.
This, at the least, is certain: that my kisses
Will be much dearer to the lasses' lips,
If I, who am Love's self, to love apply me;
So that in many an instance, she must needs
Ask after me in vain. The lips are sealed.

But to keep closer still, and to prevent her
From finding me by any sign or symptom,
I have put off my wings, my bow and quiver.
Yet not the more for that walk I unarmed;
Since this which seems a rod is my good torch,
So have I wrought deception; and breathes all
Invisible flame; and this good dart of mine,
Though pointed not with gold, is nevertheless
Temper divine; and wheresoe'er it lights,
Infixes love.

And now will I with this,
Pierce with a deep immedicable wound
Into the hard heart of the cruelest nymph,
That ever followed on Diana's choir.
No shallower shall it go in Sylvia's bosom
(Such is the name of this fair heart of rock),
Than once it went, years back, out of this hand,
Into the gentle bosom of Amyntas,
When everywhere he followed her about
To chase and sport, young lover his young lass.
And that my point may go the deeper, I
Will wait awhile, till pity mollify
The blunting ice, which round about her heart,
Cold honor has kept bound, and virgin niceness;
And wheresoe'er it turn to softness most,
There will I lance the dart. And to perform
So fair a work most finely, I go now
To mingle with the holiday multitude
Of flowery-crowned shepherds, who are met
Hard by in the accustomed place of sport,
Where I will feign me one of them; and there,
Even in this place and fashion, will I strike
A blow invisible to mortal eye.

After new fashion shall these woods today
Hear love discoursed; and it shall well be seen,
That my divinity is present here
In its own person, not its ministers.
I will inbreathe high fancies in rude hearts;
I will refine, and render dulcet sweet,
Their tongues; because, wherever I may be,
Whether with rustic or heroic men,
There am I, Love; and inequality,
As it may please me, do I equalize;
And 'tis my crowning glory and great miracle,
To make the rural pipe as eloquent
Even as the subtlest harp. If my proud mother,
Who scorns to have me roving in the woods,
Knows not thus much, 'tis she is blind, not I;
Though blind I am miscalled by blinded men.

ACT I

Scene I

Daphne *and* Sylvia.

Daphne.　And wouldst thou then indeed, dear Sylvia,
　　Pass this young age of thine
　　Far from the joys of love? and wouldst thou never
　　Hear the sweet name of mother; nor behold
　　Thy little children playing round about thee
　　Delightfully? Ah think,
　　Think. I beseech thee, do,
　　Simpleton that thou art.
Sylvia.　Let others follow the delights of love,
　　If love indeed has any. To my taste
　　This life is best. I have enough to care for
　　In my dear bow and arrows. My delight
　　Is following the chase; and when 'tis saucy,
　　Bringing it down; and so, as long as arrows
　　Fail not my quiver, nor wild deer the woods,
　　I fear no want of sport.
Daphne.　　　　　　　　Insipid sport
　　Truly, and most insipid way of life!
　　If it is pleasant to thee, it is only

From ignorance of the other. The first people,
Who lived in the world's infancy, regarded
With like good sense their water and their acorns
As exquisite meat and drink; but nowadays
Water and acorns are but food for beasts;
And grain and the sweet grape sustain humanity.
Ah! hadst thou once, but once,
Tasted a thousandth part of the delight
Which a heart tastes that loves and is beloved,
Thou wouldst repent, and sigh, and say directly,
'Tis all but loss of time
That passes not in loving.
O seasons fled and gone,
How many widowed nights,
And solitary days
Which might have been wrapped round with this
    sweet life,
Have I consumed in vain!
A life, the more habituate, the more sweet!
Think, think, I pray thee, do,
Simpleton as thou art.
A late repentance is at least no pleasure.

Sylvia.   When I shall come to thee with penitent sighs,
And say the words which thou hast fancied for me,
And rounded off so sweetly, then, why then,
The running river shall turn home again,
And wolves escape from lambs, and hounds from
    hares,
And bears shall love the sea, dolphins the hills.

Daphne.   I know too well this girlish waywardness.
Such as thou art, I was; so did I bear
My fortune and my careless countenance;
And so were my fair locks; and so vermilion
Even was my mouth; and so the white and red
Was mingled in my ripe and delicate cheeks.
'Twas then my highest joy (a foolish joy,
Now I think of it) to go spreading nets,
And setting snares for birds, and sharpening darts,
And tracking to their haunts wild animals;
And if I saw a lover look at me,
I dropped my little wild and rustic eyes,
Half blushes and half scorn. His kindliness
Found no kind thoughts in me; and all that made me
Pleasing to other eyes, displeased myself;
As if it was my crime, my shame, my scorn,
To be thus looked at, and thus loved, and longed for.

But what can time not do? And what not do
A faithful lover, and importunate,
Forever serving, meriting, entreating?
I yielded, I confess; and all that conquered me,
What was it? patience, and humility,
And sighs, and soft laments, and asking pardon.
Darkness, and one short night, then shewed me more,
Than the long luster of a thousand days.
How did I then reproach my blind simplicity,
And breathe, and say,—Here, Cynthia, take thy horn;
Here, take thy bow; for I renounce at once
Thy way of life, and all that it pursues.—
And thus I still look forward to the day,
When thy Amyntas shall domesticate
Thy wildness for thee, and put flesh and blood
Into this steel and stony heart of thine.
Is he not handsome? does he love thee not?
Is he not loved by others? does he alter so
For love of them, and not for thy disdain?
Or is his fault an humbler origin?
Thou, it is true, art daughter to Cydippe,
Whose father was the god of this great river;
Yet he is son of old Sylvanus too,
Whose father was the shepherds' god, great Pan.
There's Amaryllis: if thou hast at any time
Beheld thee in some fountain's glassy mirror,
She is as fair as thou: and yet he flies
All her delicious arts, to follow thee
And thy poor scorn. Suppose (and yet heaven grant
The supposition never may come true)
That wearied out with thee, he should repose
His joys in her who sees so much in him:
How would thy heart feel then? or with what eyes
See him become another's? happy in
Another's arms, and laughing thee to scorn?
Sylvia.   Pray let Amyntas with himself and his loves
Do what he pleases. It concerns not me.
He is not mine; let him be whose he chooses.
Mine he cannot be, if I like him not;
And if he were mine, I would not be his.
Daphne.   Whence springs all this disliking?
Sylvia.   From his love.
Daphne.   A blessed father of a child so cruel!
But come, come; when were tigers ever born
Of the kind lamb, or crows of lady swans?
Thou dost deceive me, or thyself.

Sylvia.   I hate
His love, because it hates my honesty.
I loved him well enough, as long as he
Wished nothing but what I wished.
Daphne.   Thou didst wish
Thine evil. All that he desired of thee
Was for thee too.
Sylvia.   Daphne, be still, I pray;
Or speak of something else, if thou wouldst have
An answer.
Daphne.   Oh pray mark her airs! Pray mark
The scornful little lass! Give me, however,
One answer more. Suppose another loved thee,
Wouldst thou receive his love in the same way?
Sylvia.   In the same way would I receive all love
That came to undermine my honesty;
For what thou callest lover, I call enemy.
Daphne.   And callest thou the sheep then
The enemy of his female?
The bull of the fair heifer?
Or of his dove the turtle?
And callest thou sweet springtime
The time of rage and enmity,
Which breathing now and smiling
Reminds the whole creation,
The animal, the human,
Of loving! Dost thou see not
How all things are enamored
Of this enamorer, rich with joy and health?
Observe that turtledove,
How toying with his dulcet murmuring
He kisses his companion. Hear that nightingale,
Who goes from bough to bough,
Singing with his loud heart, I love! I love!
The adder, though thou know'st it not, forgets
Her poison, and goes eagerly to her love;
Headlong the tigers go;
The lion's great heart loves; and thou alone,
Wilder than all the wild,
Deniest the boy a lodging in thy breast.
But why speak I of tigers, snakes, and lions,
Who have their share of mind? The very trees
Are loving. See with what affection there,
And in how many a clinging turn and twine,
The vine holds fast its husband. Fir loves fir,
The pine the pine; and ash, and willow, and beech,

Each toward the other, yearns, and sighs, and trembles.
That oak tree which appears
So rustic and so rough,
Even that has something warm in its sound heart;
And hadst thou but a spirit and sense of love,
Thou hadst found out a meaning for its whispers.
Now tell me, wouldst thou be
Less than the very plants, and have no love?
Think better, oh think better,
Simpleton that thou art.

Sylvia. Well, when I hear the sighings of the plants,
I'll be content to fall in love myself.

Daphne. Thou mockest my kind council, and makest game
Of all I say to thee—O deaf to love,
As thou art blind. But go: the time will come
When thou wilt grieve thou didst not mind my words.
Then wilt thou shun the fountains, where so oft
Thou makest thee a glass, perhaps a proud one;
Then wilt thou shun the fountains, for mere dread
Of seeing thyself grown wrinkled and featureless.
This will most surely be; but not this only;
For though a great, 'tis but a common evil.
I'll tell thee what Elpino, t'other day,
The wise Elpino, told the fair Lycoris;
Her, whose two eyes can do as much with him,
As his sweet singing ought to do with her;
If ought were good in love. He told it her
In hearing both of Battus and of Thyrsis,
Great masters they of love; they were conversing
Within Aurora's cavern, over which
'Tis written, "Far be ye, profane ones, far."
He told her—and 'twas told to him, he said,
By that great name that sung of Arms and Loves,
And who bequeathed him, dying, his own pipe,
That underneath there, in the infernal depth,
Is a black den, which breathes out noisome smoke
From the sad furnaces of Acheron;
And there, in everlasting punishment,
With moaning, and tormenting hold of darkness,
Are kept ungrateful and denying women.
There then expect a proper dwelling place
For thy fierce hardness.
It will be just and well that the harsh smoke
Shall wring the stubborn tears out of those eyes,
Since never pity yet could draw them down.—

Follow thy ways, go follow,
Obstinate that thou art.
Sylvia.   But what pray did Lycoris? and what answer
Made she to this?
Daphne.   Thou carest not what thou dost,
And yet wouldst fain be told what others do.
She answered with her eyes.
Sylvia.   Why how could one
Answer without?
Daphne.   They turned with a sweet smile,
And answered thus: Our heart, and we, are thine;
More thou shouldst not desire; nor may there be
More given. And surely this is all-sufficient
For a chaste lover, if he holds those eyes
To be sincere as beautiful, and gives them
Perfect belief.
Sylvia.   And why not so believe them?
Daphne.   Knowest thou not what Thyrsis went about
Writing, the time he wandered in the forests
Out of his wits, and moved the nymphs and
     shepherds
To mirth and pity at once? No things wrote he
Worthy of laughter, whatsoe'er his deeds.
He wrote it on a thousand barks, to grow
Verses and barks together; and one I read:
False faithless lights, ye mirrors of her heart,
Well do I recognize the tricks ye play!
But to what profit, seeing I cannot fly?
Sylvia.   I waste the time here, talking. I forget
That I must join the accustomed chase today,
Among the olive trees. Now pray wait for me,
Just while I bathe in our old fountain here,
And rid me of the dust I gathered yesterday
In following that swift fawn, which nevertheless
I overtook and killed.
Daphne.   I'll wait for thee;
Perhaps will join thee in the bath; but first
I must go home. The hour is not so late
As it appears. So wait for me at home
Thyself, and I'll come speedily. And pray
Bethink thee, the meantime, of what imports thee
Much more than fawns or fountains. If thou
     knowst it not,
Know thy own ignorance, and trust the wise.

Scene II

Amyntas *and* Thyrsis.

Amyntas.   In my lamentings I have found
 A very pity in the pebbly waters;
 And I have found the trees
 Return them a kind voice;
 But never have I found,
 Nor ever hope to find,
 Compassion in this hard and beautiful—
 What shall I call her? Woman or wild animal?
 But she herself denies the name of woman,
 In thus denying pity
 To one, whom nought else under heaven denies it.

Thyrsis.   The grass is the lamb's food, the lamb the
   wolf's;
 But cruel love delights to feed on tears,
 And seems to satiate never.

Amyntas.   Alas! Alas!
 Love has drained all my tears; it is my blood
 Which he must thirst for now. I hope and trust,
 He and this impious one will have it shortly.

Thyrsis.   Amyntas! dear Amyntas! talk not so:
 'Tis idle. Take good heart. This cruel one
 May treat thee ill; but thou canst find another.

Amyntas.   Ah me, another! I have lost myself.
 How can I find me joy, myself being gone?

Thyrsis.   Do not despair. Thou'lt win her heart at last.
 Patience and time enabled man to put
 His rein on lions and Hyrcanian tigers.

Amyntas.   The miserable cannot bear to wait
 Long time for death.

Thyrsis.   The time will not be long.
 Woman is soon offended, soon appeased,
 Being a thing by nature moveable
 More than the boughs by the wind, or than the tops
 Of quivering corn. But prithee, dear Amyntas,
 Let me more inwardly into the heart
 Of this your troubled love. Thou hast assured me
 Many a time that thou didst love me well,
 And yet I know not where thy yearnings lie.
 A faithful friendship, and the common study
 Of the sweet muses, make me not unworthy
 Of knowing what thou mayst conceal from others.

Amyntas.   Thyrsis, I am content to let thee hear

What the woods know, and what the mountains know,
And what the rivers know, and man knows not.
For to my death I feel myself so nigh,
'Tis fit I leave behind me one to tell
The reason why death took me. He can write it
Upon a beech tree near where they will bury me;
And when that hard one passes by the place,
She shall rejoice to trample my poor clay
With her proud foot, and say within herself,
"This is indeed a triumph!" and rejoice
To think how all whom chance conducts that way,
Native or stranger, shall behold her victory.
And there may come a day (alas! it is
Too great to hope), but there may come a day,
When moved with tardy pity, she may weep
For one, when dead, whom when alive, she killed;
And say, "Ah, would that he were here, and mine!"
Now mark me.

Thyrsis.   Pray speak on. I listen eagerly,
Perhaps to better purpose than thou thinkest.

Amyntas.   While yet a boy, scarce tall enough to gather
The lowest hanging fruit, I became intimate
With the most lovely and beloved girl,
That ever gave to the winds her locks of gold.
Thou knowst the daughter of Cydippe and
Montano, that has such a store of herds,
Sylvia, the forest's honor, the soul's firer?
Of her I speak. Alas! I lived one time,
So fastened to her side, that never turtle
Was closer to his mate, nor ever will be.
Our homes were close together, closer still
Our hearts; our age conformable, our thoughts
Still more conformed. With her I tended nets
For birds and fish; with her followed the stag,
And the fleet hind; our joy and our success
Were common: but in making prey of animals
I fell, I know not how, myself a prey.
There grew by little and little in my heart,
I know not from what root,
But just as the grass grows that sows itself,
An unknown something, which continually
Made me feel anxious to be with her; and then
I drank strange sweetness from her eyes, which left
A taste, I know not how, of bitterness.
Often I sighed, nor knew the reason why;
And thus before I knew what loving was,

Was I a lover. Well enough I knew
At last; and I will tell thee how; pray mark me.
Thyrsis.   I mark thee well.
Amyntas.   One day, Sylvia and Phillis
Were sitting underneath a shady beech,
I with them; when a little ingenious bee,
Gathering his honey in those flowery fields,
Lit on the cheeks of Phillis, cheeks as red
As the red rose; and bit, and bit again
With so much eagerness that it appeared
The likeness did beguile him. Phillis, at this,
Impatient of the smart, sent up a cry;
"Hush! Hush!" said my sweet Sylvia, "do not
    grieve;
I have a few words of enchantment, Phillis,
Will ease thee of this little suffering.
The sage Artesia told them me, and had
That little ivory horn of mine in payment,
Fretted with gold." So saying, she applied
To the hurt cheek the lips of her divine
And most delicious mouth, and with sweet humming
Murmured some verses that I knew not of.
Oh admirable effect! a little while,
And all the pain was gone; either by virtue
Of those enchanted words, or as I thought,
By virtue of those lips of dew,
That heal whate'er they turn them to.
I, who till then had never had a wish
Beyond the sunny sweetness of her eyes,
Or her dear dulcet words, more dulcet far
Than the soft murmur of a humming stream
Crooking its way among the pebble-stones,
Or summer airs that babble in the leaves,
Felt a new wish move in me to apply
This mouth of mine to hers; and so becoming
Crafty and plotting (an unusual art
With me, but it was love's intelligence),
I did bethink me of a gentle stratagem
To work out my new wit. I made pretense,
As if the bee had bitten my underlip;
And fell to lamentations of such sort
That the sweet medicine which I dared not ask
With word of mouth, I asked for with my looks.
The simple Sylvia then,
Compassioning my pain,
Offered to give her help

To that pretended wound;
And oh! the real and the mortal wound,
Which pierced into my being,
When her lips came on mine.
Never did bee from flower
Suck sugar so divine,
As was the honey that I gathered then
From those twin roses fresh.
I could have bathed in them my burning kisses,
But fear and shame withheld
That too audacious fire,
And made them gently hang.
But while into my bosom's core, the sweetness,
Mixed with a secret poison, did go down,
It pierced me so with pleasure that, still feigning
The pain of the bee's weapon, I contrived
That more than once the enchantment was repeated.
From that time forth, desire
And irrepressible pain so grew within me
That, not being able to contain it more,
I was compelled to speak; and so, one day,
While in a circle a whole set of us,
Shepherds and nymphs, sat playing at the game,
In which they tell in one another's ears
Their secret each, "Sylvia," said I in hers,
"I burn for thee; and if thou help me not,
I feel I cannot live." As I said this,
She dropped her lovely looks, and out of them
There came a sudden and unusual flush,
Portending shame and anger: not an answer
Did she vouchsafe me, but by a dead silence,
Broken at last by threats more terrible.
She parted then, and would not hear me more,
Nor see me. And now three times the naked reaper
Has clipped the spiky harvest, and as often
The winter shaken down from the fair woods
Their tresses green, since I have tried in vain
Everything to appease her, except death.
Nothing remains indeed but that I die!
And I shall die with pleasure, being certain,
That it will either please her, or be pitied;
And I scarce know which of the two to hope for.
Pity perhaps would more remunerate
My faith, more recompense my death; but still
I must not hope for aught that would disturb
The sweet and quiet shining of her eyes,

And trouble that fair bosom, built of bliss.

Thyrsis. And dost thou think it possible she could hear
  Such words as these, and love thee not some day?

Amyntas. I know not, and believe not. She avoids me,
  As asps avoid enchantment.

Thyrsis.   Trust me now,
  It gives me heart to try, and make her hear thee.

Amyntas. She will not grant thy wish, nor if she does,
  Will she grant anything to me for speaking.

Thyrsis. Why such extreme despair?

Amyntas.   I have good reason.
  Wise Mopsus prophesied my unlucky chance;
  Mopsus, who knows the language of the birds,
  And what the herbs can do, and what the fountains.

Thyrsis. What Mopsus dost thou speak of? Of that
    Mopsus,
  Who with a tongue of honey, and a grin
  Of friendship on his lips, is hollow at heart,
  And holds a dagger underneath his cloak?
  Now be thou of good heart. These evil omens,
  Which with that solemn brow of his he sells the
    unwary,
  Will never come to pass; and to convince thee,
  I tell thee that I know it. The very evil
  He has predicted, gives me joyful hope
  Of seeing thy love happy.

Amyntas.   If thou knowest
  Aught that might comfort me, I pray thee speak.

Thyrsis. Most willingly. When first my fortune brought
    me
  Into these woods, I knew him; and I thought him
  Then, what thou thinkst him now. One day meanwhile,
  Having necessity as well as wish
  To go where the great city, queenlike, holds
  The banks of the river, I told him my journey.
  This was his answer: 'Thou art going then
  To the great spot, where keen and crafty citizens,
  And courtiers in their malice, laugh at us,
  Cutting vile jokes on our simplicity.
  Therefore, my son, take my advice. Avoid
  The places where thou seest much drapery,
  Colored and gold; and plumes, and heraldries,
  And such new-fanglements. But above all,
  Take care how evil chance, or youthful wandering,
  Bring thee upon the house of Idle Babbling."
  "What place is that?" said I, and he resumed;

"Enchantresses dwell there, who make one see
Things as they are not, aye, and hear them too.
That which shall seem pure diamond and fine gold,
Is glass and brass; and coffers that look silver,
Heavy with wealth, are baskets full of bladders.
The very walls there are so strangely made,
They answer those who talk; and not in syllables,
Or bits of words, like Echo in our woods,
But go the whole talk over, word for word,
With something else beside, that no one said.
The tressels, tables, bedsteads, curtains, lockers,
Chairs, and whatever furniture there is
In room or bedroom, all have tongues and speech,
And are forever tattling. Idle babblings
Are always going about in shape of children:
And should a dumb man enter in that place,
The dumb would babble in his own despite.
And yet this evil is the least of all
That might assail thee. Thou mightest be arrested
In fearful transformation to a willow,
A beast, fire, water—fire forever sighing,
Water forever weeping." Here he ceased:
And I, with all this fine foreknowledge, went
To the great city, and by heaven's kind will
Came where they live so happily. The first sound
I heard was a delightful harmony,
Which issued forth, of voices loud and sweet:
Sirens, and swans, and nymphs, a heavenly noise
Of heavenly things; which gave me such delight
That, all admiring, and amazed, and joyed,
I stopped awhile quite motionless; there stood
Within the entrance as if keeping guard
Of those fine things, one, of a noble presence,
And stout withal, of whom I was in doubt
Whether to think him better knight or leader.
He with a look at once benign and grave,
In royal guise invited me within,
He, great and in esteem; me, lorn and lowly.
Oh the sensations, and the sights, which then
Came on me! Goddesses I saw, and nymphs
Graceful and beautiful, and harpers fine
As Linus, or as Orpheus; and more others,
All without veil or cloud, bright as the virgin
Aurora, when she glads immortal eyes
And sews her beams and dewdrops, silver and gold.
And fertilizing there, I saw act round

Apollo and the Nine; and with the Nine
Elpino sat; and at that moment, I
Felt myself greater, gifted newly, and full
Of sudden deity; and I sung of wars
And chiefs, and trampled the rude pastoral song.
And though as it pleased others, afterward
I came home to these woods, I yet retained
Something of that great spirit, nor did my pipe
Speak with its old humility; but loud
And loftier-toned filled the wide-echoing woods,
The rival of the trumpet. Mopsus heard;
And eying me with a malignant stare,
Smote fascination on me; whence I grew
Hoarse in my song, and for long time was mute.
The shepherds thought that I had seen a wolf;
And so I had; but then the wolf was he.
I tell thee this, to shew how little worthy
He is of thy belief. And now pray hope.
The more, because he would have kept thee hopeless.

Amyntas.   What thou hast told me, comforts me to hear:
To thee then I commit the only care
For which I live.

Thyrsis.   I will take care of it.
Do thou be here again in half an hour.

Chorus.   O lovely age of gold!
Not that the rivers rolled
With milk, or that the woods dropped honey dew;
Not that the ready ground
Produced without a wound,
Or the mild serpent had no tooth that slew;
Not that a cloudless blue
Forever was in sight,
Or that the heaven which burns,
And now is cold by turns,
Looked out in glad and everlasting light;
No, nor that ev'n the insolent ships from far
Brought war to no new lands, nor riches worse
    than war:
But solely that that vain
And breath-invented pain,
That idol of mistakes, that worshipped cheat,
That Honor—since so called
By vulgar minds appalled,
Played not the tyrant with our nature yet.
It had not come to fret
The sweet and happy fold

Of gentle humankind;
Nor did its hard law bind
Souls nursed in freedom; but that law of gold,
That glad and golden law, all free, all fitted,
Which Nature's own hand wrote—What pleases
  is permitted.

Then among streams and flowers
The little winged Powers
Went singing carols without torch or bow:
The nymphs and shepherds sat
Mingling with innocent chat
Sports and low whispers; and with whispers low
Kisses that would not go.
The maiden, budding o'er,
Kept not her bloom uneyed,
Which now a veil must hide,
Nor the crisp apples which her bosom bore:
And often times, in river or in lake,
The lover and his love their merry bath would take.

'Twas thou, thou, Honor, first
That didst deny our thirst
Its drink, and on the fount thy covering set:
Thou bad'st kind eyes withdraw
Into constrained awe,
And keep the secret for their tears to wet:
Thou gatheredst in a net
The tresses from the air,
And mad'st the sports and plays
Turn all to sullen ways,
And putst on speech a rein, in steps a care.
Thy work it is—thou shade that wilt not move—
That what was once the gift, is now the theft of
  Love.

Our sorrows and our pains,
These are thy noble gains!
But oh, thou Love's and Nature's masterer,
Thou conq'ror of the crowned,
What dost thou on this ground,
Too small a circle for thy mighty sphere?
Go and make slumber dear
To the renowned and high:
We here, a lowly race,
Can live without thy grace,

After the use of mild antiquity.
Go; let us love: since years
No trace allow, and life soon disappears.
Go; let us love: the daylight dies, is born;
But unto us the light
Dies once for all; and sleep brings on eternal night.

ACT II

Scene I

The Satyr.

Satyr. Small is the bee, and yet with a small sting
  Makes grave and troublesome wounds. But what
    is smaller
  Than love, who lurks in the minutest things,
  And strays in the minutest? now beneath
  The shadow of an eyebrow; now among
  Threads of fine hair; and now in the small wells,
  Which a sweet smile forms in a lovely cheek.
  And yet what great and mortal wounds are his,
  And past all remedy! Alas! all wound
  And bleeding havoc is he in my nature;
  And millions of sharp spears does he keep stored
  In Sylvia's eyes. Oh cruel love! Oh Sylvia,
  More hard and without sense, than are the woods,
  How rightly dost thou bear that sylvan name!
  What foresight his who gave it thee! The woods
  Hide with their lovely leaves, lions, and bears,
  And snakes; and thou in thy fair bosom hidest
  Hate, and disdain, and hard impiety;
  Things wilder far than lions, bears, and snakes;
  For those are tameable, but to tame thee
  Defies the power of present and of prayer.
  Ah me! when I would give thee flowers new-blown,
  Thou drawest thyself back; perhaps because
  Thou hast more lovely flowers in thy own looks.
  Ah me! when I present thee sweet young apples,
  Thou puttest them away; perhaps because
  Thou hast more sweet young apples in thy bosom.
  Alas! when I would please thee with sweet honey,

Thou treatest it as nought; perhaps because
Thou hast a sweeter honey in thy lips.
If my poor means can give thee nothing better,
I give thee my own self. And why, unjust one,
Scorn and abhor the gift? I am not one
To be despised, if truly t'other day
I saw myself reflected in the sea,
When the winds hushed, and there was not a wave.
This ruddy sanguine visage, these broad shoulders,
This hairy breast, and these my shaggy thighs,
Are marks of strength and manhood. If thou dost not
Believe them, try them. What dost thou expect
Of those young dainty ones, whose girlish cheeks
Are scarcely tinged with down, and who dispose
Their pretty locks in order—girls indeed
In strength as well as look? Will any of them
Follow thee through the woods, and up the
      mountains,
And combat for thy sake with bears and boars?
I am no brute thing; no—nor dost thou scorn me
Because I am thus shaped, but simply and solely
Because I am thus poor. Oh, that the woods
Should take this vile example from the town.
This is indeed the age of gold; for gold
Is conquered of all, and gold is king.
Oh thou, whoe'er thou wert, that first did shew
The way to make love venal, be thou accursed.
Cursed may thine ashes be, and cold thy bones;
And never mayst thou find shepherd or nymph
To say to them in passing "Peace be with ye";
But may the sharp rains wash them, and the winds
Blow on their bareness; and the herd's foul foot
Trample them, and the stranger. Thou didst first
Put shame upon the nobleness of love;
And thine was the vile hand that first did put
Bitterness in his cup. A venal love!
A love that waits on gold! It is the greatest,
And most abominable, and filthiest monster,
That ever land or sea shuddered at bearing.
But why in vain lament me? Every creature
Uses the helping arms which nature gave it:
The stag betakes himself to flight, the lion
Ramps with his mighty paws, the foaming boar
Turns with his tusks; and loveliness and grace
Are woman's weapons and her potency.
If nature made me then fitted for deeds

Of violence and rapine, why not I
Use violence for my ends? I will do so:
I will go force from that ungrateful one
What she denies my love. A goatherd, who
Has watched her ways, tells me that she is used
To bathe her in a fountain; and has shewn me
The very spot. There will I plant me close
Among the shrubs and bushes, and so wait
Until she come; then seize my opportunity,
And run upon her. What can she oppose,
The tender thing, either by force or flight,
To one so swift and powerful? She may use
Her sighs and tears, and all that is of force
In beauty to move pity. I will twist
This hand of mine in her thick locks; nor stir
One step till I have drank my draught of vengeance.

Scene II

Daphne *and* Thyrsis.

Daphne.   As I have told thee, Thyrsis, I knew well
How warmly Amyntas loved: and heaven knows
How many offices of kindness I
Have done him, and how many more would do.
Thy prayers have now been added; but as soon
Mightst thou expect to tame a sullen bull,
Or bear, or tiger, as this simple girl,
As foolish as she's fair. She never heeds,
How hot or sharp the darts may be, that strike
From her fair hands; but whether grave or merry,
Goes slaying on; and slays, and knows it not.
Thyrsis.   Nay, where is to be found the girl so simple,
That if she has but left her leading-strings,
Learns not the art of striking and of pleasing,
And killing with those pleasing arts, and knowing
What arms she wears, and which dispenses death,
And which is healing and restores to life?
Daphne.   And who is master, pray, of all those arts?
Thyrsis.   Thou feignest ignorance to try me. Well:
The master is the same that teaches birds
Their singing and their flight, fishes their swim-
     ming,
The ram his butting, tossing to the bull,
And shews the stately-loving peacock how

To open wide the pomp of his eyed plumes.
Daphne.   And this great master's name?
Thyrsis.   Daphne.
Daphne.   Fine words!
Thyrsis.   Why so? Art thou not fit to open school
For thousands of thy sex? Though, to say truth,
There is no need of master. Nature is master;
But then the mother and the nurse bear part.
Daphne.   Truly thou'rt both a simple and a sad one.—
But to our business. I must own to thee,
I half suspect that Sylvia is not quite
So simple as she seems. I witnessed something
But yesterday which makes me doubt. I found her
In those large meadows neighboring the city,
Where there's a little isle among the pools.
She looked on one of them, and hung right over
Its clear unruffled glass, as if to see
How beautiful she looked, and how to best
Advantage she might set the dropping curls
About her brow, and on her curls her net,
And on her net some flowers that filled her bosom.
And now she would take out some privet-blossom,
And now a rose, and hold it to her fair
Fine neck, or her vermilion cheeks, to make
Comparison of their hues. Then she would dart
A smile, as if in gladsome victory,
Which seemed to say, "I conquer nevertheless;
And I will wear ye, not for my adorning,
But solely to your shame, that ye may find
How I surpass ye far." As she was thus
Adorning and admiring her, she chanced
To turn her eyes, and finding I had seen her,
Let fall her flowers, and rose covered with
  blushes.
I laughed to see her blush; she blushed the more
To see me laugh; and yet, having her locks
But partly gathered up, she had recourse
Once or twice more to her fair friend, the lake,
And stole admiring glances: till afraid
That I espied her spyings, she was pleased
To let herself remain thus partly dressed,
Seeing how negligence became her too.
I saw it, and said nothing.
Thyrsis.   'Tis exactly
As I supposed. Now dost thou understand me?
Daphne.   I understand thee well. But I have heard

That nymphs and shepherdesses formerly
Were not thus knowing, yet reserved. I was not
In my own youth. The world methinks, grows old,
And growing old, grows sad.

Thyrsis. In those good times
The town, I guess, did not so often spoil
The woods and fields; nor on the other hand
Our foresters so often go to town.
Manners and tribes are mingled nowadays.
But let us leave this talk. Tell me now, Daphne,
Canst thou not so contrive, some day or other,
That Sylvia shall consent to see Amyntas
Alone—or if not so, at least with thee?

Daphne. I know not. She is now more coy than ever.

Thyrsis. And he, no doubt, more full of his respect.

Daphne. Respectful loving is a desperate trade.
He should set up another. The first step
In learning love is to unlearn respect.
The scholar then must dare, demand, entreat,
Importune, run away with; and if that
Be not sufficient, there is one thing more.
Knowest thou not the stuff that woman's made of?
She flies, and flying, would provoke pursuit:
Refuses; and refusing, would be plundered:
Combats; and combating, would be overthrown.
Ah, Thyrsis, 'tis in confidence I speak
To thee. Deride it not; nor above all,
Put it in rhyme. Thou knowest I know how
To give thee for thy verses, something better.

Thyrsis. Thou hast no reason to suspect me capable
Of ever uttering syllable thou lik'st not.
But now I pray thee, gentle Daphne mine,
By the sweet memory of thy fresh youth,
That thou wilt help me to help poor Amyntas.
He will die else.

Daphne. O gallant adjuration!
To remind woman of her younger days;
Of her delights gone by, and present sadness,
Well: what wouldst have me do?

Thyrsis. Thou wantest not
Wit nor advice, suffice it that thou wilt.

Daphne. Well then. We two (Sylvia and I) shall go
To the fountain which is call'd Diana's fountain,
Thou know'st it—where the plane tree is, that holds
Sweet shade to the sweet waters, and invites
The nymphs to seat them freshly from the chase.

There, I know well, she will engulf her fair
And naked limbs.
Thyrsis.   What then?
Daphne.   What then! O brain
Of little wit! Think, and thou'lt know what then.
Thyrsis.   I see. But then his courage——I doubt that.
Daphne.   Nay, if he have not that, he must needs stay,
And wait till people fetch him.
Thyrsis.   And even that
His nature would deserve.
Daphne.   A little now
To talk of thyself, Thyrsis. Come; hast thou
No wish to be in love? Thou art still young,
Not more than four years over the fourth luster,
If I remember rightly. Wouldst thou lead
A life of insipidity and denial?
Man knows not what delight is, till he loves.
Thyrsis.   The man that avoids love need not be ignorant
Of the delights of Venus. He but culls
And tastes the sweets of love without the bitter.
Daphne.   Insipid is the sweet undashed with bitter:
And satiates too soon.
Thyrsis.   Better be satiate
Than ever hungering—hungering during food,
And after food.
Daphne.   Not if the food so pleases,
And so possesses one, that every relish
Invites but to another.
Thyrsis.   Aye, but who
Possesses such a food, and has it always
At hand, to feast his hunger?
Daphne.   Who is he
Finds what he does not look for?
Thyrsis.   'Tis a search
Too perilous, to look for what so cheats us,
When it is found; and tortures more, when not.
No; no more love for me; no slaveries more
Of sighs and tears before his reckless throne.
I have had sighs and tears enough. Let others
Play their part now.
Daphne.   But not enough of joys.
Thyrsis.   I wish them not, if they must cost so dear.
Daphne.   Thou wilt be forced to love, whate'er thou
   wishest.
Thyrsis.   But how can he be forced, who keeps at
   distance?

Daphne. Who keeps love distant?

Thyrsis.   He who fears and flies.

Daphne. What use to fly, when the pursuer has wings?

Thyrsis. A love newborn has but small wings. He scarcely
  Can lift himself upon them, much less dare
  To spread them to the wind.

Daphne.   Man seldom knows
  When Love is born; and when he does, Love is
  Full grown at once, and plumed.

Thyrsis.   Suppose he has seen
  Love born before?

Daphne.   Well; we shall see, Thyrsis,
  Whether thine eyes will be so prompt for flight,
  As thou supposest. I protest to thee,
  That should I ever see thee call for help,
  When thou dost play the racer and the stag,
  I will not move a single step to help thee;
  No, not a finger, a syllable, or a wink.

Thyrsis. Cruel! And would it give thee pleasure then
  To see me dead? If thou wouldst have me love,
  Love me thyself. Let both be loved and loving.

Daphne. Thou mockest me, I fear; perhaps, in truth,
  Deserv'st a mistress more complete than I.
  Oh! the seductions of enameled cheeks!

Thyrsis. I mock thee not, believe me. It is thou
  That rather tak'st this method to refuse me.
  It is the way with all of ye. However,
  If thou wilt love me not, I will love on
  Without a love.

Daphne.   Be happy then, dear Thyrsis,
  Happier than ever. Live in perfect ease;
  For love takes root in ease, and flourishes.

Thyrsis. O Daphne! 'twas a God gave me that ease.
  For well may he be deemed a God among us,
  Whose mighty flocks and herds feed everywhere,
  From sea to sea, both on the cultured smoothness,
  And glad amenity of fertile fields,
  And o'er the mountainous backs of Apennine.
  He said to me, when first he made me his,
  "Thyrsis, let others guard my walled folds,
  And chase the wolves and robbers; others give
  My servants their rewards and punishments;
  And others feed my flocks, and others manage
  The dairies and the shearings, and dispense
  Their wealth. Do thou, since thou art more at ease,

Sing only." Therefore 'tis most just, my song
Turn not upon the sports of earthly love,
But sing the lineage of my great and true
(Which name am I to choose?) Apollo or Jove,
For in his works and looks, both he resembles;
A lineage worthy of Saturn and of Cœlus.
Thus has a rustic muse, regal reward;
And whether clear or hoarse, he scorns her not.
I sing not of himself, being unable
To honor his great nature worthily,
Except with silence and with reverence.
But not forever shall his altars be
Without my flowers—without the sweet uprolling
Of odorous incense. And this faith of mine,
Pure and devout, shall go not from my heart,
Till stags shall go to feed themselves in air,
And the old rivers run from out their paths,
And Persians drink the Soane, and Gauls the
    Tigris.

Daphne.   Truly thou fliest high. Now please descend
A little to our work.

Thyrsis.   The point is this;
That thou shouldst go into the fountain with her,
And try to awake her tenderness. Meanwhile
I will persuade Amyntas to come after.
And I suspect my task is not less difficult
Than thine, so let us go.

Daphne.   I will: but mind;
Forget not that we have a task besides.

Thyrsis.   If I discern his countenance at this distance,
It is Amyntas issuing there. 'Tis he.

Scene III

Thyrsis *and* Amyntas.

Amyntas.   I wish to know what Thyrsis may have done;
If nothing, then, before I pass to nothing,
I will go slay me right before the eyes,
Of this hard girl.
        She is displeased to see
        The wound in my heart's core,
        Struck by her own sweet eyes.
        She will be pleased to see
        The new wound in my bosom,

　　Struck by my own poor hand.

Thyrsis.　I bring thee comfortable news, Amyntas,
　　Dry up thy tears forever.

Amyntas.　　　　　　　　What! Ah, me,
　　What dost thou say? What bring me? Life or death?

Thyrsis.　Life and salvation, if thou darest to meet them;
　　But thou must be a man, and dare indeed.

Amyntas.　What dare, and against whom?

Thyrsis.　　　　　　　　Suppose thy lady
　　Were in the middle of a wood, which girt
　　With lofty rocks, harbored wild beasts and lions:
　　Wouldst thou go join her?

Amyntas.　　　　　　　Aye, as full of joy,
　　And more, than holiday maiden to a dance.

Thyrsis.　Suppose her too, in midst of arms and robbers,
　　Wouldst thou go join her?

Amyntas.　　　　　　　Aye, more headlong glad
　　Than thirsting stag to fountain.

Thyrsis.　　　　　　　　There is need
　　Of greater daring then, than even this.

Amyntas.　Why, I will go in middle of rapid torrents,
　　When the great snows get loose, and swell them down
　　Sheer to the sea. I will go treading fires,
　　The fires of hell itself, if she be there,
　　And hell can be where there's a thing so fair.
　　Now, tell me all.

Thyrsis.　　　　　　　Listen.

Amyntas.　　　　　　　I pray thee speak.

Thyrsis.　Sylvia is waiting for thee at a fountain,
　　Naked and alone.

Amyntas.　　　　　　Oh! what is it thou sayest?
　　Naked and alone, and me!

Thyrsis.　　　　　　　　Alone; except
　　Daphne be with her, who is in our interest.

Amyntas.　Naked? and waits for me?

Thyrsis.　　　　　　Aye, naked; but——

Amyntas.　Alas, that *but!* Thou speakest not; thou killest
　　me.

Thyrsis.　But she is not aware yet of thy coming.

Amyntas.　Oh hard conclusion, which comes poisoning
　　all!
　　What arts are these to torture me, fierce friend?
　　Does it seem little to thee I am wretched,
　　That thus thou wouldst increase my misery?

Thyrsis.　Follow my counsel, and I'll make thee happy.

Amyntas.　What counsel?

Thyrsis.　　　That thou go directly, and seize
　What friendly fortune offers.
Amyntas.　　　　　　　　God forbid,
　That I should do the least thing to displease her.
　I never did, except in loving her;
　And that I could not help: her beauty made me.
　Therefore it is not the less true for that,
　That in all things I can, I seek to please her.
Thyrsis.　Now answer me. Suppose 'twere in thy power
　To cease to love her, wouldst thou please her so?
Amyntas.　Love will not let me answer thee; no, nor
　　suffer
　The very imagination of the thing.
Thyrsis.　Then thou wouldst love her in her own despite,
　When thou couldst cease to love her, if thou wouldst.
Amyntas.　No, not in her despite; but I would love her.
Thyrsis.　Against her will then?
Amyntas.　　　　　　Yes, undoubtedly.
Thyrsis.　Why then not dare to take against her will
　That which however grievous to her at first,
　Will when 'tis taken, be at last, at last,
　Both sweet and dear to her?
Amyntas.　　　　　　Ah, Thyrsis, love
　Must answer for me. At my heart he speaks,
　At my heart's core; but I cannot repeat it.
　Custom has made thee talk of love too lightly.
　Thou art too used in art, to talk of love.
　What ties my heart, ties up my tongue.
Thyrsis.　　　　　　　　Thou wilt
　Not go then?
Amyntas.　　　Yes, I will; but not where thou
　Wouldst have me go.
Thyrsis.　　　　Where then?
Amyntas.　　　　　　　To death—if all
　Thou hast to tell me for my good, be this.
Thyrsis.　Does this then seem to thee so little? Think:
　Dost thou suppose that Daphne would have formed
　This plan herself, had she not partly known
　Sylvia's own mind? Sylvia may know of it,
　And yet not wish to be supposed to know.
　Now if thou seekest her express consent,
　Dost thou not see thou wilt displease her more?
　Where then is all this mighty wish of thine
　To please her? If she wishes thy delight
　To be thy theft, thy rapine not her gift,
　Nor favor, foolish boy, what matters it,

This mode or that?
Amyntas.   And who will make me sure
That she does wish it?
Thyrsis.   Now art thou a madman.
See if thou dost not wish the very certainty
Which she dislikes, and which she should dislike,
And which thou shouldst not look for. Oh but then,
Who is to make thee sure she does not wish!
Now grant she does, and that thou dost not go.
The doubt and risk are equal. Oh! how nobler
To die like a brave man than like a coward!
Thou'rt dumb: thou'rt conquered. Come, confess
    as much,
And thy defeat shall be thy cause of victory;
Come, let us go.
Amyntas.   Nay, stop.
Thyrsis.   Why *stop?* Time flies.
Amyntas.   Ah, let us first consider—let us think
What we should do, and how.
Thyrsis.   Upon the road then.
To think too many things, is to do none.

Chorus

Tell us, O Love, what school,
What mighty master's rule,
Can teach thine art, so doubtful and so long?
Who shall enable sense
To know the intelligence,
Which takes us heavenward on thy pinions strong?
Not all that learned throng
Among the Attic trees,
Nor Phœbus on his hill
Who sings of loving still,
Could truly tell us of thy mysteries.
Little he spoke, and cold,
Of what we would be told;
Nor had the voice of fire
Fit for the listening of our great desire.
With thee, O Love, with thee,
He raises not his yearnings equally.

It is thyself alone
By whom thou canst be shewn,
Sole manifester thou of all thy sense:
'Tis thou, that by the rude
Canst render understood

Those admirable things, deep, sweet, and wise,
Which thine own proper hand
In amorous letters writes in others' eyes:
Thou loosenest the tongues
Of those that serve thee well
Into a beauteous and a bland
Abundant eloquence.
And often (O divine
And wondrous deed of thine!)
In passion-broken words,
And a confused saying,
The struggling heart shall best
Leap forth and be expressed,
And more avail than rhetoric's whole displaying.
Thy very silence wears
The face of ended prayers.

Oh Love, let others read
The old Socratic scrolls,
Two lovely eyes outmaster all their schools:
And pens of learned mark
Shall find it but lost time.
Compared with this wild rhyme.
Which a rude hand cuts on the rude tree bark.

ACT III

Scene I

Thyrsis *and* **Chorus.**

Thyrsis.   O infinite cruelty! O thankless heart!
   O thankless woman, and thrice and four times most
   Ungrateful sex! and thou, Nature thyself.
   Negligent mistress, why in looks alone.
   And surfaces of women, dost thou put
   All that is in them of the gentle and kind?
   Ah, my poor friend! perhaps he has slain himself!
   I see him not; I have searched all the place
   In which I left him, and looked round about,
   And searched again, and found no trace of him.
   He must have slain himself! I'll ask the shepherds,

Whom I see there. Friends, have you seen Amyntas,
Or heard of him?

Chorus.   Thou seemest much disturbed:
What is it troubles thee? Why this heat and panting?
Has any ill befallen? Pray thee tell us.

Thyrsis.   I dread ill of Amyntas. Have ye seen h'm?

Chorus.   Not since he left thyself. What dost thou dread?

Thyrsis.   That he has slain himself.

Chorus.   Has slain himself,
Why? for what reason?

Thyrsis.   Oh, for Hate and Love.

Chorus.   Terrible enemies to league together!
What could they not? But tell us, pray, more clearly.

Thyrsis.   He loved a nymph too well, who too much
hated him.

Chorus.   Nay, tell us all. This is a thoroughfare;
And while thou talkest, someone may arrive
With news of him, perhaps his very self.

Thyrsis.   Most willingly. For 'tis not just that such
Extreme and strange ingratitude should miss
Its proper infamy. My friend had learned
(Alas! 'twas I that told him and conducted him;
I repent now) that Sylvia meant to go
With Daphne to a fount to bathe herself.
There then he followed, doubting and uneasy,
Moved, not by his own heart, but by my urgent
And goading importunity. Ofttimes
Would he have turned him back; and I as oft
Forced him along. Scarcely had we arrived
In neighborhood of the place, when lo! we heard
Cries of a woman in distress; and Daphne
Appeared at the same time, wringing her hands.
The moment she beheld us, she cried out,
"Help, help! Sylvia is forced!" The enamored boy,
As soon as his ear heard, sprung like the pard.
I followed him: and lo! bound to a tree
Was the fair nymph, naked as she was born.
The rope that bound her was her own soft hair,
Her very hair, twisted about the tree
In savage knots; and that bright zone of hers,
Which held her virgin bosom in its clip,
Was made to serve the outrage, and strapped fast
Her hands to the hard trunk. Nay, even the tree
Itself was forced to that vile ministry;
And a green withy of its flowering boughs

Fettered each delicate leg. Right fronting her
We saw a villain Satyr, who that moment
Was finishing his fastenings. She did all
She could to hinder him; but what was that?
The moments vanished. Amyntas with a lance
In his right hand, came on the Satyr, like
A lion. I had filled my lap with stones:
And the brute ravisher fled. His flight left leisure
To the glad lover's eyes; and round he turned them
With earnestness upon those lovely limbs,
Which looked as delicate and fair as cream
When curdled smooth it trembles in white baskets.
I saw his visage sparkle fire. But soon
Accosting her in a low voice, and modestly,
He said, "O heavenly Sylvia, thou must pardon
These hands, if it be too presumptuous bold
To come so near thy limbs of loveliness.
Necessity compels them—hard necessity
To loosen all these knots; and so I pray thee,
Let not the grace, which fortune thus concedes them,
Be painful to thee."

Chorus.   Words to mollify
A heart of stone: but what did she reply?

Thyrsis.   Nothing. But in disdain and shame kept down
Her eyes toward the earth, hiding, as much
As in her lay, her delicate bosom. He,
Assisting her aloof, began to untie
Her tresses, saying all the while, "Unworthy
Of knots so beautiful was this hard trunk.
What are the advantages of Love's own servants,
If trees and they have such fair bonds in common?
Hard-hearted tree! and couldst thou hurt the hair
That did thee so much honor?" After this
He loosed her hands with his, in such a manner
As showed how much he feared, yet longed, to
      touch them;
And then he stooped to set her ankles free;
But she, the moment she could use her hands,
Made a contemptuous gesture, and said, "Shepherd,
See that thou touch me not: I am Diana's:
Leave me to loosen them."

Chorus.   Can such pride be
In woman's heart? Oh graceless recompense
For such a graceful service!

Thyrsis.   He drew back,
And stood apart in reverence, not even raising

His eyelids to admire her, but denying
The pleasure to himself, purely to take
The trouble of denying it from her.
I, who kept close, and witnessed everything,
And heard as well, felt ready to cry out;
But I restrained myself. Now hear a wonder;
After much trouble she unloosed herself,
And scarcely had done so, than without **saying**
A bare adieu, she set off like a fawn.
Certainly for no fear; for his respect
Was too well known.

Chorus.   Why fled she then?
Thyrsis.   Because
She fain would have owed thanks to flight alone,
Not to his modest love.

Chorus.   Ungrateful still:
But what did he do then? What said he?

Thyrsis.   I know **not**;
For in my haste to finish my fine work
And bring her back, I missed both her and him.
When I returned, he was not at the fountain;
And therefore is it that I dread some evil.
I know he was disposed to slay himself,
Even before this happened.

Chorus.   'Tis the custom
And artifice of Love to threaten suicide:
But the blow seldom follows.

Thyrsis.   Heaven grant
He may be no exception.

Chorus.   Trust he will not.

Thyrsis.   I'll look into the cave of sage Elpino.
Amyntas, if alive, may have gone there;
For there he has been often used to sweeten
His bitter sufferings in the flowing sound
Of that clear pipe, which is of charm enough
To make the mountains listen, and the streams
Run into milk, and the hard trees give honey.

Scene II

Amyntas, Daphne, *and* Nerina.

Amyntas.   Pitiless was thy pity,
O Daphne, when thou didst pull back the lance;
For the more slowly my death comes, the more

His shadow will oppress me.
And why thus lead me through so many paths,
Dsicourising all the while? What dost thou fear?
That I shall kill myself? Thou fearst my comfort.

Daphne.   Despair not, dear Amyntas.
I know her well. 'Twas but shamefacedness
That made her fly, not cruelty.

Amyntas.   Ah me!
It is my safest business to despair.
Hope is my ruin. Even now, alas!
It tries to spring up in this heart of mine,
Solely because I live. What evil is there
Worse than the life of such a wretch as I am?

Daphne.   Live, live, unhappy one, in spite of wretched-
          ness:
Endure thy state, to be at last made happy.
If thou dost live and hope, thy hope's reward
Will be what thou hast seen in that bare beauty.

Amyntas.   Nay, love and fate thought not my misery
Quite perfect, till in all its perfectness
Mine eyes had seen the bliss,
Which I must ever miss.

Nerina (*coming among the trees*). Thus must I be the
          raven of bad news.
O wretched Montano! miserable forever.
How wilt thou bear thyself, when thou art told
What has befallen thine own and only Sylvia?
Poor gray bereaved old man, no more a father!

Daphne.   I hear a sorrowful voice.

Amyntas.   I hear a name
That strikes through ears and heart.

Daphne.   It is Nerina,
The gentle nymph whom Cynthia holds so dear!
She that has such sweet eyes, and beautiful hands,
And manners of such grace and friendliness.

Nerina.   Still he must know it; he must make them
          gather
Her luckless relics, should she be not whole.
Oh Sylvia, what a hard and dreadful lot!

Amyntas.   Alas! who can it be? Who speaks?

Nerina.   O Daphne!

Daphne.   Why talkest thou to thyself? and what of Sylvia,
And all these sighs?

Nerina.   A dreadful thing it is,
That makes me sigh.

Amyntas.   What horror does she speak of?

A deadly ice has shot about my heart,
And shuts up my loud spirit. Is she alive?
Daphne. Tell us, pray tell us!
Nerina. Oh God, that I should be the messenger!
But I must speak. Sylvia—she came to me—
To my house—naked. Why, thou knowest well.
When she was dressed, she asked me to go with her
And join a chase, down in the Wood of Holms:
I said I would. We went, and found a throng
Of nymphs arrived; when lo! I know not whence,
A most enormous wolf dashed right among us,
His jaws all bathed in blood. Sylvia like lightning
Fits a large arrow to a bow I had,
And draws and strikes him sheer upon the head.
He plunges back into the woods; and she,
Holding a lance in ready fierceness, follows.
Amyntas. Oh dolorous beginning! What, ah me!
Will be the end?
Nerina. I with another lance
Followed her track, but far enough behind,
Not being so swift, as soon as they had reached
The inmost part of the wood, she disappeared.
Still I pursued the track; which led so far
That I arrived at last at the most desert
And gloomy spot in the forest. There I came
Upon the lance of Sylvia—and not far off
Was a white net, which I myself had bound
Her tresses with; and as I looked about,
I saw seven wolves, busy in licking blood
Among some naked bones. They saw not me,
As it turned out, so earnest was their meal.
Brimful of fear and pity, I returned:
And this is all I know of Sylvia's fate.
Here is the net.
Amyntas. *All* which thou knowest! and the net! and
blood!
Oh Sylvia, thou art dead. (*He falls to the earth.*)
Daphne. This misery
Has overcome him. How now! Is he dead?
Nerina. He breathes again! 'Twas but a passing swoon;
He comes to himself.
Amyntas. Oh Sorrow,
Why dost thou so contrive to torture me
That death is spared me still. Thou art too merciful.
Or wouldst thou leave the task to mine own hands?
Content! Content! since thou wilt do it not,

Or cannot. Oh if this dire news be true,
And my great misery perfect, why stay longer?
What can I look for more? Oh Daphne, Daphne,
To this most bitter end 'twas thou didst keep me,
Even to this end most bitter.
A sweet and comely death might I have died,
Compared with dying now. Thou didst prevent me;
And heaven, which knew I should have so outstripped
This fiercer misery that was to follow,
May now in striking its last wound upon me,
Well grant me leave to die.
Thou too shouldst grant me leave.

Daphne.   Have patience yet till thou hast learned the
truth

Amyntas.   The truth! What truth? Did I not wait before,
And learn too much?

Nerina.   Would I had held my peace!

Amyntas.   Fair nymph, I pray thee, give me
That net—the poor remains of all that beauty.
It shall be my companion
For the small space I have to live and move,
And with its presence aggravate a martyrdom,
Which is, indeed, small martyrdom, at best,
If I have need of being helped to die.

Nerina.   Ought I to give it him or not?
The very reason which thou giv'st for asking it
Compels me to deny it thee.

Amyntas.   Deny!
Deny me at my last extremity
A thing so small! Even in this I see
The malice of my fate. I yield! I yield!
Let it stay with thee; and do ye, stay both:
I vanish, never to return.

Daphne.   Amyntas!
Amyntas! Stay!
Oh, with what desperate fury does he run!

Nerina.   So swiftly, 'tis in vain to follow him.
I will pursue my way; and it may be
Better perhaps that I do hold my peace,
And tell not poor Montano.

Chorus. There is no need of death
    To bind a great heart fast:
    Faith is enough at first, and Love at last.
    Nor does a fond desert
    Pursue so hard a fame
    In following its sweet aim;

Since Love is paid with its own loving heart.
And oftentimes, ere it work out its story,
It finds itself clasp glory.

ACT IV

Scene I

Daphne, Sylvia, *and* Chorus.

Daphne.   May the wind bear away with the bad news
That was so spread of thee, all, all thy ills,
Both present and to come. Thou art alive
And well, thank Heaven; and I had thought thee
    dead;
Fully believed it; with such circumstance
Nerina had described thy misadventure.
Ah, would she had been mute, or others deaf!
Sylvia.   Doubtless it was great chance; and she had
    reason
To think me dead.
Daphne.   But not to tell us so.
Now tell us all thyself of thy escape.
Sylvia.   Following a wolf. I found myself immersed
In such a depth of trees, I lost the track.
While I was seeking how I should return,
I saw him again; I knew him by an arrow
Which I had fixed upon him by the ear.
He was with many others, occupied
With some dead animal, I know not what,
Which had been freshly slain. The wounded beast
Knew me, I think; for with his bloody mouth
He issued forth upon me. I expected him,
And shook my lance. Thou knowest I have skill
At games like those, and seldom strike in vain.
This time, however, though I seemed to mark
My distance well, I launched the steel for nothing.
Whether 'twas fortune or my fault, I know not,
But in the enemy's stead, it pierced a tree.
More greedy then came he; and I who found him
So close to me, and thought my weapon useless,
Having no other arms, took swift to flight.
I fled: he followed. Hear now the result.
A net which held my hair got partly loose,

And fluttering to the wind, was caught by a bough.
I felt a something pull me. and retard,
And frightened for my life, would have redoubled
The swiftness of my running; but the bough
Resisted in its turn, and held me fast.
At last I tore away, leaving the veil
And some of my hair with it; and such wings
Fear lent my feet, that he o'ertook me not,
And forth I issued safe. Returning home,
I met with thee, looking all agitation;
And was not less astonished at the sight
Than thou at mine.

Daphne.   Thou art alive indeed.
Alas, that all are not so!

Sylvia.   What? Dost grieve?

Daphne. No: I am pleased to see thee safe: I grieve
Because another's dead.

Sylvia.   Dead? Who?

Daphne.   Amyntas.

Sylvia. Amyntas? How?

Daphne. I cannot tell thee how;
Nor yet indeed whether he lives, or not,
But I, myself, firmly believe him dead.

Sylvia. What do I hear? But what dost thou suppose
The reason of his death?

Daphne.   Thine own.

Sylvia.   My death?
I do not understand thee.

Daphne.   The report then
Of thy sad end he heard and he believed;
And it has certainly by this time, driven him
To some most desperate end on his own part.

Sylvia. Nay, thy suspicion will turn out as groundless,
As it has done just now. Everyone takes
All possible care of his own life, believe me.

Daphne. Oh Sylvia, Sylvia, thou hast no conception
Of what love's fierceness in a heart can do;
A heart, at least, of flesh and blood, not stone
As thine is. If thou hadst but known it half,
Thou wouldst have loved the being who loved thee
More than the very apples of his eyes,
More than the breath he lived by. I believe it,
For I have seen it. When thou didst betake thee
To flight from him (oh, fiercer creature thou
Than tigers), when thou shouldst have been
Embracing him for love and gratitude,

I saw him turn his lance upon himself.
It pierced his clothes and skin, and with his blood
Was colored; nor did he, for all that, slacken,
But would have thrust it desperately in
And pierced the heart which had been treated worse
And wounded more by thee, had I not seized
His arm and hindered him. Alas! Alas!
That shallow wound perhaps was but the exercise
Of his determined and despairing constancy,
And did but shew the way for the fierce steel
To run more freely in.

Sylvia.　　　　What dost thou tell me?

Daphne. Afterward, when he heard that bitter news.
I saw him swoon with agony; and on coming
To life again, he flung away in fury,
To kill himself; and doubtless, it is done.

Sylvia. Ah me! And thou not follow him! Let us go;
Oh, let us find him! If he would have died
To follow me, he must live now to save me.

Daphne. I followed him with all the speed I had;
But in his swiftness he soon disappeared;
And I went seeking him through all his haunts,
In vain. Where wouldst thou go, having no trace?

Sylvia. But he will die, unless we find him; die
Alas! by his own hand.

Daphne.　　　　　　　Cruel! and wouldst thou
Snatch from him then the glory of that deed,
To finish it thyself? Wouldst thou dispatch him?
And does it seem an injury done to thee
That he should die by any hand but thine?
Now, be appeased; for howsoe'er he dies,
He dies for thee: the blow is thine at last.

Sylvia. Alas! thou piercest me to my heart's core.
The grief he gives me now, doubles my bitterness
In thinking upon all that cruelty
Which I called honesty: and I called it right,
But 'twas indeed too hard and rigorous.
I see it now, and suffer for it.

Daphne.　　　　　　　　What!
What do I hear? Dost thou take pity—thou?
Thou feel at heart one touch of tenderness!
And see—what weep! Thou weeping thou the
　　proud one!
Oh wonder! What then are these tears of thine?
Real! And tears of love!

Sylvia.　　　　　　Not love, but pity.

Daphne.   Pity as surely is love's harbinger,
  As lightning is the thunder's.
Chorus.   Thus it is,
  When love would steal into a virgin heart,
  Where sour-faced honesty would have barred him
    out,
  He takes the habit and the countenance
  Of his true servant and sweet usher, Pity,
  And so beguiles the simple mistress there,
  And gets within.
Daphne.   Nay, what are all these tears
  That flow away so fast? Sylvia, thou'rt silent.
  Thou lovest? 'Tis so. Lovest; and in vain.
  Oh mighty power of Love! just chastisement
  Dost thou send down on this thy unbeliever.
  Wretched Amyntas! like the bee art thou
  Who pierces as he dies, and leaves his life
  Within another's wound. Thy death at last
  Has smitten the hard heart, which thou couldst never
  Touch when alive. If thou art now a shade,
  (As I believe) wandering about thy naked
  And poor unburied limbs, behold her tears,
  Behold them and rejoice; loving in life,
  Beloved in death. If 'twas thy destiny
  To be beloved then only, and this cruel one
  Would sell her pity at no meaner price,
  'Tis paid; and thou hast bought her love with dying.
Chorus.   Dear price to give; useless and shameless one
  To take!
Sylvia.   Oh! that I were but able with my love
  To purchase back his life, or with my life
  Itself; if he indeed is dead.
Daphne.   Oh wise!
  Too late! Oh pity, come at last in vain!

Scene II.

Messengers, Chorus, Sylvia, *and* Daphne.

Messenger.   I am so overcome with pity and horror
  That whereso'er I turn, I cannot see
  Or hear a thing that does not start and shake me.
Chorus.   Who is he
  That brings such trouble in his looks and voice?

Messenger. I bring terrible news. Amyntas
  Is dead.
Sylvia. Alas! what says he?
Messenger. The noblest shepherd of the woods is dead,
  He that was such a gentle spirit, so graceful,
  And so beloved by all the nymphs and muses:
  He in his prime is dead; and what a death!
Chorus. Tell us, I pray thee, all; that we may weep
  His loss with thee—his loss, and our own loss.
Sylvia. Ah me! why shake I thus, and stand aloof!
  I dare not hear! I dare not hear; and must.
  Oh my hard heart, my hard and impious heart,
  Why dost thou shrink! Come, meet the terrible
      darts
  Which this man carries in his tongue;
  And shew them now thy fierceness.—
  Shepherd, I come for part of that sad pain
  Thou promisest to us assembled here;
  It fits me more than thou perhaps mayst think;
  And I shall take it from thee as a thing
  Most due to me. Now keep thou nothing back.
Messenger. Nymph, I can well believe thee; for that
      hapless one
  Finished his life in calling on thy name.
Daphne. Now opens this dread history.
Messenger.   I was standing
  In middle of a hill, where I had spread
  Some nets of mine; when close to me I saw
  Amyntas pass me; looking, not as usual,
  But strangely altered and disturbed. I rose,
  And making speed came up with him. He stopped,
  And said, "Ergastus, there is a great pleasure
  Which thou mayst do me: 'tis to come with me
  And witness something I am going to do:
  But I must have thee first swear solemnly
  That thou wilt stand aloof, and by no means
  Obstruct me in my work." I, as he wished
  (For who could have foreseen so wild an accident?),
  Made fearful adjurations, and invoked
  Pallas, Priapus, and Pomona, and Pan,
  And midnight Hecate. Then did he resume
  His way, and took me to the edge of the hill,
  From which in dizzy juttings and rude crags,
  Without a path, for never foot could make one,
  There drops into the valley a precipice.
  We stopped—I looking down below, and feeling

Such headlong fear in me that suddenly
I drew me back—he seeming that small space
To smile and be serene of countenance;
A look, which doubled my security.
He then addressed me thus: "See that thou tell
The nymphs and shepherds what thou shalt behold."
Then looking up, "If I had thus," said he,
"At my command the ravening and the teeth
Of greedy wolves, as I have now the crags,
My death should be like hers who was my life.
My wretched limbs should all be torn and scattered,
As they did tear, alas! that delicate body:
But since they cannot, since the heavens deny
Even this welcome death to my desire,
I must betake me from the world
Another way, which if not what it should be,
Will join my fate to hers, at least more soon.
Sylvia, I follow thee; I come
To bear thee company, if thou wilt not scorn it:
And I should die content,
Could I at heart be certain that my coming
Would trouble thee no longer as 'twas wont,
And that thy scorn was ended with my life.
Sylvia, I follow thee! I come!" So saying,
Down from the height he went
Sheer overhead; and I remained, all ice.

Daphne.   Wretched Amyntas!
Sylvia.   Oh my heart!
Chorus.   But why
  Didst thou not stop him? did thy oath restrain thee?
Messenger.   Oh no: as soon as I discerned his mad
  And impious project, I disdained all oaths,
  Vain at such times as these, and ran to hold him;
  When, as his luckless destiny would have it,
  I caught by the scarf of silk, which girt him round,
  And which, unable to resist the weight
  And force of his wild body, snapped in my hand.
Chorus.   And what became of the unhappy corpse?
Messenger.   I know not. I was struck so full of horror
  That I had not the heart to look again,
  For fear of seeing him all dashed in pieces.
Sylvia.   Now I am stone indeed,
  Since this news kills me not.
  Ah! if the fancied death
  Of her who scorned him so,
  Bereft him of his life,

Just reason is it now
That this most certain death
Of him who loved me so,
Should take my life from me.
And if it cannot take me
With sorrow or with steel,
This scarf, this scarf of his,
Which not without a cause
Did follow not the ruin
Of its lamented lord,
Shall wreak its destined vengeance
On my most impious cruelty
For his most bitter end.
Unhappy scarf which girdled,
That kind, departed heart,
Be patient for a little
Within this hateful bosom,
Whence thou shalt soon reissue
To be my pain and punisher.
I should, I should have been
Amyntas' companion
In life; but since I would not,
'Tis thou shalt join me with him
Among the shades infernal.

Chorus. Unhappy me, take comfort.
'Tis fortune's doing this, and not thy fault.

Sylvia. Oh shepherds, do ye weep?
And are your tears for me?
I do deserve no pity,
For I was used to none.
If ye lament the loss
Of that most perfect heart,
Then is your grief too small
For such a height of sorrow.
And thou, O Daphne, lock
Thy tears up in thy heart, love,
If they are spent for me.
And yet for pity too,
Not of myself, but one
That did deserve it all.
I pray thee let us go, oh! let us go,
And gather up his limbs and bury them.
'Tis this alone restrains me
From dying instant death,
This office will I pay him,

The only one I can,
For all the love he bore me.
And though this impious hand
Will stain the sweet religion of the work,
Yet any work it did
Would still be dear to him
Who loved me past all doubt,
And shewed it with his dying.

Daphne. I will assist thee in the work; but do not
Speak thus of dying afterward.

Sylvia. 'Twas for myself till now
I lived, and for my fierceness.
What now remains of life,
I wish to live for him;
And oh! if not for him,
At least for his unhappy,
And cold, and mangled corpse.
So long then, and no more,
Shall I remain on earth.
But finish at one moment
His obsequies, and my own life. Now, Shepherd,
Which is the path that leads into the valley
Where that hill terminates?

Messenger.   The one before thee.
The place itself is but a little way.

Daphne. I will conduct and guide thee: I know it well.

Sylvia. Shepherds; farewell! Farewell, ye plains;
    Farewell,
Ye rivers, and ye woods!

Messenger.   She speaks as though
She took a last departure.

Chorus. That which Death loosens, thou, O Love, dost
    bind,
Friend thou of peace, as he is friend of war,
Over his triumphs act thou triumpher;
And leading forth two lovely souls well joined,
Openest a face of heaven upon mankind.
So dost thou fit thee for our earthly star.
They wrangle not above. Thou, coming down
Mak'st mild the human spirit, and dost ease
From the only inward hatred, all that own
Thy reign: dost ease a thousand madnesses:
And with thy heavenly touching sendest round
Our smooth and quickened sphere with an eternal
    sound.

ACT V

Scene I

Chorus and Elpino.

Elpino.   Truly the law, with which imperial Love
   Governs eternally, is not a harsh
   Nor crooked law; and wrongly are his works
   Condemned, being full of a deep providence.
   Oh with what art, and through what unknown paths
   Conducts he man to happiness; and when
   His servant thinks himself plunged down to the
      depths
   Of evil; lifts him with a sparkling hand,
   And places in his amorous paradise!
   Lo, here, Amyntas casting himself down
   Precipitous, ascends at once to the top
   Of all his joy. O fortunate Amyntas!
   By so much more the happier, as thou wert
   Unhappy! Thine example gives me hope,
   That that most fair and unaffectionate thing
   Under whose smile of pity is concealed
   An iron for my soul, may heal at last
   With a true pity what her false has wounded.
Chorus.   He who comes hither is the wise Elpino.
   I hear him talking of the dead Amyntas,
   As though he were alive, calling him blest
   And fortunate. Ah! thus it is with lovers,
   We think the lover fortunate who dies.
   And so finds pity in his lady's heart;
   And this we call a Paradise and long for!
   With what light bounty does the winged god
   Content his servants. Art thou then, Elpino,
   So miserable too, that thou esteemest
   The miserable end of poor Amyntas
   A blessing, and wouldst reach the same thyself!
Elpino.   Be joyful, friends, it was a false report
                        That told us of his death.
Chorus.   O blessed news!
   But did he not then cast himself from the hills?
Elpino.   He did; but 'twas a cast so fortunate,
   That in the shape of death, a vital joy
   Received him in its arms: and now he lies
   Lapt in the bosom of his lady adored,

Who is as kind as she was hard, and kisses
With her own mouth the sorrow from his eyes.
My business now is with Montano her father,
To bring him where they are; for his consent
Alone is wanting to their mutual love.

Chorus.   Alike their age, their gentle blood alike,
And now their wishes harmonize. The old man
Has wished, I know, for grandchildren, to make
A happy circle round about his age;
So that his wishes must conform with theirs.
But oh, Elpino, what kind God or chance
Rescued Amyntas from the perilous leap?

Elpino.   I shall delight to tell ye. Hear, then, hear,
What with these eyes I saw. I was in front
Of my own cave, which lies beside the hill,
Just where it parts on meeting with the valley,
And makes a kind of lap. I was conversing
With Thyrsis upon one, who in her net
Him first, and afterward myself, took fast;
And I was saying how much I preferred
My sweet captivity to his flight and freedom;
When suddenly there was a cry in the air;
And we beheld a man shoot headlong down
From the top of the hill, and fall upon some bushes
There grew on the hillside, just overhead,
A little queach of bushes and of thorns,
Which being closely intertwisted, made
A sort of flowering hurdle. 'Twas on that
He pitched, before the rougher juts had hurt him;
And though he weighed it down, and so came
    rolling
Almost before our feet, yet it had broken
His fall enough to hinder it from killing.
He was so much hurt, however, that he lay
An hour or more quite stunned and without sense.
The sudden spectacle had struck us mute
With pity and horror seeing who it was;
But our conviction that he was not dead,
And hopes to see him well, made the shock less.
Thyrsis then gave me all the whole recount
Of his sad story with its hopeless love;
And while we were endeavoring to revive him,
Having meanwhile sent for Alphesibœus,
To whom Apollo gave the art of healing.
When he gave me the poet's harp and quill,
Daphne and Sylvia who (as I found afterward)

Were searching for the body they thought dead,
Arrived together; but when Sylvia recognized
Amyntas, and beheld his beautiful cheeks
So lovelily discolored that no violet
Could pale more sweetly, it so smote her
That she seemed ready to breathe out her soul.
And then like a wild Bacchante, crying out
And smiting her fair bosom, she fell down
Right on the prostrate body, face to face,
And mouth to mouth.

Chorus.   Did then no shame restrain
Her who had been so hard and so denying?

Elpino.   It is a feeble love that shame restrains;
A powerful one bursts through so weak a bridle.
Her eyes appeared a fountain of sweet waters,
With which she bathed his cold cheeks, moaningly,
Waters so sweet that he came back to life,
And opening his dim eyes, sent from his soul
A dolorous "Ah me!" But that sad breath
Which issued forth so bitterly,
Met with the breath of his beloved Sylvia,
Who with her own dear mouth gathered it up,
And turned it all to sweet.
But who could tell with what deliciousness
They kept in that embrace, each of them sure
Of t'other's life, and he at least made sure
Of his long love returned,
And seeing himself bound thus fast with her!

Chorus.   And is Amyntas then so safe and sound,
His life is in no danger?

Elpino.   None whatever.
He has some petty scratches, and his limbs
Are somewhat bruised, but it will come to nothing,
And nothing he accounts it. Happy he,
To have given so great a proof of all his love,
And now to have its sweets all set before him,
Healing and heavenly food for his past toils.
The Gods be with ye, friends: I must resume
My way, and find Montano, the old man.

Chorus.   I know not whether all the bitter toil,
With which this lover to his purpose kept,
And served, and loved, and sighed, and wept,
Can give a perfect taste
To any sweet soever at the last:
But if indeed the joy
Come dearer from annoy,

I ask not, Love, for my delight,
To reach that beatific height:
Let others have that perfect cup:
Me let my mistress gather up
To the heart, where I would cling,
After short petitioning;
And let our refreshment be
Relished with no agony;
But with only pungent sweets,
Sweet disdains, and sweet retreats;
And warfare, such as still produces
Heart-refreshing peace and truces.

Giordano Bruno

THE CANDLE BEARER

(*Il Candelaio*)

"The finest learned comedy in the first half of the sixteenth century," writes Marvin T. Herrick, "is surely *The Mandrake,* written by a historian and politician. The most remarkable comedy in the second half is *The Candle Bearer,* by the philosopher Giordano Bruno." Bruno was, in fact, both less and more than a philosopher—less in that he never submitted his mind to philosophical discipline, more in that he soared above schoolbooks in speculations that time has proved not only astonishing but profound. He was also less and more than a playwright— less in that he was a playwright for a day, a playwright in his very first published book only, but more than a proficient practitioner in that, like Machiavelli, he easily transcended the everyday comedy of entertainment in a type of play that offers a searching critique, explicitly of Italian life in his time and implicitly of life in general. De Sanctis, in his great *History of Italian Literature,* censures Bruno for his aloofness. But after all Bruno did belong to society, and what is called aloofness is precisely his response to society, his rejection of it. In this sense all the satirists are aloof, and have to be. We can ask only that they know what they are rejecting—know it as artists, that is, know it in their senses and their bones—and that the angle of vision from which, in their aloofness, they see society is well chosen, enabling them to see significantly. Surely, in *The Candle Bearer,* Bruno passes these tests. And one might add that his aloofness was of a spiritual meaning. He died, after all, expressing aloofness toward all that Western culture claims to hold most dear: offered a crucifix to look at while he burned at the stake, Bruno proudly averted his gaze.

E. B.

THE CANDLE BEARER

(1582)

Giordano Bruno

ENGLISH VERSION BY J. R. HALE

Characters

BONIFACIO, *the "Candelaio"*
ASCANIO, *his servant*
BARTOLOMEO, *a miser*
POLLULA, *the favorite pupil of Manfurio*
SANGUINO, *a rogue*
MANFURIO, *a pedantic schoolmaster*
LUCIA, *a bawd and servant to Vittoria*
GIOVAN BERNARDO, *a painter*
SCARAMURÉ, *a magician*
CENCIO, *a cheating alchemist*
MARTA, *wife to Bartolomeo*
OTTAVIANO, *a gentleman*
VITTORIA, *professionally known as Porzia, a courtesan*
BARRA
MARCA } *henchmen to Sanguino*
CORCOVIZZO
MOCHIONE, *servant to Bartolomeo*
CARUBINA, *wife to Bonifacio*
CONSALVO, *a druggist*

The Scene: A square in Naples.
The Time: About 1580.

CANDELAIO

A comedy by Bruno Nolano
Academican of no Academy
Called the World Weary

In tristitia hilaris, in hilaritate tristis.

MY PLAY

To those who drink at the fount of Pegasus

You who suck the muses' breasts
And rub your noses in their sweat,
If charity can touch you yet
Grant me, I beg, my few requests:

I ask for some poetic murmur,
Some puff that lauds, some squib that rails,
Some hymn or ode to fill my sails
And waft me back to terra firma.

Alas, I fear I'll naked go,
Like Adam ere he needed pardon
In his monastery garden,
Or like philosophers who show

Their scorn of goods by going bare:
And what a quandary for a lover
To bring his cock and arse *sans* cover
Before his startled lady fair!

But even as I beg for breeches
The critics near me with their switches!

To the Lady Morgana B.,
his ever-honored lady.

And to whom shall I dedicate my *Candelaio*? To whom, Great Destiny, would you have me offer this sprightly bridegroom's page, this brave leader of my chorus? To whom shall I send what has, by Sirius' celestial influence during these burning, hour by hour more piercing, so-called Dog Days, made the fixed stars swim in my brain, the firmaments wandering glowworms pierce me like a sieve, the leader of the twelve zodiacal signs shoot my skull through and through, and the seven planets sail in my inner ear? To whom shall I turn, I say, to whom look up, where fix my gaze? On his Holiness? No. His Imperial Majesty? No. His Serenity? No. His Altitude, Most Illustrious and Most Reverend? No, no. On my faith, it is no prince or cardinal, king, emperor, or pope who shall lift up my candle in this awful ceremony. It is yours, it is for you; keep it in your inmost room or put it in your candlestick, O my lady Morgana, learned, wise, lovely, and kind beyond all others: the tender of my soul's pasture, who refined my style—breaking down the stiffness of the clods and sprinkling them with holy water from your own spirit's spring, so that the dust clouds raised by the absurd should not sting anyone's eyes—and nourished my understanding. At the time when we could not even touch hands I sent you my poems, first *Gli Pensier gai* and then *Il tronco d'acqua viva;* so now that a great chaos stretches between you, happy in Abraham's bosom, and me burning and sizzling in anguish without the solace you gave to cool my tongue, I am sending as pledge a candle in the *Candelaio*, to show you that my love can still reach out to you across the void; for me, here at home, it may help to clear up certain *Shadows of Ideas* that are making beasts run wild, leaving even asses far behind, as if they had Dante's devils after them; and abroad, where you are now, it may show my mind to many and they will see that it is not entirely off its hinges.

My salutations to that *Candelaio* of flesh and blood of whom it is said that *Regnum Dei non possidebunt,* and tell him not to rejoice too much over my reputation being battered by pigs' trotters and asses' hooves there, because the asses' ears have been cropped and the pigs, one December, will deck my table. And let him not comfort

himself with *Abiit in regionem longinquam,* for if ever
the heavens allow me to say *Surgam et ibo,* that fatted
calf will surely make part of our feast. Meanwhile let him
take pains to grow even fatter than he is; where I've fed
the hay I expect to claim the meat, if not in one way,
then in another, if not in one life, then in the next. Remember, Lady, what I know I need not teach you: "Time
takes all, and gives all; everything changes but nothing
vanishes; only one thing cannot change, is eternal, and
will be forever one, changelessly itself." With this philosophy my spirit thrives and my mind expands. So in
whatever the moment of this evening of life I wait, if
this mutation is true, I who am in the night will move on
into day, those who are in the day will move on into
night; for everything that is, is here or is there, near or
far, now or to come. Be happy, then, if you can, keep
well, and love him who loves you.

ARGUMENT AND ARRANGEMENT
OF THE PLAY

There are three main intertwined themes in this comedy: Bonifacio's love, Bartolomeo's alchemy, and Manfurio's pedantry. However, to see the subjects clearly in
the complex weave of the plot, let us characterize them
as: the insipid lover, the sordid miser, the stupid pedant,
and note that the insipid one is not without stupdiity and
sordidity, nor the sordid one without insipidity and stupidity, and that the stupid one is no less sordid and insipid than stupid.

Bonifacio, then,

in Act I, Scene i, in love with Vittoria, and seeing that
she cannot return his love—the reason being that she is,
as they say, one for the lads and the loot, and he is
neither young nor generous—stakes his chances on the
amorous effect of vain and superstitious magic, and to
this end he sends his servant to find Scaramuré, who had
been described to him as a competent magician (Scene
ii). Having dispatched Ascanio, he soliloquizes on the
virtue of that art (Scene iii). He is joined by Bartolomeo,
who artfully gets him to throw up the secret of his love
and reveals the very different objects of his own passion
(Scene iv). Sanguino, foster-father of all rogues, and
Pollula, a scholar who had studied under Manfurio, having overheard part of their conversation, discuss it, and

then Sanguino begins weaving a plot against Bonifacio (Scene vi). Enter Lucia, a procuress, with a gift sent by Bonifacio, which she describes and which she is preparing to mulct, when she is nearly taken by him unawares (Scene vii). Bonifacio comes flushed with pride over a poem he has just written to the honor and glory of his lady; in which transport he is discovered (Scene viii) by the painter, Giovan Bernardo, and is about to tell him about this new poetic effusion but is diverted into the matter of his portrait and also by a certain doubt which Giovan Bernardo leaves in his mind—and (Scene ix) he is left turning over this enigma, more or less understanding what is meant by "candlesticks," but quite in the dark as to the significance of "thimbles." While he is thus perplexed, Ascanio (Scene x) returns with the magician, who, having hoodwinked him with some nonsense, leaves him hopeful that all will be well.

In Act II, Scene ii, we see Vittoria and Lucia plotting to extract wine from this pumice stone, oil from this piece of cork: they plan, by sowing hope in Bonifacio's orchard, to get a golden picking for their own store, but the poor wretches have miscalculated, assuming that love had so far stolen his wits away that he would forget the proverb you will hear him repeat at the beginning of Act IV, Scene vi (Scene iii). Vittoria, alone, builds fine castles in the air, thinking that this flame of love will melt and precipitate precious metals, and that Cupid's hammer, working it on the anvil of Bonifacio's heart, will produce at least enough coin to enable her, when her own trade fails, to adopt that of Lucia, *iuxta ilud: "Et iam facta vetus, fit rofiana Venus."* While she feeds on air—which swells the stomach without nourishing it—Sanguino comes (Scene iv), who, in the light of what he has heard from Bonifacio, begins to think up a good scheme and goes off to discuss it with her.

In Act III, Scene ii, Bonifacio meets Lucia, who tries to wheedle something out of his purse. However, while he is chewing over this sticky situation, something happens to aid his digestion, i.e., he finds a chance of postponing a decision until he has discussed various important matters with two men who come in. These (Scene iii) are Scaramuré and Ascanio, with whom he discusses how to put magic to the best use; he gives the magician something in advance and goes. Scaramuré remains (Scene iv) and mocks at this mania of his. Lucia returns (Scene v), expecting to find Bonifacio, and Scaramuré convinces her that her hopes and labors are useless; they go off to tell Vittoria all about it, and he persuades her that she can, by pretending to love Bonifacio, get something out of him in a different way. Sanguino and Scaramuré enter (Scene ix), apparently having arranged something with Vittoria and Giovan Bernardo; they, with two other brave fellows, plan to do some mischief disguised as officers of the watch, with Sanguino as captain, a plan that (Scene xiii) delights them hugely.

In Act IV, Scene I, Vittoria comes in, bored with waiting so long. She soliloquizes on the miserly passion of Bonifacio and his idle hopes and shows herself eager to play some unsavory trick on him with the aid of the fake captain, and the watch, and Giovan Bernardo. Soon Lucia appears (Scene ii), who explains how usefully she has spent her time and effort; how she has coached Carubina, Bonifacio's wife; and in Scene iii she is joined by Bartolomeo, and they part with no love lost. Bartolomeo remains (Scene iv) and talks about his own affairs; and here comes (Scene v) Bonifacio, and they make mock of one another for a while. Meanwhile Lucia is not letting the grass grow under her feet; she meets (Scene vi) Bonifacio, who, having got rid of Bartolomeo, is only too eager to believe the tall story she brings him: i.e., that Vittoria longs to give herself to him, and that he should come and sleep with her that night if he is to prevent her pining away altogether; thanks to the spell he has been performing, he readily believes this. He agrees to disguise himself as Giovan Bernardo. Lucia takes Vittoria's clothes to disguise Carubina in, and Bonifacio stays (Scene vii), and glories in the effect his spell is having. He and Marta, Bartolomeo's wife, make fun of each other (Scene viii), until he goes off, presumably to disguise himself—like a carnival St. Cresconio. Now here comes Carubina (Scene xii), disguised and given instructions by Lucia, and describes the fine coaxings and caresses the pretended Vittoria is going to subject her infatuated sorcerer to; then she goes off to Vittoria's. Lucia is left (Scene xiii) and is about to go in search of Giovan Bernardo, when (Scene xiv) here he comes, having been as urgently about his own affairs as Lucia about hers. They decide how to spring their trap, and where the confederates should be, and when. Then Lucia goes to find Bonifacio, and Giovan Bernardo to see to the rest.

In Act V, Scene i, here comes Bonifacio, dressed as Giovan Bernardo, breathing love from his arse and every

other orifice, and after a word with Lucia, he goes off to
the chamber of his desire. While various other things
happen, Giovan Bernardo stiffens his resolve by thinking
of Carubina, and waits and waits, playing sentinel while
Sanguino plays the knave and Bonifacio takes his punishment; until (Scene ix) the distracted Bonifacio and the
still implacable Carubina come out and find, to their
mutual surprise, another problem facing them and another quagmire to cross in the shape of Giovan Bernardo.
This leads to words and is on the point of turning to
blows when (Scene x) Sanguino enters, disguised as Captain Palma, and his companions dressed as officers of the
watch; when formally charged by Giovan Bernardo, they
arrest Bonifacio and shut him in a room nearby, pretending to take him later on to the courthouse prison. Carubina is left (Scene xi) in the clutches of Giovan Bernardo,
who, like all those who are passionately in love, tries
with every Epicurean sophistry—Love lends courage to
men and gods—to undermine any scruples that Carubina,
whose appetite has never been satisfied beyond the first
course, might still have. It is left uncertain whether she
wants to conquer or be conquered; at least she is prepared
to continue the argument in a quieter spot. While all this
is going on, Scaramuré, who has a clock in his head as
well as in his stomach, comes in (Scene xiv) on the pretext of wanting to help Bonifacio. He talks (Scene xv) to
Sanguino and his colleagues and begs permission to
speak with Bonifacio, and having, by various shrewd
devices (Scene xvi), obtained it, he persuades Bonifacio
(Scene xvii) that he had brought all this confusion on
himself by making a mistake in the spell, and says he is
willing to negotiate for his freedom. He does this (Scene
xviii) by offering a bribe to the captain and is greeted
on his part (no novice in his trade) by a brusque refusal
which reduces Bonifacio and Scaramuré (keeping a
straight face as best he can) to kneel and grovel for
mercy—without, however, any effect. The captain will
only grant it if Scaramuré brings Carubina and Giovan
Bernardo and gets the charge withdrawn. This agreement
is reached after much pretended difficulty (Scenes xix, xx,
xxi, and xxii) until at last (Scene xxiii), after having
begged forgiveness on his knees from his wife and Giovan
Bernardo, thanked Sanguino and Scaramuré, and greased
the palms of the captain and the watch, he is set free by
the mercy of God and the Madonna. When he has gone,
Sanguino and Ascanio (Scene xxiv) discuss his situation.

Consider then: it was his infatuation with Vittoria that first put him in the way of being deceived, and when he tried to enjoy her, he became deceived indeed; prefigured, in fact, by Actaeon, who went hunting for horned beasts and when he thought of enjoying Diana, was turned into a stag himself. So it is not surprising that this man was ripped and torn in pieces by these ruffianly hounds.

Bartolomeo

first appears in Act I, Scene iii, where he mocks Bonifacio's passion, concluding that a passion for gold and silver, and the pursuit of these two fair creatures, is more to the point; and it is likely that when he goes, it is to practice the alchemy he studies under the guidance of Cencio. This Cencio seems (in Scene xi) to be a swindler, at least in the opinion of Giovan Bernardo, and actually reveals himself as one in Scene xii. Bartolomeo's wife, Marta, comes in (Scene xiii) and talks about her husband's labors, and is joined (in Scene xiv) by Sanguino, who laughs at both of them.

In Act II, Scene v, Barra, in conversation with Lucia, shows where Bartolomeo's money comes from; while he attends to his alchemy, his wife takes in certain articles for a good scrubbing and soaping.

In Act III, Scene i, Bartolomeo gives a panegyric on his new study and argues in his own way that there is no better occupation or doctrine than that *de minerabilibus*, and then, remembering that he must get back to work, he goes.

In Act IV, Scenes iii and v, Bartolomeo is waiting for the servant he has sent for *pulvis Christi* and (Scene iv) delivers a harangue on the tag *onus leve,* comparing gold to plumage. In Scene viii his wife shows what an honest matron she is by her conversation with Bonifacio, and how much more adept she is at her own trade than her husband at his alchemy, and (Scene ix) points out that this is not to be wondered at, as she was initiated into her business at the age of twelve; then, after revealing still more evidence of her skill in riding her own hobbyhorse, she begins a pious and touching digression on her husband's studies and how they have distracted his attention from more vital matters; finally she diligently calls on the gods to restore her husband's previous interests. She begins to see the effects of her prayers almost at once (Scene x), for his alchemy has broken down over a certain *pulvis*

Christi which cannot be obtained because it was only made by Cencio, who had produced five talents of gold out of it for every five talents he had been given. To get to the bottom of the matter, Bartolomeo sends his servant Mochione to find Consalvo.

In Act V, Scene ii, Consalvo comes with Bartolomeo, who attacks him as being privy to the trick played on him by Cencio, and having gone from insults to blows they are joined (Scene iii) by Sanguino and his companions as captain and officers of the watch. Under guise of taking them to prison, they bind their hands behind them and leave them fastened back to back in a remote spot and strip them of cash and clothes, as the conversations in Scenes iv, v, vi, vii, and viii reveal. Then (Scene xii), having staggered about looking for someone to cut them free, they come at last on Giovan Bernardo and Carubina, who are just going out. Trying to catch them, Consalvo goes too fast, trips up Bartolomeo, and is brought to the ground with him; there they remain till (Scene xiii) Scaramuré comes and releases them and sends them home by separate ways.

Manfurio

is seen speaking with pedantic presumption in Act I, Scene v; Sanguino sees him to be a dolt, and the gang decide to involve him in their plot.

In Act II, Scene i, he is made fun of by Ottaviano, who pretends first to be much impressed by his conversation and then to despise his peoms, to see how he behaves first when flattered, then when subjected to a little criticism. When Ottaviano goes, Manfurio hands a love letter to his pupil Pollula, to take to Bonifacio, for whom he has written it. In Scene vi this letter is read and commented on by Pollula and Barra.

In Act III, Scene vi he declaims a poem he has written against Ottaviano in revenge for the scant respect he showed to his verse, and is discussing it with Pollula when Giovan Bernardo comes in (Scene vii) and argues until the pedant's patience is exhausted. When he appears again (Scene xi), he talks to Corcovizzo, who manages to run off with his money. While he is weeping and wailing (Scene xii), he is joined by Sanguino, Barra, and Marca, who leading him to think they will find the thief and recover the money, persuade him to go off with them in disguise.

In Act IV, Scene xi, he comes back in his shabby disguise and laments that this second set of thieves have gone with his precious cap and gown, leaving him to kick his heels alone while they escaped on the other side of the house they took him to. Dressed as he is, he is ashamed to go home. He hides in a corner to wait for the night to draw on, till in Scene xv he comes forward and walks about reflecting on what he has seen and heard. Sanguino, Marca, and the rest, dressed as the watch, come in and, when Manfurio tries to slip away, they arrest him on this and other charges and lock him up in the house nearby.

In the penultimate scene of Act V he is asked to choose between three alternatives to going to prison: to pay a fat bribe to the officers and their captain; to have ten stripes on the palm of the hand; or fifty on his bare behind. Prepared for anything rather than to go to prison, out of the three he chooses the ten stripes on the hand, but at the third he says, "I would rather have the fifty blows on the buttocks." Having had a good number of these, and failing to keep an accurate count of them, for one reason or another, he ends by having been beaten on the hand and the bottom and made to pay over what money remained in his purse, and all he is left with is a cloak that isn't even his. After all this, stripped and deluded, he composes and recites the *Plaudite*, in the last scene.

ANTIPROLOGUE

Yes, sir; well thought out, well prepared, well arranged. Didn't I prophesy that this comedy wouldn't be ready for this evening? That bitch who was to play Vittoria and Carubina has got some sort of woman's complaint. The man who is meant to play Bonifacio is so drunk that he hasn't known the difference between heaven and earth since noon, and so as not to have to do anything he won't even get out of bed; he just says, "Leave me alone! Leave me alone! In three and a half days and seven nights, with four or two men to row me, I'll be among the moths and bats: one—out ! . . . two—out ! . . ." I've been told off to deliver the prologue, and I swear to you that it's so devilish complicated that I've been sweating over it for four days and nights and not even the combined trumpets and drums of those whores, the Muses of Helicon, can make a scrap of it stick in my head. To hell with the

Prologue. It's like one of those derelict, gaping, smashed-up, uncalked old boats that look as if they've been hauled up with hooks and grappling irons from the bottom of the sea. It lets in water like a sieve, it hasn't seen a drop of pitch, and I'm expected to get in and sail the high seas in it? Leave this snug little port, this jetty of silence? If you know the author, you'll agree that he has a sort of fuddled expression; he looks as if he spends all his time contemplating the pains of hell, as if he'd been put through the mangle. He only laughs to chime in with other people; mostly he looks disgusted, mulish, and, well, eccentric. Nothing pleases him, cantankerous as an old man of eighty, melancholy as a dog who's been whipped a thousand times. And, God's blood, there's no need to tell you how much he and all the other philosophers, poets, and pedants hate riches and possessions; while they anatomize them mentally they flee from them as if they were a hundred thousand devils, for fear of being quartered, torn to pieces, and utterly destroyed, and go hunting about for anything that can keep them sound and in one piece. And as a result of serving such miserable creatures I'm so hungry, so hungry, that if I vomited, I'd bring up nothing but wind: if I had to shit, all I could get out would be my soul, like a hanged man. In conclusion, I'm off to turn friar, and as for the prologue, whoever wants it can have it.

PROPROLOGUE

Where's that good-for-nothing rogue who's meant to say the prologue? Sirs, the comedy will have no prologue, but it doesn't matter, it's not essential; the theme, the subject, the method and arrangement and details will emerge in due order and in due order pass before your eyes; and that is much better than if you were simply told about them. The play is a sort of tapestry, with warp and woof; whoever can understand it, will, whoever wants to appreciate it, can. But I should at least tell you that you must imagine yourselves to be in the most royal city of Naples, in the district of Nilo. The house you see here will be used tonight by certain scoundrels, thieves, and tricksters—take care they don't relieve you of any of your own possessions—this is where they will set their trap:

let him touch it who dares. This way leads to the Candelaio's, that is, Bonifacio the candle-maker's, and his wife Carubina's, house, and to Bartolomeo's. This other way leads to where Vittoria lives, and the painter Giovan Bernardo, and Scaramuré, the necromancer. And here you'll keep seeing, on one pretext or another, a supersolemn pedant called Manfurio. You'll miss nothing, I assure you: the bawd Lucia will come and go on various errands; you'll see Pollula, usually with his *Magister;* it's not difficult to see just what keeps those two so close together. You'll see Ascanio, Bonifacio's page—he too provides day and night service. Mochione, Bartolomeo's boy, is neither hot nor cold, sweet nor stinking. In Sanguino, Barra, Marca, and Corcovizzo you will be able to study some parts of the discipline of thievery; from Cencio you will learn about the deceits practiced by alchemists; for diversion you will have the druggist Consalvo, Marta, Bartholomeo's wife, and the facetious Ottaviano. Watch who comes and goes, what happens and what is said, and take it as you will; there's no doubt that if you consider the speech and actions of these men with the eyes either of a Heraclitus or a Democritus, you will find plenty of occasion to laugh or weep.

You will witness purposeless purposes, feeble plots, trivial thoughts, idle hopes, bursting hearts, bared breasts, false surmises, alienation of wits, poetic furies, clouding of the senses, perturbations of the imagination, wanderings of the intellect, perfervid faith, senseless anxieties, dubious studies, untimely germinations, and the glorious fruits of madness.

In a lover you will behold sighs, tears, irresistible yawns, terrors, dreams, erections, and a heart roasted in the flames of passion; fancies, moodiness, anger, melancholy, envy, quarrels, and hope waning as desire grows stronger. In his mind you will see shackles, chains, wickedness, prisons, eternal punishment, martyrdoms, and death; in the center of the heart, arrows, bolts, darts, fires, flames, yearning, jealousy, suspicion, despair, intolerance, hatred and rage, cuts, wounds, laments, bellows, pincers, anvils, and hammers; the archer with his quiver, blind and naked; then Love's object: my heart, my hope, my life, my sweet wound and death, god, divinity, sweet vale, retreat, hope, wellspring, spirit, north star, glorious sun never to set on the horizon of my soul; and then the meeting: hard heart, column of ice, flint, diamond-breasted, this cruel hand that holds the key to my heart, my enemy, my sweet adversary, sole mark of all my thoughts, my love is of a finer stamp than any other's love. In one of the women you will observe heavenward glances, smoldering sighs, watery ideas, earthly desires, and aerial fuckings—with apologies to chaste ears— she being one of those who will leap into bed at the sight of a clean sheet. You will see her assailed by a lover armed with a will that warms, a desire that roasts, charity that kindles, love that scorches, lust that burns, and ruttishness that sends sparks into heaven. And then —so you need not fear a universal deluge—you will see the bow of Love, which is like the rainbow in that you can't see it from right below but only from a distance, for lovers can only see the folly of others and never their own. You will see another woman, a prioress of those penitents who regret the sins they can no longer commit, moaning like the ass who carries wineskins and can get nothing but water to drink. What of her? Well: an angel, an ambassadress, secretary, counselor, referee, gossip, saleswoman, weaver, factor, go-between, and guide; heart-merchant, girl-dealer who buys and sells by weight, measurement, and market value, who ravels and unravels, makes happy and wretched, hurts and heals, distracts and comforts according to whether she brings good news or bad, plump pullets or thin ones; advocate, intercessor, cloak, remedy, hope, mediator, way and doorway, who aims Cupid's bow for him, the wind behind his arrows, the knot that ties, the glue that sticks, the nail that fastens, the horizon that joins the hemispheres. All of which comes to pass *mediantibus* counterfeit goods, invented stories, fake sighs, tears on request, lamentations learned from a creaking cartwheel, sobs that die of their own cold, masculine ribaldry, jokes pedantic, flattery unromantic, excuses dithering, accusations withering, serving all and loving none at last, whetting the appetite and leaving one to fast.

You'll see, what's more, the prosopopoeia and mock majesty of a man *masculini generis;* one who wafts with him certain odorlets that would make a pig sick or a hen vomit, an institutor of the old Latin, an emulator of Demosthenes, one who summons Tullius from the deep and murky pit, singer of great deeds and great men. He'll exhibit an acumen that will make you weep, your hair stand on end, your teeth gape; you'll fart, stand, cough, and sneeze. He's one of those composers of de- serving books: margin-fillers, glossators, scissors-and-paste men, analyzers, addition-mongers, riddle-guessers, translators, interpreters, compilers, connoisseurs of obscurities, publicists with a new grammar, a *lexicon*, a *varia lectio*, a patter of authors on the head, a licensed authenticator with epigrams in Greek, Hebrew, Latin, Italian, Spanish, and French *in fronte libri*. So they all scramble on the back of immortality, as benefactors of present and future, with statues and colossi commemorating them in the Mediterranean and the ocean and in other uninhabitable portions of the globe. When they hear *lux perpetua*, they whip off their caps and bow to the earth at *saecula saeculorum;* their itch for fame makes them raise their voices from one pole to the other, deafening Boreas and Auster, the Indian Ocean, and the Mauretanian Sea, with their cries, uproar, and din. What a splendid sight it is to see—like pearls and daisies on a field of gold—Latin stuck into a passage of Italian, or Greek in one of Latin; not a page goes by without at least a vocabulary, a quotation, and some eccentric and obscure conceit. It's the last straw when, by choice or compulsion, in speaking or writing, they drag in some scrap of Plato or Demosthenes the Greek to illustrate a quotation from Homer or Hesiod. How they love to show that Saturn pissed wisdom into no one's head but theirs, that the nine handmaids of Pallas poured a cornucopia of vocables into *their* skulls and nowhere else, and how they go about mouthing their prosopopoeia, with that oh so weighty step, head erect and eyes evincing a circumspect blend of modesty and hauteur. You will see one of those who chew learning, sniff opinion, spew judgment, piss authorities, belch mysteries, crap simple-minded or lunatic interpretations, and at the same time scatter ambrosia and nectar, act as taster to Ganymede, and propose a toast to Jove the thunderer. You will see a synonymical, epithetical, appositionatorial, suppositionatorial *pubercola*, Minerva's beadle, Pallas' master of ceremonies, Mercury's trumpet, the Muses' patriarch and dauphin of the kingdom of Apollo—I am tempted to sum him up as a poll parrot.

And interspersed with all this you will see the plans of thieves, the strategems of swindlers, the acts of knaves; and besides, sweet horrors, pleasing bitterness, crazy resolution, fickle faith, faithless expectation and niggardly charity; judges grave and shrewd in the affairs of others, feebleminded in their own, masculine women, effeminate men, much talking from the head and little from the heart; the most sincere will be the most deceived, and all will worship money. From this proceed quartern fevers, spiritual cancers, idle thoughts, knavery rampant, laureate lunacy, canonized confusion; and more: will that begins, knowledge that guides, activity that reaps, and pertinacity, mother of effect. In conclusion you will see nothing certain, but much action, much weakness, little that is fine and nothing that is good. But I hear the actors. Farewell.

BIDELLO

Before I speak, I must beg pardon. I trust that the majority, if not all of you, will say: The pox eat your nose off! Whoever saw a comedy open with a beadle? To which I answer: Rot you! Before comedies existed, who saw them? And just where could they be seen before they'd been invented? Don't you really think a character like the one you're going to see this evening deserves to be introduced by something out of the ordinary? Why, a crazy fool, a thoroughgoing idiot, a weak-minded simpleton, a tropological beast, an anagogical ass like him is worthy of a field marshal, let alone a beadle. Do you want me to tell you who he is? Would you like to know? Are you really longing for me to describe him? He is—I'll tell you straight—he is—Il Candelaio! Shall I show him to you? Do you want to see him? Here he comes, then! Give way, make room; back there, if you don't want to get a taste of horns that have put the wind up better men than you.

ACT I

Scene I

Enter Bonifacio *and* Ascanio.

Bonifacio. Go and find him quickly and do your best to bring him here. Off with you, do what I say, and come back soon.

Ascanio. You're asking for speed *and* efficiency. It's better to do a thing slowly than badly. *Sat cito, so sat bene.*

Bonifacio.   Praise be to God. I thought I had a mere
servant and I see I have a majordomo, a satrap, a
philosopher, and a counselor as well; tell me I'm a
poor man after that. I tell you, in the name of the
holy ass's tail of Castello; off with you, sluggardly
rascal. And don't go inside his house. Call him to the
window and tell him what I've said—do you hear?
Ascanio.   Yes sir, and I go.

He goes.

Scene II

Bonifacio, *alone.*

Bonifacio.   Art, Bonifacio, supplies the deficiency of
nature. So, it's my luck not to be able to make this
traitress love me or even pretend to. Well, who knows,
perhaps what my words, my love, my frenzy, can't
move can be shifted by this occult philosophy. They
say magic has such force that it can turn rivers in
their courses back against nature, halt the tides, make
the mountains bellow, the abyss cry out, can blot out
the sun, veil the moon, pluck out the stars, turn day
into night. As the academician *sans* academy wrote in
that lost poem with the impossible title:

It stops the rapid rivers in their stride
And plucks the gilded stars down from the sky
Makes day of night, and turns night into day,
It makes the fixèd moon to go awry.
Changing her features from the left to right,
It makes the sea swell and stay fixed on high,
Earth, air, fire, water it confounds together
And blows about man's purpose like a feather.

Everything is open to doubt, and as far as love is
concerned we see proof of that last remark every day.
I'll wait and hear what wonders Scaramuré has to say
on this point. Ah, here's one of those cattle-stealers
who go and give the horns to charity. Let's see what
he has to say.

Scene III

Enter Bartolomeo, *then* Pollula *and* Sanguino *who listen
in hiding.*

Bartolomeo. O cruel love! Who could want your reign, unjust and tyrannous, to endure! Why make the one I respect and adore flee from me? Why isn't she as tightly bound to me as I to her? How can this be? And yet it is. What sort of trick is this that can shackle two together while leaving one as free as air?

Bonifacio. A fellow sufferer? (*He sobs.*)

Bartolomeo. Master Bonifacio? What's the matter? Are you weeping for my pain?

Bonifacio. And for my own. I recognize that pallor and distraction. I heard you lamenting and I know all too well what is making you unhappy; as a victim of the same passion, and perhaps a worse one, I can sympathize. For days now I've watched you—as I'm sure others have seen me—going about brooding and withdrawn, bewildered, lost, with tears in your eyes and sighing like a furnace. The devil, I've said to myself, he hasn't lost any near relation, or friend, or benefactor, he's not mixed up with the law, he has everything he needs, nothing's hanging over him, all goes well. And I know he's not one to dwell on his sins, yet here he is weeping and wailing, his thoughts as discordant as a pair of ill-tuned cymbals. So he must be in love: some phlegmatic or choleric or sanguine or melancholy humor—I don't know what type the cupidinous humor falls into—has got hold of him. And now I overhear your grief and conclude that you've got a bellyful of the sweet poison.

Bartolomeo. Ah, it's cruel to take me off my guard. But I'm surprised at you, Master Bonifacio, not at myself—two or three years younger than you but married to a hunchback eight years older than I am. You have a beautiful wife, only twenty-five, and you'd hardly find a lovelier in all Naples. Yet you are in love?

Bonifacio. From what I've heard you say I know you understand love's way of setting everything at sixes and sevens. If you want to know the progress, or lack of progress, of my affair, then, I beg you, listen to me.

Bartolomeo. Well, Master Bonifacio, we're not like the brute beasts who go through the act of sex simply to reproduce themselves; they have mechanical laws of time and place: donkeys, for instance, who need to be warmed up by the sun—May is the best month for them—can copulate in warm and temperate cli-

mates but can't in the north, up around the pole.
But we can do it at any time, in any place.

Bonifacio.   I had nothing to do with women until I was
forty-two, the age when the first white hairs come and
normally love cools, and bothers one less——

Bartolomeo.   Some it does, and some it doesn't.

Bonifacio.   And just when it was cooling off, like the
heat in autumn, I fell in love with Carubina. She
seemed the most beautiful of women: she heated me
until I went up in flames like so much kindling. Well,
living with her helped to put that fire out, but it's
left my heart, like embers, susceptible to fresh out-
breaks——

Bartolomeo.   A better blaze would have left you ashes,
not embers. If I'd been in your wife's place, I would
have seen to that.

Bonifacio.   Let me finish, and then say what you like.

Bartolomeo.   Very well, go on with this fine simile.

Bonifacio.   Now, since this flame turned my heart to
embers, it was easy enough for another bellows to set
it off this April.

Bartolomeo.   That was the season Petrarch fell in love,
and when goats, too, begin to get their tails up.

Bonifacio.   What's that?

Bartolomeo.   I said that's the time when Petrarch fell
in love, and when our souls, too, begin to set their
sails of contemplation again; for while in the winter
they contract with cold, and in summer disperse in the
heat, in spring, when the temperature is calm and
moderate, the body's tranquillity allows the soul to
contemplate and resume its own function.

Bonifacio.   Enough of this rigmarole: let me go on
with it. Now, it was when I was on a stroll to Posil-
lipo that I was pierced so deeply by Vittoria's glances,
so burned by her radiance, so bound by her chain,
that, alas . . .

Bartolomeo.   This animal we call love usually attacks
those who have too little to think about and even less
to do. Hadn't you gone out simply from idleness?

Bonifacio.   Now you have heard about the torments
of my love, tell me about yours. There ought to be
comfort in talking it over with someone who suffers
from the same malady, if one can call love a malady.

Bartolomeo.   Nominative: the lady Silverosa tortures
me, the lady Golderosa stabs me to the heart.

Bonifacio.   Bad luck strike the lot of you!

Bartolomeo. Genitive: I dream of the lady Silverosa, my mind is full of the lady Golderosa.

Bonifacio. May you all be full of the pox.

Bartolomeo. Dative: I bear love to the lady Silverosa, I am a slave to the lady Golderosa. I subject myself to both of them together.

Bonifacio. I'd like to know what the devil he is getting at.

Bartolomeo. Vocative: Oh, Lady Silverosa, why do you leave me? Oh, Lady Golderosa, why do you flee me?

Bonifacio. Let them flee you and leave you down and out! Go to the devil for making fun of me!

Bartolomeo. And you stay with the god who's got hold of your brains, if you ever had any. I must go and serve my mistresses.

Bonifacio. See, see with what deliberate cunning that wretch has got out of me what I'd rather have told to fifty others. That's the first time this passion has led me to pure folly. Now, in the devil's name, I'll go and arrange things with Lucia. Those knaves are laughing at me: I shouldn't wonder if they'd heard this confounded dialogue. Love and anger can't keep a secret.

He goes.

Scene IV

Sanguino *and* Pollula *come forward.*

Sanguino. (*laughing*). What a pill you've had to swallow, you poor bleating, come-and-cut-my-throat beast! It certainly didn't need the rack to get your secrets out of you! See how easily that ninny found out that he's in love, and who with, and what he suffers, and how and when and where.

Pollula You can be sure that when he says the office of Our Lady, he has no need to pray, *Domine, labia mea aperies!*

Sanguino. What does *"Domino lampia mem periens"* mean?

Pollula. "O Lord open thou my lips." I mean that for anyone who tells his secrets to every Tom, Dick, and Harry, the prayer is beside the point.

Sanguino. But didn't you see that at the end he repented of telling him? So he can't come to any harm, because as the Bible says somewhere, "Who sins and repents shall be saved."

Pollula. Here's the master. We shall be stuck here all day, the devil break his neck for him!

Scene V*

Enter Manfurio.

Manfurio. *Bene repperiaris, bonae, melioris, optimaeque indolis adolescentule: quomodo tecum agitur? ut vales?*

Pollula. *Bene.*

Manfurio. *Gaudeo sane gratulorque satis, si vales bene est, ego quidem valeo:* Marcus Tulliesque elegance in almost all the familiar letters.

Pollula. Is there anything else, *domine Magister?* I am planning something with Sanguino, so I can't stay here with you.

Manfurio. See how you have rejected the learning which in my glorious Minervan academy, illuming it with my Mars-like acumen, I have made you inscribe on snowy sheets with *attramento intincto, exarare!* Rejected, I say *in cassum, cumsit* their proper tense and place, *eorum servata ratione*, you know not their uses. While your teacher questioned you in that Latian idiom so celebrated *apud omnes, etiam barbaras, nationes*, you, *etiam dum* persisting in the *commercio bestiis similitudinario* of the ignorant mobs, *abdicaris a theatro literarum*, giving me responses composed of words which you have picked up from the wet nurse *et obstetrice in incunabulis, vel, ut melius dicam, suscepti*. Tell me, blockhead, when you intend to deadolescentificate yourself?

Sanguino. Master, with this asinine way of speaking by the grammar book, this catacombery and smellegant latinaty, you infect the air and make yourself a laughingstock.

Manfurio. True, if this megalocosmos and terrestrial machine, O contemned and unurbane one, were farced and compacted with your likenesses.

Sanguino. What's all this about Cosmo and Urbanus? Speak a language I can understand if you want an answer.

Manfurio. *Vade ergo in infaustam nefastamque crucem, sinistroque Hercule!* Should the Muses stoop to

---

*See the Appendix, p. 569, for an explanation and translation of the Latin in this scene.

contact with your porcine presences, *vel haram col-
loquii vestri?* What is your judgment on this renegade,
oh, Pollula? Pollula, *appositorie fructus eruditionum
mearum*, receptacle of my pedagogic seed, *ne te move-
ant modo a nobis dicta*, because, *quia, namque, quandoquidem—particulae causae redditivae*—I have tried
to give you the use of the idiom in which *lepidissime
eloquentissimeque* we construct objurgations, so that
you *posthac deinceps*—the Gods extending to you
what they have already entrusted to us—in contradistinction to your *erudiendi* followers, might imitate
them.

Pollula. Very well, but one must make it fit the occasion.

Manfurio. The cause of my *excandescentia* has been
your statement, "I can't stay here with you." *Debuisses
dicere, vel elegantius—infinitive antecedente subiunc-
tivum—dicere debuisses: "Excellentia tua, eruditione
tua, non datur, non conceditur mihi cum tuis dulcis-
simis musis ocium."* Then that "with you," *vel ethrus-
cius: "Vosco"; nec bene dicitur latine respectu unius,
nec urbane,* with respect to the togaed and the academical.

Sanguino. See then how the world goes: you are reconciled, and I'm left out in the cold. I beg you,
domine Magister, we too can be friends, for though
I'm not fit to be at the end of your cane, *idest*, a pupil
of yours, I might be able to serve you in some other
way.

Manfurio. *Nil mihi vobiscum.*

Sanguino. *Et con spirito tu-u-o!*

Manfurio. Ah, Pollula, how, how, how have you come
to associate with this animal?

Sanguino. Admirable or not, at your Worship's service,
most worshipful sir.

Manfurio. This creature seems not so altogether beyond trainingworthiness. Not so noneducable as he
seemed at first. He bestows on me epithets not altogether unpolite and off the mark.

Pollula. *Sed a principio videbatur tibi homo nequam.*

Manfurio. Away with that *nequam:* though it found its
way into holy writ, it has no savor of the *dictio Cicer-
oniana.*

Tu vivendo bonos, scribendo sequare peritos

says the unmatchable Giovanni Dispauterio, echoed

by my own preceptor Aloisio Antonio Sidecino Sarmento Salano, successor to Lucio Giovanni Scoppa, *ex voluntate heredis. Dicas igitur: "non aequum,"* prima *dictionis litera diphtongata, ad differentiam* of the *quadrupede substantia animata sensitiva, quae diphtongum non admittit in principio.*

Sanguino. Most learned, our master, we are compelled to bid you adieu; we have to go to Master Giovan Bernardo, the painter, without delay. Farewell.

They go.

Manifurio. Go, then, with the birds of good augury. But who is this who, with that *calatho in brachiis,* comes this way? It is a *muliercula, quod est per ethimologiam mollis Hercules, opposita iuxta se posita:* a sex frail, wavering, weak, and inconstant: the opposite to Hercules. What a sweet etymology! *Deprompta* from my own genius, this very instant! So now *propriam versus domum* I shall direct my way, as I wish to make a note of it *maioribus literis* in my *propriarum elucubrationum libro. Nulla dies sine linea.*

He goes.

Scene VI

Enter Lucia.

Lucia. My, but I'm tired. I'll stay here a bit. All night long—not that I want to be ungrateful—I've had to stay on my feet and feed off the smell of the joint and the steam from a cabbage stew. Poor me, I've been like a candlewick: lean in the midst of plenty. Now, Lucia, let's think of something else. Since there's no one around, I'll look at what Master Bonifacio has sent to Mistress Vittoria: that'll do for soup, roast, and marzipan. All sorts of goodies here, and here, at the bottom, a paper—poetry, by all that's holy! Lord's sake. He's turned himself poet! Let's see.

> Mistress with your heart of travertine
> You've slain the part of me that was divine,
> And if you'll not believe: then read this line;
> Its witness would be false did my design
> Less bright than those of other lovers shine.
> But when to your beauty I my face incline
> And dazed by grace, invoke the Muses nine,
> I send these verses—would they were more fine—

That you may see from these poor words of mine
Your Bonifacio will always pine
Unless you save him with a gracious sign.
From hour to hour, with eyelids stung by brine,
He thinks of nought but you; sleep, meat and wine,
Family and friends provide no anodyne.

What a fine conclusion and such arguments! As clever
as he is himself. For my part, I don't understand
poetry; still, if I were to pass judgment, I'd say two
things: one, that these verses are really out of the
ordinary, and the other, that they are like a tolling
bell or a braying ass—all on the same note. But I
must be off, to find a quieter place where I can take
a delivery fee out of this packet. There's no point in
his being off his head if I can't get something out of
it.

She goes.

Scene VII

Enter Bonifacio.

Bonifacio.   Great is the power of love! How else, ye
Muses, would such inspiration and genius in making
verses have come to me, without the help of any
master? Has there ever been such a sonnet before?
Every line, from first to last, ends with the same
rhyme. Read all Petrarch, read Ariosto from cover
to cover, and you won't find the like. O traitress,
traitress, my sweet enemy, at this moment you must
be reading and pondering over it—and unless your
heart is more flinty than a tiger's, this surely will
make you think more kindly of your Bonifacio! Ah,
Giovan Bernardo.

Scene VIII

Enter Giovan Bernardo.

Giovan Bernardo.   Good day and good fortune, Bonifacio. Has business gone well today?
Bonifacio.   Well? Today I did something I've never
achieved before in my whole life.

Giovan Bernardo.   What's strange in that? Is it possible for anyone to do today what he could have done yesterday, or some other day? Can you ever do again what you have already done? No: what was done yesterday can't ever be done again, and I never before painted the portrait I have painted today, and I can never paint it again, either. Another one, possibly, yes.

Bonifacio.   Spare me your sophistry. You have reminded me of the portrait. Have you seen the one I've had done of me?

Giovan Bernardo.   Oh, yes. I've seen it.

Bonifacio.   What do you think of it?

Giovan Bernardo.   It's good. It looks more like you than like me.

Bonifacio.   Be that as it may, I want you to paint me another.

Giovan Bernardo.   To give some woman friend to remember you by?

Bonifacio.   That needn't be the only thing that comes to mind.

Giovan Bernardo.   It's a good sign to have things come to one's mind. Watch out that your mind doesn't go to the things; it can get attached to one of them so that the brain, when evening comes, waits in vain for its supper. And then you're like the housewife who went about looking for reason with a lantern. As for the portrait, I'll do it at once.

Bonifacio.   Good, and on your life, make it a good one.

Gioven Bernardo.   Don't expect too much if you know what's good for you. If you want a handsome picture, that's one thing: if you want an accurate portrait, that's something quite different.

Bonifacio.   For mercy's sake, stop joking about it. Try to make a good job of it, and I'll come to your studio.

Giovan Bernardo.   Come when you want, and I'll do my best, never fear. But see that you do *your* best: I mean——

Bonifacio.   Well, what do you mean?

Giovan Bernardo.   Give up the old game.

Bonifacio.   What? What the devil do you mean by that?

Giovan-Bernardo.   Try to think less of candles and more of—thimbles.

Bonifacio.   How do you mean, candles? What thimbles?

Giovan Bernardo.   Never mind. Good-bye.

Bonifacio.   God—save you, then.

Giovan Bernardo. And grant you just what you want.
He goes.

Scene IX

Bonifacio. "Think less of candles and more of thimbles." What a state I'm in! Everybody who comes along tries to make a fool of me. What the devil he meant by thimbles I don't know. Making thimbles isn't a bad trade—the only drawback is having to dip your hands in the urine that goldsmiths use to clean their silver and gold and so forth. Ah well, perhaps one day I'll understand what he meant. Surely that is Ascanio and Scaramuré

Scene X

Enter Scaramuré *and* Ascanio.

Scaramuré. Well met, Master Bonifacio.

Bonifacio. Well met, indeed, Scaramuré, hope of my poor passion-struck life.

*Scaramuré. Signum affecti animi.**

Bonifacio. If you cannot provide a remedy, I am a dead man.

Scaramuré. I see—surely—that you are in love.

Bonifacio. You are right. I need say no more.

Scaramuré. As far as I can tell from your physiognomy, the analysis of your name, from your parentage and ancestry, the sign of your nativity was *Venus retrograda in signo masculino; et hoc fortrasse in Geminibus vigesimo septimo gradu,* which points to a certain change and alteration of circumstances at the age of forty-six—your present age, in fact.

Bonifacio. To tell the truth, I'm not entirely sure about the date of my birth, but from what I have heard, I must be about forty-five.

Scaramuré. I shall be able to fix the month, day, and hour more exactly when I have measured with my compasses the relation between the width of the great branch of your lifeline and the distance between its

* Symptom of a troubled mind.

vanishing point and the central point in the hand, which is called the field of Mars. But for the moment it is enough to have spoken in general terms. Tell me, when you saw her and felt yourself fall in love, was she cn your left side or your right?

Bonifacio. On my left.

Scaramuré. Arduo opere nanciscenda.* Toward the north or south, east or west, or at some intermediate point?

Bonifacio. Toward the south.

Scaramuré. Oportet advocare septentrionales.† Good, Enough. For the moment that's all we need. I intend to effect your business with natural magic, leaving the deeper aspects of my art for emergencies.

Bonifacio. Use whatever means you like that will help me.

Scaramuré. Don't worry yourself: leave it to me. The contact was through ocular transfixion?

Bonifacio. Ocular transfixion? I don't understand what you mean.

Scaramuré. Idest, by looking at her while she was looking at you.

Bonifacio. Yes, yes, by ocular transfixion.

Scaramuré. Transfixion follows from the action of a pure, transparent humor generated out of the purest blood by the warmth of the heart, and this, in the form of rays, when projected from eyes that are open in earnest contemplation, penetrates the object contemplated, and passing through its brain and heart, infects it, body and soul, with love—or with hatred, envy, melancholy, or some other quality of the same genus. Ocular transfixion occurs when the eyes of one transmit frequent, or if few, then very intense, observations, and the rays meet one another, and beam kindles beam. Then spirit is linked to spirit, and the more intense beam dominating the less intense, irradiates the eye, descending to penetrate the humor situated in the heart; and so begins the amorous conflagration. Thus, if one does not wish to experience ocular transfixion, one must keep the eyes under the greatest possible surveillance, for, with regard especially to love, they are the windows of the soul. Hence the saying, *Averte, averte oculos tuos.* So, enough for the present.

---

* It's hard work winning her.

† We must call to our aid the northern influence.

We will meet again on some more auspicious occasion with everything that is necessary.

Bonifacio. Sir, if this business reaches a happy conclusion, I promise you won't find you have been dealing with an ungenerous patron.

Scaramuré. Master Bonifacio, I am aware of it, I wish to be of service to you, so I am sure that if you do not feel indebted to me, at least you ought to.

Bonifacio. I am your affectionate servant, and I have the greatest faith in your skill.

Ascanio. Well, then, let's be off. Good-bye.

Bonifacio. Yes, let us go on; I see the most detestable of all nature's works coming. I don't want to have to speak to him. I will call on you.

Scaramuré. I shall expect you. Farewell.

They go.

Scene XI

Enter Cencio *and* Giovan Bernardo.

Cencio. This business must be conducted in the light of the doctrines of Hermes Trismegistus and Geber. The core of all metals is mercury: lead belongs to Saturn, tin to Jupiter, iron to Mars, gold to the sun, bronze to Venus, silver to the moon. Quicksilver is especially Mercurial, and there are traces of it in all other metals: that is why he is called the messenger of the gods: masculine among men, feminine among women. With reference to the metal mercury, Trismegistus calls the sky "father" and the earth "mother" and says that the maternal gold is impregnated in the mountains, or in the valleys or in the plains, or in the sea or in abysses and caves; I've told you what this enigma signifies. In the womb of the earth this is the essential component of all metals; together with sulfur, according to the most learned Avicenna, in his letter to Hazem. Against which opinion I cite Hermes, who claims the soul of any metal to consist of all the elements, and with Albertus Magnus I call the opinion of—according to the alchemists— Democritus ridiculous, which opines that lime and lye—he means aquafortis—are the base of all metals. Nor can I embrace the opinion of Gilgile, in his book *De' secreti,* where because he observed that *metallorum materiam esse cinerem infusum,** because he observed

*The base of metals is an infusion of ash.

that *cinis liquatur in vitrum et congelatur frigido,** an error he propounds in order cunningly to circumvent the divine Albertus's——

Giovan Bernardo. All this hairsplitting means nothing to me. I should like to see gold made, and you better dressed than you are. I'm sure that if you did know how to make gold, you wouldn't sell the formula but use it to make it; and instead of making gold for someone else, to show him the process, you'd do it yourself so that you wouldn't have to sell the formula.

Cencio. You interrupted me. You think you are the only one with a head on your shoulders, and have brought out a crushing argument, but for all the caution you have shown, Master Bartolomeo is more canny than you think he is. He knows I was held up and robbed in the woods on my way back from Airola.

Giovan Bernardo. I think he knows more from what you have told him than from what I have.

Cencio. So I, not having the means to buy the herbs and minerals I need for the work, have done what you know.

Giovan Bernardo. You could have protected yourself by saying, "Sir, I will obtain gold both for you and for me." You'd certainly get help from someone else if not from him, and with the gold you take from their purse you can double your reputation by taking it out of your furnace.

Cencio. Oh, I agree. When I am dead, what does it matter to me if the whole world knows how to make gold? Or if the world is full of gold?

Giovan Bernardo. I suppose that silver and tin will be worth more than gold is today.

Cencio. Let me tell you in the first place that Master Bartolomeo had the whole formula in his hand, giving the method of manufacture and everything about it. He sent his boy to the druggist to get what was needed. He was present throughout the operation, he did everything himself. I did no more than tell him what to do: do it like this, like that, don't do that, do this, add this, extract that, and at the end, to his great joy, he found the purest and most veritable gold in the bottom of the retort, reconstituted *luto sapientiae—*

* Ash liquefies into glass and freezes with cold.

Giovan Bernardo. Reconstituted with the sweat that runs down the legs of the fair pilgrims to Piedigrotta.

Cencio. And so, on my word, he paid me six hundred guineas for giving him the secret, by the terms of our agreement.

Giovan Bernardo. Well, now you have done one thing, do one more, and as far as you are concerned the whole business will be finished.

Cencio. What do you want us to do?

Giovan Bernardo. Since he is in the miserable state you were in before, without his six hundred guineas, and you with the six hundred guineas are in the condition he was in—since you've changed circumstances, change clothes as well: you wear his and let him have these.

Cencio. Oh, you are joking as usual.

Giovan Bernardo. All right, I'm joking. The very first time I saw you together I said: that cloak fits you, Cencio, and that one fits you, Bartolomeo. But, as an honest man, tell me truthfully: aren't you battening on him as Gigio did on Perrotino?

Cencio. And what did he do?

Giovan Bernardo. You don't know what he did? Well, I can tell you. He took a piece of wood, put some gold in it, then burned the outside so that it looked like any other piece of charcoal. And when the time came, he very skillfully took it out of his pocket and while putting two other pieces of carbon in the furnace, substitued it for one of them, and soon, as the fire consumed them, the gold went through to the bottom.

Cencio. As God's my witness, I could never have imagined such a piece of wickedness. Would I deceive? Would I deceive Master Bartolomeo? But I think someone must have warned him of that trick. Not only did he not want me to touch anything, but he made me sit six paces away from the furnace when he first came to see me, to learn how to use the formula. And the second time he insisted on being alone and would not let me even come in, and used nothing but my directions. Then after trying twice with little material and risking little, now he is determined to do his utmost and, as I told you, to sow liberally in order to reap a great harvest.

Giovan Bernardo. What, he's increased the dose?

Cencio. So much that this time he'll get five hundred guineas for the outlay of fifty shillings.

Giovan Bernardo. I'd find it easier to believe if you said fifty shillings for fifty guineas. Well, you have prophesied better than a Caiaphas. Let's wait for the confinement before we guess whether it will be a boy or a girl.

Cencio. Farewell, farewell. It is no little thing to believe in the articles of one's faith.

Giovan Bernardo *goes*.

Scene XII

Cencio. Really, if Bartolomeo had the wits of that man, and everyone were as maliciously informed, I'd spread my nets in the world in vain. Let's go about it smartly now the bird is caught; we mustn't be like those who let it get away while they are taking it out of the snare. I won't count myself sure of these guineas or call them mine till I'm out of the country. I've ordered horses and now I'm off. I've no need for more baggage. When the druggist opens the box he is looking after for me, he'll find it full of stones—and that the cover is worth more than the contents. There's no need for me to be here when Bartolomeo sends for his transmuting *pulvis Christi*. But there's his wife. I don't want her to see me dressed like this.

He goes.

Scene XIII

Enter Marta.

Marta. I think Satan, Beelzebub, and the whole pack of devils would take him for one of themselves; he'd know just how to stoke up the fires of hell and torture and roast damned souls. My husband's face is like a miner's who's been working at the coal face for thirty years. A fish isn't happier in water than he is bending over the smoke of his furnace all day. I'm not telling a lie—and then he comes to me with his eyes so raw and red he looks like Lucifer himself. Well, there's no labor so heavy but love makes it light. He's got such a vision stuck in his head of finding the philosopher's stone that he can't eat, he grudges going to bed, and the nights seem longer to him than to a girl with a new dress to put on in the morning. Everything annoys him, he's always down in the dumps, all he gets any pleasure from is his furnace. Charcoal is like precious stones to him, his idea of angels are the rows of retorts over the furnace with glass ones here and iron ones there—big, small, and middling. And there he hops and dances and sings like a cat on the tiles. Not long ago, to see what he was up to, I put my eye to a crack in the door, and there he was sitting in his chair like a professor with one leg thrown this way and the other that way, gazing at the joists in the roof and saying to them, after he'd wagged his head up and down three times, "You there, I'll have you plastered with solid gold." Then, he looked at the safe and the money box and muttered I don't know what. "Well, then," I said to myself, "so these will soon be full of golden crowns!" Oh, here's Sanguino.

Scene XIV

Enter Sanguino.

Sanguino (*sings*).   Who needs a swee-e-p, or tinker, or a ca-a-ndlestickmaker—

Marta.   What's the matter with you, Sanguino? Have you gone mad or turned street singer? Which are you going in for?

Sanguino.   I don't know. One or the other. Can't you tell?

Marta.   Not if you don't tell me.

Sanguino.   I'm the servant, pupil, and companion of your husband, who is a chimneysweep-tinsmith-tinker-blacksmith. If you don't believe me, look at my face. And see my hands. What the devil is he up to? Do you hang him up in the smoke like a sausage or a piece of green bacon?

Marta.   Oh, leave me out of it! Thanks to him I'll become the butt of every fool who wants to point his finger at me. Ask him, not me.

Sanguino.   They say Our Lord cured every other sort of infirmity, but he never tried to meddle with madness.

Marta. And go away, for I don't want to meddle with you.

Sanguino. Off you go, then, meddle with him, dear madam, but watch out if you give him something to heat up—the meal will taste of smoke.

ACT II

Scene I*

Enter Ottaviano, Manfurio, *and* Pollula.

Ottaviano. Master, what is your name?

Manfurio. Mamphurius.

Ottaviano. What is your profession?

Manfurio. Magister artium, instructor of unbearded youth, *lenium malarum, puberum, adolescentulorum: eorum qui adhuc in virga in omnem valent erigi, flecti, atque duci partem, primae vocis, apti* to sing soprano, *irrosorum denticulorum, succiplenularum carnium, recentis naturae, nullius rugae, lactei haiitus, roseorum labellulorum, lingulae blandulae, mellitae simplicitatis, in flore, non in semine degentium, claros habentium ocellos, puellis adiaphoron.*

Ottaviano. Oh, most gracious master, elegant, most eloquent, most gallant chamberlain and cup-bearer to the Muses——

Manfurio. A good apposition.

Ottaviano. —patriarch of the Apolloesque chorus——

Manfurio. Melius diceretur "Apollonian."

Ottaviano. —herald of Phoebus, permit me to bestow a salute on your left glove, unworthy as I am to kiss that sugared mouth——

Manfurio. With such ambrosia and nectar I need not envy Jove himself.

Ottaviano. —that mouth, I say, which exhales such varied and beauteous sentences, such rare phrases.

Manfurio. Addam et plura: in ipso aetatis limine, ipsis in vitae primordiis, in ipsis negociorum huius mundialis seu cosmicae architecturae rudimentis, ex ipso

*See the Appendix for an explanation and translation of the Latin in this scene.

vestibulo, in ipso aetatis vere, ut qui adnupturiant, ne in apiis quidem.

Ottaviano. Oh, master, Hippocrene fount, I beg you slay me not with sweetness before I confess my fault: say no more, I beseech you; torture me no more.

Manfurio. *Silebo igitur, quia opprimitur a gloria maiestatis,* as happened to that caitiff whom Ovid mentions in the Metamorphoses, whose thread was cut by the Fates when she saw Jove the thunderer in naked majesty.

Ottaviano. Then have mercy, spare me, by that Mercury who has so dowered you with eloquence——

Manfurio. *Cogor morem gerere.*

Ottaviano. ——have pity on me and pierce me no more with these darts that scatter my wits in pieces.

Manfurio. *In ecstasim profunda trahit ipsum admiratio. Tacebo igitur de iis hactenus, nil addam, muti pisces, tantum effatus, vox faucibus haesit.*

Ottaviano. Master Manfurio, pleasantest river of eloquence, serenest sea of learning——

Manfurio. *Tranquillitas maris, serenitas aëris.*

Ottaviano. ——have you some piece of your own composition about you? I have a great desire to have some record of your wisdom.

Manfurio. I think, sir, that *in toto vitae curriculo* and in the perusal of every sort of literary work you would not come across songs so mellifluously symmetrical, *idest* so well compounded, as these I am about to demonstrate to you *exarati.*

Ottaviano. What is their matter?

Manfurio. *Litterae, syllabae, dictio et oratio, partes propinquae et remotae.*

Ottaviano. I mean, what is their subject matter, their theme?

Manfurio. You would say: *de quo agitur? materia de qua? circa quam?* The greed, gluttony, and swag-belliedness of that trough-swilling Sanguino, the true image of Philoxenes *qui collum gruis exoptabat,* and his partners, associates, congeners, brethren, and fellows.

Ottaviano. I beg you, let me hear them.

Manfurio. *Lubentissime. Eruditis non sunt operienda arcana:* So, I *explico papirum propriis elaboratum et lineatum digitis.* But I should like you to note that the Sulmonensian Ovid—*Sulmo mihi patria est*—in the eighth book of his *Metamorphoses* describes the Caly-

donian boar with numerous epithets in a way to which
I accommodate my description of the domestic pig.

Ottaviano.   Read it at once, I beg you.

Manfurio.   *Fiat. Qui cito dat, bis dat—Exordium ab
admirantis affectu.*

> Foul fat big pig your worthless life
> Is spent in grunting
> And wallowing in the filthy trough
> For fouler fragments hunting
> And gulping what the dirty cook
> Swills on your snout
> Much-hugging grease bag: obese hag
> Or idle turded lout.

Post haec:

> Fit for every loathly wallow
> And for each disgusting swallow:
> Stomach like a bottomless pit
> Connoisseur of asses' shit:
> Stinking muzzle, throat convulsive,
> Feet unfirm and stern repulsive:
> Of soul the least that can be had
> To keep the rest from going bad.
> Thus is the pig. If this anatomy
> Displeases you, then do not flatter me.

What is your opinion of these poems? Do you think
you grasped the meter?

Ottaviano.   Clearly, as the product of one of your profession, it could hardly be lacking in ingenuity.

Manfurio.   *Sine conditione et absolute* they are worthy
of being judged in the light of the most profound
study, worthy of the fruit gathered from the choicest
plants that ever grew on Mount Helicon, were watered by the Parnassian spring, nurtured by the fair-
locked Apollo, and gathered by the Muses nine.
What do you think of that statement? Is this not
worthy, too, of your praise?

Ottaviano.   A very fine concept, and skillfully expressed.
But tell me, did you spend a great deal of time working
on these poems?

Manfurio.   No.

Ottaviano.   Did composing them exhaust you?

Manfurio.   *Minime.*

Ottaviano.   They required great thought and toil?

Manfurio.   *Nequaquam.*

Ottaviano.   You wrote and rewrote them?

Manfurio.   *Haudquaquam.*

Ottaviano.   You corrected them?

Manfurio.   *Minime gentium, non opus erat.*

Ottaviano.   You have not adapted them, or downright
stolen them, from any author?

Manfurio.   *Neutiquam, absit verbo invidia, Dii avert-
ant, ne faxint ista Superi.* You wish to pry too deeply
into my erudition. Believe me, I have absorbed not
a little from the Pegasian fount. I have drawn not a
little on her *de cerebro nata Iovis,* I mean the chaste
Minerva, the source of wisdom. And do not think
that I should have been *minus foeliciter* less effective
if I had been challenged *ad explicandas notas affirman-
tis vel asserentis.* My memory remains firm. *Sic, ita,
etiam, sane, profecto, palam, verum, certe, procul
dubio, maxime, cuidubium? utique, quidni, mehercle,
aedepol, mediusfidius, et caetera.*

Ottaviano.   I beg you, in place of that *et caetera,* tell
me another negative.

Manfurio.   Such *cacocephaton, idest* grammatical heresy,
I cannot commit, for *factae enumerationis clausulae
non est adponenda unitas.*

Ottaviano.   Well, then, which of all those affirmatives is
the one that pleases you most?

Manfurio.   The *utique* is particularly close to my heart.
It is fitting in *lingua aethrusca vel tuscia, meaeque in-
haeret menti:* it has the idiomatic elegance of the
worthier tongue.

Ottaviano.   And which negative do you prefer?

Manfurio.   The *nequaquam est mihi cordi,* and is my
favorite.

Ottaviano.   Now you ask me a question.

Manfurio.   Tell me, Master Ottaviano, did my poems
please you?

Ottaviano.   *Nequaquam.*

Manfurio.   How *nequaquam?* Are they not *optimi?*

Ottaviano.   *Nequaquam.*

Manfurio.   *Duae negationes affirmant:* you intend to say
therefore that they are good.

Ottaviano.   *Nequaquam.*

Manfurio.   You are joking?

Ottaviano.   *Nequaquam.*

Manfurio.   You are serious?

Ottaviano.   *Utique.*

Manfurio.   You don't appreciate the Martian and Minervan me?

Ottaviano. Utique.

Manfurio. Then you are envious and have turned against me. At the beginning you admired *nostra dicendi copia,* but then, *ipso lectionis progressu,* your admiration was metamorphosed into envy. Is that it?

Ottaviano. Nequaquam. Why envy? Why turned against you? Didn't you say that these phrases pleased you?

Manfurio. Ha! You are joking indeed, then, and speak *exercitationis gratia?*

Ottaviano. Nequaquam.

Manfurio. Dicas, igitur, sine simulatione et fuco: were there inharmonies, vulgarities, or inelegancies in my poems?

Ottaviano. Utique.

Manfurio. And am I to take you at your word?

Ottaviano. Utique, sane, certe, equidem, utique, utique.

Manfurio. I don't want to speak to you.

Ottaviano. If you don't want to hear what you say pleases you, what would happen if I said something that didn't please you? Farewell.

He goes.

Manfurio. Vade, vade. Adesdum. Pollula. Did you watch the behavior of that man who just left?

Pollula. He started by making fun of you in one way and went on to make a fool of you in another.

Manfurio. But don't you think that all springs from the envy that the ignorant feel for us others—*melius diceretur "alii," differentia faciente aliud*—the learned?

Pollula. Because you're my master, I'll agree with everything you say—that pleases you.

Manfurio. De iis hactenus, missa faciamus haec. Now, I intend to employ the muses against this Ottaviano, and as I have let him hear porcine epithets applied to someone else, *posthac,* for his own benefit, I intend him to hear them applied to an inept judge of another's learning. Here, this is a love letter I wrote for Master Bonifacio, who asked me to compose a letter to inflame his mistress. Give it to him from me privately, and say that I am busy with other aspects of my literary studies. Ego quoque hinc pedem referam; I see two women coming, *de quibus illud "Longe fac a me."*

Pollula. Salve, domine praeceptor.

Manfurio. Faustum iter dicitur: Vale.

They go.

Scene II

Enter Vittoria, Lucia.

Vittoria. The great bashfulness I produce in him persuades me to like him, his lust argues that we wouldn't
lose by having him as a lover, and, as a "Bonafacio,"
he could do nothing, you see, but good.

Lucia. He's not one of those madmen who suffer from
dryness of the brain—his trouble is its wetness, so he
has far more need to burn off the heavy, cloying hum-
ors than a man who is too subtle, nervous, choleric, or
jumpy.

Vittoria. Then go and thank him from me, and say that
I can never weary of reading his letter, and that during
the short time you have been with me you have seen
me ten times put it in my bosom and take it out again.
Tell him anything you want to make up, just as long
as it convinces him that I'm head over heels in love
with him.

Lucia. Leave it to me, as Gradasso said when he promised to cure the madman. I could manage a king or an
emperor, let alone him. Look after yourself.

Vittoria. Then off you go. Do what your good sense
tells you, my dear Lucia.

Scene III

Lucia *goes.*

Vittoria. Love is painted as a young boy, for two reasons: because he doesn't suit old men, and because he
turns weak-willed and fickle men into children. But it's
not in either of these ways that love has got at him,
because he's no real taste for this sort of sport, and as
for his mind, well, no one can take away what's not
there. But I'm less concerned with him than with my
own affairs. Just like the wise and the foolish virgins,
there are among us horses of a different color, foolish
ones who love the game for its own sake and don't give
a thought to the old age which follows so swiftly that
they don't see or even suspect it till all their friends
have taken to their heels. When faces wrinkle, purses
shut. They are left their own misery to hug, while their

lovers nod and pass by on the other side. So we must
resolve on using our time well. To linger is to lose. I
may wait for time, but time is not going to wait for
me. We must make use of others while others still have
need of us. Take the beast while it is after you, not
when it turns and runs; and if you can't hold onto a
bird in a cage, you're not likely to catch one in the air.
As for him, though in fact he's got neither a good
brain nor a good figure, he's got a handsome purse: the
first is his own loss; the second can't hurt me; it's the
third I must concentrate on. Wise men are for fools,
fools for wise men; if everyone was a lord, there'd be
no lords at all, so if every man was as wise as the next,
there'd be no sages, and if everyone was foolish, there'd
be no madmen. The world is very well as it is. But
now, Porzia, to business. It's the charming young thing
that must think carefully about old age, or winter will
strike in the middle of the harvest. So, how can we
pluck the feathers from this bird? Here is Sanguino.

Scene IV

Enter Sanguino.

Sanguino. I kiss your beauteous knees and feet, my most
lovely Porzia, more fragrant than sugar, cinnamon, or
ginger. Strike me dead if, were we not in the open
street, the chains of Prometheus wouldn't hold me
from planting a kiss on those lips for which I die.
Vittoria. Any news, Sanguino?
Sanguino. Master Bonifacio commends himself to you,
and I commend him to you as good fathers commend
their children to a schoolmaster, that is, if he behaves
ill, punish him well, and if you want someone who can
keep him in his place, call on me.
Vittoria. And what exactly do you mean by that?
Sanguino. You don't understand? You really don't know
what I mean? Are you really so simple?
Vittoria. I'm not as devious as you.
Sanguino. Not in the same way as I am, perhaps, but
devious enough in your own, and if you haven't my
finesse, you've got about as much as anybody else.
Now, leaving this empty chat, let's get down to busi-

ness. Once upon a time the lion and the donkey kept company, and going on a journey together, agreed that when they came to a river they would help each other over, first the donkey carrying the lion, then the lion helping the donkey. Making for Rome, then, and there being neither bridge nor boat at the river Garigliano, the donkey took the lion on his back, and as he swam toward the other bank, the lion, for fear of slipping off, dug his claws deeper and deeper into the donkey's skin till they reached the poor creature's very bones. But the poor wretch, making a virtue of necessity, went on as best he could without a word. All he did, when they came to dry land, was to twitch his coat a little and rub his back two or three times in the warm sand, and on they went. A week later, when they came back, it was the lion's turn to carry the donkey, who, to stop sliding into the water, took the scruff of the lion's neck in his teeth, and as that wasn't enough to hold him firm, he pushed his instrument, or rather his—well, you understand me—into the—let's call it the vacant space under the lion's tail so that for the lion it was worse than a woman in labor, and he cried out, "Ow! Ouch! Ouch! Eee-ouch! Traitor!" To which the donkey replied, with a straight face and dignified tone, "Patience, my brother, you know this is the only hook I've got to hang on by." So the lion had to put up with it till he got to the other side. The moral? *Omnio rero vecissitudo este,** in turn the tricked becomes the trickster, and no one is such a donkey as not to turn the tables when the chance comes. A few days ago, Bonifacio was upset by a trick I played on him: today, just as I though he'd forgotten it, he has treated me worse than the donkey did the lion, and I'm not going to leave it at that.

Vittoria. What has he done to you? And what do you want to do to him?

Sanguino. I'll tell you. Oh—company coming. Let's go and talk where we won't be interrupted.

Vittoria. Good, come home with me. I want to hear all about it.

Sanguino. Come on then.

They go.

*All things are subject to change.

Scene V

Enter Lucia *and* Barra.

Lucia. The sneeze of a crow, oysters' feet, and a leopard's egg!

Barra (laughs). Her husband was inside poking his furnace, and I was working on her in the next room.

Lucia. Working, how?

Barra. At the thimble game—now you see it and now you don't. And you'd laugh if you heard what happened.

Lucia. Go on, make me laugh. I could do with a laugh.

Barra. When I asked the old witch if she'd like me to amuse her with it, she answered, "No, no, no, no"——

Lucia. You vile rogue! So you go about seducing poor innocent women and breaking up families!

Barra. What's wrong with you? What's that got to do with it? Is that the only way men and women can amuse one another?

Lucia. Go on, then.

Barra. If she had said "no" just once, I'd not have said another word and left things there, but as she said it more than a dozen times: "No, no, no, ono, ono, noo, noo, oono, nooono"—Right! I said to myself, she wants it. We'll get across the river if we die in the attempt. So I said, like this, "O countenance of beaten gold and diamantine eyes—do you wish me, eh, to die?"

Lucia. And the poor creature answered that she didn't know what you were after.

Barra. Lucia, really, I despair of you. Can you only imagine one way in which women can make men die?

Lucia. All right, go on. What did she say to that?

Barra. She said, "Go away, go away, away, away, away, away, vile man." If she had said "go away" once, maybe I would have put down the hopes raised by all those no, no's, but as she went on fifteen times or more, "go away, go away," and I'd heard from Doctor Manfurio that two negatives made an affirmative, and still more, three, as indeed we learn from experience, so, I said to myself, "She wants to dance on three legs, and as she's only got two of her own, maybe I ought to lend her one."

Lucia. There you are! What did I say?

Barra. The black pox on you—if you'll excuse my language—if you don't take everything I say amiss.

Lucia. Go on then, and I'll keep quiet until you get to the end. What did you say then?

Barra. Then I said, in a little fainting voice, "But my love, do you want me to die? And why do you want me to die if I love you? What would you do, my life, to someone who hated you? Here is a knife—kill me with your own hand and, believe it, I shall die happy."

Lucia. Aha! And she?

Barra. "Rogue, criminal, seducer, bedwarmer! I'll tell my confessor that you have made advances to me. With all your fine words you'll never get me to give in, and use all your strength and you'll never get what you want; if you try, you'll see, I assure you. Do you think that because you're a man you're stronger than me? You treacherous cur, if I had a dagger, I'd kill you while there was no one to see me do it." Well, now, if my head was solid marble, or if I'd been a bass drum, I'd have understood what she meant. After all, even a drum responds when it's beaten—

Lucia. What sound did you produce, then?

Barra. Come inside and I'll show you.

Lucia. No, tell me here; it's too dark to see inside.

Barra. Come on, come on, we'll snap the flint so hard that we'll light a candle I always carry in my pocket for emergencies.

Lucia. You might make a bigger fire than you can manage.

Barra. Better risk death by fire than drowning.

Lucia. Well, let's get on with the story. After all this scolding and defiance, what happened? Did she go on holding out?

Barra. Poor dear, all her resistance blew out behind. She was like Alciono's mule that would have gone twice as fast with the bit in his bottom. She reminded me of when the woman was trying to work up poor good don Nicola. He said if you bother me again, I'll . . . I'll—and she replied, here I come again, what are you going to do? What next, don Nicola, how feeble can you be? Look, here I go again, what are you going to do about it? Dear don Nicola, you couldn't throw a pebble, you know, if I put my mind to it. Tell me, Lucia, there was a poor sinner who hadn't had a chance to celebrate for weeks, what was he to do? Poor don Nicola—under such pressure, I wonder which bit of him surrendered first?

Lucia. All right, all right: it's all too subtle for me. I've

got to take a letter to Master Bonifacio, and I've wasted
too much time listening to all your elaborations.

Barra. Go on then. I want to talk to this young man
anyway.

Scene VI

Lucia *goes. Enter* Pollula.

Pollula. Good day, Master Barra.

Barra. Good day, my heart. Where have you been and
where are you off to?

Pollula. I'm looking for Master Bonifacio to give him
this letter.

Barra. What is it? Can I see?

Pollula. I can't help telling you. It's a love letter which
Doctor Manfurio has written for him, which he intends to send to some flame of his. I don't know who.

Barra. Aha! Mistress Vittoria! Let's see what it's like.

Pollula. You read it. Here.

Barra. *Bonifacius Luccus D. Vittoriae Blancae S.P.D.*
"When shining Phoebus lifts in the east his radiant
head, he seems, in his celestial sphere, less beauteous
to my amative sense than thine inspiring face, O most
beauteous of the beautiful, my lady Vittoria"—What
did I tell you? Didn't I guess?

Pollula. Go on.

Barra. "So it is no marvel if, at an arching eyebrow's
disturbance of the forehead—*nemo scilicet miretur,
nemini dubium sit*—" What devil's way of talking to a
woman is this? They don't understand all this talking
by the book. Oho!

Pollula. Go on, please—go on.

Barra. —"*nemini dubium sit*, the juvenal archer, if with
that selfsame bow whose arrow has caused Jove himself to change into other shapes—*Divum pater atque
hominem rex*—has reached my very heart's heart with
arrow's tip and graved there for all time your most
gracious name. So by the Stygian waves—a vow in-
violable among the heaven-dwelling—" To the stews
with this damned pedant and his rigmaroles. What's
the fool's idea in writing this letter? Bonifacio wants
to play the professor, but she won't believe this is his
doing. This is just learned lunacy. Pooh! I've read too
much already. I don't want to see any more. If he's

no better vanguard than this, he'll get no assault moving this week.

Pollula.   I agree. Women like a good plain letter.

Barra.   Yes, in the form of banknotes, and for a portrait, the king's, in gold. Let's go, there's something I want to talk over with you. You can run your errand later.

They go.

ACT III

Scene I

Enter Bartolomeo.

Bartolomeo.   What is the name of that great bull elephant who still leads the herd with him wherever he goes? When people discuss the essence of things they make the distinction: *in verbis, in herbis et in lapidibus.** The rot strike all those who are not of my way of thinking! Why don't they set the precious metals above these senseless things? Metals like gold and silver are the source of everything: these, these are the cause of words, plants, and stones; flax, wool, silk, fruit, corn, wine, oil, everything desirable on the earth depends on them. I give them this importance because without them, you can have none of the others. This is why gold is called the substance of the sun, and silver of the moon: take these two planets from the sky and what happens to your generative power, where is the light of the universe? Take gold and silver from the earth, how does life begin, grow, and flourish? How much better it would have been if the brute had declared that there was only one true essence instead of defining the other three and leaving this one out— unless of course his intention was to protect my knowledge and possessions. Plants, words, and stones are quintessentials to crazed and feckless philosophers, hated by God, nature, and fortune, who drag out their lives without a penny piece in their pockets and die of starvation, all the time assuaging their envy by cursing gold and silver and those who possess them. Now that

*Between words, plants, and stones.

I think of it, see how they all come like dogs to the
rich man's table, just like tykes that can only get their
bread by barking for it. And where? At the tables of
the rich, those fools who for four malapropos words
from these curs with their bristling brows, popeyes,
and fawning looks, let bread fall from the table and
money from their purses, and the pedants feel that in
very truth *in verbis sunt virtutes.** But let them look
out if they expect any such reward for their babbling
from me; they'll see that I only pay words with words.
Let beasts of the field praise plants, let madmen worship stones and mountebanks words. I'll only value the
one thing that gives value to all else. Money subsumes
the very elements; he who lacks money not only lacks
stone, plants and words, but air, earth, water, fire, and
life itself. This is the whole of life, temporal and eternal, knowing how to use it, and being charitable—in
which one must be moderate, and not let your purse
lose its soul by losing count of what is in it; as the
saying has it, *Si bene feceris, vide cui.* But there is no
profit in this theorizing. I've heard that there's to be an
order lowering the exchange value of the guinea, and
before it's promulgated I want to change mine into
francs. *Interim,* my boy should be back with the *pulvis
Christi.*

Scene II

Enter Lucia *and* Bonifacio.

Bonifacio.   Master Bartolomeo! A word. Where are you
off to in such a hurry? Are you trying to avoid me, eh?

Bartolomeo.   Good day to you, Master Lightthought,
I've better to do than talk nonsense about your love
affairs.

He goes.

Bonifacio.   Go on then and pimp for your other half—I
hope you die of it.

Lucia.   What were you arguing about? Does he know
you are in love?

Bonifacio.   To hell with him. It's just that he saw me
talking to you. And now to business. What does my
sweetest Mistress Vittoria say?

*Words have their virtues.

Lucia. The poor lady is in such a pass that she has had to pawn a diamond and her beautiful emerald.

Bonifacio. Devil take it, what a piece of luck!

Lucia. I know she'd be most grateful if you could redeem them for her; it wouldn't be more than ten guineas.

Bonifacio. Enough, enough. I'll do it. I'll do it.

Lucia. The sooner the better.

Bonifacio. Yes, yes. Lucia, excuse me, good-bye. I can't plan anything now, there's an important matter I have to see a friend about. Leave me now.

Lucia. Good-bye.

She goes.

Scene III

Enter Ascanio *and* Scaramuré.

Ascanio. There is my master. Sir, here is the most worthy and most learned Master Scaramuré.

Bonifacio. Welcome. Have you started? Is this the time to come with empty hands?

Scaramuré. Empty hands? Here is an image in virgin wax, made while repeating her name. Here are the five needles to insert in five parts of the body. This one here, the longest, goes into the left breast. Mind you don't go too deep; you might kill the patient.

Bonifacio. I'll be very careful.

Scaramuré. Here, take it then. Don't let it be touched by anyone else. Ascanio, not a word, no one else must know about this.

Bonifacio. He's all right. I trust him with weightier secrets than this.

Scaramuré. Good. Make him build a fire, then, of pine or olive or laurel, or better still, of all together. Then take some exorcised or enchanted incense and throw it on the fire with the right hand and say three times: *"Aurum thus,"* and then proceed to cense and fumigate this image, holding it as you say three times, *"Sine quo nihil."* Then yawn three times with your eyes closed and then, little by little, keeping the image facing the fire—take care it doesn't melt or we lose the patient—

Bonifacio. I'll be careful.

Scaramuré. —take it three times around, saying each

time, *"Zalarath Zhalaphar nectere vincula: Caphure,
Mirion sarcha Vittoriae,"* as it's written down on this
paper. Then, placing the image facing the fire, as
before, go to the opposite side, facing west, and say,
very quietly, *"Felapthan disamis festino barocco da-
raphti. Celantes dabitis fapesmo frises omorum."* When
all this is over, let the fire die out of its own accord
and hide the image in a secret place—and not in an
unworthy one: somewhere decent and sweet-smelling.

Bonifacio. I'll do just as you say.

Scaramuré. Very good; but I must point out that I have
spent five guineas on material for the image.

Bonifacio. Here you are. It seems a lot.

Scaramuré. And my own pains deserve some notice.

Bonifacio. Take this for now, and I will see that you do
well if the scheme succeeds.

Scaramuré. Patience, then! But remember, Master Bonifacio, to launch a boat successfully you have to grease
the skids.

Bonifacio. I don't understand you.

Scaramuré. I mean you have to apply a little—you
know?

Bonifacio. In the devil's name I'm using spells in order
not to get involved in too much expense! But cash-
down magic!

Scaramuré. Don't delay. Quickly do what I say; Venus
is in the last degree of the Fish. Don't let thirty minutes
pass or she'll be in Aries.

Bonifacio. Farewell, then. Come on Ascanio. Damn
Venus and all her——

Scaramuré. Quick, strike while the iron is hot.

Scene IV

Bonifacio *and* Ascanio *go.*

Scaramuré. It's not bad at all to have squeezed seven
guineas out of that louse. It always pays with men like
that to conceal one's profit by pleading the cost of the
materials needed for the spells. Otherwise my fee to
date would be a paltry couple of guineas; the problem
now is to make sure of the rest before the Day of
Judgment!

Scene V

Enter Lucia.

Lucia. Wherever can he have got to? I let myself be
humbugged by that capon; I kept thinking he'd reach
the climax.

Scaramuré. Hallo, Lucia, where are you off to?

Lucia. I'm looking for Master Bonifacio, who I left
with you just now; I thought he was waiting for me
here.

Scaramuré. What do you want him for?

Lucia. Well, in confidence, then, Mistress Vittoria is
hoping to get some money from him.

Scaramuré. Aha! I know. I know! He's preparing to
warm her up and give her incense, but he's given the
money to me—so he can't give to her!

Lucia. How the devil can that be?

Scaramuré. Mistress Vittoria is asking too much, and
he wants to make sure of her with a mere half-dozen
guineas.

Lucia. What's happening, then? Tell me.

Scaramuré. We'll go together to Vittoria's and talk
things over with her and work out a scheme that will
make sure of my profit out of this idiot; we'll make a
regular comedy out of it.

Lucia. A good idea—especially keeping it private: there
are people coming.

Scaramuré. It's the doctor. Let's be off.

Scene VI*

Lucia *goes. Enter* Manfurio *and* Pollula.

Manfurio. *Adesdum, paucis te volo, domine,* Scaramuré.

Scaramuré. *Dictum puta*: till another occasion when I
have less on my hands.

He goes.

Manfurio. A fine response! Now, my Pollula, *ut eo
redeat unde egressa est oratio,* I shall astonish you.
Ahem!

* See the Appendix for an explanation and translation of
the Latin in this scene and the next.

Pollula.   Would you like me to read it?

Manfurio.   *Minime,* for by not emphasizing the cadence
   according to the rhythm of the phrases or delivering
   them with the energy they require you will rob it of
   its majesty and grandeur. As the prince of Greek
   orators, Demosthenes, remarked, "the principle concern of the orator is with delivery." Now, listen: *ar-
   rige aures, Pamphile.*

> Man of rude and witless cant
> Presumptuously ignorant;
> One who sloth and stupor chooses,
> Deaf to Pallas and the Muses;
> Weak of will and so unstable
> That to think you're hardly able.
> Rooting witless through the gloom
> Loathed by all: why not make room
> For someone else to take your place
> And help us to forget your face?
>
> Infirm of judgment, void of sense.
> Whelmed in mental darkness dense,
> The merest outside, lacking knowledge
> And all literary polish:
> As fit for intellectual toil
> As a peas-pudding boiled in oil.
> Myopic, brain soft as a squash,
> With Lethe water half awash:
> From birth till death prepares his sting
> You won't have learned a single thing.
>
> Childish fancy, wandering thought,
> Speculation—all of nought;
> Uncontrolled, illiterate,
> Reared to maim and obfuscate;
> Learning, none; and spirit, less:
> Epitome of gutlessness;
> Imagination none, no vision,
> Incapable of a decision;
> Born to coarsen and to worsen:
> The son of ignorance in person.

Did you ever see decades like that before? Others have
used verses of four, or of six, or of eight lines, but
mine is the perfect number, *idest, videlicet, scilicet,
nempe, utpote, ut puta,* the tencet, *authore Pythagora*

atque Platone. But who is that, or yon, man coming this way?

Pollula. Giovan Bernardo, the painter.

Scene VII

Enter Giovan Bernardo.

Manfurio. *Bene veniat ille* whose name no less deserves the brazen salute of trumpets than those of Zeuxes, Apelles, Timagoras, Polignotus, and Phidias.

Giovan Bernardo. All I understood of that was the fried ass at the end; and I think that, plus a bottle of wine, has bestowed on you the gift of tongues. If I'd dined myself, I'd answer you in kind.

Manfurio. Wine uplifts and bread sustains.

> *Bacchus et alma Ceres, vestro si munere tellus*
> *chaoniam pingui glandem mutavit arista*

says Publius Virgilius Maro, the Mantuan poet, in his first book of the *Georgics,* toward the beginning, where he utters, *more poetico,* his invocation. Therein he imitates Hesiod, the Attic poet and bard.

Giovan Bernardo. Do you know, *domine Magister*——

Manfurio. *Hoc ist magister: magi* and *ter,* the three wise men enfolded in one. *Pauci, quos aequus amavit Iuppiter, aut ardens evexit in aethera virtus.*

Giovan Bernardo. What I wanted to say is this: I would like to know the meaning of the word "pedant."

Manfurio. *Lubentissime* will I tell you, teach you, render unto you, expose for you, make plain to you, make *palam* before you, participate with you *et—particula coniunctive in ultima dictione apposita*—dissect for you; *sicut, ut, velut, veluti, quemadmodum nucem ovidianam meis coram discipulis—quo melius nucleum eius edere possint—enucleavi.* "Pedant" could be derived from *pede ante,* that is, it refers to the way he leads, places his feet before, his *erudiendi* young scholars. *Vel per strictiorem arctiorumque aethymologiam;* a stricter etymology would give us "pe" from *perfectos,* "dan," the French *dans,* or "in," "te," from *thesauros*— "perfect-in-the-knowledge of words." What do you think of these two?

Giovan Bernardo. Excellent, but neither, to my mind, is really relevant.

Manfurio. You may say that *alia meliore in medium prolata, idest,* when you have suggested a better one.

Giovan Bernardo. Very well: "ped" from "pederasty," "ant" from "eleph*ant*iasis": a pedant is an inflated pervert.

Manfurio. As the elder Cato said, *Nil mentire, et nihil temere credideris.*

Giovan Bernardo. Hoc est, id est, who says contrary, lies in his throat.

Manfurio. Vade, vade: Contra verbosos, verbis contendere noli. Verbosos contra, noli contendere verbis. Verbis verbosos noli contendere contra.

Giovan Bernardo. I'd give the whole race of pedants to the devil. Go and join all the other fallen angels with sooty faces.

He goes.

Manfurio. Join them yourself—that's all the company you're fit for! Pollula, where are you? What do you say, Pollula? Do you see how wicked, abominable, violent and depraved is this age of ours?

> This sorry world in which I find myself,
> Void of all honor, full of every pride

as Petrarch says. But let us direct our steps homeward, for I want to exercise you in the adverbs of place, *motu de loco, ad locum et per locum: Ad, apud, ante, adversum vel adversus, cis, citra, contra, erga, infra, in retro, ante, coram, a tergo, intus et extra.*

Pollula. I know them all. I've got them by heart.

Manfurio. The lesson must be frequently repeated, *et* recalled *in memoriam; lectio repetita placebit.*

> *Gutta cavat lapidem non bis, sed saepe cadendo:*
> *Sic homo sapiens bis non, sed saepe legendo.*

Pollula. If your Excellency will go on, I will follow close behind.

Manfurio. Perfectly correct *in foro et in platea.* When we are *in privatis aedibus,* this formality and protocol may be laid aside.

They go.

Scene VIII

Enter Barra *and* Marca.

Marca. What is Doctor Manfurio going off for?

Barra. He can be with the devil, for all I care. Go on with the story. We'll stop here.

Marca. Well, then, yesterday evening, at the Cerriglio inn, we had a good meal and then we sent out the land-lord to get some nuts and sweets and raisins and things, you know, to nibble at, because he didn't have any in the house. Well, when we couldn't think what to ask for next, one of the lads staged a fainting fit, and when the landlord ran up with the vinegar, I said "Aren't you ashamed, you shabby little man! Go and bring orange brandy, malmsey, and juniper bitters." The landlord started muttering I don't know what under his breath and then yelled out,"Devil take it, do you think you're dukes and marquises? Are you the sort to throw money away like this? What's to happen about the bill? I don't know. It's not right to ask for things like that in an ordinary public house." "Scoundrel," said I, "rascal, thief, do you think you have scum like your-self to deal with? Don't try to be smart, you shameless turd, you twisty liar," said I. Then, very fine, we got up from the table and grabbed ourselves a spit each, one of those ten-foot-long ones, you know——

Barra. A good start, anyway.

Marca. —with the meat still stuck on them, and the landlord got hold of a great pike, and two of the serv-ants had a couple of rusty swords. There were six of us, and our spits were longer than the pike, but we thought we'd pick up dish covers and use them as shields——

Barra. Very sensible.

Marca. —and some of us put pots on our heads to serve as helmets——

Barra. It was certainly a miracle that brought all these pots and pans to life.

Marca. —and fully armed, we backed out, defending ourselves down the stairs toward the door, though we kept pretending to attack.

Barra. A pretty attack! A step forward and two steps back, another forward and two more back: that's how a puppy attacks a bull!

Marca. When the landlord saw how bold we were and yet how we mysteriously seemed to give ground all the time, instead of triumphing over us, he began to have suspicions, and lowering his pike he called off the servants, as he didn't want to start a real quarrel——

Barra. He's rips for canonization, that man.

Marca. And he said to us. "Gentle sirs, forgive me, I've

no desire to offend you, on my honor. Pay me and go in peace!"

Barra. I hope his absolution produced some act of penance.

Marca. "And you want to kill us, traitor," said I; and with this we were outside the door. Then he realized that we weren't going to fall for his compliments and bowing and scraping, and took up his pike again and called up the servants and his sons and his wife. There was a fine racket. The landlord shouted, "Pay me! Pay me!" The others yelled, "Rogues! Rascals! Dirty thieves!" But for all that no one ran at us because the darkness was on our side. Still, not wanting to come up against the innkeeperly wrath, the fury of mine host, we took refuge in a room at the Carmelites', and we still, in fact, owe them three days' rent.

Barra. To get your own back on an innkeeper is a sacrifice to the Lord; robbing a landlord is charity; whenever you beat one soundly a soul is released from purgatory. Did you hear what happened afterward in the inn?

Marca. The place was jammed with people, some reveling in it and others protesting, some wailing, some laughing and trying to put the fight back into them: some in this state and others in that, talking this way and that way—it was like seeing a comedy and a tragedy at once, a triumph and a funeral. If you'd wanted a portrait of the world in miniature, you should have been there to watch.

Barra. Yes, that was good. For my part, not having such a flair for rhetoric, I was on my way, all by myself, from Nola to Pumigliano the other evening, and I had a meal and then didn't feel too much like paying, so I said to the landlord, "Landlord, I feel like a game." "Of what?" he said. "I've got taroccho cards here." "That cursed game?" I said; "I can never win at it because I've got such a poor memory." "Well," he said, "I've got ordinary cards." "They're probably marked," I said, "and you can identify them all. Have you any that have never been used?" He said he hadn't. "Well, let's think of some other game." "I've brisket-brasket?" "No, never heard of it." "I've got chess?" "It's a game that stirs me to blaspheme my maker." Then he began to lose his temper. "What the devil then do you want to play? You suggest something." "All right," I said, "let's play croquet." "What?" he said. "Croquet?

Where's the equipment? Where's the space to play it?"
"All right," I said, "arse-over-tip." "That's a game for
porters, plowmen, and swineherds." "Fivekins?" "What
the devil is fivekins? I've never heard of it. I'll play
threekins if you like." I said I never had any luck at
threekins. "In the name of fifty thousand devils," he
said, "suggest a game that we can both play." "Let's
play whip-me-whop-me-whipmeree." "What are you
trying to give me?" he said. "That's a kid's game.
Aren't you ashamed of yourself?" "Well, then," I said,
"let's have a race." "I see what you're after," he said.
"By the blood of the Madonna," I said, "you'd better
play!" "You'd better pay up," he said, "and if you
won't go peaceably, I'll give you a taste of the devil's
pitchfork." "By the blood of Shadrach, Meshach, and
Abednego," I said, "I want a game!" "And aren't we
playing one now?" he said. "What game?" I said. "And
if I don't want to play?" "And if I do?" "And if I
don't?" "And if I insist?" So in the end I paid him
with my heels, by running off, and lo and behold;
that brute who had just said he didn't want to play and
swore he wouldn't play, began to play and so did his
two cooks; so I increased my speed for a while till I
could only hear their voices. Since then, I swear, by
the gaping wound of San Rocco, I haven't heard them
and they haven't seen me.

Marca. I see Sanguino and Scaramuré,

Scene IX

Enter Sanguino *and* Scaramuré.

Sanguino. The very man I've been looking for. We are
planning something for this evening that'll bring us a
profit, even if it's only in having a good time. I'm
going to disguise myself as Captain Palma, you and
Corcovizzo dress up as officers of the watch; we'll meet
near here where I think we'll be able to trap Bonifacio
when he goes to see Vittoria, or when he leaves her,
and do a good turn to her as well as ourselves.

Barra. That should be really good.

Marca. Yes, by God; and there may be more happening than that.

Barra. Oh, there'll be plenty happening.

Scaramuré. As for Bonifacio, when the time comes, I

shall do him the courtesy, in return for some courtesy from him, not to turn him over to the magistrate.

Sanguino. I've heard worse ideas than that. Let's meet as soon as possible—we'll have to make ourselves ready—and we'll wait for you at Vittoria's.

> Sanguino *and* Scaramuré *go.*

Scene X

Barra. By the blood of—um! We officers must watch our language. There's a lot to be said for this plan of dressing up as the night watch, with three or four of us wearing the night watch's badge of office—carrying truncheons in our hands. And then, when we see our chance—forward!

Marca. By Saint Quintin, there's Corcovizzo himself coming.

Barra. But who is that with him?

Marca. I think it's Doctor Manfurio.

Barra. Yes, it is. Quick, Corcovizzo is telling us to move back. I think he's going to play some trick on him.

Marca. Here, where we can't be seen.

> *They hide.*

Scene XI*

Enter Corcovizzo *and* Manfurio.

Corcovizzo. You are sure that he's in love?

Manfurio. Certainly. His love love passes through these very hands: I have written an amatory letter for him which he intends to pass off as his own, so that his mistress will admire and esteem him the more.

Corcovizzo. Yesterday, as if he'd been a young blade of twenty-five, he went and ordered a pair of Spanish morocco boots from Luca, to use in town. He was overheard by that rogue Mariolo, who waited today for him to come to fit them on. When he saw him coming from Nilo toward the shop, he took off his cloak and quietly crept in after him. There, because he

---

*See the Appendix for explanation and translation of the Latin in this scene and the following two scenes.

was with Master Bonifacio, they took him to be his
servant, and because he had no cloak and his sleeves
were rolled up to the elbow, Master Bonifacio thought
he worked there. So when he started fitting the boots
on, he unsuspectingly gave him his own cloak to hold,
all swathed in velvet and studded with gold buttons.
And Mariolo standing with his arms akimbo, like a
good valet—or a good shop assistant hoping for a
tip—while Luca was busy with the fitting and Master
Bonifacio was stretching out his legs for him, he stayed
calmly watching what was going on in the shop, and
who was coming and going outside, turning this way
and that, until seeing the coast was clear, he quietly
disappeared. In conclusion: *Cappa cuius generis? abla-
tivi.* (*Laughs.*)

Manfurio. *Dativus a dando, ablativus ab auferendo*: if
you weren't entirely uneducated, you'd have a pretty
wit: I believe you had Minerva in the ascendent.

Corcovizzo. But to come back to the story: when Master
Bonifacio was finished with him and Luca had brushed
the back of his coat for him, he put out his hand and
asked for his cloak. "Your servant has it." says Luca.
"Hey, you, where are you? He must have gone out for
a chat." "There's no need for all this flattery," says
Master Bonifacio. "I know your man has it." "Devil
take me if I ever saw it," says Luca. So there they
stood, and a fine sight Master Bonifacio must have
been, all in his new boots, and his best cloak stolen!
Pah! It's unbearable living among so many fools,
knaves, and pickpockets.

Manfurio. It's one of the miserable and unfortunate results of living in this Campanian climate which *subest
Mercurio,* who is known as the god of wallet-ampu-
tators. So, my friend, keep a close eye on your purse.

Corcovizzo. Oh, I keep my money here under my arm
—look.

Manfurio. And I keep my purse neither at my back
nor by my side, but in my groin—here, in fact; that's
the thing to do in a land of thieves.

Corcovizzo. *Domine Magister,* I can see you are most
wise and have plied your studies to good purpose.

Manfurio. *Hoc non latet* my Maecenas, whose children
*ego erudio, idest extra ruditatem facio, vel e ruditate
eruo!* He has commissioned me to go to *decernere*
the price of the material and making of their clothes.

and take charge of the *elargienda pecunia*. Which, as a good steward—*Oeconomia est domestica gubernatio* —I keep in this velvet and leather wallet.

Corcovizzo.   Praise be to God! My most excellent professor, you have given me so much good counsel and advice, help me, I beg you, by doing me another favor. I was going to change six guineas at the money-changers; if you have any smaller change on you, I'll give them to you. It will save me a journey, and I'll give you the exchange fee.

Manfurio.   I do not do it *lucri causa, iuxta illud:* "*Nihil inde sperando,*" *sed,* but *ex humanitate, et officio; mitto quod* even *ego minus oneratus abido.* Here: three and two make five, seven and four make eleven; three and three, and two, that's twenty-four crowns—equals your six guineas. No, no, I take no fee.

> Corcovizzo *runs off with the money.*

Scene XII

Manfurio.   Help! Help! Hey! Help! Help! Catch him, catch him! Stop, abstractor! Wallet-amputator! Purloiner, argentirapist, ducat-knapper! Stop him! Stop him! Stop him! He's stolen my silver and gold!

Barra *and* Marca *come forward.*

Barra.   What's all this? What's he done to you?

Manfurio.   Why did you let him go?

Barra.   The poor wretch said, "My master is going to beat me, and I've done nothing wrong." So we let him go, so that when your first anger is over, you can punish him at home in your own time.

Marca.   Yes, sir, you ought sometimes to give servants another chance and not always be strict.

Manfurio.   But he's not my servant at all, he's nothing to do with me, he's a raptor who has taken six pounds out of my very hand.

Barra.   The devil! But why didn't you shout straight out, "Stop thief! Stop thief!" instead of all that incomprehensible stuff you did shout?

Manfurio.   That word which you have just enunciated is neither Latin nor Etruscan: It cannot pass the lips of one of my profession.

Barra. Why didn't you shout, "Robber! robber!"?

Manfurio. Because that word is properly used only of one who offends openly, on the highways. *Fur qui furtim et subdole,* as he did from me; *qui et subreptor dicitur a subtus rapiendo, vel quasi reperdo,* for under the guise of being an honest man, he deceived me! Oh, my precious guineas!

Barra. See where your learning has got you: if you don't want to be robbed, speak plain Neapolitan. With your Latin and Etruscan, we thought you were speaking to him, not to us.

Manfurio. Oh, ducat-knapper, fit food for vultures!

Marca. But, tell us, why didn't you run after him?

Manfurio. Do you really expect a reverend umpire of the linguistic tournament, in doctor's robes, to accelerate his pace in the public arena? I cling to the adage, *si proprie adagium licet dicere:* "*Festina lent,*" *item et illud: Gradatim, paulatim, pedetentim.*

Barra. You are right, Professor, always to have a due regard to your honor and to the dignity of your manner of progress.

Manfurio. Oh, ducat-knapper, whose bones I long to see broken on the wheel! Perhaps there is something left. But what will my Maecenas say? I will answer on the authority of Aristotle, prince of the Peripatetics, *secundo Physicorum, vel Periacroaseos:* "*Casus est eorum quae eveniunt in minori parte, et praeter intentionem.*"

Barra. I should think that would satisfy him.

Manfurio. Oh, false auxiliaries of the magistracy, if you but did your duty, there would not be such legions of malefactors! Did he leave me with anything at all? Oh, most wicked! Most wicked!

Scene XIII

Enter Sanguino.

Sanguino. Now, then, friends, what was that man rushing off for? What had he done, the knave?

Barra. Oh, I'm glad to see you. We've just had a terrible experience: we had our hands on that thief—whatever the Professor prefers to call him—and, because we aren't properly educated, he got off scot-free.

Sanguino. I don't know what you're talking about. I repeat: why was he running away?

Manfurio. He stole six guineas from me.

Sanguino. How the devil did he do that?

Marca. It's easy to see you never went to school.

Sanguino. As soon as I'd finished my ABCs my father made me page to the captain of the watch.

Manfurio. Venimus ad rem: he robbed me of six guineas.

Sanguino. Robbed? Robbed you, *Domine?* Robbed you, *Domine Magister?* Greetings, sir; do you remember me?

Manfurio. I saw you some time ago with my pupil Pollula.

Sanguino. That's right, *Domine Magister.* I am your servant, if you please, and have a great desire to help you; from this moment, then, know that your six guineas are as good as recovered.

Manfurio. Dii velint, faxint ista Superi, o utinam!

Barra. If you come to the aid of this good man, you will never have done a worthier deed. And he won't be ungrateful; I will give you a shilling myself.

Sanguino. They are recovered, I say.

Manfurio. You have them?

Sanguino. No, but they are as good as in your hands.

Barra. Do you know the man?

Sanguino. I know him.

Barra. And where he lives?

Sanguino. I do.

Manfurio. O Superi, O Caelicoli, Diique, Deaeque omnes!

Marca. Now we've got him.

Barra. We owe a helping hand to the professor in this affair for the love and duty we bear to learning and to men of letters.

Manfurio. Me vobis commendo: I humbly thank you all.

Sanguino. Let's go after him, then. I know where he hides out; we'll get our hands on him for sure. And he can't deny the theft because, though he didn't see me, I saw him as he ran away.

Marca. And we saw him running from the professor.

Manfurio. Vos fidelissimi testes.

Sanguino. No need to break his head open; either he gives us the money or we give him up to justice.

Manfurio. Ita, ita, nil melius. What you say is excellent.

Sanguino. Professor, you must come with us.

Manfurio. Optime. Urget praesentia Turni.

Sanguino. So, we'll all four go together. When we knock

at the door, it may be that we can't get in, either because he's warned the whore he lives with or because he can see us through a crack in it, or he might get out and hide himself somewhere else. Now as long as you aren't recognized, I'm sure I can get him to talk to me; I'll think of something to hold his attention. But it would be best, in fact essential, for you to change your clothes and get rid of that professorial look. You, sir, what is your name, if I may ask?

Barra. Coppino, at your service.

Sanguino. You, Master Coppino, do this service to me and the professor. He'll be grateful, I know.

Manfurio. Me tibi offero.

Sanguino. Lend him your cloak, and you wear his gown; as you're shorter, you'll look like someone else. And to divide it up better, Professor, you give him your cap, and you wear his. Then let's go.

Manfurio. Nisi urgente necessitate, nefas esset habitum proprium dimittere, tamen nihilominus, nonetheless, *quia ita videtur,* in imitation of Patroclus who deceived Achilles with altered garments, and of Corebo who took upon himself the habit of Androgeo, and of great Jove himself—*poetarum testimonio*—who adopted, in the pursuit of his designs, so many transformations, involving at times a putting off of his sublimity. I will not demur at putting off my magistral gown, *optimo mihi proposito fine,* to *animadvertere* against this abhorred criminal.

Barra. But remember, Professor, to repay the courtesy of these fine fellows. I ask nothing for myself.

Manfurio. For you *in comuni* I intend the third part of the guineas that we recover.

Sanguino. Many thanks for your generosity.

Barra. Up then and on.

Manfurio. Eamus dextro Hercule.

Sanguino.
Marca. } Come on!

ACT IV

Scene 1

Enter Vittoria.

Vittoria. To wait, and wait in vain is a sort of death.
If we wait too long, we shall have lost our chance. I
don't know if there will be another occasion so fit for
this creature to reap what his love deserves. Just as I
thought his infatuation would help me to a dowry, I
heard that he was trying to cast a spell on me, with a
wax image. Could it really happen that the spirits of
darkness, working with those of air and water, could
make me love someone who isn't lovable in himself?
If he were the very god of love, but was poor, or miserly, which comes to the same thing, than he's a cold
fish and the world can freeze with him. Yes, surely—
poor, stingy: that's a vile and shameful epithet; it can
make beauty look ugly, nobility squalid, wisdom petty,
and vitality impotent. Who do we respect more than
kings, monarchs, emperors? And even these, if they
are poor, if they haven't got money in their pockets,
are like images stripped after their festival day; no one
cares tuppence for them. Holy images and men: it's
just the same; we worship statues and paintings, we
honor holy names, but we think of men, living men.
We live in terms of those who piss and crap, though we
direct our prayers and requests to pictures and statues,
for it's these that reward the virtuous, exalt the humble,
defend the oppressed, free the imprisoned, protect
their votaries, strengthen the weak. The king, the emperor; unless he is made into a statue, is nothing. What
then of Bonifacio, who wants, as if he was the only
man in the world, to be loved for his pretty eyes? How
far can folly go? This evening he is looking forward to
being happy. And this evening I'm looking forward to
him seeing the effect of his spell. But he still hasn't
come, this bogey who tries and tries—Ah, but there you
are!

255

Scene II

Enter Lucia.

Lucia. Is that you, mistress?

Vittoria. I wanted to see you so badly I couldn't stay
   inside. Don't you see it will soon be too late to give
   these men the chance they want? Have you spoken to
   Bonifacio's wife?

Lucia. I told her everything, and more besides, and she
   wants nothing better than to revenge herself. She had
   another idea—I thought it a splendid one—to borrow
   your skirt and cloak, for two reaosns: so that she won't
   be recognized when she comes here or leaves, and also
   so that when he greets her, which we'll make him do
   in the dark, he'll thing it's Vittoria—except for the
   face: and she'll keep hers covered with her cloak, as
   everyone knows you do. And then, once inside her
   house, we'll make some excuse to keep her out of the
   light—until she gets lit up herself!

Vittoria. Yes, but she will have to answer him and say
   something. How can we keep him from recognizing
   her voice?

Lucia. It's the easiest thing in the world! I'll warn him
   to speak in a whisper because the walls are so thin the
   neighbors can hear anything you say.

Vittoria. Yes, that's good. He won't want anyone to
   overhear him. Who is that?

Lucia. Master Bartolomeo.

Scene III

Enter Bartolomeo.

Vittoria. Where are you going, Master Bartolomeo?

Bartolomeo. To the devil!

Lucia. You'll certainly find him long before you find the
   angel Gabriel.

Bartolomeo. Lady Gossip, Lady Lute-tuner, if angels
   mix less with men than devils do, they have the excuse
   of wanting to avoid the company of women like you.

Vittoria.   Well! Are you finding it difficult to come, these days? Spending all this time near the furnace has dried you out and made you so touchy that you lash out without provocation.

Bartolomeo.   Not at you, Mistress Vittoria; you I honor and respect.

Vittoria.   Not at me? You think your insult doesn't reflect vilely on me? Come, Lucia.

Bartolomeo.   Don't go in such a fury, mistress. I was joking with Lucia, who I find more tempting the more disgusted she looks.

Lucia.   Oh, yes, yes, there isn't a more malicious tongue than yours. I wish it were cut out—stirring up trouble and strife!

Bartolomeo.   In contrast with yours, all peace, concord, and harmony.

Vittoria and Lucia go.

Scene IV

Bartolomeo.   The rot strike all the whores and punks in the world! They can offer it to us in vain, as far as I'm concerned, and spiders can spin their webs there. They say that gold is the heaviest of metals, yet nothing else makes a man so agile, light-headed, and capricious. A substance to which you add gold doesn't actually become heavier; but for all its weight, if it's of the right quality, it will get lighter and more flexible. So a man, without gold, is like a bird without feathers; if you want to catch it, you can; if you want to eat it, you can. But if it has feathers, it flies, and the more feathers it has, the better it flies and soars higher, out of reach. When Bonifacio has lost his purse and his virtue, he will feel much heavier and fall back to earth again. But here comes our fine lover, pat. He's not wearing his fine cloak anymore, thanks to that rogue's thieving hands! He's in a hurry to get to the cesspit.

Scene V

Enter Bonifacio.

Bartolomeo.   Faster, Master Bonifacio, faster than that! I saw your mistress, your heart's desire, only a moment ago. I swear that when I saw her, I remembered that you were in love with her, yet as I looked again she seemed so beautiful that the great vein swelled so much it burst my breeches.

Bonifacio.   That's enough; don't make fun of me, Master Bartolomeo. I'm in love. I'm in chains. You stick to nouns and I'll live for adjectives. You've your alchemy and I've got mine; you've your fire and I've one of my own.

Bartolomeo.   Mine's Vulcan's and yours is Cupid's.

Bonifacio.   We'll see which brings the greater success.

Bartolomeo.   Vulcan is a man of sense, discreet and honest; the other is a mindless brat, a fiickle lecher; if he doesn't dishonor you, he'll damage you in some other way, and usually he does both.

Bonifacio.   Well, I wish you as much success as you've got good sense!

Bartolomeo.   And you'll need all the help that Venus, mother of madmen, can give you.

Bonifacio.   Luck, you mean. You know how, if you succeed in anything, people find some reason that really had nothing to do with it. If I rush into some business like a wild boar, and I do well, then they say, he's got a good head on his shoulders, he knew which way the land lay and made his profit. On the other hand, if I planned a piece of business with as much philosophical cunning as all the bearded hypocrites of Greece and Egypt ever had, and it turns out badly, then everyone would say what a fool I was. If things go well—who did it? who did it? Those clever French. If things go badly—who was responsible? who was responsible? Those barbarian French. Or again: What made this go so well? The rectitude of the Spaniards. And this go badly? Spanish turpitude! What conquered and maintained so many fine territories in Istria, Dalmatia, Greece, in the Adriatic Sea and in Cisalpine Gaul? What adorned Italy, Europe and the very world with a republic whose like was never seen before? The wisdom of the sage Venetians. But who lost Cyprus, who lost Cyprus? The stingy, twisty Venetians. It's only when luck brings you success that you only get praised for your wisdom.

Bartolomeo.   So you would say that, "With luck on your side, you can do without brains." Here is Lucia: I'll

leave you. I've sent my boy to Consalvo's for a powder
I need, and he still hasn't come back; I must go myself.
Bonifacio. Good; I've more to say to her than you think.

Scene VI

Bartolomeo *goes.* Enter Lucia.

Bonifacio (*aside*). She'll begin by asking me for money;
that will be her first move. And my resolution is: cash
on delivery. Besides, I don't like the idea of a woman
getting the better of me.—Welcome, Lucia, what news?
Lucia. Oh, sweet Master Bonifacio, I haven't even time
to greet you properly: you must come to my poor
lady's aid at once.
Bonifacio. You must offer me something, if you want
something back. The pox——
Lucia. She is dying——
Bonifacio. "When she is dead, then'll be the time to
bury her," as some holy father said.
Lucia. I mean our lady Vittoria is dying for you, cruel
man. Is this the life you mean her to lead, is this what
you have to offer her? You go about enjoying yourself,
and my poor lady is all sighs and tears—if you saw
her, you might not recognize her anymore, you might
not even find her so beautiful as you used to. Is your
compassion as great as your love, I wonder?
Bonifacio. Well? Does she need money?
Lucia. Who mentioned money? Who said anything
about money? Oh, perish the whole world! If you are
in need, she will give money to you.
Bonifacio. Oh, come! No, really, this I can't believe!
Lucia. Then don't believe it, you beastly, cruel ruffian!
O-ooh! O-ooh!
Bonifacio. What, tears?
Lucia. I'm crying because of your cruelty and my lady's
misery. O-ooh, misery, misery, what bad luck made
you cross our path? I never knew that love could do so
much to a woman's heart. She has loved you before now,
I swear it but o-ooh! o-ooh! the last few hours I don't
know what has got into her—it's always, "My Bonifacio, my heart, light of my life, my flame, my love,
my passion!" I swear—and I've known her for fifteen
years, since she was a child, a tiny child—I've never

really seen her moved, never seen her in love, till now;
if you could see her, you'd find her lying on her bed
with her face buried in the cushion she's clutching and
saying—so that I blush for her, and pity her—"Ah, my
Bonifacio, who keeps you from me? Oh, cruel Fortune!
When he wanted me, you kept him away, and I know
that now I long and languish for him, you in turn deny
him to me. Oh, my poor wounded heart!"

Bonifacio.   Does she really say that? Is that what is
really happening?

Lucia.   "You, you, Bonifacio, will force me to do something I have never done in my life before, you will
make me renounce—" O-ooh! o-ooh! my poor lady Vittoria, what a wretched fate! In—what hands have you
fallen into? O-ooh! Now, now at last I see you always
loved him and that there isn't another man in Naples
who behaves so deceitfully to you. O-ooh! O-oooooh!
Misery me! What cure can I offer you, poor lady?

Bonifacio.   All right, all right, I believe you, Lucia, I believe you; don't go on crying. It's not that I didn't
believe you, I was just astonished. What fresh influence
in the stars can this be, that wishes me so much good
that my diamond-hearted lady, who has always answered my love with a cruelty as great as her beauty,
has become so changed?

Lucia.   Changed? Changed? If I hadn't kept her back,
she'd have gone to find you in your house. I said to her,
"Madwoman that you are, you will offend him. What
will his wife say? What will everyone who sees you
say? They'd all say, 'What's got into her head? Is she
out of her senses?' Don't you know he loves you?
Have you forgotten all his favors to you? Unless you
are blind and out of your wits, if you must know, he'll
think himself blessed and blessed again when he hears
me say you want him to come to you——"

Bonifacio.   And you were right! You were absolutely
right!

Lucia.   —then that poor soul—as if she'd forgotten all
the evidence of your love that you'd given her and I'd
told her of—then she said, "Is it possible, O Heaven,
Heaven, cruel only to me, that you would let him
come—O happy fate—when you forbid me to seek
him out?"

Bonifacio.   Ah! And you really fear for my mistress'
life?

Lucia. You know that as desire increases, hope declines, and it may be that this great change she feels in herself makes her in the same way suspect a change in you. If you see one miracle, you can easily credit a second.

Bonifacio. Never! Whales will chase hares, devils cross themselves, Brescians learn good manners, Satan say a *Pater* and an *Ave Maria* for the souls in purgatory, before I ever fall out of love with my so much loved, so much desired lady. So, without more ado—Where are you going with all that?

Lucia. I'm returning these clothes to a neighbor, and so killing two birds with one stone—I was going on to your house, but fortune has brought me on you here. What shall we do? As soon as I've got rid of these I'll be back, as quick as I can, to comfort my poor lady and tell her I've seen you and spoken to you and that you will soon be with her.

Bonifacio. Yes, promise her that, and tell her this is the happiest day in my whole life: that I long to kiss the lovely face I so adore and that holds the key to this afflicted heart.

Lucia. Hers is the afflicted one. Don't fail to come to-night. She won't eat or sleep or rest, remember, she's more likely to die if she doesn't see you soon. If there is any pity in your heart, don't keep her on the rack, for mercy's sake; I can see her burning out like a flaring candle.

Bonifacio. I can't get away for a while, but come for me later, or, if not, I'll come to you.

Lucia. There is a point you must bear in mind. For your own reputation and for hers you musn't arouse suspicion when you enter or leave the house. You know how the neighbors are at the windows up to midnight, watching who's coming and going. So you must disguise yourself in a big cloak like Master Giovan Bernardo's; he can go in and out without making anyone talk. And it would be a good idea, in case you were seen close, to wear a little false beard like his; with this disguise we can go together and I can take you up to her room. And this would please my mistress, too, for it will show her that you think of her reputation.

Bonifacio. That's very well thought of. I am about the same height as Giovan Bernardo, and there will be no difficulty getting a cloak like his; I think I can lay my hands on one. So on my way I'll go to Pellegrino's and get the right sort of beard.

Lucia. Start now, I beg you, and be quick. Bless you for taking this weight off my shoulders!

Bonifacio. Farewell.

                                                    Lucia *goes.*

Scene VII

Bonifacio. From what she says I think I must have let the image get so close to the fire it nearly melted; I must have overdone it. See how the poor woman is tortured with love. By my faith, I can hardly keep back my own tears. If Scaramuré—and may he prosper; I can see now that he is a most worthy man—hadn't warned me: don't let it melt! I'd certainly have done something rash—I hardly dare think of it! Well, now, let's see who'd doubt the force of magic!

Scene VIII

Enter Marta.

Marta. There's that rabbit's skin; if God had filled it up with a rabbit's insides, then he'd be worth something at least. Good evening, Master Coneyfacio.

Bonifacio. Well met, Madam Marta. Your husband is a philosopher, so you must be one, too, and it's no wonder, if you analyze the meaning of words. What did you mean by calling me "Coneyfacio"? I'm your friend, wherever I am: don't you believe that? You have no cause to make fun of me.

Marta. How's your purse?

Bonifacio. When it's got no coin in, it's like your husband's head.

Marta. I mean the one lower down.

Bonifacio. Oh, a thousand thanks for your kind inquiry! You poke about for the source of the trouble like a doctor. If you could help me, I'd show you all the symptoms. If it's simply soup you're interested in, then go to the friars at Santa Maria.

Marta. D'you mean I'm food for the friars, Sir Bollocks?

Bonifacio. No, you're beyond that; you're food for

worms, for when a woman's over thirty-five, she should depart in peace, in fact, go to purgatory and there pray to God for the living.

Marta. And that's just what we say of men.

Bonifacio. But God hasn't arranged it like that; he made women for men, not men for women. They have been made to serve him, and when they can't, then to the devil with them, for they've no use in the world. No one lights candles at a dismantled altar; no one tries to push pennies into a money box with gaping hinges—

Marta. Isn't it shameful for a middle-aged man like you to be talking in this tone? Let children prattle to children, and youth talk bawdy to youth, but age should have more dignity.

Bonifacio. —so hang them up in the smoke and have them pickled in the chimney. But that isn't the advice the doctors gave to the patriarch David, or, not long ago, when they brought a young mother to a certain holy father when he was dying: "Come, come," they said, "no, no, don't just kiss her—" But he got so excited that though he should simply have sucked, he actually——

Marta. —put too much pepper on his thistle.

Bonifacio. So you see, dear madam, an old cat needs a tender mouse.

Marta. But why don't you think this applies to old women as well as to old men?

Bonifacio. Because women are made for men and not vice versa.

Marta. That's where the injustice lies: men sit as judges on their own cause. But we are thought to be out of our minds if we——

Bonifacio. Lie back under the burden?

Marta. No, no: if we try to find some just punishment and revenge.

Bonifacio. In fact, there's one law for us and another for you.

They laugh.

Marta. But what about your own wife? I gather you leave her to die of want. She's young and beautiful, and yet—? You tire of even the best meat if you have it day after day. Isn't that it?

Bonifacio. Well, is that it? Do you really know what

you are talking about? Aren't you just repeating
gossip? Now let's be a little more serious, my dear
Madam Marta. I know you have a lot of secrets and
I'd like you to help me out. You see, tonight I want
to play the game of five-posts-to-the-bed with my
wife better than ever. I beg you, tell me of some drug
or medicine that will help me ride well.

Marta.   *Recipe*: water from the kidneys, grease from the
back; liquor from the penis and manna from the
balls; *ad quantom suffrica, mesceta et fiat potum*.
And then take care to keep your feet in the stirrups,
for you'll gallop so fast the saddle bow might break
your rump for you.

Bonifacio.   By Saint Frigonius, you are a past master!
Now I must go. Farewell, you have given me what I
wanted.

Marta.   Farewell. If you meet my smoked cheese of a
husband, tell him I want to see him about something
urgent.

Bonifacio *goes.*

Scene IX

Marta.   "Nez coupé n'a faute de lunettes," as that sweet
lecher Jean de Bretagne used to say, and bless his
soul who first put the French tongue into my mouth,
when I was but twelve and a half. He used to say that
just as he was poorer than the King of France, the
king was needier than he was. The more you have, the
more you worry, the more you want, the less pleasure
you take in it. The Prince of Conca lives on an in-
come of a guinea and a half a day; the King of France
can hardly keep his kingdom by spending at times ten
thousand a day. Which of them is richer, then? And
happier? The one who has a little coming in, or the
one who has a lot going out? After his defeat at the
battle of Pavia, I've heard the King of France had to
find more than eight millions in gold; when did the
Prince of Conca ever have to find more than twenty
or twenty-five guineas? When would he ever have
need of more? So which of those two princes is the
less needy? Poor me, I know, I know, I know by experience all too well that I'll be better off when my
baboon of a husband doesn't have as much to spend
as he has now. We used to play at this side that side,

horse and mare, at your turn my turn, and suck the
lollipop, and with these games and others like them
we passed the days and nights. But now, because he's
been left all this money by Pucciolo—whose soul be
cursed, even if it's in Abraham's bosom!—he's suddenly plunged in worry, anguish, doubts, fear of losing it, fear of being robbed, fear of being deceived by
one and murdered by another. He comes and goes,
wanders around, takes it out and puts it back again,
counts it and sniffs it, huffs and puffs morning, noon,
and night. On top of everything, I could swear it's
more than seven months (apart from Barra, bless
him) since I was irrigated. Yesterday I said the Mass
of Saint Elias against drought, and this morning I
gave fivepence to have Saint Joachim and Saint Anna's
said, which has a wonderful power to bring husband
and wife together. So if the priest did his job properly,
I hope I'll soon be blessed, though it looks as though
I'm going to have a weary wait for it; instead of leaving his furnace and coming in to me, he's been out
longer than usual, and now I'm having to look for
him. Still, grace falls when you're least expecting it.
Ah, I think that's him!

Scene X

Enter Bartolomeo *and* Mochione.

Bartolomeo. Oh, misery! Oh, misfortune and desola-
tion!
Marta. Heaven, what is this weeping and wailing?
Bartolomeo. Alas! If this is really what has happened,
I have lost all, all! Tell me, rascal, that's exactly what
he said? Watch out, now.
Mochione. Yes, sir. He ended by saying, "I haven't any
of this powder and don't know where it's to be found":
he said he'd been given it by Master Cencio, and that
he doesn't even know what *pulvis Christi* is.
Bartolomeo. Ruined, ruined!
Marta. Jesus, Saint Maria of Piedigrotta, Virgin Maria
of Rosario, Our Lady of the Mount, Saint Maria Ap-
pareta, Our Lady of Scafata! Alleluia, alleluia, avert
the evil! Saint Cosmo and Saint Guiliano, avert the
evil! Evil, evil, on your way, don't come back this

many a day! Now, Bartolomeo, what's all this about?

Bartolomeo. You here, at this hour, curse you? Go home—go to the devil. Just leave me alone to find out if I'm to be ruined or not! Come on, Mochione, we'll see this man again. He was still in his shop?

Mochione. Yes, sir. This is the shortest way.

> Bartolomeo *and* Mochione *go.*

Marta. Mercy me, I'll go home and wait for news. I'm afraid my prayers have been answered, the worse for me. I daren't say what I think. Blessed Saint Bruin, keep us from ruin! *Giesu auto et transit per medio milloro mibatte.* Who's that creeping up behind me so quietly? He's surely the look-out for some band of robbers. I'll be off.

> *She goes.*

Scene XI

Enter Manfurio.

Manfurio. In Adige's Erasmus—I mean in the adages of Erasmus—I'm getting confused—I mean in the Erasmian adages, there is one, from among the others, which runs *"A toga ad pallium."* This, relating it *in me ipso,* makes today *nigro signandus lapillo* for me. *O caelum, o terras, o maria Neptuni!* After having had my money taken from my hand by a most vile raptor, three others came forward and offered themselves as desiring to advantage me, and then, *non inquam dexteritate sed sinisteritate quadam,* left me with a mangy cloak on my back, *proque capitis operculo* an old hat —which, *versus centrum et in medio, prae nimii sudoris densitudine* appeared waxed, *vel* pitched, *vel* tanned, *vel* of leather *seu* hide—and took away my cap and master's gown. *Proh deûm atque hominum fidem,* here am I fallen *a patella ad prunas.* They persuaded me by saying, "Come with us, and we will find the raptor for you." So I went with them *bona fide,* to the dwelling of—*ut facile crediderim*—certain meretrixes, where they went in, leaving me in the hall and telling me, "It is best if we go in first so that he doesn't think that we intend to confront him with you *ex abrupto;* so wait here till one of us calls you to *discernere,* with the least *excandescentia* as possible, *quod ad restitutionem atticet.*" Now, after waiting for a long period *deambulando*, rehearsing the arguments with which I would confound him, *tandem*, no one had summoned me. I ascended the stairs and knocked on the door of the first room. And there I was told to move on, because there was not, and had never been, anyone living there but the servants. *Aliquantolum progressus*, I knocked at the door of another apartment on the same floor. There I received a similar reply from a *vetula*, who said I could come in but there were only certain *minime contemnendae iuvenculae*, to which I replied that my head was occupied by purposes of a quite dissimilar nature, and thus, *ulterius progressus*, I found myself outside the house by a way which opened into another *platea*. So, *de necessitate consequentiae* I concluded: *Ergo forte* I have been deceived by them, for *domus ista duplici constat exitu et ingressu*. And having entered a second time, *per cunctatus sum*, if there were some other cubiculary receptacle in which they might be congregated, I said *in forma conclusionis* to myself: "My friend, if they entered by this door, they went out by that; if they entered by that, they went out by this." *Tunc statim*, fearful of some further assistance or counsel similar to that I had already received, I absented myself thence, and—*iuxta* the Pythagorean expression— fleeing through the popular streets and traversing their intersections, I wait for an opportunity to regain my house. *Quandoquidem*, now, with all these perambulations and contraperambulations I fear *incidere*—to the prejudice of my reputation—someone who knows me while I wear this most indecent habit. *Expedit* that I withdraw *in istum angulum* for I see approaching within propinquity two feminules.

He hides.

Scene XII

Enter Carubina *and* Lucia.

Carubina.   In the name of Saint Raccasella!
Lucia.   Our advocate.
Carubina.   Do you really think that I could be taken for Vittoria?

Lucia. I swear by the fifteen mysteries of the rosary—
which I've just this minute stopped saying—that I
have the impression of being with her at this very
minute. You remind me of her even in your voice and
the way you speak. It would be wise, though, to keep
your voice down when you speak to him, and make
him do the same, as if you were afraid of being heard
by the neighbors, and the people living in the next
rooms. As for your face, you are as young, smooth,
and plump as Vittoria herself, if not even more so.

Carubina. You won't bring any light into the room until
I signal to you, will you? So that I can confront him
with what he intended to do and what he actually
did.

Lucia. And you might as well give some comfort to
the poor beast before tormenting him. Let him empty
his wallet at least once, to see how thoughtfully we
handle him.

Carubina. As for that, you'll enjoy it more than he does!
I'll seem to be desperately in love: and to prove it
I'll give him kisses like the bites of a bear. I'll chew
his cheeks and bruise his lips so you'll hear him cry
out and be able to share the fun. And I'll say, "My
heart, my life, don't make such a noise, we'll be heard!
And forgive me, my heart, I love you so much I can't
help myself—"

Lucia. He'll believe it's all due to the power of the
spell.

Carubina. "—I melt with love: I could nibble you up
to the very bones."

Lucia. As the viper does.

Carubina. Oh, that's not all! Then I'll get him to push
out his tongue, and I'll bite it so hard that he won't
be able to pull it back before he's screeched out three
or four times.

Lucia (*laughs*). And I'll say to Mistress Vittoria, "There
goes his tongue!" He'll be able to scream but not talk
—but maybe that's going too far and will bring his
temperature right down to zero.

Carubina. And then I'll say, "My heart, sweet, cruel
life of my heart, forgive me if I seem too passionate:
but I love you so much and you excite me so much, I
can't restrain myself."

Lucia. By Saint Appollonia, you have planned it well!
He'll be thinking, "My God, what have I got hold of?"

Carubina. Then, after act two, I'll let him see that I'm

prepared to let him come in once before we get into bed. I'll get ready for him and as soon as his trousers are off I'll let him get as far as the, "Lift up your heads, O ye gates," but before the "that the king of glory may come in," I'll take his cock and balls in both hands and say, "Oh, my love, my longed-for love, oh, the only hope of my consuming passion, I would rather have my hands cut off than let you be torn from them"—and with this I'll squeeze as hard as I can, and wring him the way I wring out the washing. And I'm sure that in this case he won't be able to use his hands to push me off.

Lucia (*laughs*). That's a pain that would make take the strength out of Hercules, and in any case you're stronger than he is to start off with.

Carubina. You can be sure he'll shout out loud enough to be heard at home, and it'll be the worse for him if he doesn't: I'll pinch and twist all the harder. When you hear this third, loudest lot of cries, come quickly with the lamps and we'll all recognize one another in the light, by the grace of Saint Lucy. What happens next, we shall see.

Lucia. Everything's ready, so go to Mistress Vittoria's house, taking care, you know, to hide your face with the cloak. If you meet him in the street, don't speak to him, because that wouldn't be proper in a public place, but make him a deep curtsey, and when you've gone on a little, heave a great sigh and take the way straight to our door, which you'll find open. In the meantime I've something else to do, then I'll go and bring him along. Be careful now. Farewell.

Carubina. We'll meet again soon!

She goes.

Scene XIII

Lucia. The proverb says, "If you want Lent to go quickly, contract a debt you'll have to pay at Easter." Today has gone in a flash thinking of what has to be done to boil this kettle of fish tonight. Everything is going well. It only remains to warn Master Giovan Bernardo to get here at the right moment, and the others too. When several smiths are hammering together, they must keep time. Heaven be praised. I think he's coming now.

Scene XIV

Enter Giovan Bernardo.

Lucia. I was just looking for you.

Giovan Bernardo. What have you been doing, Lucia my dear?

Lucia. Everything. Bonifacio has gone to disguise himself and get fitted out with a beard like yours. His wife is ready, dressed in some clothes of Vittoria's. Sanguino is disguised as Captain Palma, with a long white beard, and Marca, Barra, and Corcovizzo are got up as a night patrol.

Giovan Bernardo. I've just seen them and talked to them. They are waiting in a shop just over there. I'll take care not to let this treat slip through my fingers. Have you told my lady Carubina about my idea?

Lucia. *Liberamus domino.* Do you think I'm a fool?

Giovan Bernardo. Sensible girl. I'll give you a present —here.

Kisses her.

Lucia. Many thanks, sir! But that's not what I need.

Giovan Bernardo. Take it as something on account, my dear. No one else can manage these things as well as you.

Lucia. If you knew how much ingenuity I had to use to get Bonifacio to believe this sudden passion of Vittoria's, and to disguise himself and then to bring Mistress Carubina around as well, then you really would admire me.

Giovan Bernardo. I'm sure this is nothing to what you could manage. Now it's best for me to be off: the time for talking is past. If Bonifacio came now and saw us, the soup would be spoiled for too much salt. Farewell.

Lucia. You look after the others, and I'll take care of him.

Scene XV*

Lucia *and* Giovan Bernardo *go.* Manfurio *comes forward.*

* See the Appendix for an explanation and translation of the Latin in this scene and the next.

Manfurio. Now they are gone. I will stay awhile in this *deambulatorio.* I saw two feminules conversing, and then one stayed to converse with the painter. The young woman must be some *lupa, unde derivatur lupanar*: the older, doubtless is some *lena.* Their manner of conferring together *habet lenocinii specimen.* The painter I adjudge to be *aliquantolum* fornicator. *Ergo, sequitur conclusio.* I see a cohort coming. I will *iterum* retire.

> *He goes to hide.*

Scene XVI

Enter Sanguino *disguised as captain;* Marca, Barra, *and* Corcovizzo *as officers of the watch.*

Sanguino. That man who runs away and hides is purgatory-bound; he has a guilty conscience. Apprehend him!

Barra. Stop there! The watch! Name and occupation!

Manfurio. Mamphurius *artium magister. Non sum* a criminal, *non fur, non moechus, non testis iniquus: alterius nuptam, nec rem cupiens alienam.*

Sanguino. What office are you reciting, compline or matins?

Marca. The penitential psalms or the office of the dead?

Sanguino. What is your occupation? You seem to be a priest.

Manfurio. Sum gymnasiarcha.

Sanguino. A crazy barber? Kennel him, then, before he maddens us all.

Corcovizzo. Hold out your hands, my little lost pig. Come on, we'll give you lodging for the night, and at the king's expense.

Manfurio. Domini, I am a schoolmaster and have but recently been robbed of money and garments.

Sanguino. Why did you flee the watch? You are a thief, an enemy of justice.

> *Beats him.*

Manfurio. Quaeso, don't beat me! I fled because I did not want to be seen in these garments, which are not my own.

Sanguino. Sergeant Corporal: aren't you going to arrest this man? Don't you see that this cloak of his has been stolen from Tiburolo at the customhouse?

Corcovizzo. Excuse me, Captain, your Worship is mistaken; that one had gold trimming on the collar.

Sanguino. Haven't you eyes? Are you blind? Isn't this trimming? Isn't this yellow?

Corcovizzo. By Saint Christopher's staff, you are right.

Marca. By Hercules' club, this is a hardened villain. There! There! And there! And there!

Manfurio. For pity's sake, why are you beating me? I have told you that my own garments were stolen by barbarous raptors, or, *ut more vestro loquar,* thieves.

Sanguino. You are the man we want: this cloak is stolen property. To prison, and we'll soon see there who is the thief.

Manfurio. Take me to my patron's house, near the church of the Crutched Friars, and I will prove that I am no malefactor.

Sanguino. We don't arrest a man to escort him to his own home. Take that! To prison with you, and argue your case with the jailers there.

Manfurio. What a way is this to treat a man of erudition: *Afficere me* in this unurbane manner?

Marca. Speak Italian! Speak like a Christian, in the devil's name, if you want us to understand you.

Barra. He does speak like a good Christian: it sounds like someone saying Mass.

Marca. I think we've hit on some monk in disguise.

Corcovizzo. So do I. *Domine abbas, volimus comedere fabbas?*

Barra. *Et si fabba non habbemo, quid comederemo?*

Manfurio. *Non sum homo ecclesiasticus.*

Sanguino. He's even tonsured, do you see, like a priest?

Manfurio. *Hoc est calvitium.*

Barra. You'll do penance for this, excommunicate! There! And there! And there!

Manfurio. *Dixi "calvitium," quasi calvae vitium.* Don't go on beating me *quia conquerar.* Is this the way to treat men of learning and erudition, Doctors?

Sanguino. You lie: you have no hide nor hair of the doctor about you. Take that! And that!

Manfurio. I will recite a hundred lines of the poet Virgil, *aut per capita* as much of the *Eneide* as you wish. The first book, in the estimation of some, begins, "*Ille ego qui quondam,*" according to others, who attribute those lines to Varro, it begins, "*Arma virumque cano*"; the second, "*Conticuere omnes*"; the third, "*Postquam res Asiae*"; the fourth, "*At regina gravi*";

the fifth, *"Tu quoque littoribus nostris"*; the sixth, *"Conticuere omnes."*

Sanguino. Don't try to hoodwink us, ruffian, with these Latin tags, learned by heart for homework. You are an ignoramus; if you were wise, you wouldn't be a thief.

Manfurio. Bring some doctor here, then, and I will dispute with him.

Sanguino. Cennera nomino quotta sunt?

Manfurio. That is a question for beginners, novices, tyros *et primis attingentium labellis;* which declares that *masculeum idest* masculine, *foemineum* feminine, *neutrum* what is neither the one nor the other, *commune* which is both one and the other—

Barra. Masculine *and* feminine?

Manfurio. —*epicoenum* where the sexes are not distinguished.

Sanguino. And which of all these are you? Epicene, I suppose?

Manfurio. *"Quae non distinguunt sexum, dicas epicoena."*

Sanguino. Tell me, if you are a *magister,* what's the first thing you teach children?

Manfurio. In Dispautanus' Grammar there is this line: *"Omne viro soli quod convenit, esto virile."*

Sanguino. Expound it.

Manfurio. *"Omne"*—*idest totum, quidquid, quidlibet, quodcumque universum; "quod convenit"*—*quadrat, congruit, adest; "Viro soli"*—*soli duntaxat, tantummodo, solummodo viro, vel fertur a viro; "esto"*—*idest sit, vel dicatur, vel habeatur; "virile"*—*idest* what belongs to man only is called virile.

Sanguino. That's a devil of a fine first lesson for young boys! What man only has, and woman has not, *hoc est ideste,* is called, is nominated the virile, the *membrum virile!*

Barra. A fine lesson indeed, by my faith!

Manfurio. Nego, nego. I do not mean what you think—what benefit can come of talking to those without erudition?—I mean objects that should be attached only to the masculine——

Sanguino (beats him). That's talk for women, you dirty old man.

Manfurio. —what you are thinking of is both masculine, *proprie et ut pars;* and feminine, *ut portio, et attributive vel applicative.*

Sanguino. Quick, quick, in here with him, and then we'll take him to the magistrate. You try to show us what your art consists of, and we find it's the art of buggering small boys!

Manfurio. *O me miserum! verba nihil prosunt. O diem infaustum atque noctem!*

They go within.

ACT V

Scene I

Enter Bonifacio *and* Lucia.

Bonifacio (*trembling*). Oh, oh, oh, oh, oh.

Lucia. And so, my dear Master Giovan Bernardo——

Bonifacio. I'm Bonifacio, remember? Oh, oh, oh.

Lucia. I swear I'd forgotten: you are disguised so well you seem to be Giovan Bernardo in everything but name.

Bonifacio. Oh, oh, oh, oh. You'd better call me that. If anyone heard you speaking to me, brrrh! Brrrh! It would be better if he heard you use that name. Ugh! Ugh! Brrrh!

Lucia. You're shaking all over. What's the matter?

Bonifacio. N-nothing. Brrrh! Now look, Lucia, if anyone thinks I'm Giovan Bernardo—oh! oh! oh! oh!—and wants to talk to me, o-oo-h—I shall pretend to be too f-furious and take no n-notice and you—brrrh! brrrh!—you must tell him to leave me alone because I'm out of my mind because of something that has happened—brrrh! brrrh!

Lucia. All right. There won't be any trouble.

Bonifacio. Oh, oh, oh, oh, oh.

Lucia. But tell me, why are you trembling? From cold or fear? What is it?

Bonifacio. My dear Lucia, I tr-r-remble for l-love, because I'm so n-near to my b-b-bliss. Brrrh! brrrh!

Lucia. Ah, now I understand! You are trembling with excitement like someone on the point of finding something they've long been hunting for—now you are on the point of being with her at last.

Bonifacio. Oh, oh, oh, oh, my beloved V-V-Vittoria,

my comfort, my d-diamond-hearted, who made me
s-s-suffer so.

Lucia. You are her comfort and she yours. I swear by
the saint who gave half his cloak for the love of God
that you have truly softened a diamond with your
pretty ways. You seem more handsome today than
ever before; I don't know if that's the effect of love
or of something else.

Bonifacio. Oh, oh, oh, oh. Let's hurry. I can't hold on
any longer.

Lucia. Well, don't waste it on the ground if you don't
want God's curse on you. Really! I can't help laughing.
But never mind, if you can't hold on, you can always
do it again.

Bonifacio. That's true, b-b-b-b-but—

Lucia. Come on then.

Scene II

Bonifacio *and* Lucia *go. Enter* Bartolomeo, Consalvo,
and Mochione.

Bartolomeo. Oh, traitor, thief, murderer, so you haven't
got *pulvis Christi,* or the *pulvis* of the devil? Oh, catastrophe! I am ruined, you accursed villain. You will
pay for this.

Consalvo. You'd do better to keep quiet, you fool, or
everyone will think you are mad: you'll be the laughingstock of all Naples, the children will be playing
games about you in the streets; and it does no good.

Bartolomeo. You think that's how to make me hold
my tongue?

Consalvo. If you don't want to hold it, shout till you
burst your lungs for all I care. How was I to know
anything about this affair of yours? A month ago
your friend Cencio came and asked if I had any
litharge, alum, quicksilver, red sulfur, verdigris, sal
ammoniac, and other ordinary things—I said I had.
Then he said, "Now you shall be my supplier for a
piece of work I am doing. Keep this powder, which
is called *pulvis Christi,* and send me whatever amounts
of it I ask for. Keep this cash box of mine, too, which
contains the most precious things I possess."

Bartolomeo. Has he taken all this back?

Consalvo. No; but calm down: when he comes for

them, he won't get out of my house as easily as he thinks.

Bartolomeo. Very fine—if he hadn't already left town. Isn't that what you have just heard, Mochione?

Mochione. That's what everyone says.

Consalvo. Well, what am I to do? You ought to know; he stayed in your house and worked for you more than a fortnight. Since then I don't know where he's been. You yourself have asked me for this and that, and as for the *pulvis Christi,* first you asked me for what amounted to half of it, and the next time you had the rest. Now, you send and ask for ten times as much as I ever had and so naturally I'm surprised and send back word that the alchemist Cencio hasn't given me any more.

Bartolomeo. I've no doubt left that you and he planned to stick a leek up me.

Consalvo. If you suggest that I was planning anything wrong, you are lying in your teeth, you crazy fool. There was just enough for him to trick you with. What do you expect me to know of your concerns when I haven't even spoken to you for ten years? You've sent for things to my shop, and I have sent you what I had.

Bartolomeo. Why, then, this devil's *pulvis* was gold dust mixed with some other accursed substance to disguise it! I saw it weighed more than other powders. And that's where the pieces of gold came from. Oh, curse the day I saw him! I'll hang myself.

Consalvo. Go and do it right away, then.

Bartolomeo. Not before hanging you first, you filthy traitor.

Consalvo. You've lied in your throat a hundred times! Do the worst you can. I don't give a straw for you. Go on, madman, poor stupid madman, go and find your *pulvis Christi.*

Bartolomeo. Alas! What am I to do? How can I get my guineas back?

Consalvo. Do as he did, if you can find someone else with a brain like yours and as much money.

Bartolomeo. I'll leave that sort of thing to you, you filthy old wretch.

Consalvo. Wait a bit! This'll let some of the madness or booze out of your nose—there! There! Miser! Miser!

Bartolomeo. That, too, eh? Dirty cuckold! Uh! Uh! (*Punches him.*)

Consalvo. Try these, then; they'll suit you better! Uh! Uh!

Bartolomeo. Ow, ow, ouch! Treacherous bandit! Help! Help!

Mochione. Help! Help! My master's being beaten to death!

Consalvo. Just give me time to help you knock the stupidity out of your head. Uh! Uh! Uh! Uh!

Bartolomeo. For the love of God, he's murdering me! Help! Help!

Scene III

Sanguino, Corcovizzo, Barra, *and* Marca *come out.*

Sanguino. Order in the name of the watch! What's all this noise?

Bartolomeo. This assassin had assassinated my purse— now, as you can see, he's assassinating me in person.

Sanguino. Bind them together and take them to prison.

Consalvo. But Captain, he accused me of things no decent man, with a good reputation like mine, would do.

Bartolomeo. To the magistrate, so that the law can do its duty.

Barra. Go on and quickly, it's getting late.

Sanguino. Bind them tight, so they can't escape.

Corcovizzo. If they get away from this, say I set them free myself.

Sanguino. Really tight, now! Right. Away, away there!

Bartolomeo. Oh, misery, misery! This on top of everything else! Mochione, run to Marta and tell her to come early tomorrow morning to the jail.

Mochione. Right.

Sanguino. Come on now, curse you, march! Pick up your feet, there.

All go except Mochione.

Scene IV

Mochione. "A begat B" is followed by "and B begat C" and so forth and so forth and so forth; eating one cherry leads to another; and woes and misfortunes usually come on one another's heels. It's a saying all

the world over that troubles never come singly. First
my master meets Cencio, then he lets him have six
hundred guineas; then, three, he pours out money on
retorts, furnaces, fuel, and the other things this folly
of his needed; then, four, he wastes time and, five,
labor; six, he has trouble, and there's more to come,
with this druggist; seven, he's had twelve blows like
kicks from a mule; eight, he's off to prison, and for
the ninth some other misfortune is bound to come
before he is out of it, and that will be more time and
money down the drain; last of all, he'll be made a
laughingstock over this wretched *pulvis Christi*. That
must be Master Giovan Bernardo. He'll know something about this. I'll see if I can overhear what he's
muttering.

Scene V

Enter Giovan Bernardo.

Giovan Bernardo. I've a suspicion these rogues have
their own irons in the fire and are thinking of some
other plot that will divert them from the main one, if
they can't manage the two at once. I'm afraid they're
going to spoil things. Hey there, my lad!

Mochione. What is it, Master Giovan Bernardo?

Giovan Bernardo. Have you seen anyone about here?

Mochione. I've seen all too many, worse luck.

Giovan Bernardo. Who were they?

Mochione. The captain of the watch and three of his
men, and they have taken my master off to prison, and
Consalvo the druggist. They found them fighting and
have tied them up and taken them off to the courthouse.

Giovan Bernardo. Who is your master?

Mochione. Master Bartolomeo.

Giovan Bernardo. So! Master Bartolomeo off to prison?
What a misfortune! Tell me another thing, my lad;
why was he fighting Consalvo?

Mochione. I wouldn't know, sir. And if you'll humbly
give me leave, I must get home right away.

Giovan Bernardo. Then farewell to you.

Scene VI

Mochione *goes.*

Giovan Bernardo. One trick after another, that shifty
  rogue Sanguino and his gang are about some knavery
  of their own. Bonifacio and his wife will soon be
  coming out of Vittoria's house, and I can't do anything
  on my own. How long are they going to be? When
  they come out, I shall have to delay them till the
  others leave whatever mischief they've got themselves
  into and—*Ave Maria,* my purse, *Ave Maria,* my
  cloak—grant it's them I see coming.

                                          He withdraws.

Scene VII

Enter Sanguino, Barra, Marca, *and* Corcovizzo.

Sanguino. Ha, ha! Their case is like Cola Perillo's, who
  felt ill and couldn't tell what part of the body the
  trouble was in. The doctor tapped him on the chest
  and said, "Does that hurt?" "No." Then he tapped him
  on the back. "Does it hurt there?" "No." Then in the
  kidneys. "Does it hurt there?" "No." Then the stomach.
  "Do you feel it there?" "No." Then his belly. "Does
  it hurt there?" "No." Then his bollocks. "Perhaps it's
  these?" "No." Then the doctor says, "Well, what about
  this leg, or this?" "No, sir. I beg you see if it's in the
  other one."
Barra. Ha, ha, ha!
Sanguino. So these poor souls, once in our hands, began
  to feel ill and they couldn't quite place it.
Corcovizzo. When Bartolomeo felt my hand on his
  purse, he said, "You're no more officers and I a prisoner than you are cardinals and I the pope. Take it,
  take it, and good luck to you. I'll get it all back from
  my companion." "Oh, yes?" says the other. "Someone
  is going to pay for this, all right."
Sanguino. And what did the other say when you took
  his?
Corcovizzo (*laughs*). He said, "So the judgment is already given, by Our Lady's body: we've been into

court and out again. Thanks to Saint Leonard—and
I'll pay for a Mass for him with a set of fetters—
we've already done penance for our sins with our
purses."

Sanguino. And you? What did you say then?

Corcovizzo. "This time," I said, "we'll let you off and
we won't take you to prison, and so you won't go on
creating a disturbance we'll leave you tied up. I have
to do that so you can't knock each other about before
someone else comes along. And as it's not fair that
this good turn should cost me time, trouble, and a yard
and a half of rope, I'm going to see I'm not out of
pocket. And because it's dark here, you'll have to wait
till I bring you the change."

Scene VIII

Giovan Bernardo *comes forward.*

Giovan Bernardo. Aha! What have you been doing?

Sanguino. We have punished two malefactors.

Giovan Bernardo. Do justice, and God will support you!

Sanguino. We're copying that pope—was it Pope Ha-
drian?—who sold benefices cheap rather than accept
credit and spend all day with a pair of scales seeing
if his guineas were the right weight. We're seeing what
our shares come to.

Giovan Bernardo. How have you left your prisoners?

Sanguino. Tied up safely, so that as long as they're left
alone, they can't do one another any damage.

Giovan Bernardo. Quick, quick, get back, keep out of
sight. I think Bonifacio is coming.

Sanguino. Here, Barra, Marca, Corcovizzo, get back,
back. Let them talk to Master Giovan Bernardo first.

Giovan Bernardo. I'll wait for them in here.

                                        He withdraws.

Sanguino, Barra, Marca, *and* Corcovizzo *hide.*

Scene IX

Enter Bonifacio *and* Carubina.

Bonifacio. This has all been the work of that pimping

witch Lucia and that cow of a whore her mistress.
They meant to make a fool of me, but I'll never trust
a woman again. If the Virgin Mary herself—I nearly
said something blasphemous.

Carubina. Take that accusation back, you villain: I
know them but I know you, too! Who is that coming
up?

Bonifacio. This is some other devil's plot. I think that
foul procuress has hatched four or five of them together.

Giovan Bernardo *comes forward.*

Giovan Bernardo. Either I am he, or he is me.

Bonifacio. Here's another devil—didn't I tell you?—
a bigger, fatter one.

Giovan Bernardo. Hallo there, my good man.

Bonifacio. Oh, that's all I needed!

Giovan Bernardo. Hullo, you there with the black
beard, tell me which of us two is me; me or you?
Speak up!

Bonifacio. You are you and I am myself.

Giovan Bernardo. What? I am myself? Haven't you,
you thief, stolen my person and gone about committing villainies under cover of it? What are you doing
here, what are you doing with Mistress Vittoria?

Carubina. I am his wife, Master Giovan Bernardo, and
I came here, thanks to the help of a woman friend, to
get the better of this villain.

Giovan Bernardo. So you are Madam Carubina? And
how does he come to be a Giovan Bernardo?

Carubina. I don't know. Ask him, he's old enough to
speak for himself.

Bonifacio. I changed my costume to go to bed with
my wife.

Carubina. You lie, traitor! Do you still dare, in my
presence, to deny it?

Giovan Bernardo. So, you villain: is this how you betray your wife, whom I know to be virtue itself?

Bonifacio. Giovan Bernardo, I beg you, don't let us
start arguing over this. Let me settle affairs with my
wife on my own.

Giovan Bernardo. What, villain, you think you'll wrig-
gle out of my hands like that? I want an explanation
of this disguise; I want to know what harm has been
done to my reputation. You could have used that to

commit a thousand crimes which I shall be held responsible for, if I don't keep my wits about me.

Bonifacio. Forgive me, please forgive me. I've committed no offense save against my wife, and no one else knows of it except Vittoria and her household, and they knew it was me, not you.

Carubina. For my sake, Master Giovan Bernardo, forgive him. Don't let this go any further.

Giovan Bernardo. Forgive me, madam, if I find it impossible to brush this off quite so lightly. As I don't know what he has done, I don't see how I can pardon him for it.

Bonifacio. Come, Carubina, come.

Giovan Bernardo. Stop there, stay just where you are; you're not going to escape me.

Bonifacio. Let me go, I warn you, if you don't want it to come to blows.

Carubina. Please, kind Master Giovan Bernardo, think of my reputation.

Giovan Bernardo. Mistress, your reputation is unspotted because there can be nothing wrong in what you have done, but I intend to find out what harm he has done both you and me.

Bonifacio. You shan't keep me here.

Giovan Bernardo. You shan't get away.

Scene X

Sanguino, Barra, Marca, *and* Corcovizzo *come forward.*

Sanguino. Halt there! The watch! What's going on here?

Bonifacio (*aside*). Let's try another way.—Welcome, officers. I have just met this man, disguised as myself and walking with my wife. He planned to ravish her. I charge him with it!

Giovan Bernardo. False, villain, you're a liar and I'll prove it by this disguise you're wearing.

Sanguino. The devil, we've got a case of twins on our hands!

Barra. These three, including the woman, make two in one flesh.

Marca. I think they've been trying to decide which of them is which and which is the husband of the lady.

Sanguino. This could turn out to be an important case. To prison with the lot of them.

Giovan Bernardo. Sir, he is the one you should imprison, not me.

Sanguino. What? What, rogue? You'll be the first!

Giovan Bernardo. Captain Palma, I beseech you, don't do me this injustice; I am a reputable person, I am Giovan Bernardo, a respectable citizen.

Corcovizzo. You see, Captain—you can't tell the difference between them.

Carubina. Captain Palma, sir—let's have the truth!— this man in disguise is my husband, Master Bonifacio: this is Master Giovan Bernardo. That's the truth and there's no getting away from it.

Giovan Bernardo. And to confirm it—see if that beard is his own.

Bonifacio. I admit it's a false one, but I got it to help me in a certain matter between myself and my wife.

Corcovizzo. Here is the beard of this honest man, in my hands!

Sanguino. Tell me, honest man, is this beard yours?

Barra. It must be his—he paid for it.

Sanguino. Now we know that he is the impostor, take him and his wife to prison. And as for you, Master Giovan Bernardo, we command you, in the name of the Central Magistrates' Court, to appear before the judge in ordinary tomorrow morning at nine o'clock precisely, under penalty of one hundred and fifty guineas, to give your evidence in this case.

Giovan Bernardo. I will be there, Captain Palma; I notify you that no person injured by this man should place a charge against *me*, and that I charge him for all the offenses he may have committed in this disguise.

Sanguino. Justice will be done.

Carubina. And must I be abused and sent to prison just for catching out this wretched husband of mine?

Giovan Bernardo. Captain, I will answer for this woman, and go bail for her. Although she is his wife, I know her to be of unblemished reputation. She had nothing to do with this deception.

Sanguino. You must be content with our releasing you. Was she not with her husband?

Giovan Bernardo. Yes.

Sanguino. Then she shall stay with him.

Carubina. But I was not his accomplice. I found him in shameful circumstances and was reproaching him as we came out of Vittoria's house together. Everyone there can bear witness that I'm speaking the truth. Can't we ask Vittoria and the others in her house?

Giovan Bernardo. I assure you, sir, that there is no fault on this lady's side, and if need arise, I bind myself to answer for her in every way. I am content that this man alone should go to prison: that, indeed, I insist on. But I make no charge against Madam Carubina, and I beg you again to let her go free.

Sanguino. It seems clear enough that she has nothing to do with it. She stands under your surety, then. And—what's your name?

Carubina. Carubina, your Honor.

Sanguino. —we command you, Madam Carubina, in the name of the Central Magistrates' Court, to appear before the judge in ordinary tomorrow morning at nine o'clock precisely, under penalty of sixty guineas, to give your evidence in this case.

Carubina. I will do my duty and be there without fail.

Bonifacio. I tell you, Master Giovan Bernardo, that I have not harmed you in the way you think.

Giovan Bernardo. Well, we'll see.

Sanguino. Off, then; on we go—no more discussion. Don't try to get away. We'll lock him up with the schoolmaster and take them both into court together.

Bonifacio. Be so good as to tie me up. Do this one more favor for my wife and Master Giovan Bernardo.

Sanguino. Do it, so he won't escape. So, good night.

Giovan Bernardo. Good night and good fortune, Captain and gentlemen all.

Sanguino, Barra, Marca, *and* Corcovizzo *take* Bonifacio *within.*

Scene XI

Giovan Bernardo. You see, my own, what a vile wrong this wretched fool has done your divine beauty. Doesn't it seem fair that he should be paid in the same coin?

Carubina. If he has done something he shouldn't, it doesn't follow that I should.

Giovan Bernardo. You are not doing wrong, my love, when you do what anyone else of any sense and feeling would do. Let me tell you that these men who have taken him off are not officers of the watch, but a set of

good fellows I know, and they will deal with him just
as we please. For the time being he is out of the way,
and among the other things they have in store for him
before taking him to prison is an interview with a certain Scaramuré, who will pretend to settle the matter
out of court for him, provided that he apologizes to us,
as the offended parties, and compensates the others, not
because they are really concerned about that, but to
make it look convincing. So you have nothing to lose.

Carubina.   Now I see your cunning has been behind the
whole plot. I'm beginning to understand a lot that has
happened.

Giovan Bernardo.   To serve you, my love, I would throw
myself over a thousand precipices. And now my fortune and good luck—and please the gods may you confirm it—have brought me so close to you, I beg, by the
devotion I feel and have always felt, that you will have
pity on a heart that has been so deeply wounded by
your divine eyes. I love you; I adore you. If heaven
had only granted you to me instead of this ungrateful
and stupid man who doesn't appreciate the miracle of
your beauty, my breast would never have held a spark
of love for anyone but you, who live there now.

Carubina.   Heaven, what is this? What have I fallen to?

Giovan Bernardo.   Sweet goddess, if you have ever felt
the flame of love—and what noble, generous, and affectionate heart has not?—don't take what I say amiss;
don't believe, don't entertain the thought for a single
moment, that it's because I don't value your honor—I
would shed my blood a thousand times for it—that I
ask you this: to quench the passion that consumes me
and which I cannot believe will lessen even with death.

Carubina.   Alas, Master Giovan Bernardo, my heart is
only too tender. I am not surprised by what you say—
all the world knows how much a lover's word is to be
trusted. And I would like to make you happy, but how
can I without losing my honor?

Giovan Bernardo.   Life of my life, you know what con-
stitutes honor and dishonor, I am sure. Honor is only
reputation, what people think of one. As long as they
think you honorable, you are. Honor is the good opinion other people have of us; while that continues, so
does our honor. It is not what we are or what we do
that makes us honored or dishonored, but just what
people think of us, how we stand in their eyes.

Carubina.   That may be true of mortals, but what do you

say of the angels and the saints, who see and judge everything?

Giovan Bernardo. They don't want to be seen more than they let us see them; they don't want to be feared more than they are feared just by existing; they don't want to be bothered into taking more notice of us than they want.

Carubina. I don't know what to say to that. I don't know whether I agree or not. But I feel there is something impious about it.

Giovan Bernardo. Let us stop this debate, then, hope of my life. Don't let heaven have made you lovely in vain, for though it has been lavish of beauty and grace, it has been mean as well, in not marrying you to a man who could appreciate them, and cruel to me, for making me distracted by them and die a thousand deaths each day. You should mind more about keeping me alive, my love, than about lossing some fragment of your honor. I will gladly kill myself—if grief doesn't do it for me—should cruel fortune deny me what is dearer to me than life, and which I have almost within my grasp. Oh, life of this distracted soul, your honor won't suffer if you deign to save my life, but it will, if I die because of your cruelty.

Carubina. Oh, let us go somewhere else if we are to talk like this.

Giovan Bernardo. And people are coming, Come, then, my beloved.

They go.

Scene XII

Enter Consalvo *and* Bartolomeo, *tied together, their hands behind their backs.*

Consalvo. Go on, curse you, cuckoldy fool, till we find someone who can cut us free.

Bartolomeo. Pox on you, eunuch, father of idiots! You've made me fall down.

Consalvo. Ouch! my leg!

Bartolomeo. I wish you'd broken your neck. There— now we're both down! Go on, get up!

Consalvo. We'll have to get up together.

Bartolomeo. Do what you like, jackass. I intend to spend the rest of the night here.

Consalvo. Up! Come on. It's now or never.

Bartolomeo. Oh, now you're lying down, go to sleep. See what I've suffered and still am suffering for you, you coward.

Consalvo. And will suffer again.

Bartolomeo. Double-dyed villain—grrh!

Consalvo. Ow! So you bite, do you? By Saint Cuccufatto I swear that if you take to biting, I'll rip the nose off your face or tear off an ear!

Scene XIII

Enter Scaramuré.

Scaramuré. Whoever are these fighting on the ground?

Consalvo. Get up, you swine! We'll be all the more of a joke if we're found like this.

Bartolomeo. You're a fine one to be afraid of being a joke! You can't see past the mote in your own eye, can you?

Consalvo. If I had my hands free, I'd make you squeal for help once and for all. Will you get up?

Bartolomeo. I told you; I'm going to spend the rest of the night here.

Scaramuré (*laughing*). They're tied together with their hands behind them, and one wants to get up and the other doesn't. One of them sounds like Master Bartolomeo, but it can't be: they're just a couple of roughs. Hey, you drunks, what are you doing?

Consalvo. Oh, sir, kind sir; I beg you come and cut us free. Master Scaramuré, is it you?

Bartolomeo. Leave us as we are—that's all I ask.

Scaramuré. Why, Master Bartolomeo, and Master Consalvo—I'd no idea it was you! Whatever has happened? Two sensible men in this pickle? What brought you to this pass? Have you lost your senses?

Bartolomeo. It's more serious than that—I'm ruined. Don't let us loose. I implore you.

Scaramuré. Leave it to me: let me decide. How did all this happen?

Consalvo. I had words with him and then we came to blows. The noise brought a gang of ruffians dressed as the watch, and they bound us and pretended to take us to prison. When we got to Maiella, they tied us up

like this, tail to tail. First they took our purses and
went away, then they thought better of it and two of
them came back and took our cloaks and hats and slit
the very clothes off our backs. Then we got up and
wandered about until I saw a man and a woman here.
I've been trying to hurry in order to reach them or
call out to them, dragging along this noble specimen——

Bartolomeo.   And you're a fine brute, a prize ox.

Scaramuré.   You shouldn't insult him like this.

Consalvo.   —dragging him along, till he fell like an over-
loaded ass and pulled me down with him; and now, out
of pure spite, he won't get up.

Scaramuré (*cuts them loose*).   Well, get up now; you're
free. Too much anger makes a man mad past reason.
I don't want to hear any more because it's late. Keep
away from one another: the first that tries anything
will have two of us to reckon with. Master Consalvo,
go that way, and Master Bartolomeo, you go that way.

Bartolomeo.   For tonight, well and good. Tomorrow I'll
have another word with this fine fellow.

Consalvo.   Adieu—for a hundred years. Good night,
Master Scaramuré.

Scaramuré.   Good night.

Bartolomeo.   Good night. O misery! I'm sure I'll be
happier when I'm dead and gone and disasters can't
touch me anymore!

Bartolomeo *and* Consalvo *go, separately.*

Scene XIV

Scaramuré.   That devil Sanguino gets about like a bad
coin, and he brought it off so well that Captain Palma
could hardly have acted himself as well as he did. Just
see how he treated those poor brutes! Now while Giovan Bernardo is dealing with him in his own way, I
shall work it so that this fine fellow not only has nothing to complain of, but will feel under a positive obligation to me. Here is the door of the academy of knaves.
(*Knocks.*)

Scene XV

Corcovizzo (*within*).   Who is it? Who's there?

Scaramuré.   Scaramuré, at your service.

Corcovizzo.   Scaramuré? What sort of a gypsy's name is that? What do you want? Who are you?

Scaramuré.   I want a word with Captain Palma.

Corcovizzo.   He's busy. Wait a bit: I'll ask if he wants to see you.

Scaramuré.   Ha! They really know their business, this crew. Knavery has its rules and regulations like every other art.

Sanguino (*within*).   Hey, there. Who is it?

Scaramuré.   A friend.

Sanguino.   Friend or relation, or whoever you are, come to the courthouse tomorrow.

Scaramuré.   No, listen to me: I have to speak to you tonight.

Sanguino.   Who are you?

Scaramuré.   Scaramuré.

Sanguino.   Never heard of you. What is it you want?

Scaramuré.   I want to consult you about an important matter.

Sanguino.   Then you'll have to wait. In an hour's time I shall be taking some prisoners to the courthouse and you can talk to me on the way.

Scaramuré.   I entreat you, come down if you possibly can. It's important and you'll find it to your advantage.

Sanguino.   Oh, this is too much. Wait till I come down.

Scaramuré.   Ha, the others may be students or bachelors, this one is doctor and professor, I think—Ah, there is Master Bonifacio at the window.

Bonifacio (*within*).   Master Scaramuré, can you see me? You know what has happened?

Scaramuré.   Quiet, quiet: that is why I have come.

Sanguino.   Get away from that window, curse you, presumptuous swine! Who said you could talk out of the window?

Bonifacio.   Captain, sir, pardon me, your Honor. I'll come away.

Scene XVI

Sanguino *comes out.*

Scaramuré (*laughs*). What a set of devils you are! I've just set Bartolomeo and Consalvo free. They couldn't get off the ground and were bitting and cursing each other with fury.

Sanguino (*laughs*). And if you'd seen what we've done with Master Bonifacio and the pedant, you'd have another laugh.

Scaramuré. Your comedy was fine, but as far as these men are concerned, the tragedy is becoming tiresome.

Sanguino. Very well, then. We'll get rid of the pedant when we've relieved him of any cash he's still got about him. You talk to Bonifacio and get everything settled.

Scaramuré. I'll have a word with him. I'll make him ask me to beg Giovan Bernardo to forgive him; he'll have to ask both him and Carubina for pardon. Then together we will beg you to set him free. I think he'll do all this rather than be taken to prison.

Sanguino. Right, we'll lose no time about it. I will have him brought down in chains and arrange a secret conversation with you.

He goes in.

Scaramuré. I'll wait here.

Scene XVII

Enter Sanguino, Barra, *and* Marca *with* Bonifacio.

Sanguino. You there, Coppino, keep a sharp eye on him in case he tries to get away.

Barra. No fear of that, sir.

Sanguino. And Barrelbellio, you guard the other way.

Marca. Right.

Sanguino. Give him room so he can talk comfortably to this citizen. And you, master—I can't remember your name—

Scaramuré. Scaramuré, your Honor.

Sanguino. —you, Master Scaramuré, you can talk to him privately over here.

Scaramuré. A thousand thanks, your Honor.

Sanguino. One thank at a time is all I need.

Sanguino, Barra, *and* Marca *stand back.*

Scaramuré. Master Bonifacio, come over here.

Bonifacio. Boohoo! Oh, dear, oh, dear, what a terrible day. You see the fruits of my love and your advice, Master Scaramuré.

Scaramuré. Oh, cursed be—I'm trying to think of the name of one of the biggest saints in Paradise.

Bonifacio. Who? Saint Christopher? Boohoo!

Scaramuré. I don't mean the tallest, the stoutest, but one of the most important ones. But the litany I ran off as soon as I heard what had happened will suffice; instead of saying *ora pro nobis* I cursed the lot—except for Saint Leonard, whose aid we need at the moment—and if I have to serve seven years in Purgatory for every sin, the ones I've committed in just the last two hours will keep the Day of Judgment waiting more than ten thousand years.

Bonifacio. It's wrong to blaspheme.

Scaramuré. What can you expect, what with the injury and the scandal you have suffered and it seeming to be my fault, and the fact that as things are going it looks as though we shall both be ruined?

Bonifacio. How do you know?

Scaramuré. Just as Apollonius, Merlin, and Malagigi knew of things that happened afar off.

Bonifacio. I see. Please heaven that you can set me free from these men with the same art.

Scaramuré. Leave it to me; this is why I have come. First tell me more about yourself. Don't you see that it is by my art that these men have been constrained to let me speak to you in secret like this, while they only watch you from a distance? You realize that these men would not grant so much even to their friends?

Bonifacio. I was surprised, it's true.

Scaramuré. I employed humility, entreaty, spells, and a guinea. But before we go on with that, tell me what happened to you.

Bonifacio. What do you want me to tell you? This is what your spells and conjurations have reduced me to! This is what I've been brought to by my love for that whore and by the wickedness of that bawd Lucia, who made me believe more lies than the patriarch of the consistory of devils could have done. I'd give twenty-five guineas to have the bawd's mark branded on her.

Scaramuré. But suppose the fault were not hers, nor Mistress Vittoria's, nor mine—I believe you think even worse of me than of the others, though you don't say so—suppose the fault was your own?

Bonifacio. I should like to see you convince me of that.

Scaramuré. Are you sure that those hairs I asked for to put on the image's head were really Vittoria's?

Bonifacio. I'm sure the pox can eat her for ruining me! The hairs were my wife's—and a thousand plagues on those who betrothed us, and on whoever told me she'd agreed, and on the unfrocked priest who married us! I took them from her comb on Saturday evening, without her seeing me.

Scaramuré. There: now I understand what has happened.

Bonifacio. Understand from whom?

Scaramuré. From the one who knows, and has told me. Did I ask for your wife's hair? Did I?

Bonifacio. No, you asked for a woman's hair.

Scaramuré. I asked, in the devil's name, for *the* woman's hair, not any woman's hair. Were we designing dolls for children?

Bonifacio. What difference is there between *a* woman's hair and *the* woman's hair?

Scaramuré. It's a difference a child would understand with its first moment of reason. Weren't we setting out to make the image in her name?

Bonifacio. Really, I must have a weaker head than you. You think other people can understand a thing just because you do. Well it isn't always like that.

Scaramuré. This, then, was the damnable cause of the spell going astray. The wax was chosen, and enchanted, in Vittoria's name, and the image was shaped in her name, but the hairs belonged to your wife—hence this muddling together of your wife and Vittoria: your wife magically drawn to her house while Vittoria magically fell in love; your wife in Vittoria's clothes, Vittoria without hers; your wife in Vittoria's place, in Vittoria's house, in Vittoria's bed, in Vittoria's dress; Vittoria burning and yearning with passion and, in your imagination, making love to you. And all of them, Vittoria, Lucia, and your wife, astonished at what was happening. Lucia remembers taking Vittoria's clothes to your wife but not how she did it, and she can't say what moved her to. Vittoria was astonished to find you, dressed as Master Giovan Bernardo, and your wife, dressed as her, together in her bed, and astonished at the way all the doors flew open for you and your wife when Lucia led you in, as though walking in her sleep, and astonished that she and all her household were frozen in their places and could not move until your lovemaking had come to an end. You'll find that your wife still can't explain how she came to be dressed like that and led up to that room.

Bonifacio. This is all too complicated for me.

Scaramuré. You'll understand what caused this confusion more clearly when we have left it all behind us.

Bonifacio. Well, I'm amazed. And there is still one thing: why, when my wife was brought to Vittoria's house by the part of the spell that affected her and not Vittoria, did she treat me worse than a dog?

Scaramuré. But I've explained that your wife was only led to the room because of the hairs; she could not have *loved* you, because the wax was not chosen, shaped, pricked, and heated in her name.

Bonifacio. Ah, now I see it all. I wasn't altogether clear at first.

Scaramuré. That's that, then, and we've spent too much time clearing it up. Now let us find something to give these men to let you go, so they can pretend you fled or think up some other excuse. Then we can easily solve the rest of your problems.

Bonifacio. I haven't more than eight guineas left on me. I'll offer them those; surely they won't want more?

Scaramuré. You needn't think you'll get out of their clutches for that.

Bonifacio. I can offer my cloak and my rings. I think you could get them to take less; even for one guinea they'd deny Christ and His mother and His grandmother into the bargain.

Scaramuré. You don't know Captain Palma.

Scene XVIIī

Sanguino, Barra, *and* Marca *come forward.*

Sanguino. I'd be glad to know when your little talk is over: do we have to wait here the whole night?

Scaramuré. I hope your Honor will forgive us if we have given too much trouble by keeping you so long. As you've already been so good to us, we beg you to listen to just one more word.

Sanguino. That's enough, that's enough, and now to prison. Tomorrow you can talk as long as you like. Come along, come along, Coppino. Barrelbellio, come along.

Bonifacio. Oh, no! Help me God! Glorious Saint Leonard!

Scaramuré. Have mercy on him, Captain, for the love of God.

Bonifacio. I am praying to you with crossed arms.

Sanguino. Well, I've already stood so much, I suppose I can put up with a little more.

Scaramuré. Ah, sir, what we mean is that your Honor would get no profit from the ruin of this poor man, but you would if you made both him and me your everlasting servants and slaves by accepting some small present and allowing him to go free.

Sanguino. I had a very good idea that that was what you'd come for, to try and suborn justice. I'm amazed at your daring, you unprincipled man, hoping to make me release such an important prisoner as he may turn out to be. I said as much to my men. I've given you this much rope, and listened to what you had to say, just to be able to punish you for your crime and make an example of you to others. And to make sure of it, you'll go to prison with him, chained wrist to wrist. Here, Coppino.

Bartolomeo. Yes, sir?

Sanguino. Bring manacles for this other fine fellow.

Scaramuré. I beseech you, Captain Palma, listen to me first.

Bonifacio. Oh, sir. I beseech you by the love of God, by all the angelic choirs, by the immaculate Virgin, by all the courts of heaven.

Sanguino. Get up, up! I don't want to be adored; I'm not the Grand Turk, or the King of Spain.

Bonifacio. Oh, have mercy on me and do not be angry. Remember we are all sinners and have need of the mercy of God, who promises to forgive our sins as we forgive them that trespass against us.

Sanguino (*aside*). This rogue could have been a preacher if he'd set his mind to it—Crimes must be punished. What about that?

Bonifacio. If all crimes were punished, what place would there be for mercy?

Sanguino. Off, curse you. I've more to do than stand about arguing.

Scaramuré. Be quiet, Master Bonifacio; leave it to me. Captain Palma, God would never have allowed me to think of doing this if it were to the prejudice of justice

or your good name, which in matters of the law is
most sincerely honored throughout Naples.

Sanguino.   Leave off flattering me. It is not I who deal in
mercy or severity, justice or injustice, but my superiors.
My office is only to take malefactors or suspected
malefactors to prison. And that duty I can't exceed.

Bonifacio.   Oh, oh! Poor me!

Scaramuré   If your Honor would listen, I think you
would grant my petition.

Sanguino.   I'm not one who can be trifled with and
angered with impunity. So your arguments had better
be as good as you say; otherwise you don't sleep in
your bed tonight.

Bonifacio.   O help me, Christ!

Scaramuré.   Your Honor knows that in Italy it is not as
in certain countries to the north where they make pros-
titution a crime, either because of the cold there, or
too much religious zeal, or because of the sordid ava-
rice of the officers of justice. Here in Naples, for instance, or in Rome or Venice, founts and mirrors of
every sort of nobility as they are to the whole world,
not only are whores, or courtesans, as we say, permitted——

Sanguino.   He seems to praise these three cities for being
brothels and swarming with punks: a paradox, and not
the least of them.

Scaramuré.   Listen, I beg you. Not only are they toler-
ated by the civil and municipal law, but brothels are
founded, just like convents.

Sanguino (*laughs*).   Oh, very fine! He'd like them to be
made one of the four hundred major or four minor
orders, and of course they will appoint an abbess!
(*Laughs*).

Scaramuré.   But listen to me. Here in Naples we have
the Piazzetta, the Fundaco del Cetrangolo, the Borgo
di Santo Antonio, and the street near Santa Maria del
Carmine. In Rome, because the whores were scattered
all over the city, in 1569 His Holiness ordered them all
to be brought together on pain of being whipped, and
gave them a street to themselves which was locked off
at night—which he did, not to take his part of the tax
they had to pay, but so that they could be set apart
from decent women and not contaminate them. I say
nothing of Venice, where by the magnanimity and
liberality of the most illustrious Republic—think what
you like of certain well-known Mr. Head-in-the-airs

who have themselves castrated for tuppence to improve
their voices—whores are exempted from all penalties;
they are even better off than ordinary citizens, though
there are so many—for the greater and finer the city
the more there are—that if they did pay a small tax,
there would be enough to fill a second treasury almost
as full as the first. There is no doubt that if the Senate
wished to stoop to doing as others do, it could make the
city a good deal richer than it is, but because the text
says "by the sweat of your brow" and not "by the
sweat of—" well, it has refrained from doing it. What
is more, their courtesans are highly respected, as you
can see from the recent law that prevents, under heavy
penalty, any person, base or noble, whatever his condition, from daring to reproach or insult them. And that
has never been done for any other sort of women.

Sanguino (aside). Ah, I've not heard a better sophist
than he!—You take up too much of my time; I think
you are having a game with me and this poor fellow,
who is waiting for the outcome of your oration, or
tale, or history, whatever the devil it is. But I'll hear a
little more if that brings you to the end.

Bonifacio. Please, please speak about my affair. What
has that to do with Venice, Rome, or Naples?

Scaramuré. I conclude that the true greatness of Italy
resides in these three cities, for among all the others,
even the greatest is far behind the least of these.

Bonifacio. Oh, oh, dear! I've got to go to the bathroom.

Sanguino. Hold on, hold on, man: let's see where he
gets to in the end.

Scaramuré. So we see that prostitutes in Naples, Venice,
and Rome, *ideste* in all Italy, are allowed, nay, encouraged, to have their own statutes, laws, taxes, and
other privileges——

Sanguino. And what privileges!

Scaramuré. —and so, in consequence, those who go to
prostitutes should not be hounded or punished by the
law——

Sanguino. Now I see what he's getting at.

Bonifacio. And I. We are getting to the point, praise and
glory to our Lady of Loreto.

Scaramuré. —and not only that; the law should assid-
uously refrain from troubling, persecuting, or arrest-
ing those who frequent ladies of honor, for our rulers
think it to be a barbarous thing to take the lust that a
man of reputation and standing might have in his

heart and brand it on his forehead. So be the fact as
notorious as you will, it is not done to act on it unless
the party concerned—who will invariably come from
the dregs of society—is so shameless as to insist. As to
the party visited, the law should beware of placing
its mark on her, for the ill fame that comes to the
whoremonger is far less damaging than the harm he
does by exposing the woman to the derision of the
world in general. She suffers more by the law's inter-
ference than does the offender himself, for everyone
knows that a lawsuit always makes the roving husband
more glamorous and admired. Every man of sense,
then, recognizes that this ambivalence in the law is a
healthy one; because a rake and a lecher—if one can
use words like "rake" and "lecher" about someone
whose reputation remains intact—for fear of notoriety
or, at least, because he is quite easy about sins that
aren't known about—if indeed they can then be called
sins—avoids calling on the law's revenge that would
have to follow if the offense were widely known. So
the custom in Italy and other civilized countries where
lechery is not despised not only tolerates and veils the
excesses that might trouble our——
Sanguino. Your conclusion, and quick about it.
Bonifacio. Help! I can't last much longer! I'm in
agony.
Scaramuré. In conclusion, I point out to your Honor
that Master Bonifacio's intemperance was caused by a
woman, who, be she respectable or a whore, should
not be the cause whereby a man of position and breed-
ing——
Bonifacio. Yes, I'm a gentleman and live in San Paulo.
Scaramuré. —should be exposed as a jailbird, *etcetera,*
which could lead others to be gravely compromised
into the bargain. I think I have said enough to apprise
your Honor, as a man of the world, how the matter
stands.
Sanguino. If a woman's at the bottom of this, I am certainly sorry that he should have fallen into my hands;
before God and man I protest that it's no intention of
mine to compromise the honor of anyone living. But
you ought to know, and he and my men can bear witness, that I cannot finish the matter here. He has been
charged to me by a certain Master Giovan Bernardo,
a painter, whom he impersonated in a false beard, and
still does with the cloak he's wearing. The beard is

here—one of my men has it—and if you want to see
how it suits him, you can tomorrow morning at nine
in the courthouse, and you'll have a good laugh when
the two beards confront one another.

Bonifacio. Oh, help me, help me! I beg you, for the love
of God.

Sanguino. That gentleman appealed to the law against
the offenses that this man committed, or might have
committed, while disguised as himself, which could
lead the aggrieved party to sue him for the aforesaid
offenses.

Bonifacio. There is no need, sir, to worry about that.

Sanguino. The worry, my good sir, is not mine. So you
can see, as could anyone, that I don't hold and take
him to court for my own pleasure but because I am
responsible for him. The other party has taken violently
against him, and is ready to present his charges tomorrow morning. Besides that, his wife feels strongly,
too, and Master Giovan Bernardo and the lady could
give me a very difficult time.

Bonifacio. There's no need to worry about her.

Sanguino. But it is her I worry about most. Jealousy
drives women to damage the lives and reputations of
their husbands. Well, then, sirs, what do you think I
can do for you? I can be sorry for him, but help him—
no, I can't.

Scaramuré. Captain, your Honor speaks like an angel.

Bonifacio. Like an evangelist, like a saint: one can't say
more.

Sanguino. Off we go, then. Barrelbellio, bring the *magister* down and we'll be off.

Scaramuré. Captain, I have something more to say.

Sanguino. What is it?

Scaramuré. I am sure I shall find a way—If you would
give us a quarter of an hour's grace—to reconcile Master Giovan Bernardo with Master Bonifacio.

Bonifacio. Would to God it could happen!

Sanguino. You're joking. That's impossible.

Scaramuré. But there's no other way. When he sees how
things stand, I'm sure he'll *etcetera*. He knows me so
well that even if he is asleep, I will get him up and
bring him here and try to reconcile them. But it will be
up to you, Master Bonifacio, to beg pardon and convince him by the way you do it that you are sincere,
for it's not surprising that he feels you've seriously
compromised him.

Bonifacio.　I will. I'll offer to kiss his feet and become his friend and supporter for life if he forgives this slip of mine and doesn't expose me to public shame. And not only his (*weeps*), but yours, sir Captain, your Honor, uh, uh!

Sanguino.　Get up! Wait till I'm pope before you kiss my feet.

Bonifacio.　I would be obliged if your Honor would help me by allowing a little time to bring this reconciliation about. And I beg you, Master Scaramuré, by the entrails of my heart and soul, do your best toward it; my life will be at your service forever.

Scaramuré.　I have great hopes of at least finding a way of bringing him here. When he arrives, we must do our best with your apologies and the intercession of the captain—if he is prepared to help—and my arguments, to stop the affair going any further. And you must not be ungrateful for the captain's generosity, either.

Sanguino.　For myself, I don't care about that. Just something for my men here, if only to shut their mouths. But I want him to go further than this. I want him to be reconciled to his wife, and ask for her forgiveness as well. And when I see both of them happy and content, then I shall step aside; even I can't see this poor Master Bonifacio without pitying him.

Bonifacio.　Good sir, here I am, body and soul at your service. For your men, I mean these officers, here are my rings; all I have left is my purse and this accursed cloak—which I'm only too glad to be rid of.

Sanguino.　Enough, enough; but you pay the bill without reckoning with the landlord, as the saying is. This will do you no good unless your wife and Master Giovan Bernardo are satisfied, too.

Bonifacio.　I hope they will be. Please go, Master Scaramuré.

Scaramuré.　I will bring him here; I'll think of some excuse. Your wife, I'm sure, is too concerned for her reputation to keep away.

Sanguino.　Be quick about it if you expect us to wait for you.

Scaramuré.　They don't live far apart. I'll soon be back.

Sanguino.　Let's have their "yes" or their "no" quickly, mind; don't keep me kicking my heels here for nothing.

Scaramuré.　Your Honor need have no worry.

Bonifacio.　Glorious Saint Leonard—help me!

Sanguino.　Come along, we'll go back and wait inside.

Sanguino, Barra, Marca, *and* Bonifacio *go in.* Scaramuré
goes.

Scene XIX

Enter Giovan Bernardo *and* Ascanio.

Giovan Bernardo.   And so, my son, to come back to the
point, it's commonly supposed that matters are so arranged that nature lacks no essential and admits few
superfluities. Oysters have no feet, yet in whatever part
of the sea you find them, they have all they require to
sustain them, for they live on water alone and on the
heat of the sun that strikes down to the seabed. Take
the mole; he has no eyes, for he lives entirely under the
earth; his life depends on his environment, and he
cannot change it. Where a faculty is not needed, the
tools are not provided.

Ascanio.   That's too true. I've heard that a certain critic
of Jove's action called Momus—and such critics are
essential; first, so that princes and judges watch their
step and aren't just flattered by knaves and sycophants;
secondly, so that they weigh the consequences of their
actions; and thirdly, because goodness and virtue, when
they are challenged, appear brighter, clearer, and more
visible, and are strengthened and made more confident
—this critic, then, of Jove——

Giovan Bernardo.   He is not included among the major
or nobler gods; those whose arms are abnormally short
usually have abnormally long tongues.

Ascanio.   —this critic of Jove, once upon a time dis-
puting with Mercury—who was appointed interpreter
and counsel to the gods—argued with him in this
manner: "O Mercury, sophist of sophists, false council-
lor and bravo of the All-Thunderer: as it is well, according to changes and hazards of the weather to go
faster or slower, to slacken or hoist or lower sail, how
does it come about that this mast has no halyards? Or
to put it more familiarly, why has the cunt—speaking
with all possible respect—no buttons?" To which Mercury replied, "Because the prick—no offense intended
—has no fingers."

Giovan Bernardo (*laughs*).   And what did the other gods
say to that?

Ascanio.   The chaste Diana and the modest Minerva
turned their backs and walked away, and one of the

disputants said, "To a brothel with you!" He would have said, "To the devil with you!" but that honest fellow had not yet been invented. So in confirmation of what you say, whenever this question was raised, or is raised now, or will be raised—as it was then, is now, and ever shall be—no mistakes can ever be found in the provisions of nature and the mind save in appearance only.

Giovan Bernardo. You are right. All the mistakes that happen are due to the traitress Fortune: it's she, for instance, who has favored your master, Malefacio, at my expense. She gives honor where it's not deserved, a good harvest where no seed has been sown, a fine orchard where no tree has been planted, she gives riches to one who doesn't know how to spend it, many children to those who can't rear them, dry toast to the toothless. What then? Should I pardon the poor lady because she is blind, and in trying to distribute her riches has to feel her way—and so usually bumps into fools, madmen, and knaves, of which the world is full? It's mere chance if she meets one of the few who are deserving, rarer still if she meets one of the still fewer who are more deserving, rarest of all, a matter for wonder, if in all her stumbling about she stumbles on one of the most deserving, the fewest of all. So if it is not her fault, it's the fault of him who created her. Jove denies having done it, but whether she was created or not, if she is not to blame, then nobody is.

Ascanio. And I hold, it is unfair and useless to blame Fortune or anything else. It has even been said that she is not only a help but a necessity, for a virtue is inert and useless unless it is practiced, and whoever has a chance of seeking and finding her shouldn't simply sit about and wait for her. The gods intend that our initiative should drive out bad luck and enable us to seize what we want, as in your own case. What is more, possessions and worthiness don't go hand in hand: they have to seek each other out and learn to live together. The man who is given possessions doesn't deserve them, and the deserving man isn't given them.

Giovan Bernardo. My boy, you speak well, and your sentiments are in advance of your years! What you say is true, as I know from my own case at the moment. Whatever good I have come to tonight wasn't given me by nature or the gods; Fortune was working against me, but judgment showed me my opportunity, dili-

gence enabled me to take it by the forelock, and per-
severance to hold on to it. The problem is to grasp the
forelock in time; after that, you can be sure of possess-
ing the rest of the body. From now on, as far as my
lady Carubina and I are concerned, there will be less
need of all that plotting and planning, speechifying,
argument, and persuasion.

Ascanio.   True enough, for one kiss is enough for you
to learn one another's language. Eyes see, tongues talk,
hearts understand. Sometimes what is imparted in a
moment remains forever. One Good Friday, Scipione
Savalino confessed all his sins to don Paulino, the
curate of Santa Primma, which is in a village near
Nola, and because he was on good terms with him he
had no great difficulty in getting absolution for the lot,
great and small together. And this occasion was good
for all others, for in the following years, without going
into details, Scipione would say to don Paulino,
"Father, you remember the sins of a year ago today?"
and don Paulino would reply, "My son, you know the
absolution of a year ago today; *vadde in pacio et non
amplio peccare.*"

Giovan Bernardo (*laughs*).   We've spent too much time
on this. You see that door?

Ascanio.   Yes, sir.

Giovan Bernardo.   That is where they are. We won't
knock until I've had the word from Master Scaramuré.
He must have everything arranged by now and be
looking for me. You go and get Madam Carubina to
come here quickly.

Ascanio.   Very well. Shall we find you here?

Giovan Bernardo.   Yes, it won't take me very long to
find Master Scaramuré.

Ascanio goes.

Scene XX

Giovan Bernardo.   There is an epitaph on the tomb of
Giacopo Tansillo the world-weary which goes like
this:

> Who fails one button to undo
> Will never get to number two;
> My fate I only guessed the day
> That Giacopone passed away.

The first button Bonifacio undid was when he fell in
love with Vittoria, the second when he fell for the
idea that Scaramuré could use magic to unchain Satan,
make women fly through the air whenever he wanted,
and other things against the course of nature. From
here all the other accidents followed one after the
other as each generation springs from the last. Nothing
remains now but to sew the breeches to the jacket, and
this can be done by getting him to apologize and repent
for the harm he's done to us poor innocents.

Scene XXI

Enter Ascanio, Scaramuré, *and* Carubina.

Giovan Bernardo.   Ah, here you are.
Ascanio.   They were on their way when I met them.
Scaramuré.   We are all here to free this poor soul from
    Purgatory.
Carubina.   I wish God would release him so finally that
    I shouldn't have to see him again.
Ascanio.   If that's what you want, it shouldn't be diffi-
    cult.
Scaramuré.   When I found you weren't at home, I went
    to Madam Vittoria, thinking you would be there. Then
    I sent Lucia to find you and bring you here.
Giovan Bernardo.   We don't need anyone else. You,
    Madam Carubina, and Ascanio, pretend to have come
    on your own initiative; and let Master Scaramuré and
    me begin by negotiating with Sanguino and the others;
    you can go and hide over there, around the corner.
Carubina.   A good idea. Come, Ascanio.
Ascanio.   Over here, madam, then we can listen and
    decide the best moment to join them.
Carubina.   Very well.

Carubina *and* Ascanio *hide.*

Scene XXII

Scaramuré.   We'll knock.
Corcovizzo (*within*).   Who's there?
Scaramuré.   Friends. Tell the captain we're here.
Corcovizzo.   Wait a moment, my friend.

Scaramuré. That was Corcovizzo; they're calling him
    Cappino or some devil's name like that. They call him
    or one of the others Barrelbellio.

Giovan Bernardo. Ah, so that the pedant and Master
    Bonifacio won't recognize them. Are they all wearing
    beards?

Scaramuré. All of them—it's like a real comedy. The
    pedant hasn't one, but Master Bonifacio has, if he
    decides to wear it. They know each other, but they
    don't know that the others are in disguise.

Ascanio. We only need Madam Carubina to wear her
    mask—

Sanguino (within). Are you there? Haven't you brought
    his wife? I told you there was nothing doing without
    her.

Scaramuré. She is coming now; she will be here in a
    moment, sir.

Sanguino. Wait while we bring him down.

Scaramuré. Keep out of sight for a while.

Giovan Bernardo. Let me handle my own affair.

Enter Sanguino.

Sanguino. Well met, Master Giovan Bernardo.

Giovan Bernardo. Your Honor, very well met. As soon
    as I heard from Master Scaramuré that you wanted me,
    I got out of bed and came posthaste, thinking you had
    discovered something this criminal had committed in
    my name.

Sanguino. Here is the malefactor, the Malefacio. But
    by the devil's name it wasn't I who sent for you but
    this Master Scaramuré, who begged and besought me
    to delay taking him to prison and said you would
    agree because he can throw some light on this disguise
    business. For your sake, and moved as I was by his
    pleading, and the tears and contrition of this miserable
    sinner as well, I've held my hand; but it was not I who
    sent for you.

Bonifacio. Mercy, for the love of God!

Giovan Bernardo. Master Scaramuré, didn't you fetch
    me on the captain's behalf, telling me I was needed for
    some important development in the case, and so ur-
    gently that my very hair stood on end? Why this
    treachery? Is this friendship? Is this how you value my
    friendship? You have tried, and it seems to me are still
    trying, to damage me by supporting this vile wretch.

Captain, I extend my charge to him; he has abused my name and my intentions and your name and authority in persuading me to come here and disturb you all.

Bonifacio.   Mercy, for the love of God and Our Lady!

Sanguino.   Let's take it gently, now. Let's see if this can't be smoothed over. Let's see if it's as bad as it seems. Now you're here, be careful what you do, don't let anger get the better of you.

Giovan Bernardo.   The matter can never be smoothed over, as far as I am concerned. Even when justice has run its course, there will still be an issue between this man and me.

Scaramuré.   My dear Master Giovan Bernardo, what I've done, what I do, is in no way intended to threaten your honor. If crimes had been committed during the night in your name, we would all bear witness here against Master Bonifacio, but as nothing did happen apart from a practical joke or two, because of some misunderstanding between him and his wife, you should take it more lightly.

Giovan Bernardo.   He disguised himself to let it be thought that it was me with his wife, to compromise us both and put us in danger of our lives. Didn't you know he was trying to deceive her and compromise me as thoroughly as he could?

Bonifacio.   No, no, by the love of God. Why should I do this to you, Master Giovan Bernardo? Forgive me, I beg you. Mercy, for the five wounds of Our Lord!

Giovan Bernardo.   Don't wet my feet, if you please.

Barra (*aside*).   For this occasion, at least, he treats everyone as a king or a pope.

Sanguino.   Come, come, have pity, at least until you are sure that he's done more harm than this. His is not the only intrigue we are dealing with; his wife was not wearing her own clothes, he told me; she was disguised as someone else. So he can hardly have planned to compromise you with *her*.

Scaramuré.   Besides, she was dressed in the clothes of a woman who can be seen with Master Giovan Bernardo without causing the least surprise. Come, Master Giovan Bernardo, come, my friend: I beg you to keep God's mercy in view. I knew you wouldn't have come unless I spoke to you as I did. If I misled you with regard to the captain, it was only because I knew you wouldn't hold it against me if I did an act of mercy and compassion for one, without harming the other.

Bonifacio. Master Giovan Bernardo, I pledge myself against any suit or damages that could possibly be made against you. Oh, Master Giovan Bernardo, take pity, I beg you, on this poor Bonifacio, who, if you don't will be cast out utterly. My reputation is in your hands; only do me this favor. (*Weeps.*)

Sanguino. Aha! Excellent! Here is his wife!

Scene XXIII

Carubina *and* Ascanio *come forward.*

Carubina. And there is that wife-seducer!

Sanguino. This is something really new! I doubt if those who specialize in cases of conscience have even imagined yet how a man can be a fornicator or a seducer while he's giving it to his own wife.

Scaramuré. Come, let's try to do without irony or anger. We have to settle this matter here, between us—since Captain Palma is kind enough to concern himself with your honor, Madam Carubina—assuming that your husband can't help your own reputation, nor be of any service to yours, Master Giovan Bernardo.

Bonifacio. That's right. Mercy, pity, compassion, charity, for the love of God! Master Giovan Bernardo, wife: forgive me, I beg you, just this once.

Barra. The world is a curious place. Some sin all the time and never get punished, as far as can be seen; some are punished after many offenses; others after only one; some suffer without having sinned at all, and some are even punished for the sins of others. In this man, if you think about it, you have all these varieties rolled into one.

Bonifacio. I beg for mercy and forgiveness. I beg it as Our Saviour Jesus Christ interceded for the good thief, for the Magdalen.

Barra (*aside*). By the devil's arsehole, he's a good enough thief himself!—When you are as expert as the thief who broke into Paradise, then Our Lord will have mercy on you. You're the sort of thief who takes what belongs to your wife and gives it to others, her milk, her liquor, her manna, her sustenance and joy.

Giovan Bernardo. And my identity, and my beard, and my cloak, and, perhaps, for all I know, my honor.

Barra. So he can't be pardoned like the good thief. Perhaps like the Magdalen.

Corcovizzo. Look at the pretty Magdalen, then! The pox on him and on the four hundred lice he's got in the thick on his two beards! See what precious ointment he's spreading around! By my faith, he only needs a skirt to be the Magdalen herself. If he's to be pardoned, I say it should be as the Jews pardoned Barabbas.

Sanguino. A fine way to help an unfortunate, a brave way to console an afflicted man. Be quiet, hold your tongues. Keep out of this and do nothing till you're told to.

Scaramuré. I beg you to forgive him; and he begs, too, as you see, on his knees, in the name of God or the devil, like Barabbas or Dimas.

Sanguino. Yes, you should, you should. It's right he should be forgiven.

Giovan Bernardo. What do you say, Madam Carubina?

Carubina. I would let him go this once, but let him watch out for the future, or I will make him pay for both.

Bonifacio. I promise, my Carubina, that——

Carubina. I may be your Carubina, but you belong to Vittoria.

Bonifacio. ——you will never have cause to complain again.

Carubina. Because this has taught you to be more cautious.

Giovan Bernardo. Ah, you understand him.

Bonifacio. No, you'll have no cause to complain because I'll do nothing wrong.

Barra. Women in labor say, "Never, never again; this time I'm putting a padlock on it. If you lay hands on me, you treacherous brute, I'll kill you; watch out, I'll tear you to pieces!" But as soon as the child is *out*, well, nature abhors a vacuum, and they want the other thing *in* as quickly as possible. What we have here is the repentance of childbed, the promises of parturition.

Sanguino. A fine spectacle: while others are weeping and wailing you make fun of them and treat it as a joke. Now be quiet.

Carubina. I not only forgive you, but to increase the favor, and because my own reputation is involved, I implore Master Giovan Bernardo to take you out of the captain's hands.

Bonifacio. Thank you, my dear wife. Up till today I

have loved you for one purpose and from two duties; from today on I shall love you for every reason and with all duty.

Giovan Bernardo. Master Bonifacio, I am a Christian and claim to be a good Catholic. I go regularly to confession, I take communion on all the major feast days. My profession is to paint and to bring before mortal eyes the images of Our Lord, Our Lady, and the saints in Paradise. So as I see you are penitent, I am moved to pardon you and to offer the forgiveness that any good and sincere Christian should offer in such a case. May God pardon you in heaven, as I forgive you on earth. But—I make one reservation. As it is written, "*Honorem meum nemini dabo,*" if you have committed any other misdemeanor while in this disguise, you must be prepared to make full reparation. And this you must promise the captain, as an officer of the law, and me, before your wife, Master Scaramuré, and the others.

Bonifacio. I promise and repromise it, affirm it and confirm it, and what is more I swear with both hands raised to heaven that I have not committed any other action that could possibly harm Master Giovan Bernardo apart from disguising myself as him so I shouldn't be recognized when going to Vittoria and leaving her room, and no scandal or suspicion can be attached to him for that since he rents it to her.

Sanguino. On my faith, if this is a crime, it's not a very serious one. So, up you get, Master Bonifacio, embrace Master Giovan Bernardo, be better friends in the future than you have been in the past, try to be of service to one another, rely on one another, help one another.

Giovan Bernardo. We will if all goes as it should; and with this I embrace you and greet you as a friend.

Bonifacio. I shall always be your friend and servant.

Barra. So now you've made it up.

Sanguino. What's this? Embrace your wife, kiss her.

Carubina. There is no need for that. Peace is made.

Marca. Home, let's go home. Be good to your wife, Master Bonifacio, or she and Master Giovan Bernardo will find some way of paying you back.

Sanguino. Off then, farewell all. Come this way and out through the other door. And, Master Bonifacio, perhaps you'll leave the consideration you promised my colleagues for the inconvenience you have caused them.

Bonifacio. I will, most gladly.

Scaramuré. God be praised, who has brought about this peace and union between Master Bonifacio, Madam Carubina, and Master Giovan Bernardo: three in one.

Bonifacio. Amen, amen.

Carubina. After you, Master Giovan Bernardo.

Giovan Bernardo. Never, mistress: it is for you to make the first move.

Carubina. If I must—

Giovan Bernardo. It is your duty, madam.

Carubina. Then, to obey you, and to give you pleasure, I will.

Giovan Bernardo. You after me, Master Bonifacio: keep close to me and hold on to my cloak and be careful you don't fall.

Bonifacio. I'll be careful.

Sanguino. You wait for a moment here with me, my boy; while the others are going through.

Ascanio. As your Honor desires.

Giovan Bernardo, Carubina, *and* Bonifacio, *go.* Barra, Marca, *and* Corcovizzo *go inside.*

Scene XXIV

Sanguino. Well, what do you think of your master?

Ascanio. I like what I know of him.

Sanguino. Isn't he a fine figure of a man? Wise, shrewd, courageous, worthy of admiration?

Ascanio. As other men are.

Sanguino. Do you know any who is his equal?

Ascanio. Anyone who knows neither more nor less than he, and who is worth neither more nor less.

Sanguino. Madness can take many forms; which is his particularly?

Ascanio. Madmen fall into different types; assuming that some are harmless, some wicked, and some good, he represents all three: asleep he is harmless, awake wicked, and dead, he will be good.

Sanguino. Why did he marry Carubina?

Ascanio. Because he is mad.

Sanguino. Do you think she has been good for him?

Ascanio. To judge from the opinion of that triple-piled old Madam Angela, she has been more than good, *ideste*, ideal. Angela acts as shepherdess to all the pretty girls of Naples and ahs been Carubina's confidante. Whoever needs *Agnus dei*, or consecrated incense, or water from San Pietro Martire, or the seed of San Gianni, or manna from Sant' Andrea, or oil from the marrow of the most interesting part of the remains of Saint Fornicario, or whoever wants to put up an *ex voto* to bring them good fortune, goes to Angela Spigna. Madam Carubina went and said, "Mother, they have decided on a husband for me." The old woman replied, "Take him." "Yes, but he is too old," said Madam Carubina. "Don't take him," said the old woman. "My parents want me to say yes," said Carubina. "Accept him," said the old woman. "But I don't like him," said Carubina. "Then don't accept him," said the old woman. Carubina went on, "I know he's of good family." "Take him," said the old woman. "But he's said to be stingy." "Then don't take him." "I'm told," Carubina said, "that he has a thoroughbred greyhound." "Take him," said the old Madam Angelina. "But, ahem!" she said, "they say he's a *candelaio*." "Don't take him." "Everyone thinks he's mad," said Carubina. "Take him, take him, take him, take him, take him, take him, take him," said the old woman seven times; "it doesn't matter if he's a sodomite! don't bother about his being a miser; if you don't like him or if he's too old, that doesn't matter a jot. Take him, take him because he's mad. Just be sure he's not strict or bitter or harsh." "I'm sure he's not any of those," said Carubina. "Then take him," said Madam Angela, "take him." Oh—here they come.

Scene XXV*

Barra, Marca, Corcovizzo, *and* Manfurio *come out.*

Barra. Now the other has gone, what shall we do with the *domine Magister?*

Sanguino. His guilt is written on his forehead: can't you see how he is disguised? Don't you see that this is the cloak he stole from Tiburolo? Didn't you see him try to escape from the watch?

*See the Appendix for an explanation and translation of the Latin in this scene and the next.

Marca. True, but there is something genuine about him.

Sanguino. That's just what qualifies him for prison.

Manfurio. Verum. But the accusations that are supererogated upon me will cost me the esteem of my scholars and others.

Sanguino. Do you understand what he means?

Corcovizzo. His riddles would stagger Oedipus.

Sanguino. To cut this short, decide, *Magister,* what you want to do, whether to go to prison or to give a little something to my colleagues, for instance the guineas you had left on you when the thief ran off with the ones you were changing.

Manfurio. Minime. I have none left at all. Those I had were all taken, *ita, mehercle, per Iovem, per Altitonantem, vos sidera testor.*

Sanguino. Listen to what I say. If you don't want a taste of prison discipline, and you've no money, you can make this choice: either ten blows on the palm with this stirrup leather, or fifty lashes on your bare bum; as long as, whichever you choose, you don't get away until you've apologized for your misdeeds.

Manfurio. "*Duobus propositis malis minus est tolerandum, sicut duobus propositis bonis melius est eligendum*": *dicit Peripateticorum princeps.*

Ascanio. Speak so they can understand you, Professor; these are dangerous men.

Barra. Do you think he talks like that so we can't understand?

Manfurio. Nil mali vobis imprecor: I am not abusing you.

Sanguino. Nor amusing us either.

Corcovizzo. Choose quickly which you want, or we'll truss you up and give you a double beating.

Manfurio. Minus pudendum erit palma feriri, quam quod congerant in veteres flugella nates: id non puerile est.

Sanguino. What? What in hell's name did you say?

Manfurio. I choose the palm.

Sanguino. Go ahead, Corcovizzo, and hard.

Corcovizzo. Right. Taf! One.

Manfurio. Help! *Iesus,* ouch!

Corcovizzo. Open the other hand—open it wide. Taf! two.

Manfurio. Ow—ouch! *Iesus Maria.*

Corcovizzo. Keep your hand up well, straight out, like this. Toff! Three.

Manfurio. Ouch, ooch, phew, ooooh! For the love of the Passion of Our Lord *Iesus*! *Potius* make me ride the horse; I can't stand so much pain in my hands.

Sanguino. Come on then, Barra, up on your shoulders with him. Marca, hold on to his feet so he can't move. Corcovizzo, undo his breeches and pull them well down, and let me do the beating. You, Professor, count the strokes, and just look out; if you make any mistake, we shall have to begin all over again. Ascanio, you look after that.

Marca. All ready. Start dusting him off, and don't punish his poor innocent clothes.

Sanguino. In the name of Saint Strappado, count! Toff!

Manfurio. Toff, one; toff, ow! three; toff, ouch! four; toff, oh no! oh no!—toff, oh! help! toff, for the love of God, seven!

Sanguino. Start again, back to the beginning. We'll see if "seven" comes after "four." It should have been "five."

Manfurio. What can I do? There were *in rei veritate* seven.

Sanguino. Count them one at a time then. Now, then, off we go again. Toff!

Manfurio. Toff, one; toff, one; toff, help! two; toff, toff, toff, three—four! toff, toff, five; ouch! toff, toff, six. For the love of God, toff, no more! toff, toff, no more, let's—toff, toff—look in my gown—toff—in case there is a little more money left there.

Sanguino. Back to the beginning: you let a lot go without counting them.

Barra. Let him off, Captain; he wants to go back to the other choice and pay for his freedom.

Sanguino. He has no money.

Manfurio. *Ita, ita,* I have suddenly remembered I have a little more than four guineas.

Sanguino. Down with him, then, let's see what he's got in his gown.

Barra. Blood of—there's more than seven guineas.

Sanguino. Up again, to horse again. For lying and perjury; start counting again, this time to seventy!

Manfurio. Mercy! Take the money, the gown, and whatever you want, *dimittam vobis.*

Sanguino. Very well. Take what he offers and the cloak, too, it's only right that it should go back to its poor

master. And now let's be off: good night to you,
Ascanio.

Ascanio.   Good night and good fortune to your Honor,
Captain, and Professor, good health to you.

          Sanguino, Barra, Marca, *and* Corcovizzo go.

Scene XXVI -

Manfurio.   Ecquis erit modus?

Ascanio.   Hello! Doctor Manfurio, Doctor Manfurio!

Manfurio.   Who knows me? Who can distinguish me
in this garb and this misery? Who calls me by name?

Ascanio.   Don't worry; that hardly matters anymore.
Open your eyes and look about you: see where you
are.

Manfurio.   Quo melius videam—to corroborate the
intuitive, and confirm the working of the visual power,
so that the axis of the pupil, emitting rays to the visible object, can the better bring the image back along
the line of vision and introduce it into the inner sensor,
via, idest, the governing sense located in the cell of
the visionary faculty—I wantt o put on my glasses.
Oh! A crowd of spectators sitting around!

Ascanio.   You seem to have got into a comedy, don't
you?

Manfurio.   Ita sane.

Ascanio.   You think you're on the stage, don't you?

Manfurio.   Omni procul dubio.

Ascanio.   And what point do you hope the play has
reached?

*Manfurio.   In calce, in fine: neque enim et ego risu
ilia tendo.*

Ascanio.   Well, then, invent and speak the *Plaudite*.

Manfurio.

> *Quam male possum plaudere,*
> *tentatus pacientia,*
> *nam plausus per me factus est*
> *iam dudum miserabilis,*
> *et natibus et manibus*
> *et aureorum sonitu. Amen.*

Ascanio.   Speak the *Plaudite*, I tell you, make yourself
do it, and do it well as a true teacher and man of
letters—otherwise the other characters will come back,
and the play will go on again.

Manfurio.   Hilari efficiam animo, forma quae sequitur.
As sailors, though the mast be broken, the sail lost, the
rigging and the rudder blown away and smashed by the
fury of the gale, continue nonetheless to be brought
to land, *plaudere; et iuxta* the Maronian verses:

> *Votaque servati solvent in littore nautae*
> *Glauco, et Panopeae, et Inoo Melicertae;*

similarly, *Ego Mamphurius, graecarum, latinarum vul-
gariumque literarum, non inquam regius, nec gregius,
sed egregius—quod est per aethimologiam e grege
assumptus—professor; nec non philosophiae, medic-
inae, et iuris utriusque, et theologiae doctor, si vol-
uissem*; to be brought to port after the miserable and
calamitous things that have happened to me—*posthac
vota soluturus—Plaudo. Proinde*—I must add, most
noble spectators—*quorum omnium ora, atque oculos
in me video esse coniectos*—that as I come to the end
of my supposititious tragedy, without gown or clothes,
without even hands, *corde, tamen, et animo Plaudo.*
I may more fitly say to you, *meliori hactenus acti fortuna,* who have been the happy and carefree spectators
of our weary and painful adventures, *Valete et Plaudite.*

Carlo Gozzi

TURANDOT

Turandot was written and produced in Venice in 1761. It was the fourth of ten *fiabe*, or theatrical fables, which Carlo Gozzi wrote between 1761 and 1765. Today, due chiefly to Puccini's operatic version of the story, it is the best known of the fables.

Gozzi came to write his plays under odd circumstances. He had never intended to be a playwright. By birth he was an aristocrat and the theater was beneath him. By nature he was touchy, provincial, and solitary—unsuited to the forced gregariousness of the theater. By temperament he was a sentimental classicist, an occasional poet, and an academician of sorts. But above all Gozzi was a militant conservative. His fables are the product of his conservatism.

In the middle of the eighteenth century the Venetian stage was dominated by two men: the Abbé Chiari, who wrote stiff, formal tragedies of preternatural dullness; and Carlo Goldoni, who wrote realistic comedies with Venetian settings. As his art progressed, Goldoni relied less and less on the traditional, improvised comedy of masks, the *Commedia dell' Arte*. Gozzi loved the *Commedia dell' Arte*. He loved the familiar situations, the characters, and all the old business. He thought that Goldoni meant to destroy the old comedy and managed to draw him into a literary quarrel. Goldoni, who was then at the height of his powers and the peak of his fame, was kind and reasonable. Gozzi was violent; but he was violent with such little effect that he turned imprudent. He boasted to Goldoni that he, Carlo Gozzi, a novice in the theater, could draw more people to see old fairy stories—"tales grandmothers tell their grandchildren"—acted by the comedians of the *Commedia dell' Arte* than Goldoni had ever done with his prosaic plays. Accordingly, on January 21, 1761, Gozzi produced a rambling, satiric piece based on a fairy tale and filled out with local references and improvisation. The piece was *The Love of the Three Oranges* and proved a great success. It was followed by other successes, and at the end of a few years, Gozzi had made his boast good. In the 1760's and early '70's the Venetian public did actually prefer his strange, old-fashioned fables to the modern comedies of Carlo Goldoni.

Turandot, like the other fables, is based on a fairy tale. Gozzi took the story from a French version of *A Thousand and One Nights*. But, unlike most of the other fables, *Turandot* does not depend for its effect on the fabulous. There is virtually no magic in the play—no spells, no transfigurations. Its charm and power depend on other things: on the pageant and the music; on the mixture of diction; on the transportation of the old mask characters to the court of China, and their behavior there; on the luxurious setting and the undercurrent of ritual; and on the deep, enigmatic character of the heroine.

Turandot was successful in Venice when it was produced and has been successful elsewhere since. The Germans particularly have taken to it. Schiller adapted it and so did Vollmoeller and Brecht. Versions have been done in English, French, and Russian. In Italy it has done better in the opera house than in the theater. Busoni made an opera of it, and, of course, so did Puccini.

Unfortunately, since the end of the eighteenth century the play has rarely been done in anything like its original form—and this has been a loss. For, despite the fact that many of the dramatic conventions seem dated to us, and much of the language seems artificial, the fable at the center of the play is still compelling; and consequently the play itself is still strong.

J. L.

TURANDOT

(1761)

A Tragi-Comic Fable for the Theater

Carlo Gozzi

ENGLISH VERSION BY JONATHAN LEVY

Characters

TURANDOT, *Princess of China, daughter of*
ALTOUM, *Emperor of China*
ADELMA, *sometime Princess of Tartary, now the slave and confidante of* Turandot
ZELIMA, *another of* Turandot's *slaves*
SCHIRINA, *mother of Zelima and wife of*
BARACH, *now called Hassan, once the trusted minister of*
CALAF, *Prince of Astrakhan, and son of*
TIMUR, *King of Tartary*
PANTALONE, *Prime Minister of China*
TARTAGLIA, *Keeper of the Great Seal*
BRIGHELLA, *Master of the Pages*
TRUFFALDINO, *Chief Eunuch of the Seraglio*

Eight doctors of the Divan, slaves in the seraglio, eunuchs, soldiers, citizens, and an executioner.

The action of the play takes place in and around the city of Pekin in the distant past.

ACT I

*Scene I: The entrance to the city of Pekin. On the spikes
that surmount the city gate several human heads
are impaled.*

Calaf, *then* Barach.

Calaf. There must be some charitable soul even here in
Pekin.
Barach (coming out of the city). What? What do I see?
Prince Calaf!
Calaf. Barach!
Barach. Your Highness.
Calaf. You here . . .
Barach. And you, Prince Calaf . . .
Calaf. Silence! Do not speak my name. Do you under-
stand? But tell me how you come to be here.
Barach. After the rout of your army near Astrakhan,
seeing that your forces fled in terror from the Cariz-
mani, I took refuge in the city, wounded and desperate.
There I heard that King Timur, your father, and you
yourself had been killed in the fighting. I rushed to
the palace to defend Elmaze, your mother. I sought
her everywhere, but in vain. At that moment the Sultan
of Carizmano entered the city with his men. I fled in
haste and for some months wandered aimlessly. At last
I arrived here in Pekin and soon encountered a widow
in deep misfortune. I helped her as I could. I found
her pleasing, and she, either out of gratitude or real
affection, consented to become my wife. She thinks I
am Persian and knows me by the name of Hassan. I
have lived here with her ever since. But tell me: how
is it that you, Prince Calaf, are alive and here in Pekin?
Calaf. Barach, do not pronounce my name again. That
fearful day, when the battle had been lost, I rushed to
the palace, where I found Timur, my father, and
Elmaze, my mother. We fled the city carrying a few
jewels under the vile rags in which we disguised
ourselves. We traveled secretly, at night, over dry,
interminable deserts and unimaginable mountains. Ban-
dits in the Caucausus robbed us of our jewels. Only our
most fervent prayers persuaded them to spare our lives.

Hunger, thirst, every conceivable hardship accompanied us after that. I was often forced to carry my father on my shoulders, or my poor mother, much wasted, in my arms. One day we reached the city of Jaich, where, by begging coins and bits of bread in the streets, I sustained my parents and myself. But the Sultan of Carizmano was not satisfied with the report that we were dead, as he had not found our bodies on the battlefield; and so he sent out proclamations to all kingdoms, offering a great price for proof of our deaths. Any king, even in the most debased condition, retains something of his former majesty, something that sets him apart from the common people. We were discovered. But, by a lucky accident, I had been forewarned. I went to my parents and told them we were forced to flee once again. They wept and prayed with all their hearts that death would take them first. I pleaded with them and recalled to them that the ways of heaven are hidden from us. At last they were persuaded, and we fled, suffering new deprivations, new trials . . .

Barach.   Sire, say no more. My heart is breaking. That my king and all his family should be so reduced! But, Prince, are the king and queen still alive, or . . . ?

Calaf.   They are alive, Barach. But I would never have believed to what depths a man can fall and still live. Finally we halted again, this time at the court of Ciecobad, the King of Turkestan. Once again I was forced to take on the lowest employments. Only Adelma, Ciecobad's daughter, took pity on me and showed me kindness; in fact, it seemed to me that she felt more than pity for me. I thought with her long glances she had discovered I was not what I seemed. We lived quietly in Turkestan until, on some point of honor, Ciecobad was moved to wage war on Altoum, the Emperor of China. There were, at the time, fantastic stories told among the people about the causes of that war. But whatever the cause, Ciecobad was soon vanquished, his kingdom overrun, and his entire line destroyed. I heard that Adelma, my benefactress, was drowned. My parents and I were once again forced to flee. After many months, starved and in rags, we came to the kingdom of Berlas.

Barach.   No more, sire, no more. You no longer wear rags, but fine armor. Tell me when and in what manner your fortune changed.

Calaf.   It has not changed, Barach. One day Alinguer,

the King of Berlas, lost a falcon that was very dear to
him. By chance I caught it and returned it to him at
the palace. He asked me who I was. I did not tell him
my name, but told him only that I was an unfortunate
creature obliged to carry other men's burdens to support my parents and myself. King Alinguer, in his
gratitude, ordered that my mother and father should be
taken to the almshouse, and maintained there. That,
Barach, is what has become of your king and queen.
They are kept in a public almshouse on charity.

Barach.   It is truly too much to bear.

Calaf.   As my own reward, Alinguer gave me this purse
of gold, a good horse, and the armor I am wearing.
Immediately, I went to my parents and bade them
farewell, saying that I was off to repair our fortunes;
that I could not bear to see them in the miserable condition they were in and so intended to risk everything,
even my life, to better it. They tried at first to restrain
me and then to follow me; but I could not let them. I
left them and came here to Pekin. I intend to offer
myself as a soldier to the emperor. But the city is
filled with armed foreigners who seem to have the
same intention. In fact, I could find no lodgings at all
in the city until the kind lady who owns that inn took
pity on me and agreed to give me lodgings.

Barach.   She is my wife, sire.

Calaf.   Barach, you are indeed fortunate to have found
such a good woman for a wife. But now I must go.
I am interested to see the event that has brought so
many people to Pekin. Then I will present myself to
the emperor and ask to be his soldier. (*He starts to go
into the city.*)

Barach.   Stop, Calaf. Go no further into the city. The
event you speak of is an abomination.

Calaf.   What do you mean, Barach?

Barach.   Prince, have you never heard of Turandot? Of
Turandot, the emperor's daughter?

Calaf.   I have heard that name whispered in Turkestan.
The people there told strange stories about the princess.
They said that the son of King Ciecobad died here in
Pekin on her account; and that it was for that reason
that Ciecobad made war on China. But the common
people always tell fantastic stories about their betters.
They are so eager to seem part of court life that they
invent what they could never know. No intelligent person takes their stories seriously.

Barach. Sire, this story is true; and it is deadly serious. Turandot is so inexpressibly beautiful in her person that no artist can reproduce it; so deep and subtle in her mind that no one—not the most learned doctor at court—can fathom her; and yet so hard in her heart that she despises all men, and has refused the greatest monarchs of the world in marriage.

Calaf. That is the story I heard the people tell, and I disbelieved it.

Barach. Ah, but it is true, sire. The emperor has tried again and again to tempt her with the most brilliant matches, with princes worthy of her and of her heritage. For, sire, she is heiress to an empire. But in her pride she refused them all. The emperor, who loves her to excess, would not give her in marriage against her will. He has often been forced to wage war against insulted and outraged kings; and although he has always been victorious, he is old and weary of fighting. One day he went to Turandot and spoke to her, not in anger but sadly and pensively. He said to her, "My daughter, I cannot continue in this way. Either you must marry, or else you must instruct me how I may end these wars you occasion. For I am weary of defending your intransigence. Teach me the means to end these wars and you may continue to live as you please. Otherwise you must marry." Turandot struggled to escape the choice. She pleaded with her father, but in vain. Then, poisoned by her own venom, she fell sick and was at the point of death. But when she saw that her father was still resolute, she rose from her bed and proposed a plan to him.

Calaf. That is the story I heard. Turandot requested her father to decree that any prince who so desired could sue for her hand. But on this condition: that she should have the right to put three riddles to the prince in the Grand Divan, before all the doctors and sages of the empire. If the prince answered these riddles correctly, he would have Turandot for his wife and the empire of China for his inheritance. But if he failed to answer any one of the riddles, Altoum was to be constrained by the most solemn oath of his faith to deliver the unhappy prince into the hands of the executioner. Tell me, Barach, is that your story?

Barach. I would to heaven it were only a story. At first Altoum refused to grant her the decree. But Turandot used all her guile and at last prevailed. She argued that no prince would be foolish enough to offer himself for such an ordeal; and that if one were, his death would be his responsibility and not Altoum's. Finally the decree was made, sworn to, and widely published.

Calaf. But surely no one has ever come forward to accept the challenge.

Barach. No one, sire? Look. (*He points to the row of heads affixed on the wall.*) All those are the heads of princes who came forward and failed.

Calaf. How can it be that a man would risk his life to win so barbarous a woman?

Barach. They say that anyone who sees so much as a portrait of the princess is so enthralled that he risks death gladly in the hope of gaining the original.

Calaf. Perhaps one isolated madman . . .

Barach. No. Many princes have come forward, and all have been of great nobility. The crowd here in Pekin today has come to mourn the execution of the Prince of Samarkand, the most regal, sweet, and virtuous prince the city has ever seen. Altoum is desperate with grief and curses the law and his own inhumanity; while Turandot savors the end of the spectacle in silence. (*A muffled drum is heard offstage.*) Listen, sire. That drum is the signal that the blow is about to be struck. (*The drum-roll grows louder and then ceases.*)

Calaf. How could nature have produced a creature who rejoices in such horrors?

Barach. My wife has a daughter who is a servant in the seraglio. She has told my wife stories you would never believe. Turandot is capable of extraordinary cruelty; but her deepest vice, her ruling passion, is pride. But here is my friend Ismaele, who was tutor and companion to the Prince of Samarkand.

Scene II

Ismaele *and the above.*

Ismaele (*enters crying from the city*). My prince is dead. Would that it were I instead of him.

Barach. But why did you permit it, Ismaele? You were his friend and adviser?

Ismaele. Barach, do not reproach me. I tried to reason with him but my arguments were useless. I was only his servant and could not insist. Had there been time,

I would have warned the king, his father. But there was no time. (*He cries.*)

Barach. Be reconciled, Ismaele. Philosophy will comfort you.

Ismaele. There is no comfort for me, Barach. He loved me and in his last moments wanted me near him. His last words are fixed in my mind. "Ismaele, don't weep," he said. "Since I have lost Turandot I die gladly. Ask my father to pardon me for having left his court secretly. Tell him I was afraid he would oppose my design, and that fear turned me discourteous. Then show him this picture and he will understand." (*Ismaele takes a miniature from his cloak.*) Having spoken these words, my master kissed this accursed picture a thousand times; then he bared his neck; and presently I saw his head severed from his body. (*He throws the miniature down and grinds it into the ground with his foot.*) Let this diabolical image be buried here in the earth, as its model should be. I will never carry it to my king, nor will I return to Samarkand. Instead, I will flee into the desert and mourn my dead prince there.

                                                    He exits.

Scene III

Calaf *and* Barach.

Barach. Now you have heard the truth, sire.

Calaf. Yes. And I am moved by what I heard. How is it possible that a simple miniature should have such power?

He stoops to retrieve the miniature. Barach *restrains him.*

Barach. Sire, what are you doing?

Calaf. I must see this supernatural portrait for myself, Barach.

He stoops again. Barach *restrains him forcibly.*

Barach. I cannot allow it, sire. It would be less dangerous for you to look directly into the eyes of Medusa.

Calaf. You are mad, Barach. Let me alone. (*He pushes Barach away and picks up the miniature.*) Even if you

have lost your senses, I have not. There has never been
a woman's beauty that could move me once I put it out
of my mind. Look, Barach. See if a few daubs of paint
can work the magic you fear.

As Calaf *is about to look at the picture,* Barach *covers it*
with his hand.

Barach. Don't, Prince. For the love of God.
Calaf (*pushing him away*). Let me alone, fool. I am my
own master.

Calaf *looks at the picture and is struck by it. He then*
mimes increasing enchantment.

Barach. God, I foresaw it.
Calaf. But, Barach, what is this? The cruelty you spoke
of could never dwell in such a countenance.
Barach. I will not hide the truth from you, sire. Turandot herself is infinitely more lovely than any portrait.
But it is also true that her wickedness is unfathomable.
Sire, I beg you: put that deadly image from you before
you succumb to it.
Calaf (*still staring at the picture*). You can no longer
dissuade me, Barach, or turn me from the contemplation of this face. The man who possessed such harmony
would surely be the most blessed man on earth. (*Pause.*
Then Calaf *continues, resolute.*) Barach, now is the
moment for me to tempt fortune. I will offer myself
for Turandot's ordeal; in which I shall either gain at
one stroke the most perfect woman in the world and a
great empire, or else be quickly rid of my life which,
without Turandot, has become insufferable. Turandot,
you have acquired a new victim. Have pity on me.

The sound of a muffled drum is heard closer than before.
Calaf *and* Barach *stand back to watch. A hideous*
executioner, his arms naked and bloody, appears at
the top of the city wall. He affixes the head of the
Prince of Samarkand on a spike and then retires.

Barach. Look, Prince, and be warned. That is the head
of the Prince of Samarkand who sighed and spoke of
love like you, and kissed the same portrait not two
hours ago. That grinning man you saw will be your
executioner tomorrow. Tomorrow your dear head will

be fixed on the neighboring spike, to the sound of a covered drum.

Calaf (*addressing the head*). Unhappy prince. What occult, irresistible force is it in me that compels me to join you? (*Then to Barach.*) Listen to me, Barach. I am going now to present myself to the princess and the emperor. Do not tell anyone my name, or that I am here in Pekin. Perhaps the gods at last are satisfied with all I have suffered and are about to restore me to felicity. Farewell, Barach. If the prize is mine, you too will have your reward. (*He starts to go. Barach restrains him.*)

Barach. Ah, no . . . please, sire . . . please. Schirina, help me. This boy is threatening to offer himself for Turandot's ordeal.

Scene IV

Schirina *and the above.*

Schirina (*entering*). What? Who is it? My guest! Tell me: what is it that drives you so quickly to your death?

Calaf (*showing her the miniature*). Lady, it is this countenance that drives me.

Schirina. Hassan, how could he have come by that infernal portrait?

Barach. He had it by accident. By a tragic accident.

Barach *and* Schirina *weep.*

Calaf. Hassan, kind Schirina, do me this favor. Keep my horse and my few possessions here with you. And take this purse. (*Calaf takes a purse from his robe and gives it to* Schirina.) I am sorry that in my present misery I have nothing more with which to show my gratitude. If it does not displease you, use some part of this gift in my behalf; in alms for the poor and in sacrifices to the gods; so that Heaven may intervene for me.

He exits into the city.

Barach. Sire . . . sire . . .

Schirina. Hassan, who is he? Such a regal boy, rushing to his death.

Barach. Do not be curious, Schirina. And do not despair of him so soon. He is a boy of extraordinary qualities.

Come, Schirina. Let us hurry to distribute this gold on his behalf, as he wished.

Exits.

Schirina. Not just his purse but all the gold I have shall be spent in that boy's aid. All that we mortals can do will be done. Copious gifts of oxen, fish, and grain shall be offered up to the gods. May they hear our prayers and supplications, and answer them.

CURTAIN

ACT II

Scene I: The Great Divan. There are two large doors on either side of the stage. One leads to Turandot's *seraglio, the other to the apartments of* Altoum, *the emperor.*

Truffaldino *and* eunuchs *in Chinese costume. Then* Brighella.

Truffaldino orders his eunuchs to prepare the hall. They erect two thrones and eight chairs for the eight doctors of the Divan. While his eunuchs work, Truffaldino is gay, and sings.

Brighella *enters.*

Brighella asks Truffaldino why he is preparing the Divan. Why the thrones? Why the chairs? Etc.

Truffaldino answers that the Divan has been convened at very short notice and that the emperor, the doctors, and his own dear princess should be arriving any minute. He is delighted, he continues, that things are going so well. Just think: another victim has just appeared. Isn't that splendid?

Brighella is astonished. Astonished. But it's not three hours since we lost the last prince. This haste is barbarous. He reproaches Truffaldino for his light heart and his indecorous singing.

Truffaldino replies that Life is known to be a Gamble, that Man's Will is notoriously Free, etc. There's no law that forces these silly princes to match wits with

Turandot. If they think they're equal to it, well, it's their funeral, isn't it? He continues singing.

Brighella is shocked. Truly shocked to discover such lack of feeling in another human being; particularly in another Chinese. But bad as Truffaldino is, the princess is worse. If she had a glimmer of natural female sentiment in her she would accept one of those nice little princes she's always being offered and live happily ever after.

Truffaldino disagrees. The princess is perfectly right not to marry, he says. Only fools and lunatics marry. Women, you see, are such drab, flighty, treacherous, and—let's be perfectly frank—such *useless* creatures.

Ah, says *Brighella,* for a moment I forgot I was talking to the chief eunuch. Of course you would have no use for women. Excuse the indelicacy. He pats Truffaldino on the head.

Truffaldino gets angry. There is no need to stoop to personalities, he says. He is opposed to marriage on general grounds. It is, for example, an institution calculated to fill the world with Brighellas; to proliferate little Brighellas into every crevice of the earth. What a thought!

Now *Brighella* loses his temper. If he weren't such a gentleman, he says, he would kick Truffaldino right over the Great Wall with one flick of his shoe.

Oh, would you, says *Truffaldino.* Oh, would you. You're welcome to try any time at all. Now, if you like. He assumes a ferocious pose and circles Brighella menacingly.

Come, come, says *Brighella,* blanching, be mature. What distinguishes the *homo sapiens* from the lower animals is the power of Reason.

And our prehensile thumbs, says *Truffaldino.*

Them too, of course, *Brighella* agrees. But most of all our reason. Our powers of ratiocination, which cats, for example, don't have.

That's so, says *Truffaldino,* abandoning his crouch. Poor cats.

Here's proof for you, says *Brighella.* Look at the whole question logically. If there were no such institution as marriage, Truffaldino's mother could never have married Truffaldino's father. And then there would be no Truffaldino today.

Who says my mother and father were ever married, says *Truffaldino* indignantly. They were never married a

day in their lives. And yet here I am, Truffaldino, chief
eunuch to the emperor, loaded with honors and in perfect health. He pirouettes for Brighella's inspection.
Q.E.D., says *Brighella*. The prosecution rests.

*During this argument the eunuchs have prepared the hall.
Now a march is heard. The great doors to* Altoum's
apartments open slowly. Truffaldino *and his* eunuchs,
then Brighella, *exeunt to different sides of the stage.*

Scene II

The march continues. Enter guards; *then the eight* doctors
of the Divan; then Pantalone *and* Tartaglia, *dressed
as ministers of state; and finally* Altoum, *majestic-
ally. When* Altoum *enters, all fall to their knees and
press their foreheads to the ground.* Altoum *ascends
the throne and sits.* Pantalone *and* Tartaglia *place
themselves on either side of the throne. The* doctors
*take the eight seats prepared for them. The music
ends.*

Altoum.   Friends and ministers, how much longer must
we endure this anguish? Hardly is there an end to those
solemn obsequies which are royalty's due, when the
tragic cycle begins again. No sooner are we reconciled
to one atrocity than we are compelled to do another.
We are old and mortally tired. We would gladly give
our empire to change the law, but we cannot. For we
have sworn, with the most solemn oaths of our religion,
to execute the cursèd edict in each fierce particular.
Now new victims present themselves with each fresh
wind; and Turandot is implacable. Nor is there one
among all our doctors and ministers to aid us or counsel us in our distress.

All the doctors *and* ministers *turn their faces away except* Pantalone, *who jumps to his feet.*

Pantalone.   Oh, now, your Majesty, be fair. We'd like to
help you. It's just that what you have isn't exactly what
you could call a common problem. Take me, for
example. Where I come from (you may not have
noticed it, but I am not, myself, of Chinese descent;
not that I have a thing against the Chinese, mind you)
where I come from we don't have these what-do-you-

call-'em's, these edicts. Princes, where I come from,
don't travel for months to get their heads chopped off
on the offchance of marrying some princess who hates
them and says so. Excuse me, your Majesty, but it
doesn't make good sense.

*He moves to the front of the stage and speaks directly to
the audience.*

Before certain scandals forced me to leave home in a
hurry; before I rose to the position of prime minister to
his Chinese Highness there (through slyness and trickery, of course, not merit; but you've already guessed
that); before my metamorphosis, as you might say, I
didn't know what China was. I'd never even heard the
word before, except in the sense of crockery—vases,
plates, beer mugs shaped like your favorite characters
from fiction—that kind of thing. So how can I advise
him? What I personally would do in this situation is
tell everybody to go home and forget the whole thing.
But all that would accomplish around here is to lose
me my job. I tell you, if I mentioned any of this back
home, they'd clap me in the asylum and lose the key.
They'd tie me up in a straitjacket and feed me gruel
with a wooden spoon. But here they all act as if it was
perfectly natural and normal. No. I give up. I really
do. Hard as I try, I'll never understand the oriental
mind.

Altoum. Tartaglia, tell me: have you been to see the
new prince yet?

Tartaglia. Yes, I have, your Majesty. They put him in
the same room the last one had; the one they reserve
for t-t-t-terminal princes. I tell you f-f-frankly, your
Majesty, I'll be sorry to lose this one. This one is
special. He's one prince who acts like a prince; not one
of your short, nervous, badly s-s-s-spoken princelings.
And he has such a manner about him, your Majesty.
All I can say is, it will be a great shame when this
one . . . (*He imitates a man losing his head.*)

Altoum. All the instruments have been set in motion.
May the gods grant him poise and clarity to solve the
three riddles and so preserve his life. Pantalone, attend to the sacrifices. They, if anything, will dispose
Heaven to be kind.

Pantalone. They've already been attended to, your Highness. (*He takes a list from his pocket.*) A hundred

cows have been sacrificed to the sun. A hundred sheep have been sacrificed to the moon. A hundred pigs have been sacrificed to the North Star. The last word in orthodoxy has been performed, your Highness.

Tartaglia (*aside*). If they'd listened to me, they would have sacrificed Turandot to the North Star. It would have been better for everyone concerned.

Altoum. Let the new prince be brought into our presence.

Exeunt two guards.

We will talk with him, reason with him, and attempt to dissuade him. We count on you, doctors and ministers, to come to our aid if our heavy grief should overcome us.

Pantalone. Certainly, your Highness. After all, we've been through it all before. We're experts by now. This is how it goes. We all stand around looking grave. Enter the prince, looking puzzled. We all bow. (*Business. Then aside.*) We upper-class Chinese go in for a lot of ceremony. (*Aloud.*) The prince bows. We stand up. He stands up. We kneel. He kneels. We fall down flat on our faces. He falls down flat on his face. Then everybody jumps up and the princess comes in. (*Aside.*) Nothing like exercise to shake up the brains. (*Aloud.*) The princess comes in. She asks the poor fool a riddle. He hesitates and then answers wrong. We shake our heads. No, sorry, we say, that's wrong. Then they take him out and kill him.

Tartaglia. Don't be too sure, Pantalone. This one is different from the others, I tell you frankly, this time I'm hopeful.

Pantalone. If you're hopeful, you're a bigger fool than you look. You know as well as I do; it's always the same old story and it always has the same ending.

Scene III

Calaf, guards, *and the above.*

Calaf *enters, kneels, and touches a hand to his forehead.*

Altoum. Rise, Prince.

Calaf *rises and assumes a noble attitude.* Altoum *studies him before continuing.*

(*Aside.*) This boy awakes great compassion in me. How fine his bearing is. (*Aloud.*) What is your name, Prince? Tell us your name and lineage.

Calaf. Sire, I entreat you: for the present, permit me to keep my name a secret.

Altoum. What? Do you dare to pretend to our daughter's hand without disclosing your name and lineage? Sir, you presume on our courtesy.

Calaf (*grandly*). I am a prince, sire, and my father is a king. My word should suffice for you. It is not gracious of your Majesty to imagine I would aspire to so high a connection if any but royal blood ran in these veins. If Heaven has ordained my death, you will learn my name and lineage soon enough. But for the present, sire, I entreat you: permit me to keep them secret.

Altoum (*aside*). What nobility he has. He moves me extraordinarily. (*Aloud.*) But, Prince, suppose you should succeed? Suppose the gods should come to your aid and help you to solve the riddles; and then, afterward, you should prove to be of low birth? What then, Prince? The law . . .

Calif. Sire, the law applies only to princes. I know that. But, if it will put your mind at ease, let me propose this condition to my suit: if Heaven should grant me victory (as I pray it may) and if thereafter my birth prove ignoble, let my head be the forfeit. And let my corpse lie unburied like carrion for the dogs and predatory birds. There are those here in Pekin who know me, and could testify for me. But, sire, I entreat you: for the present, permit me to keep my name a secret.

Altoum. We grant what you ask, Prince. We cannot find it in ourself to deny anything to your nobility. We would only that you were equally disposed to charity. We, Altoum, Emperor of China, implore you from the lonely eminence of our throne; implore you, Prince: ponder your rash decision. Turn back. Abandon this unequal contest. Your virtues are patent and need not be put to any test. Instead, remain with me. Stay, and be companion to my failing majesty. And when death claims me (as soon it must), you may expect the very highest legacy from me. But do not force me to further wrongs. Do not compel me, who am so near my ultimate peace, to abet my barbarous daughter in her cruelties. (*He weeps.*)

Calaf. Sire, calm yourself. You malign yourself. No

child could have learned any but the gentlest qualities
from your example. Your only fault, if fault it is, is to
have loved a daughter beyond the commands of reason.
But, sire, you have brought into the world a daughter
who transcends the dry laws of reason; a daughter of
such overwhelming beauty that men are grateful for
the opportunity to risk their poor lives to possess it. I
thank you for your kindness and your magnanimity,
sire. I thank you profoundly but I cannot rule or be
your heir. My choice is clear: I must win Turandot or
die.

Pantalone. Oh, but look, sonny—your Highness, whatever you are. Look. You saw those heads up on the
wall. They were all live princes once, and now they're
dead curiosities. After you saw them, I can't imagine
why you didn't turn right around and go home. Who
do you think you are? I mean, why do you think you're
different from the others? You'll end up on that wall,
too. Look. Maybe you don't understand what's happening to you. Maybe you're an imbecile, a good-looking imbecile. (*Aside.*) That's a common type. (*Aloud
very slowly.*) Now listen. What's going to happen is
this. The princess is going to come in here and she's
going to ask you three riddles—three rid-dles. You
understand so far? Good. Well, it would take a cabinet
of wizards, a parliament of oracles, to answer those
riddles; and even *they* wouldn't get more than two out
of the three right. Sounds like baby stuff, doesn't it;
riddles? Well, it isn't. Believe me, it isn't. They'll kill
you for a missed riddle around here quicker than for
anything else. And another thing. Wait until you see
the princess. Even I—me, Pantalone, man of the
world, born and bred around courts—even I sometimes get a little nervous when Turandot fixes me with
those steely green eyes of hers. Listen to me, sonny.
Take my advice. Go away for a few weeks in the
country somewhere. Rest up. Because, believe me, if
you stay here, they'll have you up on that wall before
you know what's happened.

Calaf. You are wasting your time and breath, old man.
I am resolved: I will have Turandot or die.

Tartaglia. T-t-turandot. T-t-t-t-turandot. You've got a
one-track mind, boy, an obsession. That's probably
why you're not thinking clearly. What you don't seem
to realize is that Turandot isn't joking. This is life or
death, boy. You're playing riddles for your head. It's

such a pretty head and they're such hard riddles. Listen.
Even I, T-t-t-tartaglia, a notorious intellectual—brought
up around books, been to all the best universities; why,
even now I'm never without a novel or two on my
bed-table—even I, boy, with all my formal training,
haven't been able to guess one of those riddles yet. And
I'm not in love with the princess. (*Aside.*) In fact, I
hate her. (*Aloud.*) So be a good boy. Don't be so
stubborn. Go away now and the whole thing will be
f-f-f- . . . dismissed.

Calaf.   Sir, I know you mean well and you are very
kind. But I am resolved: I will have Turandot or die.

Altoum.   So be it. Prince, since you persist despite all
our pleas, you may die as you choose. Your obstinacy
begins to try our charity. (*To a* guard.) Inform the
princess that we await her. Tell her that still another
suitor has taken up her challenge.

The guard *exits.*

Calaf (*aside*).

You eternal gods, protect me. Guard me, lest her presence overwhelm me. Make me lucid and unafraid. For
you in your omniscience see what I have hidden from
the others; my inward doubts and waverings; that I
halt, falter, and vacillate. Stay with me and keep me
resolute. (*Aloud.*) And you, doctors, ministers, and
judges: I beg you to pardon me any lapse of protocol
or any dumb discourtesy I may show you during the
ordeal. Understand me and be lenient. I am driven
into this deadly contest by powers that I cannot comprehend.

Scene IV

*Drums. Then a slow march. The door to the seraglio
opens. Enter* Truffaldino, *a scimitar over his shoulder, followed by his eunuchs. Then other* slaves *of
various duties and degrees. After them enter two
veiled* slaves. *The first,* Adelma, *is dressed luxuri-
ously in the Tartar fashion; the second,* Zelima,
modestly in the Chinese fashion. Zelima *carries a
small chest in which are three sealed scrolls. All
make obeisance to* Altoum—*the eunuchs by pressing
their foreheads to the ground, the slaves by gestures
with their hands. Pause. Enter* Turandot, *veiled and
richly dressed. Her manner is at once bold and*

severe. The doctors *and* ministers *throw themselves to the ground. Altoum stands, and* Turandot *bows to him. She then ascends her throne and sits. Zelima stands on her left side, Adelma on her right. Calaf, who has been kneeling throughout, stands and is entranced. The other courtiers return to their places. Truffaldino executes several ceremonial bows. He takes the chest containing the scrolls from Zelima and, with more ceremony, presents it to the chief doctor. Truffaldino exits. The music ends.*

Scene V

All the above except Truffaldino.

Turandot (*haughtily*). Who is it that importunes us? Which one is it who refuses to learn from the past?

Altoum. It is he, daughter. (*He indicates* Calaf, *who bows.*) Finally a prince worthy of you has presented himself; a prince to whom you should extend great tenderness and offer gifts of love. He comes as your pilgrim, filled with charity; for which, in return, you taunt him and destroy him.

Turandot (*low to* Zelima). Zelima, never before has any suitor moved me to feeling. But this one moves me.

Zelima (*low*). Then, Princess, receive his suit. Accept him. And if, for reasons of honor, you must persist in the ordeal, ask him three simple things. In that way you will both maintain your honor and satisfy the letter of the law.

Turandot. Do you think I could deceive myself with such a stratagem? Do you think my honor would be content with the letter of the law? You do not know me, Zelima.

Adelma (*to herself*). O you gods, it is not possible! It is too cruel! Can this be the same low menial who served Ciecobad, my father, when he lived and ruled in Turkestan? How can a slave transfigure to a prince? And yet my heart assures me it is the same man.

Turandot. Prince, abandon this fatal enterprise. Be warned and flee. I know my father and the court call me barbarous; but I am not. I have no pleasure in this ordeal. But if you press me, I promise you I will see you destroyed with equanimity. I must defend myself

with every weapon I have and hold myself distant by
every means. For, Prince, know that I abhor your sex:
hate and abhor it, and make no exceptions. Do not
think that I am cruel without a motive or heartless to
no purpose. No. If my prayers have any power to
move you, I beg you be moved. Go. Do not challenge
me. I am intractable in this one thing alone. My
weapons may seem light ones—wit and ritual—but I
have learned to wield them expertly; and, depend on it,
I will have no pity. Do not force me to destroy you.
Go now. Later you will repent in vain.

Calaf (aside). Far from dissuading me, her pride and
majesty only make me more steadfast. (*Aloud.*) Princess, forgive me. I must persist, although it pains me
to deny you anything.

Zelima (low to Turandot). Be lenient with him. This
one is worthy of you.

Adelma (aside). Had I but recognized his true condition before fortune made a slave of me! Now, at this
moment, my love is stronger than ever before and I am
helpless.

Turandot (to herself). Can it be that this one prince
alone can move me to tenderness? No. I will not permit
it. I will not yield. (*Aloud.*) Rash Prince, prepare
yourself.

Altoum. Do you persist, my son?

Calaf. Sire, it distresses me to rebuff your clemency
once again. But I am resolved: I will have Turandot
or die.

Altoum. Let the decree be read.

Pantalone *takes a book from the folds of his robe. He
touches it first to his chest and then to his forehead.
He then hands it to* Tartaglia, *who takes it and reads
aloud.*

Tartaglia. By the terms of this solemn and unalterable
statute, the prince who would have Princess Turandot
for his wife must consent to answer three riddles, put
to him by the princess and of her making. If the prince
is able to answer these three riddles to the satisfaction
of the learned doctors of the Divan, Turandot must
agree to be his wife. If, however, he fails to answer
any part of any one of the three riddles correctly, he is
to be delivered forthwith into the custody of the public
executioner, who will be charged to sever his head

from his body. Affirmed and sworn to by his Majesty Altoum, Emperor of China, with the most secret and holy covenant of our religion.

Tartaglia *kisses the book and touches it first to his chest and then to his forehead. He then returns it to* Pantalone. Pantalone *hands the book to* Altoum, *who touches it reverently, then takes it back and replaces it in the folds of his robes. The Divan is silent.* Turandot *stands.*

Turandot (*in a grave voice*). Say, Prince:
What creature, though of common birth,
Rules his own realm and moves among
Us freely; who, though very young,
Is known to every man on earth.

No man can gain what he has got.
He is unique in every act.
His way is wide. He is, in fact,
Here now, and yet you know him not.

Calaf. Princess, I will be fortunate indeed if none of your riddles is more difficult than this one. The creature that is of low birth and yet is free to move among all men; who is young and yet known to all; who is peerless, unperceived, ubiquitous; who performs acts each day that no one else has done, can do, or will do, is, of course—the sun.

Pantalone. Tartaglia, he got it.

Tartaglia. He did. He got it. He certainly did.

The doctors *open the first sealed paper.*

Doctors (*together, ad. lib.*). The sun! It's the sun! Etc.

Altoum. Prince, may Heaven continue to aid you.

Zelima (*aside*). You mighty gods, stay by him and protect him.

Adelma (*aside*). Ah, no, you gods, keep victory from him.

Turandot (*to herself*). He will not answer my next riddle. (*Aloud.*) Hear me once again, rash Prince. (*She rises and continues in a grave voice.*)
There is a tree that you have seen
Of unknown height and breadth untold.
It always seems both fresh and green
But is incalculably old.

Its leaves are white as ivory
And bright as the most radiant light.
But when the brightness fades we see
The undersides are black as night.
Tell me, Prince, in charity,
The name of this mysterious tree.

Calaf *ponders a moment, then bows to* Turandot.

Calaf. Princess: this tree of unknown and unknowable
size, which is forever young and old; whose leaves are
bright in flower and black in sere; like night and day,
sweet Princess, is the year.

Pantalone. Tartaglia, he got it again!

Tartaglia. Two out of two. This gets better all the time.

The doctors *open the second sealed paper.*

Doctors (together, ad. lib.). It's true. The year. The
year. Etc.

Altoum. Now there is only the third riddle left.

Zelima. Would that had been the last.

Adelma (aside). God, I am losing him. (*Low to* Turandot.) My lady, in one instant all your past triumphs
and renown are wiped out. He will vanquish you.

Turandot (low). I would rather that the world fall to
pieces and the entire human race perish in the debris.
(*Aloud.*) Know, Prince, that I loathe you the more
with each of your little victories. Go from the Divan.
Flee the last riddle and save your life.

Calaf. Princess, your anger only strengthens my resolve.

Altoum. Desist, my son. Or you, daughter; refrain from
asking the last riddle. Accept this noble boy for your
husband.

Turandot. My husband? No, Father. You have sworn
that the law will be performed in its every particular.
Let us continue.

Calaf. Sire, she is right. Do not try to dissuade her. I
am resolved: I will have Turandot or die.

Turandot. Then die, Prince. (*She stands and continues
in a grave tone.*)

There is a curious and ancient beast
Whose strength diminished as its size increased.
The beast is loved by some, by some despised,
But those who trust it often are surprised.

It nurses what it knows
And weakens as it grows.
Its own intestines are its only food;
It gorges on itself and is renewed.

It dies, is born, and always stays the same.
Now tell me, Prince: what is this strange beast's name?

Having finished reciting the riddle, Turandot *removes the veil from her face.*

Now, Prince, answer my last riddle or die.

Calaf, *blinded by* Turandot's *beauty, covers his face with his hands.*

Calaf. Ah, what splendor!
Altoum. My son, come to your senses or you are lost.
Zelima (aside). He cannot answer.
Adelma (aside). He is mine. Love will teach me how to save him and, by saving, win him.
Pantalone. Come on, oh, come on, sonny. I'd help you if they'd let me.
Tartaglia. If it weren't for the s-s-s-solemnity of the occasion, I'd run to the kitchen and take a drink.
Turandot. I am waiting, Prince.
Calaf (coming back to himself). Princess, your beauty blinded me, but I am myself again. The contest is not yet finished. The treacherous beast which is both loved and hated; which hides its wisdom and grows smaller as it grows older; which feeds on itself; which is always changing and yet always the same is, Princess, life!
Pantalone. Oh, you lovely boy. I can't restrain myself anymore. (*He rushes to* Calaf *and embraces him.*)
Tartaglia. He's done it, your Majesty. No doubt about it.

The doctors *open the third and last sealed paper.*

Doctors (together, ad. lib.*).* Life. He's right. It's life itself. Etc.

The sound of cheering and the clamor of instruments is heard offstage. Turandot *collapses on her throne.* Zelima *and* Adelma *attend her.*
Zelima. Princess, he has won.

Adelma (aside). I have lost you, my love. But still . . .

Altoum, *assisted by* Pantalone *and* Tartaglia, *descends from the throne. The* doctors *draw back.*

Altoum. There, Turandot, is the end of your barbarities. Beloved Prince, come to me so that I may embrace you.

Altoum *embraces* Calaf. Turandot *rushes off her throne in a fury.*

Turandot. Stop. Stop, Father. I will not have him for my husband. Never let him imagine I will. If he thinks he has vanquished me, let us renew the ordeal tomorrow. Today I had no time to reflect . . .
Altoum. No, daughter. There will be no more ordeals. The law has been satisfied.
Pantalone. Princess, be sensible. The thing is finished. You asked your riddles, and this young boy answered them. That's all there is to it. It's as the emperor said, the law is satisfied. Let's all go have some wedding cake and forget the whole thing. (*To* Tartaglia.) What's your opinion, Chancellor?
Tartaglia. If the law is s-s-satisfied, I'm s-s-s-satisfied. That's my opinion. What do the doctors say?
Doctors (together, ad. lib.*).* It's finished. Solved and done with.
Altoum. Let us proceed to the temple where, once the unknown prince has revealed his name and lineage, the high priests will solemnize . . .
Turandot (desperate). No, Father. Reconsider . . .
Altoum. There will be no reconsideration, Turandot. You will not find us so compliant in the future as we have been before.
Turandot (falling to her knees). Father, grant me one more day. A little time, Father. I would rather die than submit to this man.
Altoum. Daughter, we will admit no more argument. Come, ministers. Follow us.
Calaf. Listen, sire. For charity's sake, suspend your orders. I cannot accept a victory that renders her miserable. I cannot permit my love to be the cause of her suffering. Princess, I will not compel you to be my wife. Sire, if you would please me, grant her the second trial she requests.

Altoum. No, we are resolved. We will not grant another trial. Come. The high priests await us.

Turandot. Father, I promise you I will not live to reach the altar.

Calaf. Sire. Princess. I pray that you will grant me this kindness. Tomorrow morning, here in the Divan, permit me to put a riddle to the princess. And, lest she say she had no time to reflect on it, I will tell her the riddle now. Princess Turandot: there is a certain prince from a high and noble line who was reduced to begging bread and carrying vile burdens to maintain himself; who, having unexpectedly attained the height of human happiness, was then cast down lower than he had been before. Tomorrow at dawn, here in the Divan, you must tell me both the name of this prince and of his father. If you fail to tell me these names, Princess, you must consent to become my wife, willingly and without delay. If, however, you do tell me the correct names, I once again offer my head as forfeit.

Turandot. I accept the challenge and am content.

Zelima (aside). There is still danger.

Adelma (aside). There is still hope.

Altoum. But we do not agree to the challenge. The law will be performed as it is written.

Calaf (falling to his knees). Sire, if there is charity in your heart, grant my wish. Let us have this second trial tomorrow. For without her good will, I can never be content.

Turandot (aside). My rancor vanishes and I am charmed.

Altoum. Prince, you do not know what you have asked. You do not know what means she has, what resources. . . . Nevertheless, we grant a second trial. If Turandot succeeds in guessing the two names you ask, she shall be free once again of all obligation. We do not, however, agree to the second part of your plea. Whatever occurs here tomorrow, you shall go free. I will permit no more outrages. Rash prince, I do not think you know what you have set in motion.

The march begins again. Altoum *and his guards,* the eight doctors, *and* Pantalone *and* Tartaglia *exeunt through the door through which they entered.* Turandot, Adelma, Zelima, Truffaldino *and his eunuchs, and* the slaves *from the seraglio, exeunt through the other door.*

ACT III

Scene I: A room in the seraglio.

Adelma *and a Tartar slave, her confidante.*

Adelma. I forbid you to say any more to me. Your
advice is useless, for my heart speaks to me irresistibly;
and my heart commands me to love the unknown prince.
It is insupportable that I must serve as a slave to his
beloved. For five years I have nursed hatred in my
heart for her who is the cause of all my suffering. Yet
all the while I obeyed her and pretended to love her.
Royal blood flows in my veins. I am in no way Turandot's inferior. But fortune overthrew me; and has reduced me ever since, like snow in the winter sun. Tell
me: do you still know me? Do you still recognize
Adelma? No. I am resolved to use all the art and
cunning I have to flee my slavery.

Slave. But, my lady, it is too dangerous . . .

Adelma. Go. Do not speak another syllable to me. You
cannot persuade me to suffer a single day longer.

The slave *bows, raises a hand to her forehead, and exits,
terrified.*

Here is my enemy, torn between rage and shame. The
moment has come to triumph or to die. I will conceal
myself. (*She hides.*)

Scene II

Turandot *and* Zelima. *Then* Adelma.

Turandot. Zelima, I can endure no more. The memory
of my shame is like a violent fire at my heart.

Zelima. But, my lady, how is it that such a man as he is
—so noble yet so humble—can arouse such hate in
you?

341

Turandot. Do not torment me, Zelima. You must know that . . . that he wakens in me certain feelings I have never known . . . feelings, feelings of . . . But no. It is disgraceful. All I feel for him is loathing. He was the cause of my disgrace in the Divan. Throughout the empire it will soon be known that Turandot has been vanquished. My defeat will be the object of every rustic's coarse wit. Help me, Zelima. My father has ordered the assembly of doctors to convene at dawn tomorrow. He intends that the marriage follow the trial directly if I fail to answer the prince's riddle. *Who is the prince and who is his father who was reduced to begging bread and carrying vile burdens to sustain his life; who, having reached the peak of felicity, is now cast down lower than before?* I am sure that the unknown prince himself is the prince in question. But how shall I discover his name, and his father's name? The emperor permitted him to keep both his name and lineage secret today in the Divan. Suppose he permits it tomorrow? I shall be disgraced again. Zelima, what shall I do?

Zelima. My lady, there are those in Pekin who are expert in magic, adepts of the cabala. Go to one of them. See whether he can tell you . . .

Turandot. No, Zelima. Those charlatans, who prey on the ignorance of the vulgar, are beneath my notice. Can you suggest nothing else to me?

Zelima. Yield, my lady. Recall the prince. Remember how he was. Remember with what grace and sweet humility he acted. Remember that he threw himself at the emperor's feet.

Turandot. No more, Zelima. Know that in my heart I . . . No. It is not so. I know too well how treacherous men are; all men, without exception. I know that they are false despite their protestations, changeable despite their promises, and shallow. They dissimulate to trap us; and when they have vanquished us, they love us no longer. Then they lightly break the vows they once swore to. No, there is no constancy in them, Zelima. No dignity. No pride.

Zelima. My lady, you will learn what real unhappiness is when you have lost him. Then you will repent in vain. Tell me, my lady: why do you not accept him? I do not understand it.

Adelma (*coming forward*). Princess, anyone born of common blood would think like Zeiima. It is not her fault. Zelima, I mean no offense. I realize you cannot understand the feelings of a princess vanquished in front of her people, disgraced in her own court. With my own eyes I saw the vulgar laugh and exult in her defeat. And, in the love I bear the princess, I was mortified for her.

Turandot. Enough, Adelma. I already know all you can tell me.

Zelima. But where is the disgrace? Where is the misfortune?

Adelma. There is no reason that you should comprehend a regal sensibility, Zelima. But does it truly seem a small thing to you that the princess should be constrained to answer questions in front of a rude and hostile crowd? And suppose she should answer incorrectly?

Turandot. Know, Adelma, that I will not submit quietly to defeat. Failing all else, I will turn this dagger on myself.

Adelma. No, Princess. We must find some way of learning those two names.

Zelima. If Adelma understands your Highness so well, perhaps she will help you.

Turandot. Dear Adelma, do help me.

Adelma. Princess, the prince said this morning to your father that there were people here in Pekin who knew him and can testify to his nobility. It is these people you want, Princess. You must use all your resources, your entire treasury, if necessary, to find them.

Turandot. I will put the treasury at your disposal, Adelma. Use it all; but find me those names.

Zelima. But where should the money be spent? Where should the search be begun? And even if you are successful, how could you hide the fact that you discovered the names by trickery?

Adelma. Perhaps you, Zelima, would be the one to betray us?

Zelima (*angry*). How could you think that? I am much offended, Adelma. Princess, you can save your treasury. Earlier I hoped to calm you, to persuade you to yield. But since you are determined to find the prince out, learn now that it is I who am your true servant and friend, and not Adelma. Schirina, my mother, came here to visit me and, overjoyed at what she believed was the end of the ordeals, told me in confidence that the unknown prince is a guest at her inn; also, that Hassan, my stepfather, knows him from another time and loves him. I asked my mother the prince's name, but she protested that Hassan had not told her; that, in fact, he had refused to tell her. Then she left me, but she promised she would do what she could to discover the name. Now doubt my love if you will, Princess.

She exits.

Turandot. Zelima. Dear Zelima, where are you going?

Adelma. Princess, Zelima has given us precious information, but she is too weak to help us further. It is clear that it is Hassan we want; but we cannot suppose he will reveal the names willingly even if he knows them. Princess, let us retire to a more private place where, if you trust my love for you, I will tell you how we can make best use of what we have learned.

Turandot. Come, then. And do not doubt that I trust you.

She exits.

Adelma. You god of love, strengthen me. Help me, for now is my moment to rise from slavery. The arrogance and blindness of my enemy have given me the means.

Scene III: *A room in the palace.*

Calaf *and* Barach.

Calaf. But Barach, you are the only one in Pekin who knows me, and you are incorruptible. My father's kingdom is distant and for many years now has been ruled by others. The report was spread that our entire family perished in battle; and we have lived secretly. Barach, the world quickly forgets those who have fallen from high places.

Barach. No, sire. Pardon me, but what you did was imprudent. The unfortunate man must learn to fear every contingency, even such as seem impossible. When the gods forget us, the trees, the walls, every inanimate thing becomes our enemy. I cannot be easy, sire. All that you had gained at the risk of your life—the most beautiful woman in the world and a kingdom vaster than the one you might have had by inheritance—you now may lose because of one instant of mistaken charity.

Calaf. Barach, love cannot be judged by such standards. You yourself heard what loathing Turandot expressed for me this morning in the Divan.

Barach. But Turandot was compelled by law to be your wife. Excuse me, sire, but this morning you should have thought less about Turandot's displeasure than your parents' misery.

Calaf. Do not reproach me, Barach. I had to yield to her. I suspect she did not find my gesture displeasing. If she feels even a spark of gratitude toward me, I am well rewarded.

Barach. Turandot? Do not deceive yourself, sire.

Calaf. Everything you say is true, Barach, and yet I cannot lose her. Tell me: are you certain you haven't told anyone who I am?

Barach. No, sire, no one, not even my wife. Though I do not think you have acted wisely in this affair, you are still my prince and I will obey your orders. But, Prince, be cautious. I feel a presentiment and I am frightened.

Scene IV

Pantalone, Tartaglia, Brighella, soldiers, *and the above.*

Pantalone (*entering busily*). Oh, so there you are, sonny.

Tartaglia. Who is this man, your Highness?

Calaf. I don't know him. I met him here accidentally and took the opportunity to ask him about the city, the court, and other trivial matters.

Tartaglia. Excuse me, your Highness, but if you've got any fault at all, it's that you're too polite. I noticed it this morning in the Divan. With things the way they are, with the danger you're in, what the devil made you stand around talking with a perfect stranger?

Pantalone. All right, Tartaglia, that's enough. What's done is done. But, sonny, you know he's right. You're in terrible danger. If it wasn't for responsible citizens like us looking out for you, you'd give yourself away twenty times a day. (*To* Barach.) This is no place for you, friend. You don't know it, but you've wandered in among some very important people—that boy, this stout gentleman, myself. All very highly placed. Now do go away and save yourself a lot of social embarrassment. (*To* Calaf.) If your Highness will be good enough to follow us. We have orders to take you to a certain apartment and make sure you're comfortable. Brighella here has two thousand soldiers to guard you, to make sure no one can get in to see you. These orders come from the very top. The emperor himself. You know, the emperor has taken a great liking to you. I can't imagine why, but it's so. He's scared to death something will happen to you before he becomes your father-in-law. (*Low to* Calaf.) Listen, sonny, what you did yesterday was very foolish. But everything will still be all right if you are sure, absolutely sure, not to tell those two names to anybody. Not to anybody at all. On the other hand, if you feel you have to tell somebody, get it off your chest, there's always me. If you'd just like to whisper those names in my ear . . . I'm absolutely trustworthy. Never been a word said against Prime Minister Pantalone's honesty. Come on. What do you say? Just one little whisper . . .

Calaf. Old man, you do not know how to obey your master's orders.

Pantalone. That's right. That's right. Righteous indignation. That's the thanks I get. You talk to him, Brighella.

Brighella. No more talk. What we need is action.

Tartaglia. I wouldn't be so impetuous if I were you, Brighella. Just because you're h-h-highly placed in the government, it doesn't mean you're out of danger, you know.

Brighella. Don't worry, Tartaglia. I know just what I'm doing.

Tartaglia. Oh, you do. Well, that's all right then. It's more than some people around here know. His Highness is absolutely right not to give himself away to old Pantalone. Absolutely right. (*Low to* Calaf.) But you could tell me, your Highness. I'm dying to know. What the devil is your name? If you tell me, I won't tell a living soul.

Calaf. You will know in the morning. All of you.

Tartaglia. Good. That's the right answer, Prince. I was just testing you.

Pantalone. Your obedient servant, sonny. (*To* Barach.) As for you, my good friend, I'll tell you just once more. Go away. Go far away before the dogs get wind of you.

He exits.

Tartaglia (to Barach). It's true, you know. You do have an untrustworthy look about you I took an immediate dislike to. I'm not sure whether it's the tight mouth or

the small, piglike eyes. But I'm sure it's been mentioned
to you before.

He exits.

Brighella. Your Highness, if you will be good enough
to follow, we will lead you to your apartment.

Calaf. Yes. I'm coming. (*To* Barach.) My old friend,
we will see one another soon under happier circumstances.

Barach. Always your servant, sire.

Brighella. Please, your Highness, come along. I must
obey my orders.

Exeunt.

Scene V

Barach, *then* Timur. Timur *is a feeble old man, dressed
in rags.*

Barach. Heaven help you, Prince. For my part, I will
do as you ask.

Timur (entering, frantic). My son! My son! Has the
Sultan of Carizmano followed us this far? Has the
usurper pursued us to Pekin? Wait, Calaf. Wait. I'll
come with you.

Barach, *hearing the prince's name pronounced, half draws
his scimitar and catches* Timur *by the arm.*

Barach. Old man, be quiet. Who are you? Where are
you from? How is it that you know the prince's name?

Timur. Barach. So even you are a rebel. You, who used
to be so loyal, can now raise a sword against your
king.

Barach. Timur!

Timur. Yes, traitor. But go on. Strike. My life has indeed lasted too long when I see my most trusted minister turned against me.

Barach (falling to his knees). Sire, forgive me. But
believe me, what I did was in your interest. Listen,
sire: if you hold your son dear, never utter either his
name or your own in this city. And you must not call
me Barach, but Hassan. (*He rises.*) Tell me, sire, has
Elmaze, my queen, come here with you?

Timur (crying). Please do not recall my dear wife's
name to me. In Berlas, overcome with our present grief

and our past misfortunes, she laid her head on my breast and, with the name of her dear son on her lips, gave her soul up to Heaven.

Barach. Ah, my queen.

Timur. I set out desperately from the city, seeking my son, seeking death, not caring which I found. Now, scarcely arrived in Pekin, I see my son, my only hope, led off by soldiers.

Barach. Do not grieve for your son, sire. Tomorrow he will reach the heights of felicity, and you will reach them with him. But I beg of you; for the present, you must not pronounce either his name or your own in any public place.

Timur. But what are these mysteries? I do not understand.

Barach. Come away from here, sire, and I will explain everything to you. But here is Schirina, my wife. Schirina, what is the matter? Where are you going?

Scene VI

Schirina *and the above.*

Schirina. I have just come from the seraglio, Hassan. I went to rejoice in our victory with Zelima, my daughter.

Barach. Foolish woman. I warned you against going to the seraglio. What did you tell Zelima? That the unknown prince was staying at our inn? That I knew him and loved him?

Schirina. Would there be any great harm done if I did?

Barach. Don't put me off, Schirina. Did you tell your daughter that I knew the prince?

Schirina. Yes, I did. She even asked his name, and to tell you the truth . . .

Barach. We are lost. Hurry, sire, we must flee from here, find a way to escape Pekin. . . No. There is no time. Turandot's guard is upon us. Listen, Schirina: there is no time for me to escape. But you go. Take this old man with you and hide him.

Timur. Tell me the reason for our haste.

Barach. Later. (*Low to* Timur.) Remember. Tell no one your name, or your son's. (*To* Schirina.) You, Schirina: if you want to repair some of the harm you've done, go with this old man and hide him. Not in the

inn. Find some other place. Keep him hidden until past
noon tomorrow.

Schirina. Hassan . . .

Timur. If there is some danger, you should flee with us,
Hassan.

Barach. That would only betray us all. I am the one
they're looking for. I am the one whose name they
know. Go. Go quickly.

Timur. But can't you . . .

Barach. Quickly.

Schirina. In what did I do wrong?

Barach. Remember. Never speak your name. Quickly,
now. Quickly. (Timur *and* Schirina *start off.*) It is too
late.

Scene VII

Truffaldino, *the* eunuchs, *now armed with spears, and the
above.*

Truffaldino *deploys the* eunuchs *about the stage to block
all exits.*

Barach. I am Hassan. I know you are looking for me
and I will come with you.

Truffaldino tells them not to make any noise. He says
they should all be delighted, as he has come to do
them a great favor.

Barach. Yes. You have been sent to bring me to the
seraglio. I am ready.

Truffaldino expatiates on Barach's good fortune. He explains how rigorous they are in the seraglio. How, if a
mosquito should fly in by accident, they catch it and
examine it to see whether it's male or female. If it
turns out to be male, they kill it on the spot. He
gives other examples of their scrupulousness. He then
asks who the old man is.

Barach. I don't know him. He must be some unfortunate
beggar.

Truffaldino says he is in a generous mood and has decided to take the old man along to the seraglio, too. He
then asks who the woman is.

Barach. I have never seen her before. I met them both
here by accident. But come. I know your lady sent you

to find me. Let us go. There is no need to bother with the old man or the woman.

Truffaldino is very angry. He says that Barach has been lying to him. He, Truffaldino, knows the lady is Barach's wife and Zelima's mother. He has seen her in the seraglio many times with her daughter. He orders his eunuchs to take all three prisoner.

Timur.   What will they do with us, Hassan?

Barach.   What will they do with us? Old man, you have suffered much; but you must now prepare yourself to suffer more. Yet even in the most desperate circumstances do not forget what I told you.

Truffaldino, with much blustering, has them lined up and marched out.

ACT IV

Scene I: A room in the seraglio. In the center of the room is a chest filled with gold.

Turandot, Barach, Timur, Schirina, Zelima, *and* eunuchs.

Barach *and* Timur *are tied to columns.* Zelima *and* Schirina *are on one side of the stage, crying.* Turandot *is on the other.*

Turandot.   There is still time to save yourselves. If you reveal the names of the prince and his father, you will go free and that chest of gold will be yours. But if you persist in your silence, I will be compelled to set my slaves on you. (*To the* eunuchs.) You there, make yourselves ready.

The eunuchs *bow to* Turandot *and arm themselves with whips.*

Barach.   Turandot, I will never reveal the names to you, although I know them. I will suffer all your tortures and even death, but I will not tell you the names. (*To* Schirina.) Schirina, do not weep for me. If the princess can be moved by tears, you should weep for this innocent old man whose only fault was to be found with me. He should not be touched.

Schirina.   Please, my lady. For pity's sake . . .

Timur. Do not beg for me, Schirina. For me, death means only liberation from my misery. I welcome it. But there is no reason that this man should also die. Turandot, if you want the names . . .

Barach. No, my friend. If you tell her the names, the unknown prince is lost.

Turandot. Then you know the names too, old man.

Timur. Yes, I know them. (*To* Barach.) But tell me why I must not reveal them.

Barach. Because if you do, it will mean the prince's certain death, and ours as well.

Turandot. He is lying to you, old man. He is trying to frighten you. Come, slaves. Come teach him to keep silent.

The eunuchs *approach* Barach.

Schirina. God, no! Stop. My husband . . .

Timur. Stop. Princess, swear to me your most solemn oath that you will spare this man's life if I tell you the names.

Turandot. I swear by all the gods in heaven that, once you have told me the names, both his life and your own will be spared.

Barach. She is lying. Tell her nothing, old man. Her oath is treacherous. Princess, swear instead that once you know the names you will have the unknown prince for your husband. And swear further that not only will you spare our lives but that you will set us free. If you swear to that, Princess, I myself will tell you the names, and gladly.

Turandot. Hassan, I have grown tired of your obstinacy. (*To the* eunuchs.) Take them. They are yours. I do not wish either of them to survive.

Schirina. Pity, my lady. Have pity.

Barach. Old man, now the method behind her charity should be clear to you.

Timur (*preparing himself for death*). My son, I willingly give my life for yours. Your mother is in heaven, and I follow her gladly.

Turandot. Stop. (*To* Timur.) Are you the father of the prince? Is it possible that you are a king?

Timur. Yes, Turandot. I am his father and a king.

Barach. What have you done?

Schirina. Is it possible that a king should be so reduced?

Turandot (*to herself*). A king. This poor old man a

king, and the father of the prince whom I should hate
mortally, but . . . What am I saying? The unknown
prince caused my shame and disgrace, and this is his
father. (*Aloud.*) Who are you, old man? I will no
longer permit this silence.

Timur (*to* Barach). Friend, what shall I do?

Barach. Endure. Remember, Turandot, this man was a
king. Do not debase yourself. Do what you will to me,
but respect his royalty.

Turandot. He will be respected. My vengeance will
spend itself on you alone.

She signals to the eunuchs, *who approach brandishing
their whips.*

Schirina. Ah, no. My husband. My husband.

Scene II

Adelma *and the above.*

Adelma. Stop, Princess, the emperor is coming here to
speak with you. He has already left his apartments.
Have these two taken to the dungeons and hidden
there. While your father is here with you, I will take
this gold and use it to buy the prince's guards, who I
know are corruptible. Schirina, if you value your husband; Zelima, if you love your mother; you will do just
as I say. If everyone follows my instructions, Turandot
will soon be restored to her original glory.

Turandot. My friend, I trust you. Take the gold. Let
Zelima and Schirina go with you so that you may instruct them more fully in what they are to do. I put all
my hope in your hands.

Adelma. Come with me. (*Aside.*) When I know the
names, I will have absolute power over both the prince
and her, my enemy.

Adelma, Zelima, Schirina, *and two* eunuchs *carrying the
chest of gold between them, exeunt.*

Barach. Wife. Daughter. Do not betray us. Do not yield
to her.

Turandot. Let these two be imprisoned in the dungeons
underneath the palace. Quickly. Secretly.

Timur. Turandot, do what you will with me but, for
pity's sake, do not harm my son.

Barach. Pity? By now you should know there is no pity
in her. Your son is already betrayed. And you and I
will be locked forever in her dungeon lest her treachery
come to light. But, Turandot, you may be certain we
will not go unrevenged. Heaven sees you clearly and
will punish you.

Timur *and* Barach *are led off by* eunuchs.

Scene III

Turandot, *alone.*

Turandot. If Heaven sees me clearly, I am not afraid.
Men, alas, do not see with equal clarity; they stumble
on appearances. Who, after all this, will speak anything
but bad of me? What will become of my name, of my
reputation? And yet, how sweet it will be to say those
names tomorrow in front of my father, the doctors, and
all my people. How sweet it will be to see him sent
from the Divan, shamed and defeated. Yet my triumph
is not as pure as it should be. When I picture his
despair to myself, when I picture it . . . But no, I will
continue in my design. Surely the joy of victory will
follow the fact.

Scene IV

Altoum, Pantalone, Tartaglia, guards, *and* Turandot.

Altoum (*to himself*). Who could have foreseen it would
come to this? That Calaf, son of Timur, should have
at last come to Pekin; and that it is here that he is to
be recompensed for his past miseries. O you gods: who
can refuse you his love once he has seen the just work-
ings of your providence?

Pantalone (*low to* Tartaglia). What the devil is the
matter with the emperor? He's whispering to himself
like a shy lunatic.

Tartaglia (*also low*). Shh. He had a visit from a secret
messenger a little while ago; some kind of spirit, or

demon, or whatever. I tell you frankly, Prime Minister, when that thing arrived—whoosh—in a billow of black smoke, clutching a scroll in its paw; well, to tell you the honest truth, I left in something of a hurry.

Altoum. Daughter, the dawn is quickly approaching and you have not yet been able to learn what you seek. Yet I have learned it, just now, without effort. (*He takes a scroll from his robe.*) The two names you seek are written here on this paper. A messenger from a far place came and spoke with me. When he departed, he left me this scroll on which are inscribed the two royal names along with much other information, both grave and glad. I have promised to keep the scroll to myself until the ordeal is over. But I may tell you that the unknown prince is a king's son, and that the prince himself will one day be a king. Daughter, why expose yourself a second time to public ridicule and derision? Why shame yourself again tomorrow?

Altoum *signals* Pantalone, Tartaglia, *and the* guards *to leave. They make reverences to him and exeunt.*

I have come to you with a plan by which you can preserve your good name and your honor.

Turandot. My good name and honor! Thank you, Father, I will see to them myself tomorrow in the Divan.

Altoum. Believe me, daughter, it is impossible for you to learn the names. I see in your eyes that you are desperate. I am your father and I love you. We are alone. Tell me truthfully; do you know the two names?

Turandot. You will learn that tomorrow, Father.

Altoum. Turandot, if you have somehow managed to learn the names, tell me, and I will inform the prince and see that he leaves Pekin secretly tonight. I will spread the report abroad that you had pity on him and refused to shame him in public. In that way you will please the people, who hate your unwavering pride; and you will give me infinite consolation. Daughter, do not deny me this favor.

Turandot. He had no pity on me today. It is only just that he should suffer equal humiliation tomorrow.

Altoum. He shamed you to save his life, because he loves you. Turandot, for once be compassionate. Listen. Listen to my plan. I want you to know how much your

father still loves you. I am sure you do not know the
names you seek. I know them. They are written here
on this paper. If you agree to my plan, I will tell them
to you. You may confront the prince with them tomorrow and see his shame and anguish, if that will
please you. In return I ask you this: that after your
triumph you relent and consent to be his wife, not from
any obligation but of your own free will. If you promise to do this, I will tell you what you want to know
immediately, and our transaction will forever remain
a secret between us. In this way you will satisfy your
pride; gain the eternal love of your subjects; win the
most noble prince in the world for your husband; and
console your father, who has suffered so much on your
account.

Turandot (*aside*).   How clever my father is to tempt
me thus. What shall I do? Where shall I turn? Shall I
trust Adelma's strategems or shall I half capitulate,
take the names on my father's terms, and so spare
myself total humiliation tomorrow? Surely it is wiser
to do as my father suggests. And yet Adelma was so
sure, so confident. What if she should succeed after
I have given my word to my father?

Altoum.   Why do you hesitate, daughter? After such a
display of indecision how can you ask me to believe
you know the names? Come, Turandot, do as I ask.
Agree.

Turandot (*aside*).   My father is too insistent. He and
the prince must have conspired together to tempt me.

Altoum.   Come, Turandot, yield.

Turandot.   I am resolved. Let the Divan be assembled
at dawn tomorrow as was agreed.

Altoum.   You are resolved to be shamed publicly again.

Turandot.   I am resolved the ordeal will take place.

Altoum (*angry*).   Obstinate, arrogant woman! So be it.
So be it. Know, so that your disgrace will be the
greater, that as soon as you are vanquished the Divan
will be transformed into a temple; and there, amidst
the raucous shouts and laughter of the multitude, you
and the prince will be wed. And when you cry for time,
for pity, for mercy, I will recall your obstinacy and refuse.

Altoum exits.

Turandot.   Adelma, my friend, I now depend wholly
on you for my deliverance.

Scene V: A magnificent room in the palace. In the middle of the room is an oriental sofa that serves as Calaf's bed.

Calaf *and* Brighella, *holding a torch. A clock strikes nine.*

Brighella. Your Highness, that was nine o'clock. In the last half hour you've paced up and down this room three hundred and forty-four times. I'm exhausted and I've just been watching you. Why don't you rest a little?

Calaf. I cannot rest, but there is no reason for you to stay with me. Go. Leave me.

Brighella (going). Just one last word of advice, your Highness. If you should happen to be visited by any, ah, apparitions during the night, you'll be very careful, won't you? Promise me.

Calaf. Apparitions? What do you mean?

Brighella. Oh, my. It's worth my life to be more explicit. Listen. We have orders, strict orders from the emperor himself, not to let anyone into this room tonight. But—now here's the delicate part—the emperor is the emperor, of course, but Princess Turandot has her authority, too. Do you understand what I mean? I'm being very subtle. You see, we poor bureaucrats are caught between them, between the hammer and the anvil, so to speak. Believe me, you have no idea how hard the diplomatic life is. You can't displease anyone, anyone at all. In addition to which you have to smile all the time. *(Aside.)* I think it's the smiling that's the hardest part. *(Aloud.)* We'd like to have our morality, too, but you understand, we're in an impossible position.

Calaf. Go on. Are you saying it isn't safe here tonight, even with guards at every door?

Brighella. Oh, my no, I'm not saying that. Not at all. Remember, I never said anything like that. But you know how anxious the princess is to find out who you are. Well, it's possible, barely possible, that someone, some friend of hers perhaps, might slip by my men during the night. It's so dark, you see, it wouldn't be their fault. You understand? All right. Just be careful.

Calaf. Go, and don't be afraid. I will be on my guard.

Brighella. That's fine. Now don't give me away, please, Prince. I'm at your mercy now. *(Aside.)* I've done everything in my power. It's not my fault if nothing I ever do ever has the least effect. I'm a man of good will, as you've just seen, but unfortunately completely without influence. Like so many men of good will. And you know something odd? I'm not at all sure I'd like it if all my little criticisms and suggestions were instantaneously turned into law. No. I don't think I'd like it in the least.

Brighella exits.

Calaf. It was good of him to warn me. Now I am prepared to defend myself against hell itself. But the dawn is not far off. I will try to rest.

He lies down on the sofa.

Scene VI

Schirina, *disguised as a soldier,* and Calaf.

Schirina (entering hesitantly). Sire . . . sire . . . my heart trembles in my breast.

Calaf. Who are you? What do you want?

Schirina. I am Schirina, Hassan's wife. I slipped past your guards in this disguise. I come to you with grave news, Prince. I can hardly bring myself to speak for fear, for grief . . .

Calaf. Tell me your news, Schirina.

Schirina. Hassan, my husband, has been captured. Somehow Turandot learned that he knew you. She has had him brought to the seraglio to force him to reveal your name. She has threatened him with torture, but he said he would die rather than betray you.

Calaf. My loyal minister. That you should be subjected to this for my sake!

Schirina. But there is more. At this very moment your father is in my house. He is inconsolable over the loss of his wife, your mother . . .

Calaf. O God. What are you saying, Schirina?

Schirina. He knows that both you and Hassan have been taken. He is desperate. He threatens to come to the palace and reveal his identity, and so die with you; for he believes you are condemned to die. I restrained him by promising to bring him a letter from you saying that you are well and that there is nothing to fear.

Calaf. My mother dead and my father here in Pekin!
Is it possible? Are you telling me the truth, Schirina?
Schirina. If I am lying, may Heaven destroy me on the
spot.
Calaf. Ah, my unfortunate parents. I should not have
left them.
Schirina. Don't delay, Prince. If your father is not
reassured immediately, fresh tragedies will follow.
Here. I have brought paper, pen, and ink. You need
write only a few lines. Tell him that you are well
and that he should remain where he is. Just the sight of
your signature will cheer him immeasurably.
Calaf. Let me have the paper. (*He is about to write.
He stops.*) What am I doing? (*He throws the pen
and paper at* Schirina's *feet.*) Schirina, go to my
father and tell him that he may go to the emperor if
he wishes and confess whatever he likes. In short, tell
him he may do whatever he will to reassure himself.
Schirina (*confused*). But don't you want . . . how
. . . Prince, one line will be enough.
Calaf. No, Schirina. Not one word. Tomorrow at
dawn my name will be revealed and not before. I
am grieved that Hassan's wife should try to betray
me.
Schirina. Betray you, Prince. What are you saying?
After I have risked so much for you. I will go now and
tell your father what you said. (*Aside.*) May Adelma's
other schemes fare better. She is very shrewd, but
he is a match for her.

                                        Schirina *exits.*
Calaf. Brighella did well to warn me there might be
apparitions tonight. Yet Schirina swore a solemn oath
that my mother is dead and that my father is here in
Pekin. That much must be true. Misfortune after
misfortune . . . (*A shape moves at another door.*)
Another apparition. We will see what this one wants.

Scene VII

Zelima *and* Calaf.

Zelima. Prince, I am one of Turandot's slaves and come
on her errand, bearing good news.
Calaf. I cannot imagine that the news you bring is the

news I most desire. The princess's heart is too hard and unyielding.

Zelima. I have always thought that so. You, Prince, are the first ever to kindle affection in her. I know it does not seem possible, but I am convinced the princess loves you. I am sure of it, Prince. If I am not telling the truth, let the earth open and swallow me.

Calaf. Slave, I believe you think you are speaking the truth. But what else have you come to tell me?

Zelima. Just this: that Turandot is more than willing to become your wife, but she is also frantic to preserve her name and reputation. She realizes that she accepted an impossible challenge and she is mortally afraid that she will be shamed again tomorrow in the Divan. I promise you that is her only concern. If I am not telling you the truth, let the earth open up and swallow me.

Calaf. Do not call down such prodigies on yourself. I believe you. If Turandot has sent you to ask if I will agree to call off tomorrow's ordeal, go back to her and tell her I will. Her reputation will increase enormously when the people see she is capable of pity; when they see that she is willing to become my wife, and so console her father, her people, and myself. Tell me, was that the news you were sent to bring me?

Zelima. Not precisely, sire. You must forgive us certain female vanities. The princess sent me to ask a favor of you. She says her only thought is to regain her reputation by answering you with the correct names tomorrow. Once she has done that she promises to descend from the throne and herself ask the priests to join you in marriage. Prince, we are alone here. The revelation of the names will cost you nothing, but it will assure you of the princess's eternal gratitude.

Calaf (*smiling*). You neglected to end this speech with the usual words.

Zelima. What words, sire?

Calaf. "If I am not telling you the truth, let the earth open and swallow me!"

Zelima. Do you doubt that I am telling you the truth, sire?

Calaf. Yes, I doubt it. I doubt it so strongly that I will not tell you what you ask. Return to Turandot and tell her that I withhold the names from her not from malevolence but from an excess of love.

Zelima (*dropping the pretense*). Impudent Prince, you

do not realize what your obstinacy can cost you.

Calaf. It can cost me my life.

Zelima. When it does, I will feel myself well rewarded.
(*Aside.*) It was all in vain.

Zelima exits.

Calaf. Leave me. Let us have an end to these apparitions. Schirina's words still torment me. My mother
. . . my father . . . It is almost too much. In a few
hours I will know all, for better or worse. Now I will
try to rest.

He lies down on the sofa and sleeps.

Scene VIII

Truffaldino *and* Calaf, *asleep.*

Truffaldino enters gaily and says, *sotto voce,* that he has
been promised two bags of gold if he manages to learn
the two names from the prince, who luckily is sleeping. He continues that for this purpose he has brought
a mandrake root which he bought from Dr. Archimedias, a celebrated magician who has a shop in the
piazza. It is common knowledge, he adds, that if a
mandrake root is placed under the pillow of a sleeping
man, the man will answer truthfully any question put
to him in the proper manner. Truffaldino proves this
by reciting all sorts of strange and wonderful cases
which Dr. Archimedias told him of. He approaches
Calaf with great caution, slips the root under his pillow, steps back, and waits. He then recites a short
spell with appropriate gestures. Calaf does not speak,
but he does make certain movements with his arms
and legs. Truffaldino triumphantly imagines that these
movements have been caused by the mandrake root
and are therefore significant. He postulates that each
movement stands for a different letter of the alphabet.
With great care he derives two outlandish names from
the prince's movements. Then, thinking he has got
what he came for, he exits gleefully.

Scene IX

Adelma, *veiled and carrying a lamp; and* Calaf, *asleep.*

Adelma (*to herself*). All my emissaries have failed me,
but I will succeed. Now is the moment I have long
awaited. Love, you who have quickened my intelligence; and you, fortune, who have made my opportunities; come help me now, that all my desires may
be realized in a single moment. (*She holds the light
near* Calaf *and studies him.*) He is asleep. (*She puts
down the lamp. Then aloud.*) Unknown prince, awake!

Calaf. Who wakes me? Who are you? Why don't you
leave me in peace?

Adelma. Prince, why this anger? In me you see only
an unfortunate slave, not a spy come to trick secrets
out of you. But you are wondering who I am. Sit where
you are and I will tell you.

Calaf. I warn you. I will not let myself be betrayed.

Adelma. I, betray you! Tell me, Prince: did Schirina
come here tonight and ask you to sign a letter?

Calaf. Yes, Schirina was here.

Adelma. But, Prince, you didn't sign her letter, did you?

Calaf. No, I am not that foolish.

Adelma. Thank Heaven. And after she had left, did
another slave come and try, with many traps and
subterfuges, to make you reveal yourself?

Calaf. One did. But she left here as ignorant as she
came, as you will.

Adelma. You are unjust, Prince. You do not know
me. Sit down and listen. Once you have heard what
I have to say, call me traitor if you like.

Calaf. What do you want of me?

Adelma. First, look at me closely and tell me if you
recognize me.

Calaf. Your carriage and patrician manner lead me to
believe you are of high birth. But your dress is that
of a slave, in which condition I remember seeing you
this morning in the Divan. I pitied you.

Adelma. As I pitied you five years ago when I saw you
reduced to carrying vile burdens for your bread. My
heart told me you were not born to such base work,
and I did everything in my power to help you. I tried
to convey to you in covert glances the tenderness I
felt. It is not always possible for a princess to say what
she feels. (*She removes her veil.*) Now tell me, Prince:
have you ever seen my face before?

Calaf (*astonished*). Adelma!

Adelma. Yes, Adelma, the daughter of Ciecobad, the

King of Turkestan; born to reign but condemned to
serve.

Calaf. Adelma, we all believed you dead. But can it
be that the daughter of great King Ciecobad, so recently a queen, is now a slave?

Adelma. Yes. I am a slave. You must not be amazed
when I tell you the cause of my degradation. I had
a brother who was as blindly in love with Turandot as
you are yourself, Prince. He, too, faced her ordeal,
but he was less fortunate than you. You will have
seen his head on the city wall among the others. Ah,
my dear brother. (*She cries.*)

Calaf. Had I heard this from anyone else, Adelma, I
would not have believed it.

Adelma (*composing herself*). Ciecobad, my father,
was a valiant and honorable man. Enraged at his son's
pointless death, he assembled his armies and waged war
on Altoum. But Fate, who holds all men's destinies pre-
cariously in her hands, proved to be against him, and
he was vanquished and killed. One of Altoum's generals, a pitiless, hard man, resolved to destroy our
entire family, down to the youngest child. He put
my three remaining brothers to the sword; and had
my mother, my sisters, and myself hurled into a
raging river and left to drown. But Altoum himself
happened to see us from the bank and ordered his
men to drag us from the river. My mother and sisters
were already dead. I, less fortunate than they, was
still alive. The emperor's physicians used all their
art and brought me back to health. When I was completely well, I was given to Turandot as a slave for
her seraglio. Prince, if you have any compassion, you
will see how cruel an irony this was: to be compelled
to serve the very one who was the first cause of my
misfortunes.

Calaf. Adelma, I do pity you. But you are wrong to
blame Turandot for your misfortunes. Surely it was
your brother's passion and the pride and imprudence
of your father which brought you so low. (*Adelma
cries.*) And what can I do to repair your fortunes?
You see I am powerless. If I should triumph tomorrow, I promise, you will have your freedom and whatever other aid it is in my power to give. But, Adelma,
do not say any more now. It is futile to recite miseries
it is not possible to redress.

Adelma. You know my name, my lineage, and my tragic history. You know I was born a queen and meant to rule. I hope this knowledge, quickened by compassion (for I cannot hope for your love), will move you to be equally open with me. But perhaps it is too much to hope that you who are so blind with love for Turandot will trust one who speaks against her.

Calaf. Adelma, do not press me.

Adelma. I have more to tell you, Prince. Much more, if you trust me.

Calaf. I trust you, Adelma.

Adelma (aside). O you gods, make him believe me. *(Aloud.)* Prince, your beloved Turandot has given secret orders that you are to be murdered before dawn tomorrow. That is the way she returns your love.

Calaf. Murdered!

Adelma. As you leave these rooms tomorrow, twenty of her assassins will intercept you and see that you never reach the Divan.

Calaf. I must warn the guards.

Adelma. The guards are her men, Prince. They are the assassins.

Calaf (desperate). Ah, Calaf, is this the end then? Is my death the only succor I can bring you, Timur?

Adelma (aside). The lie was well chosen. He is in my power. Calaf, the son of King Timur. Now, even if he will not yield to me, I have the price to buy myself out of slavery.

Calaf. Fortune, what more can you do to me? What more harm can you bring me? It is unbearable that Turandot should be so treacherous; that so lovely a person should harbor such a treacherous heart. But, Adelma, what you have told me cannot be the truth.

Adelma. I knew you would doubt me, Prince. But everything I told you is true. You do not know how desperate Turandot is. She knows that what she has undertaken is impossible. She paces back and forth through the seraglio, half mad, speaking unintelligible things to herself. Her face is discolored and distorted with rage. You would not recognize her, Prince. She is no longer the divine creature she seemed this morning in the Divan. I tried to calm her. I praised you to her, listed your qualities and virtues. In short, I did everything I could to reconcile her to becoming your wife. But all my efforts were in vain. She cut me off rudely

and then gave orders to the two slaves you saw tonight.
In case their deception failed, she gave alternative
orders to her soldiers.

Calaf.   Brighella was speaking the simple truth when he
told me to trust no one, no one at all. At last I understand how the world is. I no longer have the will to
flee my destiny.

Adelma.   Prince, I will show you how to escape it forever; and, at the same time, find a way for me to
escape my slavery. Several of the guards are in my
pay. They have two swift horses saddled and waiting
for us, and they themselves are prepared to escort us
as far as the city walls. From there we can ride to the
frontier without danger. Once out of China I will re-
assemble my army, which is still loyal to me. Together
with the armies of Alinguer, Emperor of Berlas, who is
my kinsman and my ally, we will reconquer my kingdom. That kingdom will be yours, as I will be if you
desire it. But if you do not, there are princesses among
the Tartars who surpass Turandot herself in beauty, and
who are gentle and womanly as well. If you choose one
of them, I will be your subject. So long as you are
freed from the threat of death, and I from the odium of
slavery, I will be content. But it is almost day, Prince.
Hurry. Let us flee.

Calaf.   Adelma, you are most kind. I am truly sorry
that I cannot help you reach freedom. If I flee with
you, Altoum will call me traitor, and rightly so. I cannot betray or bargain or abuse his trusut.

Adelma.   But the emperor's daughter can abuse it. And
does.

Calaf.   Adelma, you must realize that I am no longer
my own master. You must understand that I would
gladly die to fulfill Turandot's slightest wish. Flee by
yourself, Adelma. I am resolved to stay and, if she
desires it, to die for her.

Adelma.   Are you that blinded by your love?

Calaf.   So much so that I can imagine no alternatives but
to gain Turandot's love or to die.

Adelma.   Prince, I am aware that she surpasses me in
intellect, in beauty, in everything. I believed I could
inspire some gentler feeling in you. But I do not mind
your neglect and disesteem. All I want is to save your
dear life. Come. Flee with me.

Calaf.   Adelma, I am resolved to stay and, if necessary,
to die.

Adelma.   Stay, then. Die. I will stay, too, and remain a slave for life. Since the Heavens are still hostile to me, we will see which of us can be truer to his love. Farewell, Calaf, son of Timur.

Adelma exits.

Calaf.   When has any mortal man ever spent a crueler night? Ringed with spies and beset with traitors, tortured by an impossible love; informed of his mother's death and his father's desperation; brought nearly within reach of his desire only to learn that he is to be betrayed by his beloved You were right, Zelima. My obstinacy has cost me more than I imagined. Well, the sun is up. Her spies have failed. It is time for her alternative orders to be carried out. At least my anguish will be ended once and for all. (*Rises as the door opens.*)

Scene X

Brighella, guards, *and* Calaf.

Brighella.   Prince, the time has come.

Calaf.   So it is to be you, Brighella. Come. Carry out your orders. Take my life. I no longer have any use for it.

Brighella.   Orders? What orders? What the devil are you talking about, your Highness? The only orders I have are to take you to the Divan. The emperor will be there in a minute. He's just finished combing his beard and adjusting the tilt of his crown.

Calaf.   Then let us go to the Divan. I am certain I will never arrive there alive. (*He throws down his sword.*) See that I can face death calmly and without any defense. Let the princess know that even at the last I refused to interfere with the execution of her orders.

Calaf exits.

Brighella.   Poor boy. Obviously went crazy during the night. All those ladies, in and out, in and out; declaiming, posturing, beating their breasts, tearing their hair. Finally, they drove him crazy. Ah, well. He's not the first lunatic in a high place, and I daresay he won't be the last. (*To the* guards.) Guards. Attention. Shoulder arms. Double-time, march. Catch that prince if you know what's good for you.

Exeunt to the sound of drums and other instruments.

ACT V

Scene I: The scene is the Great Divan. Everything is arranged as in Act II, except that a large curtain upstage has been added. The doctors, guards, *etc. are placed as In Act II.* Altoum *is seated on his throne.*

Altoum, Pantalone, Tartaglia, doctors, *and* guards. *Then* Calaf.

Calaf *enters, still suspicious. He bows to Altoum.*

Calaf (to himself). I have come the whole way fearing death at each corner, but I am still alive. Either Adelma lied to me, or else Turandot has learned the names she sought and suspended the order for my death.

Altoum. My son, I see you are still uneasy. You need not be. You have nothing more to fear. I have wonderful news for you. Turandot has consented to become your wife. Three of her emissaries have just left me. I had sent her numerous pleas, offering to suspend the ordeal if she would agree to the marriage. Here is her answer. Read it, if you need reassurance.

Pantalone. It's true, your Highness. I took two of the messages in person. I've been running around all night in the freezing cold, half dressed. I've carried questions, queries, and clarifications—offers and counteroffers. No, don't thank me. It's all in the line of duty. I'm glad it all worked out so well. Although I must say it would have been nice to see the princess really humiliated.

Tartaglia. I was there half the night myself. She got really frantic when the dawn broke. She kept me half an hour in a draft asking me to do things and then changing her mind. I tell you, what with the early hour, the cold, and those ridiculous questions, I'm afraid I used some bad language in front of the princess. (*Aside.*) And I wish I'd used worse. Much worse.

Altoum. See how slow she is. I gave my men orders
that if she refused to come willingly, she should be
brought by force. I am no longer disposed to be gentle
with her. (*Grave music is heard offstage.*) Here she is
at last. Now let her suffer all the shame I offered to
spare her. Rejoice, my son.

Calaf. Pardon me, sire. I am tortured with remorse that
she should suffer this great shame on my account. I
would prefer . . . no. I cannot live without her. Perhaps she will never love me, but I hope that time and
kindness will teach her affection.

Altoum. Ministers, we will wait no longer. Let the hall
be transformed into a temple, so that Turandot may
learn when she enters that we intend to perform what
we promised in every detail. The time has come for
her to pay for all the anguish she has caused. Let the
people be admitted, and let there be general rejoicing.
Prepare the altar.

*The curtain upstage is opened, revealing an altar and two
priests.*

Pantalone. Look, Chancellor, she's coming. It looks as
if she's been crying.

Tartaglia. It certainly is a melancholy entrance. This
looks more like a funeral to me than a wedding.

Scene II

*Turandot, Adelma, Truffaldino, eunuchs, slaves, and the
above. The grave music grows louder. Enter* Turandot *and her retinue, dressed in mourning. They go
through the same ceremonies and take the same positions as in Act II.* Calaf *remains immobile at the
center of the stage.*

Turandot. Prince, the sad air of my retinue must glad-
den your heart. I, for my part, look on the marriage
altar and am unutterably sad. Know that I have used
all the art at my disposal to revenge myself for the
shame I suffered yesterday at your hands. But now I
realize it is no use and that I must at last submit to my
destiny.

Calaf. Princess, I wish I knew the way to turn your
sadness to joy. I would to Heaven that you took the

hundredth part of the pleasure in this union that I do.
But since you do not, I can only ask your pardon.

Altoum.   My son, she does not deserve such courtesy.
The time has come for her total humiliation. Let the
sound of joyful instruments be heard; and let the marriage follow.

Turandot.   No, Father. The time for my humiliation has
not yet come. The day, after all, is mine. I could have
had no better vengeance than this; to seem defeated,
to all but yield, and then to dash the prince once again
to the depths of misery. (*She stands.*) Now listen, all
of you. Calaf, son of Timur, quit the Divan. You
have been vanquished. Find some other woman for
your wife. Know that Turandot cannot be bested.

Altoum.   What is this? What do I hear?

Pantalone.   She got it! By the six horns of Confucius, she
got it.

Tartaglia.   But how could she have known?

Calaf.   Now all is indeed lost. Nor can I find any comfort, since I myself am the cause of my downfall. It
would have been far better had I failed yesterday, for
this augmented pain is insupportable. Altoum, the law
must run its course. Our bargain was that I should die
if Turandot guessed the names I asked. And she has
guessed them.

Altoum.   Slowly, Calaf, slowly. My age cannot absorb
all this at once.

Turandot (*low to* Zelima). Zelima, he moves me more
in his misery than he ever did triumphant. I can no
longer contradict the commands of my heart.

Zelima (*low*). Then yield to them, my lady.

Adelma (*to herself*). Now is the moment that means
life or death to me.

Calaf.   Princess, I want your victory to be complete. It
cannot be while I am alive. (*He approaches her
throne.*) Here at your feet you see Prince Calaf, your
newest victim. You will have forgotten him by now;
but he cannot live without your love.

He draws a dagger and is about to stab himself when
Turandot *rushes from her throne and restrains him.*

Turandot (*tenderly*). What would you do, Calaf?

Altoum.   Can it be possible?

Calaf.   Turandot, why do you impede a death that you
yourself brought about? Can my desperation have

moved you? Ah, no. I see. You want me to live, since you know it will be more painful for me to live without you than to die. But let me die. (*He tries to stab himself again, and again* Turandot *restrains him.*)

Turandot. No, Calaf. You must live for my sake. I yield to you. I confess I am vanquished. Zelima, go to the prisoners. Console the old man and his minister with this joyful news.

Zelima. Yes, my lady, with pleasure.

Adelma (*to herself*). There is no hope left. It is time for me to die.

Turandot. Calaf, know that I would never have discovered the names had you not revealed them last night in some strange transport to Adelma, my slave. I would never profit from such an accident. But, Calaf, even if I had won your challenge honorably, your speech, your gentleness, and your nobility have so touched me that even then I would have gladly consented to become your wife.

Calaf (*throwing the dagger to the ground*). Princess, your words have brought me to the summit of happiness.

Adelma (*to herself*). The lowest depths of misery are at last attained.

Altoum (*descending from his throne*). My dear daughter, I forgive you all your past offenses. You have atoned for them all in this one moment.

Pantalone. A wedding! We're going to have a wedding. Give them room, Doctors.

Tartaglia. That's right, Doctors. Spread out.

The doctors *retire to the back of the stage.*

Adelma. Yes. Take her. May you be happy with her. (*She comes forward.*) Princess, learn that all I seemed to do on your behalf I did only to gain the prince for myself. I loved him five years ago at my father's court and I have loved him ever since. Last night I tried to persuade him to flee with me by slandering you, Princess. But it was in vain. When the two names fell by some accident from his lips, I told them to you, hoping that you would drive him from the city and that I might follow. But that, too, has come to nothing. There is now only one way left to me, and I will take it. I was born of royal blood. It has been my shame to live these five years in subjugation. Turandot, I hate the barbarous creature you were and which, under that mask of repentance, you still are. You took my father from me, and my brothers; my mother and my sisters; the kingdom I was born to rule; and finally the only man I have ever loved. I will suffer no more losses or indignities. My life is the only thing you have left me, Princess, and that I will take myself. (*She picks up* Calaf's *dagger.*) Here is one way to escape slavery. (*She tries to stab herself, but* Calaf *restrains her.*)

Calaf. Stop, Adelma.

Adelma. Leave me alone. I want to die. (*She tries to stab herself again.* Calaf *takes the dagger from her.*)

Calaf. No, Adelma. Dear as you are to me, you must understand that my love for Turandot overwhelms all.

Adelma. No. By my treachery I have made myself unworthy of your affection.

Turandot. Adelma, what made you betray me? You were always more friend to me than servant.

Adelma. It should be clear to you, Princess. You were about to take Calaf from me. If I betrayed you, it was for his sake. Now, Princess, since Calaf has just taken my last means of escape from me, grant me one thing: let me leave Pekin. Do not force me to remain here to witness your marriage. I could not bear it. (*She cries.*)

Altoum (*aside*). I pity you unhappy Princess.

Calaf. Adelma, you need cry no longer. I can now repay you in part for what you did for me. Turandot, Altoum: if my words can influence you, let this unhappy woman have her freedom.

Turandot. Father, I too ask that favor. She abused all the love and confidence I had in her. I can no longer be her friend. And I would not be her mistress. Let her go free.

Altoum. On such a joyful day we will not measure our charity. We desire Adelma to share our happiness. She shall go free; and, also, her kingdom will be restored to her. Let her chose a consort to rule with her who will help her to reign wisely and justly.

Adelma. Sire, I am overcome. Overcome with remorse, with gratitude, and with love. Pardon me. I cannot speak.

Calaf. Timur, my father, is here in Pekin. Where can I find him to tell him of our great good fortune?

Turandot. My servants are caring for him. He knows the news already and rejoices with us.

Altoum. Timur here in the palace? Let him be told that he has still another reason to rejoice. His kingdom has been freed. The Sultan of Carizmano, widely hated for his tyranny, has been overthrown and killed. The people are still loyal to Timur and his family. One of your former ministers is keeping the kingdom and is searching for Timur or Calaf in all the countries of the earth, calling you back to rule. In this document you may read in what manner it all took place. (Altoum *hands* Calaf *a scroll.*)

Calaf (*having glanced at the scroll*).   Your Majesty, Turandot: excuse what must seem like ingratitude, but it is not to you or indeed to any mortals that I must address my thanks, but to the gods in heaven. It is to them I kneel and give thanks. For the gods can transform us in an instant against all human probability. I ask their pardon for my past complaints and lamentations. Their ways are truly unknowable. All we poor mortals can do is live, and pray, and await the just evolution of our destiny.

Turandot.   I have seen Calaf risk his life for love and have seen a loyal minister risk his rather than betray his lord. I have seen a subject who might have been a king search the world patiently for his monarch, and have seen that monarch, old and suffering, face death heroically for his son's sake. And also, I have seen a woman who I thought my dearest friend betray me. You eternal gods, pardon me for the obstinate, unjust hatred I have had for the male sex until this moment. I beg you, pardon my numerous cruelties, which were the fruit of my ignorance. I have been deaf to your commands and blind to nature. Hereafter I swear to love and revere the whole sweet race of men, and never again to trust one of my own sex.

She steps forward to the front of the stage.

If you believe my change of heart sincere
And my repentance worth your commendation
I pray you, signify it. Let us hear
Some token of your gentle approbation.

Luigi Pirandello

THE EMPEROR

(*Enrico IV*)

The great Italian theater of the nineteenth century, and of the early twentieth century, was the operatic theater, the theater of Verdi and Puccini—a circumstance not wtihout its logic if one traces the previous history of opera back, as one can, to such Italian pastoral dramas as the *Amyntas*. The work of the leading Italian dramatist of around 1900, Gabriele D'Annunzio, may be regarded as a kind of opera *manqué*. Italian dramatic literature proper was renewed for the twentieth century, not by D'Annunzio, but by Luigi Pirandello.

According to some accounts, the idea for *The Emperor* came to Pirandello when he was thumbing through an illustrated magazine and happened upon a picture of a cavalcade. One account specifies that it was the Roman hunt club riding to Villa Doria in medieval costume. But a translator of Pirandello's quotes the Maestro as giving a different version. "Henry IV has its origin in an episode of Italy's movie world during the manufacture [sic] of a now famous play. An Italian actor, called upon to assume the role of Dante, threw himself so wholly into his work that he broke down under the strain. Thereafter, as Pirandello says, he was unable to 'de-dantify' himself, and is to this day living a placid life in an Italian insane asylum as the immortal poet of Beatrice."*

Another translator of Pirandello's, Benjamin Crémieux, tells what books the Maestro consulted about the German Emperor Henry IV, namely, the appropriate volume in

* Arthur Livingston's Essays on Modern Italian Literature. New York: S. F. Vanni, 1950.

Wilhelm Oncken's *Allgemeine Geschichte* (a history of civilization in many volumes) and an early-nineteenth-century life of Pope Gregory VII, also by a German scholar (Johannes Voigt). Having looked up these books myself, I cannot report that Pirandello drew upon them for more than he could have found in any textbook, or even in encyclopedia articles, though it is of interest that the Oncken contains pictures of Henry's palace at Goslar and of the Abbey of Cluny.

More significant than Pirandello's reading on the theme is, I think, his choice of it. He had been a student at the University of Bonn, and undoubtedly German culture had exercised a powerful influence on him, perhaps even a fascination. The philosophy that people call "Pirandellian" could be regarded as his own little digest of the German contribution to metaphysics from Kant on. If we have heard, in our time, of a Rome-Berlin axis, we might speak, as students of Pirandello, of a Palermo-Bonn axis, for Pirandello spent much spiritual energy endeavoring to fuse within himself the Sicilian and popular elements with the European and intellectual elements. He naturally makes his Henry a spokesman for "German idealism," for "Pirandellianism"; whether this philosophy embraces the total vision of the play is another question.

Pirandello is wise enough to put into the play itself any historical details he wishes his audience to be aware of, but he does assume the spectator's prior knowledge of "Canossa." "We shall not go to Canossa," Bismarck had said in Pirandello's lifetime. For any educated European, Canossa is a permanent symbol of papal supremacy and, contrariwise, of the subjection of the temporal to the ecclesiastical power. In the year 1077, eleven years after William the Conqueror set foot in England, the Holy Roman Emperor knelt two days in the snow at Canossa, doing obeisance to the Pope and begging his Holiness for an audience. His wife, the Empress Bertha, knelt with him, and Bertha's mother Adelaide went with the Abbot of Cluny, another friendly witness, to plead with the Pope and his ally the Countess Matilda of Tuscany.

Such is the scene, which has remained indelibly imprinted upon the memory of Europe. Or perhaps one should say upon the fantasy of Europe. For the incident did not actually signify—as it is often taken to—that in the Middle Ages emperors always took their orders from popes. There is evidence that this very emperor, Henry

IV, knelt there, not in sincere submission, but because it was "the smart thing to do." In 1076 at Tribur the German princes had proposed the deposition of Henry. In kneeling at Canossa, the latter was heading off the prospect of having to face his accusers. Pirandello draws on very little of this material, but does remind us that the pseudo-humble Henry remained the Pope's fierce enemy and, in the year 1080 at Brixen, would declare Pope Gregory VII deposed. Pirandello was no doubt interested also in the insecurity of Henry's position—and the insecurity of a world in which not only the Pope but also the Emperor lived in daily danger of deposition.

If the Canossa symbol is clear, and the reference to it at least understandable, all the history the reader need bother his head with, concerns, I think, the situation of Henry in his childhood. Even at Canossa he is only 26 years old. He had succeeded to the throne as a child, and his mother Agnes had had to be Regent. But she had come under suspicion of adultery with Henry Bishop of Augsburg. Pirandello adds a touch of his own in suggesting that it was one of the Pope's henchmen, Peter Damiani, who pointed the accusing finger at the pair. Agnes is removed as Regent, and Henry IV himself rules—under the tutelage of Anno Bishop of Cologne and Adalbert Bishop of Bremen. Pirandello brings up the curtain at the point where Adalbert, as Henry believes, has been driven away by rival bishops.

Pirandello does not work out any point-for-point analogy between the eleventh-century story and the twentieth-century one, so that the reader to whom an historical reference here or there means nothing need not feel he is missing clues. When Pirandello wishes his audience to know that Matilda of Tuscany corresponds to Matilda Spina, he will say so. He will also let it be known that while the historical Matilda of Tuscany was simply the enemy of the Emperor, "our" Henry harbors a secret love for her. . . . And so on.

The play is, after all, about the twentieth century, nor is it a mere exposition of the "Pirandellian philosophy." To begin with, it is a study in insanity. And while we need not take Pirandello too literally as a pathologist, he stays, in essentials, close to well-known symptoms. Let me cite two sentences about insane delusions from Bernard Hart's standard introduction to the subject, *The Psychology of Insanity:*

Delusions may be of all kinds, but there are two types which call for special mention on account of their great frequency, *grandiose* and *persecutory* . . . The two types are frequently combined: for example, a patient may maintain that he is the king but that an organized conspiracy exists to deprive him of his birthright.

I do not believe that Pirandello himself was committed to the "absolute relativism" which is preached by his protagonists and *raisonneurs*. His plays, in fact, imply objective standards (as perhaps plays have to). For example, they imply a clear distinction between delusion and nondelusion. Without such a distinction, it would be meaningless to say that Henry ceased being mad after twelve years. Similarly, in the play which professes in its title that a thing "*is* so if it seems so" to anyone, it is definitely implied that "seeming" may be an unreliable guide to truth, since the person to whom something seems thus and so may be crazy. (The most serious characters in *Right You Are*—Signora Frola and the two Ponzas— do *not* believe that "it is so if you think so," they protest constantly that it isn't so *though* you think so . . .)

No major playwright—and Pirandello is one—deals chiefly in opinions *per se*. He deals in experience—and therefore in opinions only insofar as they are not merely spoken or held but experienced. The doubts about reality and identity with which Pirandello's works bristle are not, for this author, chiefly an intellectual matter, they are a psychological matter. And a clinical approach to Pirandello can be of service as a challenge to the intellectualistic analysis of him, as a recent study of *Six Characters in Search of an Author* has shown.* Some of the very same clinical "material" is present in *The Emperor*, notably, the fantasy of a father embracing his daughter, and indeed the whole play can reasonably be taken as a realistically intended study of both neurotic and psychotic phenomena. If anyone seriously doubts this, I would ask him to reread just the expository part of Act One, particularly what Belcredi and Matilda say about themselves and about Henry. The language is not that of psychiatry in the mid-twentieth century; but this is beside the point.

---

* "A Psychoanalytic Study of Pirandello's 'Six Characters in Search of an Author,'" by Charles Kligerman. *Journal of the American Psychoanalytic Association*, October, 1962.

It even makes sense to set aside the talk of "relativity" and conclude at the end that Henry *is* insane, that the unlucky experiment, though it went wrong, has produced the result that was feared and driven him back into insanity. The experiment, that is, plus the unfortunate turn taken by the conversation after it. What, after all, is going on here? It is not possible to take the murder of Belcredi as one is invited to take the murder of Claudius in *Hamlet,* namely, as a just retribution, willed by God. It is naked revenge at best, and committed in a peculiarly ignoble, unimperial way: would the medieval emperor have run an unarmed man through—and, at that, through the belly!? I see the ending of this play not as "romantic" and of vague import, nor yet as a rather forced illustration of a metaphysical thesis, but as just brutally what it seems—either immoral or insane, probably the latter. In either case, Pirandello's *Hamlet*—and the play might be considered such—is a *modern* Hamlet, that is, an anti-Hamlet, a savage and serious parody. In genre, then, it is not tragedy but tragi-comedy. And it belongs to the modern and extreme form of this: tragic farce.

In its substance, *The Emperor* is not *merely* psychological, not, at any rate, if the term psychology is limited to what the psychoanalytic journals limit themselves to—hunting for primal scenes and unacknowledged Oedipal relationships and the like. To understand it, one would need a psychology with a psyche—that is, a psychology which finds in the traditional terms *spirit* and *soul* a good deal more than can be reduced to the sexual mishaps of infancy or later. Pirandello writes of a sickness of the human creature which can scarcely be put down solely to the misadventures of the bedroom or the nursery. To diagnose this sickness one would need, I should think, the instruments of other disciplines than the clinical, and even within the field of psychology, men of religious interests and great intuition can contribute more in the interpretation of Pirandello than men who rely on current therapeutic science. St. Augustine, for instance, said: "Every disordered spirit is a punishment to itself," which might stand as an adequate motto for *The Emperor*. And Blaise Pascal has a passage that seems to put the Pirandellian view of things in the best perspective: "It is imagining . . . that makes people happy, unhappy, healthy, sick, rich, poor . . . mad or wise . . . How many invalids owe to their imaginings their cure, how many healthy people their illness. . . . Riches are no use to the man who imagines he is not rich enough."

E. B.

THE EMPEROR

Luigi Pirandello

(1922)

ENGLISH VERSION BY ERIC BENTLEY

Characters

FIRST VALET
SECOND VALET
HARALD (*whose real name is Franco*)
LANDOLF (*whose real name is Lolo*) } *supposed Privy*
ORDULF (*whose real name is Momo*) } *Councillors*
BERTOLD (*whose real name is Fino*)
GIOVANNI, *the butler*
MARQUIS CARLO DI NOLLI
BARON TITO BELCREDI
DR. DIONISIO GENONI, *a psychiatrist*
COUNTESS MATILDA SPINA, *the Baron's mistress*
FRIDA, *her daughter, engaged to the Marquis*
"HENRY THE FOURTH, EMPEROR OF GERMANY," (*the Marquis' uncle*)

The scene is laid in a solitary villa in the
Umbrian countryside.
The time is "the present"—the play was
first performed in 1922.

ACT I

*A hall in the villa got up in every way to pass for the
throne room of the German Emperor Henry the
Fourth in his imperial residence at Goslar, Hanover.
But in the midst of the ancient furnishings two large
modern oil paintings—life-size portraits—stand out
from the back wall. They are supported, not far
above the ground, on a sort of pedestal or ledge of
carved wood which runs the whole length of the
wall. (It is broad and protrudes so you can sit on it
as on a long bench.) Between the two portraits is
the throne itself—the imperial chair and its low
baldachin—which is, as it were, inserted in the
pedestal dividing it into two parts. The two portraits represent a lady and a gentleman, both young,
rigged up in carnival costumes, one as the Emperor
Henry the Fourth and the other as Countess Matilda
of Tuscany. Doors to left and right.*

*Two valets, in eleventh-century costume, are lying on
the ledge. Suddenly they jump down, in surprise,
apparently, running to place themselves, stiff as
statues, at the foot of the throne, one on each side,
with their halberds. Soon afterward, by the second
door on the right,* Harald, Landolf, Ordulf, *and*
Bertold *come in. These young men are paid by the
Marquis Carlo Di Nolli to pretend to be privy councillors—regal vassals, belonging to the lower aristocracy, at the court of the Emperor. They are
therefore dressed as German knights of the eleventh
century. The last of them,* Bertold *(his real name is
Fino), is doing the job for the first time. His three
companions are amusing themselves telling him
everything. The whole scene should be played with
extreme vivacity.*

Landolf (*to* Bertold, *as if following up an explanation*).
    And this is the throne room!

Harald.   At Goslar!

Ordulf.   Or, if you'd prefer that, in his castle in the
    Harz Mountains!

379

Harald.   Or at Worms.

Landalf.   It jumps around a bit. According to the scene
we're acting out. Now here, now there——

Ordulf.   Now in Saxony——

Harald.   Now in Lombardy——

Landolf.   Now on the Rhine.

First Valet (holding his position, hardly moving his lips).
Sss, Sss!

Harald (hearing and turning).   What's the matter?

First Valet (still like a statue, in an undertone).   Well, is
he coming or isn't he? *(The allusion is to the Emperor.)*

Ordulf.   He isn't. He's sleeping. Take it easy.

*Second Valet (dropping the pose as his partner does so,
taking a long breath, and going to lie down again on the
ledge).*   Well, for Christ's sake, why didn't you say so
before?

*Bertold (who has been observing everything in mixed
amazement and perplexity, walking around the room
and looking at it, then looking at his clothes and his
companions' clothes.)*   But look . . . this room . . .
these clothes. . . . *What* Henry the Fourth? . . . I
don't quite get it—is it Henry the Fourth of France
or Henry the Fourth of England?

At this demand, Landolf, Harald, *and* Ordulf *burst into a
roar of laughter.*

Landolf (laughing all the time and pointing at Bertold
*as if inviting the others—who also go on laughing—to
continue making fun of him).*   Is it Henry the Fourth
of France?

Ordulf.   Or Henry the Fourth of England?

Harald.   Why, my dear child, it's Henry the Fourth of
Germany!

Ordulf.   The great and tragic emperor——

Landolf.   —who repented and knelt in the snow before
the Pope at Canossa! And day by day in this room we
keep the war going—the terrible war between Church
and State——

Ordulf.   —between Pope and emperor!

*Bertold (covering his head with his hands to protect him-
self against this avalanche of information).*   I see, I see!
I just didn't get it. Clothes like this. A room like this.
I was right: these are *not* sixteenth-century clothes!

Harald.   Sixteenth century, indeed!

Ordulf. We're between the year 1000 and the year 1100.

Landolf. Count it up yourself: if we're in the snow at Canossa on January 25, 1077. . .

Bertold (*more distressed than ever*). My God, this is a disaster!

Ordulf. It certainly is, if you thought it was the *French* court.

Bertold. The *English* court, I studied up on *English* history, I was reading Shakespeare and everything . . .

Landolf. My dear man, *where* were you educated? Still, you're only a couple of centuries out.

Bertold (*getting angry*). But why in God's name couldn't they have told me it was Henry the Fourth of Germany! I had two weeks to study the thing up—I can't tell you the number of books I've had my nose in!

Harald. Look, dear boy. Didn't you know that poor Tony was called Adalbert, Bishop of Bremen, in this house?

Bertold. Adalbert, Bishop of . . . ? How'd I know that?

Landolf. Well, you see how it was: when Tony died, the Marquis . . .

Bertold. Ah, so it *was* the Marquis. Then why on earth didn't he tell me . . .

Harald. Maybe he thought you knew, dear boy.

Landolf. He wasn't going to take anyone else on. There were three of us left, and he thought we'd be enough. But then *he* took to shouting, "Adalbert driven out, Adalbert driven out!" Poor Tony, you see, it didn't seem to *him* Tony had died, it seemed to *him* the bishops of Mainz and Cologne had driven Adalbert out!

Bertold (*taking his head in his two hands and keeping it there*). But I never heard a word of all this!

Ordulf. Then you're in a fix, my dear fellow.

Harald. And the trouble is that we don't know who *you* are either, dear boy!

Bertold. Even you don't know? You don't know what part I'm to play?

Ordulf. Well, um—Bertold.

Bertold. Bertold? Who's he? *Why* Bertold?

Landolf. "They've driven Adalbert away from me? Then I want Bertold, I want Bertold!"—He took to shouting *that*.

Harald. The three of us just stared at each other. Who the devil could this Bertold be?

Ordulf. So here you are, my dear fellow—Bertold.

Landolf. And what a wonderful job you'll make of it.

Bertold (*rebelling and starting to go*). Oh, no! Not for me, thank you! I'm going, I'm going.

Harald (*while he and* Ordulf *hold him back, amid laughter*). Calm down, dear boy, calm down!

Ordulf. You won't be the Bertold of the story.

Landolf. Comfort yourself with the thought that even we don't really know who we are. He's Harald, he's Ordulf, I'm Landolf. . . . That's what we're *called,* and by now we've got used to it, but who *are* we? Names. Names of the period. And that's what you'll be—a name—of the period: Bertold. Only one of us, the late lamented Tony, ever had a good part, a part out of the story—the Bishop of Bremen. He looked like a real bishop, he was marvelous, poor Tony!

Harald. God, how the dear boy would study: read, read, read!

Landolf. And he gave orders. Even to his Majesty. Oh, yes, he knew how to put himself over. Guided him. Was a tutor. An adviser, in effect. *We're* privy councillors, for that matter. But with us it's just for appearances: because the history books say the Emperor was hated by the *higher* aristocracy for surrounding himself at court with young men of the *lower* aristocracy.

Ordulf. That's us, my dear fellow.

Landolf. It really is a shame, because, well, with these clothes we could make a sensational appearance on the stage. In a costume play. They go over big these days. The Life and Loves of Henry the Fourth—what a story! Material not for one but for half a dozen tragedies! And now look at us! Just look at the four of us—and those two unfortunates standing by the throne like stuck pigs. (*He points at the two valets.*)—No one —no one puts us on stage, no one gives us scenes to act. We've got the—what do you call it?—we've got the *form*—but we don't have the *content!* We're worse off than the Emperor's real privy councillors because, well, it's true no one had given *them* a part to play either, but they didn't know they *had* to play one, they played it because they played it, it wasn't a part, it was their life, see what I mean? They acted in their own interests, they fought their rivals, they sold investitures, and so forth, while we . . . here are we in this beautiful court, dressed up as you see, and for what? To do what? To do nothing. . . . Six puppets hanging on the green room wall.

Harald.   No, no, dear boy, pardon me, but our replies do have to be in character.

Landolf.   Yes, as far as that goes—

Bertold.   And you said we do nothing! How'm *I* going to reply in character? I've got myself all prepared for Henry of England, and now someone calling himself Henry of Germany comes . . . comes butting in!

Landolf, Ordolf, Harald *start laughing again.*

Harald.   You'd better attend to it, dear boy—

Ordulf.   —and we'll help you, my dear fellow—

Harald.   —we've lots of books in there, my dear man— but first we'll just run through the main points—

Ordulf.   —so you'll have a general idea—

Harald.   Look at this! (*Turns him around and shows him the Countess Matilda's portrait on the back wall.*) Who's that, for example?

Bertold (*looking*).   That? Well, in the first place, if you don't mind my saying so, it's out of place. Two modern paintings in the midst of all this medieval stuff?

Harald.   You're right, dear boy. And as a matter of fact they weren't there originally. Behind the pictures there are two niches—for two statues they were going to put in—in the style of the period. The niches stayed empty —then they were covered by these two canvases——

Landolf (*interrupting and continuing*).   —which would certainly be out of place—if they really were paintings!

Bertold.   They're not paintings? What are they, then?

Landolf.   If you go and touch them, yes, they're paintings. But for *him* (*He points mysteriously out right, alluding to the* Emperor.)—since he does *not* touch them . . .

Bertold.   He doesn't? What are they, then—for him?

Landolf.   Well, this is just my interpretation, don't forget. All the same, I think it's pretty good. They're— images. Images—like, um, like images in a mirror, you see? That one there is him (*pointing*), the living image of him, him in this throne room—which is also—as it should be—in the style of the period. What are you so amazed about, may I ask? If we place you in front of a mirror, won't you see *your* living image? Won't you see the "you" of today in the trappings of yesteryear? Well, then, it's as if we had two mirrors here—two

living images—in the midst of a world which . . . well,
you'll see for yourself, now you live with us, you'll see
how this world, too, every part of it, will come to life.

Bertold. Now, really, I didn't come here to go mad!

Harald. Go mad, dear boy? Ts, ts. You're going to have
fun!

Bertold (*to Landolf*). You certainly have quite a line in
philosophy!

Landolf. My dear man, you can't go behind the scenes
of history—eight hundred years of it—and not bring
back a bit of experience!

Harald. Let's be going, dear boy. We'll fix you up in no
time—

Landolf. We'll fasten the wires on and have you in full
working order: the perfect marionette!

Ordulf. Let's go. (*Takes him by the arm, to lead him
off.*)

Bertold (*stopping and looking toward the other portrait*).
Just a minute. You haven't told me who *she* is. The
Emperor's wife?

Harald. No, dear boy. The Emperor's wife is called
Bertha of Susa.

Ordulf. The Emperor can't stand her. He wants to be
young like us. He's planning to get rid of her.

Landolf. That's his fiercest enemy: Countess Matilda. Of
Tuscany.

Bertold. Wait. Wasn't it her castle the Pope was staying
in . . .

Landolf. At Canossa.

Ordulf. Precisely.

Harald. Now *do* let's get going!

*They are all moving over toward the door on the right
by which they had entered when the old butler Giovanni, in modern cutaway, comes in at the left.*

Giovanni (*in a great hurry, and worked up*). Sss, sss!
Franco! Lolo!

Harald (*stopping and turning*). Hey! What do *you*
want?

Bertold (*amazed to see him come into the throne room in
his modern coat.*) What's this? *He* comes in *here*?

Landolf. A visitor from the twentieth century! Away!

*He and his two comrades make a joke of running over to
threaten him and drive him out.*

Ordulf. The Pope's ambassador—away with him!

Harald. Away with the rogue!

Giovanni (defending himself, annoyed). Oh, come on, stop this!

Ordulf. No, you're not allowed in here!

Harald. Get away, old man!

Landolf (to Bertold). It's witchcraft! He's a demon conjured up by the Great Magician of Rome! Out with your sword! (*And he reaches for his own.*)

Giovanni (shouting). Stop this, I say! This is no time for fooling; the Marquis is here, and there's company with him . . . .

Landolf (rubbing his hands). Oh, wonderful! Ladies?

Ordulf (doing the same). Old? Young?

Giovanni. Two gentlemen.

Harald. But the ladies; who are they, dear boy?

Giovanni. Countess Matilda and her daughter.

Landolf (amazed). What? (*Pause.*) What's that?

Ordulf (also amazed). The Countess, you say?

Giovanni. Yes, yes, the Countess!

Harald. And the two men, dear boy?

Giovanni. I don't know.

Harald (to Bertold). Landolf told you we have form without content in here, but keep your eyes open, dear boy.

Ordulf. The Pope has sent a whole *bevy* of ambassadors! We'll have fun all right.

Giovanni. Will you let me speak?

Harald. Speak! (*Pause.*) Speak, dear boy!

Giovanni. Well, one of the two men seems to be a doctor.

Landolf. Oh, sure, we're used to *them*.

Harald. Many thanks, Bertold, you bring us luck!

Landolf. You'll see how we'll manage *him*.

Bertold. I'm walking into a fine old mess, I can see that.

Giovanni. Now, listen. They'll be coming into this room.

Landolf (in amazement and consternation). What? Is that true? Even she? The Countess will come in here?

Harald. This is content—with a vengeance, dear boy.

Landolf. This'll be a real tragedy!

Bertold (his curiosity aroused). But why? What are you talking about?

Ordulf (pointing to the portrait). The Countess is the woman in the portrait.

Landolf. Her daughter is engaged to the Marquis.

Harald. But what have they come for? That's the question.

Ordulf. If *he* sees her, there'll be fireworks.

Landolf. Maybe he won't recognize her anymore.

Giovanni. If he wakes up, you'll just have to keep him in there.

Ordulf. Are you joking? How'd we do that?

Harald. You know what he's like, dear boy!

Giovanni. Good heavens, use force if need be! Those are the Marquis's orders. Now get going! Get going!

Harald. Yes, we'd better go; he may be awake already.

Ordulf. Let's go.

Landolf (*leaving with the others, to* Giovanni). You must explain it all later!

Giovanni (*shouting after them*). Lock the door on that side and hide the key! This other door, too. (*He points to the other door at right.*)

Landolf, Harald, *and* Ordulf *leave by the second door on the right.*

Giovanni (*to the* two valets). You must go, too; go on, that way! (*He points to the first door on the right.*) Lock the door and take the key out of the lock!

The two valets *leave by the first door on the right.* Giovanni *goes to the door on the left and opens it for the* Marquis Carlo Di Nolli.

Marquis. You have given the orders properly, Giovanni.

Giovanni. Yes, Marquis. Certainly, Marquis.

The Marquis *goes out again for a moment to bring the others in. First comes* Baron Tito Belcredi *and* Dr. Dionisio Genoni, *then* Countess Matilda Spina *and her daughter* Frida. Giovanni *bows and goes out. The Countess is about forty-five, still beautiful and shapely, though she too patently repairs the inevitable ravages of time with a violent if expert makeup which gives her the haughty head of a Valkyrie. This makeup stands out in high and painful relief from her mouth, which is very lovely and very sad. Many years a widow, she now has* Baron Tito Belcredi *for friend. Neither she nor other people have ever taken him seriously, or so it appears. What the* Baron *really means to her, he alone fully knows. He can*

*therefore laugh if she needs to pretend she doesn't
know, can laugh at the laughter of other people,
caused, as it is, by the Countess's jests at his expense.
Slim, prematurely gray, a little younger than she, he
has a curious, bird-shaped head. He would be very
vivacious if his agility—which makes him a formid-
able swordsman and is in itself live enough—were
not actually encased in a sleepy, Arab laziness that
comes out in his strange voice, which is rather nasal and drawling.* Frida, *the* Countess's *daughter, is
nineteen years old. Having grown sad in the shade to
which her imperious and showy mother relegates her,
living in this shade she is also offended by the easy
gossip which the mother provokes to the detriment of
them both equally. And yet, as luck will have it, she
is already engaged—to the* Marquis Carlo Di Nolli,
*a stiff young man, very indulgent toward others, yet
rigid and shut up in the small space of what he
thinks he can be, of what he thinks he is worth, in
the world, though at bottom even he doesn't know
what this worth is. At any rate his consternation is
great at the many responsibilities which he believes
weigh him down. Yes, the others can talk, the others
can have their fun, lucky they. He cannot. Not that
he wouldn't like it. Just that he cannot. He is dressed
in the deepest mourning for the death of his mother.*
Dr. Dionisio Genoni *has a fine, satyr's face, insolent
and rubicund, with protruding eyes, a short, pointed
beard that shines like silver. He has refined manners
and is almost bald. They enter in a state of consternation, almost afraid, looking with curiosity about
the room—all except the* Marquis. *And at first they
speak in low voices.*

Baron. Splendid, it's very splendid!
Doctor. Most interesting, how one can see the madness
  in the room itself, in inanimate objects, it really *is*
  splendid, quite splendid!
Countess (*who has been looking around the room for her
  portrait, finding it, and moving toward it*). Ah, so here
  it is! (*Looking at it from a certain distance while different feelings arise within her.*) Yes, ye-e-s . . . why,
  look . . . heavens . . . (*She calls her daughter.*) Frida,
  Frida. . . . Look . . . .
Frida. Ah! Your portrait?
Countess. No, just look, it's not me at all, it's you!

Marquis. It's true, isn't it? I told you so.

Countess. I'd never have believed it—to this extent. (*She shakes with a sudden tremor along the spine.*) Heavens, what a strange sensation! (*Then, looking at her daughter.*) What's the matter, Frida? (*Slipping an arm about her waist, she pulls her close.*) Come here, don't you see yourself in me—in that picture?

Frida (*with a gasp*). But it's me, why . . .

Countess. Wouldn't you think so? You couldn't miss it, could you? (*Turning to the* Baron.) You look, Tito, and *you* tell me!

Baron (*not looking*). I say it's not you. I know without looking.

Countess. How stupid, he thinks he's paying me a compliment. (*Turning to the* Doctor.) You tell me, Doctor!

Doctor (*starts to come over*).

Baron (*with his back turned, pretending to speak to him secretly*). Sss! No, Doctor! For heaven's sake, have nothing to do with it!

Doctor (*bewildered, smiling*). But why not, why not?

Countess. Pay no attention to him, just come. He's insufferable.

Frida. Don't you know he's a professional fool?

Baron (*to the* Doctor, *seeing him go*). Watch your feet, watch your feet, Doctor, your feet!

Doctor (*as above*). What's wrong with my feet?

Baron. You've got hobnailed boots on!

Doctor. What?

Baron. And you're walking toward four little feet of delicate Venetian glass.

Doctor (*laughing out loud*). What nonsense! There's nothing staggering, it seems to me, in the fact that a daughter resembles her mother . . .

Baron. Crash! Now it's over.

Countess (*exaggeratedly angered, coming toward the* Baron). What do you mean: Crash! What is it? What has he been saying?

Doctor (*sincerely*). Don't you think I'm right?

Baron (*answering the* Countess). He said there's nothing staggering in it. While *you* are extremely staggered. Why?—if it's all so natural?

Countess (*still more angered*). You fool! It's *because* it's so natural. Because it's *not* my daughter. (*Pointing to the canvas.*) That is *my* portrait. To find my daughter in it instead of myself is a staggering experience.

Believe me, I was quite sincerely staggered, I can't
let you say I wasn't!

After this violent outburst there is a moment of embar-
rassed silence.

Frida (*quite annoyed*). Always the same story: arguments about absolutely nothing.

Baron (*also quiet, almost with his tail between his legs,*
apologetically). I wasn't saying anything of the sort.
(*To* Frida.) I simply noticed that, from the outset,
you weren't . . . staggered like your mother. If *you're*
staggered, it's merely because the portrait resembles
you so strongly.

Countess. Obviously! Because there's no way for her
to see herself in *me*—as I was at her age. Whereas I,
the girl in the portrait, can perfectly well see myself
in her—as she is now.

Doctor. True. A portrait stays just as it is. Fixed! It
can't move away from the moment when it was made,
a distant moment now, and, for the young lady, a
moment without memories. Whereas for her mother
it brings back many things: movements, gestures, looks,
smiles, things that aren't *in* the portrait at all . . .

Countess. Exactly.

Doctor (*continuing, turning to her*). For you, naturally,
the same things are to be found in your daughter,
too.

Countess. It's so seldom I give way to my feelings, and
when I do, *he* has to come and spoil it for me! Just
for the pleasure of hurting me!

Doctor (*impressed with his own perspicacity, starts up*
again in a professional tone, turning to the Baron).
Resemblance, my dear Baron, oftentimes has its roots
in intangibles. On these lines, it seems eminently ex-
plicable that . . .

Baron (*to interrupt the lecture*). Someone might find a
resemblance between you and me, my dear professor.

Marquis. Drop it now, drop it, I beg you. (*He points*
to the doors on the right, indicating that someone is
there who might hear.) We've been sidetracked too
much already, coming . . .

Frida. Of course! With him here . . . (*Indicating the*
Baron.)

Countess (*promptly*). That's why I so much wished
he wouldn't come.

Baron. Now you've had a lot of fun at my expense. Don't be ungrateful!

Marquis. Tito, please, that's quite enough. The doctor is with us, and we're here for a very serious purpose. You know how much it means to me.

Doctor. Precisely. Now let's see if we can't begin by getting certain points quite clear. This portrait of yours, Countess, may I ask how it comes to be here? Was it a gift from you? Did you make him a present of it—I mean in the days—before . . .

Countess. Oh, no. How could I have given him presents in those days? I was just a girl—like Frida now—and not engaged at that. No, no, I let him have it three or four years after the accident. I let him have it because his (*indicating the* Marquis) mother urged me to.

Doctor. His (*with a gesture toward the doors on the right, the reference being to* Emperor Henry) sister, that is to say?

Marquis. Yes, Doctor: my mother was his sister. She died a month ago. It's for her sake we've come here— the payment of a debt to her, you might say. In the normal course of events, she (*indicating Frida*) and I would be traveling . . .

Doctor. On business of quite another sort, hm?

Marquis. Please! My mother died in the firm conviction that her beloved brother's recovery was imminent.

Doctor. You couldn't tell me, perhaps, from what evidence she reached this conclusion?

Marquis. I believe it was from certain strange things he said to her not long before she died.

Doctor. Strange things? Aha! It would be terribly useful to me to know what those things were, by Jove!

Marquis. I don't know myself. I only know Mother came home after that last visit extremely upset. It seems he'd shown her a most unusual tenderness, as if he foresaw the coming end. On her deathbed she made me promise never to neglect him, to make sure that people see him, visit him . . .

Doctor. I see. Very good. Now, to begin with . . . Oftentimes the most trivial causes lead . . . well, take this portrait . . .

Countess. Heavens, Doctor, how can you attach such overwhelming importance to the portrait? It happened

to make a big impression on me for a moment just
because I hadn't seen it in so long.

Doctor. Just a minute, please, just . . .

Baron. But it's so. It must have been there fifteen
years . . .

Countess. More! More than eighteen by now!

Doctor. I beg your pardons, but you don't yet know
what questions I'm going to ask. I set great store—
very great store—by those two portraits. I fancy
they were painted before the famous—and most unfortunate—cavalcade, isn't that so?

Countess. Why, of course.

Doctor. So it was when he was . . . normal . . . quite
sane . . . that's what I'm really getting at.—Was it he
who suggested having it painted—to you?

Countess. No, no, Doctor. Lots of us were having
them done. I mean, of those who took part in the
cavalcade. They were something to remember it by.

Baron. I had one of me done!

Countess. We hardly waited for the costumes to be
ready!

Baron. Because, you see, it was proposed to collect
them all in the drawing room of the villa that the
cavalcade came from. As a memorial. A whole gallery of pictures. But afterward each of us wanted to
keep his own picture for himself.

Countess. As for mine, as I told you, I let *him* have it
—and without very much regret—because his mother
. . . (*Indicating the* Marquis *again.*)

Doctor. You don't know if he actually asked for it?

Countess. No, I don't. Perhaps he did. Or perhaps it
was his sister—as a loving gesture . . .

Doctor. Just one other point: the cavalcade—was it
his idea?

Baron (*promptly*). Oh, no! It was mine!

Doctor. Now, please . . .

Baron. The idea was mine, I tell you! After all, there's
nothing to boast of in *that*—seeing how it all turned
out! It was . . . oh, I remember it well: one evening,
early in November, at the club, I was leafing through
an illustrated magazine, a German one—just looking
at the pictures, you understand, I don't know German—and there was a picture of the German Emperor in . . . what was the university town he'd
been a student in?

Doctor. Bonn, Bonn.

Baron. Possibly, Bonn. He was on horseback and dressed in one of the strange traditional costumes of the oldest student fraternities. He was followed by a cortege of other students of noble birth, also on horseback and in costume. Well, the idea came to me from that picture. I should have told you some of us at the club had been thinking of possible masquerades for the next carnival. I proposed this . . . historical cavalcade. Historical, in a manner of speaking. It was really a Tower of Babel: each of us was to choose a character, from this century or that, king or emperor or prince, with his lady beside him, queen or empress. All were to be on horseback. With the horses harnessed and dressed up—in the style of the period of course. Well, my proposal was accepted.

Doctor. So *he* chose the character of Henry the Fourth?

Countess. Because—thinking of my own name—and, well, not taking the whole thing any too seriously—I said I'd like to be Countess Matilda of Tuscany.

Doctor. I don't . . . I don't see the connection . . .

Countess. I didn't understand it myself in the beginning —I just heard him saying, "Then I'll be at your feet at Canossa—like Henry the Fourth." Oh, yes, I knew about Canossa, but to tell the turth I didn't remember much of the story, and it made quite an impression on me when I studied it. I found I was a loyal and zealous friend of the Pope in the fierce struggle he was waging against the German Empire. I now understood why *he* wanted to be next to me in the cavalcade—as the Emperor.

Doctor. Ah! You mean because . . .

Countess. . . . because I'd chosen to present his implacable enemy.

Doctor. Ah! Because——

Baron. Because he was courting her all the time! So she (*indicating the* Countess) naturally . . .

Countess (*stung, fierily*). Yes, naturally! I *was* natural in those days . . .

Baron (*pointing to her*). You see: she couldn't abide him!

Countess. That's not true! I didn't even dislike him. Just the opposite! But with me, if a man wants to be taken seriously——

Baron (*finishing her sentence*). —he gives the clearest proof of his stupidity!

Countess. Don't judge others by yourself, Baron B. *He* wasn't stupid.

Baron. But then *I* never asked you to take me seriously.

Countess. Don't I know it! But with him it was no joke. (*Changing her tone and turning to the* Doctor.) My dear Doctor: a woman has a sad life, a silly life. And some time or other it's her lot to see a man's eyes fixed upon her, steady and intense and full of—shall we say?—the promise of enduring sentiment! (*She bursts into a harsh laugh.*) What could be funnier? If only men could see their looks of enduring sentiment!—I've always laughed at them. More at *that* time than any other.—And let me tell you something: I can still laugh at them, after more than twenty years.—When I laughed like that at *him*, it was partly from fear, though. Perhaps one could have believed a promise in *those* eyes. It would've been dangerous, that's all.

Doctor (*with lively interest and concentration*). Aha! I'd be interested to know about *that*.—Why dangerous?

Countess (*with levity*). Because he wasn't like the others. And because I too am . . . I can't deny it . . . I'm a little . . . more than a little, to tell the truth, more than a little (*She searches for a modest word.*) intolerant, that's the word. I don't like stuffiness, I don't like people who take life hard.—Anyway, I was too young at that time, you understand? And I was a woman: I couldn't help champing at the bit.—It would have needed *courage*, and I didn't have any.—So *I* laughed at him, too. With remorse. With real self-hatred eventually—my laughter mingled with the laughter of fools, and I knew it. With the laughter of all the fools who made fun of him.

Baron. More or less as they do of me.

Countess. My dear, you make people laugh at your . . . your perpetual affectation of self-abasement—they laughed at him for the opposite reason: it makes a difference, hm?—And, with you, people laugh right in your face!

Baron. Better than behind my back, *I* say.

Doctor (*coughing nervously*). Ahem, yes, um . . . he was already rather . . . strange . . . exalted, as it were —if I've been following you properly?

Baron. Yes. But after a very curious fashion, Doctor.

Doctor. Namely?

Baron. Well, I'd say . . . he was damned cold-blooded about it—

Countess. Cold-blooded? What nonsense! This is how it was, Doctor. He was a little strange, it's true, that was because there was so much life in him. It made him—eccentric.

Baron. I don't say this . . . exaltation was just an act. Not at all. He was often genuinely exalted. But I could swear, Doctor: he was looking at himself, looking at his own exaltation. And I believe the same is true of every move he made, however spontaneous: he *saw* it. I'll say more: I'm certain it was this that made him suffer. At times he had the funniest fits of rage against himself.

Countess. That is true.

Baron (*to the* Countess). And why? (*To the* Doctor.) As I see it, the lucidity that came from acting all the time . . . being another man . . . shattered, yes, shattered at a single blow the ties that bound him to his own feelings. And these feelings seemed—well, not exactly a pretense, no, they were sincere—but he felt he must give them an intellectual status, an intellectual form of expression—to make up for his lack of warmth and spontaneity—so he improvised, exaggerated, let himself go, that's about it, to deafen his own ears, to keep his eyes from seeing himself. He seemed fickle, silly, and sometimes . . . yes, ridiculous, let's face it.

Doctor. Was he . . . unsociable?

Baron. Not in the least. He was a regular fellow. He was famous for his *tableaux vivants*, he was always getting up dances, benefit performances, all just for fun, of course. He was an awfully good actor, believe me.

Marquis. And he's become a superb and terrifying one —by going mad.

Baron. Even before that. I still remember how—when the accident happened—and he fell from his horse, you know——

Doctor. He hit the back of his head, didn't he?

Countess. Oh, what a horror! He was next to me. I saw him between the horse's hooves. The horse reared up——

Baron. At first we'd no idea any great harm was done. There was a stop—a bit of a scrimmage in the cavalcade—people wanted to know what had happened. . . . But he'd been picked up and carried into the villa.

Countess. There was *nothing*, you understand: not a sign of a wound, not one drop of blood.

Baron. We all believed he'd merely fainted——

Countess. —so, about two hours later, when ——

Baron (*nervously*). —that's right, he reappeared in the hall of the villa—this is, what I was going to say——

Countess. His face at this moment! I saw the whole thing in a flash.

Baron. No, no, *that's* not true, nobody had the least idea——

Countess. You didn't—you were all behaving like madmen!

Baron. Everyone was performing his own part! As a joke! Oh, it was a real Tower of Babel——

Countess. You can imagine our horror, can't you, Doctor, when we realized *he* was playing his part—in earnest?

Doctor. Oh, so he too . . .

Baron. Exactly. He entered. Came into the midst of us. We assumed he'd recovered and that he was just acting—like the rest of us . . . only better—he was a fine actor, as I told you—in short, we assumed he was joking.

Countess. Some of the others started fooling with him, jostling, fighting . . . and at a certain point he was hit . . .

Baron. At that instant . . . —he was armed—he drew his imperial sword and bore down on a couple of us. What a moment! Scared the pants off us.

Countess. I shall never forget the scene: all those masked faces, distorted, panic-stricken, turned toward that terrible mask, which was now no mask at all, but the very face of lunacy!

Baron. The Emperor! It was Henry the Fourth himself in a moment of fury!

Countess. His obsession with the masquerade was taking effect, Doctor. He'd been obsessed with it for over a month. And everything he did was an obsession of this sort.

Baron. The things he studied for the purpose! Down to the smallest details . . . minutiae . . .

Doctor. Yes, I see. What with the fall, and the blow on the head that caused the damage to his brain, the momentary obsession was perpetuated. Became a fixation, as we say. One can go raving mad, one can become simpleminded. . .

Baron (*to* Frida *and the* Marquis). You see the tricks life plays, my dears? (*To the* Marquis.) You weren't more than four or five. (*To* Frida.) It seems to your mother that you've taken her place in the portrait though at the time she hadn't even dreamed of bringing into the world. I have gray hair now. And as for him—(*He clicks finger and thumb.*)—he was hit in the neck—and he's never moved since. He is the Emperor—Henry the Fourth!

Doctor (*who has been lost in thought, now takes his hands from before his face as if to focus everyone's attention upon himself, and starts to give his scientific explanation*). Well, ladies and gentlemen, it all comes down to this . . .

But all of a sudden the first door on the right—the one nearest the footlights—opens, and Bertold emerges, his face very excited.

Bertold (*rushing in like a man at the end of his tether*). Excuse me, everybody . . .

But he stops directly when he sees the confusion that his entry has created.

Frida (*with a cry of horror, drawing back.*)   My God, it's he!

Countess (*stepping back, upset, with an arm raised so as not to see him*).   It's he. He?

Marquis (*promptly*).   No, no, no! Don't be excited!

Doctor (*astonished*).   Then who is it?

Baron.   A fugitive from the masquerade!

Marquis.   He's one of the four young fellows we keep here to . . . um, back him up in his lunacy.

Bertold.   I beg your pardon, Marquis . . .

Marquis.   So you should! I'd given orders for the doors to be locked! No one was to come in!

Bertold.   Yes, I know, Marquis. But I can't bear it! I've come to beg off! I want to quit!

Marquis.   Ah! So you're the one who was to start work this morning?

Bertold.   Yes, Marquis. But I can't bear it, I tell you—

Countess (*to the* Marquis *in lively consternation*).   Then he *isn't* calm—you said he was!

Bertold (*promptly*).   That's not it, madam, it isn't him! It's my three comrades. You say they "back him up," Marquis. Back him up! They don't back him up—because it's them that's mad! I come here for the first time, and instead of helping me, Marquis . . .

Landolf *and* Harald *come to the same door on the right, in haste, anxiously, but stopping at the door.*

Landolf.   May we come in?

Harald.   May we, dear Marquis?

Marquis.   Come in then! But what on earth is the matter? What are you all up to?

Frida.   O God, I'm going, I'm scared out of my wits! (*She starts to go toward the door on the left.*)

Marquis (*who at once holds her back*).   No, no, Frida!

Landolf.   Marquis, this dumbbell . . . *Indicating* Bertold.)

Bertold (*protesting*).   No: thanks very much, my friends! I'm not staying!

Landolf.   What do you mean, you're not staying?

Harald.   He's ruined *everything,* Marquis, running in here like this! Ts, ts, ts!

Landolf.   He's driven him absolutely crazy. We can't keep him in there any longer. He's given orders for this fellow's arrest. Wants to pass judgment on him. From the throne. What's to be done?

Marquis.   Lock the door of course! Go and lock that door!

Landolf *starts to do so.*

Harald.   But Ordulf won't be able to hold him all by himself!

Landolf (*stopping*).   Marquis, if we could just announce your visit: it would be a distraction for him. Have you gentlemen thought what you'll wear in his presence . . .

Marquis.   Oh, yes, we've thought the whole thing out. (*To the* Doctor.) Doctor, if you think we can make the call at once. . . .

Frida.   I won't, I won't, Carlo! I'm leaving. You come with me, Mamma, please!

Doctor.   Tell me, Marquis . . . he won't be armed, will he?

Marquis.   Armed? Of course not, Doctor. (*To* Frida.) Forgive me, Frida, but these fears of yours are really childish. You wanted to come . . .

Frida.   I didn't! I didn't at all: it was Mother!

Countess (*firmly*).   Well, I'm ready! So what are we to do?

Baron.   Is all this dressing up really necessary?

Landolf. Oh, yes, Baron, it's essential! Unhappily, he just sees *us* . . . (*He shows his costume.*) He *mustn't* see you gentlemen in modern dress!

Harald. He'd think it was some devilish travesty, dear Baron!

Marquis. Just as these men seem a travesty to you, to him *we*—in our modern clothes—would seem a travesty.

Landolf. And maybe it wouldn't much matter, Marquis, only he'd think it was the work of his mortal enemy!

Baron. The Pope?

Landolf. Right. He says he's a pagan.

Baron. The Pope a pagan? Not bad!

Landolf. A pagan who conjures up the dead! He accuses him of all the black arts. Lives in constant fear of him.

Doctor. Ha! Persecution mania!

Harald. Oh, he'd be furious, dear sir—

Marquis (*to the* Baron). But you don't have to be there, if I may say so. We'll leave that way. It's enough if the doctor sees him.

Doctor. You mean . . . just me?

Marquis. They'll be present. (*Indicating the three young men.*)

Doctor. It's not that . . . I mean, if the Countess . . .

Countess. That's right: *I* want to be there! I want to see him!

Frida. But why, Mother? Come with us, do!

Countess (*imperiously*). Leave me alone, I came for this! (*To* Landolf.) I shall be his mother-in-law, Adelaide.

Landolf. Marvelous. Yes. Adelaide, the Empress Bertha's mother. Marvelous! Your ladyship need only put on a cloak—to hide these clothes. And the ducal crown on your head, of course. (*To* Harald.) Go on, Harald, go on!

Harald. Just a moment, dear boy, what about this gentleman? (*Indicating the* Doctor.)

Doctor. Oh, yes . . . they told me the Bishop, I believe . . . the Bishop of Cluny.

Harald. You mean the Abbot, dear sir? That'll be simply divine: the Abbot of Cluny!

Landolf. He's been here so often before . . .

Doctor (*astonished*). He's been here before?

Landolf. Don't be afraid, sir. I only mean it's an easy disguise and . . .

Harald. And it's been used *often*, dear sir.

Doctor.   But . . . but . . .

Landolf.   No, no, he won't remember. It's the clothes he looks at—not the man inside them.

Countess.   That'll be just as well. For me, too.

Marquis.   You and I'll be going, Frida. You come with us, Tito.

Baron.   What? Oh. No, no, if she stays, um, (*indicating the Countess*) I'll stay, of course.

Countess.   I don't need you in the least, my dear Baron.

Baron.   I didn't say you needed me! But you're not the only one who wants to see *him.* Surely I can stay if I want?

Landolf (*helping out*).   Yes, um, maybe it's better if there are three!

Harald.   Then the gentleman will surely——

Baron.   Yes, I'll need a disguise. Make it an easy one.

Landolf (*to Harald*).   I have it! *He* can be from Cluny, too.

Baron.   From Cluny; how do you mean?

Landolf.   The cassock of a monk from Cluny Abbey. He can be in attendance on the Abbot. (*Still to Harald.*) Now, go, go! (*To Bertold.*) You go too, and keep out of sight all day today! (*But as soon as he sees him going.*) Wait! Bring the clothes he gives you! (*To Harald.*) And you go and announce the arrival of his mother-in-law and the Abbot of Cluny.

Harald.   It shall be done, dear boy.

Harald *shepherds* Bertold *out by the first door on the right.*

Marquis.   Now we can go, Frida.

With Frida *he leaves by the door on the left.*

Doctor (*to* Landolf).   I take it he should think rather well of me—when I'm the Abbot of Cluny?

Landolf.   Quite right, you can count on it, sir. The Abbot has always been received with great respect. So have you: *you* needn't worry either, my lady. He hasn't forgotten it was due to the intercession of the two of you that he was admitted to the castle at Canossa and brought before the Pope, who hadn't *wanted* to receive him at all. Kept him waiting in the snow for two days —he almost froze.

Baron.   What about me, may I ask?

Landolf. You, sir? Oh, yes. You should, um—stand deferentially apart.

Countess (*irritated, very nervous*). Oh, why didn't you leave?

Baron (*quietly, but nettled*). You're certainly very worked up over . . .

Countess (*with pride*). I am as I am! Leave me in peace!

Bertold returns with the clothes.

Landolf (*seeing him enter*). Oh, good, here are the clothes!—This cloak for the Countess.

Countess. Wait, I must take my hat off.

She does so and gives it to Bertold.

Landolf. Put it over there, Bertold. (*Then to the* Countess, *preparing to place the ducal crown on her head.*) May I, Countess?

Countess. But, heavens, isn't there a mirror here?

Landolf. There are mirrors in there. (*He points through the left entrance.*) If your ladyship would prefer to put it on yourself?

Countess. Oh, yes, it'll be much better, give it to me, it won't take a minute.

She takes the hat back and goes out with Bertold, *who is carrying the crown and the cloak. In the meantime the* Doctor *and the* Baron *put on the monks' cassocks as best they can.*

Baron. Well, I must say, I never expected to be a Benedictine monk! Think what a heap of money this madness is costing!

Doctor (*defensively*). Oh, well, my dear Baron, lots of other kinds of madness cost . . .

Baron. Surely, if you have a fortune to put into them!

Landolf. Yes, indeed. In there we have an entire wardrobe of costumes of the period. Tailored to perfection after ancient models. It's my special job—I commission theatrical costumers, experts. It costs plenty.

The Countess *reenters, wearing cloak and crown.*

Baron (*immediately, in admiration*). Ah, magnificent, truly royal!

Countess (seeing the Baron *and bursting out laughing*). Good God, no! Take it off! You're impossible! You look like an ostrich in monk's feathers!

Baron.   Well, look at the doctor for that matter!

Doctor.   Don't be hard on *me*, Countess.

Countess.   Oh, you'll do, *you're* all right. (*To the* Baron.) But you're ludicrous!

Doctor (to Landolf).   You have many receptions here then?

Landolf.   It depends. Many times he gives orders for such and such a person to be presented to him. Then we have to hunt up someone who'll serve the purpose. Women, too . . .

Countess (touché but trying to hide the fact).   Ah! Women, too?

Landolf.   At one time there were rather a lot of women.

Baron (laughing).   Wonderful! In costume? (*Indicating the* Countess.) Like that?

Landolf.   Well, you know: any women who'd . . .

Baron.   Who'd serve the purpose? I see! (*With innuendo, to the* Countess.) Take care, it may get dangerous for you!

The second door on the right opens and Harald *appears. First he gives a furtive sign to stop all conversation in the room. Then he announces, solemnly*

Harald.   His Majesty the Emperor!

First, the two valets enter, taking up their positions at the foot of the throne. Then, between Ordulf *and* Harald, *who hold themselves back a little, deferentially,* Emperor Henry *enters. He is nearly fifty, very pale, and already gray at the back of his head—while on the temples and forehead he seems blond because of very obvious, almost childish hair dye. High on each cheek, in the midst of that tragic pallor, is a patch of red, doll makeup, this too very obvious. Over his regal habit he wears a penitent's sack, as at Canossa. His eyes are characterized by a horrifying, convulsive fixity. At the same time he expresses the attitude of a penitent who wishes to be all humility and repentance. One feels that the humility is as ostentatious as the humiliation is deserved.* Ordulf *carries the imperial crown in both hands,* Harald *the scepter and eagle and the globe and cross.*

Henry (blowing first to the Countess, *then to the* Doctor).
My Lady . . . My Lord Abbot . . .

He then looks at the Baron, *starts to blow to him, too, but
turns to* Landolf, *who has gone over to his side, and
asks, suspiciously, and in an undertone,*

Is it Peter Damiani?
Landolf. No. your Majesty, it's a monk of Cluny: he
came with the Abbot.
Henry (turns to scrutinize the Baron *with increasing suspicion and, noting that the latter, hesitant and embarrassed, turns to the* Countess *and the* Doctor *as if to
take counsel from their eyes, draws himself up very
straight and shouts).* It is the Pope's henchman Father
Damaini—It's no use, Father, looking at her like that!
(Suddenly turning to the Countess *as if to ward off a
danger.)* I swear, my lady, I swear to you, my mind is
changed toward your daughter, though I confess that
I'd have divorced her if he *(indicates the* Baron*)*
hadn't come to stop me. Oh, yes: there were people
prepared to favor such a divorce. The Bishop of
Mainz would have arranged it in return for one hundred and twenty farms. *(Steals a look, rather perplexed, at* Landolf *and then suddenly says:)* But at this
time I should say nothing against the bishops. *(Humble now, he is in front of the* Baron*).* I'm grateful to
you, believe me, Peter Damiani, I'm glad you stopped
me!—My whole life is made up of humiliations! My
mother, Adalbert, Tribur, and now Goslar with my
young men of the lower aristocracy! *(Of a sudden he
changes his tone and speaks like someone who, in a
clever parenthesis, runs through a part he is rehearsing.)* But it doesn't matter! Clarity in one's ideas, insight, firmness in behavior, and patience in adversity!
*(Then he turns to them all and with contrite gravity
says.)* I know how to correct my errors, and I abase
myself even before you, Peter Damiani! *(Bows low to
him, and then stays with his back bent, as if under the
impulsion of an oblique suspicion. It is new, but it
makes him add, almost in spite of himself, in a threatening tone,)* Except that it was you who started the
obscene rumor about my mother Agnes and Henry,
Bishop of Augsburg!
Baron (since Henry *stays bent over, with one finger
pointed threateningly at him, places his hands on his*

breast and then speaks in denial). No . . . no, it was
not . . .

Henry (*straightening up*).   You say it wasn't? Sheer
infamy! (*Glares at him and then says,*) I wouldn't
have thought you could! (*Approaches the* Doctor *and
pulls at his sleeve a little, winking with some cunning.*)
It's them! It always is, isn't it, my Lord Abbot?

Harald (*quietly, whispering, as if prompting the* Doctor).
That's it: the rapacious bishops!

Doctor (*turned toward* Harald, *trying to stick to his
"part"*). Oh, them . . . of course, them!

Henry.   They were insatiable!—When I was a little
child, my Lord Abbot—even an emperor has a childhood—he doesn't know he's an emperor in fact—he's
just a kid at play, letting time go by . . . I was six
years old and they snatched me from my mother and
made use of me against her without my knowing,
against her and against the dynasty itself, profaning,
robbing, marauding, one greedier than the other—
Anno greedier than Stefan, Stefan greedier than Anno!

Landolf (*in a persuasive undertone, to get his attention*).
Your Majesty . . .

Henry (*turning of a sudden*).   You're right! At this time
I shouldn't speak ill of the bishops.—But this infamous
slander against my mother, my Lord Abbot, goes beyond the bounds! (*Melting, as he looks at the* Countess.) And I may not even weep for her, my Lady.—
I turn to you, you are a mother, you must feel it here.
(*Indicates the pit of his stomach.*) She came from her
convent to seek me out a month ago now. They had
told me she was dead. (*Sustained pause, dense with
emotion. Then with a most mournful smile,*) I cannot
mourn her because if you are here and I am dressed
like this (*shows his sackcloth*), it means I am twenty-
six years old.

Harold (*almost in an undertone, sweetly, to comfort
him*). It means she is still alive, your Majesty.

Ordulf (*in the same manner*).   And still in her convent.

Henry (*turns to look at them*).   True. So I can postpone
my grief to another occasion. (*Almost coquettishly he
shows the* Countess *the dye on his hair.*) Look, I'm
still blond . . . (*Then quietly, confidentially,*) for you!
—*I* wouldn't need it, but externals do help. Milestones
of time, aren't they, my Lord Abbot? (*He returns to
the* Countess *and, observing her hair*) Ah, but I see
that . . . you too, my Lady . . . (*He winks, makes an*

expressive sign with one hand as if to say her hair is false—but without a hint of scorn, rather with mischievous admiration.) Heaven keep me from amazement or disgust!—O vanity of human wishes: we try to ignore the obscure and fatal power that sets limits to our will! What *I* say is, if one is born and died—did you wish to be born, Lord Abbot, did you will your own birth? I didn't—and between birth and death, both of them independent of our will, so many things happen that we all wish wouldn't happen. Willy-nilly, we resign ourselves to them.

Doctor (*just to say something while he scrutinizes* Henry). It's true, alas!

Henry. But when we're not resigned, we always start wishing and willing! A woman wishes to be a man, an old man wishes to be young. . . . None of us is lying, there's no conscious deception in it, it's simply this: in entire good faith we are fixed in some fine conception of ourselves, as in a shell or a suit of armor. However, my lord, while you keep this firm grip on yourself, holding onto your holy cassock with both hands, something is slipping away from you unnoticed, slithering down your sleeves, gliding off like a serpent. That something is LIFE, my lord. And when you see your life suddenly taking shape, coagulating outside you in this way, you are surprised. You despise yourself, you're furious with yourself. And the remorse, the remorse! How many times I've seen my own remorse— with a face that was my own and yet so horrible I couldn't behold it! (*He returns to the* Countess.) Has this never happened to you, Countess? You can recall being always the same, can you? But, once upon a time, I tell you . . . how can it be? How *could* you do such a thing? (*He looks her so sharply in the eyes, she nearly faints.*) Such a thing as . . . precisely . . . we understand each other. But don't worry, I won't breathe a word to anyone! And you, Peter Damiani, how could you be a friend to *that* man . . .

Landolf (*as above*). Your Majesty . . .

Henry (*at once*). No, no, I won't name him, I know it would be too annoying for you. (*Turning on the* Baron, *as if by stealth.*) What an opinion, what an opinion you had of him, eh?—All the same, every one of us clings to his idea of himself—like a man who dyes his hair when he grows old. What if the color of the dye in my hair cannot, for you, be that of my real hair? You, Lady, certainly don't dye your hair to deceive others or even yourself. You only deceive—and ever so little at that—your own image in the glass. I do it as a joke. You do it in earnest. But, however much in earnest, you too are in disguise, Lady, and I don't mean the venerable crown that rings your forehead and which I bow before, I don't mean your ducal mantle, I mean you wish to fix a memory in your mind, artificially, the memory of your blond hair as it was when, one day, it pleased you—or of your dark hair if you were dark—the fading image of your youth. With you it's different, isn't it, Peter Damiani? You're not interested in *fixing* your memories, are you? For you, to remember what you have been, what you have done, is but to recognize the realities of the past which have lived on inside you, isn't that so? Like a dream. Like a dream! *My* memories are like that too, inexplicable to me as I think them over. . . . Oh, well, don't be amazed, Peter Daminai: it'll be the same tomorrow with your life of today! (*Suddenly getting into a rage and seizing his sackcloth.*) This sackcloth here! (*With almost fierce joy he begins to take it off while* Harald *and* Ordulf *at once run up in horror to stop him.*) Oh, God! (*Drawing back and taking off the sackcloth he shouts to them.*) Tomorrow, at Brixen, twenty-seven German and Lombard bishops will sign with me the deposition of the Pope!

Ordulf (*with the other two, imploring him to be silent*). Your Majesty! In God's name!

Harald (*motioning to him to put the sackcloth on again*). Take care, your Majesty!

Landolf. The Abbot is here with the Countess Matilda to intercede in your favor! (*Furtively makes urgent signs to the* Doctor *to say something at once.*)

Doctor (*worried*). Um, yes, of course . . . we came to intercede . . . sire . . .

Henry (*repenting at once, almost terrified, lets the three of them put the sackcloth back on for him. He pulls it down over him with convulsive hands*). Pardon! That's it: pardon, pardon, my Lord Abbot, pardon, Lady! . . . I swear to you, I feel the weight of the anathema, I do!

He bends down with his head in his hands as if expecting something to fall and crush him. He stays like this a moment. Then, in a changed voice but in an unchanged position, he says softly and confidentially to Landolf, Harald, *and* Ordulf,

I don't know why, but somehow I *can't* be humble
before that man! (*Indicating the* Baron *quasi-secretly.*)

Landolf (*in an undertone*).   But, your Majesty, why do
you persist in believing it's Peter Damiani? It isn't at
all!

Henry (*looking at them askance, fearfully*).   It isn't
Peter Damiani?

Harald.   No, no, it's just a poor monk, your Majesty!

Henry (*mournfully, with plaintive exasperation*).   Perhaps you, Lady, can understand me better than the
others because you are a woman. This is a solemn and
decisive moment. I could, look you, accept the aid of
the Lombard bishops, capture the Pope, run to Rome,
and set up a pope of my own choosing!—But I do not
give way to the temptation, and believe me, I'm right.
I know the drift of the times. I know the majesty of a
man who *can* be what he should be, a pope!—Would
you be inclined to laugh at me in my present situation?
You're stupid if you do. You don't understand the
political shrewdness which enjoins this penitential habit
upon me. I tell you that, tomorrow, the roles could be
reversed. And then what would you do? Would you
laugh to see a pope in captive's clothes?—No.—Yet the
two cases are the same. Today I wear the mask of a
penitent, tomorrow he wears the mask of a prisoner.
Woe betide the man who knows not how to wear his
mask, whether of pope or emperor!—Perhaps his
Holiness is, at present, a little too cruel, that's true.
Think, Lady, how Bertha—your daughter and my wife
—toward whom, I repeat, my heart is changed (*He
turns suddenly on the* Baron *and shouts in his face as
if the latter had said him nay.*) changed, CHANGED
—because of the affection, the devotion she was able
to show me in that terrible moment!

*He stops, convulsed by his angry outburst, and makes an
effort to hold himself in, a groan of exasperation in
his throat; then, with sweet and mournful humility,
he turns again to the* Countess.

She has come with me, Lady. She is below, in the
courtyard. She insisted on following me as a beggar.
And she is frozen, frozen from two nights in the open,
in the snow. You are her mother. May the bowels of
your compassion be moved: with his aid (*indicating*

the Doctor) beg the Pope's pardon! Induce him to receive us!

Countess (*trembling, a thin thread of voice*).   Yes, sire, at once, yes . . .

Doctor.   Yes, sire, we'll do it!

Henry.   And one more thing, one more! (*He summons them round about him and speaks quietly, as if telling a great secret.*) You see me? I am a penitent, and I swear I'll remain one till the Pope receives me. But it's not enough that he receive me. (*Pause. He starts again.*) You know how he can do anything, literally anything, even to calling up the dead? Now, my Lord Abbot, now, my Lady: my real punishment is (*pointing to himself*)—here—or (*pointing to the picture of himself*) if you like, *there*—for it consists in the fact that I cannot cut myself loose from that piece of magic! When the excommunication is revoked, I want you two to make another request of him who can do everything, namely, that he cut me loose from that picture and let me live! Let me live my poor life, the life I've been excluded from, let me have it intact, entire! One cannot go on being twenty-six forever, Lady! I ask this favor for your daughter, too. So that, well disposed as I am toward her, and so deeply affected by her compassion, I may love her as she deserves. That's all. Just that. I am in your hands. (*He bows.*) My Lady! My Lord Abbot!

Still bowing, he starts to withdraw by the door through which he entered. The Baron, *who had come forward a little to hear the proceedings, now turns to go back again to his place.* Henry *assumes he wishes to steal the imperial crown which is on the throne. Amid general concern and astonishment,* Henry *runs over, takes it, hides it under his sackcloth, then, with a cunning smile on his lips and in his eyes, he starts bowing again and disappears. The* Countess *is so deeply disturbed she falls into a chair with a crash, almost fainting.*

ACT II

Scene I

*Another room in the villa. Antique and austere furniture.
On the right, about eighteen inches from the floor,
is a raised platform very like a church choir, with a
ring of wooden pilasters around it, the ring being
broken at the front and sides by two steps. On the
platform are a table and six stools of the period, one
at the head and two on each side. The main door is
at the rear. On the left there are two windows looking out on the garden. On the right there is another
door.*

It is later in the afternoon of the same day. The Countess,
the Doctor, *and the* Baron *are on stage. They are
conversing, but the* Countess *stands gloomily on one
side, clearly very irritated by what the other two are
saying, though she can't help listening because in her
present disturbed state everything interests her in
spite of herself—so that she can't concentrate on
perfecting the plan which hovers before her mind's
eye and beckons and is stronger than she is. The
words which she hears the others speak attract her
attention because she instinctively feels something
like a need to be held fast in the present.*

Baron. Well, my dear Doctor, you *may* be right, but
that's my impression.
Doctor. I won't gainsay you but I rather think it's
only . . . well, yes, an impression.
Baron. But he said it in so many words, my dear Doc-
tor! (*Turning to the* Countess.) Didn't he, Countess?
Countess (*interrupted in her thoughts, turning*). Said
what? Oh, yes . . . But not for the reason you think.
Doctor. He was referring to the clothes we'd put on.
(*To the* Countess.) Your cloak, our Benedictine cas-
socks. The whole thing is childish!
Countess (*in a little burst, indignant, again turning*).
Childish? Doctor, what are you saying?
Doctor. On the one hand, it's childish—let me speak,

408

Countess, I beg—and on the other hand, it's much more complicated than you could possibly imagine.

Countess. Not at all. To me, it's crystal-clear.

Doctor (with the expert's pitying smile for the nonexpert). All the same! One must take account of that special psychology of madmen according to which, you see, one can be sure that the madman sees, sees right through the disguise we confront him with, sees through it and at the same time accepts it, believes in it, like a child, to whom it is both reality and a game. That's why I said it's all childish. But then it's highly complicated, too—in this respect: that he is, he must be, perfectly aware of being—an image. To himself, I mean. In his own eyes. He is an image. The image in the picture. *(He points out left where the picture is.)*

Baron. He said that!

Doctor. Precisely.—Now: to this image, other images have just presented themselves. Ours. The images we created in those clothes. Don't imagine he isn't clever and clear-sighted in his lunacy! On the contrary, he was at once aware of the difference between his sort of image and ours. He knew there was in ours an element of deliberate fiction. So he was suspicious. All madmen are fortified by constant, vigilant suspicion. Not that he could see any further than that. He couldn't see compassion in the way we adapted our game to his. His own game seemed the more tragic to us the more he tried to reveal that it was only a game. Coming before us with paint on his cheeks and temples! To tell us he'd done it on purpose, as a joke! That's how suspicious he is! And how defiant!

Countess (again breaking out). No, Doctor, that's not it, that's not it at all!

Doctor. What do you mean, that's not it?

Countess (positively trembling). I am quite sure he recognized me.

Doctor. Out of the question, out of the question!

Baron (at the same time as the Doctor*).* Nonsense, nonsense!

Countess (even more positively, almost convulsed). He recognized me, I tell you. When he came over to talk to me at close quarters, he looked me in the eyes, deep in the eyes, and recognized me!

Baron. But if he talked of your daughter . . .

Countess. He didn't!—It was me, he was speaking of me!

Baron. Perhaps so, when he said . . .

Countess (*at once, without restraint*). About my dyed
hair? But didn't you notice how he right away added:
"or the memory of your dark hair if you were dark"?
—He remembered perfectly well that in those days I
was dark.

Baron. Nonsense, nonsense!

Countess (*taking no notice of him, turning to the* Doctor). My hair is dark really, Doctor, like my daughter's. *That* is why he started talking of her!

Baron. But he doesn't even know your daughter; he's
never seen her!

Countess. Exactly! You understand nothing. By my
daughter, he meant me. Me—as I was "in those days"!

Baron. Great heavens, this is catching!

Countess (*quietly, with contempt*). What's catching?
You fool!

Baron. Tell me, were you ever his wife? In his lunacy
your daughter is his wife, Bertha of Susa.

Countess. That's precisely it! Not being dark anymore—
as he remembers me—but like this, blond, I was introduced to him as his wife's mother.—For him my
daughter doesn't exist—he never saw her—you said so
yourself. So how can he know if she's blond or dark?

Baron. Oh, he just happened to say dark, sort of in
general, for heaven's sake. Like anyone who wants to
tie down a memory of youth with the color of a girl's
hair—blond, brunette, what have you. As ever, you go
off into foolish fantasies.—Doctor, you say *I* oughtn't
to have come here, but what about *her?*

Countess (*is defeated for a moment by the* Baron's *argument. She has been lost in thought but now she takes
hold of herself, the more excited because she is unsure
of herself*). No . . . no, he was speaking of me . . .
He talked *to* me, *with* me, *of* me . . .

Baron. Not so bad! He never left *me* for a moment, I
couldn't *breathe,* and you say he was talking with you
the whole time? Maybe you think he was alluding to
you when he spoke with "Peter Damiani"?

Countess (*defiantly, almost breaking the bounds of de-
corum*). Who knows?—Can you explain to me why,
from the very first moment, he felt an aversion to you,
to you in particular?

(*The answer must be almost explicitly expressed in the*

tone of the query. It is: "Because he understood that you are my lover." The Baron *gets the point. Discomfited, he stands there emptily smiling.)*

Doctor. May I say the reason could also be that only two persons' arrival had been announced: the Emperor's mother-in-law, Adelaide and the Abbot of Cluny. When he discovered a third person who hadn't been announced, suspicion at once . . .

Baron. Of course: suspicion at once made him see in me an enemy, Peter Damiani.—But if *she's* got it into her head that he recognized her . . .

Countess. There's not the least doubt of it!—His eyes told me, Doctor. There's a way of looking at someone that leaves no doubt whatsoever, *you* know that. Perhaps it was only for an instant, but what more do you want?

Doctor. It's entirely possible he could have a lucid interval . . .

Countess. It's possible—you admit it! But that's not all. His talk seemed to me full, brim-full, of regret for my youth and his, regret for the horrible thing that happened to him, the thing that has held him here in a mask he can't cut from his face. But he'd like to, Doctor. Oh, how he longs to cut loose!

Baron. Yes: and why? He wants to start loving your daughter. Or even you. Softened, as you think, by the pity you feel for him.

Countess. Which is great, don't make light of it.

Baron. I won't, my dear Countess. I'm sure a faith healer would consider the miracle more than likely.

Doctor. May *I* speak? I don't perform miracles. I am not a faith healer. I am a doctor. I've been listening to everything that's been said, and I must repeat what I've told you already. Every elaborate or, as we say, systemized form of lunacy is characterized by what we call analogical elasticity. In him this elasticity is no longer . . . well, um, elastic. It has worked loose, it's limp. In short, the various elements of his lunacy aren't holding together. Years ago he superimposed a second personality upon himself, but now it's proving next to impossible for him to maintain his equilibrium within it—because (and this is very reassuring) of the attacks this second personality is being subjected to. Sudden recollections are wrenching him free from what has been his state of mind hitherto, a state of

mind we call incipient apathy—no, that's not right
either, it's really a morbid wallowing in reflective
melancholy, accompanied by, yes, considerable cerebral
activity. Very reassuring, I say. And now, if by the
trick—I should say, the shock treatment—we've
planned . . .

*Countess (turning toward the window, in the tone of a
querulous invalid).* How is it the car hasn't come
back yet? In three and a half hours . . .

Doctor (stunned). What do you say?

Countess. The car, Doctor. It's more than three and a
half hours now!

Doctor (taking out his watch and looking at it). Yes,
more than four, for that matter!

Countess. They could have been here half an hour ago
at least, that chauffeur . . .

Baron. Perhaps he couldn't find the dress.

Countess. But I told him exactly where it was. *(She is
very impatient.)* And where's Frida?

Baron (leaning out of the window a little). Maybe she's
in the garden with Carlo.

Doctor. He'll talk the fear out of her!

Baron. It isn't fear, Doctor, don't you believe it: It's
just that she's annoyed.

Countess. Do me the favor of not asking her to do this!
I know how she is!

Doctor. Let's wait. Patiently. Anyhow, it'll only take a
moment, and it has to be in the evening.—If, as I was
saying, our shock treatment shakes him up till, at a
single blow, he breaks the threads that still bind this
fiction of his together, threads that are slack enough
as it is, if, I say, we give him back what he himself
demands—"One cannot go on being twenty-six forever," he said—namely, liberation from this punishment, which even he regards as a punishment, in short,
if we can help him regain, all at once, his sense of time,
his sense of duration——

Baron (stepping in). He will be cured! *(Then underlining his words with irony.)* We shall have cut him
loose from his delusion!

Doctor. We can hope he'll start going again—like a
clock stopped at a certain hour. Here we stand, so to
speak, watch in hand, waiting for that watch to start
up. A shake, like this! And now let's hope it'll begin
to tell the time again, it's been stopped quite long
enough.

At this point the Marquis *enters by the main door.*

Countess.   Carlo . . . where's Frida? Isn't she here?
Marquis.   Yes, Countess. She'll be in at any moment.
Doctor.   The car got back?
Marquis.   Yes, Doctor.
Countess.   He found the dress, that chauffeur?
Marquis.   Yes, yes, he found it.
Doctor.   Well, that's a relief!
Countess (*shuddering*).   Then where is it? Where is it?
Marquis (*shrugging his shoulders and smiling sadly with the air of one who lends himself unwillingly to a jest that is out of place*).   You'll see soon enough, Countess. (*Indicating the direction of the main entrance.*) Watch . . .

Bertold *presents himself at the threshold solemnly announcing,*

Bertold.   Her Ladyship the Countess Matilda—of Canossa!

Magnificent and very lovely, Frida *at once enters. She is dressed in her mother's old dress, that is, as the Countess Matilda of Tuscany, and appears a living version of the dead image we have seen in the throne-room portrait.*

Frida (*as she passes the bowing figure of* Bertold, *says to him with contemptuous gravity*).   Of Tuscany, Matilda of Tuscany, please! Canossa is just a castle of mine!
Baron (*admiring her*).   Ah! Well! She looks like some-one I know!
Countess.   Like me!—God in heaven, do you see?—Stop, Frida!—Do you see? It's my picture come to life!
Doctor.   Yes, yes . . . to a T, to a T! The portrait!
Baron.   No question of that, the portrait! Just look at her: what a girl!
Frida.   Now don't make me laugh or I'll burst. Heavens, what a wasp waist you had, Mamma! I could hardly squeeze myself into it.
Countess (*convulsed, helping to fix the dress*).   Wait . . . keep still . . . Now these pleats . . . Does it really feel so tight?
Frida.   Stifling! For heaven's sake, let's be quick . . .
Doctor.   Oh, but we must wait till evening . . .

Frida. No, no, I can't! I can't hold out that long!

Countess. But why on earth did you put it on so early?

Frida. When I saw it . . . the temptation . . . was irresistible . . .

Countess. At least you could have taken me with you. Or had someone help you. . . . It's all crumpled—oh, dear! . . .

Frida. I know, Mamma, but they're such old creases . . . it'd be hard to get them out.

Doctor. It doesn't matter, Countess. The illusion is perfect. (*Then, approaching and asking her to stand in front of her daughter, though without concealing her.*) Pardon me. We place them . . . thus . . . at a certain distance . . . will you stand a little further forward? . . .

Baron. And in this way we learn to appreciate the passage of time!

Countess (*turning slightly to him*). Twenty years after: isn't it a catastrophe?

Baron. You exaggerate, my dear Countess.

Doctor (*highly embarrassed, trying to put matters to rights*). No, no! I meant . . . I mean, the dress . . . I wanted to see . . .

Baron (*laughing*). For the dress, Doctor, it's *more* than twenty years: it's eight hundred. An abyss. You want to make him jump across? You'll hit him that hard? From here (*pointing to* Frida) to here (*pointing to her mother*). You'll need a basket to pick up the pieces. My friends, just think for a moment: joking aside, for us it's a matter of twenty years, two dresses, and a disguise. But, for him, if, as you say, Doctor, time is fixed, if he's really living back there with her (*indicating* Frida) eight hundred years earlier, I tell you the jump will simply make him dizzy, make his head reel. He'll fall in our midst like a . . . (*The* Doctor *shakes a finger in dissent.*) You deny it?

Doctor. Yes, Life, my dear Baron, renews itself. *Our* life—here—will at once be real—even to him. It will take hold of him and, at a blow, strip him of his illusion and reveal your eight hundred years as a bare twenty. It will be like certain practical jokes—the leap into space, for example, as the Freemasons do it: you think you're making a tremendous jump, then you find you've taken a single step down.

Baron. Now we're onto something. Doctor: look at Frida and her mother. We say youth goes on ahead.

We imagine youth to be in front. But it isn't true, is it, Doctor? We oldsters are ahead, we are in front, we are rightly called "advanced in years," for—time is something we have a lot more *of*.

Doctor.   Except that the past is all the time receding from us.

Baron.   No, no, the point is this. They (*indicating* Frida *and the* Marquis), have still to do what we have already done, they have still to grow old, they have still to do more or less the same foolish things . . . The idea that you start out in life ahead of those who've already started—this is the great illusion, the great untruth! You are no sooner born than you start dying. He who started first is therefore furthest along of all, *he* is ahead, *he* is in front. The youngest of men is our common father Adam. Behold the Countess Matilda of Tuscany: (*Shows* Frida.) She is eight hundred years younger than any of us! (*He makes a low bow before her.*)

Marquis.   Please, Tito, this is no laughing matter.

Baron.   Oh, if you think I'm joking . . .

Marquis.   Certainly I do, for heaven's sake . . . ever since you arrived . . .

Baron.   What? I've even dressed up as a Benedictine . . .

Marquis.   Why, yes, for a *serious* purpose . . .

Baron.   That's what I'm saying . . . if it's been serious for the others . . Frida, now, for example . . (*Then, turning to the* Doctor.) Doctor, I swear I still don't understand what you wish to do.

Doctor (*annoyed*).   Give me a chance!—Naturally, with the Countess in the wrong costume——

Baron.   You mean, she too must . . .

Doctor.   Surely; she must wear a dress exactly like that one. (*Indicating* Frida's.) The young lady enters, he sees Matilda of Tuscany, then the Countess enters, and——

Baron.   There'll be two Matildas of Tuscany!

Doctor.   Two Matildas of Tuscany. Precisely. Such is our shock treatment. After that, the watch starts going again.

Frida (*calling him to one side*).   Doctor, one moment, please!

Doctor.   Here I am.

He goes over to Frida *and the* Marquis *and is explaining things to them during the following dialogue.*

Baron (quietly, to the Countess). Good heavens, then . . .

Countess (turning on him with a firm expression). Then what?

Baron. Are you really interested? You'll lend yourself to . . . this sort of thing?

Countess. I owe it to *him*!

Baron. What you're doing is an insult to me, my dear.

Countess. Who's thinking of *you*?

Marquis (coming forward). That's it, yes, that's what we'll do . . . *(Turning toward* Bertold.) You! Go and call one of the other three, will you?

Bertold. Yes, sir.

He leaves by the main door.

Countess. But first we must pretend to take our leave!

Marquis. Exactly. I'm sending for a valet to prepare the leave-taking. *(To the* Baron.) *You* needn't bother, of course, you can just stay here.

Baron (nodding ironically). Of course, *I* needn't bother!

Marquis. So as not to arouse his suspicions again, you understand?

Baron. I'm a negligible quantity. Of course.

Doctor. His certainty that we've gone away must be absolute. Absolute.

Landolf, *followed by* Bertold, *enters by the door on the right.*

Landolf. May we come in, Marquis?

Marquis. Yes, come in. Now . . . you're Lolo, are you?

Landolf. Lolo or Landolf, as you please, Marquis.

Marquis. Good. Now look. The Doctor and the Countess are about to take their leave . . .

Landolf. Very good. All we need say is that the Pope has agreed to receive him as a result of their entreaties. He's in his apartment, groaning at the thought of what he's been saying. He's penitent, but quite sure the Pope won't oblige him. Will you come in to him? . . . You must be good enough to put those clothes on again . . .

Doctor. Yes, let's be going.

Landolf. One moment, Doctor. May I make another suggestion? You should say that Countess Matilda of Tuscany implored the Pope to receive him.

Countess.   So he did recognize me!

Landolf.   No! I beg your pardon, Countess. It's because he so fears Matilda——fears her dislike. The Pope was staying in her castle. It's strange—in the version of the story I know—though doubtless you all know the truth of the matter better than I do—there's nothing about Henry being secretly in love with Matilda, is there?

Countess (*at once*). Nothing at all! Quite the reverse!

Landolf.   That's what I thought. But *he* says he loved her—he's always saying so . . .—And now he fears that her indignation on this score will hurt him with the Pope.

Baron.   We must make him understand she no longer dislikes him.

Landolf.   That's it! Precisely!

Countess (*to* Landolf). Yes, yes, quite! (*Then, to the* Baron.) Because, in case you didn't know, it was to the prayers of Matilda and the Abbot of Cluny that the Pope yielded. And let me tell you this, my dear Baron: at that time—the time of the cavalcade, I mean—I was going to exploit this fact—I was going to show him my heart was no longer so unfriendly to him as he imagined.

Baron.   Well, isn't that marvelous, Countess? You're just following history . . .

Landolf.   Yes. So my lady could easily spare herself the trouble of wearing two disguises and present herself from the start, with the Abbot here (*indicating the* Doctor) in the costume of Matilda of Tuscany.

Doctor (*at once, with force*).   No! No! For heaven's sake, not that! That would spoil everything! His impression of the confrontation must be instantaneous. A sudden blow. No, Countess, let's be going: you will again appear as his mother-in-law, Adelaide. And we'll take our leave. The essential thing is that he know we've gone. Come on now, don't let's waste any more time, there's still plenty to be done.

Exeunt the Doctor, *the* Countess, *and* Landolf *by the door on the right.*

Frida.   I'm beginning to be terribly afraid, Carlo——

Marquis.   All over again?

Frida.   Wouldn't it have been better if I'd seen him before? . . .

Marquis. Believe me, Frida, there's nothing to it! All you've got to do is stand there.

Frida. But isn't he raving?

Marquis. No, no, he's quite calm.

Baron (*with an ironic affectation of sentimentality*). He's melancholy, poor chap. Haven't you heard he loves you?

Frida. Thank you, but that's *why* I'm afraid.

Baron. He won't want to hurt you!

Marquis. And it'll only be a matter of a moment anyway . . .

Frida. Yes. But to be in the dark! With him!

Marquis. For one moment. And I'll be at your side. And the others will be in ambush at the door, ready to run to your assistance. As soon as he sees your mother, understand? As soon as he sees your mother your part is finished . . .

Baron. I'm afraid what we're doing is like digging a hole in water.

Marquis. Oh, don't start *that* again, Tito! I think the doctor's remedy will work perfectly!

Frida. So do I! I can feel it in me already . . . I'm trembling all over!

Baron. That's all very well, my friends, but madmen— little, alas, as they know it—are blessed with a certain characteristic which we're forgetting——

Marquis (*interrupting, annoyed*). What characteristic is that?

Baron (*forcibly*). They do not reason things out!

Marquis. What's reasoning got to do with it, for heaven's sake?

Baron. Why, what else is he supposed to do but reason out the situation we're confronting him with—seeing her (*indicating* Frida), and her mother at the same time? That's how we planned it, hm?

Marquis. Not in the least, it's not a matter of reasoning at all. We're confronting him with . . . "a double image of his own fiction." That's what the doctor said.

Baron (*suddenly taking off*). I've never understood why they graduate in medicine.

Marquis (*stunned*). Who?

Baron. The psychiatrists.

Marquis. Heavens above, what should they graduate in?

Frida. They're psychiatrists, aren't they?

Baron. They're psychiatrists, my dear: an exact legal

definition! And all they do is talk. The best talker, the best psychiatrist. "Analogical elasticity," "the sense of time, of duration!" They tell you right off the bat they can't work miracles—when a miracle is precisely what we need. Of course, the more they say they're not faith healers, the more people believe they're serious —and don't they know it! They don't work miracles —but they always land on their feet—not bad, huh?

Bertold (*who has been spying at the door on the right, looking through the keyhole*). Here they are! They're coming!

Marquis.   They are?

Bertold.   I think he wants to show them out . . . Yes, yes, here he is!

Marquis.   Let's get out then, get out at once! (*Turning to* Bertold *before leaving.*) You stay here!

Bertold.   I'm to stay?

Without answering him, the Marquis, Frida, *and the* Baron *make their escape by the main door, leaving* Bertold *lost and irresolute. The door on the right opens.* Landolf *enters first and at once bows. Then the* Countess *enters with cloak and ducal crown as in Act One, the* Doctor *in the cassock of the Abbot of Cluny.* Emperor Henry, *in regal robes, is between them. Behind,* Ordulf *and* Harald.

Henry (*continuing what we suppose him to have been saying in the throne room*). Now I ask you, how could I possibly be clever, as you now describe me, if I'm also considered obstinate . . .

Doctor.   Obstinate, sire? Nothing of the sort . . .

Henry (*smiling, pleased*).   For you, I'm really clever?

Doctor.   Neither obstinate nor clever, sire, no . . .

Henry (*stops and exclaims in the tone of someone who wishes, benevolently yet ironically, to observe that matters can't rest here*). My Lord Abbot, if obstinacy is not a vice that consorts with cleverness, I did hope that in denying it to me you might have conceded me a little cleverness instead. I assure you I could use some! But if you insist on keeping it all for yourself . . .

Doctor.   I? You think me clever, sire?

Henry.   Oh, no, my Lord, what are you saying? You don't seem very clever to me! (*Cutting this short, so he can turn to the* Countess.) With your permis-

sion—a word in confidence with our Empress' lady
mother. Here on the threshold. (*He draws her a
little on one side and with a great air of secrecy
anxiously asks her,*) Your daughter is very dear to
you, is she?

Countess (*lost*).   Why, of course . . .

Henry.   Would you like me to make amends for the
grave wrong I have done her—by offering all my love,
all my devotion? Of course you mustn't believe what
my enemies say about my debauches.

Countess.   I don't believe it, no, I never have . . .

Henry.   So you *would* like it?

Countess (*lost again*).   Like—what?

Henry.   You *would* like me to love your daughter again?
(*He looks at her and at once adds in a mysterious
tone of mingled admonition and pain,*) Don't be
friendly to Matilda of Tuscany, please don't!

Countess.   But I tell you again she has begged the Pope,
she has pleaded with him, as much as we have . . .

Henry (*at once, quiet, trembling*).   Don't say that, don't
say that, in heaven's name, don't you see how it affects
me?

Countess (*looks at him, then very quietly indeed as if
in confidence*).   You love her still?

Henry (*dismayed*).   Still? You say *still*? How do you
know? No one knows, no one *must* know!!

Countess.   But wouldn't *she* know? She who has been
on her knees for you?

Henry (*looks at her for a moment, then says*).   Do you
love your daughter? (*A short pause. Turns to the* Doctor, *laughingly*.) Ah, my Lord, it was only afterwards
I realized my wife existed, and that was rather late
in the day . . . . Even now, well, I suppose I have a
wife, yes, I certainly have a wife, but I assure you
I hardly ever give her a thought. It may be a sin, but
I don't feel her, I don't feel her in my heart. It's an
extraordinary thing but her own mother doesn't feel
her in her heart either. She doesn't mean very much
to you, does she, Lady, confess! (*Turning to the* Doctor, *in exasperation*.) She talks to me of another
woman, *the* other woman. (*Getting more and more
excited.*) She *insists* on talking of her, she insists, I
can't understand it!

Landolf (*humbly*).   Perhaps, Majesty, you have formed
an unfavorable opinion of Matilda of Tuscany and
my Lady would like to remove it? (*Upset at having al-*

lowed himself this remark, he at once adds,) I mean
of course at this particular time . . .

Henry. *You* maintain that she's my friend?

Landolf. At this time, yes, your Majesty!

Countess. Yes, of course, that's the reason . . .

Henry. I see. So you don't believe I love her. I see, I
see. No one ever did believe it, no one ever dreamed
of it, so much the better, let's change the subject. (*He
breaks off, turning to the* Doctor, *his face and mind
completely different.*) My Lord Abbot, have you noticed? The Pope will revoke the excommunication on
certain conditions. Have you noticed that these conditions have nothing, nothing to do with the original
reason ʰe had for excommunicating me? Go tell
Pope Gregory I'll settle accounts with him at Brixen!
And you, Lady, should you chance to meet your
daughter--let's say down in the courtyard of your
friend's castle—your friend Matilda of Tuscany—
well, what shall I say? Have her come up. And we'll
see if I don't succeed in keeping her at my side: wife
and empress. Many women, before now, have come
here telling me, assuring me, they were she—the wife
I knew I had . . . and, well, sometimes I actually tried
—there's nothing shameful in that, is there?—with one's
wife—But every one of them, when she tried to say
she was Bertha, that she came from Susa, I don't
know why, burst out laughing! (*As if in confidence.*)
We were in bed, understand? I didn't have these clothes
on. For that matter, well, she had no clothes on
either . . . heavens, it's natural, isn't it? For a man
and a woman? At those moments we don't think who
we are, do we? Our clothes, on the hook, are—phantoms! (*Changing his tone again, to the* Doctor, *in
confidence.*) In general, my Lord, I think phantoms
are nothing but slight disorders of the spirit, images
we don't succeed in holding within the bounds of
sleep. They come out even in the daytime when we're
awake and frighten us. I'm always so afraid when I
see them before me at night. A confused mob of
images, alighting from their horses, laughing! Sometimes I'm afraid of my own blood: it pulses in my
arteries like the dull sound of footsteps in distant
rooms in the silence of the night! But enough! I have
kept you far too long on your feet. Your humble
servant, Lady. Your servant, my Lord.

*He has accompanied them to the threshold of the main
    door. He takes his leave of them and they bow.
    Exeunt Matilda and the Doctor. He shuts the door
    and at once turns. Another change of expression.*

The clowns, the clowns, the clowns! Like a color organ: touch it and, look! White, pink, yellow, green. . . .
And the other fellow, Peter Damiani, ha-ha! He's hit,
a bull's-eye. He's scared even to appear before me
now!

*He says this with gay, bursting frenzy, pacing and look-
    ing first in this direction, then in that, till of a sudden
    he sees* Bertold, *more than astounded and terror-
    struck by the sudden change. He stops in front of
    him and points him out to his three comrades, who
    also are lost in astonishment.*

Just look at this idiot here! He stands gaping at me
with his mouth open! (*Shaking him by the shoulders.*)
Don't you understand? Don't you see how I dress
them up, how I fool them, how I like to have them
parade before me like terrified clowns! What is there
to be terrified by? The fact that I tear off the comic
mask and reveal all their trappings as mere disguises?
As if it were not I who had forced them to wear the
mask in the first place—because it pleased me to
play the madman!

Landolf ⎫   (*their heads swimming, flabbergasted,
Harald ⎬   looking from one to the other*). What?
Ordulf ⎭   What do you say? Then . . . ?

Henry (*when they speak, turning at once, and shouting
    imperiously*). Enough, then, let's have done with it!
The whole thing annoys me! (*Then at once, as if on
    second thought, he isn't satisfied, he can't believe it.*)
God, the effrontery of the woman, coming here, to
me, now, her gigolo on her tail . . . Pretending they
were doing me a favor, coming out of pity, to keep
me within bounds—as if I weren't beyond everything
already, beyond this world, beyond life, beyond time!
The other fellow, their Peter Damiani, wouldn't have
permitted such presumption, but *they* would. They
would: every day, every minute, they claim that other
people are what they would have them be. That isn't presumption, is it? Oh, dear no! It's their way of thinking, their way of seeing, of feeling, every man has

his own! You have yours, haven't you? By all means. But what can yours be? That of a flock of sheep: miserable, frail, uncertain . . . They profit by this, they make you swallow their way, so you'll see and feel what they see and feel, or at least so they can kid themselves you will. For what, after all, do they manage to impose on you? Words! Words which each of you understands and repeats in his own fashion. That's the way so-called public opinion is formed! Woe betide the man who, one fine day, finds himself labeled with one of the words that people have been repeating. The word Madman for instance. Or the word—what's another example?—the word Idiot. Tell me something: if someone went around persuading people you are as *he* sees you—went around fixing his own judgment of you in the minds of others—could you stand idly by? "Madman, madman!"—I'm not saying right now that I do it as a joke. Earlier, before I hurt my head falling from a horse . . . (*He stops short, noting their agitation, more than ever upset and astounded.*) You're looking each other over? (*With bitter mimicry he mocks their astonishment.*) Ha? Huh? What's the revelation? Am I or am I not? —I'll tell you: I am! I am mad! (*Becoming terrible.*) And so, by God, down on your knees, down on your knees before me! (*One by one he forces them to kneel.*) I order you all to kneel before me! That's it! Now touch the floor three times with your foreheads! Down! That's how everyone should be before madmen! (*At the sight of the four kneeling men, he feels his fierce gaiety evaporate at once. He is indignant now.*) Off your knees, you cattle, get up!—You obeyed me when you might have put a straitjacket on me?—Is a word heavy enough to crush a man with? It's a mere nothing, it's . . . like a fly!—Yet words are heavy enough to crush us all. Oh, the weight of the dead!—Here am I. Can you seriously believe Henry the Fourth is still alive? And yet: I speak and give orders to you, the living! I want you that way!— Do you think this a jest, too—the way the dead continue to take part in life? *Here*, yes, it is a jest. But go outside. Into the living world. Day is dawning. Time lies before you. Break of day. The day that lies before us, you say, will be of our own making. Hm? Of your own making? What about tradition then? Time-honored customs? Come on: speak for yourselves. You will not utter a word that has not been uttered thousands of times before. You think you are living? You are remasticating the life of the dead! (*He is now right in front of* Bertold, *who by this time is completely stupefied.*) You don't get it, do you, my boy?—What's your name?

Bertold. Me? . . . er . . . Bertold.

Henry. Bertold? You fool! Between the two of us, what's your name?

Bertold. My . . . um . . . real name . . . is Fino . . .

No sooner have the other three started to give signs to Bertold, *advising and chiding him, than* Henry *at once turns to silence them.*

Henry. Fino?

Bertold. Fino Pagliuca, yes sir.

Henry (*turning again to the others*). I've heard the names you use among yourselves so many times. (*To* Landolf.) You are called Lolo?

Landolf. Yes, sir. (*Then, with a burst of joy.*) Heavens! . . . So you . . .?

Henry (*at once, very abrupt*). So what?

Landolf (*straightaway growing pale*). Nothing . . . I mean . . .

Henry. So I'm not mad anymore? No. You see me, don't you?—It's all a joke on those who believe it. (*To* Harald.) I know your name's Franco . . . (*To* Ordulf.) And yours—one second now—

Ordulf. Momo.

Henry. Momo, that's it! A nice state of affairs, hm?

Landolf (*still hesitant*). Then . . . then . . . heavens.

Henry (*not changing*). What? No: not in the least! Let's all have a big, long, lovely laugh about it . . . (*And he bursts out laughing.*)

Landolf ⎫ (*looking each other over, uncertain,*
Harald ⎬ *lost between joy and pain*). He's cured?
Ordulf ⎭ It's true? What?

Henry. Sh, sh! (*To* Bertold.) You don't laugh? Are you still offended? I wasn't addressing you in particular, you know.—*Everybody* finds it convenient, understand? everybody finds it convenient to believe certain people mad—as an excuse for keeping them locked up. You know why? Because they can't bear to hear what they say. What do I say of these people who've just left? That one is a harlot, another a lecher,

another an impostor . . . "It's not true! No one can
believe it!"—All the same, they listen to me. Ter-
rified. *Why* do they listen—if what I say is untrue?
One simply cannot believe the words of madmen.
And yet they listen! Their eyes goggling with terror.
Why? You tell me, you tell me why. I am calm, look!

Bertold.   Well, because . . . maybe they think . . .

Henry.   No, my dear fellow, no! Look at me, look me
right in the eyes . . . I don't say it's true, don't
worry! Nothing is true! But just look me in the eyes!

Bertold.   Very well, how's that?

Henry.   There: you see, you see! You, too! You have
terror in your eyes!—Because you think I'm mad.—
That's the proof!

He laughs.

Landolf (*representing all four, plucking up courage, ex-
asperated*). What's the proof?

Henry.   The distress you're all in because again you
think I'm mad!—And, by God, you know it! You believed me: up to now you believed I was mad. Didn't
you? (*Looking at them for a moment, he sees the
alarm they are in.*) You see this distress? You feel
how it can turn into terror? Terror at something that
takes the ground from under your feet, that deprives
you of the air you breathe? You *do* see it, you *must*
feel it! For what does it mean to find yourself face
to face with a mad man, eh? It means being face
to face with one who takes what you have painstakingly
constructed within yourself, takes it and shakes it,
shakes it down to the very foundations! Your logic—
the logic of all these constructions of yours—totters!
—Well? Who is it that constructs without logic? The
madman! Blessed are the mad—they construct without logic. Or with a logic of their own that floats
on air like a feather. They chop and change. Like this
today, but tomorrow who knows?—You stick to your
guns, they take to their heels. Choppers and changers!
—You say: this cannot be! For them, anything can
be.—You say it's not true, because—because what?
—because it doesn't seem true to (*indicating three of
them in turn*) you, you, you, or to a hundred thousand
others! Then, my dear friends, we'd have to see what
seems true to a hundred thousand others, a hundred
thousand who're *not* considered mad. We'd have to

see what account *they* can give us of the things they
agree on—the fruits of their logic. But this I know:
when I was a child, the moon in the pond was . . .
true . . . to me. Lots of things were true. People told
me about them; I believed; and I was happy. Hold
fast to whatever you think true today! Hold fast
to whatever you think true tomorrow—even if it's
the opposite of what you thought true yesterday! Or
woe betide you! Woe betide you if, like me, you are
swallowed up by a thought—a thought that will *really*
drive you mad. You are with no other human being,
you're at their side, you look into their eyes—how
well I remember doing it, that day—and . . . you might
as well be a beggar before some door you must never
pass through! Open it if you wish: the man who enters is not you, will never be you, will never carry
your world within him, the world you see, the world
you touch. You don't know the man. He is another
person like *any* other person who, from his own impenetrable world, sees you, touches you . . .

*A long, sustained pause. The shadows in the room be-
gin to thicken, increasing that sense of distress and
deepest consternation which fills the four masquer-
aders, increasing also the distance between them and
the great masquerader, who is lost in the contemplation of a terrible misery which is not his alone but
everyone's. Then he pulls himself together, and, not
feeling their presence around him, starts to look for
them, and says,*

It's been getting dark in here.

Ordulf (*at once, coming forward*). Shall I go and get
the lamp?

Henry (*with irony*). The lamp, yes . . . . Do you think
I don't know that as soon as I turn my back and go
off to bed, oil lamp in hand, you switch the electric
light on! Both here and in the throne room!—I pretend not to see it . . .

Ordulf. Ah! Then you want me to . . .

Henry. No! It would only blind me.—I want my lamp.

Ordulf. Very well, it'll be here at the door, ready. (*He
goes to the center door, opens it, goes out, and returns at once with an ancient oil lamp, the kind you
hold by a ring on top.*)

Henry (*taking the lamp and pointing to the table on the platform*). There, a little light. Sit there, around the table, all of you. No, not like that! In special attitudes, handsome attitudes! (*To* Harald.) You, like this. (*Putting him in position. Then to* Bertold, *putting him in position, too.*) You, like this. That's right. I'll sit here. (*Turning his head toward one of the windows.*) One should be able to say: "O Moon, shed your light on us! Give us one little ray, a pretty one!" The moon is so good for us, so good! For my part I feel the need of the moon. I often spend my time gazing at her from my window. To look at her, who would think she knows eight hundred years have passed and that this man seated at the window moon-gazing cannot really be the Emperor Henry the Fourth? But look, look at the scene: what a picture! a nocturne! "The Emperor Henry with his trusty councillors." Don't you relish that?

Landolf (*quietly to* Harald *so as not to break the spell*). You see now? To think that it wasn't true . . .

Henry. True? What?

Landolf (*wavering, as if to apologize*). Nothing . . . I mean . . . (*pointing to* Bertold) he's only just started work here—and I was telling him only this morning what a pity it was . . . with us dressed up like this . . . and with all the other fine clothes in the wardrobe . . . and a room like that one . . . (*Pointing to the throne room.*)

Henry. Well? What's a pity?

Landolf. That . . . that we never knew . . .

Henry. That it was all just playacting, a comedy, a jest?

Landolf. Because we thought . . .

Harald (*coming to his assistance*). It was all done in earnest, dear sir!

Henry. And wasn't it? Don't you really think it was?

Landolf. Well, sir, if you say . . .

Henry. I say you are fools. Call it a deception, if you wish. The point is you should have been smart enough to accept this deception—for your own sakes. Not just as a play to enact before me or those who came to visit me from time to time. For your own sakes, for your natural selves, day in, day out, before nobody. (*Taking* Bertold *by the arms.*) For your own sake, my boy, so you can eat, sleep, within a . . . a piece of fiction that's your own—so you can scratch your

back when it itches! (*Turning again to all four.*)
Feeling alive, really alive in the eleventh century,
here, at the court of your Emperor, Henry the Fourth!
And, from this vantage point, the vantage point of
an age long past, sepulchral, yet colorful, to think that
nine centuries down the road of time, down, down, the
men of the twentieth century live in the utmost confusion. Their life is all strain, all anxiety to know
what will happen to them. To see to what issue the
crises will come that keep them in such anguish and
turmoil. Whereas—you are history already! With me!
What has happened to me may be sad, the situations
I've found myself in may have been horrendous, oh,
yes, there were bitter struggles, painful vicissitudes
. . . BUT they are history! They have stopped changing! They cannot change anymore! You understand?
Fixed forever! You can take your ease and marvel at
every effect as it follows from every cause in perfect
obedience, with perfect logic, at the unfolding of
every event—precise and coherent in every particular!
The pleasure of history, in fact, the pleasure of history!
And how great that is!

Landolf. Wonderful!

Henry. Wonderful! But over with. Now that you know,
I can't go through with it. (*He takes the lamp in order
to go to bed.*) Nor can you, for that matter. If you've
never understood the real reason. It gives me nausea
to think of! (*Almost to himself, with violent, contained rage.*) By God, I'll make her sorry she came!
In a mask of a mother-in-law, pah! With him as
Father Abbot!—And they bring me a doctor with
them—to study me! Who knows if they don't even
hope to cure me? . . . Clowns!—How nice it would
be to smack one of them in the face, at least one—
that one!—A famous swordsman, is he? He'll run me
through, will he? We'll see about that. (*He hears a
knocking at the center door.*) Who is it?

Giovanni's voice. Deo Gratias!

Harald (*delighted at the thought that here's a trick one
could still play*). It's Giovanni the butler. He comes
here every evening. As a monk!

Ordulf (*rubbing his hands, lending himself to the jest*).
Yes, let him do his act as usual, sir, let him do his act!

Henry (*at once severe*). You fools! Play a prank on a
poor old man who's doing this for love of me? Why?

Landolf (*to* Ordulf *and* Harald, *whispering*).   It must be
   as if it were true, don't you see?

Henry.   Oh, very good—*as if it were true.* Only in
   that way does the truth cease to be a jest. (*He goes
   and opens the door and lets* Giovanni *in. The latter
   is dressed as a humble friar with a roll of parchment
   under his arm.*) Come in, Father, come in! (*Then,
   taking on a tone of tragic gravity and deep resentment.*)
   All the documents of my life, of my reign, that were
   favorable to me have been destroyed, deliberately destroyed, by my enemies. All that has escaped de-
   struction is this one—my life, as written by a humble
   monk who is devoted to me. And you would laugh at
   him? (*With love in his eyes, he turns again to* Giovanni *and invites him to sit at the table.*) Be seated,
   Father, sit there. With this lamp beside you. (*He places
   at his side the lamp he is still carrying.*) Now write,
   write!

Giovanni (*unrolls the parchment and prepares to write
   from dictation*). Ready, your Majesty!

The lights fade, but go up almost at once on

Scene II

Henry *is just finishing the dictation.*

Henry.   ". . . the proclamation of peace issued at Mainz
   was of benefit to the poor and good while it did
   harm to the bad and powerful. It brought prosperity
   to the former, hunger and poverty to the latter."
   Henry's voice is tired. He notices that Giovanni *and
   the four young men are drowsy. Quietly:*) Enough!
   (*As he rises, the five others are suddenly alert and on
   their feet.*) No, No! Just stay where you are, I can
   manage! Good night! (*They continue to watch him
   as he leaves the room.*)

*At this point the revolving stage starts to rumble. The
   throne room set is being brought on. Henry is on the
   turntable walking in the direction opposite to its
   movement and at the same speed; hence, in relation
   to the audience, he is stationary. The rumbling
   stops; we are in the throne room.**

* These stage directions are an interpolation by the translator, designed to eliminate the need for a second inter-
mission. In the original, what follows is Act III.—E. B.

In the dark, the back wall is hardly visible. The canvases have been removed from the portraits. Within the frames which are now in the two empty niches, in exact imitation of the two portraits, are Frida, *dressed as Matilda of Tuscany (i.e. as we saw her in Scene I) and the* Marquis *dressed as Henry the Fourth.*

Frida (*as soon as she sees* Henry *has just passed the throne, whispering from her niche like someone who feels she's about to faint with fright*).   Henry! . . .

Henry (*stopping at the sound, as if by some treachery he has suddenly received a knife in his back. In his alarm he turns his face toward the back wall and instinctively starts to raise his arms as if in self-defense*).   Who's calling me?

It is not a question. It is an exclamation which slipped out in a tremor of terror and which asks no answer from the darkness and terrible silence in the room, a darkness and silence which have for him been suddenly filled with the suspicion that he is mad in earnest.

Frida (*at this act of terror is the more alarmed at what she is to do. She repeats a little more loudly*).   Henry! . . .

But although she wishes to stick to the part they have assigned her, she stretches her head out a little from the one niche toward the other.

Henry (*gives a mad yell, lets the lamp fall in order to shield his head with his hands, and starts to flee.*)

Frida (*jumping from the niche onto the ledge and shouting as if she'd gone mad*).   Henry . . . Henry . . . I'm afraid . . . I'm afraid! . . .

The Marquis *jumps onto the ledge and then to the floor, running over to* Frida, *who continues to shout convulsively, on the point of fainting. Meanwhile the others rush in from the door on the left: the* Doctor, *the* Countess *who is also dressed as Matilda of Tuscany, the* Baron, Landolf, Harald, Ordulf, Bertold, Giovanni. *One of them suddenly turns on the light: a*

*strange light emanating from small bulbs hidden in
the ceiling and arranged in such a fashion that only
the upper part of the stage is brightly lit. Without
paying attention to* Henry, *who, after the moment
of terror is past (though it continues to vibrate
through his whole body), just stays looking on,
astonished at the unexpected inrush of people, they
anxiously run to support and comfort* Frida, *who
still trembles and groans and rages in her fiancé's
arms. General confusion of voices.*

Marquis.   No, no, Frida . . . *I* am here . . . I am with
you!

Doctor *(coming up with the others).*   That will do!
Nothing more is needed . . .

Countess.   He's cured, Frida, look! He's cured, do you
see?

Marquis *(astonished).*   Cured?

Baron.   The whole thing was a joke, don't worry!

Frida *(unchanged).*   I'm afraid, I'm afraid.

Countess.   Afraid of what? Look at him! It wasn't true,
it isn't true!

Marquis *(unchanged).*   It isn't true? What are you saying? He's cured?

Doctor.   It seems so, Marquis. As for myself . . .

Baron.   Yes, yes, *they* told us . . .

Countess.   He's been cured for some time. He told those
four attendants about it.

Marquis *(now more indignant than astonished).*   What?
Up to a short time ago . . .

Baron.   My dear Marquis, he put on an act so he could
have a good laugh behind your back, behind the backs
of all of us who—in good faith——

Marquis.   Is it possible? He even deceived his own
sister on her deathbed?

Henry *(who has stayed apart, peering now at one, now at
another, as he feels their accusations and their ridicule;
for all now believe it has been a cruel jest on his part,
and that it is at last unveiled. His flashing eyes have
shown that he is pondering a revenge, though up to now
his scorn, in tumult within him, has prevented him
seeing precisely what it will be. Wounded, he bursts
forth at this point with one clear idea: to accept as
true the fiction which they have insidiously worked
out. He shouts to his nephew).*   Go on talking, go on!

Marquis (stopped by this shout, stunned). What, go on?

Henry. Your sister isn't the only one who's dead.

Marquis (unchanged). *My* sister? I'm talking of yours. To the very end you forced her to come here as your mother Agnes!

Henry (again having regard to the Marquis's present disguise). And she wasn't your mother?

Marquis. *My* mother, *my* mother, exactly.

Henry. To the old man, old and far away, that I am, your mother is dead. But you're newly come down out of that niche! How should *you* know that I've not mourned her in secret—mourned her year in, year out—even in these clothes?

Countess (in consternation, looking at the others). What's he saying?

Doctor (very disturbed, observing him). Quiet, for heaven's sake, quiet!

Henry. What am I saying? I'm asking everyone if Agnes wasn't the Emperor's mother! *(He turns to Frida as if she were really Matilda of Tuscany.)* It seems to me, my Lady, you should know!

Frida (still scared, holding on to the Marquis). I? Oh, no, no!

Doctor. Here's the lunacy back again . . . Be careful, everyone!

Baron (scornfully). Lunacy? That's not lunacy, Doctor, it's the same old play acting!

Henry (at once). I? You have emptied those two niches, and it's *he* that stands here as the Emperor!

Baron. Oh, let's have done with this perpetual jesting!

Henry. Who says it's jesting?

Doctor (to the Baron, loudly). Don't excite him, Baron, for the love of God!

Baron (taking no notice of him, more loudly). They said so! *(Pointing at the four young men.)* They said so!

Henry (turns to look at them). You said that? You said it was all a jest?

Landolf (timidly, embarrassed). No . . . what we said was, you were cured.

Baron. Very well, let's have done! *(To the Countess.)* His appearance—*(pointing to the Marquis)* and for that matter yours, Countess—is coming to seem insufferably childish, don't you see that?

Countess. You be quiet! Who cares about clothes if he's really cured?

Henry. Cured? Yes, I'm cured! (*To the* Baron.) Oh, but not to make an end of things all at once as you think! (*Attacking him.*) Do you know that for twenty years no one has ever dared to appear before me here like you and this gentleman? (*Indicating the* Doctor.)

Baron. Of course I know. Only this morning, after all, I myself came in dressed.

Henry. Dressed as a monk, yes . . .

Baron. And you took me for Peter Damiani. And I didn't even laugh, thinking of course . . .

Henry. That I was mad. It makes you laugh to see her like that—now I'm cured? And yet you might have realized that in my eyes, her present appearance . . . (*He interrupts himself with a burst of scorn and an:* Ach! *He turns at once to the* Doctor.) You are a doctor?

Doctor. Yes, I . . .

Henry. And you dressed *her* as Matilda of Tuscany, too? (*Indicating the* Countess.) Don't you know, Doctor, that in that moment you risked driving my poor brain back into the night? By heaven, to make the portraits speak, to make them jump, living, from their frames . . . (*He contemplates* Frida *and the* Marquis, *then he looks at the* Countess, *finally he looks at his own costume.*) Oh, quite a coincidence: two couples. Not bad, Doctor, not bad—for a madman . . . (*With a gesture in the direction of the* Baron.) He thinks it's a carnival out of season, does he? (*Turns to look at him.*) Then away with my masquerade costume, I'm coming with you, why not?

Baron. Why not indeed?

Henry. Where shall we go? To the club? White tie and tails? Or home with the Countess—a happy threesome?

Baron. Wherever you like, my dear fellow. I can quite see you wouldn't want to stay here—perpetuating, by yourself, what was after all only the unhappy joke of a carnival day! It's incredible, it's incredible to me that you've been able to do it—even before today—once the effects of the accident were over.

Henry. Surely, but it was like this, don't you see? After I fell from the horse and was hit on the head, I was *really* mad for quite a time . . .

Doctor. Aha! A long time?

Henry (*very quickly to the* Doctor). Yes, Doctor, a long time: about twelve years. (*Then, at once, turning to the* Baron.) Can you imagine how it was, my dear

fellow, to see nothing of what happened after that carnival day, what happened for you and not for me—
how things changed, how friends betrayed me? Can you
imagine having your place taken by others? Maybe . . .
let's say . . . in the heart of the woman you loved? Not
knowing who had died, who had disappeared! It wasn't
such a . . . jest to me as you think!

Baron. Pardon me, but that's not what I meant, I meant
afterwards!

Henry. Did you? Afterwards? Well, one day . . . (*He
stops and turns to the* Doctor.) A fascinating case,
Doctor, study me, study me carefully! (*He shakes from
head to foot while speaking.*) One day, all by itself,
heaven knows how, the trouble here (*he touches his
forehead*) shall we say? stopped. Little by little I
opened my eyes again. At first I didn't know if it was
sleep or wake. Why yes, I was awake. I touched one
thing, then another, I could see clearly again . . . (*He
breaks off and makes a gesture toward the* Baron.) I
agree with him! away with these clothes, they're a mask,
an incubus! Let's open the windows, let in the breath
of life! Come on, let's run out of doors! (*Putting the
brakes on.*) But where? To do what? To have everyone
secretly pointing at me and whispering "Emperor
Henry!" when I'm no longer like this but out there in
the streets with my friends and arm in arm with you?

Baron. Not at all! What are you talking about? What
makes you think that?

Countess. Who could conceive of such a thing? An
accident is an accident.

Henry. They all said I was mad—even before—all of
them! (*To the* Baron.) And you know it! No one was
more furious than you if anybody defended me!

Baron. Oh, come, that was only a joke!

Henry. Look at this hair. (*Shows the hair on his neck.*)

Baron. I have gray hair, too.

Henry. There's a difference: mine went gray here! While
I was Emperor! Understand? I never noticed it. I
noticed it all at once—one day as I opened my eyes—
I was terror-struck! For I realized that my hair wasn't
the only thing that was gray, I must be gray all
through, decayed, finished! Hungry as a wolf I would
arrive at the banquet after it had been cleared away!

Baron. That's all very well, my dear man, but you
couldn't expect other people . . .

Henry (*at once*).   —to wait till I was cured. I know.
(*Pause.*)
Not even those who came up behind and pricked my
horse, harnessed and dressed up as he was, with their
spurs . . .

Marquis (*disturbed*).   What? What was that?

Henry.   Pricked my horse, with their spurs! To make
him rear up! Treachery, don't you see? So I'd fall!

Countess (*at once, with horror*).   It's the first I've heard
of that!

Henry.   That must have been a joke, too!

Countess.   But who was it? Who was behind us?

Henry.   No matter who. All of them! All who went on
with the banquet, all who would now leave the scraps,
Countess—the scraps of their piddling pity! Whatever
leavings of remorse have stuck to their filthy plates
they'll give to me! No thanks! (*Turning to the* Doctor
on a sudden impulse.) So you see, Doctor: isn't this
case absolutely new in the annals of madness? I preferred to stay mad. Everything had been prepared
for this new kind of pleasure: to *live* my madness,
to live it with the clearest consciousness of it, and so
avenge myself on the brutality of a stone which had
struck me on the head: to take solitude—*this* solitude—
squalid and empty as it seemed when my eyes reopened
—to take solitude and straightway clothe it in all the
colors and splendors of that distant carnival day when
you—(*he points* Frida *out to the* Countess) ah! there
you are, Countess!—when you had your day of triumph: to oblige all those who came to see me, to live
out, by God, that famous masquerade of long ago
which—for you but not for me—was the jest of a single
day! To make it last forever—not a jest, no, a reality,
the reality of a true madness! So here we were with
our masks on—here was the throne room—here were
my four privy councillors—traitors, of course! (*He
suddenly turns in their direction.*) I'd like to know
what you hoped to gain by letting out the fact that I
was cured!—Once I'm cured, I don't need *you* anymore, you're fired!—To confide in anyone, now *that,*
that is really the act of a madman!—But now it's my
turn, and I accuse you! (*He turns to the others.*) Do
you know, they thought they and I could play the
joke on you now, take *you* in! (*He bursts out laughing.
The others manage to laugh, embarrassed, except the*
Countess.)

Baron (*to the* Marquis). Just think . . . not bad, hm? . . .

Marquis (*to the four young men*). You?

Henry. We must forgive them. For me, these clothes (*indicating his own costume*) are a caricature, a voluntary and overt caricature, of that other masquerade, the one that's going on all the time. You take part in it whether you know it or not. If without knowing it you wear the mask of what you think you are, you are still a puppet in this masquerade, though an *in*voluntary one. That's why we must forgive these four young men if they don't yet see these clothes of theirs as in character. (*Again he turns to the* Baron.) You know this? One soon gets used to it. And one walks around like this—(*He does so.*) a tragic character—there's nothing to it—in a room like this!—Look, Doctor. I remember a priest—an Irish priest undoubtedly—good-looking, too—and one November day he was sleeping in the sun in a public park. He'd laid his arm along the back of the seat for support. He was basking in the delight of a golden warmth which to him must have seemed almost like summer. One can be sure that at that moment he didn't know he was a priest anymore, he didn't know where he was. He was dreaming, who knows of what?—A small boy passed. He was carrying a flower he'd plucked, with a long stalk. In passing, he tickled the priest, right here in the neck.—I saw laughter in the priest's eyes as they opened. His whole mouth laughed with the happy laughter of his dream. He'd let himself go, he had escaped. But I must tell you, he soon put himself together again, he soon belonged to his priest's cassock again. He grew rigid. And back into his eyes came the same seriousness that you have seen in mine—for Irish priests defend the seriousness of their Catholic faith with the same zeal I felt for the sacred rights of hereditary monarchy.—I am cured, gentlemen, for I *know* I'm playing the madman, I do it quite calmly.—Woe betide you if you live your madness unquietly, without knowing it, without seeing it!

Baron. So the obvious conclusion is—that *we* are the madmen!

Henry (*with a little outburst that he manages to check*). If you were not mad—you and she—would you have come?

Baron. Actually, I came here believing the madman to be you.

Henry (*loudly of a sudden, indicating the* Countess). And she?

Baron. She? I don't know. I see that she seems bewitched by what you have to say, fascinated by this conscious madness of yours! (*He turns to her.*) Dressed as you are, I'm sure you could stay here and live it out, Countess . . .

Countess. You are impertinent!

Henry (*at once, placating her*). Don't mind him, don't mind him. He's determined to provoke me—though that was just what the doctor told him not to do. (*Turning to the* Baron.) Do you think I'll trouble myself any more about what happened between me and you—about the part you played in my misfortune with her—(*Indicates the* Countess, *then turns to her, indicating the* Baron.) the part he is now playing in *your* life?—My life is like this! Yours is not!—The life you have grown old in—I have not lived at all! (*To the* Countess.) Is that what you wanted to say, to prove, to me? You were even prepared to take the doctor's advice and dress like that? Well done, Doctor, I say again. Two pictures: "Before and After: what we were then, and what we are today!"—But I'm not mad in your way, Doctor. I well know he (*indicating the* Marquis) can't be me because *I* am Henry the Fourth. I've been Henry the Fourth for twenty years, understand? Fixed in this eternity of masquerade! (*Indicating the* Countess.) She has lived them, she has enjoyed them, the twenty years, and she's become—a woman I can't recognize. For I know her thus—(*indicating* Frida *and going over to her*) in my eyes, this is she, forever . . . You seem like a child that I can frighten as I will. (*To* Frida.) You've been badly frightened, haven't you, my child, by the joke they persuaded you to play? They didn't understand that, to me, it could hardly be the joke they intended, it could only be this terrible prodigy: a dream come alive—in you! More alive than ever! For there (*pointing to the niche*) you were an image. They have made you a living creature. You are mine, mine, mine! And by right!

He takes her in his arms, laughing like a madman while the others are scared out of their wits and shout.

But, when they try to tear Frida *from his arms, he
becomes terrible and shouts to his four young men.*

Hold them back, hold them back, I order you to hold
them back!

*Stunned, yet fascinated, the four young men automatically
set about holding back the* Marquis, *the* Doctor, *and
the* Baron.

Baron (*liberates himself at once and rushes toward*
Henry).   Leave her alone! You are *not* mad!
Henry (*drawing the sword, swift as lightning, from the
side of* Landolf, *who is next to him*). Not mad? We'll
see about that! (*And he wounds him in the belly.*)

A general yell of horror. The Marquis *and* Bertold *run
to support the* Baron.

Marquis.   He's wounded you?
Bertold.   He's wounded him! He's wounded him!
Doctor.   I told you so!
Frida.   God, God!
Marquis.   Frida, come here!
Countess.   He's mad, he's mad!
Marquis.   Hold him!
Baron (*while they carry him out by the door on the left,
fiercely protesting*).   No! He's not mad! He's not mad!
He's not mad!

*They are shouting as they leave by the door on the left.
And they keep on shouting until, amid the general
din, is heard a more piercing shout from the* Countess. *Then silence.*

Henry (*is left on stage with* Landolf, Harald, *and* Ordulf.
*His eyes are starting from his head. He is thunderstruck
at the life of the fiction he himself created. In a single
moment it has driven him to crime.* This time . . . we've
no choice. (*Calls them around him as if to defend himself.*) We're here . . . forever!

Eduardo de Filippo

FILUMENA MARTURANO

I.

Both in technique and in philosophy, Eduardo de Filippo is traditional. At the same time he strikes me as one of the three or four original figures in the theater today. Let me tell something about his plays, beginning with the two latest: *La Grande Magia* (*The Big Magic*) and *La Paura numero uno* (*Fear Number One*).

Calogero di Spelta is so jealous he will hardly let his wife, Marta, out of his sight. Her friend Mariano has to resort to stratagem to be alone with her. He bribes a visiting conjurer to use Marta in a disappearing act. The conjurer thus brings her where Mariano is—but instead of returning after fifteen minutes, as arranged, the young couple run off to Venice. Meanwhile the conjurer must save face before his audience. He tells Calogero that his wife can be produced out of a small box—which he shows the company—*if* he, the husband, has complete faith in her—that is, is sure she is "faithful" to him.

Otto, the conjurer, saves the occasion. But days pass, and weeks, and months, and the waiting husband is not to be appeased by the improvisation of a moment. He has to be convinced of the truth of the whole magical philosophy of life: what seems real is only illusion. Thus, while Calogero has the illusion of time passing, he yet, under Otto's influence, has faith that no time has passed: all this is but a dream happening in the moment before Marta's reappearance at Otto's performance.

The idea grows on Calogero. It is a game, which he is more and more determined to play out to the end. He is

From *In Search of Theatre*, by Eric Bentley (New York: Alfred A. Knopf, Inc., 1953). Copyright 1953 by Eric Bentley.

so eager to agree to the basic premise (time is not passing) that he tries to do without eating and excreting.
Otto, who had practiced conscious deceit from the start,
takes pity on him and urges him to open the box and
finish a losing game. Calogero, however, is determined to
win. He will open the box only when his faith is complete.
He is just reaching this point and is bracing himself to
open the box, "one, two . . ." when Otto cries ". . . and
three!"—Marta has returned, after four years. But it is a
moment too soon. The box is still closed, and Calogero's
faith still untested. He cannot accept Marta on these
terms. He clings to the box and does not open it.

When this story was first placed before a metropolitan
audience, in Rome last February, everyone cried "Pirandello!" Like the Sicilian master, Eduardo had insisted
that illusions were needed because the truth was more
than we could stand. Like Pirandello in *Il Piacere dell'
onestà* (*The pleasure of Honesty*) and *Ma non è una cosa
seria* (*But It Isn't a Serious Matter*), Eduardo had shown
an idea beginning as fiction, an escape from life, and
later incorporated into life. There are even more specific
resemblances to *The Emperor* (*Enrico IV*). At the beginning of each play a man retires from the bitter reality of
sexual rivalry into a deliberate unreality in which time
is supposed to stand still (though its not doing so is in
both cases indicated by the protagonist's graying hair).
At the end of each play reality irrupts into the illusion
in a way calculated to shatter it; but the result is the
opposite; the illusion is accepted by the protagonist in
perpetuity.

Whether Eduardo was influenced by Pirandello or was
simply nourished from the same sources and interested in
the same problems was not discussed. Worse still: the
word *Pirandello*, as such words will, prevented people
from seeing things that would otherwise have been
evident. For all the superficial "Pirandellism" of *La
Grande Magia*, the play is really a much simpler, more
commonsensical affair. Pirandello in his despair toys with
a nihilistic relativism. The veiled lady at the end of *Così è*
(*se vi pare*) is one person or another as you choose; in
which proposition the law of contradiction itself (that a
thing cannot both be and not be) is flouted. In Eduardo,
on the other hand, no such devilry is thrust upon the universe. If one man has an illusion, another sees it as such.
The apparent magic in even his spookiest play *Questi
Fantasmi* (*These Phantoms*) is all explained away as the

chicanery of a servant or the secret generosity of a friend. So in *La Grande Magia*, Otto's "little magic" is rather brutally exposed from the beginning as mere charlatanism. The "big magic"—the magic not of the parlor but of life itself—is magic only honorifically. The word *magic* is a figure of speech. Illusions, mad ideas (we are given to understand), may be instrumental in a man's moral development. Thus Calogero's sin had been jealousy, lack of faith in a woman. Once he has entered upon the great moral game of life, he must not be deflected from it until he has ceased to be jealous, until he has found faith. Otto's assumption that it would be enough to produce Matra—as out of a hat—shows to what a degree his understanding is limited to the realm of the little magic. His actually producing her is the completest betrayal of the greater game. Now Calogero will never open the box: his faith is locked in it.

La Grande Magia, then, is not about the nature of reality, it is about faith in one's wife. Eduardo likes to use some big, much discussed subject as a kind of come-hither. It turns out to be incidental. He may almost be said to have tried this once too often with *La Paura numero uno*, where the big, much discussed subject is right now so bothersome that, once mentioned, it is not easily shaken off. This subject—our "fear number one"—is the third world war. Eduardo deals so cleverly with it in his first act, and even his second, that the third, in which it is definitely pushed into the background, seemed pretty much of an anticlimax to the audience that gathered to see the play at the Venice Festival in July. We should have to be as free of "fear number one" as Eduardo wishes us to be to recognize all at once that the subject of his play is parenthood.

Eduardo shows ua a father and a mother. Matteo Generoso, paterfamilias, is so possessed with fear of the third world war that all business on hand, and notably his daughter's wedding, keeps being postponed. The young people decide to put his soul at rest by faking a radio announcement that war has actually broken out. . . . The mother of the play is the bridegroom's mother, Luisa Conforto. She also is an obstacle in the young couple's way since she resists the loss of her son. She has lost his only brother already and his father. In the fanaticism of her maternal love she contrives to postpone the marriage for eleven days by walling her son up in a little room where she feeds him all his favorite dishes.

In the end the marriage is celebrated, and war has not broken out; the play is a comedy. What of the delusions and distortions in the minds of the two parents? The conclusion enforced by the action of the play is that the father's case, though "normal," is more deplorable because it disqualifies him from being a father. The mother's case, though a psychiatrist would take a stern view of it, is found excusable, a case of virtue driven into a corner. One recalls the conjurer's accurate description of Calogero in *La Grande Magio*. "[He] is not mad. He is a man who knows he has been stricken and reaches after the absurdest things in order not to confess it even to himself." Calogero will continue his fight for faith if he has to "reach after the absurdest things" in the process. Luisa Conforto will continue to be a mother even if she too does the absurdest things in the process.

In calling Eduardo traditional, I had in mind, among other matters, that drama has so often and over so long a period been a defense of family piety. In Greek tragedy it is the desecration of this piety that horrifies us. In the comedy of Molière it is the desecration of this piety that we find ridiculous. Then in modern times there has been that enormous assault upon all our intimate relations which Balzac described through all the volumes of his great comedy and which Marx and Engels announced in their tragic rhapsody of a manifesto.

Italy has written its own sad chapter in this story. After the heroism of Garibaldi and his thousand, the indignity of the millions. The Fascist era was but the lowest point of a deep descent, and whether the long climb up again has really got under way since 1945 seems doubtful. Abroad, people know about the brutalities of Fascism, far more indeed than the citizens of Fascist countries. What they know less about is something evident in every institution and every social group where Fascism has secured a foothold—the corruption, the petty knavery, the bottomless indignity, the dishonor.

There is no politics in Eduardo, but in play after play he has put his finger on the black moral spot. Perhaps *Le Voci di dentro* (*The Voices from Within*), famously written in seventeen hours, is its most devastating diagnosis. A man accuses a whole family of murdering a friend of his. Later he realizes that he dreamed it all, perhaps not even dreamed it. The friend is alive. But the accuser is not mad. He has sound intuitions ("voices from within") and they crystallized into a single clear hallucination. Eduardo's main point is in the subsequent behavior of the family. They accept the charge because each thinks it quite possible that one of them *has* committed the murder. As their accuser cries:

> I accused you and you didn't rebel though you were all innocent. You thought it—possible—normal—you have written Murder in the list of daily events, you have put Crime in the family book of accounts. Respect, mutual respect, that puts us on good terms with ourselves, with our conscience . . . what shall we do to live, to look ourselves in the face?

In *Questi Fantasmi* it is the petit-bourgeois protagonist who has lost self-respect:

> If you knew how humiliating it is, and sad, for a man to have to hide his poverty and pretend to be playful with a joke and a laugh. . . . Honest work is painful and miserable . . . and not always to be found. . . . Without money we become fearful, shy, with a skyness that is embarrassing, bad. [To his rich rival:] With you I don't feel envy, pride, superiority, deceit, egoism. Talking with you I feel near God, I feel little, tiny . . . I seem to be nothing. And I *like* destroying myself, seeming nothing . . . in this way I can free myself from the weight of my own being which oppresses me so.

In *Napoli milionaria* (*Millionaire Naples*), Eduardo shows how common folk are dehumanized, how a family is ruined and divided—mother from father—by blackmarketeering. In *Natale in Casa Cupiello* (*Christmas with the Cupiellos*), he portrays a father who lacks paternal maturity and we realize to what a large extent the childishness of the "little man" may contribute to catastrophe.

> Luca Cupiello, your father, was a big baby. He took the world for an enormous toy. When he saw it was a toy you couldn't play with as a child any more but only as a man . . . he couldn't make it.

The special relevance of Eduardo's defense of the pieties may now be clearer. They are the bedrock above which everything else, even sanity perhaps, has been shot away. The sane are only hypocritical parties to the general offense. Humanity has taken refuge in the crazy and infirm. Uncle Nicolo in *Le Voci di dentro* has vowed himself to silence because he holds that mankind is deaf. From time to time he spits. Old Luisa Conforto in *La Paura numero uno* needs no convincing that war has broken out because she holds that it was in full swing already! Deprived of both her sons, she now has nothing much to call her own—"*rrobba mia*"—save her jams and conserves. How these can mean so much is perhaps explained by a longish quotation. The passage is worth exhibiting also because, however simple, it could be by no playwright but Eduardo.

MATTEO: *Now, I swear, if twelve wars broke out one after the other, they'd make no impression on me. But you never believed it was just a story, an invention. You're always sure we're at war! I don't know how I'd convince you. . . .*

LUISA: *Don Mattè, you're a darling! I'm old now as you see—you are much younger than I am—but I assure you I wouldn't change my brain for yours!*

MATTEO: *Why not?*

LUISA: *Why, because you believe a thing when the radio says it. I mean: to you the radio is more important than your own thoughts. You want to convince me there isn't a war on while you yourself talk of it—as a "tragic problem that makes you sick of life itself": you complain of the chauffeur who forces you into selling your car so as to be rid of a nuisance, of the maid who doesn't take a liking to you and robs you; you complain of your struggle with the tradespeople; you complain of the tailor who drives you into the poorhouse, of frauds, extortions, betrayals. . . . Come here.* (She goes toward the cupboard where the conserves are. Matteo follows her automatically.) *Do you like jam?*

MATTEO: *Yes. I'm not mad about it, but a little once in a while. . . .*

LUISA (opening the cupboard doors and showing Matteo the little jars): *These I made myself.*

MATTEO: *And what precision!* (Reading some of the labels) *Amarena, strawberry, apricot. How nice to keep all these things at home!* (Fastening his attention on a jar of cherries preserved in spirits) *Oh, those! I'm crazy about them! In winter they're a real comfort.* (Reading) *"Cherries in spirits."*

LUISA: *I've taken to these jams. I love them. As if they were my children. When I'm alone and a longing for a bit of amarena comes over me, for example, I talk to it as to a living soul.—"How good you are! How tasty you are! I made you with my own hands. How happy I am you've turned out well!"—And they answer, they comfort me a little with their sweetness. The only sweetness a poor woman like me can expect in life. And I understand . . . I understand now why my good soul of a mother did the same and turned the house upside down if someone in the family helped themselves without asking her permission.*

MATTEO: *Oh, yes. Says she: "That's mine!"* ["Chello è rrobba mia!"]

LUISA: *Surely. But it's hard. The jam is really mine and nobody must touch it. The same with the flowers. You see this balcony. . . . They're all plants I grow with my own hands.* (Pointing to a plant) *That one, I don't know, I don't recall how many years I've had it. Just think, I was a young lady. Many's the move I've seen. Like that piece.* (She points to a small casket.) *It was my grandmother's, then my mother's . . . when we lived at Foria . . . then at Riviera . . . then near the Church of the Conception . . . I can't tell you how many different houses that table has lived in.* (In a good-natured tone, thoughtful) *Not long ago your wife said: "Blessed be you that can take life so easy!" Don Mattè, I never let my sons breathe. From the time they began to use their reason I'd interfere with any of their pleasures rather than lose their company even for a moment. If they ever came home a half-hour later than they were expected, I was thinking of a disaster. I used to think out ways of keeping them in the house. No good, I simply couldn't. And sometimes they openly let me know my presence annoyed them. They ran out. They went away. They found excuses, pretexts. They told me a pack of lies to get away, to leave me, to live their own life, which was to be no concern of mine. . . . Don Mattè, I shut Mariano up! You see now? With a wall of brick and cement . . . he couldn't get out! And if one of you had gone and reported it, wouldn't the authorities have shut me up in the madhouse? "Crazy!" "See her, she's crazy!" "You know what*

*she's done? She shut her son up in a room and built
a wall in front of the door!" "And why?"—Because
I wanted to have him near me, because I didn't want
to lose him! . . . You yourself, in the family circle,
haven't you said almost these very things?* (At this
point she can't control her feelings. Her voice becomes thick. But a quick succession of sobs, at once
repressed, puts her to rights.) *Don Mattè, before
God you must believe me. If what I say is a lie may
I never see tomorrow's light! I am not sorry for what
I did. For fifteen days I felt him to be once more—
my son. Like when I had him here.* (With both hands
open she strikes her stomach.) *Don Mattè take good
note: here!* (She repeats the gesture.) *Like the nine
months of pregnancy when I found a way of being
alone with him, lying on a couch with my hands
like they are now, to talk to him. And he moved inside me and answered. As the jam answers me today.
And I ate—I ate more than I wanted, so he'd be born
strong and healthy. . . . For fifteen days I slept peacefully—as I'd never managed to sleep since he came
into the world. So many things to keep me busy,
thoughts, responsibilities. . . . Ever since he started
to walk. "If he falls. . . If he hurts himself badly.
. . ." And the vaccinations, the fevers, the ill-
nesses. . . . And then the war. . . . You remember hearing the Germans giving instructions over
the radio? . . . "All men who do not present themselves at German headquarters will be punished with
death." . . . "Parents hiding their sons will be shot
at sight." . . . For fifteen days he was my son again.
Shut in! And in bed with my hands here* (repeating
the gesture) *I went to sleep happy because I felt him
inside me once more. . . .*

II.

It is sometimes debated how far we need to know an
author's background in order to judge his work. I should
think we need to know it whenever we should otherwise
be in danger of taking something as his personal contribution when it is a representative product of his time and
place. Thus some of Eduardo's attitudes, as I have described them, may seem forced when we take them as an
assertion of his will, whereas as an expression of a social
tradition we might let them pass. I have in mind the im-

pression probably produced by the foregoing pages that
what Eduardo principally does in a play is to put his own
special ideas across—the impression, in short, that he
writes laborious *drames à thèse*.

The extreme individualism of Matteo's final attitude to
war—"if twelve wars broke out one after the other they'd
make no impression on me"—may be open to criticism
but, in context, is an expression of a traditional group
feeling and not a pet idea of the author's. It belongs to
Naples, where the state is regarded as an enemy—and
whose regionalism the Fascist state did in fact try to sup-
press. To tell people to forget the newspapers and get on
with their private lives, valid or not as a piece of advice
to us all, has somewhat different meaning in a city that
for so long has had to consider how to survive under
different masters and amid recurrent conflagrations. Eduardo is true to this situation when he shows people, such
as Luisa, achieving dignity in their apartness. When he
longs for dignity, moreover, he is not an aristocrat or
would-be aristocrat bemoaning the inundation of aristocratic culture by plebeian hordes. On the contrary, it is
the dignity of the plebs he is championing, the *urbanità*
of the poor who throng the alleys and docksides of Naples
while the aristocrats and their wars come and go.

Not that Eduardo sees the life of "the other half" as
uniformly dignified. The lower depths of Naples form as
fantastic a society of adventurers and desperadoes as can
well be imagined. Living by the skin of their teeth, a
dreary past behind and a blank future ahead, they accept
the present with peculiar vehemence. Familiar with death,
they do not take life too seriously. They are willing to
see it as a joke, a paradox, a fantasy, a show, a game. As
absurd, the existentialists would say. There is something
existentialist, in one of the popular meanings of the word,
about *La Grande Magia:* the world is lawless, ethics are
at best improvised, yet the imperative remains to improvise them. Perhaps it was occupation by the Germans
that precipitated the anguish of the French writers and of
this Italian. To Eduardo's credit it must be said that he
gives also the sense of emerging from under the incubus
and looking about him. A recurrent character in his plays
is coming to be the man in midpassage through life, tortured, perplexed, deflected from normal paths, but unde-
feated, questing. But Eduardo has never stuck in the
quagmire of Teutonic lugubriousness. Here again plebeian Naples came to his aid. There is a philosophy of

the absurd, after all, in plebeian humor in general: your life is hopeless but you laugh, you are cheerful, and morally positive, against all reason. Thus, while *La Grande Magia* is one of Eduardo's most somber pieces, it is also his most ambitious projection of the idea that life is a game. And it is when we feel the fairy-tale quality of the story that we get it right—when, that is to say, we talk less of *Pirandellismo* and more of Naples.

Naples is the reservoir on which, consciously and unconsciously, Eduardo draws. Not only the city as a whole but the Neapolitan theater in particular. It is a popular as against an art theater. This means, to begin with, that it is a dialect theater and not an "Italian" one. It uses a popularly spoken language and not an official, national, bourgeois language—in this respect resembling Synge and O'Casey rather than Pinero and Galsworthy. The lack of a national theatrical repertoire in Italy may be deplorable, but the quality of the defect is—the regional repertoire.

The next most salient feature of Neapolitan popular theater as I have seen it is the style of acting. In Paris today you hear much about *commedia dell'arte*. What they show you is Jean-Louis Barrault and the Piccolo Teatro di Milano (the latter being more the rage in Paris than in Milan). These things are very fine, but they are art theater, and the *commedia dell'arte* was nothing if not popular theater. You would find a much more authentic version of its famous artificial clowning in the Neapolitan comedian Totò. And for another side of the tradition—not famous at all, unfortunately—you must go to Eduardo.

It is no slur on his playwriting to say that he is first and foremost an actor, perhaps the finest actor in Italy today, the son of a fine actor, the brother of a fine actor and an even finer actress. For anyone who comes to Italy with normal preconceptions, for anyone who has seen any of the great Italian stars of recent times or who today catches the last echo of D'Annunzio's generation in the voice of the aged Ruggeri, Eduardo on the stage is an astonishment. For five minutes or so he may be a complete letdown. This is not acting at all, we cry; above all, it is not Italian acting! Voice and body are so quiet. *Pianissimo.* No glamour, no effusion of brilliance. No attempt to lift the role off the ground by oratory and stylization, no attempt to thrust it at us by force of personality. Not even the sustained mesmerism of big Ibsen performances. Rather, a series of statements, vocal and corporeal.

When the feeling of anticlimax has passed, we realize that these statements are beautiful in themselves—beautiful in their clean economy, their precise rightness—and beautiful in relation to each other and to the whole: there are differentiations, sharp or shifting, between one speech and the next; there is a carefully gauged relationship between beginning, middle, and end.

My point here is not so much to praise Eduardo as to observe that here is an actor more likely—for demonstrable historical and geographic reasons—to be the heir of *commedia dell'arte* than any other important performers now living and that his style is distinctly different from anything I expected. It is a realistic style. It makes few large departures from life. No oratory, no stylization. Both in speech and in gesture, rhythm, accent, and tempo are an imitation of life. The "art" consists of the skill of the imitation, the careful registering of detail and nuance, and a considered underlining of the effects—the outline is firmer, the shape more sure. The assumption is that there is more drama in real speech and gesture—for these are arts and not raw material like a sculptor's clay —than in invented speech and gesture. That this realism is not just Eduardo's personal style or due—God save the mark!—to the influence of Stanislavsky you may prove by visiting the grubby popular theaters of Naples, notably the Apollo and the Margherita, any day of the week.

One of the persistent heresies about *commedia dell'arte*, often as Italian scholars denounce it as such, is the idea that the actors made up their lines as they went along. The nearest they ever got to this is probably that they sometimes wrote their lines, the script being the fruit of a collaboration between various members of the cast. At any rate, Eduardo de Filippo began his career as an actor doing this sort of writing. From reports I gather the impression that the plays he acted in must have been rather like Chaplin shorts. There would often be several to an evening, and they would represent incidents in the life of the little man, the *povero diavolo*. A play like *La Grande Magia* is of course as far from a one-act farce or melodrama in a popular Neapolitan theater as *Monsieur Verdoux* is from a Keystone Comedy. In each case, however, the later work is made up to a surprising extent of elements from the earlier. And it is these elements that save both film and play from polemical aridity, that give them a tang and an identity, that make them dramatic art.

They would not do so if they operated as mere comic relief or melodramatic seasoning; their function is to lend definition to the author's subject. Thus in *La Grande Magia,* the idea of life as a game, the world as a show, is given body and form by, among other things, the brilliant theater of Otto's conjuring, in which we get a back-stage glimpse of all the mechanism of magic. To be told, as my reader has been, that Otto had to convince Calogero of the reality of magic is very little compared to actually seeing Otto play his phonograph record of applause and persuade Calogero it is the sea. To be told, as my reader has been, that Matteo in *La Paura numero uno* is tricked into believing war has broken out is very little compared to actually seeing the enactment of the ruse with the microphone and the comic sequences that follow. Matteo talks at cross-purposes with the other tenants: he thinks they are talking about the war, they think he is talking about the house. Another sequence ends with Matteo's mistaking a multi-national group of pilgrims for an invading army. These two sequences lead up to a climax of laughable absurdity at the conclusion of acts one and two respectively.

For, though Eduardo's plays are chock-full of amusing and imaginative details—minor characters, bits of business, meditations as of an unsophisticated Giraudoux—they have a solid overall structure, usually in three clearly marked phases or acts. If the sequences within the acts often derive from popular farce, the act-structure is even more often that of popular melodrama. Eduardo likes to bring the curtain down, especially the curtain of Act II, on a terrific moment—which means "at the psychological moment," a moment when two lines of narrative suddenly intersect by amazing coincidence. Thus in *Natale in casa Cupiello,* the ugly rivalry of husband and lover reaches boiling-point just as Luca Cupiello's idyll, the adoration of the Magi, comes to actual performance —a big curtain for Act II! In *La Grande Magia,* it is the denouement in Act III where the arm of coincidence is longest and most active: it just happens that Marta, absent for four years, reappears one second before Calogero is to open the box. Eduardo is saying not only "such is the wonder of fairyland" but also "such is the perverseness of reality." He has not surrendered to melodrama; he has exploited it. For him it is not a jazzing-up of otherwise inert and tiresome elements. It is a legitimate accentuation of the fantastic character of life.

This purposeful manipulation of fable is nowhere more striking than in Eduardo's most popular play, *Filumena Marturano*. Since this play is also one of his most realistic works, the reader may be interested to hear in more detail how the apparently curious mixture of realism and its opposite actually works out. Since, moreover, the play is Eduardo's most powerful tribute to mother love, a note on it may serve to bind together the first and second parts of this note and leave us with a rounded if not complete impression of Eduardo's playwriting.

The story is the unprepossessing one of the man who makes an honest woman of a prostitute. What stands out in Eduardo's play is the prostitute herself, a heroic plebeian, a tigress of a mother. The portrait derives half its life from the language—which in translation can scarcely be shown. But, as already intimated, the mode of the narrative is a contributory factor.

Filumena comes from the lower depths of Naples. She is rescued from poverty by a prolonged liaison with a rich man, Domenico Soriano. When they are both getting along in years, and he wants to marry a younger, more beautiful, and more respectable girl, Filumena pretends to be dying and arranges a deathbed marriage. The ceremony over, she jumps lightheartedly out of bed, and Domenico realizes he has been had. It is at this point that Eduardo raises the curtain on his first act! The stormy exposition is followed by a revelation. Filumena has not been acting selfishly. Unknown to Domenico, she has three grown-up sons: they are now legitimized!

The first act ends with Domenico rushing off for a lawyer to rescind a marriage held under false pretenses. In the second, it seems that he will have his way, and Filumena, crushed for the moment, accepts the hospitality of her son Michele. As a parting shot, however, she tells Don Domenico that he is the father of one of the three sons. Another melodramatic revelation! Further: with a secrecy at once melodramatic and realistic, she will not tell him which one, because she wants no discrimination against the other two. End of the second act.

Act III is a happy epilogue. In the time between the acts Domenico has come around. The old marriage has been rescinded, but a new one is now being celebrated. He gladly accepts Filumena as wife and all three young men as sons. "I am fifty-two, you are forty-eight. We are two mature souls in duty bound to understand what they are about—ruthlessly and to the depths. We have to face it. And assume full responsibility."

The sententiousness is naïve, but the language, sunny and bland in the original, implies some unworried awareness of the fact. There is an irony about this happy ending (as there is about many others). What stays with us is the conclusion arrived at and, far more, the sense of danger and disaster this time—perhaps not next time— narrowly averted. What stays with us is Filumena's cry: *"Il tenero amor filiale lo abbiamo perduto!"*

A traditional playwright, then, in technique and philosophy. But do we understand what it means to live in a tradition—as against merely believing in tradition, professional traditionalism? Eduardo de Filippo started with an infinitely suggestive and dramatic milieu, Naples, and with a theater which, if not great, had yet a real existence —in a sense in which our broadways and boulevards and west ends are deserts of unreality. These circumstances conduced to a concentration of energy which stands in direct contrast to that dissipation of energy by which talents elsewhere are frittered away. They conduced to a growth so natural and green that most art theaters seem hothouse products by comparison. In short, they brought Eduardo to the threshold of great theater; his own gifts took him across it; and it is thus that one of the most traditional artists of our time became one of the most original.

E. B. (1950)

FILUMENA MARTURANO

A Mother's a Mother

(1946)

A COMEDY IN THREE ACTS BY

Eduardo de Filippo

ENGLISH VERSION BY ERIC BENTLEY

Characters

FILUMENA MARTURANO
DOMENICO SORIANO
ALFREDO AMOROSO, Domenico's *crony*
ROSALIA, Filumena's *friend*
DIANA, Domenico's *mistress*
LUCIA, *the maid*
UMBERTO ⎫
RICCARDO ⎬ Filumena's *sons*
MICHELE ⎭
NOCELLA, *a lawyer*
TERESINA, *a seamstress*
TWO WAITERS
    The Place: Naples
    The Time: Not long ago

ACT I

The style of Domenico's *dining room is decidedly twentieth century. The room is showily furnished in mediocre taste. Certain pictures and ornaments, carefully placed on the walls and furnishings, violently conflict with this modernism. They doubtless belonged to* Domenico's *father.*

The door downstage left leads to the bedroom. Upstairs left, a large French window set across the corner of the room looks out on an ample terrace that is provided with plants and flowers and shaded by a colored, striped awning. The main door is in the back wall on the right. Upstage right there is an archway; and through partly drawn curtains one can descry what Domenico *dares to call his study. Here also his penchant for modernity shows itself. It is a "modern" cabinet which protects and exhibits a vast number of cups of various metals and divers forms and dimensions; these are the First Prizes his racehorses have won.*

On the opposite wall, behind a desk, two crossed banners bear witness to victories at the Festa di Montevergine. Not a book, not a journal, not even a piece of paper. The study is orderly and decent, but lifeless.

In the center of the dining room is a table laid with considerable care and taste for two. In the middle are fresh red roses.

It is the time of year when spring is turning into summer. It is the time of day when afternoon is turning into evening. The sun is shedding its last rays on the terrace.

AT RISE: *Four people are on stage*—Filumena, Domenico, Rosalia, *and* Alfredo.

Filumena *is wearing a long white nightgown. Her hair is in disorder, though a hasty attempt has been made to set it to rights. Her feet are stockingless in her old bedroom slippers. This woman's face shows signs of torment: we can see her past has been sad and stormy.* Filumena *doesn't look coarse, but she cannot hide her humble origin, nor would she want to. Her gestures are broad and open. Her tone of voice is can-*

*did and forceful: she is someone to reckon with, rich
in instinctive intelligence and moral force. After her
own fashion she knows life and its laws—and after
her own fashion confronts them. A strand or two of
silver on the temples announce her forty-eight years;
not so her dark eyes, which have preserved all the
youthful vitality of the dark Neapolitan type. She is
pale as a corpse, partly from the role she has just
been playing (she has pretended to be dying), partly
because of the storm she knows is coming. But she
isn't afraid. On the contrary, she is waiting like some
wounded beast to leap on her adversary.*

Domenico Soriano *is a strong, healthy man of about fifty.
He has lived well. Money and an easy time of it
have kept him lively in spirit and youthful in appearance. His father, Raimondo Soriano, was one of
the richest and most rascally confectioners in Naples;
he had bakeries at Vergini and Forcella and very
popular stores in Toleda and Foria. And* Domenico
*was the apple of his eye. The caprices of Don Dom-
enico—as a boy he was Signorino Don Mimì—knew
no bounds either for originality or extravagance;
they were famous and even today are the talk of
Naples. A passionate horse fancier, he can spend
half the day with his cronies going over the athletic
feats of the leading champions who have passed
through his well-fed stables. And now here he is,
wearing only a pair of pants and a quickly buttoned
house jacket, pale, convulsed, facing this "thing of
naught,"* Filumena Marturano, *whom for so many
years he has treated as a slave, but who now holds
him in the palm of her hand, ready to crush him like
an insect. Not that he knows it; he sees no limits to
his will. He is sure of the triumph of his godlike
reason. He is sure he can expose the outrage, lay
bare before the world the baseness which has deceived him. He feels offended, insulted, and, in a
certain sense which he can't explain and wouldn't if
he could, desecrated. The fact that he seems publicly discomfited turns his head; he is going berserk.*

Rosalia *is mild and humble. She is seventy-five. Her hair
is of an uncertain color, rather more white than gray.
She is wearing a dark dress of no definite color. A
little bent but still full of life. She used to live in a*
BASSO—*the name the Neapolitans give to ground
floor living quarters in the slums. This was in San*

Liborio Street, right opposite where the Marturanos
lived: that's how she came to know all about them.
She has known Filumena from earliest childhood.
She was with her in her saddest moments, and did
not spare those words of comfort, understanding,
and tenderness which the common women of Italy
have to offer, and which are a balsam to the suffering heart. From harsh experience she knows the
effects of this man's irascibility and is petrified.

Alfredo is an agreeable fellow of some seventy years,
solidly built, vigorous, muscular. He was a fine
coachman, and it was in this capacity that Domenico
first took him on, keeping him ever after at his side
as handyman, scapegoat, spy, and friend. He has
come to symbolize his master's past. You can see how
loyal and devoted he is to Domenico, and how great
his self-abnegation, in the way his eyes follow his
master. He is wearing a gray jacket of perfect cut,
if a little frayed, trousers of another color, and a
beret worn jauntily on one side. On his portly belly
he displays a gold chain. He is simply waiting—perhaps the calmest of the four people in the room, for
he knows his Domenico, he hasn't fetched and carried for him for nothing.

As the scene opens, Filumena is standing by the bedroom
door with her arms folded a posture of defiance.
Downstage right is Domenico, facing her. Upstage
.. left, near the terrace, stands Rosalia. Upstage right is
Alfredo. They are standing in the four corners of the
room as if playing a children's game. A long pause.

Domenico (slapping himself repeatedly, vehemently).
Fool! Fool! Fool!!!
Alfredo (intervening with a slight gesture).   Now really,
Don Do . . .
Domenico.   Am I a man? I should go to a mirror and
spit in my face! (To Filumena.) Married to you? I've
wasted a lifetime with you already: twenty-five years
of health and strength and youth and effort! And you
want that, too? And Don Domenico has no choice but
to give it to you? For twenty-five years you've done
what you liked with me, you've all done what you
liked with me! (To himself.) You thought you were
Jesus Christ our Lord, and they've all done what they
liked with you! (He turns to the three of them one

after the other.) You, you, you—in our street—in our precinct—in Naples—throughout the world—you've planned my downfall! (*Now he is quiet again*.) It won't bear thinking about. But I might have known. A woman like you *had* to get where you've got. But don't think you've heard the last of this. I'll murder you! And all your accomplices, too! The doctor, the priest, and (*pointing at* Rosalia *and* Alfredo) those two reprobates who've lived off me and grown fat off me, I'll murder you all! (*Looks for his revolver*.) Where's my revolver? Give me my revolver.

Alfredo (*calmly*). It's at the gun shop. I took it to be cleaned. Like you told me.

Domenico. I've told you plenty in my time, haven't I? And it's beginning to look as if I was telling you what you wanted me to tell you, isn't it? Well, that's all over: My eyes have been opened! (*To* Filumena.) You will leave this house. And if you don't leave quietly, you'll leave dead. No law can stop me! Not *God* can stop Domenico Soriano!! I'll denounce you in the streets, I'll send you to the galleys! I can pay the piper and I'll call the tune! And when I tell them who you were and where you lived when I picked you up, I'll win my case all right! I'll annihilate you!!

Pause.

Filumena (*not at all overwhelmed, sure of herself*). Are you through now?

Domenico (*still roaring*.) And don't speak to me. I can't stand it!!!

Filumena (*calmly*). When I've said my say, I'll never set eyes on you again. And you'll never hear my voice again.

Domenico (*still bellowing*). A harlot: that's what you were and that's what you are!!!!

Filumena (*still quiet*). Why do you shout so? It's no secret. Everyone knows who I was and where I lived. But—you—came—there. Like the others. And I treated you like the others. Why should I treat you different: aren't men created equal? What I've done . . . well, I'm sorry for it. But now I'm your wife, Domenico. The army and the navy can't change that.

Domenico. My—wife?

Filumena. Your wife.

Domenico. You're crazy! It was the most barefaced piece of trickery you ever heard of. You were sick, were you? You must take to your deathbed, must you? A trick: and I have witnesses! (*He indicates* Rosalia *and* Alfredo.)

Rosalia (*hastily, not wanting to be dragged in*).   I know nothing. All I know is, Donna Filumena got sick, she got so bad she was going to die, but she never said nothing. I know nothing neither.

Domenico (*to* Alfredo).   You know nothing either, huh? You didn't know this dying was just an act?

Alfredo.   By the Holy Virgin, Don Mimì! If Donna Filumena wanted to tell somebody, it certainly wouldn't be me: she can't stand the sight of me!

Rosalia.   What about the priest? Who told me to call the priest? You did!

Domenico.   Because she wanted him . . . I wanted to please her . . .

Filumena.   Oh, of course—you didn't believe I was passing on, did you? Oh, no! You weren't thinking how nice it would be to get rid of me, were you?

Domenico.   Yes, I was! And you were whispering in the priest's ear. And the priest said, "Marry her! Marry her in extremis, poor woman! It is her one remaining wish! With the good Lord's blessing, tie the bridal knot!!"

Filumena (*continuing*).   And you said to yourself, "After all, what have I got to lose? It's only a question of hours, it won't cost much." When the priest left, I hopped out of bed and said, "Wish us luck, Domenico, for now—we're husband and wife!" It must have been quite a shock.

Rosalia (*hysterical*).   I nearly jumped out of my skin. And laugh! I couldn't stop! (*In fact, she starts again.*) I can't get over it, I could have sworn she was sick . . .

Alfredo.   On her deathbed in fact . . .

Domenico.   If you two don't be quiet, *you'll* be on your deathbed!! (*Pausing.*) But I still don't get it: how could she . . . (*He has a thought.*) What about the doctor? A qualified doctor could come here and not notice she's in perfect health and making a fool of him?

Alfredo.   I think . . . er . . . maybe he made a mistake.

Domenico. (*stung*).   Shut up, Alfredo! (*Thinking hard.*) That doctor needn't think he'll get away with it, he'll pay for this as sure as God's in heaven! He couldn't

have acted in good faith, he was in on the deal sure as
fate, *you* cut him in on it, you *bought* him, huh?

Filumena. Bought! The only idea in your head: everything you ever wanted you bought. Including me. Because you were Don—Mimi—Soriano. You wore the
best shirts, you went to the best tailors, your race
horses ran for you, and you did quite a bit of running
yourself, didn't you, after one thing and another?
And sometimes I set the pace, Don Mimi, and you
didn't know it, and you've a long way to run yet, Don
Mimi, there's blood and sweat ahead, before—you—
know—what—a—gentleman—is! (*She is quiet again
now.*) The doctor knew nothing about it, he thought I
was dying, too: why shouldn't he? (*Another change
of tone.*) Any woman would be on her deathbed after
twenty-five years with you. (*To* Rosalia *and* Alfredo.)
For twenty-five years I've been his servant. You know
that. He just used to go away and have a good time.
In London. In Paris. Or at the race tracks. So I was
his policeman. I went to the bakeries at Forcella and
Vergini, I went to the stores in Toledo and Foria.
If I hadn't he'd have been robbed right and left. (*She
imitates his hypocritical tone.*) "I don't know what
I'd do without you, Filumena, you're—a woman!"
(*Shouting.*) I've kept house for him better than a . . .
then a legitimate wife! (*Dropping her voice*). I've
washed his feet. Not just since I've got old. Even
when I was young—I washed his feet. (*Raising her
voice again.*) I might have been a housemaid he could
fire from one moment to the next!

Domenico (*sullenly*). You never tried to understand
how things stood between us. Always mooning around
the house with that sullen, resentful face. You said
to yourself, "Well am *I* in the wrong? Have I done
anything to him?" (*Slowly.*) I have never seen a tear
in those eyes. Never. In all the years we've lived
through together, I have never seen her cry!

Filumena. I should have cried then? For you maybe?
For this fine . . .

Domenico. Never mind about me. You were a soul in
torment that knew no peace! A woman who doesn't
cry, doesn't eat, doesn't sleep—I never saw you sleep
but once! A damned soul, that's you!

Fulumena. When did you want to see me sleep? You
never came home. I was always alone. Even at Easter.
Even at Christmas. Like a lonely old dog. Do you know

when a woman cries. Don Mimì? When she catches
sight of the good thing and can't have it. Filumena
never caught sight of the good thing. And when all
you know is the bad thing, you don't cry. It's good to
cry, I know that, crying is a blessing, a blessing Filumena wasn't to know. A harlot you call me, and
well you might—you always treated me as one. (*To*
Rosalia *and* Alfredo, *sole witnesses of the sacred
truth of what she is saying.*) And let's not talk of his
youth and his wild oats. In those days you could say,
"Well, he's rich, he's spoiled, he'll get over it." But
now he's fifty-two and he still comes home with lipstick on his handkerchiefs. Pah! Where are they, Rosalia?

Rosalia (*reassuringly*). In the cupboard, Donna Filumena.

Filumena. A considerate man would say to himself,
"She mustn't find them, I must hide them someplace."
What this man thought was, "What can she do when
she finds them? Who is she, anyway? What rights has
she?" And off he goes after his little . . .

Domenico (*caught out and furious.*) His little—who?

Filumena (*not in the least intimidated, more violent
than he*) . . . . after his little floozy! You think I didn't
catch on? You can't even tell good lies, that's what's
wrong with you. Fifty-two years old and he's still
after girls of *twenty*-two! He isn't ashamed of himself
either. He sets her up in *my* home. We all pretend she's
a nurse. Because he believed—oh, yes, he believed—
I was dying. (*This is true but incredible.*) Not more
than one hour ago, before the priest came to marry
us, they thought I was just going to give my soul to
God, and I'd lost my sense of sight, so, at the foot of
my bed, they started kissing and caressing! . . . (*She
can't hold her nausea back.*) Madonna, you make me
feel sick to the stomach! Why, suppose I'd *really* been
dying—with you carrying on like that at the foot
of my bed!! Me dying in there, the table laid in here.
For two: him and the corpse, I suppose!

Domenico. You mean, when you're dying, I'm not
supposed to eat? I had to have food, didn't I?

Filumena. With roses on the table?

Domenico (*passing it off as normal*). With roses on
the table.

Filumena. Red roses?

Domenico (*losing patience*). Red, blue, green, good

God, can't I have roses if I want to? (*He is blustering now.*) If I want to, can't I be glad you're dead?

Filumena.   Only I'm not dead, Domenico. (*Defiantly.*) I changed my mind.

Domenico (*to himself*).   "So put that in your pipe and smoke it." (*Pause.*) But there's something I don't get. If you've always treated me just like all the others, if men are all alike, if, as you put it, they're created equal, why did you have to marry me? And if I'm in love with this girl and want to marry her—and I will marry Diana, mark my words—what does it matter to you whether she's twenty or a hundred and fifty?

Filumena.   You're right: that girl doesn't matter. (*She buckles down to explain.*) Did you really think I'd done it for you? You didn't enter into my calculations at all. You never have. A woman of my type—you've said it yourself, you've always said it—a woman like me has it all figured. (*Underlining each word.*) It so happens I can use you. (*A break.*) Or did you really believe—after the lifetime of sacrifice I've lived—that I'd simply pick up and go?

Domenico (*thinking he understands, jubilant*).   Money! I knew it! But couldn't you have had it? (*Pompously.*) You think a son of the Sorianos would have failed to provide for you? Failed to set you up in a home of your own? Failed to make you a woman of independent means?

Filumena (*humiliated by his lack of understanding, with scorn*).   Oh, stop! Will you men never understand anything? As for your money, Domenico, you can keep it. Keep it. It's something else I want of you right now. And you're going to give it to me. (*Pause.*) I have three sons.

Domenico *and* Alfredo *are astonished.* Rosalia *is not.*

Domenico.   Three sons? What are you talking about, Filumena?

Filumena (*repeating herself almost mechanically*).   I have three sons.

Domenico (*bewildered*).   But . . . whose children are they?

Filumena (*what* Domenico *fears not having escaped her, coldly*).   Their fathers are men like you.

Domenico (gravely). Filumena, Filumena, you're play-ing with fire. What do you mean, men like me?

Filumena. Men are created equal.

Domenico (to Rosalia). You knew about this?

Rosalia (feelingly). I certainly did!

Domenico (to Alfredo). You, too?

Alfredo (eager to get out of it). No! Donna Filu-mena hates me. I told you!

Domenico (not yet convinced, as if to himself). Three sons?

Filumena. The eldest is twenty-six.

Domenico. Twenty-six?

Filumena. You needn't pull such a face about it. They're not yours.

Domenico (somewhat relieved). Do they know you? Do they see you? Do they know you're their mother?

Filumena. No, but *I* see *them.* Often. I talk to them.

Domenico. What do they do? Where do they live? What do they live *on?*

Filumena. They live on your money.

Domenico (surprised). They live on my money?

Filumena. They live on your money. I stole it from you. From your wallet when necessary. Under your very nose.

Domenico. So you're a thief!

Filumena (boldly). I sold your suits, I sold your shoes, you never noticed. Remember that diamond ring? I said it was lost? Well, I'd sold it. I've raised my family on your money. I'm a thief.

Domenico (appalled). What sort of woman *are* you?

Filumena (goes on as if he hadn't spoken). One of them has a store in the next street. He's a plumber——

Rosalia (correcting her). An engineer: sanitary and high-droolic!

Domenico (who hasn't followed this). What!?

Rosalia (pronouncing the word right this time). A san-itary and *hydraulic* engineer! Fixes faucets and all that. . . . The second boy, what's his name? (*Searches for the name.*) Riccardo . . . he's the handsome one, a real lady killer, lives on Via Chiaia, he has a shop too, number seventy-four, he's a shirtmaker, and what shirts, and what customers . . . Then, there's Um-berto——

Filumena. He wants to study. He's always wanted to study. He's a thinker! Writes in the papers!

Domenico (*ironically*). So we have a writer in the family——

Rosalia. And what a mother she's made them! They've never wanted for anything. I am old and I may find myself at any moment in the presence of Him who beholdeth all things, comprehendeth all things, and forgiveth all things, so it's true, what I say, and don't you go listening to no gossip! From the time they was in their baby clothes, she's fed them on milk and honey!

Domenico. Paid for with Don Domenico's shirts, shoes, and diamond rings!

Rosalia (*blurting it out*). You threw your money to the four winds of heaven——

Domenica (*severely*). And whose business was that, may I ask?

Rosalia (*frightened, but unable not to drive her point home*). But, saints above—you never even noticed!

Filumena (*with contempt*). Take no notice of him, it's no use.

Domenico (*controlling himself*). You're trying to provoke me, Filumena, you're going too far. Do you realize what you've done? You've made me look like a man of straw! Take these three young men I haven't even met, whose existence I hadn't even dreamed of, in fact—tomorrow or the next day, they can laugh in my face and say to themselves, "Fine, so that's Don Domenico. The man who foots the bill."

Rosalia (*eagerly*). No, no, Don Mimi, what do they know about it? Donna Filumena, she does everything the right way, she has a head on her shoulders. It was the lawyer who sent the money when Michele—he's the engineer—set up shop in the next street. He told him it came from "a lady who wishes to remain anonymous!" (*She has difficulty with the last word.*) It was the same with Riccardo, he's the shirtmaker. And the lawyer has to send Umberto his monthly allowance, so he can finish up his studies. You don't come into it at all!

Domenico (*bitterly*). I only pay for it!

Filumena (*on a sudden impulse*). I should have got rid of them, then? Is that what I should have done, Domenico? I should have put them out of the way, as other women do, is that what you mean? You'd admire a Filumena of that sort, wouldn't you? (*More excited.*) Answer me! Tell me I should have done what the other girls said. "What are you waiting for?"

they said, "it's one worry too many!" But I'd have
worried to all eternity! How could I have lived with
that on my conscience? And then, when I talked with
the Madonna, the little Madonna at the end of our
street . . . (*Turning to* Rosalia.) Remember?

Rosalia (*almost insulted at the idea that she could forget*). Do I remember? It's the Madonna of the Roses!
And does she shower her favors upon us? One a day!

Filumena (*re-creating the scene, as if talking to herself*). It was three o'clock in the morning. I was alone,
walking down the street. Six months had passed since
I left home. It was the first time. Where could I turn?
Who could I confide in? I heard the other girls. "What
are you waiting for?" "Just one worry too many." "I
know a good one." Without knowing it, as I walked
along, I'd come to "my" little street, with the little
altar on the corner, the altar of the Madonna of the
Roses. I went up to her. This way. (*She plants her
fists on her hips and, raising her eyes to an imaginary
effigy, speaks as one woman to another.*) What am I
to do? Thou who knowest all things, who knowest why
I have sinned, tell me: what am I to do?" But the Madonna didn't reply. She didn't say a word. "So that's
it?" I said. "The more you don't talk, the more people
believe in you. But I'm speaking to you. (*Arrogantly.*)
Answer me!" And a voice answered me. It said:
(*Now she imitates the tone of voice of someone not
known to her; she hasn't been able to tell where the
voice comes from.*) "A mother's a mother!" I froze.
I was riveted to the spot—like this. (*She grows rigid
and fixes her eyes on an imaginary effigy.*) If I'd
turned around, maybe I'd have seen where the voice
had come from, a house with a balcony, the next street,
an open window. . . . But then I said to myself, "Why
at this particular moment? What do other people know
of my affairs?" (*Pause.*) Then . . . it was she, was it?
It was the Madonna? I'd faced right up to her, so
she agreed to talk? And of course, the Madonna
makes use of *us* when she wants to talk. . . . So when
they said, "One worry too many," it was the Madonna
speaking, the Madonna wanted to test me? (*Slowly.*)
I don't know if it was me, I don't know if it was the
Madonna of the Roses, who went like this (*she nods
as if to say, "I have understood"*) and said, "A
mother's a mother," but I swore an oath. I swore to
bring up my children. (*She turns to* Domenico.) And

that's why I've been around you all these years! For
their sake. For their sake I've put up with the way
you've treated me, I've put up with . . . everything.
And when that young fellow fell in love with me and
wanted to marry me . . . remember? We'd been together
five years then, you and I. At home you had your wife
and out at San Potito you had me with three little
rooms and a kitchen. It was the first apartment you
found for me after you'd taken me out of the——that
place, four years after we first met. Well, this young
fellow wanted to marry me. But you acted jealous. I
can hear you now, "I'm married, I can't marry you. But
if this other fellow marries you, I'll . . ." And you burst
out crying. *You* can cry, even if *I* can't. You can cry
all right. And I said to myself, "Go slow, Filumena, it
can't be helped. Domenico loves you yet, just stick
to San Potito and your three little rooms . . ." Two
years later your wife died. Time passed. I was still
at San Potito. I said to myself, "He's still young, he
wouldn't want to tie himself to another woman for life,
the day will come when he'll settle down, when he'll
realize what sacrifices I've made . . ." So I waited.
And sometimes I'd say, "Domenico, do you know
who's just got married? The girl across the way. In
the house with the little windows." And you'd smile,
you'd burst out laughing, just like when you came to
the . . . other place with your friends. Before San
Potito. The wrong kind of laugh. I'd hear it on the
stairs. It wasn't always the same man laughing, but it
was always the same laugh. (*Bearing up.*) I waited.
I waited twenty-five years. Waited for Don Domenico's
pleasure. He's an old man of fifty-two now, but that's
nothing . . . (*With a change of tone, vehemently.*) I
could die with the shame of it! This old man of fifty-
two thinks he's a schoolboy, runs after every skirt he
sets eyes on, goes around with lipstick on his handkerchiefs, and installs in my house his latest little . . .
(*threatening*). Well, try it again, bring her to this
house, now I'm your wife, I'll throw you out, both of
you. We're married. Married by the holy priest. And
this is my house!

A bell rings offstage. Alfredo *leaves upstage right.*

Domenico. Your house! Ha! ha! ha! (*He laughs with
forced irony.*) You make me laugh!
Filumena (*passionately*). All right, laugh! I don't mind

hearing you laugh now. You wouldn't know how to laugh as you did then.

Alfredo returns. He gives everyone a good look. He's bothered by what he has to say.

Domenico (noticing him, ill-humoredly). What do *you* want?

Alfredo. Me? I just wanted to say they've brought that supper . . .

Domenico. Why in God's name do you all think I shouldn't eat?

Alfredo (as much as to say: I wash my hands of this). Very well, Don Domenico. *(Talking out through the door.)* Come in!

Two Waiters from a restaurant come in with a wicker hamper and other supplies for a cold supper.

First Waiter (rather unctuous and servile). Your supper, signore! *(To his companion.)* Put it here.

(Second Waiter puts the hamper down on the spot indicated.)

First Watier. Signore, I've only brought one chicken. It's such a big one. Enough for four, signore. All best quality goods! *(He starts opening up the supplies.)*

Domenico (stopping him with a gesture, annoyed). Do you know what you can do? You can leave!

First Waiter. Yes, signore, yes, indeed. *(Taking a dessert out of the hamper and placing it on the table.)* This is the dessert the young lady is so fond of. And this is the wine . . . *(There is silence all around. To remind Domenico of a promise, he adopts a playful tone.)* You haven't forgotten, have you, signore? Our little . . .

Domenico. What?

First Waiter. You *have* forgotten? Well, signore, when you came over to order the supper, don't you recall? I asked if you happened to have any old clothes you didn't need, and you said, "Come this evening, and if things turn out the way I'm expecting, I'll have a brand new suit. I'll make you a present of it."

The atmosphere is glacial. After a pause, in a tone indicating ingenuous disappointment, the waiter continues.

First Waiter. Things did *not* turn out the way you
wanted? (*He waits, but when* Domenico *still doesn't
answer, he is impatient.*) You didn't get the good
news you expected?

Domenico (*aggressively*). I told you to leave!

First Waiter (*amazed at his reception*). We're going,
signore. Let's go, Carlo. The good news never came.
Just my luck.

     The Two Waiters *leave, upstage right.*

Filumena (*after a pause, ironically*). Eat, Don Mimì!
What's the matter with you? You're not eating? Have
you lost your appetite?

Domenico (*angry*). Sure, I'll eat. I'll eat *and* drink—
later on!

Filumena. When the corpse comes to keep you company!

Enter Diana *by the main door. She is a good-looking
girl of twenty-two. That is, she tries to look twenty-
two; actually she's twenty-seven. She dresses rather
snobbishly—with affected elegance. She looks them
all up and down. As she enters, she is talking to
everyone in general and no one in particular. She
evidently despises everybody. She doesn't even notice Filumena's presence. She is carrying medicinal
packages, which she places on the table near the
door. She takes a nurse's white coat from a chair
and puts it on.*

Diana. There was *such* a *mob* in the pharmacy, I just
couldn't get waited on, I had to go to another one,
couldn't get waited on there either, went from one
pharmacy to another, must have been to *eight* in all,
I'm sweating *all* over, Rosalia. (*In a bossy tone.*) *Do*
get my bath ready, there's a good girl. Oh! (*seeing the
roses*) roses, *red* roses, thank you, *thank* you, Domenico, you're a *dear*, what an *odor*. I'm working up quite
an appetite, too. (*Picks up one of her packages.*) I've
found the *camphor* . . . and the *adrenalin* but *oxygen*
isn't to be had for a *million* lire!

Domenico is fuming. Filumena *isn't batting an eyelash,
she's just waiting.* Rosalia *and* Alfredo *seem pretty
amused and happy.* Diana *lights a cigarette and sits
by the table, facing out front.*)

Diana. I was just *thinking*, if she—heavens, how I *hate* to say the word—but, here goes, if she *dies* tonight, I'll leave, early in the morning. A girl friend of mine has room for me in her car. I'd just be in the way here, whereas at Bologna I've a *hundred and one* little things to do! I'll be back in just about ten days, and we'll be together again. Now tell me, how is she? Out of her pain yet? Has the priest come?

Filumena (*controlling herself, with affected courtesy, slowly approaching*). The priest has come. (*Diana is taken completely by surprise. She stands up and backs away several paces.*) And seeing that I was on my deathbed . . . (*Breaking off*). Take that coat off! (*Though almost stunned* Diana *does as she is told.*) Put it on that chair. (Diana *does so.*) Seeing that I was in extremis, the priest advised Don Domenico Soriano to tie the bridal knot with the good Lord's blessing.

Not knowing what attitude to take, and trying to find something to do, Diana *takes one of the roses and raises it to her nose.* Filumena *is furious and shouts harshly.*

PUT THAT ROSE DOWN!

(Diana *puts the rose down like a German soldier obeying an order.* Filumena *is polite again.*)

Don Domenico found the priest's advice good. He said to himself, "Fair enough: the poor woman has stood by me for twenty-five years"—and lots more that we haven't time or inclination to tell you. He came to the bedside and we were married—with two witnesses and the priest's blessing. Weddings must do people a lot of good, signorina, this one certainly did me. I felt better right away. I got up and put off dying till another time. As for you, young lady, you can't be a nurse where no one needs nursing!

Filumena *sticks out the index finger of her right hand and on every emphatic word strikes* Diana *on the chin with it. Each time* Diana *shakes her head in an involuntary* "No."

And as for all those nasty goings-on, making love be-

side the deathbed and so forth, you better go and do
it in someone else's house!

Diana (*has now backed practically to the entrance with
an idiotic smile on her face*). Yes, I see. Oh, yes!

Filumena.   And if you can't think of a good place to go,
you can go . . . can go . . . where I used to live . . .

Diana.   Where's that?

Filumena.   Ask Don Domenico. He used to frequent
such places. In fact he still does.

Diana (*dominated by* Filumena's *vehement eye, almost
mechanically*). Thank you. (*And she leaves, upstage
right.*)

Filumena.   Don't mention it. (*And takes up her position
again at left.*)

Domenico (*who has been lost in his own thoughts,
snaps back again*). So that's the way you treat her,
is it?

Filumena.   I treat her as she deserves.

Domenico (*taking up the thread of his previous argument*). You're a devil, Filumena, it isn't easy to deal
with you, it isn't easy to understand what you say. But
now I know you: you're like some poisonous moth—
that destroys whatever it lights on. A short time ago
you said something I've been thinking about. You said,
"It's something else I want of you, and you'll give it
to me!" It can't be money, you know I'd have given you
money. (*He can't bear not knowing.*) What is it then?
What are you holding back? What *do* you want of me?
Speak!

Filumena (*simply*).   A mother's a mother.

Domenico.   What in heaven's name do you mean by
that?

Filumena.   Children should know who their mother is.

Domenico.   So?

Filumena (*her heart overflowing now*). My children
must know I'm their mother. They must know what
I've done for them. I want them to love me. And they
mustn't feel ashamed before other men, they mustn't
be made to feel bad every time they fill out a blank!

Domenico.   But why should they?

Filumena.   Why should they? Why should they?! Don't
you see, they've never had a family. And if you don't
have a family, what's your family name? You can
make one up, but what does it mean, with no relations
to show, not even an uncle or an aunt? You have no
name! But this is going to stop for my boys, Domen-

ico, it's going to stop. You've given your name to *me*.
Now I want it for my boys.
Domenico.   My name?
Filumena.   Your name's Soriano. Since this afternoon,
*m*y name's been Soriano, too. And now my children
will be called Soriano.

Pause.

Domenico (*swallowing the bitter pill*).   I see. In fact
I saw it coming. But I had to hear you actually say
it. (*Now he is in a rage.*) You snake in the grass!
(*Now he is shouting his head off.*) Adder, viper, cobra,
python, boa constrictor! (*Lowering his voice a little.*)
And you want to bring your brood into my nest, do
you? The house of the Sorianos is to be a house of
another color, the son of the Sorianos'll play host to
the sons of a . . .
Filumena (*has kept calm but has no intention of letting
him say "prostitute" again*).   The sons of . . .?
Domenico.   The sons of Filumena Marturano. The sons
of Filumena Marturano and I don't know who. *You*
don't know who. You thought you'd put your conscience to rest and live down your sinful past by
presenting me with three strangers to live with! I'd die
first! They will never set foot in this house! I swear
by the sacred memory of my father . . .
Filumena (*with a rush of genuine feeling and deep
earnestness.*)   Don't swear! I swore an oath twenty-five
years ago, and I've stuck to it. Don't swear an oath
you wouldn't stick to. The day will come when you'll
want something from me, Domenico, so don't go
swearing you'll never accept it, don't swear that,
Domenico, or you'll never forgive yourself!
Domenico (*overawed by* Filumena's *words, but angry*).   What's in your mind now, you witch? I don't
fear you, understand! I'm not afraid of *you!*
Filumena.   Then why do you have to say so?
Domenico.   Oh, be quiet! (*Taking off his house coat.*)
Alfredo, bring me my coat.

Alfredo *goes into the study.*

You'll leave tomorrow. This marriage is a clear case
of fraud. I'll bring suit against you. I have witnesses,
remember. (*He's working himself up again.*) And if

I lose, I'll destroy you anyway, Filumena. I'll chop you up in little pieces!

Filumena (ironically). May I ask where you want to send me?

Domenico (very far gone, and aggressive about it). Back where you came from! (Alfredo *comes back with* Domenico's *coat.* Domenico *grabs it and puts it on.*)

(*To* Alfredo.)
Tomorrow morning you'll go for my lawyer: you know who that is? (Alfredo *nods. To* Filumena.) Then we'll talk.

Filumena. Then we'll talk.

Domenico. And bring your secret weapon, if you have one. You'll need it.

Filumena. I do have a secret weapon. I'll bring it.

Domenico. Well, a harlot's a harlot, Filumena Marturano! (*He leaves, laughing horribly, outrageously.*)

Rosalia. You hear that laugh, Donna Filumena, you remember that horrible laugh? And what a horrible, nasty thing to say, too! (Rosalia *is weeping.*)

Filumena (relaxing). Sit down, Rosalia. (*As* Rosalia *sits at the opposite end of the table,* Filumena *realizes that the cold supper is before them.*) Our supper's all ready, you see. (Rosalia *dries her tears and begins to smile.*) And that wasn't what the voice said, it said: "A mother's a mother," Rosalia Solimene! (*She is enjoying the food.*)

ACT II

The next day at nine in the morning. In order to clean the floor the maid has put all the chairs out of the way; some are on the terrace, others upside down on the table in Don Domenico's study. The carpet, in the center of which stands the dining table, is folded back upon itself from all four sides. It is a fine, sunny morning.

Lucia, *the maid, is an agreeable, healthy girl of about twenty-three. She has completed the job, and is squeezing out her scrub mop in the bucket for the last time. Then she takes mop, stick, and bucket and puts them on the terrace. She starts setting the room to rights by turning down the four sides of the carpet.*

Alfredo (*comes in from the outer door, tired, sleepy*). Hi, Lucia.

Lucia (*stopping him dead with the tone she uses—and the gesture*). Don't come walking on my floor with those feet of yours!

Alfredo (*yawning*). All right, I'll walk on these hands of mine.

Lucia. So that's your tune, is it? I've been sweating blood over this floor and . . .

Alfredo. Tune, what tune? I—am—dead. Dead! Don Domenico kept me chasing around after him the whole night. Or sitting with him on the sea wall at Mergellina—which isn't the warmest place in the world. What made the Lord God send me to *him?* But I'm not grumbling. He's not treated me bad. No, I've seen life! Madonna! The times we had together! (*Enthusiastically.*) May the Lord let him live to be a hundred, a thousand! . . . (*Misgiving strikes him.*) But—quietly, peacefully! I wasn't born yesterday. These all-night sessions are getting to be a bit much! (*He takes a chair and sits at the table—all of which is a preparation for a daring demand.*) Lucia, can I have some hot coffee?

Lucia (*who has put the chairs back without paying attention to* Alfredo's *outpouring*). No. There isn't any.

Alfredo (*put out*). What d'you mean, there isn't any?

Lucia. There isn't any. There were three cups. I drank one. Donna Rosalia didn't want the second one so I gave it to Donna Filumena. The third cup I'm keeping for Don Domenico—in case he comes back!

Alfredo (*glaring and not convinced*). In case he comes back!

Lucia. In case he comes back! Donna Rosalia hasn't made any coffee today.

Alfredo. I suppose you couldn't make any youurself?

Lucia. No, I couldn't. I don't even know how. Coffee's none of my business.

Alfredo. Well, why didn't Donna Rosalia make any?

Lucia. She went out. Early. She said she had to deliver three urgent letters. For Donna Filumena.

Alfredo (pricking up his ears). Deliver three letters for Donna Filumena? (*About to repeat himself, shouting.*) Deliver three let . . .

Lucia. Deliver three letters for Donna Filumena.

Alfredo (deciding to remember his state of dire exhaustion). Lucia, I *must* have some hot coffee!! Know what you can do, Lucia? Pour Don Domenico his cup of coffee. Pour it right now. Go on, fill the cup, fill it to the brim! Then take the cup between finger and thumb like this and—easy, easy—pour a drop, a little drop (*He makes the gesture of pouring quite a bit of coffee from one cup to another*) into another cup that just happens to be standing by and feeling lonely! And don't you rob your master, Rosalia Solimene! Go to your ketcle of lovely steaming water and fill up his cup!

Lucia (dryly). And when he notices it?

Alfredo. But he won't! His mind is on . . . higher things. Anyway, he may not come. (*He pulls himself together heroically.*) And age before beauty, my dear! (Lucia *doesn't get this. So* Alfredo *tries a simpler line.*) I need it more than he does!

Lucia (submitting). Well, let me go and heat it up for you.

She is leaving left, but seeing Rosalia enter right, she stops and tells Alfredo.

Here's Donna Rosalia. You still want this coffee?

Alfredo. Donna Rosalia's here? Well, good: she can make Don Domenico some fresh coffee, can't she? Anyway, bring me that half cup.

Rosalia *comes into the room. She sees* Alfredo *but pretends not to. Full of her mission, she makes a beeline for* Donna Filumena's *bedroom door.*

Alfredo (Rosalia's *attitude not having escaped him, letting her get right to the door before he calls attention to himself*). Rosalia, what is this? Have you lost your tongue?

Rosalia (indifferently). Oh, I didn't see you.

Alfredo. I'm the invisible man.

Rosalia. Too bad. Little boys should be seen and not heard.

Alfredo (*grandly ignoring this last*). You went out early this morning, didn't you?

Rosalia (*an enigma*). Did I?

Alfredo. Where were you?

Rosalia. I was at Holy Mass, if you must know, Mr. Invisible Man!

Alfredo (*incredulous*). At Holy Mass. (*Remembering.*) You took Donna Filumena's three letters and placed them on the holy altar, I suppose?

Rosalia (*trapped but controlling herself*). Why d'you ask—if you know?

Alfredo (*also simulating indifference*). I was just wondering. (*Pause.*) Who did you take them to?

Rosalia. Some little boys *like* to be heard, don't they?

Alfredo (*this being too deep for him, he starts to bluster*). Little boys? Little . . .

Rosalia. You talk, Alfredo Amoroso, you talk a lot. What's more, you're a spy.

Alfredo (*huffily*). And when did I ever spy on you, I'd like to know!

Rosalia. Spy on me? What'd be the use of that? My record's as clear—as water from the crystal spring! What do *I* have to be ashamed of? (*She starts to reel off her life story: the singsong expression tells us she has done so very often before.*) Born in '70. Figure for yourself how many years I have to my name—of poor but honest parents, my mother Sofia Trombetta Solimene was a washerwoman, my father, Antonio Procopio Solimene was a blacksmith. Rosalia Solimene, myself in person, entered into the holy state of matrimony with Vincenzo Bagliore, who could fix anything from an umbrella to a fireplace, on the first day of April, 1887.

Alfredo. All Fool's Day.

Rosalia (*stopped cold, turns a little shrill*).

Alfredo (*very lah-di-dah*). Oh, no. (*With a gesture that says, "Pray continue, my dear madam."*) Go on!

Rosalia. Three children were born of the union, three children came into this world, and all at the same time. When the midwife took the news to my husband, who was at work in the very next street to ours, she found him with his head in a bucket . . .

Alfredo. Full of water from the crystal spring . . .

Rosalia (*repeating her last phrase with severity*). With his head in a bucket, due to a stroke—which brought

him down in sorrow to the grave. Bereft of my husband, bereft of my parents every one . . .

Alfredo. All three of them . . .

Rosalia (as before). My parents every one, and with
three children to raise, I came with the good Lord's
help to San Liborio Street—number eighty, and there
I made my living by selling flyswatters, alms boxes and
hats for the carnival at Piedigrotta, especially flyswatters, which I manufactured myself, thus earning
the necessary cash for the upkeep of the family. Donna
Filumena lived at number seventy-nine. She was a
little girl then, she played with my three boys, but
when they were twenty-one they went away. They
couldn't find work here. One went to Australia, two
went to America. Haven't had word of them since.
So here was I—with my flyswatters and my paper hats,
and I don't wish to talk of it, or the blood rushes to
my head, and if by good fortune Donna Filumena
hadn't taken me on when Don Domenico came into
the picture, I'd have ended up on the steps of a church,
begging. *(Pause.)*

Alfredo (sighing ironically). I suppose I'll go down in
sorrow to the grave not knowing *who* you gave those
letters to.

Rosalia (stiffly). The secret mission that has been entrusted to *me* cannot be made public at this time.

*Alfredo (disappointed, and with the intensity of words
carefully prepared).* You are not a nice woman, Rosalia Solimene, you aren't nice! You have a warped
mind. And an ugly, evil face.

Rosalia. (undismayed). I'm not looking for a husband.

Alfredo (as if nothing unpleasant had been said). Now,
how about sewing this button on for me? *(He shows
her the place on his coat.)*

*Rosalia (making for the bedroom, turning ever so
slightly).* Tomorrow. If I have time.

Alfredo. And you might put some new elastic in my
shorts . . .

Rosalia. Buy the elastic, and I'll put it in. Good-bye!
                          Exit left, with dignity.

Lucia *enters upstage left. On a small plate she carries
the half cup of coffee. But she is stopped in her
tracks by the doorbell. She turns her back on Alfredo
and goes out right to answer the door. After a pause*

Domenico *comes in, pale and sleepy,* Lucia *behind him. He sees the coffee.*

Domenico.   Is that coffee?

Lucia (*looking meaningfully at* Alfredo, *who has got up at the first sound of* Domenico's *voice*). Yes, signore.

Domenico.   Give it to me. (*She does so.* Domenico *drinks it right off.*) Just what I needed.

Alfredo.   Just what *I* needed.

Domenico (*to* Lucia).   Bring him a cup of coffee.

He sits at the center table, covering his face in his hands, lost in his own thoughts. Lucia *is making signs to* Alfredo *to tell him that the other half cup of coffee has already been diluted.*)

Alfredo (*shouting out in impatience and anger*). Bring it all the same!

Domenico.   What?

Alfredo (*with a forced smile.*) She said the coffee's cold, and I said, bring it all the same.

Domenico.   You went to the lawyer's?

Alfredo.   Yes.

Domenico.   When's he coming?

Alfredo.   Whenever he can fit it in. Today for sure.

Lucia *comes in upstage left, carrying the full cup of diluted coffee. She gives it to* Alfredo *and enjoys herself doing so. She leaves. Suspicious,* Alfredo *goes through the motions of drinking.*

Domenico (*continuing a thought aloud, with some fearfulness*). It's no good!

Alfredo (*thinking he means this diluted coffee, but resigned*). No good at all, Don Mimi, I'll have to get some at a café when we go out . . .

Domenico (*disoriented*). Some what?

Alfredo (*with conviction*).   Some coffee.

Domenico.   What's coffee got to do with it? I was just saying that if the lawyer says I don't have a case, it's no good. I'm powerless.

Alfredo (*is not listening. He is trying a sip of the coffee. He grimaces with disgust*). No good? It's impossible!

Domenico.   What do *you* know about it?

Alfredo (*a wise guy now*). What do *I* know? I know it turns my stomach!

Domenico. It makes *my* stomach turn! What a mess she's always made of things! She'll never make it!

Alfredo. She doesn't know *how* to make it!

Domenico. So I'll take it to court, I'll take it to one court after another, I'll take it to the Supreme Court!

Alfredo (*astonished, wondering if* Don Domenico *is crazy*). Heavens, Don Mimi, as God's above, all for one little cup of coffee?

Domenico. Cup of coffee? You idiot, I'm talking about Filumena . . .

Alfredo (*groping*). Hm . . . (*Then it dawns.*) Ah!!! (*Then he is amused.*) Ha! Ha! (*But fearing* Don Domenico's *anger, he suppresses his laughter and becomes a model of gravity.*) Oh, yes, of course!

Domenico (*realizing what has been going on in* Alfredo's *mind, accepts his incomprehension affectionately*). What's the use of talking about this with you? I could talk to you about the past, but this present business . . . ? (*Domenico* looks at Alfredo *as if seeing him for the first time. He analyzes his present unhappy state.*) Look at him, what has he come to? White hair, drooping eyes, baggy cheeks! Alfredo Amoroso in his second childhood!

Alfredo (*would never contradict his master, so he pleads guilty to all and resigns himself as to fate*). Dear God!

Domenico (*realizing that he himself has undergone changes*). Do you remember a certain Don Domenico Soriano, Don Mimi—do you remember him?

Alfredo (*his mind has been wandering and maybe he wouldn't have understood anyway*). Who's that? Who's dead? Don Domenico? . . .

Domenico (*swallowing the pill*). That's it, precisely: He's dead, Don Mimi Soriano is dead!

Alfredo (*getting it now*). Oh, you mean . . . *you*, Don Mimi . . . you . . . good God!

Domenico (*seeing himself young in his mind's eye*). With black moustaches, thin as a rail, made night into day, never slept . . .

Alfredo (*gaping*). You think I don't know?

Domenico. Remember that girl up on Capodimonte, that girl Gelsomina? She was terrific! "Let's elope, Mimi, *do* let's elope!" I can hear her voice still. Do you remember the vet's wife?

Alfredo. Could I ever forget her? What a woman! Her sister-in-law was quite something too: what was her job? Wool carding. Ran after her a bit myself. Pity we

weren't . . . er . . . what do you call it? Compatible?
(*Enjoying the word.*) We weren't compatible!

Domenico.   You remember the old horse trail down to
the villa? And me driving the best pair in Naples?

Alfredo.   You looked like a statue!

Domenico.   Horses! Horses, buff and gray, *my* colors,
my riding cap on my head, my whip in my hand, the
finest horses in . . . remember Silver Eye?

Alfredo.   Unforgettable beast! (*Nostalgically.*) Silver
Eye the gray mare! She had a rump like a full moon!
When you looked at that rump, you kept right on looking. It was the rising of the moon, the rising of the full
moon. I fell in love with that horse. That's why I had
to break off with the little wool carder. And when you
sold her, oh! the soul of Alfredo Amoroso was grievous
sick!

Domenico.   Paris! London! I was God Almighty! I was
master of my fate, not God Himself could change my
place in the world, I was monarch of all I surveyed,
king of the mountains, king of the seas, king of my
own life. And now? Now, I'm through. No will, no
enthusiasm, no passions, and if I do try anything, it's
only to prove to myself that it isn't so, that I'm still
strong, that I can still get the better of other men, that
I can get the better of death itself. And I do so well I
believe it! I convince myself, I surprise myself, and
I go on fighting! You always have to go on fighting!
Domenico Soriano never gives up and never gives in!
(*Coming down to earth decisively.*) Now what's been
going on here? Have you found anything out?

Alfredo (*tentatively*).   Nothing for certain. They keep
me in the dark. As I told you, Donna Filumena can't
stand the sight of me. I don't know what I'm supposed
to have done to her. As for Rosalia, Lucia tells me—
and Rosalia confirms it—she's been delivering three
urgent letters from Donna Filumena.

Domenico (*to whom this precise number of letters seems
not without significance*).   To whom?

Filumena *enters in her house dress, ungirt, followed by
Rosalia, who is carrying sheets and clean pillowcases.
She notices the two men but pretends not to. She
has heard their last words but ignores them. Concen-
trating on her work, she calls in the direction of the
main door.*

Filumena. Lucia! (*To* Rosalia.) Give me the key.

Rosalia (*offers her a bunch of keys*). Here you are.

Filumena (*pockets the keys*). Where is that girl? (*Shouts a bit louder.*) Lucia!

Lucia (*entering upstage left, hurriedly*). Yes, signora?

Filumena (*cutting her short*). Take these sheets. (Rosalia *consigns the sheets and pillowcases to* Lucia). In the little room next to the study, there's an ottoman, make it up as a bed . . .

Lucia. Yes, signora.

She starts to go. Filumena *stops her.*

Filumena. Wait! I need your room, too. These are the clean sheets. You'll fix up a hammock in the kitchen.

Lucia (*dismayed*). All right . . . but what about my things? Must I take them all out?

Filumena. I've told you: I need the room!

Lucia. But where'm I to put my things?

Filumena. You can use the closet in the hall.

Lucia. All right.

                         She leaves upstage right.

Filumena (*pretending to be seeing* Domenico *for the first time*). You're here?

Domenico (*coldly*). May I ask what all these changes mean in my house?

Filumena. Certainly. There are no secrets between man and wife. I need two more bedrooms.

Domenico. You need . . . for whom?

Filumena (*with precision*). For my sons. There should have been three of them, I know. But one's married, and they have four kids, so he's staying put.

Domenico. They have four kids, do they? And what's this tribe called, if I may ask?

Filumena (*still sure of her ground*). For the time being they have my name. Later on they'll have yours.

Domenico. *Not* without my consent.

Filumena. But you'll give your consent. (*Almost vengefully.*) You'll give your consent, Domenico.

                         She exits down right.

Domenico (*unable to control himself any longer*). I'll throw them out, understand? I'll *kick* them out!

Filumena (*offstage*). Close the door, will you, Rosalia?

Rosalia *shuts the door in* Domenico's *face.*

Lucia (*enters upstage right, turning to* Domenico,

quietly). Signore, Signorina Diana is outside . . .
with a man.

Domenico (*interested*).   Show them in.

Lucia (*who has obviously tried to show them in already*).
She doesn't want to come in, signore. I said she should,
but she said you should come outside to her . . .
(*With conviction.*) She's afraid of Donna Filumena.

Domenico (*put out*).   Now look, *I* wear the pants in this
house! Tell them to come in, tell them I am here!

                    Lucia *leaves upstage right.*

Alfredo.   As soon as she sees her, she'll beat her to a
pulp!

Domenico (*shouting so as to be heard on the other side
of the closed door of the bedroom*). She will not.
Alfredo, the time has come for me to make clear who
is the master in this house! She is nothing: you can
all put that in your pipe and smoke it.

Lucia (*returning apologetically*).   Signore, she won't
come in. She says she can't answer for her nerves if
she does.

Domenico.   Who is it that's with her?

Lucia.   Just a man. I think she called him attorney somebody. (*Giving her private opinion.*) If you ask me, he's
scared, too!

Domenico.   Ridiculous! There'll be three grown men
here! . . .

Alfredo (*earnestly*).   Don't count me! In the state you've
reduced me to I'm not worth a nickel. (*Firmly.*) No,
you can all have the discussion in here. I'll go
wash my face in the kitchen. (*At the door.*) When you
want me, don't hesitate to call!

                              He exits up left.

Lucia.   Well, signore, what's it to be?

Domenico (*swallowing*).   I'll go out.

Lucia *exits up left,* Domenico *up right.* Domenico *returns, bringing* Diana *and attorney* Nocella *with him,
insisting.*

Domenico.   But good heavens, I tell you, this is my
house and mine alone!

Diana (*who has remained on the threshold with Attorney
Nocella behind her, very excited*). Please, Domenico!
After the scene of last night, I refuse to face that
woman again!

Domenico.   But, Diana, please, you're humiliating me.
Come in, there's nothing to be afraid of!

Diana.   Afraid! *Me?* Why, I don't know what fear *is!* I simply can't be a party to *disgusting* behavior!

Domenico.   Well, you won't be: *I* am here!

Diana.   You were here last night.

Domenico.   Well, er, that was all . . . unexpected. Today, I assure you, you have nothing to fear. Come in. Attorney Nocella, do sit down.

Diana (*taking several paces forward*).   Where is she?

Domenico.   I tell you again, don't worry. Just sit down, relax!

They sit at the center table, Diana *to the left, the lawyer in the middle,* Domenico *on the right, facing* Diana, *who doesn't want to let the bedroom door get out of sight. She isn't at ease.*

Domenico.   Now!

Nocella *is a man of forty, average, rather a nonentity. Dresses with a certain sober elegance. He's discussing the Soriano case because* Diana *has dragged him in here. His tone of voice indicates a certain lack of interest.*

Nocella.   I live in the same *pensione* as the signorina, that's where we got acquainted some time ago . . .

Diana.   Attorney Nocella can tell who I am, what sort of life I lead.

Nocella (*who doesn't want to get involved*).   We see each other at table in the evening. Of course, I'm not in the *pensione* very much. I go to court, I see my clients, and then again I'm not much of a mixer . . .

Diana.   Domenico, would you mind *awfully* if we changed seats, *would* you? (*She wants a better view of the door, so they change.*) Now, last night, at table, I told this whole story of you and Filumena.

Nocella.   That's right. We nearly laughed our heads off!

Domenico *looks daggers at him.*

Diana.   Not at all. *I,* for one, *never* laughed!

Nocella *is amazed but holds his tongue.*

Domenico (*indicating* Diana).   She was here because I had her pretend to be a nurse.

Diana (*up in arms*).   Pretend, *pretend!* But, great heavens, I *am* a nurse! With diplomas and *everything!* Didn't I ever tell you, Domenico?

Domenico.   No! Well, I mean . . .

Diana (*interrupts him by clearing her throat loudly*). Well, of course, I didn't *have* to tell you, did I? The thing is, I've explained your position to Attorney Nocella, I've told him how you can't *bear* the idea of having to stay *tied* to a woman you never chose to be tied to, and Attorney Nocella has explained to me *at length* . . .

A bell rings offstage.

Domenico (*who hears it*).   Excuse me, but I'll have to ask you to go into my room. There's the bell.

Lucia crosses from left to right upstage.

Diana (*getting up*).   Yes, I suppose we should.

The Attorney *gets up, too.*

Domenico (*shows them into the study and follows*). Please sit down.

Nocella.   Thank you. (*Goes out first.*)

Diana (*following* Nocella, *whispers to* Domenico). You're pale as a sheet!

> Diana *and* Domenico *leave.*

Lucia (*brings* Umberto *in*).   Sit down, please.

Umberto *is a tall, well-built young man, dressed with modest dignity, serious looking. He loves study. His way of speaking, his sharp, observant eye, inspire respect.*

Umberto.   Thank you. (*He opens a notebook and makes some corrections in pencil.*)

Lucia.   Won't you sit down. Donna Filumena may be a few minutes yet.

Umberto.   I'd like to. Thanks.

He sits on the left, by the terrace. The bell rings again. Lucia goes to answer it. Pause. Then she reenters with Riccardo.

Lucia. Come in here, please.

Riccardo is likable, lithe, lively, with very mobile black eyes. Dressed with rather showy elegance. Looks at his wristwatch as he enters. Lucia *starts to go down left.*

Riccardo. Hey! One moment. (Lucia *turns back.*) How long have *you* been here?

Lucia. Eighteen months.

Riccardo (*quite a lad*). You're a damn goodlooking girl, you know.

Lucia (*flattered*). But I'll spoil with time!

Riccardo. Why not stop by at my store some day . . .

Lucia. You have a store?

Riccardo. Number seventy-four, Via Chiaia, next to the porter's lodge. I'm a shirtmaker.

Lucia. Really? And what would I do with a man's shirt? Get along with you!

Riccardo. I take care of men *and* women. I put the men's shirts on, and I take the women's shirts off! (*With this last pronouncement he embraces her fervently.*)

Lucia (*disentangling herself, offended*). Hey, stop it! (*She frees herself.*) Are you crazy? What do you take me for? I'll tell the signora! (*Thinking of* Umberto *who, however, isn't interested.*) And with him in the room!

The bell rings. Lucia *starts to go.*

Riccardo (*noticing* Umberto *for the first time, amused*). Why, look! And I never even saw him!

Lucia (*right back at him*). You don't see much. Except bad women . . .

Riccardo (*with an insinuation*). You'll come to the store?

Lucia (*holding her ground*). Number seventy-four? (*Looking at him admiringly.*) Via Chiaia? (*At a sign from* Riccardo *meaning "yes."*) I'll be there. (*Exit* Lucia *upstage right. In the doorway she throws him a meaningful smile.*)

Riccardo (*walks up and down a little. A couple of times his eyes meet* Umberto's. *He is slightly uncomfortable.*) Nice girl. (*Pause.*) Don't you think so?

Umberto.   It's all one to me.
Riccardo.   How's that? Studying to be a priest?

Umberto *pays no attention to him. Goes on writing.*

Lucia (*bringing in* Michele).   Step this way, please.

Michele *is dressed in his blue plumber's overalls. He carries a bag of tools. In good health, flourishing, rather fat. He takes off his beret as he comes in.*

Michele.   What goes on here, Lucia? Is it that bathroom faucet again? I thought I soldered it good.
Lucia.   No, it's working.
Michele.   Then what is it this time?
Lucia.   Nothing, nothing at all. The faucets are fine. Just wait while I call Donna Filumena.

Exit Lucia *down left.*

Michele (*speaks deferentially to* Riccardo).   Good morning, sir.

Riccardo *nods curtly.*

There's nobody to mind the shop!

Riccardo *gives him another look.* Michele *consents to be more explanatory.*

I mean, I hope she'll come soon. (*He takes a cigarette butt out of his pocket.*) Anyone got a light?
Riccardo (*haughtily*).   Sorry, no.
Michele.   Smoking strictly prohibited. (*Awkward pause.*) You're a relative?
Riccardo.   Is this a court of inquiry?
Michele.   How d'you mean?
Riccardo.   My friend, I can see you're crazy about discussions. I'm not.
Michele.   You should remember your manners, *you* should!
Umberto (*intervening*).   He forgot them years ago.
Riccardo.   Now look here . . .
Umberto.   Excuse me, you come in here as if you owned the place, you throw your arms around the housemaid, while doing so you see me, and aren't in the least embarrassed, and now you spit on this poor creature.
Michele (*coming right back at* Umberto).   Poor crea-

ture, am I? If anyone spits on me, *he'll* get an eyeful! (*Turning to* Riccardo.) You can thank your stars we're indoors.

Riccardo. You *annoy* me, understand? Indoors or out!

Michele (*puts his tool bag down, turning pale*). Let's see then! (Michele *comes slowly toward* Riccardo.)

Riccardo (*comes toward him with the same stealth*). Sure, let's see!

Umberto *now tries to intervene. He aims at stopping either of them taking the initiative.*

Michele (*angry at* Umberto). You little sonofa . . .(*He aims a blow at* Umberto, *but the latter, too quick for him, only receives half its force.*) You get out of the way!

Now there's a real scuffle at close quarters with many blows and kicks that miss their mark and with words, or rather half-words, spoken in rage between clenched teeth.

Filumena (*comes in from down left, her tone brisk*). What's going on here?

Rosalia *follows at her heels.*

The Three Sons *pull out of the scrimmage at the first sound of* Filumena's *voice. They are now ranged in front of her trying to look as if nothing had happened.*

Filumena. Now, where do you all think you are?

Umberto (*rubbing a sore nose*). I was trying to keep them apart.

Riccardo. So was I.

Michele. Me, too.

Filumena. So who was doing the fighting?

The Three Sons (*in unison*). Not me!

Filumena. You ought to be ashamed. (*Pause. She has momentarily lost her briskness. Is at a loss.*) Boys, I, er . . . (*trying again*) well, how *is* everything?

There is another slight pause till Michele *decides to be the first to speak up.*

Michele. I've nothing to gripe about—thanks be to God.

Filumena. How are the children?

Michele. Pretty good. Last week the middle one had a bit of fever, now he's okay. He ate four pounds of grapes. Mamma wasn't looking, I wasn't home, his tummy was like a big drum, but you know how it is with four kids. If it isn't one, it's the other, there's always something. Take the way all of mine like castor oil. When we give it to one of them, the other three shout the house down till we give it to them too. Two hours later there they all are on their little pots—in a row!

Umberto (*breaking up this low conversation*). I got your note, signora. I'm afraid your name didn't mean a thing to me. It was the address that started me thinking. I realized that this Donna Filumena was someone I see nearly every evening on my way to the newspaper office. One time I even walked her home—to this address—she had a sore foot and couldn't walk properly. It was a pleasure to help her . . . (*Drawing breath for an eloquent paragraph.*) My reconstruction of the story . . .

Filumena. I had a sore foot, that's right.

Riccardo (*to bring things to a point*). Now what's it all about?

Filumena (*to* Riccardo). How's the store doing?

Riccardo. Fine, why shouldn't it? Though if all my customers were like you, I'd have to shut up shop in a month. Excuse my frankness, signora, but when *you* come there, I feel like running for cover. You give me such a time. You make me unpack every piece of merchandise in the place. "No, not this, I'll take that, no, not that, I must think it over!" And you leave the store in such a mess it'd take a staff of fifty to put it straight.

Filumena (*maternally*). I simply mustn't trouble you in future, must I?

Riccardo (*taken aback*). I don't mean that, signora! The customer's the boss, after all. I just meant I can only sweat through one shirt at a time.

Filumena (*at ease now*). Well, now, I've called you all together for a serious reason. If you'll step in here (*pointing to her bedroom*) for a moment, we can talk it over . . .

Domenico (*comes in from the study followed by* Nocella. *He again speaks in his normal tone, that of a man who*

is sure of himself. He turns to Filumena *with good-
natured energy*). That won't be necessary, Filumena,
let's not mix things up even worse than they are already. (*To the* Attorney.) I'm no lawyer, but I said it
would be this way. I thought of it before you did, it
was as plain to me as the nose on your face! (*To*
Filumena, *who is looking doubtingly at* Nocella.) This
is Attorney Nocella. He's going to clarify this whole
situation. (*To the three sons.*) The signora made a
mistake. She has brought you here for nothing. You
may go—we're sorry for the inconvenience.

Filumena. Just a moment! I made no mistake, sending
for these boys, and what business is it of yours anyway?

Domenico (*meaningfully*). You think we can say it all
before strangers?

Filumena (*grasps the fact that somehow the whole course
of things has changed,* Domenico's *tone makes this
unmistakable. She turns to the* three boys). Will you
be patient for another five minutes, boys? Wait for me
on the terrace, will you?

Umberto *and* Michele *start off in that direction with a
little hesitation.*

Riccardo (*looking at his watch*). Listen, signora. I think
you take advantage of people. I've got things to do . . .

Filumena (*losing her temper*). Didn't I say there was a
serious reason? (*Treating him as a little boy, in a tone
that admits of no reply.*) Go out on the terrace. The
others are waiting, you'll wait too!

Riccardo (*disconcerted by her firmness*). Well, all right.
(*He will leave with the other two.*)

Filumena (*to* Rosalia). Give them some coffee, Rosalia.

Rosalia. Yes, Donna Filumena. (*To the three of them.*)
Go out on the balcony and sit down (*Showing them
where to sit.*) And I'll be right out with some lovely
coffee!

*She exits upstage left, while the boys go out on the ter-
race.*

Filumena. Well?

Domenico (*loftily*). This gentleman is a lawyer. Suppose you talk to *him.*

Filumena (*impatiently*). What good ever came of the
law?

Domenico *clears his throat audibly.*
  Well, what is it?
Nocella. It's like this, signora, as I said, this . . . er . . .
  situation is no business of mine . . .
Filumena. Then what d'you want?
Nocella. That's just it. It's no business of mine in the
  sense that this gentleman isn't my client, nor has he
  summoned me . . .
Filumena. Were you sent? Or did you just come?
Nocella. Well, now, signora, I could *never* permit my-
  self to be *sent* . . .
Domenico (*to* Filumena). For God's sake, let him
  speak!
Nocella. The signorina told me about the case. (*Looking
  back toward the study.*) Where is she?
Domenico (*rather irritated, and trying to bring the discussion back on the rails*). Attorney Nocella, I think,
  well, who told you is beside the point. State your conclusions.
Filumena (*looking toward the study*). She's in there, is
  she, she just hasn't the courage to show herself! Go on,
  Mr. Lawyer!
Nocella. In the situation described by this gentleman . . .
  no, by the young lady . . .

Domenico *coughs peremptorily.*

  . . . dealing with cases of this sort . . . well, I've found
  a CLAUSE. (*He is a drowning man, the CLAUSE is a
  straw.*) Clause Number 101! (*He takes a paper from
  his pocket.*) "Matrimony under imminent peril of
  death." (*Starting to reel it off.*) "In the case of imminent peril of death . . . "

Another cough from Domenico *stops him.*

  It explains all the different possibilities. But then this
  was *not* a case of imminent peril of death—because
  your imminent peril was peril pretended or peril
  feigned, that comes under another heading . . .
Domenico. I have witnesses: Alfredo, Lucia, the janitor,
  Rosalia . . .
Filumena. The nurse.
Domenico. The nurse. All of them. No sooner was the
  priest out of the room than she bounced out of bed

and shouted, "We're man and wife, Domenico Soriano!"

Nocella. So the clause we want is Number 122: *"Violence and error."* (*He digs another paper out of his pocket and reads.*) "The validity of a marriage may be impugned by one or other of the parties if his or her consent has been extorted by violence or granted in error." The consent of this gentleman, having been granted in error, I submit, on the basis of Clause 122, that the validity of this marriage . . .

Filumena. Attorney Nocella, I don't know what you're talking about.

Domenico (*confident that he has understood*). Don't you see? I married you because you were about to die . . .

Nocella. No! Matrimony is unconditional! Clause 164. (*He recites by heart this time.*) "Should the aforesaid parties add, spend, or otherwise affix restrictions, qualifications, modifications, or other conditions, no priest of the church, no official of the state may proceed to the celebration of matrimony."

Domenico. But you said, if there was no imminent peril of death . . .

Filumena. Be quiet, you don't understand it any more than I do. Mr. Lawyer, explain it to us.

Nocella (*offering her the papers*). Read it for yourself.

Filumena (*after a moment's hesitation, takes the paper and tears it very deliberately in two. Her voice is low*). What use is paper to me? The likes of Filumena Marturano can't read, Mr. Lawyer!

Nocella (*roused*). Signora, since you were *not* dying, your marriage is annulled, your marriage is not valid.

Filumena. What about the priest?

Nocella. The priest says it was a desecration of the Sacrament. The marriage is not valid.

Filumena (*livid*). Not valid! I had to die?

Nocella. Exactly.

Filumena. If I *had* died . . .

Nocella. The marriage would have been valid.

Filumena. And he could have married again, he could have had children?

Nocella. Naturally. This hypothetical wife would have been marrying the deceased Signora Soriano's widower.

Domenico. You *would* have been Signora Soriano . . . but dead.

Filumena.   The idea appeals to you, doesn't it? (*Changing her tone.*) All I've ever wanted is a family. I spend a lifetime at it, and now the law says "no." Is that justice, Mr. Lawyer?

Nocella.   The law, my dear signora, cannot uphold *your* principles—however human they may be—if it thereby becomes accessory to measures operating to the detriment of a third person. Domenico Soriano has no intention of marrying you.

Domenico.   And if you don't believe Attorney Nocella, consult any lawyer you do believe.

Filumena.   I believe him. Not because you say the same thing—you have your own fish to fry. Not because *he's* a lawyer, I don't know lawyers. I believe him because you can look me in the face. D'you think I don't know you by this time? Why, you're your old self again, you're cocky, you're the boss, when I look at you, you look right back. That means you're telling the truth, Domenico. When you tell a lie, you don't know *where* to look, you start looking for flies on the ceiling!

Domenico.   Attorney Nocella, proceed.

Nocella.   As you wish, Signor Soriano.

Filumena (*is still pondering the lawyer's sentence, "Domenico Soriano has no intentio nof marrying you." Through the following speech she becomes more and more wrought up*).   Domenico Soriano has no intention of marrying me. I've no intention of marrying him either. I don't want you. Go on, Mr. Lawyer, I don't want him anymore! It's not true I was dying, I admit it, I just wanted to cheat him. I'd stolen from him before, and now I wanted to steal—a name, a family name! But, as for the law, there's the sort of law that makes people cry, isn't there, Mr. Lawyer? I want you to know there's another law—that makes people *laugh*—and that's the law for me! (*In the hard tone of Act One*). You boys, come in now!

Domenico (*who'd like to smooth things over*).   Filumena, stop!

Filumena (*violently*).   You be quiet!

The Three Sons *come in from the balcony, rather disoriented, and take up their positions in the center of the stage. Rosalia comes in upstage left with the coffee. She sees that this isn't the right moment and puts her tray on a sideboard. She listens. She gets gradually nearer* Filumena *down the left side of the stage. Now the stage is set.* Filumena *continues.*

Filumena.   Now listen to what I have to say. (*Indicating* Domenico *and the* Lawyer.) That's people, that's the world. The world with its rights of men, and laws, and clauses, the world that defends itself with pen and paper: Attorney Nocella and Don Domenico Soriano. (*Striking herself on the chest.*) And I am Filumena Marturano. A woman who doesn't know the law. A woman who wants a law of her own. A woman who can't cry. You see my eyes, how dry they are? Like tinder. (*Looking straight at the* three boys.) I am your mother.

Domenico.   Filumena!

Filumena (*grimly*).   Who are you to stop me telling them? (*To* Nocella.) Can I tell 'em or not? What does the law say to that? (*More aggressively than emotionally.*) You are my children. I am Filumena Marturano —there's no need to explain *that* name, young fellows like you will have heard of me. (*They are petrified.*) I have nothing to say of Filumena Marturano. But I remember a girl of seventeen . . . (*Her mind fills with memories. Pause.*) Do you know the slums of Naples, Mr. Lawyer? San Giovaniello, Vergini, Forcella, Tribunale, Pallonetto. Do you know the smoke, the blackness? In summer you can't breathe for the heat, there are too many people. In winter the cold makes your teeth chatter. The narrow streets swarming with grimy children, the hovels they live in, dark even at noon. In one of those ratholes, San Liborio Street, lived the Marturanos, a mob of Marturanos. What became of them all later, what the end was, I don't know, I don't want to know. But I can see us as we were then, I can see the sullen faces, the crowded beds. We went to sleep without a good night, we got up without a good morning. I can only remember one thing my father ever said, and I wish I could forget that. I was thirteen, and he said, "You're a big girl now: do you know there's nothing to eat?" How hot it was! You could hardly breathe! I can see us sitting around the table every evening. The table had one large dish on it and forks all around, nothing but forks. There was no pleasure at those meals. If I dropped my fork, I felt I'd been caught stealing.

Pause.

I don't know when I found out that some people aren't poor. I used to stand on the corner of some big street downtown and look at all the people with good shoes on, good clothes, and the good girls on the arm of their good husbands-to-be. One evening—when I was seventeen—I saw a girl I knew. I hardly recognized her, she was so dressed up—though maybe any decent clothes seemed dressy to me at that time. She told me things. (*Pause.*) I didn't close my eyes all night. How hot it was! (*Abruptly.*) That's how I got to know you. There. Remember? Maybe you didn't think much of the place —to me it was a palace. One evening I went to see the family on Liborio Street. I was all of a tremble. I said to myself: "They won't look me in the face, they'll throw me out!" No one said a thing. Someone offered me a chair. Someone even stroked my cheek. I was a visitor from the great world, so they scraped the floor before me. Only my mother . . . well, when I went over to say good-bye, there were tears in her eyes. That was Filumena's last homecoming. (*Pause.*) Not a pretty story, is it? All I'll say for myself is this: I didn't murder my children. For twenty-five years I've thought of nothing else. My family! (*If there's a light in her eyes at this moment, she comes down to earth at once and addresses herself directly to the* three boys.) And here you are! I've raised you, I've made men of you, I've stolen from him (*indicating* Domenico) to bring you up . . .

Michele (*comes over to* Filumena, *full of emotion*). All right, all right, that's enough . . . (*He is almost too moved to speak.*) What more could you have done?

Umberto (*also coming over, gravely*). There are so many things I wish I could say. I'm not much good at talking, though. I'll write you a letter.

Filumena (*simply*). I don't know how to read.

Umberto (*quietly*). I'll read it to you.

Pause. Filumena *waits for her third son to come over, but* Riccardo *goes out through the door without a word.*

Filumena (*after a pause*). He's gone.

Umberto (*with sympathy*). Oh, that's just him. He didn't understand. Tomorrow I'll stop by and talk to him.

Michele. You can come with me, signora. It's a small

place, but there's a room. There's a terrace. (*Cheer-fully.*) The kids are always asking me, "Where's granny? Where's granny?" And I always have to make something up! Now I'll go home and say, "She's here!" and it'll be like the carnival of Piedigrotta. (*Urging her.*) Let's be going!

Filumena (*firmly*). Yes. I'll come.

Michele. Fine, let's go then.

Filumena. Just a moment. Wait for me at the gate (*To* Umberto.) You can go down together. I need ten minutes—to tell Domenico something.

Michele (*happily*). Good, I'll do that. (*To* Umberto.) You're coming?

Umberto. Sure I'll come with you.

Michele. Good-bye, everybody! (*To* Umberto.) I could tell there was something, that's why I wanted to talk!

They leave.

Filumena. Mr. Lawyer (*she points to the study*), give us two minutes.

Nocella. No, I think I'll be leaving.

Filumena. No, no, just two minutes, you should be here when I'm through talking to Don Domenico. Go and sit down.

Nocella reluctantly goes into the study. Without a word, Rosalia exits down left.

Filumena (*after a pause, calmly*). I'm going, Domenico. Tell the lawyer to do whatever a lawyer does. I deny nothing. I leave you free.

Domenico. I should think so. You could have just asked for money instead of making all this song and dance.

Filumena (*still very calm*). Tomorrow I'll send for my things.

Domenico. You're crazy, if you ask me. What do you want to do to those three boys? Destroy their peace of mind? Who put you up to it? *Why* did you say that?

Pause.

Filumena (*coldly*). Because one of those three boys is your son.

Domenico *turns to stone. A long pause.*

Domenico. Do you know what you're saying?

Filumena (without change in manner). One of those three boys is your son.

Domenico (not daring to shout. Intensely). Quiet!

Filumena. I could have said they were all your sons, you'd have believed it, I'd have made you believe it, but it isn't so. I know what you're thinking, you're thinking I could have told you. But I couldn't. Because you wouldn't have treated the other two right. Men are all alike, Domenico, and children are all alike. Children are created equal, too.

Domenico. You're lying!

Filumena. No, Domenico, no! Let me remind you. You can't remember because you were always going off . . . London, Paris . . . the races . . . other women . . . Let me remind you. Remember how much you paid me? You used to leave a hundred lire bill on the dressing table. Do you remember the night you said to me, "Filumena, we love each other," just before you put the light out? You didn't love me, Domenico, but I loved you. You were joking, and when you switched the light on again, you gave me the usual hundred lire bill. I put the date on it—I know numbers even if I don't know writing. Then you went on another trip. I waited. Like Our Lady of the Sorrows. You don't remember what happened, I didn't tell you, I told you my life was still the same, and it was true: when I saw you hadn't understood, I went back to—the old life.

Domenico (half to himself, slightly less convinced). It isn't true.

Filumena. Domenico, I swear it by the Madonna of the Roses!

Domenico (believing without hesitation). Ah! (*Pause.*) Which one is it, then?

Filumena (firmly). I won't tell. (*Trying to smile it off.*) Men are created equal.

Domenico (after a short pause, firmly). You're lying, the whole story is a lie! You'd have told me at the time, so you could keep me, so you could hold me in the hollow of your hand. You'd have told me at the time. *That* would have been a secret weapon, Filumena Marturano, and you want me to believe you wouldn't have used it?

Filumena. I wouldn't have used it. Because you wouldn't have let my children live. I thought that then, and I think it now. You'd have had me murder them, Domenico, so I didn't dare tell you. But for me your son would be dead.

Domenico. Which of them is he?

Filumena. Children are created equal.

Domenico (*at his wits' end, nasty*). They're equal all right—your children. ⊥ don't want to see them. Get out! I don't know them. I don't know—my son.

Filumena. Yesterday I said, "The day will come when you'll want something from me, so don't go swearing you'll never accept it." Remember? Now you know *why* I said it. Good-bye, Domenico. But let me promise you one thing: If you tell my children what I've told you, I'll kill you. And I don't just talk about killing the way you do. A promise is a promise to Filumena Marturano. (Filumena *breaks off. Calls briskly in the direction of the study.*) Mr. Lawyer! Come out of hiding, I won't hurt you. You've won your point, and I'm going. (*In the direction of the bedroom.*) Rosalia! I'm going. Tomorrow I'll send someone for my things.

The Lawyer *comes out of the study followed by* Diana. *From the left comes* Rosalia *and from upstage right comes* Alfredo.

Filumena. Good luck to you all! Patience, Rosalia! Good-bye to you, Mr. Lawyer! And no ill feelings! (*To* Domenico, *good-humoredly.*) You've understood, haven't you, Domenico? I'll say it again in front of everyone: what I've told you is a secret. Tell nobody nothing. (*She takes a locket from her breast, opens it, and takes out a hundred lire bill, folded very small. She tears a piece off and puts it back in the locket.*) Here's a hundred lire bill. I'm tearing off one corner, there's something written on it that I may need one day. (*Throwing the bill in* Domenico's *face.*) The hundred lire are for you, I hope you'll find it useful—even if you can't buy a son with it, Domenico Soriano!

ACT III

Ten months later. Flowers everywhere. Many of them in beautifully arranged baskets with the donors' names sticking out on cards. The flowers are of delicate shades: not red, but not white either. The whole house breathes an atmosphere of festivity. The curtains between the dining room and the study are closed. It is almost evening.

Rosalia *enters in her best black silks from upstage right. At the same time* Domenico *comes in from the study: he is wearing a smart blue suit. This man has undergone a complete change. There is no sign now —in gesture or tone of voice—of his old domineering nature. He has become mild and humble. His hair is a shade whiter, too.* Rosalia *is moving across down left when he stops her.*

Domenico.   You've been out already, Rosalia?

Rosalia.   I've been doing an errand for Donna Filumena.

Domenico.   What errand's that?

Rosalia (with good-natured insinuation).   Are you jealous, Don Domenico? I've been to San Liborio Street.

Domenico.   San Liborio Street? What for?

Rosalia (playfully).   Ah! So he *is* jealous!

Domenico (with quiet irony).   Terribly jealous, I've noticed it myself.

Rosalia (not wishing to needle him).   Nonsense, it's just old Rosalia's little joke. (*Looking apprehensively toward* Filumena's *room.*) I'll tell you, but you mustn't tell Donna Filumena I've told you, she doesn't want you to know . . .

Domenico.   Then don't tell me!

Rosalia.   Silly man! I'm doing a good deed, telling you, it's something that does Donna Filumena credit. (*Then in a dramatic whisper.*) She had me carry a thousand lire and fifty candles to the Madonna of the Roses in San Liborio Street. (*Becoming more explanatory.*) You know the old crone who lives on the corner and looks after the lamp and the flowers and everything? I had to go to her and say, "Donna Filumena wants you to light these candles at six this evening—on the nose!"

496

Domenico. Six o'clock on the nose?

Rosalia. Don't you know the time of your own wedding, Don Domenico? At six o'clock on the nose, you and Donna Filumena will be man and wife. Good and proper this time. And while you're getting married in here, the candles will be lit in San Liborio Street at the feet of the Madonna of the Roses.

Domenico. I see.

Rosalia. You're marrying an angel from heaven, Don Domè. A young girl of an angel, too. She gets younger and lovelier every day. I knew everything was all right. "You think Don Domenico'll forget you?" I said to her. "Him getting the marriage annulled, that was just one of his tantrums, the marriage bells haven't stopped ringing for *you*, Donna Filu . . ."

Domenico. That will do, Rosalia. Now suppose you go to your mistress.

Rosalia. I'm going, I'm going. (*But* Rosalia *can't be hustled.*) You're marrying an angel from heaven. If it wasn't for her, I'd have come to a bad end. She took me in, and here I stayed, and here I am, and here I shall die. I have everything ready for the day, a lovely long white shirt with a fine piece of lace to it, white stockings, nice underclothes, a bonnet on my head, I have it all ready in the oak chest, and Donna Filumena knows about it, too, she's going to lay me out herself, she's all I have, of course my boys may come back, where there's life there's hope . . . (*Checking herself with a big sniff.*) You don't mind if I leave now, do you, Don Domè?

Exits down left.

(*Alone,* Domenico *walks around the room a little, looking at the flowers, reading the cards. Then he involuntarily completes his thoughts aloud.*)

Domenico. Well, this is it!

(*From upstage right are heard the voices of the* Three Sons.)

Michele. Six o'clock, the ceremony is at six o'clock.

Riccardo. But you were supposed to be there before . . .

Umberto. *I* was on time anyway!

(*They enter.*)

Michele. I guess we said five, but I was only three quaters of an hour late.

Riccardo. And you didn't let us know.

Michele. Now look. When you say meet me at five, that means sort of *around* five, and what's around five? Five-twenty, five-thirty, quarter of six . . .

Riccardo. A quarter past eight the morning after, the following month, two years later : . .

Michele. Oh, come on. It's like this. We got a clock as a wedding present. But how long d'you suppose it lasted when the first kid started walking?

Umberto (*seeing* Don Domenico). Hello—Don Domenico.

Riccardo (*greeting him in the same deferential way*). Don Domenico.

Michele. Don Domenico.

They are again ranged across the center of the stage, silent.

Domenico. Hello to you! (*Long pause.*) Well? Why've you stopped talking? You were discussing . . .

Umberto (*confused*). Yes, that's right . . .

Riccardo (*starting off confidently but collapsing*). Why, sure, we were just saying . . . just saying . . .

Michele (*cheerfully*). Well, you have to stop talking sometime!

Domenico. As soon as you see me, in fact. (*To* Michele.) You were late for your appointment?

Michele. Yes, sir, Don Domenico.

Domenico (*to* Riccardo). But you were on time?

Riccardo. Yes, sir, Don Domenico.

Domenico (*to* Umberto). How about you?

Umberto. Right on time, Don Domenico.

(*Pause*).

Domenico. Well, sit down anyway.

They sit facing him.

The ceremony is at six. (*Pause.*) So there's time. (*Pause.*) At six the priest will be here. (*Pause.*) No guests, just ourselves, that's how Filumena wanted it. (*Pause*). I just want to tell you . . . (*Pause.*) I think I even did tell you once before . . . (*Pause.*) This "Don Domenico" stuff isn't . . . right.

Umberto (*tentatively*). No—it isn't.

Michele. It isn't right at all.

Umberto. But . . . er . . . you haven't said . . . . what you want us to call you.

Domenico. Well, you see, I couldn't help hoping— you'd come to your own conclusions. This evening I'm marrying your mother. And as for . . . the part of it that concerns you, I've been to my lawyer about it, and by tomorrow you'll all be called Soriano.

The three of them look at each other to decide who should speak first.

Umberto (*plucking up courage*). Well, you see . . . I know I can answer for the three of us, we all feel the same way. (*Bracing himself for a statement.*) We're not children, we're men, so it isn't easy for us to . . . er . . . call you . . . what you wish to be called, generous and fair as that wish is. . . . There are certain things you have to feel, here. (*He presses his hand to his heart.*)

Domenico (*scrutinizing* Umberto *intently.*). As for you, then, you don't feel this . . . er . . . desire, this need to call someone—me, for instance—father?

Umberto. I wouldn't want to lie to you, you deserve better than that of me, so—for now at least—I'll have to say—No!

Domenico (*is disappointed, and his interest shifts to* Riccardo). What about you?

Riccardo. The same with me.

Domenico (*turning his inquiring eyes on* Michele). And you?

Michele (*coming straight out with it*). Not me, Don Domenico.

Domenico. I see. (*He is discouraged.*) Such things come with time. You get used to them gradually. (*Cheering up a bit.*) Well, boys, it's good to be with you, you're fine fellows, you all know how to look after yourselves. (*He is thinking hard now.*) One in one field, another in another, fine fellows! (*Turning abruptly on* Umberto.) You work on a paper, don't you? From what they tell me, you're keen on your work, too, you take pride in it, you're a writer, you do articles . . .

Umberto. Short stories, too, once in a while.

Domenico. Stories, too. Your ambition is to be a great writer?

Umberto. Oh, I wouldn't say great.

Domenico. Why not? It's early days yet. (*Very interested now.*) Of course, to succeed in a field like yours, you have to have it in you from the start, don't you? Genius has to run in the family, so to speak.

Umberto. I don't know if I do have it in me. You don't know how discouraged I get. I say to myself, "Umbè, don't fool yourself, this isn't what you're cut out for at all."

Domenico (*wonders now what he is cut out for*). Then what *is*? What do you really *like* to do?

Umberto. Lord knows! You have dreams of all sorts—when you're young.

Riccardo (*rather grandly*). It's all coincidence. For instance: how is it I have a store in Via Chiaia? Because I made love to a girl. Because the girl was a shirtmaker. Because . . .

Domenico (*jumping at this chance*). You've made love to a lot of girls?

Riccardo. So so. I've not done bad.

(*Domenico's interest is aroused. He gets up to have a better look at* Riccardo. *He is on the lookout for any gestures or inflection that he can attach to his own youth.*)

Riccardo. Fact is, I have trouble finding the right type. I see a girl, I like her, I say, "That's for me, I'll marry her." But then I see another, and I seem to like her even more. I just can't explain it, there's always this other girl—the one I like better than the one I've got . . .

Domenico (*switching back to* Umberto). Whereas *you* keep calm. You don't lose your head about the girls. You think it over.

Umberto. Well, yes—and no. There isn't much to think over in the girls of today. There are good-looking girls everywhere. It's choosing that's hard. What can you do? You *have* to run through quite a few—just to find the one you really want!

Domenico *concludes that there's the same tendency in* Riccardo *as in* Umberto, *so he turns to* Michele.

Domenico (*to* Michele). What about you? Do you go
for women?

Michele. I asked for trouble and I got it. I met my wife,
and . . . good-bye, Michele! So now I live with both
feet in one slipper. With my wife there's no fooling
around, if you follow me: it isn't that I don't like the
other girls, I don't like trouble, that's what . . .

Domenico (*discouraged*). So you like women, too.
(*Pause. Now he's off on another tack.*) When I was a
young fellow, I used to sing. We all used to get together, seven or eight of us. We used to go and ser-
enade the ladies. Or we'd have supper on the terrace
in summer, and the supper would turn into a concert,
we'd sing Neapolitan songs to the mandolin or the gui-
tar. . . . Which of you can sing?

Umberto. I can't.

Riccardo. Nor me neither.

Domenico (*happy at having eliminated two from the contest. To* Michele). And you?

Michele. I can! I couldn't work without it. I sing all
the time!

Domenico (*getting excited*). Come on, then, let's hear
you!

Michele (*already sorry he spoke up*). What shall I sing?

Domenico. Anything you like, go ahead, sing!

Michele (*swallowing hard*). I'm . . . er . . . ashamed!

Domenico. But you said you sang all the time!

Michele. I do. In the shop. Okay, you know "Monastery
of Santa Chiara," it's good. (*He sings. His voice is
negligible in volume and hideous in quality.*) "Munastero 'e Santa Chiara, tengo 'o core scuro scuro . . ."

Riccardo (*at a certain point interrupts him*). If that's
singing, *I* can sing, too!

Michele (*insulted*). What d'you mean, *if* that's singing?

Umberto. So can I! If that's singing, *I* can sing!

Domenico (*to* Riccardo). Let's hear you first.

Riccardo. Naw, naw, impossible, I don't have the gall
he has, of course I know the tune . . . (*He stops awk-
wardly.* Domenico *is silent, waiting for him to sing.
So he strikes up.*) "Munastero 'e Santa Chiara . . ."

When he comes to the second line, Umberto *joins in.*
Michele *follows suit on the third. When they come to
the top note of the song, loudly but not in unison and
not together in rhythm,* Domenico *interrupts.*

Domenico (roaring the first words after which they stop). All right! *(Quietly.)* That will do, thank you. *(Sighing.)* Three Neapolitans, and not one of them can sing: what are we coming to?

Filumena *comes in wearing lovely new clothes in comely colors. Skirt and blouse: the blouse of golden-yellow taffeta with flowers sewn into it, all this in two lighter tones, the skirt to be taffeta, too, but black. Her hair is piled high on her head in Neapolitan style. A few jewels, two ropes of pearls, a gold necklace, earrings. She looks almost youthful.)*

Filumena. You're just refusing to see it, Rosalia, it *is* wrong . . .

Teresina *comes in followed by* Rosalia *and* Lucia. *She is a dressmaker of the Neapolitan type. She is impassive, her customers' insults are just water on a duck's back, and her tranquillity irritates.*

Teresina. It's all your imagination, Donna Filumena, and after all the years I've worked for you . . .
Filumena. You have the gall to say it's right when you know very well it's all wrong?
Teresina. I should say it's all wrong just to please you, I suppose!
Michele (approaching). Hello—Mother!
Umberto. Hello—and congratulations.
Riccardo. Congratulations!
Filumena. You're all here already? Hello! *(To* Teresina.*)* Now you know what's wrong with this skirt as well as I do: it's too tight! And why is it too tight? Because you didn't use enough silk. And why didn't you use enough silk? Because whenever you pick up a nice piece of silk, you cut a slice off for your little girl.
Teresina (bridling). I do, do I?
Filumena. I was in your house myself, and I saw your little girl all dressed up in the silk you'd cut out of my skirt!
Teresina. I'll really have to get mad at you, Donna Filumena! Course, if there's some left over, I'm not saying . . . But you're right, the customer comes first, that's always been my motto!

Rosalia. Donna Filumena, you're the loveliest bride I ever saw!

Filumena (*shrilly*). I won't have you stealing from *me*, understand!

Teresina (*imperturbable*). Now you're going *too* far, Donna Filumena! I swear by all that's holy . . .

Domenico. Filumena, can I speak to you for a moment?

Filumena (*limping a little in her new shoes*). Madonna, what shoes!

Domenico. Do they hurt? Maybe you should wear another pair.

Filumena. What is it you wanted to tell me?

Domenico (*to* Teresina). That'll be all for now, Teresina.

Teresina. Yes, sir, I was just going. (*She folds the piece of cloth that she carries dresses in and puts it under her arm.*) And best wishes from your humble servant! (*Leaving upstage right, to* Lucia.) What was wrong with the dress, I'd like to know, why . . .

Her voice trails on until she is out of hearing. Lucia *has gone with her.*

Domenico (*to the* three boys). You boys go into the . . . er . . . drawing room and entertain the guests— let the revels commence! And you go with them, Rosalia.

Rosalia. Yes, sir. (*To the* boys.) Come along!
                              Exit Rosalia *into the study.*

Michele (*to the other two*). Come on!

Riccardo. You've missed your vocation, you should have been a tenor at the San Carlo opera!
                They go into the study, laughing and talking.

Domenico (*after looking* Filumena *over*). You're a beautiful woman, Filumena, and you're a *young* woman, too, a slip of a girl. If I weren't such a confused old slob . . I know a man who could fall for you, hook, line, and sinker.

Filumena (*already has guessed what is on* Domenico's *mind and doesn't want to discuss it*). Well, everything seems to be in order now. I never thought it would be.

Domenico (*not to be deflected*). I'm not easy in my mind, Filumena . . .

Filumena. How could either of us be easy in our minds with only Lucia to depend on? Alfredo and Rosalia are old . . .

Domenico. Don't change the subject, Filumena, you know perfectly well what I'm getting at. . . . You can put my mind at rest, you can bring me peace, Filumena.

Filumena. Can I?

Domenico. I've done everything you asked. After the marriage was annulled, I came around to the house—not once, many times, because you always said you weren't home—I came and I said, "Filumena Marturano, will you marry me?"

Filumena. And I said, "Domenico Soriano, I will."

Domenico. And now it's your wedding day, and you're happy—I hope.

Filumena. I am happy.

Domenico. Then make *me* happy. Sit down, Filumena, I have something to say. (*She sits.*) I wish you knew how many times I've wanted to speak to you in these last months. I couldn't, that's all, I was too shy or embarrassed or something, I just couldn't. And for that matter I couldn't bear to embarrass *you* and force you to talk about things that . . . aren't easy to talk about. But now we're to be man and wife. A boy and a girl think they love each other when all they feel is an emotion that can be exhausted by a single physical act, so they get married. But the two people who're coming before God this afternoon aren't children. They've *had* their lives. I am fifty-two, you are forty-eight, we should know what we're doing. (*Pause.*) Now you do know why you're marrying me. But I don't know why I'm marrying you. I only know you said one of those boys is my son.

Filumena. Is that your only reason for marrying?

Domenico (*gently*). No, it isn't. I'm terribly fond of you, Filumena. We've been together twenty-five years. Twenty-five years is a lifetime, a lifetime of memories, yearnings . . . I found out for myself, I couldn't just cut loose from it. Let me tell you my trouble, Filumena. (*Short pause.*) I don't sleep nights. Ten months have passed since . . . that evening. And I've had no peace. I don't sleep, I don't eat, I don't live. You know, Filumena, I don't even breathe. I go like this . . . (*he opens his mouth to take a deep breath of air*) and the air doesn't go down into my lungs, it stops here (*pointing to his throat*). You can't let this happen, Filumena, you're a woman, you have a heart, you can't let this happen. I remember your saying the day would

come when I'd want something from you and I
mustn't swear I'd refuse it, and I didn't swear, Filumena, and the day *has* come, and I do want something
from you, as you hoped I would. I am on my knees
before you, Filumena, I kiss your hands, I kiss your
clothes, and I implore you: which is my son, my flesh,
my blood?

A very long pause.

Filumena (*still looking intently at her man*). I'll tell you:
it's that one. And now what happens? You'll pick
"that one" out, he'll be closer to you than the others,
you'll make sure he has a better future, and you'll figure
out how to make him richer . . .

Domenico. What if I do?

Filumena (*with gentle cunning*). *Take* that one, then,
he certainly needs you, with his four kids . . .

Domenico (*very involved in this*). It's the . . . me-
chanic?

Filumena (*nodding*). The . . . hydraulic engineer, yes.

Domenico (*half to himself, getting progressively more
excited*). A good lad, well set up . . . But why did he
get married so young? With a little shop to take care
of. . . . I must take matters in hand. With a little
capital he could open a real repair shop, take on a
few workers, learn to boss the place, he needs some
modern equipment . . . (*A suspicion strikes him.
Looking at Filumena.*) Now look, the plumber is
the poorest of the lot, he's the one with the family, he
needs help . . .

Filumena (*pretending to be crestfallen*). What can a
mother do? She must help the weakest! But you didn't
believe me, you're too smart. What would you say to
Riccardo?

Domenico. The shirtmaker?

Filumena (*teasing him all the time*). No, no! It's Umberto, the writer!

Domenico (*very put out and violent*). You're at it again!
Putting me against the wall! Crucifying me!

Filumena (*touched by the tone of real trouble and exhaustion* in Domenico's *voice, she tries to put her innermost feelings into words, to find the formula, the
synthesis, which will make the situation clear to him*).
Listen to me, Domenico. And then let's never speak of
this again. (*The love she has held in so long comes*

welling up.) I always loved you with all my heart and
soul. In my eyes you were a god. And you are dear
to me still—perhaps dearer than ever. (*She breaks
off, thinking of his thoughtlessness, his failure to understand.*) What have you done with your life? Did
you *want* to suffer? The Lord God gave you everything. Good looks, good health, money . . . and me.
I'd have done anything for you. To save you the
slightest pain I'd have made a vow of perpetual silence and kept it! And if you'd been . . . different,
you'd have taken on three children and thought nothing
of it. But you were you. (*Pause.*) Never ask me again
which is your son. I won't tell. I can't tell. And you've
got to be a gentleman and not ask, or I might give way
in a moment of weakness, and that would be the end.
Don't you see? I told you it was the plumber, and within two seconds you were talking about money, a little
capital, a real repair shop. . . . You have money, you
have a right to think of it, but what would you think
of next? "Why shouldn't I tell him he's my son?"
you'd think. "And who are these two other chaps?
Intruders!" An inferno. Brother against brother.
There'd be murder in this house, Domenico. (*Pause.*)
Don't think of yourself, don't think of me, Domenico.
Think of them: it's the children that count, Domenico.
We must never forget it. When they're tiny, we take
them in our arms, we fret over them when they're
sick and can't explain what the matter is. A little
later, they come rushing at you with their arms out,
shouting: Papa! Then they come home from school
in winter with their hands freezing and their noses
running and asking if you've remembered that surprise you promised. . . . But when they're grown up,
when they're men, what are they? They're . . . just
sons. Or else enemies. I have three grown-up sons,
Domenico, decide whether you want them. You still
have time. And there'll be no ill feelings. We needn't
go through with this. If you say so, we're free to pick
up and go each his own way.

The organ starts to play in the study.

Rosalia (*enters from the study followed by the* three
boys). He's come! The holy priest is here!

Domenico *gets up and looks at them all very slowly.*

Provoked by Filumena's *last remark, he is trying to force himself to break with her.*

Domenico. "We're free to pick up and go each his own way!" (*To the* three boys.) I have something to say to you. (*Suspense.*) I am a gentleman and I don't want to cheat you. Listen.

The Three Sons. Yes, Father.

Domenico (for this "Yes, Father" has settled it). Thank you, boys. I like the sound of that expression. I like it very much. (*Brightening up, now that this weight is off his mind.*) Now, then, the usual thing is for the bride's father to take her to the altar. There are no parents with us today. There are sons, instead. Two of them will accompany the bride. The third, the bridegroom.

Michele (firmly). We'll go with mother. (*Inviting* Riccardo.)

Filumena (suddenly remembering). What time is it?

Riccardo. Five minutes to six.

Filumena *gives* Rosalia *a meaningful look.*

Rosalia. Don't worry. At six o'clock on the nose those candles will be lit!

Filumena (leaning lovingly on Michele *and* Riccardo). Let's go in!

Domenico (to Umberto). And you'll go with me.

Forming a procession they go into the study. We hear the "Oh! which greets the happy pair as they enter and the handclapping of the guests. Rosalia *stays in the dining room, watching the ceremony through the curtains, clapping when the others clap, etc. We hear voices at first, then silence, then the wedding march. At this point* Rosalia *weeps copiously.* Alfredo *comes in upstage right as if looking for somebody; he sees* Rosalia *and goes over to her.* Lucia *comes in and joins the other two.*)

Here a change of lighting indicates a passage of time.

Filumena *comes in from the study, followed by* Umberto, Michele, *and* Rosalia; *goes to sit downstage left.*

Filumena. Phew, I'm tired!

Michele. You can rest now, Mamma. We'll be going. I have to work tomorrow.

Rosalia. It was so lovely! May you live to be a hundred, child of mine, for child of mine you are and ever will be!

Riccardo (comes in from the study). It *was* a lovely ceremony, too!

Filumena (taking her shoes off and relaxing in her armchair). Rosalia, bring me a glass of water, will you, dear?

Rosalia. Oh, yes, Donna Filumena. *(Exit left.)*

Domenico *comes in from the study carrying a bottle of special white wine, the cork covered with sealing wax.*

Domenico. No guests, no banquet, just a bottle of wine among the family. *(He takes a corkscrew and five glasses.)* The perfect nightcap. (Domenico *uncorks the bottle.*)

Rosalia (comes in with a glass of water on a plate). Here's the water.

Domenico. What do we want with *water,* for heaven's sake?

Rosalia. It's for the signora!

Domenico. Tell the signora that water on an occasion of this sort is bad luck. Get two more glasses, and bring Alfredo Amoroso, jockey and coachman, connoisseur of the racetrack.

Rosalia (calling). Alfredo! Alfredo! Come and have some wine with your master! You, too, Lucia! *(She brings* Domenico *two more glasses from a sideboard.)*

Alfredo (coming in, followed by Lucia*).* Here I come!

Domenico (has filled the glasses and now he is handing them around). Here, Filumena, drink this. *(To the others.)* Drink, everybody!

Alfredo. Alla salute! *(He raises his glass.)*

Domenico. You remember the horses, don't you, Alfredo, the way they ran?

Alfredo (thrilled). Madonna!

Domenico. They've stopped running. They stopped some time ago. I just didn't wish to believe it. And in my mind's eye I went on seeing them. But now I realize they stopped—a long time ago. *(Indicating the three boys.)* It's their turn now. For them the race is

just beginning. We'd better keep out of their way, you
and I, Alfredo Amoroso, we can't compete with all
this young blood.

Alfredo (quite overcome).   Madonna!

Domenico.   Drink up, Alfredo.

All drink.

I have just one thing left to say. It often happens in
a family that a father with three or four children takes
a special liking to one of them, maybe the ugly one,
or the sick one, or the strong one, whichever it is, he's
"father's boy," and the other kids don't mind. "Papa
has a right to feel that way," they say. In our family
this can never happen. Our family was . . . well,
formed too late in the day. Maybe that's better. What
I mean is, I'll still feel that special liking, but . . .
I'll have to divide it among the three of you. So: alla
salute!

They drink.

Now, boys, tomorrow you're coming for dinner.

Three Boys.   Thank you, Father.

Riccardo.   But now I'll be going. It's late, and Mamma
needs a rest. Good-bye—and all the best!

Umberto.   All the best!

Michele.   And the same from me!

They all kiss and embrace Filumena.

Umberto (coming over to Domenico, *smiling affectionately).*   Good night, Papa!

Riccardo.   G'night, Papa!

Michele.   Sleep well, Papa!

*Domenico (is terribly happy. But one Italian custom
remains).*   Come on, boys! *(He stretches out his arms,
embraces them, one after the other, kissing them on
both cheeks).* Till tomorrow!

Three Boys.   Till tomorrow!

They leave upstage right, followed by Alfredo, Rosalia,
and Lucia.

*Domenico follows them out with his eyes, then thought-
fully returns to the table and pours himself some
more wine.*

Filumena (*is still sitting in the armchair, has changed her shoes*). Madonna, how tired I am! It comes over me all at once.

Domenico (*understandingly, lovingly*). You've been on your feet all day. And with all the strain of it! Now you can rest. (*He takes his glass over to the terrace.*) What a lovely evening!

Filumena *has been feeling something in her throat that makes her groan slightly: at any rate a sound like sobbing comes out of her. Her eyes are staring out into nothingness. She seems to expect something. Her face is lined with tears.*

Domenico (*concerned, comes over*). What's the matter, dear?

Filumena (*with deep joy*). I'm crying, Domenico, I'm crying! And, oh, how *sweet* it is to cry!

Domenico (*holding her lovingly to him*). You'll be all right, Filumena, you'll be all right. *You've* done some running in your time, too, it's been a hard race, there's been a fall or two, but you always picked yourself up again somehow. And now it's time for a rest. (*He returns to the table for yet another glass of wine.*) A mother's a mother, and sons are sons, Filumena Soriano. (*He is drinking as*

THE CURTAIN FALLS)

THE ESSAYS

Baldassare Castiglione

THE FIRST PRODUCTION OF THE FOLLIES OF CALANDRO

It is some time since I received a letter from your Excellency, to which I did not reply at first, out of curiosity to see if you would become my debtor for more than one letter! At length I must confess that you have won the day, and in reply I will tell you that I cannot recollect the precise date on which I gave you those hundred ducats to send to Naples. But I know this, that it was when our two lady duchesses left Rome and I stayed behind for ten or twelve days, intending to go to Naples, and then changed my mind and gave you the money, and returned to Urbino with the Cardinal of Pavia. Now you will remember the whole thing!

I send you my Marine Elegy, which please pass on to M. Pietro Bembo. I beg you to read it and give me your opinion on the poem. I know not if it is worth your perusal, but I know well that it cannot possibly equal your expectations or be worthy of your praise. As for my delays, you are aware how many reasons I have to excuse them. Our comedies have gone off well, most of all *The Follies of Calandro*, which was represented in a truly magnificent style, which I need not describe, since you will have heard full accounts from many who were present. But I will tell you this much. The scene represented

From J. Cartwright, *Baldassare Castiglione: His Life and Letters*. New York: E. P. Dutton & Company.

was an outer street of the town, between the city wall and its last houses. The wall with its two towers was represented in the most natural way possible, rising from the floor of the stage to the top of the hall. One tower was occupied by the pipers, the other by the trumpeters, and between the two there was another finely constructed rampart. The hall itself, where the audience sat, occupied the place of the moat, and was crossed as it were by two aqueducts. The back of the wall above the tiers of seats was hung with the tapestries of the Trojan War. Above these was a large cornice in high relief, bearing the following inscription in large white letters on a blue ground, running the whole length of the hall:

Both in wars abroad and in games at home, Caesar displays his strength, for both alike are fit work for great minds.

From the roof of the hall hung great bunches of foliage, almost hiding the ceiling, and from the rosettes of the vault wire threads were suspended, to which two rows of candelabra in the shape of letters were fastened, from one end of the hall to the other. These thirteen rosettes made thirteen letters, spelling the words *Deliciæ Populi*, and these letters were so large that they held seven or ten torches, which lighted the hall brilliantly.

The scene was laid in a very fine city, with streets, palaces, churches, and towers, all in relief, and looking as if they were real, the effect being completed by admirable paintings in scientific perspective. Among other objects there was an octagon temple in low relief, so well finished that, even if all the workmen in the duchy of Urbino had been employed, it seemed hardly possible to think that all this had been done in four months! This temple was completely covered with beautiful stucco reliefs, the windows were made to imitate alabaster, the architraves and cornices were of fine gold and ultramarine blue, with glass jewels here and there, looking exactly like real gems; there were roundels of marble containing figures, carved pillars, and much more that would take me too long to describe. This temple stood in the center of the stage. At one end there was a triumphal arch about two yards from the wall, marvelously executed. Between the architrave and the vault an admirable representation of the story of the Horatii had been painted to imitate marble. The two niches above the pillars supporting the arch were filled with little Victories bearing trophies in their hands made of stucco. On the top of the arch stood a most beautiful equestrian statue of a figure in armor, striking a vanquished man at his feet with his spear. To right and left of this rider were two little altars with vases of burning flame that lasted to the end of the comedy.

I will not describe everything, as I feel sure you will have heard a good deal already; nor will I tell how one of the plays was composed by a child and recited by children, who perhaps put their elders to shame. They certainly acted marvelously, and it was a new thing to see little old men, not a foot high, preserving a gravity and severity of manner worthy of Menander. Nor will I attempt to describe the strange music of these comedies, played by minstrels who were all out of sight and placed in different corners; but I will come at once to our Bernardo's *Follies of Calandro*, which gave the greatest pleasure. And since the prologue arrived very late, and the actor who had to recite it could not learn it by heart in time, another which I had written was recited in its place, and met with general approval. Otherwise little was changed, only a few scenes which, perhaps, were not fit for recitation, but little or nothing else, and it was performed exactly as it is written.

These were the *intermezzi*. First a *moresca* by Jason, who appeared on one side of the stage, dancing in antique armor, looking very fine, with a splendid sword and shield. On the other came two bulls, so lifelike that several of the spectators took them for real animals, breathing fire through their nostrils. The good Jason yoked them to the plow and made them draw it, and then sowed dragon's teeth in the furrows. Presently ancient warriors sprang upon the stage in a way that was, I think, excellently managed, and danced a fiery *moresca*, trying to kill Jason all the while. As they were leaving the stage, they fell upon each other and were slain, without being actually seen to die. Then Jason appeared again, dancing exquisitely with the golden fleece on his shoulders; and this was the first interlude, or *moresca*. The second was a very beautiful chariot of Venus, with the goddess seated and holding a lighted taper in her hand. The car was drawn by two doves, who certainly seemed to be alive, and who were ridden by two Amorini with lighted tapers in their hands and bows and quivers on their shoulders. Four Amorini went before the car, four followed after, all bearing lighted tapers in the same manner, dancing a *moresca* and flourishing their burning torches. Having reached the end of the stage, they set fire to a door, from which nine gallants issued all ablaze with light, and danced another most beautiful *moresca*. The third *intermezzo* was a chariot of Neptune drawn by two sea horses with fish scales and fins, wonderfully well imitated. Neptune himself rode in the car with his trident, attended by eight monsters, four before and four behind, all as well done as it is possible to imagine, and dancing a sword dance with the chariot all aflame. These beasts were the strangest creatures in the world, but no one who did not see them can have an idea what they were like. The fourth was a car of Juno, also ablaze with light. The goddess, wearing a crown on her brow and a scepter in her hand, appeared seated on a cloud which encircled the chariot, and surrounded by numberless heads blowing the winds of heaven. This car was drawn by two peacocks so beautiful and lifelike that I could not believe my eyes, and yet I had seen them before, and had myself given directions how they were to be made. In front were two eagles and ostriches, behind two sea birds and two large parrots, with gaily colored plumage. All of these were so well done, my dear Monsignore, that I am quite sure no imitation ever came so near to reality, and they all danced a sword dance with a grace that it is impossible to describe or imagine.

When the comedy was ended, one of the Amorini, whom we had already seen, appeared suddenly on the stage, in the same habit, and explained in a few verses the meaning of these *intermezzi*, which was a separate thing from the comedy itself.

First of all there was the battle between earth-born brothers, when, as we see today, there is war between those nearest of kin, who ought to live at peace, as set forth in the fable of Jason. Then comes Love, who kindles first mankind and earth, then the sea and air, with his sacred flame, and seeks to drive away war and discord and join the whole world in blessed concord. This indeed, you will say, is rather a hope and devout aspiration, but the vision of war, alas! is all too real for our misfortune! I did not mean to show you the verses that Love sang, but yet I send them, and you can do what you like with them. They were written in great haste, by one who was struggling all the while with painters and carpenters, with actors and musicians and dancers. When the verses were ended, Love disappeared. The sound of hidden music, proceeding from four viols, was heard, and then four voices singing a verse to the strains of a beautiful melody, as it were an invocation to Love. So the *festa* ended, after giving the greatest satisfaction and pleasure to the spectators. If I had not praised the whole thing so much, I would have told you what share I had in it; but I will not do this, for fear your Excellency should think that I flatter myself!

(1513)

Carlo Goldoni

ON PLAYWRITING

TRANSLATED, COMPILED AND WITH NOTES
BY F. C. L. VAN STEENDEREN

God forbid that I should set up for a teacher! I purpose merely to confide to my readers what little I may have learned or may be trying to do, reminding them, meanwhile, that even in the least important books one sometimes finds little matters deserving attention.[1] I have no mind to write an academic treatise on the Art of Comedy. Why offer oracularly, like a pedant, what has so often been repeated by valiant men of every cultured nation?[2] Nor do I mean to lay down rules for others to follow. My plan is just to make known that I have at last, through long-continued observation and practice, succeeded in blazing a path for myself which I can travel with some degree of security, offering as proof for the statement the favor which my plays enjoy among the frequenters of theaters.[3]

Reprinted by arrangement with the Brander Matthews Dramatic Museum, Columbia University, by whom this compilation was originally published, in 1919, as "Goldoni on Playwriting."

[1] *Memoirs*, p. 313. Memoirs = *Memorie di Carlo Goldoni riprodotte integralmente dalla edizione francese. Con prefazione e note di Guido Mazzoni.* Two vols., Florence, 1907.

[2] Pasquali I, p. ix. Pasquali = Giambattista Pasquali's edition of Goldoni's Works in 17 vols., begun in 1761 and finished sometime after 1777. Only the Introduction in Vol. I is cited here.

[3] *Teatro comico*, Introduzione. *Il teatro comico* is a play first performed October 5, 1750. It embodies the author's ideas about playwriting.

It must be confessed that all men carry with them from their birth a natural disposition peculiar to themselves which leads them rather into one than another sort of study or profession, and in which they may succeed with admirable facility if they will apply themselves. As for me, I certainly have felt since my tenderest childhood the forward drive of an internal, almost insuperable power toward theatrical affairs. Whenever a play fell into my hands, I found delight in it. I remember that I wrote, merely as a result of reading some of Cicognini's dramatic works at the age of nine, a comedy, such as it was, before ever having seen one performed on the stage.

This native inclination became still stronger when I began to go to the theaters, nor did it abandon me in my various journeys among Italian cities, undertaken either for reasons of study or to accompany my father in the course of his wanderings as a physician. At Perugia, Rimini, Milan, or Pavia, while in the midst of the disgusting work of that calling which he wished to compel me by main force to enjoy, as well as later, during my study and profession of the law, my pleasure in dramatic poetry was always finding an outlet, whether through the writing of dialogues and comedy sketches or by representing some dramatic character at an aristocratic academy.

Having finally returned to Venice, I was obliged to devote myself to the legal profession in order to earn a living, my father having departed this life. My genius continued to lead me to the theater, however, and I fulfilled with painful reluctance the duties of my calling and the really honorable positions which were derived from it.[4] Thus, three or four times I have lost the luckiest opportunities for bettering my state, but abandoning myself without reflection to the blandishments of the stage, I always allowed myself to be caught in the same trap.[5] In fact, I never applied myself with more delight and diligence to dramatic writing than in those faraway days of my youth. So it came about that, though I could hope for a prosperous future in the noble profession of advocate in an important court, I nevertheless denied myself to the city of my birth, resolved as I was to yield wholly to the power within me which claimed me outright for Dramatic Poetry. Intent upon learning the various

---

[4] Pasquali I, p. ix.
[5] *Memoirs* I, p. 291.

usages and customs which flourish in plentiful variety in this our delightful corner of Europe, I visited many Italian cities; and, stopping finally in Milan, I began to write seriously for the Italian stage.

I have ingenuously related all this with the single view of emphasizing the true and only incentive I felt for devoting myself to the drama. It was nothing short of an invincible call of nature. I could not withstand it. Is it a wonder then that in all my journeys, amid all the vicissitudes of life, in my amusements even, my mind remained fixed and observant in the direction of this interest? Involuntarily I gathered abundant material, an inexhaustible mine of substance, ready and adapted for eventual use on the stage.[6]

What, you may ask, can be accomplished by one not naturally endowed with this spontaneous inclination? After developing through ample study a fair knowledge of the drama, he may be able to judge correctly other men's plays but this by no means insures his producing a successful one himself. He may, it is true, succeed in constructing plays according to rule; he may even write in the purest vernacular; yet he will have the misfortune of not pleasing on the stage. Neither, as a consequence, can he teach, for if the spectator, coming as he does to the theater primarily for recreation, is to be induced to accept a moral lesson, it must be conveyed to him *en passant*, sweetened by poetic grace and comic wit. In short, whoever does not possess the comic genius will be unable to exercise that joyous animation which sustains the sprightliness of the characters; moreover, he will be at a loss in trying to infuse his work with that humor which is the flower of a fine mind, as well as of the peculiar talent which comedy demands.[7]

However, the selfsame ardor which made me a most attentive observer of the plays which were being performed in the various theaters of Italy made me recognize and also lament their corrupted taste. I fancied, besides, that the public would derive no little benefit, and he who should succeed no small praise, if some man of talent, inspired by the spirit of comedy, should attempt to lift the Italian stage out of its abasement. The hope of this glory finally enlisted me in the undertaking.

Indeed, the Comic Stage in our Italy had been so cor-

[6] Pasquali I, p. ix.
[7] Pasquali I, p. xi.

rupt for more than a century that among the transalpine nations it had become an object of contempt. Upon her public boards only unseemly harlequinades and scandalous jests were in vogue. The plots were poor in conception and worse—even uncivil and ill ordered—in the performance, since far from correcting vice as the first and most noble aim of comedy, they but fomented it. Arousing the laughter of the ignorant plebeians, dissolute youths, and the most debauched of the population, the comic stage disgusted, then irritated the educated and the well-bred, who, if they sometimes attended so poor a theater, and were there dragged out of boredom, took good care not to take with them their innocent families, lest their hearts should be corrupted. The Fathers of the Church justly anathematized such plays, and they were in fact very proper subjects for the loathing of the wise.

Many tried to purify the stage and bring back good taste to it. Some attempted to do so by means of comedies translated from the Spanish or the French; but mere translations cannot be successful in Italy.[8] The stage must be imbued with national life, brought within the sphere of everybody,[9] for national points of view differ as do customs and languages. Seeing, in spite of their purblindness, the force of this truth, our mercenary actors set about altering these foreign pieces and reciting them in improvised form; yet they so disfigured them that they could no longer be recognized as works of such celebrated authors as Lope de Vega and Molière, who, beyond the mountains where better taste flourished, had happily written them. They treated with the same cruelty the comedies of Plautus and Terence; nor did they spare any of the other ancient and modern comedies which chanced to fall into their hands. Meanwhile the educated chafed, the public wearied. All exclaimed in accord against bad comedies; yet most people had no idea of what good ones were like.

Noticing this universal discontent, actors tried to find profit in innovation. They introduced elaborate paraphernalia, transformation scenes and magnificent stage sets, but beyond increasing their expenses inordinately, they did not succeed at all, for the attendance of the public soon decreased. Then they tried to save comedy by means of musical interludes. This expedient succeeded well for

[8] Pasquali I, p. xii.
[9] *Memoirs* I, p. 354.

a time, and I was among the first to contribute to the number of such pieces. Since actors are not musicians, however, it was not long before it became evident how little relation there is between comedy and music. What kept the theaters open were tragedies and operas, the applause lavished upon them signifying the abasement of comedy, and offering convincing proof of its extreme decadence.[10]

The germ of comedy, however, had not been utterly killed in the prolific heart of Italy. Those who were among the first to strive toward its revival, unable as they were to find in a century of ignorance the necessary skillful writers, boldly constructed plots themselves, divided them into acts and scenes, and recited extempore the phrases, thoughts, and witticisms they had agreed upon among themselves. During the last two centuries this kind of play had amused all Italy; in fact, my country had become distinguished because of it, no nation having been able to imitate Improvised Comedy. In my time it was the Bolognese who clung more tenaciously than other Italians to this form of play. There were among them people of merit who found pleasure in constructing these *commedie dell'arte,* and certain of their citizens played them very well, giving delight to their countrymen.

Before explaining what I think about this matter, I should like to entertain my readers for a few minutes with remarks on the origin, the use, and the effect of Improvised Comedy and the Four Masks which constituted its staple cast.

Those who knew how to read Latin found that in the comedies of Plautus and Terence there were always duped fathers, debauched sons, amorous daughters, rascally valets, and doltish servants. As they traveled through Italy, the actors took the fathers from Venice and Bologna, the valets from Bergamo, the lovers—male and female—and the soubrettes from Rome and Tuscany. Indeed, I have in my possession a manuscript of the sixteenth century, well preserved and bound in parchment, containing one hundred and twenty plots of Italian plays, called Art Comedies, and the dramatic foundation of them is always Pantaloon, Merchant of Venice; the Doctor, Jurisconsult of Bologna; Brighella and Harlequin, Bergamesque Valets, the one clever, the other dull.

Pantaloon is a merchant of Venice, because Venice was

[10] Pasquali I, p. xii.

in former days the state which carried on the richest and most extensive commerce in Italy. He has always worn the ancient Venetian costume; the black cloak and woolen bonnet being still in use in that city, while the red waistcoat, the breeches resembling drawers, the red stockings and slippers represent in a lifelike way the habiliments of the lagoons of the Adriatic. Nowadays his beard, which in remote times was an adornment, is scorned and ridiculed.

The second old man, called the Doctor, was taken from among the gentlemen of the robe in order to contrast the educated man with the man of commerce, and Bologna was adopted as his home because there existed in that city a university which, in spite of the ignorance of the times, continued to conserve the duties and emoluments of the professors. The costume of the Doctor is nearly the dress still in use at the University and the Law Court of Bologna, while the singular mask which covers his forehead and nose is supposed to imitate a purple birthmark which marred the face of a certain jurisconsult of earlier days. Lovers of this sort of comedy are attached to this red spot as to a tradition.

Brighella and Harlequin, also called the two Zani, were taken from Bergamo because, the first being extremely adroit and the second completely dull, it is only in that region that one finds these extremes among the lower classes. Brighella represents an intriguing, tricky, cunning valet. His costume is a species of livery; his tawny mask exaggerates the complexion of the mountaineer of Bergamo, burned by the heat of the sun. Harlequin's costume shows him to be a poor devil who will pick up pieces of divers colors in order to mend his coat; his hat corresponds to his beggarly habits, while the rabbit's scut which is its ornament is even to this day the trimming common to the headgear of Bergamesque peasants.

This will explain sufficiently the origin and the use of the four principal masks. It remains for me to speak of the effects they produce.

The masks cannot but hamper the art of the actor. Whether he try to express joy or grief, whether he show passionate or gentle love, it is always the same leather that intrudes. He may gesticulate and vary the tone of his voice as much as he will; yet he can never express through his features, which are the interpreters of the heart, such passions as the character he represents may feel. The public demands that the actor interpret a soul, but a soul under a mask is like fire under ashes. Any plan of reform must therefore include a gradual obliteration of the masks, as well as a substitution of pure comedy for slapstick farce.[11]

My first play, *Belisario*, was performed amid extraordinary silence, an almost unknown phenomenon in Italian theaters. Yet, used as it was to hubbub, the audience made up between the acts for its quiet with cries of joy, handclappings, and reciprocal signals repeated from the pit to the boxes. At the end of the performance the unusual outbursts of satisfaction increased to such a din that the actors wept and laughed in turn. When the leading man appeared to make the customary announcement for the following evening, the audience cried in chorus, "No, this one, this one!" and the curtain fell. The play was not worth all this admiration. I myself think so little of it that it shall never appear in the printed collection of my works. But my heroes were men, not demigods. They showed human foibles in the way we all know them to be; they did not carry their virtues and vices to fantastic excess.[12]

I had, however, not yet acquired sufficient experience to do aught but ponder the ways and means of reform. But I observed. And, for instance, I saw that even in poor comedies there is often something that will call forth applause from the pit and approval from the boxes; I noticed that this occurs mostly at a moment of intense seriousness, of delicate humor, or when a good situation is shown, when some noteworthy character is being truthfully revealed, or some noteworthy character worth correcting is being exposed in its results. Above all I remarked that, more than the marvelous, it was the simple, the natural that won the heart of an audience.[13]

When I brought my bride home to Venice, the company of actors for whom I had been writing more or less were glad to see me, the more so since I brought them a new play.[14] What made this troupe exceptional was the presence in it of a famous Harlequin, Sacchi by name, whose wife played the Second Lady very well, and whose sister was a good soubrette.

"There you are," I said to myself; "you can now give

---

[11] *Memoirs* II, p. 37.
[12] *Memoirs* I, p. 204.
[13] Pasquali I, p. xii.
[14] *Memoirs* I, p. 228.

free rein to your imagination. You have worked on hack-
neyed material long enough; now you must create,
invent. You have promising actors, but in order to get
out of them what is in them, you must study them, for
each has his own natural bent. Success will almost be
assured if you give them characters to act which are
analogous to their own. Come," I went on reflecting,
"this is perhaps your chance to attempt the reform you
have had in mind so long. Yes, you must handle character
subjects, they being the source of all good comedy. This
is what Molière did, thus developing his art to a degree
which the ancients only indicated, and which the moderns
have not yet equaled."

In accordance with these musings I searched in the
company for the actor best suited to playing a maskless
character. I chose the Pantaloon Colinetti, because I had
formed a high opinion of his manner in the society of
people among whom I had studied him. I believed I could
make him an excellent portrayer of a gentleman, and I
was not mistaken. Therefore I wrote for him a comedy
entitled *Momolo Cortesan*, or *L'Uomo di Mondo, The
Man of the World.* "Are there many such in Venice?" you
will ask. Yes, there are not a few, and some possess, more
or less, the very qualities I depicted in Momolo. To present such a character to the public, however, one has to
pad it, and I dressed mine in all the perfection of the
species.

In order to bring out a character I have always thought
it necessary to place it in direct contrast with another
whose nature is the opposite of it. I therefore introduced
into my play a Venetian good-for-nothing. My gentleman
defends the dupes of this scoundrel against his snares,
finally unmasking him. Thus the Harlequin in this piece
is no longer a slapstick valet, but becomes a rascal fun-
damentally characterized by the fact that he insists upon
his sister's maintaining him in his vices by her shame.

This comedy enjoyed excellent success, and I was content. My compatriots were beginning to give up their anti-
quated taste for farce. My reform was started. Yet I
could not boast of it. The play was not dialogued. Nothing
but the part of the leading man was written out, all the
rest being left in improvised form. Indeed, the smoothness of style which distinguishes classical authors was not
there. I could not reform everything at once without
antagonizing the lovers of Improvised Comedy; but I
awaited the favorable moment for a frontal attack, when

I could deliver it with more vigor and greater effect.[15]

My experience goes to prove that the reputation of a playwright often depends upon the performance of the actors. There is no use hiding this truth from oneself.[16] I always took time, therefore, and sought opportunity to study the divers natures of my players. When I began to work for Medebac's troupe, I soon observed in Darbes, one of its members, two contrasting but habitual facial expressions, to which his manner and action corresponded. He would be the jolliest, wittiest, and most energetic man in the world, then suddenly assume the expression, the speech, and the ways of an imbecile or bumpkin, and these changes would take place in him quite naturally, without apparent effort. This discovery gave me the idea of making him appear under these two different aspects in the same play. Another successful comedy, *I aue Gemelli Veneziana*, was the result.[17]

As long as I continued working over the time-worn materials of the Improvised Comedy and produced only partly written plays, I was permitted to enjoy in peace the applause of the pit; but as soon as I laid claim to being a regular author, a poet, a creator, people awoke from their lethargy and considered me worthy of their criticism. Indeed, my countrymen, for so long a time accustomed to trivial farces and elaborate scenery, suddenly became severe censors of my work. They made the names of Aristotle, Horace, and Castelvetro resound throughout their clubs, and my plays became the talk of the town.

I might today refrain from recalling these verbose disputes, which drifted away with the wind and which my successes made harmless, but I am glad to refer to them now, because of the opportunity thus afforded of telling my readers about my way of thinking in regard to the rules of comedy and the method I planned to follow when writing a play.

The unities required for the greater perfection of theatrical work were at all times open to discussion among authors and critics. The censors of my character comedies had no reproach to make concerning the unity of action, nor in regard to the unity of time, but they asserted that I had failed to satisfy the requirements of the unity of place. Yet the action in my comedies always transpired in

[15] *Memoirs* I, p. 230.
[16] *Memoirs* I, p. 239.
[17] *Memoirs* I, p. 301.

one city. The characters might move about, it is true, in different parts of it, but they remained within the limits of the same walls. I believed then, and believe now, that the unity of place is thereby satisfactorily observed.

In every art, in every discovery, experience has ever preceded precept. Authors have later laid down methods for the practical guidance of inventiveness, but the moderns have ever reserved the right to interpret these methods of the ancients. As for me, since I do not find either in Aristotle's or Horace's *Poetics* a clear, absolute, and vigorously worked-out principle regarding the unity of place and comedy, I have indeed been glad to conform whenever my subject lent itself to the idea, but I have never sacrificed a comedy which had a chance to turn out well to a prejudice which would have rendered it unsatisfactory.[18] If Aristotle were now alive, he would cancel the obnoxious rule, for a thousand absurdities, a thousand blunders and improprieties are caused by it.

There are, it seems to me, two kinds of comedy, pure comedy and comedy of intrigue. The first can be written while observing the unity of place, the second cannot be thus constructed without crudity and incongruity. The ancients had not, as we have, a way to shift scenery, and for this reason they observed all the unities. We comply with the unity of place when the action occurs in the same city, and all the more when it remains in the same house. I conclude, therefore, that if comedy can be constructed in compliance with the unity of place without hairsplitting and unseemliness, it should be done; but if, because of it, absurdities must be introduced, it is better to change the plot and observe the rules of probability.[19]

Like Aristotle, Horace has been made to say more than he intended. I refer particularly to the precept that not more than three persons should act at the same time in one scene. He says, *"Nec quarta loqui persona laboret."* Some think this to mean, "Let no more than three work." What he must have intended to say is that, if there are four persons, one of them should not exert himself; that is, the four actors should not be simultaneously in action with one another, as happens in improvised scenes, in which four or five persons immediately cause confusion. For that matter, scenes may be arranged for eight or ten

[18] *Memoirs* I, p. 310.
[19] *Teatro comico*, Act III, Scene 3.

persons, provided their action is carefully regulated and that they allow one another to speak in turn.[20]

For this reason, when certain fanatic admirers of antiquity demand of me either a scrupulous application of the unity of place or an adherence to the idea that not more than three persons should speak in one scene, or any similar finicality which has no relation to the constituent beauty of comedy, I answer them by pointing to the contrary usage of many authors approved by the fame of centuries. There are things in ancient comedy which, though pleasing in their day, would prove intolerable in ours. I hold, therefore, that one should obey the laws of national and contemporary characteristics in a spectacle designed to divert, delight, and incidentally to instruct, rather than comply with certain precepts attributed to Aristotle or Horace. Those haters of novelty who insist on a complete accord with bygone standards appear to me like physicians who refuse to prescribe quinine for the sole reason that Hippocrates or Galen had not yet adopted it.[21]

My countrymen, I think, would never have been so severe with me but for the ill-balanced zeal of my partisans, on whom they reacted. Well-informed people merely condemned the fanaticism of those who set too high a value on my work. Meanwhile, disputes waxed ever warmer,[22] complaints and compliments coming thick and fast. To me the two opposing parties were a thorn in the flesh. Trying to content both, I submitted to the task of constructing improvised plays without ceasing to write character comedies. I had the inveterate mask actors do their work in one class, and employed the more capable and adaptable human material in the other. Thus each party had its innings, and in the course of time, with patience, I slowly led them into a common understanding. After a few years I enjoyed the satisfaction of seeing myself authorized to follow my own ideas, and they became the most generally accepted and the most popular in Italy.[23]

But before I was able to write comedies which could pass muster, I, too, constructed bad ones. I wrote some plays after the Spanish manner—that is to say, comedies

[20] *Teatro comico,* Act III, Scene 9.
[21] Pasquali I, p. xiii.
[22] *Memoirs* I, p. 311.
[23] *Memoirs* II, p. 40.

of intrigue with considerable complexity in their plots. They met with unwonted success through a certain logical texture and regularity which distinguished them from the usual pieces of that sort, as well as through an undeniable naturalness and plausibility that made them worthy of note. I thought that if they succeeded so well when only the principal characters were provided with the proper directions and words, and the others were left to improvisation, with a resulting unevenness and precariousness in the performance, these plays would have turned out considerably better if all the roles had been written out. Thereby more variety could be introduced, all the characters could be smoothed on the lathe of Nature, national taste could be completely met. The success of *The Clever Woman, The Prudent Man, The Artful Widow, The Respectable Girl, The Cavalier and the Lady, The Antiquarian's Family,* and others belonging to my debut proved that I was right and that efforts to restore manners and decency to the stage of Italy were not likely to be in vain.[24]

I cannot boast that I developed to this degree of better sense through an assiduous and methodical study of the best ancient and modern writers and poets. Although I have not neglected reading them, thus receiving as from good teachers the best examples and precepts, I must confess that the two books upon which I have meditated most and which I shall never repent having used are the World and the Stage. It is a fact that no one becomes a master in playwriting who neglects the study of these books. The first of the two, the World, shows me so many characters, and depicts them to me so invitingly, that it seems to have been created expressly to provide me with plots for pleasing and instructive comedies. It presents to me the depth, the power, the effect of every human passion; and calling my attention to curious happenings, it informs me concerning current customs; furnishing me with knowledge of the foibles and defects common in our century and nation, it indicates to me, through the medium of some excellent person, how virtue resists corruption. Hence I draw upon this book as upon a bank, returning again and again and meditating upon whatever I take from it under all the circumstances of life. My experience shows how indispensable it is to anyone who would exercise my profession.

[24] Pasquali I, p. xiv.

The second, that is the book of the Stage, makes me see with what colors the characters, the passions, the action we read about in the book of the World should be bodied forth, how these must be painted and shaded to throw them in relief, and how varied to render them grateful to the discerning eye of the spectator. I learn from the stage what is most likely to impress the minds of men, what will awaken wonder and laughter, and what will cause that delightful sensation which people come to enjoy in the theater. It teaches me that this is provoked mainly by filling comedy with natural images and by tactfully placing before the vision of the audience those foibles and ridiculous delusions which can be seen in what happens all the time.

The stage shows me through the fate of my comedies how to estimate the character of the nation for which I write. Some of my productions which I held in no esteem at all have aroused great praise, while others, from which I expected no ordinary applause, gained but a languid interest, if they did not receive adverse criticism. Through this experience I have learned that if I would make my plays more practically useful, I must regulate my ideas in accordance with those that prevail universally, without paying much attention to the dicta of men who assume the right of prescribing rules of taste for a whole people, nay, for the entire world and for all centuries to come, and who do so upon a foundation of mental arguments only. These do not reflect that in certain nonintrinsic respects tastes and ideas change with impunity, and that the public is the arbiter in this case, as it is in the matter of clothes and language.[25]

This then is what I have learned from my two great books, the World and the Stage. My comedies are in the main regulated upon the precepts found in them only, and I shrewdly surmise that the first authors of comedy consulted no others. "Whatever is represented on the stage ought to be a copy of what occurs in the world," says Rapin. Comedy is what it should be when we seem to be in a company of neighbors or taking part in some familiar conversation, while in reality we find ourselves in the theater. Nothing must be shown that has no counterpart in everyday life.[26]

I have read, it is true, all manner of treatises on Poetics,

[25] Pasquali I, p. xv.
[26] Pasquali I, p. xvii.

on Tragedy and Comedy, but only after having formed my own style, or during the process of developing it in the light which the World and the Stage provided. Afterward I perceived that I had unconsciously conformed very largely to the most essential precepts of the art as recommended by the great masters: like that physician who, having discovered partly by chance, partly through experience, a wholesome medicine, subsequently applies to it the accepted principles of his art, regulating and systematizing it.[27]

Comedy was invented to expose foibles and ridicule disagreeable habits. When the ancients wrote comedies on that plan, the whole world liked them, for on seeing the facsimile of a character upon the boards, everybody saw the original in his neighbor or himself. When comedy became merely ridiculous, however, the most extravagant absurdities were gradually introduced under the pretext of causing laughter. Now that we are again fishing in the *mare magnum* of nature, men find themselves searching their hearts anew and identifying themselves with the persons presented, for they know how to discern whether or no a passion is well depicted, a character well developed and sustained: in short, they observe.[28]

My play of *The Punctilious Ladies* afforded me a striking illustration of this fact. I wrote this comedy in Mantua and had it performed on the local stage in order to try it out. It pleased greatly, but I ran the risk of drawing upon my head the wrath of one of the first ladies of the region. I learned later that she had not long before been in the situation of the countess in the play, who introduced Rosaura into society for a pecuniary consideration. Everybody stared in the direction of her box, but luckily for me, the lady was too broad-minded to lay herself open to the malice of the audience, applauding as she did every passage that might apply to her. Similar incidents occurred in Florence and Verona: in each of these cities it was thought that I had found my subject on the spot.[29]

Yet I always direct my criticism at social foibles in general, never at any sinner in particular; besides, it never becomes satire.[30] While writing a play I always strive to please the land of my fathers, to make it novel and yet

---

[27] Pasquali I, p. xviii.

[28] *Teatro comico*, Act II, Scene 1.

[29] *Memoirs* I, p. 329.

[30] *Teatro comico*, Act III, Scene 9.

keep it national, to win hearts through the attractiveness
of virtue rather than by the sorry sight of vice. Indeed, a
comedy which is truly an imitation of nature need not
shun clean and pathetic sentiment, provided that it be not
barren of those comic and witty features which are the
fundamental basis of its existence.[31] I have had no other
care than to please the average man, to induce people to
frequent the theater, and to procure profit for him who
pays me for my work.[32]

For you must know that during most of my career I
have placed my muse and my pen at the disposal of the
owners or directors of theaters. Such engagements may
be thought peculiar. A man of letters, you will say, must
be free, and should despise servitude and restraint.

If an author is well-to-do, like Voltaire, or cynical, as
is Rousseau, I have nothing to reply; but if he be one of
those who do not refuse a share in the receipts or in the
benefits of publication, if he enjoy no emolument from a
court, no pension or gifts, and yet is disposed to contribute products of his brain, he has no other resource in
Italy.[33] After all, when one possesses a talent, I do not
see why one should make no practical use of it.[34]

My contracts with theatrical managers were generally
quite satisfactory. My reputation once established, my
work was accepted before being read and paid for before
the first performance.[35] And this is bound to be, for if
the public applauds a play, it may be said without a doubt
that the author has done a good piece of work. The box-
office receipts show the manager whether a comedy has
drawing power,[36] and while he will respect a poet as a
man of education, he will not read his manuscript or listen to him through mere curiosity. What a manager looks
for is a good new idea.[37] In the drama novelty is of prime
importance.[38]

To make a play succeed, many things of beauty must

[31] *Memoirs* I, p. 312.

[32] Lettera dell' Autore dell' opera intitolata *Nerone* scritta
ad un suo amico che serve di prefazione all' opera stessa.
Venice, December 28, 1748. See also *Memoirs* I, p. 455.

[33] *Memoirs* I, p. 290.

[34] *Memoirs* II, p. 213.

[35] *Memoirs* I, p. 291.

[36] *Teatro comico*, Act I, Scene 7.

[37] *Teatro comico*, Act I, Scene 6.

[38] *Teatro comico*, Act I, Scene 2.

be united. The least flaw may make it a failure.[39] Though lacking an interesting story, a comedy may have nevertheless many beautiful details; yet if there is no complication and suspense in the action, it cannot be other than a poor play.[40] The style, too, must be proper to comedy, that is to say simple and natural, not academic or elevated. The great art lies in adhering to nature in all things, never deviating from it. Sentiments must be true, not affected; expression within the comprehension of all. The commonest traits please more than delicate conceits.[41] Moreover, it is with national morals and customs, with our own foibles and absurdities, that comedy should be concerned.[42]

My *Campiello*, for instance, gave great pleasure. Everything in it was copied from the lower classes, to be sure, but the whole action was of a truth which all recognized, the great and the small being interested in the story, for I had substituted simplicity for tinsel and nature for the phantasmagoria of a diseased imagination. My *Buona Famiglia*, on the other hand, may be one of those plays of mine which, if taken to heart, might benefit society morally. It was enjoyed by well-bred folk, by virtuous households, wise fathers, and prudent mothers; but as these do not belong exactly to the sort of people who make managers rich, it had but few performances. Though revived occasionally by amateurs, it died a speedy death on the public stage,[43] for when the groundwork is not felicitous, there is no remedy that avails, the structure being unable to rise with vigor.[44]

Indeed, writing comedies is a difficult business, and I do not flatter myself with the illusion that I shall ever learn just in what comic perfection consists.[45] But this I know, that in order to create wholesome laughter, one must first laugh oneself.[46] When things are said and done with grace, they get a double value. The shorter, therefore, and the more unexpected comic scenes are, the more they please. The principal comedian should act

[39] *Memoirs* II, p. 211.
[40] *Memoirs* I, p. 376.
[41] Pasquali I, p. xviii.
[42] *Memoirs* II, p. 42.
[43] *Memoirs* II, p. 89.
[44] Pasquali I, p. iv.
[45] *Teatro comico*, Act III, Scene II.
[46] *Teatro comico*, Act I, Scene 8.

copiously and speak sparingly. When he speaks, he should deliver his thrust pungently and at the right time, not cynically, as if under stress. He may be allowed to mutilate expressions naturally, as in dialect, but he must not twist and murder words. Especially should he beware of that cheap innuendo in which so many would-be comedies abound. In order to succeed, you must create something of your own, and to create you must study.[47]

I have also learned not to seek my subject in the association of crime, but rather to choose it among the merely ridiculous,[48] and to know that while improbability will kill a play,[49] an artistic mixture of the pathetic and the comical is ever an element of surprise.[50] The catastrophe, too, must be in accordance with human nature.[51] Although one may ridicule changes in fashion, headdress, or summer life in the country, in order to make woman a fit subject for comic attack the ridicule must be supplied by the vagaries of her mind, not by the whimsies of her heart. Even so, though the presentation of a female character may thus be comic in its own right, it has to be propped up by interesting and pleasing situations, else it may easily bore.

Rosaura in *The Fickle Woman* is such a comic character. She falls in love at one moment, and in the next falls out again; now she utters with apparent conviction certain principles and maxims, then flies, with lightheaded calculation, after passions which contradict them quite. The situation at the end of the play fits the ridiculous but not vicious folly under attack. Rosaura has finally made up her mind to marry, but all now avoid her; no man wants her for a wife.[52]

To the benefit of the public, and through the influence of my example, the evil stage manners that once were customary have at last been banished, and scandalous scenes have been abolished. No longer does one hear obscene expressions, filthy ambiguities, or depraved talk.[53] Yet I had to spend many years in dramatic labor before I was allowed to do things worthwhile. I did not become a comic author suddenly, but succeeded little by little,

[47] *Teatro comico*, Act III, Scene II.
[48] *Memoirs* I, p. 235.
[49] *Memoirs* I, p. 278.
[50] *Memoirs* I, p. 279.
[51] *Memoirs* I, p. 337.
[52] *Memoirs* I, p. 354.
[53] *Teatro comico*, Act III, Scene 3.

after long and arduous practice and a continuous, untiring study of reality.[54] Let no one think, however, that I have the temerity to believe that my plays are devoid of defects. Far from that presumption,[55] I am always a-tremble when a new comedy of mine goes on the boards,[56] and I take daily pains to improve my methods of writing.[57]

It may indeed interest some readers how I progressed in that respect. My rules cannot be safe to follow, however, for in mental work the result frequently depends on the state of mind in which one happens to be, rather than upon established and proved ability. Hence it is that among the works of any author the first are often better than the last, and sometimes the last better than the first; while again and again one may notice that variety of good and bad which is the despair of Olympus.

Perhaps more than anyone I have fallen into inequalities of manner, style, and verve, because of the quantity of plays I have produced in a short space of time or the haste with which I have many times been forced to write, and because of the consequent disinclination I have often felt for creative work. Revision for purposes of publication may have imparted a little more evenness, producing better results in language and expression, but the shrewd reader will nevertheless be able to say, "This was a stroke of genius, that was written when the author was apathetic."[58]

Indeed, how many comedies have I not dashed off in six or seven days! How often, when pressed for time, have I not sent away a first act for rehearsal and, without seeing it again, written the second, the third being done with the same celerity! In the course of time, however, I would notice the effect which my plays made upon the public. I heard the criticism and the censure, and when some of them were about to go to press, I would reconstruct them, better them, and sometimes change them completely.[59] Yet I am bound to say that experience and habit by degrees so familiarized me with the art of playwriting

[54] *Teatro comico*, Act III, Scene 2.
[55] Pasquali I, p. xviii.
[56] *Teatro comico*, Act III, Scene II.
[57] Pasquali I, p. xviii.
[58] Pasquali I, p. iv.
[59] Lettera dell' avvocato C. G. ad un suo amico in Venetia. Florence, April 28, 1753. In *Lettere di C. Goldoni*, ed. by G. M. Urbani de Ghelthof, Venice, 1880, p. 65. See also *Fogli Sparsi*, ed. by A. G. Spinelli, Milan, 1855, p. 25.

that, when the subject was once thought out and the characters determined upon, the rest finally became mere routine. I knew I possessed a good deal of aptitude, and I knew I could work with greater ardor when under pressure.[60]

To illustrate this point, the time when I had promised the Venetian public sixteen comedies may be cited. Only one play remained to be written to fill my engagement. We had reached the last Sunday but one of the Carnival, and I had not done a single line of the last one of the series. I had nothing in mind for it yet. I left my house for a walk about St. Mark's Square, seeking distraction. I looked about to see if any of the masks or jugglers might furnish me with the subject of a comedy or farce for Shrovetide. I met, under the arcade of the clock, a man with whom I was instantly struck, and who provided me with the subject of which I was in quest. This was an old Armenian, ill dressed, very dirty, and with a long beard, who went about the streets of Venice selling the dried fruits of his country, which he called Abagigi. This man, who was to be seen everywhere, and whom I had myself frequently met, was so well known and so much despised that when anyone wished to tease a girl seeking a husband, he proposed to her Abagigi.

Nothing more was needed to send me home satisfied. I entered my house, shut myself up in my closet, and began a popular comedy, which I called *I Pettegolezzi delle donne,* or *Women's Tittle-tattle.* I could not get it performed until Shrove Tuesday, and it closed the Carnival season. The crowd was so great that day that the price of boxes tripled and quadrupled, and the applause so tumultuous that the passersby did not know whether it was an effect of satisfaction or a general riot. I sat quietly in my box, surrounded by friends who wept for joy. Then a crowd came for me, bade me come out, and carried me in spite of myself to the Ridotto, where, dragging me from room to room, they forced me to accept a series of compliments which I would gladly have avoided.

I was too tired to bear the ceremony; besides, not knowing whence came the enthusiasm of the moment, I was vexed that this play should have been placed above so many others which I liked better. Little by little, however, I unraveled the motive of this general acclaim: it

[60] *Memoirs* II, p. 119.

was the triumph of having fulfilled what I had contracted to do.[61]

At another time, after the success of *Pamela*, my friends insisted that, in order to save myself the trouble of inventing a plot, I should again write a play based on some novel. Tired of their importunings, I finally said that I should prefer to construct a comedy from which a novel might be made. Some began to laugh, while others took me at my word. These said, "Then write us a novel in action, a piece as complicated as a novel." "I'll make you one," I replied. "Will you?" "I will." "On your word?" "On my word." So I went home and, excited by my wager, I began the play—and the novel at the same time, without having a plot for either.

I need, so I said to myself, a lot of action, surprise, bewilderment, and an interesting situation, with comical and pathetic elements besides. A heroine would interest more than a hero. Where shall I look for her? We shall see. In the meantime, let us take an unknown lady for protagonist. So I wrote on the paper: *The Unknown*, a Comedy, Act One, Scene the First. This woman must have a name; yes, let us call her Rosaura. But will she enter alone to announce the argument of the piece? No, that's just where comedy used to fail. Let her enter with— Yes, with Florindo. Rosaura and Florindo.

This is how I began *The Unknown*, and how I continued writing it, thus building a large structure without knowing whether I was building a temple or a barn. Each scene led to another, one incident produced the next, and the next. At the end of the first act the plot was outlined; I merely had to fill it in. I was astonished at the quantity and the novelty of the events with which my imagination provided me. At the end of the second act I bethought myself of a catastrophe, and from then on all my skill was exerted to make it unexpected and surprising, yet so that it would not fall from the clouds, as it were. The play pleased my friends and the public, and everybody averred that it could supply the material for a novel of four volumes in octavo.[62]

It was not always success and friendship, however, which spurred me on to bursts of speed. I had thought that *The Whimsical Old Man*, for instance, would have had at least the success of *The Man of the World*, but I

[61] *Memoirs* I, p. 355.
[62] *Memoirs* I, p. 351.

was horribly mistaken. Rubini had never played without
a mask and was so uncomfortable and so embarrassed
that he lost all his grace, as well as his wits and his common sense. The play fell flat, most humiliatingly for himself and for me. It came to an end under difficulties, and
when the curtain fell, hisses arose on every side.

I escaped quickly in order to avoid backhanded compliments, and went to the Ridotto. Concealed beneath
my mask, I mingled with the crowd which collects there
after the theater, and had the time and the opportunity
to listen to the eulogies lavished upon me and my piece.

Passing through the gaming rooms, I saw groups everywhere in earnest discussion, and they were all talking
about me. "Goldoni is through,"some said, "Goldoni has
emptied his bag." I recognized the voice of a mask who
spoke through his nose, and who said in a loud voice that
my portfolio was exhausted. He was asked to what portfolio he referred. "It is the collection of manuscripts," he
answered, "that has furnished Goldoni with everything
he has done till this day." In spite of the wish of all to
make fun of me, everybody began to laugh at the nasal
voice. I was looking for criticism, and found only ignorance and animosity.

I went home, passed the night somehow, and searched
the while for a way to avenge myself upon the mockers.
I found one at last, and at sunrise began a comedy in five
acts and in verse, entitled *The Ball.*

Act by act I sent it to the copyist. The actors learned
their roles as they came forth; on the fourth day the play
was announced on a poster, and it was performed on the
fifteenth day. It was, indeed, a case of *facit indignatio
versus.* The gist of the piece was again a phase of *cicis-
beatura,* a husband forcing his wife to give a ball for his
cicisbea. I arranged for a gathering of tired dancers in a
drawing room adjacent to the ballroom. There I caused
the conversation to fall on *The Whimsical Old Man.* I had
all the ridiculous talk which I heard at the Ridotto repeated; I made all the characters argue for and against
the piece, and my defense was approved by the applause
of the public. It was evident that Goldoni was not
through, that his bag was not empty, that his portfolio
was not exhausted. Listen, my fellow authors, there is no
other way for us to take revenge on the public than to
force it to applaud us.[63]

[63] *Memoirs* II, p. 34.

I used to go through four processes before taking up the construction and final polishing of a play. The first step was the making of the outline with its division into the three principal parts: the exposition, the arch of the plot, and the catastrophe. The second step consisted in the apportioning of the action among acts and scenes; the third in the dialoguing of the most interesting incidents, the fourth in the general dialoguing of the whole.

It often happened that, when the last process was reached, I had by that time changed everything I had done in the second and third, for ideas succeed one another, one scene produces the next, a word found by chance suggests a new thought. After a time, therefore, I came to combine the four operations into one. With the plot and the three divisions constantly in mind, I now begin at once: Act One, Scene One; so I proceed to the end, ever remembering that the lines must converge toward a single point, determined beforehand; that is to say, toward the climax of the action, which is the principal part of the play and for which it appears that all the machinery of planning and constructing has been set in motion.

In my climaxes I have rarely been mistaken. I can say this with assurance, for the whole world has told me so. Besides, the problem does not seem difficult to me. It is, on the contrary, quite easy to find a satisfying solution when you provide for it at the beginning of the play and do not lose sight of it in the course of the work.[64] Tastes, however, keep on changing from day to day, and my comedies, which are now triumphant, will surely become mere rubbish in the course of time.

Indeed, all comedy becomes old-fashioned in the long run, however well it may have been written, or revamped and revived. But the manner of writing it, I hope, always has room in which to improve. True and recognizable characters never grow stale, and although their number is not infinite in kind, it is infinite in species, since every virtue, every vice, every custom, every defect assumes its hue from the continuously varying circumstances which surround it.[65]

---

[64] *Memoirs* II, p. 119.
[65] *Teatro comico*, Act III, Scene 9.

E. Gordon Craig

CARLO GOLDONI

Carlo Goldoni was born in Venice on the 25th of February, 1707, in a house at the corner of the Ca' Cent'Anni.

For forty years he was doing everything, going everywhere. He was Advocate, Candidate for Holy Orders, Coadjutor of the Criminal Chancellor, Clerk of the Procurator, Consul of the Republic of Genoa at Venice, writer, compiler of almanacks, once nearly a monk—no kind of "adventurer," and always having adventures; and for forty years meeting every kind of person from diplomats and ladies of pleasure to swindlers and poets: utterly young in a quiet old way—old in that he seldom gave way to despair. Not sentimental, not tragic, smiling always —a good little disposition; absentminded, yet living entirely in the present; frank, but neither vain nor proud; full of good qualities—what we should call a dear little man. No more like the other Venetians of those skeptical times than Voltaire was like the disbelievers of his land— a child like Voltaire, but less roguish; and very fond of the theater.

The reason I do not say he was passionately fond of it is that this is just what he was *not*.

In those days every Italian went to the theater and went into raptures or furies with what he saw. But every Italian was not passionately fond of the theater. *Only the actors were that*, and the theater of Italy in the eighteenth century was still the theater of the actors.

Unless you know something about the European theater of the sixteenth, seventeenth, and eighteenth centuries you will not know that the Italian actors practically made it. Some poets and architects lent it a generous hand, dowered it with a superb setting: but the heart, the fire,

Originally published as the Introduction to *The Liar*, by Carlo Goldoni. Reprinted by permission of the Hutchinson Publishing Group, London.

and the voice of the European theater from 1550 to 1780 were given to it by the actors.

By 1564 they had swept all over Europe, these magicians; and so tremendous was their force, so countless were their numbers, they were able to wander far afield and yet leave at home many thousands of their kind to enchant the princes and the people in Siena and in Rome, in Florence, in Perugia, in Naples, Pisa, and Verona.

They traveled far and wide—no trains, no motorcars then, and yet these men of energy and genius carried their companies to Lyons, to Paris, to Madrid, to London, to Germany, to Vienna, and to Russia. For them the Seine and the Tagus and the Thames were willing to be set on fire. They inspired Molière, Shakespeare, and Lope de Vega; and having done all this, they had the amazing audacity to permit themselves to feel tired.

Then arose a good man and did an awful amount of harm. To be brief, he killed the great actors.

When actors grow lazy and loose they may expect defeat from a man who will take pains.

Carlo Goldoni was the good man who took pains.

Unless Molière had been actor first and foremost, he could never have evolved the comedies which later on flowed from him like extemporaire.

Now compare Goldoni for a moment with Molière.

Molière never took pains—was no good man. Molière was a kind of *gamin*, so passionately fond of the theater that he made plays rather than wrote them: acting all the time—always acting and finally writing drama. Goldoni did not act in his own plays.

Goldoni was of a literary turn of mind and of a theatrical inclination. He wished very naturally to invent new characters for the Italians to see and hear. So the little advocate persuaded the chief actors to take it easy and he wrote up the parts of the minor actors until it was these that the folk came to know, while they came to forget the principal figures of the Italian comedy.

These principal figures were: Arlecchino, Pantalone, il Dottore, Brighella, il Capitano, Pulcinella, Scaramuccia, Tartaglia, Coviello.

Two or more of these appeared in all comedies; they ruled the stage; they had been the glory of the drama; they were not in any way like anything we have ever seen. They were at once actors and dramatists. They had but to decide the evening beforehand what tale they would act

tomorrow, and all was done. A chair, a bottle, three rings,
and a letter was all the paraphernalia they needed to complete their scene, which was a backcloth and four to six
side wings.

And the performance would be a remarkable one,
remember. Not something one would suppose might
easily result from such haste. For if there was rapidity in
executing the work, beginning at 7 o'clock on Monday
evening and being ready by 2 o'clock the following afternoon, we have it on record that these Italians had long
been perfecting the whole art of spontaneous acting. They
had given some centuries to it.

So conceive the astonishment and indignation of these
masters of the stage on finding a little advocate on their
boards, writing for them what they considered milk-and-
water plays with pretty enough dialogue, but lacking all
the ancient virility of the masters of dramatic art—the old
actor-dramatists of the sixteenth and seventeenth centuries.

But astonishment and fury gave way to sadness as these
poor lazy descendants of the giants perceived that this
same milk-and-water dramatist offered only the purest
milk and the cleanest water. Then they recognized that
the wine they had been serving out was but the dregs,
the lees, of the old vat—and not too clean at that.

Goldoni was in the best sense of the word a respectable
little Venetian gentleman. Molière, highly unrespectable,
was just an inflammable torch set alight by the actors
with whom later on he is willing to share his fire as theirs
dwindles.

Not so Goldoni. Much as he is devoted to the theater,
he is never of it. There is therefore no more meaningless
phrase to use to Goldoni than to call him the "Molière of
Italy."

He is just what he is—the Goldoni of Italy—and there
is one only.

While Molière is purer "Commedia dell'arte," more
genuine theater of the grand and traditional manner,
Goldoni is pure Italian comedy and of a little kind which
has never been equaled: it is the best of its kind.

Do I exaggerate when I say that I consider Goldoni the
father of all good modern comedy, not only in that he is
respectable—beyond reproach—but because he is mild
and beautiful?

The days of fierce passions were past, it would seem.
No longer was fun to be so terrible and so excruciating.

The tears were no longer to be wrung from us as we rocked in our seats. The slapstick and the sack were all right in those ages when single combats between men counted: but when propaganda and the lie came into fashion as weapons the comedy had to change its tone. The old joke was of no more use.

Occasionally the old joke will even nowadays evoke the old roar; but that it is not popular with dramatists is, after all, some sort of a sign.

Goldoni has the true gaiety of a lovely mind.

And his characters are all so new to us, and his settings so original—so varied.

The very last thing anyone can call the author of *The Liar* is the "Molière of Italy"—the very last thing.

That is perhaps why everyone does it first of all. It is innocent and charming after all:

For who knows whether to know is as happy as to not know?

The wise really know nothing—and the fools too—and can anyone discern one from t'other? A clever man is he who can—yet not a wise one. Goldoni is not known by us—and Molière not known any better.

"Who is that?" asks a Turk, pointing to a portrait of the author of *Tartuffe*.

"Why, Molière! The great Molière—don't you recognize him?"

"Ah, Molière? Of course, Molière—one of the *best* of Bonaparte's generals."[1]

And from the other end of the earth comes a young and charming lady to visit the Comédie Française to witness *Les Precieuses Ridicules*, and at the end of Act II turns with every sign of vivid emotion to her host and asks, "This Molière—how much will he accept to come and lecture at Stratford-upon-Avon?"

I fear that I may be put down as a *clever* man, for I seem to know quite a lot about Goldoni—whereas really I know nothing about him—so in which category am I?

Well, being in the company of the charming translators, I'll assume the title of wise man to please them.

---

[1] Adolphi Thalasso, *Molière en Turquie*.

Arthur Symons

CARLO GOLDONI

Carlo Goldoni's genius is essentially Venetian. He himself, however, declared he was a mongrel, half Modenese and half Venetian. Giacomo Casanova's sinister genius is essentially Venetian and Spanish. Goldoni in his youth was fascinated by certain strolling players who took him by boat from Venice to Chiozza. Casanova, who was born in Venice of Spanish and Venetian parentage on April 7, 1725, was the son of two strolling players. His father, Gaetano Casanova, showed the adventurous spirit of the family by running away at the age of nineteen with a young actress, Fragoletta, becoming himself an actor, before he married Zanetta Farusi. Casanova, among his infinite passions, was always ardent after young actresses: Manon Balletti, for instance, the daughter of Silvia and Mario Balletti, the famous actors of the Comédie Française.

Goldoni met, in Venice, a beautiful woman who was called Zanetta Casanova and La Buranella: she played young lover's parts in comedies, she did not know one note of music, she had a perfect ear, and she pleased the public. Goldoni mentions the fact that, being in Mantua, April, 1747, his friend the Director of the Theatre Medebac secured rooms for him in the house of Madame Balletti: "C'étoit une ancienne Comédienne, qui sous le nom de Fravoletta, avoit excellé dans l'emploi de Soubrette, qui jouissait, dans sa retraite, d'une aisance fort agréable, et conservoit encore, à l'âge de quatre-vingt-cinq ans, des restes de sa beauté, une lueur assez vite et piquante de son esprit." Fragoletta and Fravoletta have the same meaning in Italian. So it is the glorious Goldoni who

From *Good Humoured Ladies*, by Carlo Goldoni (London: C. W. Beaumont, 1922).

discovers, without perhaps being aware of the fact, the girl Casanova's father had loved and left and who was the grandmother of Manon Balletti.

The very existence of Casanova's manuscripts at Dux was known only to a few, and to most of those only on hearsay; and thus the singularly good fortune was reserved for me, on my visit to Count Woldstein in September, 1899, to be the first to discover the most interesting things contained in these manuscripts. Among those I found in one of the bundles carefully preserved by Casanova a whole series of letters in French, very affectionate and intimate letters, usually unsigned, occasionally signed "B." These I knew for certain were written by Manon Balletti; Casanova refers to them on Christmas Day, 1759, when he allows Esther to read Manon's letters. "These letters," he says, "numbered more than two hundred, and the shortest were of four pages." In 1910 Aldo Ravà printed all her letters, which amount to forty-one, in *Lettres de Femmes à Casanova*; these, which are imaginative, passionate, exquisite, seem to have been written between April, 1757, and February 7th, 1760. Her last letter is dated Paris. The one before ends: *Addio, viscere mie, Coré, coré, coré*. The last, 3 *basi per jiacomo*.

In 1716 the Duc d'Orléans ordered Louis André Riccoboni to find a new company of actors. He, under the name of Lelio, and the Ballettis, played the principal parts. In 1750 Casanova arrived in Paris. Riccoboni's wife, Virginia Balletti (Flaminia), who was by no means young, the daughter of Fragoletta, who had been the mistress of Casanova's father, apart from her acting, had the vanity of imagining that she was "une femme savante." Soon after that Goldoni arrives in Paris: he stays in the house of the Riccoboni's. "C'étoit Madame Riccoboni, qui, ayant renoncé au Théâtre, faisoit les délices de Paris, par des Romans, dont le pureté du style, la delicatesse des images, la vérité des passions, et l'art d'interesser et d'amuser en même temps, le mettoient au pair avec ce qu'il a d'estimable dans la littérature Française. C'est à Madame Riccoboni que je m'adressoit pour avoir quelques notices préliminaries sur mes Acteurs Italiens."

The first Italian comedies were Bibbiena's *Calandra*, 1508, and Ariosto's *Cassaria*, which appeared in the same year. Suddenly, sweeping away the *Commedia Erudita*, surged the *Commedia dell' Arte*. Goldoni began by creating his comedies out of the old comedy of masks before, by some sudden instinct, he demolished them; so that, up to 1750, he met with no serious opposition, until two rivals rose up against him, Chiari and Gozzi; Chiari, an arrant impostor, bombastic in style, a prolific scribbler of third-rate melodramas: in a word, to use a phrase Swift would have used, a mere windbag. Just then Venice the irresponsible divided itself into factions for Chiari and Goldoni. This quarrel raged for more than five years: Goldoni's unpardonable vice in Gozzi's eyes was to have declared war on the *Commedia dell' Arte;* in Chiari's eyes the unpardonable sin was that Casanova had hissed his comedies, which he revenged in 1755 in a novel named *La Commediante in fortuna,* where Casanova was venemously depicted under the name of M. Vanesio. Among the various reasons for Casanova's arrest and subsequent imprisonment in the *Piombi,* one was that Casanova had not only hissed Chiari's comedies but had sworn to go to Padua and kill him. Casanova says to Laurent, his jailer, "There were others besides myself who might have been arrested on the same charge. I wanted to go to Padua and kill him; but the Jesuit Origo insinuated that I had other ways for avenging myself for his attack on me in his miserable novel. So as I praised Chiari's comedies in the cafés my vengeance might have been perfect."

Meredith—I have his signed copy of the *Commedie Scelte* of Goldoni—says, sweepingly, "Goldoni sketched the Venetian manner of the decadence of the Republic with a French pencil, and was an Italian Scribe in style." There are two kinds of imagination that which embodies and that which disembodies. Gozzi's glittering talent, Goldoni's more glittering talent, are singularly lacking in that imagination which disembodies, filling mortal things with unearthly essences or veiling them with unearthly raiment. From time to time, as Venice flashes before our vision, the misty clouds of some fabulous midnight are lifted and you are shown the moon's mocking image in the depths of a magic lantern.

To those who have seen Duse only across the footlights, Duse must be impenetrable, almost the contradiction of herself. Her face is a mask for the tragic passions, a mask which changes from moment to moment, as the soul models the clay of the body after its own changing shape. Imagine Rodin at work on a lump of clay. The shapeless thing awakens under his fingers, a vague life creeps into it, hesitating among his forms of life; it is desire, waiting to be born, and it may be born as pity or anguish, love or pride. The face of Duse is like the clay under the fingers of Rodin. But there are moments, in any crisis, when the soul seems to stand back and look out of impersonal eyes, seeing things as they are. I have seen Duse act in *La Locandiera* of Goldoni: she was wonderful. Duse is always a chalice for the wine of imagination, but in Goldoni the chalice remains empty. In the delicious part she acted she had certain little caresses; the half-awkward caresses of real people who are always very much awake, which enchants me more than any mimetic movements I have ever seen; such as a certain gentle and pathetic gesture of her apparently unconscious hand, turning back the sleeve of her lover's coat over his wrist, while her eyes fasten on his eyes, in a great thirst for what is to be found in them. Mimi Aguglia would have made Mirandolina a stinging thing that bites when it is stepped on: she always caught you in a fierce caress like a tiger-cat.

There was another play in which Duse turned slowly backward from her somber exit and breathed out one word: "Nulla!" That is not only fine art, it is great genius. And, as I have written, even in a Goldoni comedy or in the *Fédora* of Sardou, her acting completes our admiration of her genius, as it proves to us that she can act to perfection a part in which the soul is left out of the question—as indeed in I know not how many plays—in which nothing happens according to nature, and in which life is figured as a long attack of nerves, relieved by the occasional interval of an uneasy sleep.

What is acting? Is it to be oneself with the utmost intensity and to put that self into every character, or is it to have no self and be a speaking mirror? In *La Città Morta* it is Duse seen through a temperament, and the temperament is her own. Thus it is, for good and evil, to be greater than one's art. Was Rodin ever greater than his art? Never. Was Goldoni ever greater than his art? Yes, often the man was greater than his art. But Duse—who can create life in an isolation from life— has in her nature a great personal force, a force of beauty, subtlety, intelligence, intensity; she has nothing to do but to be herself and to rest from the destroying energy of imitation. So she flings herself into the soul and body of Magda, as if a new vitality had entered into her, a new force of will. I write these notes from the remembrance of when, in 1903, the days I spent in Zurich were so intolerable that I could not disentangle my sensations, setting apart the weariness of all the hours when I did not see Duse, on the stage or off, living over again all the hours in which I was conscious of nothing but the actress or the woman.

Every dramatist has his own method of invention or of creation. The desire of every dramatist is to create over again a more abundant life, and to create it through poetry or through humor; through some force, as it were, of the imagination. It is quite possible to write poetic drama in prose—as Goldoni mostly did—though to use prose rather than verse is to write with the left hand rather than the right. Shakespeare and the Elizabethans used prose as an escape or side issue, for variety, or for the heightening of verse. Molière used prose as the best makeshift for verse, because he was not himself a good craftsman in the art. The most magnificent play Molière wrote, *Don Juan, ou Le Festin de Pierre* (1665) is written entirely in prose; he found the subject in the masterpiece of Tirso da Molina: *El Burlador de Sevilla y Convidado de Piedra*. The *Don Juan* of Goldoni was acted for the first time in Venice during the Carnival of 1736 under the name of *Don Giovanni Tenorio Ossia il dissoluto, Commedie*. In *Tartuffe* we get a form of comedy which is almost tragic, the horribly serious comedy of the hypocrite. I said somewhere that Molière knew he was not a poet. When he ventured to write the most Shakespearean of his comedies, *L'Avare*, in prose, "le même préjugé." Voltaire tells us, "qui avait fait tomber *Le Festin de Pierre*, parcequ'il était en prose, nuisait au succès de *L'Avare*. Cependant le public qui, à la longue, se rend toujours au bon, finit par donner à cet ouvrage les applaudissements qu'il mérite. On comprit alors qu'il peut y avoir de fortes bonnes comédies en prose."

Goldoni wrote, "It was left to Molière to ennoble and render useful the comic stage, in exposing the vices and the laughable side of man to ridicule, for the purpose of correction. I was not yet acquainted with the works of that great man, for I did not understand French; but I made up my mind to learn it, and meantime I acquired the habit of drawing men more carefully, and never lost sight of an original character. So, acting upon the maxim of comedy, *ridendo castigat mores*, I imagined that the theater might be converted into a school for the prevention of abuse and the consequences resulting from it."

I have referred to methods. Writing on Beardsley I

said, "Every artist has his own secret, beyond the obvious one, of why he works. So far as it is not the mere need of earning one's living, it is generally some unhappiness, some dissatisfaction with the things about one, some too desperate or too contemptuous sense of the meaning of existence. At one period of his life a man works at his art to please a woman; then he works because he has not pleased the woman; and then because he is tired of pleasing her. Work for the work's sake it always must be." Yes, every artist, from Leonardo da Vinci to Vladimir de Pachmann, has his own secret, which he guards as jealously as he guards his life and his genius. Like the art of Verlaine, the art of Pachmann is one wholly of suggestion; his fingers state nothing, they evoke. There is not a note he does not create for himself, to which he does not give his own vitality. Is it through his nerves or through ours that this communion takes place? Could Pachmann himself explain to us his own magic? I have often asked him, "What is your method?" He always evaded the question; he could no more explain his magic than his method.

Denis Diderot, in his "Essay on Dramatic Poetry," said, "There is one method I have adopted of going about work, a successful one to which I turn whenever habit or novelty obscures my judgment—both produce this effect—and it is to seize the very thought of certain objects, transport them bodily from nature to my senses, and examine them from a point of view where they are neither too far from me, nor too near. Whether you write or act, think no more of the audience than if it had never existed. Imagine a huge wall across the front of the stage, separating you from the audience, and behave exactly as if the curtain had never risen." Now, this is exactly what Wagner did, who, as a matter of fact, set *La Donna Serpente* of Gozzi to music in 1833, which was performed in Munich; not only in his operas, but in Bayreuth, which is his creation in the world of action, as the music-dramas are his creation in the world of art; in a word, exactly what I saw in Bayreuth; where the solemnity of the whole thing makes one almost nervous, for the first few minutes of each act; but, after that, how near one is, in this perfectly darkened, perfectly quiet theater, in which the music surges up out of the "mystic gulf," and the picture exists in all the ecstasy of a picture on the other side of it, beyond reality, how near one is to being alone, in the passive state in which the flesh is able to endure the great burdening and uplifting of vision.

In the method of all artists, one requires, above all, illusion. We find illusion in the *Mona Lisa*; we find illusion in one of Augustus John's pictures; we find illusion in the Russian ballets. I found illusion, a wonderful illusion, the first time I was in Venice when I gazed at midnight on the miraculous and many colored façade of St. Mark's, on the pale, faintly tinged marble of the Doge's Palace: the illusion almost, of a ballet. Again, in Sarah Bernhardt, is it reality, is it illusion, when she plays *La Dame aux Camélias?* Trick or instinct? there it is, the power to make you feel intensely. Has Goldoni this trick and this instinct? That is a question I am not inclined to answer. "The æsthetic critic's end is reached," wrote Pater, "when he has disengaged that virtue, and noted it, as a chemist notes some natural element, for himself and others, and the rule for those who would reach this end is stated with great exactness in the words of a recent critic of Sainte-Beuve: *De se borner à connaître de près les belles choses et à s'en nourir en exquis amateurs, en humanistes accomplis.*"

So, as certain people have desired to die in certain ways —*mourant de maux bizarres*—and as Russian women are as uncertain of their souls as if the black earth were secretly alive, or if sleeping were not better than thinking, I give my notes on one of the Russian ballets.

"It struck me as I saw the Goldoni ballet, *Le Donne di Buon Umore*, and heard the music of Domenico Scarlatti, that all of the costumes and much of the effect of the miming—which were the most delicious and capricious that I have ever seen—had been designed after Longhi's paintings and drawings; for in many of these he gives a wonderful sense of living motion; but certainly nothing of what is abominably alive in the great and grim and sardonic genius of Hogarth.

"In Venice I have often spent delightful hours before his innumerable drawings, such as painters at the easel, ballet girls with castanets, maid-servants holding trays, music and dancing-masters (indeed, is not Enrico Cecchetti in the ballet a most admirable and most Italian dancing-master?), tavernkeepers, street musicians, beggars, waiters; the old patrician lolling in his easy chair and toying with a fan; the *cavalieri* in their fantastic dresses; the women with their towering headdresses. The whole sense of Venice returned to me as I saw Lydia Lopokova —always so birdlike, so like a butterfly with painted wings, so witty in gestures, so absolutely an artist in every dance she dances, in every mime she mimics, in her wild abandonment to the excitement of these shifting scenes, where all these masked and unmasked living puppets have fine nerves and delicate passions—putting powder on the face of the Marquise Silvestra and mocking her behind her back. I saw then Casanova's favorite haunts: the *ridotti*, the gambling-houses, the cafés in San Marco's, the carnivals, the masked balls, the intrigues; the *traghetti*, where I seemed to see mysterious figures flitting to and fro in wide miraculous *bautte* beneath the light of flickering flambeaux.

"I see before me, as I write, the night when I went from the Giudecca to the Teatro Rossini, where a company of excellent Italian comedians gave one of Goldoni's comedies, and, as when the chatter in the gallery ends, the chatter begins on the stage, I found for once the perfect illusion; there is no difference between the one and the other. Voluble, like Venice, with its unchanging attitude toward things, the prompt gaiety and warmth of its temperament finds equal expression in the gallery, and in the interpretation of Goldoni, on that stage. Going to the theater in Venice is like a fantastic overture to the play, and sets one's mood properly in tune. You step into the gondola, which darts at once across a space of half-lighted water, and turns down a narrow canal between walls which seem to reach more than halfway to the stars. Here and there a lamp shines from a bridge or at the water-gate of a house, but with no more than enough light to make the darkness seen. You see in flashes: an alley with people moving against the light, the shape of a door or balcony, seen dimly and in a wholly new aspect, a dark churchfront, a bridge overhead, the water lapping against the green stone of a wall which your elbow all but touches, a head thrust from a window, the gondola that passes you, sliding gently and suddenly alongside, and disappearing into an unseen quiet."

We have to distinguish in Goldoni's comedies those that are written in pure Italian, among which may be comprised those written in Martellian verse; those, the majority, that are written partly in dialect and partly in Italian; those, there are eleven, which are written entirely in the Venetian dialect. It has been wittily said that some of his comedies recall one of Louis Chardon's articles in Balzac's *Grand Homme de Province à Paris*, beginning, *on entre, on sort, on se promène*. Only, in Balzac, money and the passions rule the world of *La Comédie Humaine*; and, at the root of the passions, determining their action, he saw those nervous fluids, or that unknown substance which, in default of another term, we must call the will. Money, the passion, the will, the nerves—these were some of the most essential qualities in Casanova: to Goldoni they were practically unknown. Goldoni, who says beautifully in his *Memoirs* that the Venetians sang all day long, "the shopkeepers laying out their wares; the workmen coming home from work, the gondoliers waiting for their masters," adds: "Gaiety is at the root of the national character, and jesting is at the root of the Venetian language." The day is past when the gondoliers sang Tasso: they still sang in Venice, when I was there, strange and haunting songs, one of which haunted the imagination of Wagner when he was writing *Tristan and Iseult* in one of the Palaces on the Grand Canal—those wonderful nine notes of the sailors' chorus, which always ring in my ears when I am on the sea, for they have in them all the exultation of all life that moves upon the waters.

Everyone who walks from the Piazza de San Marco in the direction of the Rialto cannot fail to see, in the Campo S. Bartolommeo, Goldoni's statue. This is my own vision of the statue when I first saw it. He stands there, looking down on the people as if he saw in them one of his comedies; firmly planted, wearing his court dress with an air, and with an intensely self-satisfied smile of amused interest on his face. If he could only turn his head, he would look right up the steep, broad stairs of the Rialto, which lie there, to the right, bright with moving crowds of color, winding up and down on each side of the central row of stalls, between the shops, hung with long colored stripes. He stands there, looking down upon the people.

Harold Acton

EDUARDO DE FILIPPO

Dramatic critics have a way of splashing about their superlatives, and Italy teems with actors and actresses who really deserve them. Of all these versatile artists who devote so much more of their talent to the theatre than to the films in which they are tempted to appear surely none is more remarkable than Eduardo de Filippo, both as actor-manager and playwright.

Physically, as Henry James wrote of the great Coquelin, "he offers no bribe whatever, none of the lures of youth or beauty or sex or of an insinuating aspect." He wears a corrugated mask of careworn comedy pierced by smouldering heavy-lidded eyes. Perhaps this is insinuating in the sense that it kindles sympathy: it is the last mask surviving from the *Commedia dell' Arte*—that of Pulcinella grown older, sadder and wiser. He belongs to the tradition dating from the sixteenth century when theatrical companies were assembled under a *capocomico* or principal comedian who kept a collection of skeleton plots which the players developed with dialogue or miming. But Eduardo, as he is generally styled, writes his own plays, most of which have been published. A few have been filmed with success but they are stage-plays first and foremost, and in order to appreciate them fully they should be seen in Eduardo's own theatre, the San Ferdinando in Naples, where the audience adds zest to the performance. In other regions of Italy there is a lingering prejudice against the Neapolitan dialect though it is quite as comprehensible as the Venetian of Goldoni's best comedies. Basically the language is Italian, but it contains a multitude of words and expressions which, if

From *The London Magazine*, June, 1962. Copyright © 1962 by Harold Acton.

less elegant than the Tuscan, are more highly coloured and to some ears more melodious. It is scarcely surprising that Eduardo prefers to write in his native dialect.

Neapolitan poets, apart from the popular songsters, had discovered the flexible beauty of this instrument when it was already threatened with decay by the unification of Italy, though it had long been exploited in *opera buffa* and on the comic stage. Now its days are numbered owing to the combined assault of the ubiquitous radio, television, cinema, journalism, and the freemasonry of sport. The transformation of feminine manners and fashions since the last war has accelerated the levelling process all over Italy. But the lower-middle-class and the proletariat still converse in dialect, diluted in ever larger doses with Italian, and the cultured often have recourse to it for the *mot juste* which Italian could not supply.

The golden age of Neapolitan dialect poetry lasted from 1880 till 1930 when "regional" literature flourished as never before. Salvatore Di Giacomo and Ferdinando Russo were its most inspired exponents: they ran the whole gamut of its moods. Eduardo de Filippo, who was born in 1900, belongs to the age of transition or dilution. Consequently most of his characters mingle dialect with Italian, alternating the pungency of the one with the suavity of the other and extracting all the flavour, fun, and rich tonality of their utterance. Whether they are trying to be "refained" like a Cockney emulating the accent of a BBC announcer, or whether they are blissfully illiterate, he shows us how they revel in the syllables of their own speech. Hence his best plays defy the translator's exertions.

To take a small instance of this in the first act of *Napoli milionaria*, the neighbour Adelaide's raptures over Rituccia (whom we never see on the stage), the little daughter of Gennaro and Amalia Jovine: "What a sight for sore eyes is that daughter of yours! And what intelligence she shows! . . . She seems quite a little old lady! (*Pare na vicchiarella!*) Just how old is she?" Amedeo: "Turned five." Adelaide (tenderly): "A saint as well as old! (*Santa e vecchia!*) And how well she talks! What a splendid pronunciation! Just to put it on trial I asked her: Who do you love best, dearie? My mamma, she answered." Gennaro: "She positively adores her mother." Adelaide: "And what about your papa? I went on. He's a goose. (*E' fesso*) But with such a perfect pronunciation. Her 's' is quite beautiful. (*La esse la tiene proprio bella. . . .*)"

Here the rude word *fesso*, which has a different shade of meaning in Naples, produces a shock similar to Eliza Doolittle's "Not bloody likely!" in Shaw's *Pygmalion*, but it also helps to summarize his family's attitude towards Gennaro, the hero of the play.

Napoli milionaria, Questi fantasmi and *Filumena Marturano* are Eduardo's ripest achievements, but some experience of Naples is required to appreciate their manifold subtleties. *Napoli milionaria* is a poignant record of how the last war affected the poorer population, represented by the Jovine family in their *basso* or ground floor room opening on to a typical alley, such as Eduardo's predecessor Raffaele Viviani had celebrated in *'O Vico* (1917). The curtain rises on the squalid interior, the "matrimonial" brass bed, the rickety straw chairs in the early morning light. Maria Rosaria, the eldest daughter, is wearily washing coffee-cups in an earthenware jar; there is an altercation in the alley and the shrill voice of her mother Amalia predominates. The bombardments have started: it is the end of 1942. Thanks to her activities on the black market, including the sale of coffee and other rare provisions, Amalia keeps her family afloat. Her law-abiding husband Gennaro disapproves, but Maria Rosaria remarks that if they paid attention to him they would die of hunger. "You belong to another age," says his son Amedeo. The first act, in which the downtrodden Gennaro is made to lie down and sham dead in order to hoodwink the police, is riotously farcical.

The Allied landings were followed by an explosion of euphoria and in the absence of Gennaro, who had vanished, his wife had prospered on the black market. In the second act the *basso* had been transformed, repainted and redecorated in *art nouveau* style, of which Naples is the last refuge. Amalia, all spick and span is silk with dangling earrings, appears to have been rejuvenated. She sprays herself lavishly with eau-de-Cologne and even sprinkles the room with it. The cheerful cries of street-vendors coming and going create an atmosphere of liberation.

Maria Rosaria and her girl friends are picked up by American soldiers who are less innocent than they seem. One of the girls expatiates on Maria Rosaria's good luck: her boy friend has proposed to marry her and take her to the States. "He—John—first made love to me. Then he met Maria Rosaria and said that he fancied her much more. He told me to my face: *'Tua frenda più nais!'* I answered *'Okei.'* The same evening he brought another friend along with him who promptly fell for me and I for him. . . . Then I told him I had a *frenda* called Margherita: hadn't he got a *frendo* for her too? So he brought one along. . . ." But Margherita's companion did not appeal to her: he was too short. Amalia tells her cynically: "What does it matter? Tell him straight out: 'Look here, you're not my type. Fetch somebody with more allure.' " (Her expression *"non mi nais,"* from the English "nice," loses its savour in translation.)

On her side Amalia is courted by her black-marketing associate Errico, nicknamed Settebellizze, an up-to-date version of the handsome *camorrista.* He is all the more confident because she has had no news of her husband for more than a year. Gennaro must be dead, he maintains. But a letter recently addressed to him indicates that he is still alive. Amalia's conscience pricks her: his return would hamper her activities. In spite of material prosperity her family is going to the dogs. Her son Amedeo has become a car thief; Maria Rosaria has been jilted; little Rituccia is in bed with a temperature. Engrossed in her profits, she has turned a blind eye to these facts: about the little girl's fever she is fatalistic. A dinner is being prepared to celebrate Settebellizze's birthday—the occasion for which she is dressed up in her finery. At this point Maria Rosaria confesses that she has been seduced and there is a violent scene between mother and daughter, who accuses her of neglecting her children for Settebellizze. They have come to blows when there is a sudden commotion in the alley, an excited chorus of greetings: Gennaro, whom everybody had given up for dead, has returned.

What might be a mere figure of farce is transmuted into a tragic wreck, a spectral victim of war, by Eduardo's interpretation of the role of Gennaro. The battered Harlequin in his ragged garb—an Italian hat, American trousers, German camouflaged jacket—seems to have strayed from one of Picasso's early canvases. The prospect of seeing his family again makes his eyes glitter in his haggard face. But on crossing his threshold he is dazed at the sight of so much luxury. Surely he must have mistaken the house. "Excuse me, madam," he says deferentially, and goes out. The good neighbour Adelaide persuades him to step in. He hesitates, still dazed. His wife is thunderstruck. All at once she guesses what he has been through. Each stammers towards an embrace. Each breaks down in turn while Gennaro mutters: "A century, Ama', a century. . . ."

The practical wife is the first to recover. Gradually he relates his past experiences, but once the flood has started it cannot be dammed. The catalogue of horrors so vividly related in his soliloquy falls like a bomb on this festive environment—a bomb that fails to explode. He is still haunted by his hairbreadth escapes. Food is brought in for the feast, roast kid and potatoes, green peppers and Parmesan cheese, which remind him of his recent pangs of hunger. The irony of contrast is heightened by his description of how he hid in a ditch beside a couple of corpses during a bombardment without eating or drinking for three days. His audience show signs of boredom. "Tell us about it later," says his wife. "Dinner's ready." The gangsterish guests—the men in Sunday suits, the women in fur coats over their usual sloppy attire—shower gifts on the complacent Settebellizze, who behaves like a patronizing film star. "Thanks, but the party is not for me. It is for don Gennaro," he informs them.

But Gennaro is like a ghost from another world. He apologizes for his beggarly appearance; he cannot help harping on the war but nobody wishes to hear him. "Don't brood on misfortunes. Now that you're home we shall make you forget them." While the others are chattering gaily he sits bemused. "Life is certainly a cinematograph!" he exclaims. "I can't believe my eyes." Again he reverts to his ordeal in the ditch, and the others beg him to change the subject: "Consider your health. . . . Now all that's over and done with." "What are you saying? What's over?" says Gennaro, tragically aware that the war is still on. Unable to conceal his dejection he leaves the party, amid protests, to sit beside his feverish little daughter.

In the last act Amalia tries to defend herself against her own conscience and her husband's accusing gaze: "Why do you stare at me? I have done the same as others. I have had to defend myself and help myself. . . . How can you blame me? What have they been telling you?" And Gennaro gently explains that he blames the war. His sick little daughter puts him in mind of his country.

When he had come back from the first world war, every man, woman, and child was eager to hear all he could tell them, he even had to invent more anecdotes to satisfy them. Why didn't they want to hear about this war? First because it was not their fault—they had not asked for it—and secondly because profiteering had made them lose their heads. . . . All these thousand *lire* notes collected by his wife seemed to him a joke, sheer madness. But perhaps he too might have lost his head had he stayed at home. . . .

Eduardo is a poet as well as an actor and playwright, and he has written plays more poetical than *Napoli milionaria* such as *Questi fantasmi* (*These Ghosts*) and *Le voci di dentro* (*Inner Voices*) which make strenuous demands on their interpreters. Who but Eduardo can so mesmerize an audience with half a word, a pregnant pause, a light gesture, and the immobility of those features which express anguish and defeat more often than joy and success? A master of self-control, he is the antithesis of the conventional stage Neapolitan.

The gifts he inherited from his versatile father Eduardo Scarpetta have been polished and perfected for fifty years, since he started acting at the age of ten. In his youth the public was less sophisticated: people went to the theatre to laugh and cry and forget themselves. Eduardo chose to make them laugh though the same characters that roused their mirth were apt to sadden him. His first company was formed in 1932, supported by his incomparable sister Titina and his brother Peppino, and the first plays he wrote for it were crackling farces whose apparent spontaneity was the result of patient artifice. Technically he followed in the footsteps of his father, whose comedies were included in his repertory, but before he reached maturity Pirandello crossed his path. The influence of Pirandello and the impact of war extended his range and gave a new depth and complexity to his form and content, but he was saved from drifting into metaphysical allegory by his firm roots in the paternal tradition.

As a good Neapolitan the family unit remains at the core of his inspiration and he is an insatiable observer of its minutest particularities. It is extraordinary what subtle variations he can play on this perennial theme in *Natale in casa Cupiello, Mia famiglia,* and best of all in his more recent *Sabato, domenica e lunedi.* The latter's title is explained by one of the protagonists: business men incapable of relaxing were inclined to fish for trouble on a Sunday when they had nothing else to do.

The clouds begin to gather on Saturday evening. Peppino and Rosa have been married for many years with three grown children and a profitable business but their nerves are on edge. Peppino is tortured by a secret obsession: he is convinced that his wife is having an affair with Luigi, a respectably married neighbour of exuberant disposition. As he becomes increasingly offensive poor Rosa's temper is also rather frayed.

The storm breaks suddenly during the Sunday repast when the chorus of guests led by Luigi congratulate Rosa on her culinary genius. Peppino's exasperation boils over: he accuses his wife of indulging in a liaison with Luigi, who protests his complete innocence while Rosa gives loud vent to her outraged feelings. Peppino realizes too late that he has made a public fool of himself. Rosa suffers from an emotional crisis. The party disperses in pained embarrassment though the younger generation is amused.

On Monday morning Peppino is conscience-stricken about Rosa, who has spent a feverish night. Self-pity makes her exaggerate her nervous prostration. Peppino is crestfallen. Explanations follow, and we see how a series of trivial irritations become ingrown and cause festering sores. One day Peppino seemed to prefer his daughter-in-law's cooking to that of Rosa; another she seemed to have neglected him on account of the children. Why had she ceased to prepare a clean shirt and handkerchief for him in the morning? Owing to such trifles they had drifted apart. In the course of this heart-to-heart dialogue they are drawn together with a deeper understanding.

In outline the play sounds trite, yet it is richly embroidered with touching and humorous episodes. The aroma of the savoury stew—*il ragù*—which is an essential part of the family's Sunday ritual pervades the first two acts and lingers over the third. The onions being sliced for it almost bring tears to one's eyes when the curtain rises. "The more onion you put into it, the richer the sauce," says Rosa to her maid who thinks there is already quite enough, and she treats the audience to a recipe worthy of Brillat-Savarin. And the moment when all sit down to the meal, the sighs of pleasure, glad sniffs, gurgles, tucking in of napkins, the crescendo of enjoyment (contrasting with Peppino's exasperation) is wonderfully effective. The lyricism evoked by humble things is one of the charms of this comedy, but substituting roast beef or some local dish for the *ragù* it might happen almost anywhere.

Eduardo's more recent *Il Sindaco del rione Sanità* (*The Mayor of the Sanità District*) is specifically Neapolitan. The district in question, poor but picturesque, extends below the ancient catacombs of San Gennaro. Saint Vincent Ferrer is its celestial patron: its worldly patron and unofficial mayor is Antonio Barracano, the hero of the play, a genial old *camorrista* with his own code of justice, to whom the people take their troubles rather than to the courts of law. "The law is well made but men devour each other . . . the cunning devour the ignorant. I protect the ignorant," he says. How he does this and gets killed before he retires is the subject of the plot.

As it is unlikely to be performed in England a summary of the first act may not be supererogatory. The scene represents Antonio Barracano's country house at the foot of Vesuvius before dawn in early September. A bell is tinkling and the family maid Immacolata enters hurriedly in her dressing-gown to answer it. This she does through a speaking trumpet concealed behind a picture on the wall. Through a second speaking trumpet she tells the porter to open the gate, then proceeds to waken the other inmates. Geraldina, Don Antonio's daughter, appears in her dressing-gown, yawning and doing up her hair. She spreads a square of white muslin on the central table and puts a surgeon's overall on the chair beside it. Gennarino, her brother, joins her, a young man tousled and sleepy in pyjamas. He produces a tin box containing surgical instruments, bottles of iodine and disinfectant, a sterilizer, and other hospital paraphernalia. Immacolata contributes a couple of basins, bandages, a roll of cotton wool and towels. The household doctor Fabio della Ragione, a kindly veteran of sixty-five, toddles in half dressed and inspects the preparations. Immacolata helps him into his overall and the surgical instruments are sterilized. The porter Catiello and another lusty fellow lug in the groaning patient, who has been shot in the right leg. "Shut up, we've arrived," says Catiello. The patient moans and invokes the Madonna of the Carmine while he is lowered on the operating table.

Each inmate is familiar with his allotted task: it has happened so often before. "Who are you?" the doctor asks the patient's companion as he dons his rubber gloves. "I'm O'Nait, the one that wounded him." "Then what are you doing here?" While the doctor gives an injection O'Nait explains that he and his mate had fired at each other but after all they were pals: he hadn't had the heart to leave him bleeding on the ground and had brought him here by taxi. "Thanks," says the patient. His assailant clasps his hand and tells him naïvely: "It was just my duty. Now you must try to get well again." "As soon as I recover I'll shoot you," retorts the patient. "A fine system!" comments the disgusted doctor, "I'll shoot you! We'll shoot each other! Well, it is no fault of yours. Ignorant you are and ignorant you'll remain." (In Italian the word ignorant is more insulting than in English. But these simple heirs of the lazzaroni are accustomed to such treatment.) After a cup of coffee served by Immacolata, the doctor proceeds to operate. "How is he?" asks O'Nait anxiously when it is over. The doctor hands him the bullet he has extracted, remarking "Calibre six." "It should be taken to Pompeii," says O'Nait, alluding to his friend's miraculous escape, for the shrine of the Madonna of Pompeii is immensely popular. "But not to the sanctuary," the doctor retorts. "I doubt if the Madonna wants to enrich her collection of bullets with another sample. You should put it among the ruins to show the gigantic strides of civilization."

The patient is escorted outside for a little fresh air. Both he and his assailant wish to speak to Don Antonio, but the maid tells them that the mayor is still asleep: his slumber is sacred. The devoted awe with which Don Antonio is regarded transpires from the ensuing dialogue. As he suffered from insomnia nobody had dared to waken him in spite of his wife's accident. She had been bitten by one of the watch-dogs but had gone to be medicated at a first-aid station and had spent the rest of the night with her elder son in Naples rather than disturb her husband. Gennarino threatens to shoot the dog, but the doctor reminds him significantly that his father dotes on the beast. Immacolata observes that Don Antonio also adores his wife.

The operating table is dismounted and the room is restored to normal. Even in the country Don Antonio holds his court and people come all the way from the Sanità district to have their cases settled. A dozen had applied for interviews this morning but Don Antonio had rejected seven of these as he felt he needed a rest. At a quarter to six he enters in pyjamas and dressing-gown, a lean, sturdy and erect old man with watchful half-closed eyes. The doctor rises to greet him with a courtly bow. The maid steps backward with a shy grin, waiting for a word or sign to enlighten her about his state of humour. Don Antonio gives each a regal nod, sits down, and beckons to the doctor to join him. He is clearly the monarch of all he surveys. The shooting affray, the mastiff's attack on his wife, and other topics are reported to him as he sits at his breakfast and proceeds to dress for the day like one of the Bourbon kings, with Immacolata and his children in attendance.

"So you have made up your mind?" he asks the doctor. After thirty-five years of collaboration with the mayor the doctor has decided to join his brother in America. He is sick and tired, as he says, of "turning in a vacuum." He has given notice before but this time he means it. Don Antonio has no intention of letting him go and frightens him with a sinister hint: "I shall see that you are met at the airport by friends who will give you a suitable reception."

While the doctor ponders this threat we are shown the lighter side of Don Antonio's character. His son is to select a necktie for him. "Gennarino has good taste," he remarks. "He brings half a dozen for me to choose from . . . then makes me wear the tie that he prefers." "A tie is a personal thing," says Gennarino. "Papa never needed advice." However, Papa leaves the choice to him and of course he selects the flashiest. Don Antonio reminds him that he is seventy-five. "But you do not look it." "I may not look it but I feel it." His daughter embraces him effusively: "My Papa is still young!"

In spite of the dog's attack on his wife he will not allow his son to shoot it. He resumes his argument with the insubordinate doctor, who repeats that he is tired of helping a horde of delinquents who were the real bane of society. "Its real victims, you mean," says Don Antonio. Society exploited the ignorance of these people. But the ignorant at least understood that "he who has saints goes to Heaven." If he took a dispute to law knowing he was in the right, his adversary might either apply to his "saints in Heaven" or produce a number of false witnesses, who were always ready to be bribed. Whatever proofs were available were conjured away by money; if the false witnesses were impugned they brought suits for slander. Consequently the ignorant took the law into his own hands. He might be sent to jail for it but his opponent was sent to the cemetery. The ignorant, "who had no saints," came to him for justice and, as the doctor admits, he had prevented many crimes in the last thirty years. Don Antonio wins the argument. The doctor is reduced to hysterics. He curses the day they first met. For the last thirty years he had been kept as a prisoner, a hostage. This was the third time his brother had paid for his ticket to America. "Come on, kill me now!" he cries. "My father held the chair of medicine at the university . . . I have dishonoured my name. . . . I'm a stinking sewer." He is trembling all over; his teeth chatter. He feels his pulse: he must be feverish! Gennarino and Geraldina help him off to bed while Don Antonio remarks impassively: "If you're feverish, hadn't you better wait till you're quite well before leaving?"

Several clients come in and Don Antonio settles their disputes. His method of dealing with them betrays an intimate knowledge of their psychology. Peace is restored between the trigger-happy pals, but as O'Nait is a member of the mayor's community his face gets slapped. One hopes this will teach him a lesson. His first instinct is to fire, but he hesitates and pockets his revolver.

A more difficult case follows—that of Rafiluccio Santaniello, the cast-off son of a prosperous baker, accompanied by his pregnant fiancée. "If you wait much longer you'll have a wedding and a baptism at the same time," says Don Antonio. And the girl, who worships Rafiluccio, takes this as a compliment. Their discussion is interrupted by the arrival of Donna Armida, the lady of the house, much bandaged over her left bosom. She is pale, dishevelled and tottering. Her sons whip out their revolvers to shoot the culprit. "Wait a minute," says Don Antonio. Had the dog attacked her in her room? he inquires. "No."—"When did it happen?"—"At one o'clock, when I went to the hen-coop to collect the eggs." Even in this case justice must be done. Though he protests his devotion to his wife with fervid eloquence he points out that the dog was there to protect the house, the family, the hens. His wife had provoked the animal. "Put away your revolvers," he tells his sons. "The dog was right." Donna Armida is satisfied with his verdict.

Rafiluccio, who has been waiting with a tense expression, insists on an interview. Don Antonio is inclined to put him off till the morrow, but he declares: "To-morrow I must kill my father." Don Antonio realizes the seriousness of the situation. "You seem to have made up your mind," he remarks. Rafiluccio replies calmly in the affirmative. "Then the discussion will be long. Can you return in a couple of hours?" "Yes," says the desperate young man. So ends the first act.

Don Antonio is stabbed by Rafiluccio's father in the last act, but he lives long enough to save the young man and his fiancée from penury. The wealthy baker is kidnapped and forced to sign a big cheque in favour of the son he had disowned. This takes place at a farewell dinner for the doctor—and for Don Antonio, who knows he is dying of the knife-wound but wishes his death to seem natural and avoid further bloodshed. One of the mayor's protégés, a man who had been profuse in his expressions of gratitude, denies having witnessed the stabbing. His cowardly denial happens to suit Don Antonio, and he will not agree with the doctor that such scum were not worth his assistance. At dinner he collapses after announcing his retirement from the Sanità district in a speech that serves as an apologia. During the last thirty-five years he had at least "shortened a chain to which many other links might have been added": he hoped that in future there would be no need of an Antonio Barracano.

The doctor emerges from Antonio's bedroom with a moral tirade. "Here we have got the habit of sending our conscience to the laundry. . . . Am I scrupulously to carry out Don Antonio's will? To save whom? Two rotters afraid of telling the truth. . . . It suits your convenience that an Antonio Barracano should die of a heart attack after spending a lifetime in shortening the chain of felony. He should have spent his life prolonging it, as I shall spend my last years. I'm not going away: I shall stay put. . . . All of you will relate what you have seen and heard tonight if you wish to. I shall write the death certificate which my conscience dictates." Perhaps a better world—"less round but a little more square," as Antonio used to say—would evolve from the ensuing blood-bath.

The human details are infinitely finer than the plot, which is conceived and executed in brilliant dramatic terms. The scene where the pregnant girl is offered some soup with boiled meat in it: her timid reluctance to quench her hunger in public and her desire to save the meat for her fiancé is as delicately moving as it is true, and it is a perfect piece of acting. Some of the dialogue would be rhetorical in another language, not in Neapolitan. Where else would a working-man describe his peckishness as "a slight languor of the stomach"? For sheer rhetoric one must go to M. Sartre, to such a melodrama as *The Condemned of Altona*. It is interesting to compare Franz von Gerlach's last speech in that play with Don Antonio's about men devouring each other. (Don Antonio had also killed in legitimate self-defence.) According to M. Sartre's German officer: "The century might have been a good one had not man been watched from time immemorial by the cruel enemy who had sworn to destroy him, that hairless, evil, flesh-eating beast—man himself. One and one make one, there's our mystery. The beast was hidden, and suddenly we surprised his look deep in the eyes of our neighbours. So we struck. Legitimate self-defence."

Apart from the pleasure of skilled performance, Eduardo's success is due to the fact that he reflects the experiences of his public and establishes a closer contact with it than his predecessors. Filumena Marturano has the full-blooded maternal instincts of a typical woman of the people. The poor lost Pierrot of *Questi fantasmi* who settles in the vast haunted palace, which the owner is unable to let on that account, resembles many a disillusioned Italian during the paulo-post-war years. The haunted palace seemed the symbol of an Italy over-populated by the historical figures of the past. Even Eduardo's most fantastic characters are authentic. But his humour is of the painful kind that laughs at its own suffering. As Henry James said of Coquelin, he shows "a mastery of that mixture of the appeal to the pity of things with the appeal to their absurdity" which succeeds with Italians as well as with the French. This should also succeed with the English, and I hope that Eduardo's company will soon bring Naples to London. The portents would seem to favour a triumphant visit.

Suggestions for Further Reading

I. ITALIAN DRAMA IN ENGLISH TRANSLATION

The natural companion volume to the present one is Eric Bentley, *Classic Theatre*, Vol. I., New York: Doubleday & Co., Inc., 1958, which contains Machiavelli's *Mandrake*, Beolco's *Ruzzante Returns from the Wars*, a play of the *commedia dell'arte* based on the scenario *The Three Cuckolds*, Goldoni's *Servant of Two Masters*, Goldoni's *Mirandolina [La Locandiera]* Gozzi's *King Stag*.

Those opera librettos which constitute Italian dramatic literature in so great a measure are chiefly found in program booklets sold only in the lobby of opera houses, but two recent paperback books contain the principal masterpieces of Da Ponte, Piave, and Boito:

Mozart's Librettos. Translated by Robert Pack and Marjorie Lelash. New York: Meridian Books, 1961.

Verdi Librettos. In new English translations by William Weaver. New York: Doubleday & Co., Inc., 1963.

Also recommended:

Alfieri, Vittorio, *Tragedies*. Translated by Charles Lloyd. London: Longman, *et al.*, 1815, 3 vols. (Later in the nineteenth century the Lloyd translations were revised by E. A. Bowring and published in Bohn's Standard Library.)

Anonymous, *La Venexiana, A Sixteenth-Century Venetian Comedy*. With Introduction and English translation by Matilde Valenti Pfeiffer. New York: S. F. Vanni, Inc., 1950.

Aretino, Pietro, *The Courtezan*, in *The Works of Aretino*, Vol. I. Translated by Samuel Putnam. New York: Covici-Friede, 1933.

Betti, Ugo, *Three Plays*. Translated by Henry Reed. New York: Grove Press, Inc., 1956. (*The Queen and the Rebels, The Burnt Flower Bed, Summertime.*)

————, *Crime on Goat Island*. Translated by Henry Reed. San Francisco: Chandler, 1961.

————, *Corruption in the Palace of Justice*. Translated by Henry Reed. In *The New Theatre of Europe*, edited by Robert W. Corrigan. New York: Delta Books, 1962.

D'Annunzio, Gabriele, *The Dead City*. Translated by G. Mantellini, Chicago: Laird and Lee, 1902.

——, *The Daughter of Jorio*. Translated by C. Porter, P. Isola, and A. Henry. Boston: Little, Brown, & Co., Inc., 1907.

——, *A Dream of an Autumn Sunset*, and *A Dream of a Spring Morning*. Translated by Anna Schenck. In *Poet Lore*, Boston, 1902.

——, *Francesca da Rimini*. Translated by Arthur Symons. New York, Frederick A. Stokes, 1902.

——, *Gioconda*. Translated by Arthur Symons. New York: Russell, 1901.

de Filippo, Eduardo. *Oh, These Ghosts!* Translated by Marguerita Carrà and Louise H. Warner. *Tulane Drama Review*, Spring, 1964.

Goldoni, Carlo, *The Comedies of Carlo Goldoni*. Edited with Introduction by Helen Zimmern. London: David Stott, 1892. (*A Curious Mishap, The Beneficent Bear, The Fan, The Spendthrift Miser*.)

——, Four Comedies. Edited by Clifford Bax. London: Cecil Palmer, 1922. (*Mine Hostess, The Impresario from Smyrna, The Good Girl, The Fan*.)

——, *Three Comedies*. New York: Oxford University Press, 1961. (*Mine Hostess, The Boors, The Fan*.)

——, *The Good-humoured Ladies*. Translated by Richard Aldington. London: C. W. Beaumont, 1922.

——, *The Liar*. Translated by C. Lovat Fraser. London: Selwyn and Blount, 1922.

(Samuel French's catalog lists Henry B. Fuller's translations of *The Coffee House* and *The Fan*, and Barrett H. Clark's *Beneficent Bear*. For anthologies containing Goldoni items, see John H. Ottemiller's *Index to Plays in Collections*, 4th ed. New York: Scarecrow Press, 1964.)

Gozzi, Carlo, *The Blue Monster*. Translated by Edward J. Dent. New York: Cambridge University Press, 1951.

——, *The Love for Three Oranges*, after Carlo Gozzi's Comedy. An Opera in Four Acts by Serge Prokofieff. Libretto: Free adaptation and translation by Victor Seroff. New York: Boosey and Hawkes, 1949.

——, *The Love of the Three Oranges*. Reprinted from J. A. Symonds' edition of Gozzi's Memoirs in the magazine *Chrysalis*, Boston, 1959. (Symonds' book also contains a lengthy summary of Gozzi's *The Green Bird*.)

————, *Turandot, Princess of China,* A Chinoiserie in Three Acts, by Karl Vollmoeller, Authorized English Version by Jethro Bethell. New York: Duffield and Company, n.d.

Machiavelli, Niccolò, *Clizia.* Introduction and translation by Oliver Evans. Great Neck, N.Y.: Barron's Educational Series, Inc., 1962.

————, *The Literary Works.* Edited and translated by J. R. Hale. New York: Oxford University Press, 1961. (Includes *Mandragola* and *Clizia.*)

Metastasio, Pietro, *Dramas and Other Poems.* 3 vols. Translated by John Hoole. London: Otridge & Son, 1800.

Pirandello, Luigi, *Naked Masks, Five Plays.* Edited by Eric Bentley. New York: E. P. Dutton & Co., Inc., 1952. (*Liolà, It Is So [If You Think So], Henry IV, Six Characters in Search of an Author, Each in His Own Way.*)

————, *Plays.* Edited by E. Martin Browne. Baltimore: Penguin Books, 1959. (*The Rules of the Game, The Life I Gave You, Lazarus.*)

————, *To Clothe the Naked and Two Other Plays.* Translated by William Murray. New York: E. P. Dutton & Co., Inc., 1962. (*The Rules of the Game, The Pleasure of Honesty.*)

————, *The Mountain Giants and Other Plays.* Translated by Marta Abba. New York: Crown Publishers, Inc., 1958. (*The New Colony, When Somebody Is Somebody.*)

————, *The Man with the Flower in His Mouth.* In *One Act: Short Plays of the Modern Theatre,* edited by Samuel Moon. New York: Grove Press, Inc., 1961.

————, *Right You Are.* A stage version, with introduction and notes by Eric Bentley. New York: Columbia University Press, 1954.

The following plays by Pirandello, translated by Marta Abba, are separately printed by Samuel French, Inc.: *Diana and Tuda, The Wives' Friend, As You Desire Me, Tonight We Improvise, When One Is Someone, No One Knows How.*

Politian (Poliziano), Angelo, *The Orpheus, a Tragedy.* Translated with an essay on the Pastoral by Louis F. Lord. London: Oxford University Press, 1931. (The volume also includes Lord's translation of Tasso's *Aminta [Amyntas].*)

Scala, Flamineo, *The Faithful Friend.* Translated by W.

Chambers. In *The Drama,* edited by Alfred Bates. London: Athenian Society, 1903-4.

————, The Portrait. Translated by Ethel Van Der Veer. In *World Drama,* edited by Barrett H. Clark. New York: Dover Publications, 1956. Also in *Plays for the College Theatre,* edited by Garrett H. Leverton. New York: Samuel French, 1932.

Secchi, Nicolo, *Self-Interest.* Translated by William Reymes, edited by Helen Andrews Kaufman. Seattle: University of Washington Press, 1953.

Tasso, Torquato, *Aminta.* Edited with an essay on Renaissance Pastoral Drama by Ernest Grillo. London: J. M. Dent & Sons Ltd., 1924. (Contains both the Italian original and, on facing pages, Grillo's prose translation.)

Verga, Giovanni, Cavalleria Rusticana. In *The Modern Theatre, Vol. I,* edited by Eric Bentley. New York: Doubleday & Co., Inc., 1955.

————, *The Wolf Hunt.* In *Plays of the Italian Theatre.* Boston: Luce, 1921. (Also contains Lopez' *The Sparrow,* Morselli's *Gastone the Animal Tamer* and *Water upon Fire,* Pirandello's *Sicilian Limes*).

II. ABOUT ITALIAN DRAMA

The best quick introduction to the field in English is probably the entry under "Italy" in *The Oxford Companion to the Theatre.* The only "complete" history of Italian drama is one that does not cover the modern period and is out of print: J. S. Kennard, *The Italian Theatre,* 2 vols. (New York: W. E. Rudge, 1932). The memoirs of Goldoni, Gozzi, and Da Ponte have all been translated, and those of Gozzi and Da Ponte have also been reprinted of recent years. Students of theater history will wish to consult A. M. Nagler, *Source Book in Theatrical History* (New York: Dover Publications, 1959), for its chapters on "Italian Renaissance" and "Venetian Comedy." Students of dramatic theory (Trissino, Cinthio, Minturno, Castelvetro, Mazzoni, Guarini) will need Allan H. Gilbert, *Literary Criticism: Plato to Dryden* (Detroit: Wayne State University Press, 1962). There exists one survey in English of twentieth-century Italian drama: Lander MacClintock, *The Age of Pirandello* (Bloomington: Indiana University Press, 1951). A rather extensive Pirandello bibliography is included in *Naked Masks,* as cited above.

Appendix

Translation of the Latin in
The Candle Bearer

The Latin in The Candle Bearer does not really have to be understood; it was meant to create the impression of pompous sterility. The pedantry of the classical scholar is being ridiculed, and it would miss the point being made by Giordano Bruno to translate into English that which was left in Latin in the original Italian version. So it was the translator's decision to let stand the original Latin in the version of the play beginning on page 197.

In certain areas, however, a full translation of the Latin does help the reader understand the action of the play. But to footnote each meaningful phrase would be to make a textbook of what is essentially an entertainment. Thus this Appendix. Here will be found complete scenes and large parts of scenes with translations of the pertinent Latin included in the speeches. These sections are indicated by asterisks throughout the text.

The translation of these difficult passages has been made by Mr. J. T. Christie, Principal of Jesus College, Oxford.

J. R. H.

ACT I

Scene V

Enter Manfurio.

Manfurio. I hope I see you well, you positively, comparatively, superlatively pleasant young man. How are things with you? Well?

Pollula. Well.

Manfurio. I rejoice and congratulate you. If you are well, good enough; I too am well.

Pollula. Is there anything else, *domine Magister?* I am planning something with Sanguino, so I can't stay here with you.

Manfurio. See how you reject the learning which in my glorious Minervan academy, illuming it with my Mars-like acumen, I have made you inscribe on snowy sheets with reed pen tinctured with black ink! Rejected, I say; all in vain my observance of the rules of time and place, you know not their uses. While your teacher questioned you in that Latian idiom so celebrated among all peoples, even the barbarous, you, by still persisting in the brutish medium of the ignorant mob, forswear the arena of polite letters, giving me responses composed of words which you have picked up from the wet nurse, the midwife, even in your cradle, or, rather claimed as your own. Tell me, blockhead, when do you intend to de-adolescentificate yourself?

Sanguino. Master, with this asinine way of speaking by the grammar book, this catacombery and smellegant latinatry, you infect the air and make yourself a laughingstock.

Manfurio. True, if this megalocosmos and terrestrial machine, O contemned and unurbane one, were farced and compacted with your likenesses.

Sanguino. What's all this about Cosmo and Urbanus? Speak a language I can understand if you want an answer.

Manfurio. To hell with you, then, and to the gallows, and the curse of Hercules go with you! Should the Muses stoop to make contact with your porcine presences, or with the pigsty of your conversation? What is your judgment on this renegade, oh, Pollula? Pollula, fruit of my instruction and my nominative in apposition, receptacle of my pedagogic seed, in case you were not stirred by my remarks just now, because, since, for, inasmuchas (particles expressing causation) I have tried to give you the use of the idiom in which most wittily and eloquently we construct objurgations, and I hope that you, hereafter and in due succession—the Gods extending to you what they have already entrusted to us—in contradistinction to your erudiend followers, might imitate them.

Pollula. Very well, but one must make it fit the occasion.

Manfurio. The cause of my blazing ire has been your statement: "I can't stay here with you." It behooved you to say, or rather (infinitive before subjunctive) to say it behooved you: "Your excellence, your learning allows me not, grants me not, to linger idly with your sweet Muses." Then that "with you," or, more in the Tuscan style, "Vosco"—though the plural is not the Latin idiom in respect of one person nor is it polite with respect to the togaed and the academical!

Sanguino. See then how the world goes: you are reconciled, and I'm left out in the cold. I beg you, *domine Magister,* we too can be friends, for though I'm not fit to be at the end of your cane, that is, a pupil of yours, I might be able to serve you in some other way.

Manfurio. I'll have nought to do with you.

Sanguino [*mocking*]. And with thy sp-i-i-r-r-it.

Manfurio. Ah, Pollula, how, how, how have you come to associate with this animal?

Sanguino. Admirable or not, at your Worship's service, most worshipful sir.

Manfurio. This creature seems not so altogether beyond trainingworthiness. Not so uneducable as he seemed at first. He bestows on me epithets not altogether unpolite and off the mark.

Pollula. But from the first you thought him a worthless fellow.

Manfurio. Away with that *nequam:* though it found its way into holy writ it has no savor of the Ciceronian style. "For living let the good man be your example, for writing the skilled writer," says the unmatchable Giovanni Dispauterio, echoed by my own preceptor Aloisio Antonio Sidecino Sarmento Salano, successor to Lucio Giovanni Scoppa, his willing heir. Now, what you should say is "non aequum," the first syllable a diphthong to distinguish it from *equus*, horse, quadruped, noun substantive, animal, sentient, which does not admit a diphthong in the first syllable.

Sanguino. Most learned, our master, we are compelled to bid you adieu; we have to go to Master Giovan Bernardo, the painter, without delay. Farewell.

They go.

Manfurio. Go, then, with the birds of good augury. But who is this who, with that basket in her arms, comes this way? It is a *muliercula*—little woman—by etymology a gentle Hercules by juxtaposition of opposites: a sex frail, wavering, weak, and inconstant: the opposite to Hercules. What a sweet etymology! All out of my own genius, this very instant! So now to my own abode I shall direct my way as I wish to make a note of it in larger letters in my personal book of night thoughts. "Never a day without writing a line."

He goes.

ACT II

Scene I

Enter Ottaviano, Manfurio, *and* Pollula.

Ottaviano. Master, what is your name?

Manfurio. Mamphurius.

Ottaviano. What is your profession?

Manfurio. Master of arts, instructor of unbearded youth, of soft cheeks, tender and youthful: those who are still but saplings and can be directed, bent, and guided into any quarter; their voices are childlike, fit to sing soprano, their teeth unblemished; their flesh full of sap, creatures but newly born, unwrinkled, with milky breath and lips like roses, their little tongues so winning, as fresh as honey, in the flower not the seedtime of their life, bright-eyed and maidenly.

Ottaviano. Oh, most gracious master, elegant, most elo-quent, most gallant chamberlain and cup-bearer to the Muses——

Manfurio. A good apposition.

Ottaviano. —patriarch of the Apolloesque chorus——

Manfurio. One had better say "Apollonian."

Ottaviano. —herald of Phoebus, permit me to bestow a salute on your left glove, unworthy as I am to kiss that sugared mouth——

Manfurio. With such ambrosia and nectar I need not envy Jove himself.

Ottaviano. —that mouth, I say, which exhales such varied and beauteous sentences, such rare phrases.

Manfurio. I will say yet more: upon life's threshold, in the very dawn of their days, taking first steps in their ex-perience of the structure of this world, this universe; coming from its very vestibule they are in the springtime of life, so eager to wed you would not find their like even in a hive of bees.

Ottaviano. Oh, master, Hippocrene fount, I beg you slay me not with sweetness before I confess my fault: say no more, I beseech you; torture me no more.

Manfurio. Then I will hold my peace; he is overcome by the brightness of my glory, as happened to that caitiff whom Ovid mentions in the Metamorphoses, whose thread was cut by the Fates when she saw Jove the thunderer in naked majesty.

Ottaviano. Then have mercy, spare me, by that Mercury who has so dowered you with eloquence——

Manfurio. I am compelled to humor him.

Ottaviano. —have pity on me and pierce me no more with these darts that scatter my wits in pieces.

Manfurio. His deep admiration casts him into an ecstasy. I will be silent from now onward. I will say no more, ye dumb fishes. I have said my say, my voice sticketh fast.

Ottaviano. Master Manfurio, pleasantest river of eloquence, serenest sea of learning——

Manfurio. "Calm" of the ocean, "serenity" of the air.

Ottaviano. —have you some piece of your own composi-tion about you? I have a great desire to have some record of your wisdom.

Manfurio. I think, sir, that in the whole course of your

life and in the perusal of every sort of literary work you would not come across songs so mellifluously symmetrical, so well compounded, as these I am about to demonstrate to you which I have penned.

Ottaviano. What is their matter?

Manfurio. Letters, syllables, diction, power of speech, the parts related directly or indirectly to the whole.

Ottaviano. I mean, what is their subject matter, their theme?

Manfurio. You would say: What is the subject treated? the source of the material? the central theme? The greed, gluttony, and swag-belliedness of that trough-swilling Sanguino, the true image of Philoxenes who longed for a swine's neck, and his partners, associates, congeners, brethren, and fellows.

Ottaviano. I beg you, let me hear them.

Manfurio. Most gladly. Mysteries are not to be hidden from the learned. So, I expound the manuscript, worked and ruled with my own hand. But I should like you to note that the Sulmonensian Ovid—"Sulmo is my native land"—in the eighth book of his Metamorphoses describes the Calydonian boar with numerous epithets in a way to which I accommodate my description of the domestic pig.

Ottaviano. Read it at once, I beg you.

Manfurio. So be it. Who giveth quickly giveth twice over. *Exordium*: expressive of admiration.

[verses]

What is your opinion of these poems? Do you think you grasped the meter?

Ottaviano. Clearly, as the product of one of your profession, it could hardly be lacking in ingenuity.

Manfurio. Unconditionally and absolutely they are worthy of being judged in the light of the most profound study, worthy of the fruit gathered from the choicest plants that ever grew on Mount Helicon, were watered by the Parnassian spring, nurtured by the fair-locked Apollo, and gathered by the Muses nine. What do you think of that statement? Is this not worthy, too, of your praise?

Ottaviano. A very fine concept, and skillfully expressed. But tell me, did you spend a great deal of time working on these poems?

Manfurio. No.

Ottaviano. Did composing them exhaust you?

Manfurio. Not in the least.

Ottaviano. They required great thought and toil?

Manfurio. By no means.

Ottaviano. You wrote and rewrote them?

Manfurio. Oh, no.

Ottaviano. You corrected them?

Manfurio. Not at all, no need.

Ottaviano. You have not adapted them, or downright stolen them, from any author?

Manfurio. Neither, God save the mark, heaven forfend, God forbid. You wish to pry too deeply into my erudition. Believe me, I have absorbed not a little from the Pegasean fount. I have drawn not a little on her that was born of Jove's brain. I mean the chaste Minerva, the source of wisdom. And do not think that I should have been less felicitous, less effective, if I had been challenged to expound any marks of approval or agreement. My memory remains firm. Yes, just so, even so, by all means, of course, obviously, truly, certainly, doubtless, surely, beyond doubt, why not? by Hercules, by Pollux, by Jove, etcetera.

Ottaviano. I beg you, in place of that etcetera, tell me another negative.

Manfurio. Such solipsism, that is, grammatical heresy, I cannot commit, for there is no uniform type of *clausula* in concluding an enumeration.

Ottaviano. Well, then, which of all those affirmatives is the one that pleases you most?

Manfurio. The "certes" is particularly close to my heart. It is fitting in the Etruscan or Tuscan tongue, and it is fixed in my mind: it has the idiomatic elegance of the worthier tongue.

Ottaviano. And which negative do you prefer?

Manfurio. The "by no means" is much to my taste, and is my favorite.

Ottaviano. Now you ask me a question.

Manfurio. Tell me, Master Ottaviano, did my poems please you?

Ottaviano. By no means.

Manfurio. By no means? Are they not the best?

Ottaviano. By no means.

Manfurio. Two negatives make an affirmative; you intend to say therefore that they are good.

Ottaviano. By no means.

Manfurio. You are joking?

Ottaviano. By no means.

Manfurio. You are serious?

Ottaviano. Utique.

Manfurio. You don't appreciate the Martian and Minervan me?

Ottaviano. Utique.

Manfurio. Then you are envious and have turned against me. At the beginning you admired the abundance of my style, but then, as the speech proceeded, your admiration was metamorphosed into envy. Is that it?

Ottaviano. By no means. Why envy? Why turned against you? Didn't you say that these phrases pleased you?

Manfurio. Ha! You are joking indeed, then, and talk for the sake of talking.

Ottaviano. By no means.

Manfurio. Would you say, without pretense or disguise; were there inharmonies, vulgarities, or inelegancies in my poems?

Ottaviano. *Utique.*

Manfurio. And am I to take you at your word?

Ottaviano. *Utique, sane, certe, equidem, utique, utique.*

Manfurio. I don't want to speak to you.

Ottaviano. If you don't want to hear that what you say pleases you, what would happen if I said something that didn't please you? Farewell.

He goes.

Manfurio. Away, away. Come hither, Pollula. Did you watch the behavior of that man who just left?

Pollula. He started by making fun of you in one way and went on to make a fool of you in another.

Manfurio. But you don't think that all springs from the envy that the ignorant feel for us others—we had better say "alii"; "aliud" denotes difference of quality—the learned?

Pollula. Because you're my master, I'll agree with everything you say—that pleases you.

Manfurio. Thus far for these matters; let them go for the present. Now, I intend to employ the muses against this Ottaviano, and as I have let him hear porcine epithets applied to someone else, *posthac,* for his own benefit, I intend him to hear them applied to an inept judge of another's learning. Here, this is a love letter I wrote for Master Bonifacio, who asked me to compose a letter to inflame his mistress. Give it to him from me privately, and say that I am busy with other aspects of my literary studies. I will withdraw from hence: I see two women coming and say to them: "Keep far away from me."

Pollula. Hail, my master, my teacher.

Manfurio. For a happy journey you should say: "Fare well."

They go.

ACT III

Scene VI

Lucia *goes. Enter* Manfurio *and* Pollula.

Manfurio. Here a moment, a word with you, Master Scaramuré.

Scaramuré. Take it as said; till another occasion when I have less on my hands.

He goes.

Manfurio. A fine response! Now, my Pollula, that my discourse may return to its starting point, I shall astonish
you. Ahem!

Pollula. Would you like me to read it?

Manfurio. Not at all, for by not emphasizing the cadence
according to the rhythm of the phrases or delivering
them with the energy they require you will rob it of its
majesty and grandeur. As the prince of Greek orators,
Demosthenes, remarked, "the principle concern of the
orator is with delivery." Now, listen: prick up your ears,
Pamphile.

[verses]

Did you ever see decades like that before? Others have
used verses of four, or of six, or of eight lines, but mine
is of the perfect number, that is, *videlicet,* forsooth, to
wit, as it were, the tenset, according to Pythagoras and
Plato. But who is that, or yon, man coming this way?

Pollula. Giovan Bernardo, the painter.

Scene VII

Enter Giovan Bernardo

Manfurio. Let him be welcome, whose name no less deserves the brazen salute of trumpets than those of Zeuxis,
Apelles, Timagoras, Polygnotus, and Phidias.

Giovan Bernardo. All I understood of that was the fried
ass at the end; and I think that, plus a bottle of wine,
has bestowed on you the gift of tongues. If I'd dined
myself, I'd answer you in kind.

Manfurio. Wine uplifts and bread sustains.

Bacchus and bountiful Ceres, if it be by your gift that
the earth has exchanged acorns for full ears of corn

says Publius Virgilius Maro, the Mantuan poet, in his
first book of the Georgics, toward the beginning, where
he utters, *more poetico,* his invocation. Therein he imitates
Hesiod, the Attic poet and bard.

Giovan Bernardo. Do you know, *domine Magister——*

Manfurio. *Hoc ist magister*: *magi* and *ter,* the three wise
men folded into one. Some few there are whom Jove the
just hath loved, or whom their own bright valor raised
to Heaven.

Giovan Bernardo. What I wanted to say is this: I would
like to know the meaning of the word "pedant."

Manfurio. Very gladly will I tell you, teach you, render
unto you, expose for you, make plain to you, make open
before you, participate with you, and—keeping the con-
junctive particle for the last number of a series—dissect

for you; even as, just as, in the same way as, I have before my class of pupils eNucleated Ovid's *Nut* to enable them the better to devour the nuceus, or little nut. "Pedant" could be derived from *pede ante,* that is, it refers to the way he leads, places his feet before, his *erudiendi* young scholars. Or by a closer, more exact etymology: a stricter etymology would give us "pe" from *perfectos,* "dan," the French *dans,* or "in", "te," from *thesauros*—"perfect-in-the-knowledge-of-words." What do you think of these two?

Giovan Bernardo. Excellent, but neither, to my mind, is really relevant.

Manfurio. You may say that when you have put forward a better one, when you have suggested a better one.

Giovan Bernardo. Very well: "ped" from "pederasty," "ant" from eleph*ant*iasis"; a pedant is an inflated pervert.

Manfurio. As the elder Cato said, "Tell no lies, believe nothing lightly."

Giovan Bernardo. Hoc est, id est, who says contrary, lies in his throat.

Manfurio.

> Against the wordy, strive not thou with words;
> Strive not with words against the wordy, thou.
> With words against the wordy do not strive.

Giovan Bernardo. I'd give the whole race of pedants to the devil. Go and join all the other fallen angels with sooty faces.

He goes.

Manfurio. Join them yourself—that's all the company you're fit for! Pollula, where are you? What do you say, Pollula? Do you see how wicked, abominable, violent, and depraved is this age of ours?

> This sorry world in which I find myself,
> Void of all honor, full of every pride

as Petrarch says. But let us direct our steps homeward, for I want to exercise you in the adverbs of place, motion from, to, and through a place: to, among, before, opposite, on this side, against, toward, below, behind, in presence of, from behind, within, without.

Pollula. I know them all. I've got them by heart.

Manfurio. The lesson must be frequently repeated and recalled, and committed to memory, the lesson oft repeated will please.

> As water drops by constant fall wear out the hardest stone,
> So constant reading makes men wise, not once or twice alone.

Pollula. If your Excellency will go on, I will follow close behind.

Manfurio. Perfectly correct in the marketplace and in the

town square. When we are in my private house, this formality and protocol may be laid aside.

They go.

Scene XI

* * * * *

Corcovizzo. Domine Magister, I can see you are most wise and have plied your studies to good purpose.

Manfurio. This escapes not my Maecenas, whose children I *erudio;* I take out (or *eruo,* dig out) from their rude state. He has commissioned me to decide the price of the material and making of the clothes and take charge of the disbursement of money. Which, as a good steward —economy is the government of the household—I keep in this velvet and leather wallet.

Corcovizzo. Praise be to God! My most excellent professor, you have given me so much good counsel and advice, help me, I beg you, by doing me another favor. I was going to change six guineas at the money-changers: if you have any smaller change on you, I'll give them to you. It will save me a journey, and I'll give you the exchange fee.

Manfurio. I do not do it for the sake of gain, according to the saying, "hoping for nothing therefrom," but from my humanity and sense of duty. I make nothing of the fact that even shall I go my way with a lighter purse. Here: three and two make five, seven and four make eleven; three and three, and two, that's twenty-four crowns—equals your six guineas. No, no, I take no fee.

Scene XII

* * * * *

Barra. Why don't you shout, "Robber! robber!"?

Manfurio. Because that word is properly used only of one who offends openly, on the highways. *Fur* is a thief who steals by stealth and strategem, as he did from me; one that is termed also a filcher in that he seizes on or creeps upon his prey from below, for under the guise of being an honest man, he deceived me! Oh, my precious guineas!

Barra. See where your learning has got you: if you don't want to be robbed, speak plain Neapolitan. With your Latin and Etruscan, we thought you were speaking to him, not to us.

Manfurio. Oh, ducat-knapper, fit food for vultures!

Marca. But, tell us, why didn't you run after him?

Manfurio. Do you really expect a reverend umpire of the linguistic tournament, in doctor's robes, to accelerate his pace in the public arena? I cling to the adage, if it can properly be called a proverb, "hasten slowly:" to the same effect "step by step," "little by little," "one foot at a time."

Barra. You are right, Professor, always to have a due regard to your honor and to the dignity of your manner of progress.

Manfurio. Oh, ducat-knapper, whose bones I long to see broken on the wheel! Perhaps there is something left. But what will my Maecenas say? I will answer on the authority of Aristotle, prince of the Peripatetics, in his second lecture on physics: "There is a category of things that happen in a minority of cases and contrary to any intention."

Barra. I should think that would satisfy him.

Manfurio. Oh, false auxiliaries of the magistracy, if you but did your duty, there would not be such legions of malefactors! Did he leave me with anything at all? Oh, most wicked! Most wicked!

Scene XIII
* * * * *

Manfurio. May it be God's will, may Heaven accomplish it. O that 'twere possible.

Barra. If you come to the aid of this good man, you will never have done a worthier deed. And he won't be ungrateful; I will give you a shilling myself.

Sanguino. They are recovered, I say.

Manfurio. You have them?

Sanguino. No, but they are as good as in your hands.

Barra. Do you know the man?

Sanguino. I know him.

Barra. And where he lives?

Sanguino. I do.

Manfurio. O powers above, heavenly ones, all ye gods and goddesses.

Marca. Now we've got him.

Barra. We owe a helping hand to the professor in this affair for the love and duty we bear to learning and to men of letters.

Manfurio. I commend myself to you: I humbly thank you all.

Sanguino. Let's go after him, then. I know where he hides out; we'll get our hands on him for sure. And he can't deny the theft because, though he didn't see me, I saw him as he ran away.

Marca. And we saw him running from the professor.

Manfurio. Ye most trusty witnesses.

Sanguino. No need to break his head open; either he gives us the money or we give him up to justice.

Manfurio. Yes, yes, nothing could be better. What you say is excellent.

Sanguino. Professor, you must come with us.

Manfurio. Excellent. The presence of Turnus presses hard upon us.

Sanguino. So, we'll all four go together. When we knock at the door, it may be that we can't get in, either because he's warned the whore he lives with or because he can see through a crack in it, or he might get out and hide himself somewhere else. Now as long as you aren't recognized, I'm sure I can get him to talk to me; I'll think of something to hold his attention. But it would be best, in fact essential, for you to change your clothes and get rid of that professional look. You, sir, what is your name, if I may ask?

Barra. Coppino, at your service.

Sanguino. You, Master Coppino, do this service to me and the professor. He'll be grateful, I know.

Manfurio. I am in your hands.

Sanguino. Lend him your cloak, and you wear his gown; as you're shorter, you'll look like someone else. And to divide it up better, Professor, you give him your cap, and you wear his. Then let's go.

Manfurio. Save when we are hard-pressed by necessity, it should be reckoned a crime to doff one's proper attire, howbeit, nonetheless, since it seems good, in imitation of Patroclus who deceived Achilles with altered garments, and of Corebo who took upon himself the habit of Androgeo, and of great Jove himself—*poetarum testimonio*—who adopted, in the pursuit of his designs, so many transformations, involving at times a putting off of his sublimity. I will not demur at putting off my magistral gown, in furtherance of an excellent aim, to take steps against this abhorred criminal.

Barra. But remember, Professor, to repay the courtesy of these fine fellows. I ask nothing for myself.

Manfurio. For you to share I intend the third part of the guineas that we recover.

Sanguino. Many thinks for your generosity.

Barra. Up then and on.

Manfurio. Let us go, with Hercules to aid us.

Sanguino. } Come on!
Marca. }

ACT IV

Scene XV

Lucia *and* Giovan Bernardo *go.* Manfurio *comes forward.*

Manfurio. Now they are gone. I will stay awhile in this

promenade. I saw two feminules conversing, and then one stayed to converse with the painter. The young woman must be some whore, whence comes the word whore-shop; the older, doubtless, is some bawd. Their manner of conferring together looks very like bawdry. The painter I judge to be some degree of fornicator. So, the conclusion follows. I see a cohort coming. I will *iterum* retire.

He goes to hide.

Scene XVI

Sanguino *disguised as* Captain, Marca, Barra, *and* Corcovizzo *as officers of the watch.*

Sanguino. That man who runs away and hides is purgatory-bound; he has a guilty conscience. Apprehend him!

Barra. Stop there! The Watch! Name and occupation!

Manfurio. Mamphurius, master of arts. I am not a criminal, I am not a thief, not an adulterer, not a false witness; nor do I covet another man's wife or his possessions.

Sanguino. What office are you reciting, compline or matins?

Marca. The penitential psalms or the office of the dead?

Sanguino. What is your occupation? You seem to be a priest.

Manfurio. I am a schoolmaster.

Sanguino. A crazy barber? Kennel him, then, before he maddens us all.

Corcovizzo. Hold out your hands, my little lost pig. Come on, we'll give you lodging for the night, and at the king's expense.

Manfurio. Domini, I am a schoolmaster and have but recently been robbed of money and garments.

Sanguino. Why did you flee the watch? You are a thief, an enemy of justice.

Beats him.

Manfurio. Quaeso, don't beat me! I fled because I did not want to be seen in these garments, which are not my own.

Sanguino. Sergeant Corporal: aren't you going to arrest this man? Don't you see that this cloak of his has been stolen from Tiburolo at the customhouse?

Corcovizzo. Excuse me, Captain, your Worship is mistaken; that one had gold trimming on the collar.

Sanguino. Haven't you eyes? Are you blind? Isn't this trimming? Isn't this yellow?

Corcovizzo. By Saint Christopher's staff, you are right.

Marca. By Hercules' club, this is a hardened villain. There! There! And there! And there!

Manfurio. For pity's sake, why are you beating me? I have told you that my own garments were stolen by barbarous raptors, or, as you would put it, thieves.

Sanguino. You are the man we want: this cloak is stolen property. To prison, and we'll soon see there who is the thief.

Manfurio. Take me to my patron's house, near the church of the Crutched Friars, and I will prove that I am no malefactor.

Sanguino. We don't arrest a man to escort him to his own home. Take that! To prison with you, and argue your case with the jailers there.

Manfurio. What a way is this to treat a man of erudition: *Afficere me* in this unurbane manner?

Marca. Speak Italian! Speak like a Christian, in the devil's name, if you want us to understand you.

Barra. He does speak like a good Christian: it sounds like someone saying Mass.

Marca. I think we've hit on some monk in disguise.

Corcovizzo. So do I. Father abbot, we would eat beans.

Barra. And if there are no beans, what then?

Manfurio. I am no ecclesiastic.

Sanguino. He's even tonsured, do you see, like a priest?

Manfurio. That's my bald patch.

Barra. You'll do penance for this, excommunicate! There! And there! And there!

Manfurio. Dixi "*calvitium*," *quasi calvae vitium.* Don't go on beating me because I am protesting. Is this the way to treat men of learning and erudition, Doctors?

Sanguino. You lie: you have no hide nor hair of the doctor about you. Take that! And that!

Manfurio. I will recite a hundred lines of the poet Virgil, *aut per capita* as much of the *Eneide* as you wish. The first book, in the estimation of some, begins, "*Ille ego qui quondam,*" according to others, who attribute those lines to Varro, it begins, "*Arma virumque cano*"; the second, "*Conticuere omnes*"; the third, "*Postquam res Asiae*"; the fourth, "*At regina gravi*"; the fifth, "*Tu quoque littoribus nostris*"; the sixth, "*Conticuere omnes.*"

Sanguino. Don't try to hoodwink us, ruffian, with these Latin tags, learned by heart for homework. You are an ignoramus; if you were wise, you wouldn't be a thief.

Manfurio. Bring some doctor here, then, and I will dispute with him.

Sanguino. How many genders are there?

Manfurio. That is a question for beginners, novices, tyros, and just tasting it with their lips; which declares that *masculeum idest* masculine, *foemineum* feminine, *neutrum* what is neither one nor the other, *commune* what is both one and the other——

Barra. Masculine *and* feminine?

Manfurio. ——*epicene* where the sexes are not distinguished.

Sanguino. And which of all these are you? Epicene, I suppose.

Manfurio. "Things which do not separate the sex one calls Epicene."

Sanguino. Tell me, if you are a master, what's the first thing you teach children?

Manfurio. In Dispautanus' Grammar there is this line: "All that befits the man alone, let this as masculine be shown."

Sanguino. Expound it.

Manfurio. "All," that is, the whole, whatsoever [etc.]; "that befits"—squares with, harmonizes with, appertains to; "man alone"—i.e., men only, uniquely or coming from a man; "let this"—let it be said, or held to be; "masculine"—that is, what belongs to man only is called virile.

Sanguino. That's a devil of a fine first lesson for young boys! What man only has, and woman has not, that is, is nominated the virile, the *membrum virile!*

Barra. A fine lesson indeed, by my faith!

Manfurio. *Nego, nego.* I do not mean what you think—what benefit can come of talking to those without erudition?—I mean objects that should be attached only to the masculine——

Sanguino (beats him). That's talk for women, you dirty old man.

Manfurio. —what you are thinking of is both masculine, properly speaking and as part of man; and feminine, as the woman's portion, in attributed or applied sense.

Sanguino. Quick, quick, in here with him, and then we'll take him to the magistrate. You try to show us what your art consists of, and we find it's the art of buggering small boys!

Manfurio. Miserable me! Words are of no use. O unlucky day, unlucky night!

                                                      They go within.

ACT V

Scene XXV

Barra, Marca, Corcovizzo, and Manfurio *come out.*

Barra. Now the other has gone, what shall we do with the *domine Magister?*

Sanguino. His guilt is written on his forehead: can't you see how he is disguised? Don't you see that this is the cloak he stole from Tiburolo? Didn't you see him try to escape from the watch?

Marca. True, but there is something genuine about him.

Sanguino. That's just what qualifies him for prison.

Manfurio. *Verum.* But the accusations that are supererogated upon me will cost me the esteem of my scholars and others.

Sanguino. Do you understand what he means?

Corcovizzo. His riddles would stagger Oedipus.

Sanguino. To cut this short, decide, *Magister,* what you want to do, whether to go to prison or to give a little something to my colleagues, for instance the guineas you had left on you when the thief ran off with the ones you were changing.

Manfurio. *Minime.* I have none left at all. Those I had were all taken. That this is so, I swear by Hercules, by Jove, by the Thunderer, and you, ye stars.

Sanguino. Listen to what I say. If you don't want a taste of prison discipline, and you've no money, you can make this choice: either ten blows on the palm with this stirrup leather, or fifty lashes on your bare bum; as long as, whichever you choose, you don't get away until you've apologized for your misdeeds.

Manfurio. "Of the choice of two evils, endure the lesser; of two goods, choose the greater," says the prince of the peripatetic school.

Ascanio. Speak so they can understand you, Professor; these are dangerous men.

Barra. Do you think he talks like that so we can't understand?

Manfurio. I call down no curse on you: I am not abusing you.

Sanguino. Nor amusing us either.

Corcovizzo. Choose quickly which you want, or we'll truss you up and give you a double beating.

Manfurio. There is less shame in a caning on the hand than what the scourge can inflict on elderly posteriors: this is no matter for childish punishment.

* * * * *

ACT V

Scene XXVI

Manfurio. Will there be any limit?

Ascanio. Hallo! Doctor Manfurio, Doctor Manfurio!

Manfurio. Who knows me? Who can distinguish me in this garb and this misery? Who calls me by name?

Ascanio. Don't worry; that hardly matters anymore. Open your eyes and look about you: see where you are.

Manfurio. The better to see—to corroborate the intuitive,

and confirm the working of the visual power, so that the axis of the pupil, emitting rays to the visible object, can the better bring the image back along the line of vision and introduce it into the inner sensor, that is, the governing sense located in the cell of the visionary faculty —I want to put on my glasses. Oh! A crowd of spectators sitting around.

Ascanio. You seem to have got into a comedy, don't you?

Manfurio. Yes, indeed.

Ascanio. You think you're on the stage, don't you?

Manfurio. Past question.

Ascanio. And what point do you hope the play has reached?

Manfurio. Its end; its termination, for in truth I do not split my sides a-laughing.

Ascanio. Well, then, invent and speak the *Plaudite*.

Manfurio.

> To beg applause I'm but ill qualified,
> With all my sufferings so sorely tried.
> Their plaudits* long have echoed, as you see,
> All to the cost of miserable me.
> My hands, my rump, chastized without remorse,
> My clinking golden guineas reft perforce. Amen.

Ascanio. Speak the *Plaudite*. I tell you, make yourself do it, and do it well as a true teacher and man of letters— otherwise the other characters will come back, and the play will go on again.

Manfurio. I will do it with a cheerful heart, in the following form. As sailors, though the mast be broken, the sail lost, the rigging and the rudder blown away and smashed by the fury of the gale, continue nonetheless to be brought to land, *plaudere;* and according to the Maronian verses:

> Safe landed mariners their vows will pay to Glaucus, Panope, and Meliserta, daughter of Ino.

Similarly I, Mamphurius, of Letters, both classical and vulgar, Professor, not Regius, nor yet gregious (which signifies "taken from the herd") but Egregious; doctor also of philosophy, medicine, canon and civil law and theology—had I wanted to be; to be brought to port after the miserable and calamitous things that have happened to me—hereafter to pay my vows—I applaud. And therefore I must add, most noble spectators—whose eyes and faces I see turned upon me—that as I come to the end of my supposititious tragedy, without gown or clothes, without even hands, yet in heart and soul I applaud. I may more fitly say to you, thus far guided by a happier fortune, who have been the happy and carefree spectators of our weary and painful adventures: *Valete et Plaudite.*

---

* *Plaudere* means "to beat" as well as "to clap the hands."